W9-BOE-706

wisher that we send him a female Cook

KOSHER RESTAURANT
AND EUROPEAN HOTEL
MAX HERZOFF, Prop.

711 Fourth Street

Auto Phone 3025   SIOUX CITY, IOWA

STIEBEL'S
Importer and Manufacturer of
Human Hair Goods.
A large stock of BRAIDS, CURLS, FRIZZES, &c., &c., in Stock and Made to Order.

345 SIXTH AVE.,   NEW YORK.

Bet. 21st and 22d Sts.

Tel. 156 W'msburg

ש. פרידבערג 693
חזן, מוהל, ומסדר קדושין
פראדוויי, ניער דעבעוואיז סט. ברוקלין. נ. י.

S. FRIEDBERG
693 BROADWAY,   Near Deberoise St.   Brooklyn, N. Y.

ברוך אתה
מלך העולם אשר קדשנו במצוותיו וצונו להכניסו
בבריתו של אברהם אבינו

H. D. SWARD
FINE TAILORING
UP-TO-DATE

Opp. 5 and 10c Store   GOSHEN, INDIANA

Estimates Given on Cargoes.   Telephone Connection

ETZEL & SON,
Coal Wharf PIER 61 EAST RIVER   **COAL**   Office 88 Mangin St.

POCKETS { 88, 90, 92 MANGIN STREET, and
79 81, 83, 85, 87 TOMPKINS ST.

Bet. Rivington and Stanton Streets.   Henry Fereles,   NEW YORK.

ESTABLISHED 1909   S. FREILICH, Prop

GLOBE SIGN CO.
ALL KINDS OF **SIGNS** & SHOW CARDS

59 THIRD AVENUE

NEAR 11TH STREET   NEW YORK

'PHONE 5453 ORCHARD

H. WAGNER
MANUFACTURER OF

KNEE PANTS,   BOYS' & YOUTH'S OVERALLS.

108 ARCTIC ST.

BRIDGEPORT.   CONN.

Russian Hand Beaten Copper
Sent by JRO
Lookholder & Siegel
55 Pearl Street
We take all kinds of copper orders of Russian articles, Electric Lamps, Lamp Shades, Candle Sticks, Wine Pitchers, Jardinieres, Smoking Sets, Cigar Boxes, Flower Vases, and everything else.

'PHONE ...   SUITS MADE TO ORDER AT REASONABLE PRICES

D. KOHN
LADIES' AND GENTLEMEN'S CUSTOM TAILOR
CLEANING, PRESSING, REPAIRING AND ALTERING A SPECIALTY

SIMS STREET   DICKINSON, N. D.

BRIDGEPORT JUNK YARD
SOUTH OF B. & O. DEPOT

A. BALL, Prop.

Dealer in...Scrap Iron, Metal, Rope, Rubber, Hides, Tallow, Furs, Wool and Rags.

SECOND-HAND TOOLS, ENGINES AND BOILERS

WE PAY CASH

BRIDGEPORT, - - - ILLINOIS

BUYING AND SELLING SHOES

COMMERCIAL STREET SHOE SHOP
M BORETSKY, Prop

SHOE REPAIRING DONE WHILE YOU WAIT

REASONABLE PRICES

No. 9 Commercial Street   SALT LAKE CITY

Braslavsky & Wise
Repairing   **Shop**

The Lowest Prices Consistent with Good Work   Boot and Shoe Repairing Neatly Done

124 Monument Street, : PORTLAND, ME.

PHONE 1373 RED.

Sam Ferman

J. Katz Rye Bread Bakery
Parties and Weddings Supplied

2684 West Colfax

Look for our Label KATZ RYE BREAD.   Denver, Colorado.

Telephone Dry Dock 0472

A. NESOVETSKY

Tinsmith, Roofing
All Kinds of
Ice Boxes and Stoves
REPAIRED

139 Division Street   (Apt. 1)   New York City

DROP US A POSTAL AND WE WILL CALL

M. ROSENBERG & S. ELDRICH
BUYERS AND DEALERS IN

All Kinds of Second Hand Goods
UMBRELLA REPAIRING A SPECIALTY

BUSINESS RES.
527 DRYADES STREET   NEW ORLEANS, LA.

A. REGEN, PROPRIETOR   A. S. SOLMONSON, MANAGER

New York Pawnbrokers Sales Store
and Installment House

WATCH AND JEWELRY REPAIRING
A FULL LINE OF HOUSEHOLD GOODS

Highest Price Paid for Old Gold and Silver

238 PROCTER STREET   PORT ARTHUR, TEXAS

BELL PHONE, MAIN 174   MANSFIELD PHONE 829

J. Cousin,
Wholesale Dealer in
Rags, Rubber, Scrap Iron and Metals.

253 N. Diamond St.   Mansfield, Ohio.

TEL. CONNECTION

The O. K. Pants Co.
Manufacturers of all kinds of

PANTS AND KNICKERBOCKERS.

127 SO. MAIN ST.,

2 FLIGHTS UP.   FALL RIVER, MASS.

THE
AMERICAN JEWISH
ALBUM
1654 TO THE PRESENT

Jacob Franks, about 1740: Husband of Abigail Franks; one of the wealthiest merchants of New York City in his day. Served as parnas (president) of Congregation Shearith Israel. *Credit:* AJHS

Bilhah Abigail Levy Franks, about 1740: Wife of Jacob Franks, mother of Naphtali and Phila Franks, daughter of Moses and Richea Asher Levy. *Credit:* AJHS

David and Phila Franks, about 1735: Two of the nine children of Abigail and Jacob Franks. Phila shocked her parents by secretly marrying a gentile, Oliver Delancey. *Credit:* AJHS

Girl with Basket of Cherries, by Micah Williams, 1832: The child might have died in the cholera epidemic of 1832. *Credit:* RUAG

Mizrach, about 1825: A mizrach is a visual ornament with religious significance, which hangs on the eastern wall of the house in the direction of Jerusalem. This one was made in Pennsylvania by an unknown artist. *Credit:* Collection of Stephen Gemberling

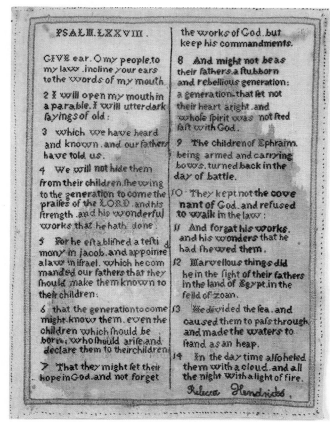

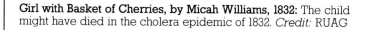

Sampler, by Rebecca Hendricks, about 1780: This cross-stitched sampler is of the Seventy-eighth Psalm. *Credit:* AJHS

Isaac Leeser, by James Peale, about 1840: One of the foremost leaders of American Jewry of his time; in 1829 he became the religious leader of Congregation Mikveh Israel in Philadelphia. In 1843 he initiated publication of *The Occident and American Jewish Advocate,* a journal which gave unity to Jews living throughout the United States. *Credit:* JM

Colonel Isaac Franks, by Gilbert Stuart, 1802: Colonel Franks served under George Washington during the entire Revolutionary War. He was the son of Moses and Sarah Franks of New York City and later lived in Germantown, Pennsylvania. *Credit:* PAFA

Uriah Phillips Levy, about 1815: First Jew to reach the rank of Commodore in the United States Navy, fought in the War of 1812
Credit: AJHS

Rebecca Gratz, by Thomas Sully, 1830: The prominent Philadelphia educator and communal figure. She is said to be the model for Sir Walter Scott's Rebecca in his novel *Ivanhoe*. In 1819 she was one of the founders of the Female Hebrew Benevolent Society and in 1838 she established the Hebrew Sunday School Society. *Credit:* DAM

Ketubah, written by Moses Levy Peixotto: This ketubah recorded the marriage of Eveline Leon to Joseph B. Nones on July 23, 1823. Private collection of Joseph Lyon Andrews, Jr., M.D.

Torah Binder, 1869: This detail of a torah binder incorporates an American flag and was made in New York. *Credit:* JM

L.J. Levy & Company, about 1857: In 1842 Adam Gimbel opened the first department store in Vincennes, Indiana. Jewish merchants were active in dry goods in cities along the Eastern Seaboard, the Midwest and the California coast. The L.J. Levy & Company dry goods store was in Philadelphia. *Credit:* HSP

Newspaper Cartoon, 1906: The "Katzenjammer Clowns Crash," and their adventures in Africa appeared in Yiddish in *The Jewish American.* Because this cartoon strip was a translation from English the panels are numbered left to right rather than right to left.
Credit: AJHS

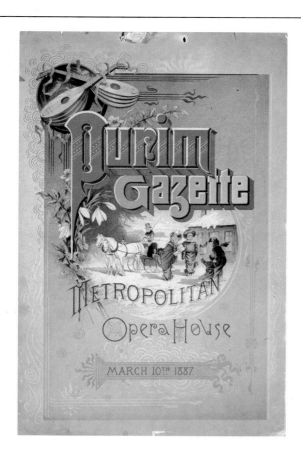

Purim Gazette, 1887: Balls and dances have often been organized as part of the Purim celebrations. On this occasion, the Metropolitan Opera House in New York was the center of activity. *Credit:* SI

Sears, Roebuck and Co. Catalogue Cover, about 1900: In 1895 Julius Rosenwald acquired an interest in the recently established mail order firm of Sears, Roebuck and Co. Under his leadership it supplied the latest merchandise to families through its indispensable catalogue, and became the largest retail merchandising organization in the world. *Credit:* SI

Jewish New Year's Card, about 1910: Such elaborate cards were common at this time. *Credit:* Author

Sheet Music, 1904: *Credit: AJHS*

Yiddish Theater Poster, about 1920: Yiddish theater came here with the tide of Eastern European immigration from 1875 to 1900. It was one of the most popular forms of entertainment for newly arrived immigrants. *Credit:* AJHS

Yiddish Theater Poster, about 1915: Boris Thomashefsky was one of the leading actors of the Yiddish theater. *Credit:* AJHS

Yiddish Film Poster, about 1930: A lively Yiddish film industry in the United States produced numerous films in the 1930s and 1940s. Ludwig Satz, one of the leading actors, appeared in the first Yiddish talking picture. *Credit:* AJHS

Benny Goodman, about 1950: Known as the "King of Swing," he was one of the most popular and acclaimed band leaders and clarinetists of his day. *Credit:* FD

Bob Dylan, about 1964: The folk-rock musician whose songs became the symbol of his generation. *Credit:* FD

Barbra Streisand, about 1975: Singer, actress and acclaimed entertainer. *Credit:* FD

Isaac Stern, about 1978: The violin virtuoso who is one of the most honored concert musicians. *Credit:* CBSR

Leonard Bernstein, about 1975: Composer, conductor and musician with an international reputation. *Credit:* FD

Richard Tucker, about 1965: The outstanding lyric tenor of the Metropolitan Opera Company. *Credit:* FD

Oscar Levant, about 1960: A fine pianist who became widely known as a panelist on television shows in the 1950s. *Credit:* FD

Arthur Fiedler, about 1970: The venerable conductor of the Boston Pops. *Credit:* FD

Peter Nero, about 1965: Popular pianist and entertainer. *Credit:* FD

Louise Nevelson, 1980: The world-renowned sculptor standing in front of one of her recent works. *Credit:* Photograph by Hans Namuth

Bar Mitzvah, 1977: Invitation to Dan Brown's Bar Mitzvah at the Fairmount Temple, Cleveland. *Credit:* Photograph by Jim Brown

Beauty Contest, 1982: Winners of the "Yiddishe Grandma Beauty Contest" in Brooklyn. *Credit:* Photograph by Ricki Rosen

XV

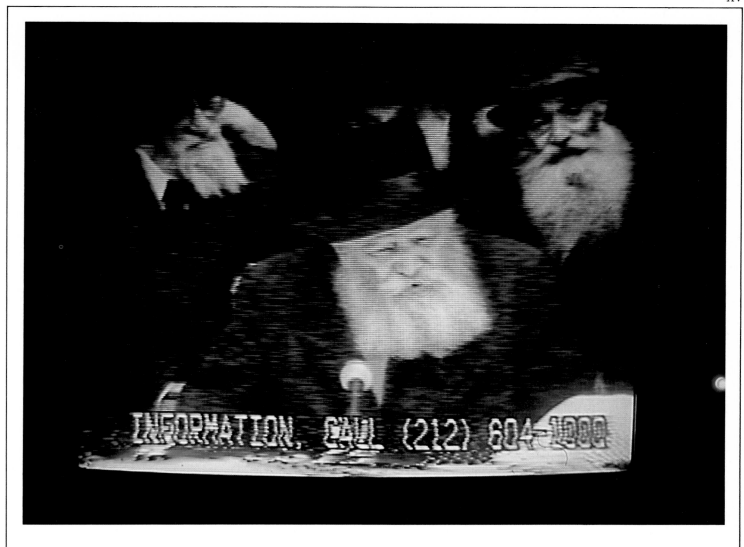

"The Rebbe" on Cable Television, 1982: The Lubavitcher Rebbe Schneerson as he appeared on cable television transmitted by the World Lubavitch Communication Center in Brooklyn. *Credit:* Photograph by Ricki Rosen

Hassidim in Purim Costumes, 1982: Two members of the Hassidic community in Brooklyn in holiday garb. *Credit:* Photograph by Ricki Rosen

Newly Arrived Soviet Immigrants, 1981: He was a captain in the Red Army and displays some of his medals; she was a bacteriologist, holding her diploma. They are being assisted by a Jewish organization and both are studying English. *Credit:* ISP/Photograph by Charles Steiner.

Passover: Philadelphia, 1945: The Aron family at the Passover table. Bill Aron, the photographer, can be seen second from the right as a child. *Credit:* Bill Aron

Author's Family, Vermont, 1982: From left to right: Rebecca, Allon in the back row; Mary and Abraham in the front row. *Credit:* Photograph by Wendy Martin

THE
AMERICAN JEWISH ALBUM
1654 TO THE PRESENT

ALLON SCHOENER

With an introduction by Henry Feingold

RIZZOLI
NEW YORK

Published in the United States of America in 1983 by
RIZZOLI INTERNATIONAL PUBLICATIONS, INC.
712 Fifth Avenue, New York, NY 10019

Copyright © 1983 Allon Schoener

All rights reserved.
No part of this publication may be reproduced in any manner
whatsoever without permission in writing by Rizzoli
International Publications Inc.

Library of Congress Cataloging in Publication Data
Main entry under title:

The American Jewish album.

  Bibliography: p.
  1. Jews—United States—History—Sources.   2. United
States—Ethnic relations—Sources.   I. Schoener, Allon.
II. Title.
E184.J5A367   1983   973'.04924   83-42934
ISBN 0-8478-0500-X

Design by Martin Stephen Moskof & Associates, Inc.,
New York
Composition by Trufont Typographers, Hicksville, New York
Printed and bound by Arti Grafiche Amilcare Pizzi, S.p.A.,
Milan, Italy

Copyright Acknowledgements and Text Permissions

Appreciation is expressed for permission from the designated
sources to publish the following:

Peter Stuyvesant Wants Portuguese Jews to Leave New
Amsterdam, AJHS; A Dutch Priest Complains about the Jews,
AJHS; Amsterdam Jews Petition West India Company on
Behalf of the Portuguese Jews in New Netherlands, AJHS;
Permission Granted for Jews to Remain in New Amsterdam,
AJHS; Jews Given Permission to Establish Their Own Ceme-
tery, AJHS; Abigail Franks Laments Her Daughter's Marriage
to a Gentile, AJHS; Michael Gratz on his Departure for
America, HSP; Mordecai Sheftall Describes his Capture by
British Troops, AJHS; Description of a Jewish Wedding, AJA;
I Do Not Want to Bring Up My Children as Gentiles, AJA; The
Blessings of Living in the United States, AJHS; Establishing a
Fund for the Sick and Poor, Congregation Shearith Israel;
Will Religion Affect Admission to Harvard? Edwin Wolff 2nd;
Rebecca Gratz Writes to her Brother in Kentucky, AJHS; Social
Gaieties in Philadelphia, AJHS; The Benefits of White Sulphur
Springs, AJHS; Dedication of the New Synagogue for Mikveh
Israel in Philadelphia, AJHS; Ararat, A City of Refuge for
American Jews, AJHS; Philanthropy and Jewish Community
Life, AJHS; Introducing a Messenger from the Holy Land,
Congregation Mikveh Israel, Philadelphia; An Immigrant
Writes to Relatives in Germany, AJHS; Joining the "Gold Rush"
to California, Western States Jewish Historical Quarterly; A
Call to Action Concerning the Mortara Affair, AJHS; From
Otterberg, Bavaria to Talbotton, Georgia, from *The Auto-
biography of Isidor Straus*, reprinted with permission from
John W. Straus; Beginning a Business Career, from *The
Romance of a Mining Venture*, reprinted with permission from
William Friedlander; Reactions to General Grant's General
Orders No. 11, AJHS; A Lavish Jewish Wedding, AJHS; From
Vilna to New York, AJA; "I Married Wyatt Earp" by permission
from *I Married Wyatt Earp*, Glenn G. Boyer, Editor, Tuscon:
University of Arizona Press, Copyright 1976; "Straight to
Lafayette, Indiana," The Indiana Jewish Historical Society; A
Russian Immigrant's Odyssey, AJHS; "A Baptism of Fire" on The
Lower East Side, AJA; Idealism from Russia to America, from
The Education of Abraham Cahan reprinted with permission
from Leon Stein; How the New York Cloak Union Started,
Working in a Sweatshop, The Cloakmaker's Strike and Reac-
tion to the Triangle Fire, from *Out of the Sweatshop*, reprinted
with permission from Leon Stein; A Family's Fortune's Rise and
Fall, reprinted with permission from David Lyon Hurwitz; "The
South is a Very Good Place to Live," AJHS; The Galveston Plan,
AJHS; We Need a "First Class Dry Goods Store," AJHS; The
Lynching of Leo Frank, from *Louis Marshall: Champion of
Liberty* reprinted by permission from The Jewish Publication
Society of America; How to "Relieve the Tremendous Conges-
tion in the Seaboard Cities," from *Jacob H. Schiff: His Life and
Letters*, reprinted by permission of Doubleday & Company,
Inc.; "My First Big Deal" from *Baruch: His Own Story* by
Bernard M. Baruch, Copyright © 1957 by Bernard M. Baruch,
reprinted by permission of Holt, Rinehart and Winston, Pub-
lishers; Brandeis on The Protocol of Peace, from *Letters of
Louis D. Brandeis*, Volume II, edited by Melvin I. Urofsky and
David W. Levy, reprinted with permission from State Univer-
sity of New York Press; Woodrow Wilson on Admission to
Princeton, AJHS; Yiddish Theater from Hutchins Hapgood,
The Spirit of the Ghetto, reprinted by permission of Harper &
Row, Publishers, Inc.; Growing Up in Boston in the Twenties
and Thirties, from *In Search of History: A Personal Adventure*
by Theodore H. White, A Cornelia and Michael Bessie Book
Copyright © 1978 by Theodore H. White, reprinted by
permission of Harper & Row, Publishers, Inc.; The Early
Struggles of Hadassah, from *Henrietta Szold: Life and Letters*
by Marvin Lowenthal, copyright © 1942 by The Viking Press,
Inc., copyright renewed 1969 by Herman C. Emer and Harry
L. Shapiro, Executors of the Estate of Marvin Lowenthal,
reprinted by permission of Viking Penguin, Inc.; The Jewish
Heritage in America, from *A Dreamer's Journey* by Morris
Raphael Cohen, reprinted by permission of Macmillan,
copyright © 1948, renewed 1977 by The Free Press, a Division
of Macmillan Publishing Company; Early Days in Hollywood,
from *Minority Report* by Elmer Rice, © 1963 by Elmer Rice;
How the Columbia Broadcasting System Began, excerpt from
As It Happened by William S. Paley, copyright © 1979 by
William S. Paley, reprinted by permission of Doubleday &
Company, Inc.; American Art and Artists in the Early Thirties,

from *My Life* by William Zorach, reprinted by permission of
Tessim Zorach; What to Do About the Depression, from
Sidney Hillman: Labor Statesman by George Soule, copyright
© 1939, renewed 1967 by George Soule, reprinted by permis-
sion of Macmillan Publishing Company; Hitler's Challenge to
Civilization: Attack on World Jewry, AJHS; Is There a Jewish
Point of View? from *Ideas and Opinions* by Albert Einstein,
copyright © 1954 and renewed © 1982 by Crown Publishers,
Inc., used by permission of Crown Publishers, Inc.; Appeals
for Help, AJHS; From Vienna to Havana and Finally to New
York, included by permission of Dr. Adolph Mechner; Darius
Milhaud's Escape from France, from *Notes Without Music* by
Darius Milhaud, translated by Donald Evans and edited by
Rollo H. Myers, copyright 1952, 1953 by Alfred A. Knopf, Inc.
reprinted by permission of publisher; How "Refugees"
Adapted in Baltimore, AJHS; An American Soldier's Encoun-
ters in Europe, YIVO; Working With Roosevelt, from *Working
With Roosevelt* by Samuel Rosenman, copyright © 1952
by Harper & Row, Publishers, Inc., reprinted by permission of
Harper & Row, Publishers, Inc.; Growing Up Radical, from *The
Romance of American Communism* by Vivian Gornick,
copyright © 1977 by Vivian Gornick, reprinted by permission
of Basic Books, Inc., Publishers; Making It: From Brownsville to
Columbia, from *Making It* by Norman Podhoretz, copyright
© 1967 by Norman Podhoretz, reprinted by permission of
Harper & Row, Publishers, Inc.; The State of Israel and Its
Impact on American Jews, from the magazine article *Amer-
ican Zionism at an Impasse*, reprinted by permission of
Commentary and Arthur Hertberg Jewish Migration to the
Suburbs, from the magazine article *The Jewish Revival in
America*, reprinted by permission of *Commentary* and Nathan
Glazer; Becoming a Successful Writer, from *Advertisements
for Myself* by Norman Mailer, copyright © 1959 by Norman
Mailer, reprinted by permission of G.P. Putnam's Sons; Minding
the Store, from *Minding the Store: A Memoir* by Stanley
Marcus, copyright © 1974 by Stanley Marcus, reprinted by
permission of Little, Brown and Company; Journals of the
Sixties, from *Journals Early Fifties Early Sixties* by Allen
Ginsberg, copyright © 1977, reprinted by permission of Grove
Press, Inc.; Bodies of Three Civil Rights Workers Found, from
Three Lives for Mississippi by William Bradford Huie, © 1965
by I.H.T. Corporation, reprinted by permission; In the Light of
Israel's Victory, from a magazine article with the same title,
reprinted by permission of *Commentary* and Milton Himmelfarb; A Woman's Struggle for a Career in Science, from an
article by Ruth Weiner, permission granted by New York
Academy of Sciences; Louise Nevelson Talks About Herself,
from *Dawns and Dusks: Louise Nevelson*, by Diana MacKown
reprinted with the permission of Charles Scribner's Sons,
copyright © 1976 Diana McKown; The Children of Holocaust
Survivors, reprinted with permission from Abraham Peck;
Welcome to Jewish L.A., from a magazine article with the
same title, reprinted by permission of *Moment Magazine* and
Neil Reisner; A Recent Examination of American Jewish
Suburbia from *Jewish Identity on the Suburban Frontier:
Second Edition* by Marshall Sklare and Joseph Greenblum, ©
1967, 1979 by The American Jewish Committee, reprinted by
permission of The University of Chicago Press; Jewish Immi-
gration Today, from *Understanding American Jewry* edited by
Marshall Sklare, copyright © 1982 by Brandeis University,
published by permission of Transaction, Inc.; Rise of the Day
School Movement, from *The World of the Yeshiva: An Intimate
Portrait* by William Helmreich, copyright © 1981 by William
Helmreich, reprinted by permission of Macmillan Publishing
Company; Return to His Jewish Heritage, from *An Orphan in
History* by Paul Cowan, copyright © 1982 by Paul Cowan,
reprinted by permission of Doubleday & Company, Inc.

For explanation of Abbreviations used see page 328.

Dedicated to my family—

Abraham Schoener
(1865-1925)
Born in Vilna, Poland

Ida Lichtenstein Schoener
(1870-1942)
Born in Vilna, Poland

Aaron Finkelstein
(1843-1929)
Born in Eurburg, Lithuania

Toba Bloch Finkelstein
(1845-1924)
Born in Eurburg, Lithuania

Harry Schoener
(1892-1973)
Born in Vilna, Poland

Ida Finkelstein Schoener
(1895-1976)
Born in Port Clinton, Ohio

Allon Schoener
Born 1926 in Cleveland, Ohio

Mary Heimsath Schoener
Born 1929 in Cincinnati, Ohio

Abraham Schoener
Born 1961 in Cincinnati, Ohio

Rebecca Schoener
Born 1963 in Cincinnati, Ohio

Contents

Foreword

The Author with his Grandfather, Cleveland, 1929

While a student at Yale in the 1940's, I found myself drawn to New York on weekends visiting relatives and roaming the Lower East Side to savor the foods and investigate what remained of that historic Eastern European Jewish immigrant environment. My father was a Lower East Side boy. Around the turn of the century his family arrived in New York from Vilna where my grandfather had been a timber broker; in New York my grandfather worked in a sweatshop operated by his brother-in-law and developed a fatal case of tuberculosis. My father, as one of the army of "schleppers," the kids who carried garments from one sweatshop to another, was initiated into the clothing business which he pursued for the rest of his life. Following traditional patterns of upward mobility for Eastern European Jews, his family moved from the Lower East Side to Harlem and then to The Bronx. Seeking greater opportunities, my father went west to Cleveland where he established himself in the wholesale dry goods business.

My fondest recollections of childhood during the first three years of my life involve an intimate relationship with my mother's father who lived with us until his death at the age of eighty-six. He was the personification of the Eastern European shtetl Jew transferred to America. While in his late forties he brought his wife and seven children to Cleveland from a small town in Lithuania. When he landed in Baltimore, a relative was at the boat to meet him. In the old country my grandfather's name was Aaron Samovich; the cousin implored him to adopt an American name so he changed it to Finkelstein, his concept of a "real American name." From Baltimore he went to Northern Ohio where he began his career as a peddler with a pack on his back selling notions to farmers and small town residents. In Cleveland he graduated to a horse and wagon as a junk dealer touring neighborhoods where he feared mischievous children who would climb on his wagon to taunt him by pulling his beard. My grandfather Aaron was a living link with our Eastern European past. In our "second settlement" neighborhood on East 105th Street, he would push me around in my stroller to visit his cronies: the shoemaker with whom he shared lunch and the delicatessen owner who permitted us to sample delicious kosher pickels and rich black olives right from the barrel.

As a teenager I worked in my cousin's hardware store located on Woodland Avenue in the heart of what had been the "first settlement" Eastern European Jewish community in Cleveland. By the time I got there, all vestiges of Jewish life had disappeared and it had become a Black neighborhood. When my grandfather died, an important link with my past disappeared. My parents were members of the generation who wanted to become Americans and were willing to sacrifice some of their cultural heritage in the process. As a result,

Yiddish, which they could speak fluently, was used only with the older generation, never with their children. Given these experiences, my sense of Jewish history both in Eastern Europe and America was clearly truncated. This, I believe, is an experience that I share with many other American Jews of my generation as well as some who are both older and younger.

Coming directly from a "second settlement" Eastern European Jewish neighborhood in Cleveland to the Yale campus in New Haven, I was thrust into a citadel of the class-conscious White Anglo-Saxon world with which I had no previous experience. Although my fellow students made our cultural differences obvious, it was of critical importance for me to find the source of those differences. Why was I so different from people whose relatives had been in this country for hundreds of years and sent their sons to Andover and Exeter for generations? Since the Lower East Side embodied the last vestiges of my historical cultural consciousness, it was important for me to investigate the place where my father made his entry into American life. Could the Lower East Side have been my ancestral Exeter?

Without a traditional religious education, I am aware that I failed to be exposed to facets of the continuity of Jewish culture and history. As my visits to the Lower East Side filled a void in my immediate background, preparing this book decades later has brought me closer to a fuller comprehension of my Jewish heritage. It has provided me with the opportunity to undertake explorations into territories representing American Jewish life and history which emphasize intellectual pursuits, artistic creativity, moral values and philanthropy with which I have tried to identify, both consciously and unconsciously, throughout my entire life.

After completing graduate work in the history of art at Yale and the Courtauld Institute in London, I began my professional career at the San Francisco Museum of Art. Knowing that there was a long established Jewish community active as patrons of the arts, I felt more secure moving to this distant city. When I arrived in San Francisco in the 1950's, the most evident members of the Jewish community were the German Jews. Although my family had made periodic references to German Jews and I had encountered some at Yale, my contacts with them had been peripheral. Having grown up in a world of bagels, lox, pastrami and corned beef sandwiches at neighborhood delicatessens, I began to search for a familiar equivalent in San Francisco. There was none to be found; however, I did locate a kosher restaurant and was perplexed by its menu because it served unfamiliar dishes. Evidently this was a German Jewish restaurant with none of the spicey foods to which I had been accustomed. Through my work at the museum I came to know many of the German Jewish families who had been in San Francisco since the Gold Rush; they were established in department stores, banking, brokerage, law, medicine, clothing, textiles, coffee, tea and spices.

From San Francisco I continued my personal odyssey through American Jewish history when I moved to Cincinnati, another bastion of American Jewish heritage. During the last half of the 19th century Cincinnati was the leading German

Jewish community in this country. Descendants of these notable families whom I came to know as a result of my professional association with the Cincinnati Art Museum were among the principal partons of the arts. Their families were involved in traditional Jewish businesses: department stores, banking, clothing, textiles, brokerage, printing and meat packing. A considerable number were eminent physicians, surgeons, lawyers and university professors.

When I moved back to New York with my family in the 1960's, the Lower East Side, that eternal symbolic image, reentered my life. As a family we regularly went to Rappoport's, a restaurant on Second Avenue, for supper on Sunday evenings and shopped in the neighboring delicatessens. In 1966 I created an exhibition, *The Lower East Side: Portal to American Life,* for The Jewish Museum which gave me the opportunity to research systematically the lost world of the Lower East Side twenty years after my first explorations. The exhibition was a phenomenal success because it presented realities of an historical epoch of great significance to the Eastern European Jews who migrated to this country at the end of the 19th century and beginning of the 20th century.

The Holocaust obliterated all traces of ancestral Jewish life in Central and Eastern Europe. For American Jews—whether our descent is from Spanish and Portuguese Jews, German Jews or Eastern European Jews—there is little left in Europe with which many of us feel that we can identify. Perhaps our lineage does not carry us back to the first Jews who arrived in 1654 or those who followed subsequently in the 17th and 18th centuries, but our lives are established in this country and we are the beneficiaries of the efforts of our collective American Jewish ancestors. At this juncture in world Jewish history I believe that it is particularly important for American Jews to comprehend our continuity in this country.

Although my personal experiences had provided me with opportunities to understand some aspects of American Jewish history—"first settlement" Eastern European Jewish communities like the Lower East Side in New York and Woodland Avenue in Cleveland, "second settlement" communities like East 105th Street in Cleveland and the established German Jews of San Francisco and Cincinnati—I never had the opportunity to put all of the pieces together into a coherent whole. Having been trained as an art historian, I have learned to examine layers of cultural history in foreign cultures. This book has made it possible to apply those techniques to my own cultural history and assemble images and text which demonstrate the continuity of American Jewish life from the 17th century to the present day as it has not been seen before.

The principles of collage, a selective organization of fragments of reality into a new totality, have governed my organization of this book. Intentionally it does not read like a linear history, moving from one event to another. It is a portrait in which images dominate text. First I completed the picture research and organized thousands of photographs which I had located from all parts of the country into a series of logical categories that followed the patterns of American Jewish history. Then I searched for first person accounts which would provide

text complements to the images. One does not have to read this book from beginning to end; the reader can be selective in investigating those particular aspects of American Jewish life which are of most interest to him or her either in a sequential or non-sequential manner.

Although my intention has been to provide a comprehensive view of American Jewish life from the 17th century to the present day, I am certain that questions will be raised about inclusions and omissions. Why was one photograph included and another one neglected? Why was one person's account printed and another one's excluded? The images and text provided here do not offer an encyclopedic documentation; that was not my intention. Should Beth Hatefusoth (Museum of the Diaspora in Tel Aviv) complete its ambitions, perhaps it will have on file millions of photographs of American Jews. I prefer to describe this book as both a personal and intimate portrait of American Jewish life. In the sense that it is personal, this is my view; in the sense that it is intimate, I have sought as much as possible to locate images and text that give a sense of the immediacy of the situation. For that reason, I have avoided historical analyses and interpretations. I am more interested in how people have been portrayed by their contemporaries and what they have said as direct witnesses to history.

Having dedicated three years to the creation of a collective American Jewish family album, I offer here the culmination of my efforts. The investigations of archives across the country as well as securing precious family photographs have provided a bewildering variety of enriching experiences. The preparation of this book has been a joyous personal voyage of discovery. I want to share it with Jews and non-Jews alike with the hope that all of us can acquire a better understanding of each other.

Allon Schoener

Introduction

Henry Feingold, 1980

Jews are enjoined to record their history, to "remember the days of old." (Deutoronomy 32:7). It may well be that part of the secret of their mysterious millenial survival is their adherence to that wisdom. In the absence of normal safeguards of their cultural tradition, national sovereignty, an army, a distinct language, history becomes the guardian of the corporate memory of the Jewish people which is one key to their survival. Jews assign history an awesome responsibility because it sits astride the sacred obligation to "choose life," to survive.

This intimate portrait adheres to the injunction in Deutoronomy in a new and different way. Jews are a people drunk with language. But while it has served them well throughout their long history, it can render their past only incompletely. It is strictly limited to relating events sequentially when in actual life things happen together. That spatial aspect of history is rendered in this album by the use of photos combined with narrative and documents. The result is a composite historical portrait which brings up the fire still smoldering in the ashes of the past.

Withal the problem of a full rendering of the past is not solved since photos raise problems too. What do these eyes peering at us across four centuries have in common? Here there is a photo of an elderly couple, Florida snow birds, dancing as if to stave off the ravages of time; there a stiff, sober German-Jewish burgher in his office, here a newly rich Jew proudly displaying his worldly goods; a well-known sad-eyed physicist, discoverer of the theory of relativity, peers out at us; and there a heavily bearded Orthodox Jew, with eyes just like Einstein's, only he learns the rules of the universe from his rebbe whom he is convinced knows everything. Is it possible that such disparate types belong to the same people? What binds them together?

The answer cannot be gleaned by examining each picture individually and reading the narrative and document related to it. It lies in the single composite image rendered by the album. It actually describes a remarkable field of cultural energy to which they all belong. The passion and intensity discernible in so many of these pictures and letters is characteristic of a people, who after having their abundant energy suppressed for centuries behind thick ghetto walls, found in America a society based on the love of what is free and the welcome of what is new and different, which encouraged them to release those pent-up energies. American Jewry has done so in all areas of endeavor from new temple architecture to better forms of bookkeeping. This album shows that passion for life and living which Jews were able to fully heed only in America.

The fact that many of these pictures and documents relate to the immigration process which brought Jews to American shores was predictable since historical circumstance has compelled Jews to be a wandering people in order to survive. The modern immigrant is merely the ancient "wandering Jew" transmuted. The process of transplantation, of uprooting and rerooting, is perhaps the most central aspect of the millenial Jewish historic experience. The American Jewish community, like prior communities in the long flow of Jewish history, is the product of one such transplantation. From the Jewish historical perspective it is merely another diaspora community in a history full of diasporas. But it is also a vibrant sub-culture in a benevolent American society. It is in fact subject to and suspended between two historical streams, the original Jewish and the adopted American. It takes cues from both, delicately balancing the one against the other.

If immigration is a Jewish habit, the provincial lad of seventeen, soon to become an immigrant who had never been far away from home, did not know it. For him crossing an ocean to experience a strange new world was frightening and not to be undertaken for light and transient reasons. While it may on the surface have seemed to be voluntarily undertaken there was in fact a subtle coercion beneath, the absence of a reliable source of livelihood caused by the prohibition against Jews learning craft skills and the presence of a pervasive animosity which crushed all hope of living a normal life. There were then forces pushing the immigrant to leave his familiar world and forces pulling him to America, an idealized image of which had taken shape in the underclass of Europe. Letters sent back from those who had braved the unknown in former years did much to generate that image of America. It was so affirmative that good will towards this nation in Eastern and Western Europe persists despite strenuous propaganda efforts to undo it. Sometimes these letters were read in the local synagogue or club or published in the Jewish press so that their contents became widely known. They contained not only a hopeful picture of life in America but the necessary "how to" information to make the trip a reality, the price of the ship tickets, news of the employment situation, what the danger points were and where a friend who might help in case of trouble lived. For frightened people moving into the unknown such information was crucial. People of flesh and blood do not, as a rule, make basic life decisions on the basis of abstract reasons such as the desire for political freedom or religious liberty or the many ideological causes presented by historians as standard motivations for immigration. These reasons are present primarily as background factors. But for the immigrant to take the actual plunge there must also be present a modicum of security, an opportunity for a livelihood and a guide to see them through the process. The latter is very important. Most immigrants actually moved along the links in a chain of relatives and friends until they reached their final destination. He came to an uncle or cousin, who willingly or unwillingly, was compelled to serve as his host until the immigrant could "get on his feet." For the Jewish immigration process the existence of such a chain of relatives and friends acted, perhaps more than the actual dire circumstances of their lives, as an enabler. It made solution by immigration a practical possibility. The reason why a greater proportion of Jews immigrated during the 19th and 20th centuries was not only persecution and the quest for freedom but the fact that the dispersion of Jews in every known part of the world was in itself an accelerator of the immigration process. That was especially true of America where Jews were virtually "present at the creation." It gave American Jewry something rarely experienced in Jewish history, a sense of belonging. That sense of security first manifest during the colonial period, when the precedents for a pluralistic society were established, was carried forward to this day.

There were three separate Jewish waves of immigration to America, the Iberian (Sephardic) of the seventeenth and eighteenth centuries, the Central European primarily of the nineteenth century and the Eastern European immigration of the nineteenth and twentieth centuries. The reader will note that the organization of the first half of this volume is based on these three waves of immigration which serve as the accepted periodization of American Jewish history. Periodization is a technique used by historians to divide the historical canvas so that they can better focus, much the way a surgeon isolates the area of the operation from the remainder of the anatomy. The fact that American Jewish history, unlike general American history, prefers to anchor its periodization in the three waves of immigration informs us at a glance how central the immigration experience is to that history. It is also evidence of the connectedness of Jewish history since it was events occuring elsewhere on the Jewish historical stage which triggered the immigration which created the American Jewish community.

The paradox, from the historical perspective, is that while the individual Jewish immigrant who populated this country possessed courage and vitality and usually a strong Jewish identity the collective American Jewish community lacked strength of numbers and cultural cohesiveness. It required constant renewal from without. The Sephardic community would probably have been swallowed up by the majority culture had it not been for the timely arrival of German speaking Jews. They in turn would not long have been able to sustain a distinct Jewish culture without the impetus provided by the Jews of Eastern Europe. These 2.4 million Jews furnished a sufficient critical mass to assure immediate survival but they did not permanently solve the problem of sheer physical continuance. Jews have maintained the lowest birth rate in the nation, and today American Jewry is on the way to becoming again the inconspicuous minority it was in the Colonial period. This demographic diminution is the most ominous portent that American Jewry cannot take its survival for granted.

By 1920 American Jewry might have been described as a stew the recipe for which read: take three waves of immigration stemming from different national cultures and at different stages of historical development, place in a large American pot, mix well and allow to simmer for a century. We are now in the midpoint of that simmering process and it appears that the ingredients have blended well. But it was not always so. Throughout the first half of the twentieth century American Jewish life was marked by deep cultural and class conflict as well as political strife. It made the notion that there was such a thing as a unified community which shared common values and aspirations a dubious one. Except for a common adherence to Judaism, which they nevertheless approached differently, American Jews appeared to have little in common. Moreover the conflict among them tended to be exacerbated by the fact that the immigrants acted as cultural agents for the very nations that had rejected them. Although sometimes overstated, the conflict between the "uptown" Jews who stemmed from Central Europe and the later arrivals from Eastern Europe, the "downtown" Jews, was in some respects a replay of the familiar conflict between Teuton and Slav played out in a Jewish arena. Ironically in the American setting Jews gave ample evidence that they were loyal adherents to cultures which rejected them for not being good Germans or Slavs.

Each wave of immigration made a distinctive contribution to the Jewish enterprise in America. The early arrival of the Sephardic Jews has given American Jewry a sense of its legitimacy and since these Jews had a long historical experience of living in a devout Christian world they were able to pass on a skill in accommodation which contributed to the relative ease American Jewry feels in being at home in America. In their turn the German speaking Jews from Central Europe displayed a special talent for organization. It is largely to them that American Jewry owes its orginizational structure which is probably the most elaborate of any sub-culture in America. They also brought with them the Reform branch of Judaism which continued a survival strategy first conceived in Germany of adjusting the ancient Jewish religious culture so that it could better function in a free post-emancipation society. The Jews from Eastern Europe which may have been in the majority as early as 1870 finally gave American Jewry the numbers it required to generate a distinct culture. Perhaps even more important, it carried with it a prouder less conflicted approach to Jewishness as well as a more direct link to k'lal Yisrael, the sense of connectedness that binds Jews everywhere together in time rather than space. That sense of Jewish peoplehood, which today is the basis of Jewish ethnic identity, is most evident in the Conservative and Orthodox branches of Judaism. It is found in secular form in Zionism. It embodies the idea that being Jewish transcends the notion of being merely a religion or denomination, which was the position of the classical Reform movement. The sense of being part of a special Jewish community with its own culture which has survived for millenia means that totally secular Jews who do not adhere to the religious precepts of Judaism are still able to feel Jewish and belong to the Jewish people. It is largely through Zionism, or its peculiar American version which we might call Israelism, that this sense of belonging is transmitted to American Jews. It is the major plank in a new civil religion which today determines the way most American Jews come to terms with their Jewishness.

Each wave of immigration gave American Jewry its own distinctive gift. Yet American society observing Jews from the outside did not notice these differentiations. They viewed the Jewish community in its totality and they were able to do so because of the commonalities in Jewish culture. In all the various branches and factions which compose the Jewish enterprise there is a quest for transcendent purpose, a sense that living a worthwhile life requires more than concern only for the self. "If I am not for myself then who will be for me," states a well known Jewish proverb. "But if I am only for myself then what am I?" Despite the crucible of recent Jewish history which took the life of one out of every three Jews, Judaism continues to generate confidence in the inevitability of progress. The assumption that progress is possible may be naive considering Jewish experience but it has a practical aspect. It releases enormous energies and talents which might otherwise remain latent. For modern secular Jews it is transmuted to a sense of mastery and a drive for achievement in all fields of endeavor. It is that hope for better things which may account for the remarkable fact that American Jewry has produced a commercial elite in each of the periods we have mentioned.

Each of the three groups demonstrated in its own way an audacity in pioneering new areas of the economy. They were courageous enterprisers. The Sephardic Jews participated in risky ocean commerce when the economy was overwhelmingly rural and confined to local trade. They were also owners of "industrial secrets," craft and professional skills developed elsewhere, which in the New World permitted them to pioneer such industries as soap making, trading in precious stones, wigmaking and ultimately a new process for making candles with spermaceti oil, rather than the more expensive tallow. The Indian fur trade, the mainstay of the colony of New Amsterdam, had a goodly Jewish representation. Jewish peddlers were among the earliest to fill in the merchandizing vacuum that naturally developed between the large seacoast towns and the moving cutting edge of the frontier.

The established pattern of economic pioneering was sustained by the second wave of immigrants from Central Europe. The center of economic gravity for Jews continued to be merchandizing of all sorts. It began with peddling because of the relative ease that difficult trade allowed for capital formation and because one could take advantage of the internal credit network which had developed among Jews. In some rare cases there was movement from lowly peddler to department store owner in one, or more likely, two generations. German Jews were fortunate in the time of their arrival since the 19th century was a period of almost uninterrupted economic expansion. They demonstrated an unerring instinct for developing new areas of the economy, mining, shoe manufacturing, the export of wheat and beef, a fishing industry on the Great Lakes and of course importing special products, such as lace, from the old country. At the pinnacle of their remarkable success is the well known "Crowd" which has become the popular name for the second commercial elite generated by American Jewry. It was composed of the most successful members of the German Jewish migration who formed a self conscious group, welded together by common culture and background. At its core were those few families who successfully negotiated the move to commercial banking, the Seligmans, the Warburgs, Schiffs, Lehmans, Baches, Kuhns and others, some of whom made their fortunes in America and others whose families were in banking in Germany. Their

orientation to service and philanthropy can still be noted today by the frequency with which their largess is cited in the establishment of the great cultural institutions of America. The character of this "Crowd" can be easily misunderstood. Like all social sets, they produced some miscreants and milder trespassers of established social mores. But they were for the most part a sober, service-oriented patriciate who gave American Jewry a remarkably high quality of leadership. The fact that the "Crowd" became the subject of an overdramatized popularized account has contributed to an exaggeration of their wealth and concealed the fact that many German Jews were not commercially successful. Most considered themselves fortunate if they attained a standard of Victorian middle class comfort. The "Crowd" was actually the tip of an iceberg, an outward manifestation, that considerable capital formation had taken place in the Jewish community of both Europe and America. Such capital investment was entitled, and actually required, Jewish representation on the boards of directors of investment institutions. Had non-Jewish banking houses invited such representation Jewish banking houses might not have been established. When that representation did finally occur, Jewish banking houses virtually vanished as a distinct entity in American money markets.

The process of generating a commercial elite was repeated by the Eastern Jews who arrived in greater numbers after 1881. But the changed American economic scene combined with the distinctive character of these Jews gave a different, perhaps more interesting twist, to their success story. In business they continued to favor merchandizing but for the first time a sizable proportion of Jews became workers, predominantly, but not exclusively, in the garment industry. That development led in turn to the establishment of a separate Jewish labor movement, the only American sub-culture to do so on such a large scale. With the Jewish Labor Movement there also emerged a remarkable group of leaders and a farsighted social welfare program for the rank and file which became a model for the welfare state associated with the New Deal. The contribution of this "Crowd" is no less noteworthy.

Yet Eastern Jews became workers by circumstance rather than by choice and most sought a rise in station at the first opportunity. They made certain that their sons and daughters attained a formal education even while they passionately spoke of rising with their class. It was intended that the children should rise above it. Many were successful beyond their wildest imagination and certainly beyond prior Jewish immigrant groups. That was so because their hopes of mobility were not exclusively confined to a business conduit. By the second and third generation the descendants of the Eastern European immigrants were well into the process of professionalization especially in the field of medicine and law. Strangely enough it was this group which challenged the notion that merchandizing or business, customarily presented as evidence of a Jewish "levantine instinct," was somehow generic. After World War II a small group the descendants of the Eastern immigration successfully combined their professional skills with traditional experience and acumen in business. The result was a continuation of the entrepreneurial pattern already noted. They struck out for undeveloped areas of the industrial economy, and played a key role in pioneering in small industries such as air conditioning, plastics, audio equipment, consultant engineers, computer technology and many others. All required some professional skill in engineering, accounting, or communications and a willingness and insight to exploit the marketing opportunities. Many of these small businesses grew and some few earned fortunes, producing a new "Crowd" fondly called the Jewish "egghead millionaires."

The relation between America and its Jews has been singular. America has gained a highly active, energetic, achievement oriented group who demonstrates a high talent for mastering those skills required to make complex modern societies function. Jews in turn have finally found a society which encourages them to express the full spectrum of their abundant talents. They have done so and earned thereby the rewards this society holds out for such achievements; Jews rank near the top in per-capita income, formal education, job status, and health and longevity in America. In 1923 the noted sociologist Robert Parkes noted with admiration that Jews, more than any other group in America, act out the success ethos which serves as the driving force of American society. That appears to be even truer six decades later.

The many photos in this album of Jews in western garb, of farmers as well as merchants, is evidence that pioneering by American Jews was not only in business. Although less well known, the Jewish participation in the westward movement and the farming of the sod-house frontier, the ranching of the cattle kingdom and the mining of the mining frontier is interesting in its own right. There seem always to have been a trickle of Jews who tried their hand at farming. Effected by the agrarian fundamentalism which touted the nobility of contact with the soil, a Tolstoyan populist version of which had swept the Jewish Pale in Russia, the number of Jews who chose farming as their avocation increased in the last quarter of the nineteenth century. In America that renewed interest corresponded in time with the Populist movement which sought desperately to hold back the commercialization of agriculture so that the noble tradition of husbandry could be preserved.

The primary effects of the new Jewish interest in farming were felt in Palestine where Eastern Jews fused the Russian populist tradition to Zionism. The pioneering Zionism which resulted produced the *kibbutzim,* perhaps the most innovative attempt at planned social organization in the twentieth century. There were similar experiments in Russia, Argentina and America. Like the Kibbutz, these Jewish pioneers were as enthusiastic about experimenting with new forms of communal organization as they were about the possibility of being renewed and purified by contact with the soil. Jewish pioneers were thus radically different than their counterparts in America who took great pride in their individualism and self-reliance. Like the Mormons they preferred to do their pioneering as part of a communal unit armed with a transcendent purpose usually couched in mystical terms.

It is difficult to determine with any precision how many

American Jews were involved in farming at any one period. It probably never came to more than two thousand souls. Most farming experiments succumbed in less than half a decade. We have noted that the time Jews chose to become farmers was particularly inappropriate. It was at the historical juncture when the agricultural sector of the economy was contracting and changing its character into what such pioneers, influenced by a fundamentalist ideology, abhorred—a business venture whose raw material was soil. It would be the laws of the market, not those of Proudhon and Marx, which were most applicable to these ventures. They failed for other reasons as well. There was little in the Jewish historical experience to draw on for potential farmers. One literally started from cultural scratch. Moreover most of these utopian experiments were poorly planned and rigid anti-commercial ideologies which motivated their establishment made the adaptation to new conditions problematic. An untimely storm or a chronic shortage of women could be sufficient cause to dissolve a once promising settlement. A sprinkling of the survivors of these failed ventures undoubtedly remained in the vicinity but most probably drifted back to the cities from which they came.

Yet the ample number of place names of Jewish origin, the prominence of Jewish officials, judges, sheriffs, state senators in the history of the West, bear mute evidence of a considerable Jewish input to development of the West. They stem from Jews, many of them merchants, who struck out for the West, like so many other Americans, to seek their fortunes. Undoubtedly a small portion of these became farmers or ranchers or miners but most retained some link to the traditional Jewish avocation of merchandizing. In the end it was the traditional Jewish merchant pioneer who established a Jewish presence in the West. These small communities were in many cases supplemental and sustained by the Galveston movement which brought about 10,000 Jews to the West through the port of Galveston between 1901 and 1914. A massive attempt at social engineering by "uptown" stewards led by Jacob Schiff, was behind the Galveston plan. It was hoped that such a dispersion would relieve the congested ghettos of the Eastern seaboard cities where most immigrants preferred to settle. More important a diminishing of such Jewish aggregations would prevent the Old European culture from renewing itself and thereby hasten the acculturation process. That hastening of Americanization was the much desired objective of men who were concerned that Eastern Jews, by their very cultural distinctiveness, would raise questions about Jewish loyalty. In the end it was neither the ideologies associated with communalism nor the social engineering, motivated by fear of rejection, which brought Jews to the West, but opportunity and hope for improvement in their position. It is the same motivation which brings an increasing number of Jews and their religious congregations to the southwest today. An American, rather than an Americanizing motivation, proved to be the more powerful one in the long run.

One of the mysteries concerning American Jewry is the difficulty sociologists encounter in classifying it. American Jewry is an ethnic group but it is not only an ethnic group. The same is true if one classifies it as a religious denomination or a hyphenate group or even a racial group. None are satisfying because by themselves none are fully accurate. Jews fit into all these categories and none of them. It may well be that American Jewry simply cannot be neatly categorized. For simplicity's sake we refer to them as a sub-culture, but that hardly suggests all the elements that enter into Jewish group identify formation. Without some heed to the Judaism which lies at the heart of being Jewish, the religious component, it is virtually impossible to understand what American Jewry is. That is true despite the fact that most American Jews are avidly secular and have placed purely denominational matters on a low-flame back burner. The many photos we are shown of synagogues and temples, and the dozens of rabbis who lead Jewish congregations, give no hint of the turmoil within. The rich organizational structure of American Jewry is anchored in the religious congregation which reaches into every facet of Jewish life by dominating the primordial rituals concerned with birth, *rites de passage,* marriage and death, to which most Jews, no matter how secular, still adhere. The religious congregations are complemented by a network of philanthropic, fraternal, social service, defense, political and dozens of other kinds of organizations. One can only speculate as to why Jews have generated every kind of organization human flesh is heir to. Some have attributed it to the fact that, like all Americans, Jews are joiners. Not only did they establish their own organizations but they became disproportionately prominent in the organizations of other ethnic groups, especially the German-Americans during the 19th century, but also general organizations like the Citizens Union. Rabbi Isaac M. Wise, the founder of the Reform branch, thought that Jews were bored and formed organizations to safely vent the frustrations they could not freely articulate outside. In the 19th century most of the social and fraternal orders, with the exception of the Masons, did not welcome Jews in any case. That accounts for the establishment of B'nai B'rith in 1843 and a full panoply of duplicate Jewish organizations. Important too is the fact that the Jewish community assumes an exceptional number of obligations, especially regarding the welfare of their brethren abroad, which can only be discharged by organizations. Then too, Judaism departs slightly from Christianity in its corporate nature. Quorums are required for prayer and most religious ceremonies, and a critical mass is necessary to support certain religious requirements, ritual slaughter and bath, philanthropy and Jewish education. One cannot really be a fully observant Jew while living apart from other Jews; communalism is inherent in the religion. In recent times the growth of professionalism has in some cases given rise to separate organizations, such as those for Jewish lawyers or accountants.

It should not be assumed, however, that this organizational infrastructure is necessarily a sign of health or strength. The reverse may actually be the case. The diversity of Jewish organizational life is a reflection of the diversity of American Jewry itself. Each religious faction, each political ideology, every random grouping of Jews, requires its own organizational expression. As American Jewry becomes more uniform the need for separate organizations will also diminish.

A similar diversity exists within the Jewish religious scene where Judaism is divided into three branches. (If the Reconstructionist movement continues to flourish there may soon be a fourth.) They differ in the emphasis they choose to give to various aspects of a broad religious culture and in how they confront modern post-emancipation conditions. The emancipation process or transaction which held out the promise of granting complete civil and political rights for Jewish citizens of a modern secular state is really where any examination of this religious diversity has to begin. American Jewry is different from most other Jewish communities, outside Israel, in that its development occurred largely after emancipation within a society itself established and heavily influenced by the same principles of the Enlightenment. One can find in it no chief rabbi or hierarchical organization, nor is there sanction to compel individual congregations or congregants to adhere to temporal or for that matter divinely ordered laws and regulations. Congregations adhere to one of the three branches on a voluntary basis. Consequently American Judaism is essentially congregational. Power lies within the congregation, with the individual worshippers. Sometimes in such a situation it appears as if the interests of the laity take precedence over those of the deity. It is the trustees who manage the congregation so that a rabbi is not technically the counterpart of a minister or priest. There were two priestly tribes in ancient Israel but today ten adult Jewish males are all that is required to hold religious services. (An increasing number of congregations now accept females for a quorum.) A rabbi is most nearly the teacher of the congregation because ideally he is most learned in Judaica. If he has leadership ability he can exercise enormous power but he is never considered a mediator between the laity and God. In contemporary America his function is much more mundane. He performs the functions of a religious administrator and serves as the Jewish community's agent to the non-Jewish world.

The characteristic denominational diversity rather than uniformity is the surest sign that American Jewry lives in a free, post-emancipation society. Partly due to the secularization inherent in modern life, which weakens all churches, and partly because the diversity which follows in the wake of being free has made the religious enterprise appear uncertain and lacking in coherence, the synagogue is not as powerful as it once was. Like all modern people, Jews no longer take their behavioral cues from their religious leaders. But the synagogue remains and important fraternal and communal center crucial for the functioning of local Jewish communities. The religious sensibility once so prominent in the Jewish community has not disappeared but as with all modern people who cherish autonomy, it has been internalized. The modern secular Jew does for himself what the tribe used to do for him, from selecting his own profession to choosing his mate and his style of life. He is his own, often lonely, tribal chieftain. That marks a radical change for a group whose hallmarks were corporateness, communalism and piety.

Yet those who know American Jewry are aware that the passionate state of mind which has always characterized Judaism has not altogether vanished. In contemporary America it seems merely to have been transmuted to secular form. They are avid creators and consumers of secular culture but behind their remarkable political activism which amplifies their voice beyond the 2.6% of the population they compose, the concern for moral elevation persists. The disproportionate number of Jews who have gained prominence in all fields of endeavor are a tribute to the emphasis on study, learning and mastery inherent in the religious culture. Many of the qualities which make Judaism distinctive has been lost in the acculturation process, much has been subsumed beneath a bland and sometimes vulgar *embourgeouisement*. But much remains that is distinctive.

There are those who wonder whether there remains sufficient energy to retain a distinctive Jewishness in America. They want to know if American Jewry can somehow exempt itself from melding into a benevolently absorbent majority culture. The decline in proportion of the population is viewed with gravity. Survival of a culture requires numbers as well as carriers. We have noted that formerly it was immigration that made up the biological and cultural deficit. The restrictionist immigration policies which began in the 1920s partially blocked this infusion. They were strictly adhered to so that during the thirties and forties not even the certain knowledge that death was the alternative for those who would not find a haven in America could convince the American Congress to change its mind. Jewish children in Europe were not exempt from the quota provisions and were allowed to perish. Only in the year 1939 was the quota fully utilized. Immigration restriction thus dealt a double blow to the American Jewish enterprise. It helped destroy the population pool whose overflow traditionally supplemented the American Jewish deficit and created a gap in the Jewish demographic curve which cannot be filled. That does not mean that the demise of American Jewry because of a paucity of numbers is imminent, but a proportionate diminution, with all that implies, is already underway. Compared to the size of the Hispanic or Black community, American Jewry will be small and its voice therefore less audible.

It is from the context of the declining Jewish proportion of the population that the burgeoning intermarriage rate, perhaps as high as one of three, takes on special importance. Intermarriage represents something of a paradox for American Jewry. Throughout their experience in America they have fought tenaciously for full acceptance in American society. They have wanted, and largely achieved, all the good things, which American society promises. Little of importance remains in American society that is not fully accessible to them. They are in fact as fully accepted as they have wanted to be, and the intermarriage rate is in fact the most certain sign of that acceptance. Not only are Jews no longer the despised or radical "other" they once felt themselves to be, they have become positively desirable as mates. Yet survivalists feel that it is a type of success that may ultimately mean the failure of a distinct culture in America to survive. The numerical loss of Jews through intermarriage is negligible since Jews have been fairly successful in convincing their non-Jewish mates to convert, although the loss becomes somewhat more ominous when added to the low birthrate. But it is not the declining number which disturb Jewish survivalists but the decline in cultural distinctiveness. Intermarriage is at once a product of the loss of that distinctiveness and an accelerator of it. How much intermarriage can a sub-culture abide, queries the survivalist, before an irreversible cultural dilution sets in.

Nevertheless even amidst this gradual crisis there persists a hope for survival. That hope lies for many in the very multi-facetedness of the Jewish religious civilization which makes its proper classification so difficult. We see two poles in Judaism. A religious core which feeds into an ethnic identity we call Jewishness. That duality permits several alternate shifting models for being Jewish. Some derive its sense merely from eating a Jewish cuisine while others live their Jewishness twenty-four hours a day by adhering strictly to the myriad rules of Jewish law. The survival of Jews as a distinct people in modern times has been at least partly due to flexibility inherent in the model and the adaptability of the Jewish people itself. That adaptability includes a skill in balancing the requirements of living in a secular world, with its own values and demands, while retaining something of the preexisting religious civilization from which, we have seen, Jews also receive behavioral cues. In America the duality is particularly interesting because the majority society is itself partly a Hebraic culture. This ability to be nurtured by two related cultures while enriching both might be called "American Jewish exceptionalism." Nothing like it can be found among the other sub-cultures which dot the American social landscape.

In one sense American Jewry can be viewed as the latest manifestation of an ancient evolving religious civilization. Much of what makes American Jewry distinctive, its elevated ethical principles, its belief in the perfectability of man and the society in which he lives, are drawn from this preexisting/coexisting religious civilization. Its influence is felt everywhere in the Jewish enterprise and particularly in the sense of concern and kinship for Jews everywhere which binds Jews into being the people of Israel. It has had a profound impact on the way Jews acculturate and the terms of the transaction. No one can doubt that acculturation is occurring. There is no sub-culture which can avoid fully the siren song of a benevolent American society. But the terms American Jewry has chosen set it apart.

It is an apartness permitted, indeed welcomed, by a pluralistic American society which offers space for the development and expression of what is distinct. Yet the fear in all subcultures, not only the Jewish, that despite the largess of America, perhaps because of it, they will not be able to retain and transmit to future generations their sense of distinct pride. America, to be sure, does not demand total amalgamation but neither does it block the flow of its own powerful solvent which gradually overpowers and mutes the call of that other culture. The impact of that solvent is felt by American Jewry which anxiously searches through its long historical record to find an antidote. So far none has been found because there is no prior society which has dared to fully carry out the promise of emancipation as America has. It is a new leaf in Jewish history.

Henry Feingold
New York, April, 1983

Dutch Merchant Ships, 17th century: In 1654 twenty-three Jews from Brazil landed in New Amsterdam, establishing the first Jewish community
Credit: LC

in North America. In 1655 the Dutch West India Company decreed that Jews could remain over the protests of Governor Peter Stuyvesant.

A Few Among the First Settlers

Jewish history in North America dates back to 1654 when twenty-three Spanish and Portuguese Jews from Brazil landed in the Dutch colony of New Amsterdam. Since the fifteenth century, when the Spanish Inquisition led to their expulsion from Spain and Portugal, Iberian Jews had wandered throughout the Mediterranean basin, to Western Europe where Holland became a haven, and finally to South America where they found refuge in the Dutch colony of Recife, Brazil. Under the Dutch rule of Brazil they seized new economic opportunities there, but after the Portuguese conquest in 1654, when a provision of the peace treaty permitted them to leave, some returned to Holland, and the group of twenty-three arrived in the Dutch West India Company colony of New Amsterdam.

Soon after the immigrants arrived, they were met with a hostile reception by Peter Stuyvesant, governor of the colony, who petitioned the board of directors of the West India Company to "require them in a friendly way to depart; praying also most seriously . . . that the deceitful race . . . be not allowed further to infect and trouble this new colony." A counter petition raised by Portuguese Jews, who had arrived in Holland earlier and had become principal stockholders in the West India Company, compelled the directors to refuse Stuyvesant's request. The Jews were granted the right to "live and remain" in New Amsterdam.

Shortly thereafter, the embryo of what would become the largest Jewish community in the world was further granted the right to bury its dead in private cemeteries. After repeated petitioning, and in some cases, court actions, they later won the right to conduct trade, to hold property, to serve in the militia and to become citizens of the emerging republic.

Although the nature and size of the Jewish community has drastically changed since the Colonial and Revolutionary periods, the patterns established then still prevail. A look into the documents and illustrations of the times reveal a certain constancy as well as a uniqueness to the Jewish experience in America. Most of all we understand that this experience is but a part of the warp and woof of a rich fabric, a pluralistic ongoing process called the American experience.

Five Jewish communities existed during the Colonial Period: New York, Philadelphia, Charleston, Newport and Savannah. As the economy grew, Jews, with previous experience of commerce and shipping, joined the New American merchant class. Most successful were the families of the Lopezes, the Gomezes, the Hendrickses, the Seixases and Riveras who had family branches conveniently located in the principal trading centers along the Atlantic coast as well as across the ocean in other lands. Taking advantage of expanding commercial opportunities, they formed extensive trade networks based on these connections.

By this time there were approximately two thousand Jews in America, some were of Sephardic (Spanish and Portuguese) origin, others were Ashkenazim (Jews of Western, Central, and Eastern Europe) yet Sephardic religious conventions prevailed. The synagogue had become a focus of the community's activities, a place where its members met to discuss the community's needs, for example, how to care for its sick, poor and aged. In 1799 Congregation Shearith Israel in New York created a fund "to assist such poor or sick persons of our society as might be of want during the time our trustees should be absent from the city." They were continuing the tradition of tzedakah (acts of kindness) established long ago by their ancestors.

Jewish traders and land speculators helped to developed the frontier that lay West of the Alleghenies. In the 1740's for example, Joseph Simon opened up a general store in Lancaster, Pennsylvania. Trading with the Indians, he accepted land as payment for commodities and then supplied the settlers in the new territories with essential goods. In a letter written in 1769 to his brother Barnard, Michael Gratz, a member of a prominent Philadelphia family, speaks of some goods shipped by his family to the Illinois territory as "turning out to great advantage." Although there was a request for more goods, he was "not sorry that we did not send any more, as I am afraid of what we have there already, if an Indian war should happen. . . ." Although it

1654-1819

was only a few years before the Revolutionary War, there was scarcely a mention of any tension between the colony and England, only a reference to the repeal of the "difficult Acts" hints at the approaching imbroglio. Michael concluded his letter with a request for a lottery ticket participation "in one-half or a quarter in two tickets." In 1793 Jacob Myers placed an advertisement in the *Pittsburgh Gazette* offering passage on armed packet boats for anyone wishing to make the hazardous journey on the Ohio River from Pittsburgh to the wilds of Cincinnati. Declaring his "love of philanthropy and desire of being serviceable to the Public," Myers assures all prospective passengers that "No danger need be apprehended from the Enemy, as every person on board will be under cover, made proof against rifle or musket balls and convenient portholes to fire out of."

Several decades later, perhaps in a time of less danger, but nevertheless an age when distances were still of great consideration, Rebecca Gratz, a Philadelphian, exhorted her brother Benjamin to return from Lexington, Kentucky where he had gone to seek his fortune. Is it worth giving up "the society and habits of home" for the unknown of the "western wilds?" asks the concerned sister. She could accept this separation if only he would find a city where he could live in the manner to which he had become accustomed. But, she warned "the *ideal good* which of late has been so inticing to our young men of clearing land, building huts—cultivating soil with the sweat of their brows, and waiting till it should grow into a populous city and seeing themselves great proprietors of lots and the wealth of ages is too chimerical for realization, and I could not bear that you should waste the flower of your days . . ."

The Jewish population in America enjoyed greater freedom under the Constitution and Bill of Rights than anywhere else in the world. Gershom Mendes Seixas, the hazan (minister) of Congregation Shearith Israel in New York stated in 1798: "It hath pleased God to have established us in this country where we possess every advantage that other citizens of these states enjoy." At the same time they did not escape incidences of anti-Semitism. In 1800, for example, Benjamin Nones of Philadelphia responded eloquently in the *Gazette of the United States* to an anti-Semitic slur directed against him the week before by the printer of that journal. Nones, who had fought with Pulaski in defense of Charleston and served as an aide to both Lafayette and Washington proudly proclaimed that as a Jew he could be nothing else but a republican. "Kingly government was first conceded . . . [to] the Jewish people as a punishment and a curse, . . . and so it has been to every nation, who have been as foolishly tempted to submit to it. . . . In the monarchies of Europe, we are hunted from society—stigmatized as unworthy of common civility, thrust out as it were from the converse of men. . . . Among the nations of Europe, we are inhabitants everywhere—but Citizens no where, *unless in Republics.*"

Anti-Jewish sentiment was not always so blatantly displayed, sometimes it manifested itself in the pernicious policy of exclusion from higher educational institutions. In a letter to his sponsor William Meredith in 1815, a young Jew named Nathan Nathans anticipated rejection by Harvard. "I would wish to know," he writes, "whether it is your wish for Doctor Allen to prepare me, for the Cambridge college or the University at Phila as I think there will be some difficulty about my religion at Cambridge, as I think they are very strict."

It would take another one hundred and fifty years for the exclusionary policies toward Jews to disappear from American universities. By then the American Jewish community, whose embryonic seeds lay in the Colonial and Revolutionary past, had multiplied, flourished and changed its ethnic mix significantly. But its pride and sense of itself owes much to that small band of Spanish and Portuguese Jews who arrived on the shores of New Amsterdam more than three hundred years ago. It was then that the concept of separation of church and state was introduced, and also a time when a community which had previously been outside the public realm was given the responsibility of citizenship which they immediately and wholeheartedly accepted.

Peter Stuyvesant Wants Portuguese Jews to Leave New Amsterdam

September 22, 1654. Peter Stuyvesant, Governor of the West India Company's Colony of New Amsterdam, wrote to the Amsterdam Chamber complaining about the presence of Jewish refugees from Brazil who had recently arrived in New Amsterdam.

The Jews who have arrived would nearly all like to remain here, but learning that they (with their customary usury and deceitful trading with the Christians) were very repugnant to the inferior magistrates, as also to the people having the most affection for you; the Deaconry also fearing that owing to their present indigence they might become a charge in the coming winter, we have, for the benefit of this weak and newly developing place and the land in general, deemed it useful to require them in a friendly way to depart; praying also most seriously in this connection, for ourselves as also for the general community of your worships, that the deceitful race,—such hateful enemies and blasphemers of the name of Christ,—be not allowed further to infect and trouble this new colony, to the detraction of your worships and the dissatisfaction of your worships' most affectionate subjects.

Sugar Plantations, Brazil, 17th century: When the group of twenty-three Jewish settlers who landed in New York in 1654 left Brazil as a result of the Portuguese conquest of the Dutch colony there, they were compelled to abandon enterprises such as this which they had established. *Credit:* AJHS

A Dutch Priest Complains about the Jews

March 18, 1655. Reverend John Megalpolensis wrote to the governing body of the Dutch Reformed Church in Amsterdam describing the attitude of his congregation toward the Jews in New Amsterdam.

Now again in the spring some have come from Holland, and report that a great many of that lot would yet follow and then build here their synagogue. This causes among the congregation here a great deal of complaint and murmuring. These people have no other God than the unrighteous Mammon, and no other aim than to get possession of Christian property, and to win all other merchants by drawing all trade towards themselves. Therefore, we request your Reverences to obtain from the Lords Directors that these godless rascals, who are of no benefit to the country, but look at everything for their own profit, may be sent away from here. For, as we have here Papists, Mennonites and Lutherans among the Dutch; also many Puritans or Independents, and many Atheists and various other servants of Baal among the English under this Government, who conceal themselves under the name of Christians; it would create a still greater confusion, if the obstinate and immovable Jews came to settle here.

Amsterdam Jews Petition West India Company on Behalf of the Jews in New Netherlands

January 1655. Portuguese Jews who escaped the Inquisition arrived in Holland in 1593. Some of them were investors in the West India Company, and their petition, with its persuasive arguments, affected the final decision.

The merchants of the Portuguese Nation residing in this City respectfully remonstrate to your Honors that it has come to their knowledge that your Honors raise obstacles to the giving of permits or passports to the Portuguese Jews to travel and to go to reside in New Netherland, which if persisted in will result to the great disadvantage of the Jewish nation. It also can be of no advantage to the general Company but rather damaging.

There are many of the nation who have lost their possessions at Pernambuco and have arrived from there in great poverty, and part of them have been dispersed here and there. So that your petitioners had to expend large sums of money for their necessaries of life, and through lack of opportunity all cannot remain here to live. And as they cannot go to Spain or Portugal because of the Inquisition, a great part of the aforesaid people must in time be obliged to depart for other territories of their High Mightinesses the States-General and their Companies, in order there, through their labor and efforts, to be able to exist under the protection of the administrators of your Honorable Directors, observing and obeying your Honors' orders and commands.

It is well known to your Honors that the Jewish nation in Brazil have at all times been faithful and have striven to guard and maintain that place, risking for that purpose their possessions and their blood.

Yonder land is extensive and spacious. The more of loyal people that go to live there, the better it is in regard to the population of the country as in regard to the payment of various excises and taxes which may be imposed there, and in regard to the increase of trade, and also to the importation of all the necessaries that may be sent there.

Your Honors should also consider that the Honorable Lords, the Burgomasters of the City and the Honorable High Illustrious Mighty Lords, the States-General, have in political matters always protected and considered the Jewish nation as upon the same footing as all the inhabitants and

New Amsterdam about 1650: The Dutch West India Company colony on Manhattan Island was a small frontier settlement that served as an outpost for a trading empire. *Credit:* MCNY

burghers. Also it is conditioned in the treaty of perpetual peace with the King of Spain that the Jewish nation shall also enjoy the same liberty as all other inhabitants of these lands.

Your Honors should also please consider that many of the Jewish nation are principal shareholders in the Company. They having always striven their best for the Company, and many of their nation have lost immense and great capital in its shares and obligations.

The Company has by a general resolution consented that those who wish to populate the Colony shall enjoy certain districts of land gratis. Why should now certain subjects of the State not be allowed to travel thither and live there? The French consent that the Portuguese Jews may traffic and live in Martinique, Christopher and others of their territories, whither also some have gone from here, as your Honors know. The English also consent at the present time that the Portuguese and Jewish nation may go from London and settle at Barbados, whither also some have gone.

Permission Granted for Jews to Remain in New Amsterdam

April 26, 1655. This extract from the reply of the Amsterdam Chamber of the West India Company instructed Peter Stuyvesant to permit them to stay.

We would have liked to effectuate and fulfill your wishes and request that the new territories should no more be allowed to be infected by people of the Jewish nation, for we foresee therefrom the same difficulties which you fear, but after having further weighed and considered the matter, we observe that this would be somewhat unreasonable and unfair, especially because of the considerable loss sustained by this nation, with others, in the taking of Brazil, as also because of the large amount of capital which they still have invested in the shares of this company. Therefore after many deliberations we have finally decided and resolved to apostille upon a certain petition presented by said Portuguese Jews that these people may travel and trade to and in New Netherland and live and remain there, provided the poor among them shall not become a burden to the company or to the community, but be supported by their own nation. You will now govern yourself accordingly.

Jews Given Permission to Purchase Land for Their Own Cemetery

July 1655. Establishing a cemetery has always been a primary need for a Jewish community.

Abraham deLucena, Salvador Dandrada and Jacob Cohen, Jews, in the name of the others, petition the Honorable Director General this day to be permitted to purchase a burying place for their nation, which being reported to the meeting and voted on, it was agreed to give them the answer that inasmuch as they did not wish to bury their dead (of which as yet there was no need) in the common burying ground, there would be granted them when the need and occasion therefor arose, some place elsewhere of the free land belonging to the Company.

New Amsterdam, 1660: This map describes the character of the Dutch settlement which has left its imprint on New York City today. *Credit:* MCNY

New York City as seen from Long Island, 18th century: In 1750 the Jewish population of New York City was estimated to be 300 persons, or 2.3 percent of the total. Ashkenazim (Jews of Western, Central and Eastern Europe) became a majority of the New York Jewish community, even though Sephardic (Spanish and Portuguese) rituals were maintained. *Credit:* LC

Philadelphia, 1754: In 1737 Nathan Levy of the prominent New York merchant family arrived in Philadelphia to open a branch of the family business. In 1747 Mikveh Israel Synagogue was organized. This illustration is from *An East Prospect of the City of Philadelphia,* engraving after George Heap and Nicholas Scull. *Credit:* LC

Newport, 1795: In 1678 the recorded purchase of land for a cemetery was the first definite proof of the existence of a Jewish community. In 1763 the Touro Synagogue, designed by Peter Harrison, was dedicated. In 1774 the Jewish population of Newport was estimated to be 200 of a total population of 9,000. *Credit:* NYPL

Charles Town, 18th century: First Jew definitely known to have arrived in Charles Town, South Carolina, was recorded as serving as interpreter for governor. In 1749 the first congregation, Kahal Kadosh Beth Elohim, was organized. The Jewish population of Charles Town was about 200 in 1776. *Credit:* LC

Savannah, 1734: In July 1733 a group of 43 Jewish colonists arrived from England to join the colony established by James Oglethorpe. Later that year another group arrived bringing the total to about 70. In 1735 a congregation calling itself Mickve Israel was established. *Credit:* LC

The 18th Century Communities: During this period five separate Jewish communities were established along the Eastern seaboard in New York, Pennsylvania, Rhode Island, South Carolina and Georgia.

Bilhah Abigail Levy Franks, about 1740: Wife of Jacob Franks, mother of Naphtali and Phila Franks and daughter of Moses and Richea Asher Levy. *Credit:* AJHS

Jacob Franks, about 1740: Husband of Abigail Franks. One of the wealthiest merchants of New York City in his day. Served as parnas (president) of Congregation Shearith Israel. *Credit:* AJHS

David and Phila Franks, about 1735: Two of the nine children of Abigail and Jacob Franks. Phila shocked her parents by secretly marrying a gentile, Oliver Delancey. *Credit:* AJHS

Abigail Franks Laments Her Daughter's Marriage to a Gentile

June 7, 1743. In this letter to her son, Naphtali, living in London, Abigail Bilah Levy Franks described the disappointment she experienced when her daughter, Phila, married Oliver Delancey.

I am now retired from town and would from my self (if it where possiable to have some peace of mind) from the severe affliction I am under on the conduct of that unhappy girle [your sister Phila]. Good God, wath a shock it was when they acquainted me she had left the house and had bin married six months. I can hardly hold my pen whilst I am writting it. Itt's wath I never could have imagined, especialy affter wath I heard her soe often say, that noe consideration in life should ever induce her to disoblige such good parents.

I had heard the report of her goeing to be married to Oliver Delancey, but as such reports had offten bin off either off your sisters [Phila and Richa], I gave noe heed to it further than a generall caution of her conduct wich has allways bin unblemish'd, and is soe still in the eye of the Christians whoe allow she had disobliged us but has in noe way bin dishonorable, being married to a man of worth and charector.

My spirits was for some time soe depresst that it was a pain to me to speak or see any one. I have over come it soe far as not to make my concern soe conspicuous but I shall never have that serenity nor peace within I have soe happyly had hittherto. My house has bin my prisson ever since. I had not heart enough to goe near the street door. Its a pain to me to think off goeing again to town, and if your father's buissness would permit him to live out of it I never would goe near it again. I wish it was in my power to leave this part of the world, I would come away in the first man of war that went to London.

Oliver has sent many times to beg leave to see me, but I never would tho' now he sent word that he will come here [to Flatbush]. I dread seeing him and how to avoid I know noe way, neither if he comes can I use him rudly. I may make him some reproaches but I know my self soe well that I shall at last be civill, tho' I never will give him leave to come to my house in town, and as for his wife, I am determined I never will see nor lett none of the family goe near her.

He intends to write to you and my brother Isaac [Levy] to endeavour a reconciliation. I would have you answer his letter, if you don't hers, for I must be soe ingenious to conffess nature is very strong and it would give me a great concern if she should live unhappy, tho' its a concern she does not meritt . . .

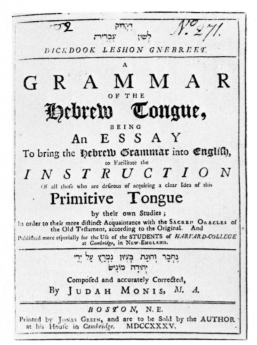

Hebrew Grammar, 1735: Title page of Hebrew Grammar by Judah Monis, published in 1735. In 1720 Judah Monis arrived in Boston and received a Master of Arts degree from Harvard. In 1722 he converted to Christianity and received an appointment as instructor in Hebrew at Harvard. *Credit:* AJHS

Circumcision Book of Barnard Itzhak Jacobs, about 1765: Barnard Itzhak Jacobs was born in Germany and was known to have been in Lancaster County, Pennsylvania, in 1757. In partnership with Isaac Levy he ran a general store. This page is from his circumcision book which records rituals that he performed as a *mohel* (person who circumcises male infants). *Credit:* CMIP

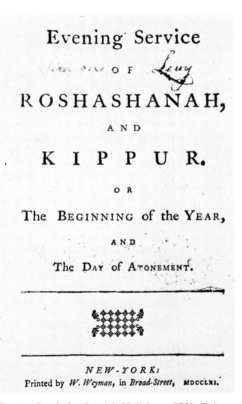

Prayer Book for Jewish Holidays, 1761: Title page of the first prayer book for Jewish holidays published in the American colonies. *Credit:* AJHS

Hechsher (rabbinical endorsement of food products), 1767: Michael Gratz of Philadelphia obtained this *hechsher* for shipment of kosher beef from Philadelphia to Barbados from Abraham I. Abrahams of Shearith Israel in New York, the nearest religious authority, in 1767. *Credit:* AJHS

מצבת

קבורת האשה הנכבדת מרת
רבקה בת יהודה זצ"ל שהלך
לעולמה עש"ק כ"ח אדר ראשון
שנת תקכ"ד לפק שניחייה סה
שנ'ים ו חדשים יח ימים

תנצב"ה

Rebecca, the Wife of
Zachariah Polock,
died March 2d. 1764,
Aged 65 Years
6 Mo. & 18 Days

Tombstone Rubbing, 1764: Rubbing made from the tombstone of Rebecca Polock of Newport, Rhode Island, who died on March 2, 1764.
Credit: Touro Synagogue

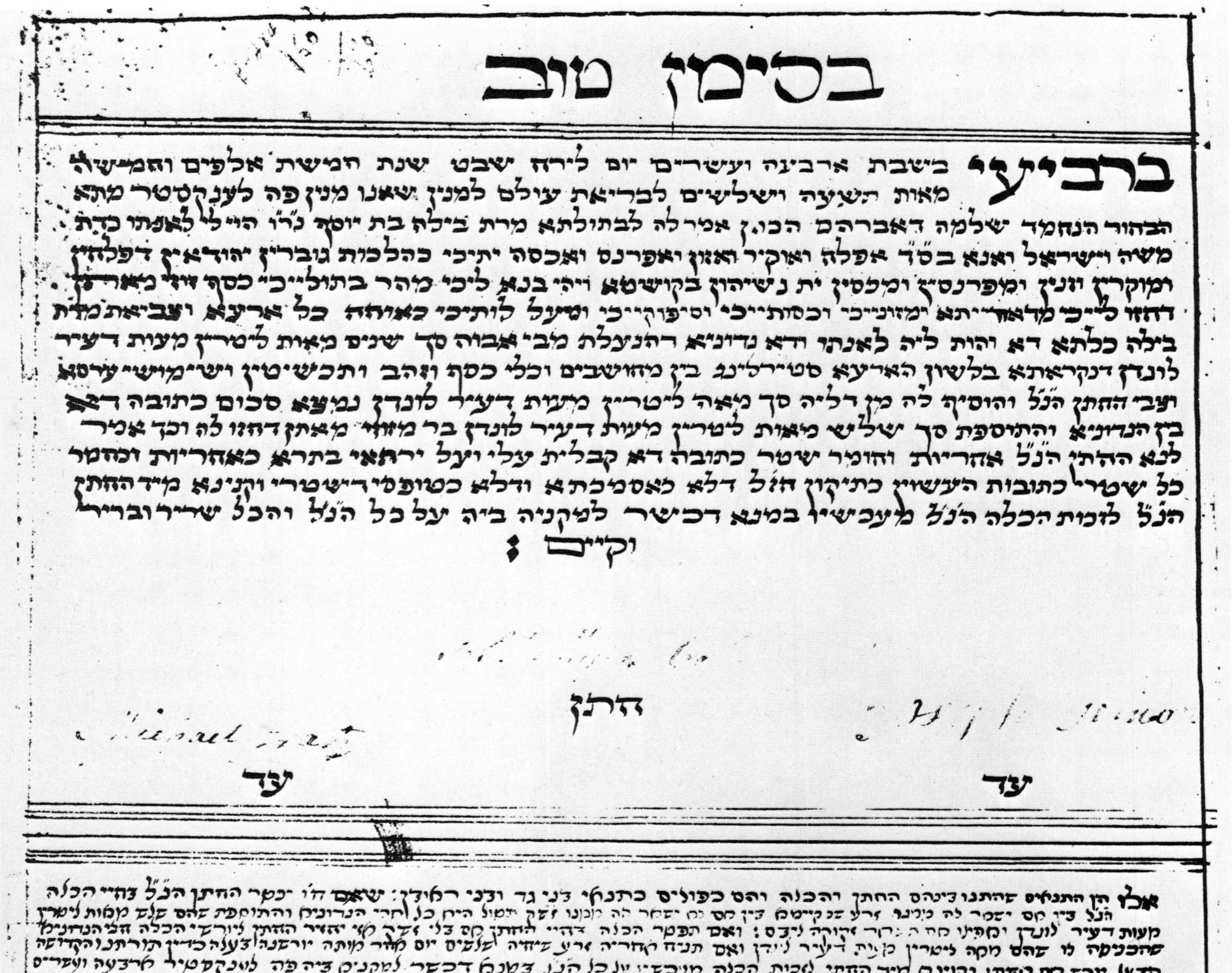

בסימן טוב

ברביעי בשבת ארבעה ועשרים יום לירח שבט שנת חמשת אלפים וחמשׁ׳ה
מאות התשעה ושלשים לבריאת עולם למנין שאנו מנין פה לענקסטר מתא
הבחור הנחמד שלמה דאברהם הכהן אמר לה לבתולתא מרת בילה בת יוסף נרו היי לי לאנתו כדת
משה וישראל ואנא בס״ד אפלח ואוקיר ואיזון ואפרנס ואכסה יתיכי כהלכות גוברין יהודאין דפלחין
ומוקרין וזנין ומפרנסין ומכסין ית נשׁיהון בקושׁטא ויהי בנא ליכי מהר בתוליכי כסף זוזי מאתן
דחזו ליכי מדאורייתא ומזוניכי וכסותיכי וסיפוקיכי ומעל לותיכי כאורחא כל ארעא וצביאת מרת
בילה כלתא דא והות לה לאנתו ודא נדוניא דהנעלת ליה מבי אבוה סך שנים מאות ליטרין מעות דעיר
לונדן דנקראתא בלשון הארעא סטירלינג בין מזומשבים וכלי כסף וזהב ותכשיטין ויש מׁושׁי עׁרסׁא
וצבי החתן הנ״ל והוסיף לה מן דיליה סך מאה ליטרין מעות דעיר לונדן נמצא סכום כתובה דא
בין תנדוניא והתוספת סך שלש מאות ליטרין מעות דעיר לונדן בר מזואי מאתן דחזו לה וכך אמר
לנא החתן הנ״ל אחריות והזמיר ישטר כתובה דא קבלית עלי ועל ירתאי בתראי כאחריות ומזמר
כל שטרי כתובות העשוין כתיקון חז״ל דלא לאסמכתא ודלא כטופסי דישטרי ותנינא מיד החתן
הנ״ל לכלת הכלה הנ״ל מעכשיו במנא דכשר למקניא ביה על כל הנ״ל והכל שריר ובריר
וקיים ؛

[signature]
חתן
[signature]

[signature Michael Gratz]
עד   עד

אלו תן התנאים שהתנו דינהס החתן והכלה והט כפולים כתנאי בני גד ובני ראובן שאם ה׳ יכפר החתן הנ״ל בחיי הכלה
הנ״ל דין מס ישמר לה מינגו ארע שכקיים בין מס בו ישאר לה מזונו וסך יטמול היק כל לחדו הנרונינ והתוספת שלם שלם ממות ליטרין
מעות דעיר לונדן ינחמיו מח ה גרור ויהיה לידבס ; ואם הפטר הכלה דהיי החתן קם צלי ירך שמי יזאיר הזמן לירשׂי הכלה חבי הנחנמל
שהכנפית מי שהם מקא מקה ליטרין סך הנ״ל דעיר ליידן דעיר ליידן ואם תנה אחריה ארע שׁיזיה שלשׂים יום מהר מותה יורשׂנה לשעלה בזדיין תרׁתני הׁקׁדיׁשה
חדען יורע קת ושׁתוׁ וקנינא סיד החתן הזדן לכית הכלה מעכשׁי על כל הנ״ל צמנא דכשׁר למקנין ביה פה למקׁטׁיר ארבעה ועד׳ים
יום לירח שבט שנ. התרקנ״ט שני ; והכל שריר ובריר וקיים ؛

[signature]
חתן
[signature]

[signature Michael Gratz]
עד   עד

Ketubah (marriage contract), 1779: This is the second oldest recorded *ketubah* in the United States. It is a document that accompanied the marriage of Solomon Myers-Cohen to Belah Simon and is dated February 10, 1779. It is signed by Solomon Myers-Cohen, Michael Gratz (brother-in-law of Belah) and Joseph Simon (father of the bride). *Credit:* AJHS

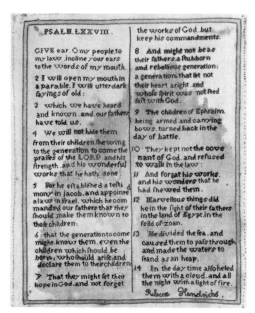

Sampler, about 1780: Embroidering samplers was a common practice for American women at this time. Rebecca Hendricks made this cross-stitched sampler of the Seventy-eighth Psalm. *Credit:* AJHS

Description of a Jewish Wedding

June 27, 1787. Dr. Benjamin Rush of Philadelphia wrote to his wife describing the marriage of Rachael Phillips to Michael Levy.

Being called a few days ago to attend in the family of Jonas Phillips, I was honored this morning with an invitation to attend the marriage of his daughter to a young man of the name of Levy from Virginia. I accepted the invitation with great pleasure, for you know I love to be in the way of adding to my stock of ideas upon all subjects.

At one o'clock the company, consisting of sixty or forty men, assembled in Mr. Phillips' common parlor, which was accommodated with benches for the purpose. The ceremony began with prayers in the Hebrew language, which were chaunted by an old rabbi and in which he was followed by the whole company. As I did not understand a word except now and then an Amen or Hallelujah, my attention was directed to the haste with which they covered their heads with their hats as soon as the prayers began, and to the freedom with which some of them conversed with each other during the whole time of this part of their worship. As soon as these prayers were ended, which took up about twenty minutes, a small piece of parchment was produced, written in Hebrew, which contained a deed of settlement and which the groom subscribed in the presence of four witnesses. In this deed he conveyed a part of his fortune to his bride, by which she was provided for after his death in case she survived him.

This ceremony was followed by the erection of a beautiful canopy composed of white and red silk in the middle of the floor. It was supported by four young men (by means of four poles), who put on white gloves for the purpose. As soon as this canopy was fixed, the bride, accompanied with her mother, sister, and a long train of female relations, came downstairs. Her face was covered with a veil which reached halfways down her body. She was handsome at all times, but the occasion and her dress rendered her in a peculiar manner a most lovely and affecting object. I gazed with delight upon her. Innocence, modesty, fear, respect, and devotion appeared all at once in her countenance. She was led by her two bridesmaids under the canopy. Two young men led the bridegroom after her and placed him, not by her side, but directly opposite to her. The priest now began again to chaunt an Hebrew prayer, in which he was followed by part of the company. After this he gave to the groom and bride a glass full of wine, from which they each sipped about a teaspoonful. Another prayer followed this act, after which he took a ring and directed the groom to place it upon the finger of his bride in the same manner as is practised in the marriage service of the Church of England.

This ceremony was followed by handing the wine to the father of the bride and then a second time to the bride and groom. The groom after sipping the wine took the glass in his hand and threw it upon a large pewter dish which was suddenly placed at his feet. Upon its breaking into a number of small pieces, there was a general shout of joy and a declaration that the ceremony was over. The groom now saluted his bride, and kisses and congratulations became general through the room. I asked the meaning, after the ceremony was over, of the canopy and of the drinking of the wine and breaking of the glass. I was told by one of the company that in Europe they generally marry in the open air, and that the canopy was introduced to defend the bride and groom from the action of the sun and from rain. Their mutually partaking of the same glass of wine was intended to denote the mutuality of their goods, and the breaking of the glass at the conclusion of the business was designed to teach them the brittleness and uncertainty of human life and the certainty of death, and thereby to temper and moderate their present joys.

Mr. Phillips pressed me to stay and dine with the company, but business . . . forbade it. I stayed, however, to eat some wedding cake and to drink a glass of wine with the guests. Upon going into one of the rooms upstairs to ask how Mrs. Phillips did, who had fainted downstairs under the pressure of the heat (for she was weak from a previous indisposition), I discovered the bride and groom supping a bowl of broth together. Mrs. Phillips apologized for them by telling me they had eaten nothing (agreeably to the custom prescribed by their religion) since the night before.

Upon my taking leave of the company, Mrs. Phillips put a large piece of cake into my pocket for you, which she begged I would present to you with her best compliments. She says you are an old New York acquaintance of hers.

During the whole of this new and curious scene my mind was not idle. I was carried back to the ancient world and was led to contemplate the passovers, the sacrifices, the jubilees, and other ceremonies of the Jewish Church. After this, I was led forward into futurity and anticipated the time foretold by the prophets when this once-beloved race of men shall again be restored to the divine favor and when they shall unite with Christians with one heart and one voice in celebrating the praises of a common and universal Saviour. . . .

Adieu. With love to your mama, sisters, and brothers, and to our dear children, I am your affectionate husband . . .

Family Genealogy, 1795: The family genealogy of Samuel Beals and Rebekah Wilkerson indicating that their last son, Isaac Nunis Cardozo Beals, was born in 1795 and that Samuel Beals died in the same year. *Credit:* Private Collection

Michael Gratz, about 1805: He was a member of the wealthy Philadelphia family. Born in Silesia, he later moved to London and finally to Philadelphia. Active in Jewish communal affairs, he served as president of Congregation Mikveh Israel. Portrait by Thomas Sully. *Credit:* AJHS

Michael Gratz on his Departure for America

1759. Michael Gratz, then living in London, wrote to his brothers, Hyman and Jonathan, in Silesia, before departing for Philadelphia.

Now, my dear brothers, I inform you that I have safely received your letters of the 21st of the month Shebat on the 29th of the Month Nisan, and I greatly rejoice to hear that you are in good health, for I have no greater pleasure than that. In the fulness of my heart, I cannot wish a greater, since I left and came here from India, and I hope we shall always hear good news ["joy"] from one another.

And, moreover, my dear brothers and sisters, I beseech you very much that you will not be selfish hereafter *about me*, and that you will pardon me because I am again going beyond the ocean,—to Philadelphia. I vow by my soul that everything I do is for the good of our family, even if it is not pleasant for me. I must learn the ways of the world and learn something of how things are done in the world. With what I now have, I cannot support a family in our country, and not in this country. But there I hope to get standing when I get there with peace [after the peace?]; and not only that, but I have already paid over my passage to the Captain, so that I must, with God's help, make the voyage, and this cannot now be altered.

But I assure you that if the Lord shall enlarge my limits, I will return to my country with the first opportunity, because I wish to visit the graves of my parents. I have always had it in mind to visit them, but now as it is a time of war, it will be better to put it off to some other time. And I beseech you again my brother,—may you live,—that you will pardon me because it is now impossible to do it. Had I received your letter six days earlier, we might be able to do otherwise, as also our cousin, the Honorable Reb Solomon [Solomon Henry] can inform you. But now it is too late and I hope everything will turn out for the best, with the help of God. Amen.

What you tell me of the engagement with Reb Joseph Tost,—if he could postpone it for some years,—is all right; but if he cannot, I think we must give it up Thanks to my lord, my brother, for his thoughtfulness and attention.

Accept my best wishes for my honored brother, with *my* love, on the betrothal of his son and daughter. I greatly rejoice in my heart. There is seldom such a good betrothal. I have no doubt that you, my brother,—may you be blessed,—will provide for everything.

And about our sister, Mistress Leah,—I cannot say anything about it when you inform me that you wish to betroth her to her cousin Feibel. I hope with God's blessing, if it takes place, that you, my brother, will see he can support himself and that he will not make the mistake of thinking he can depend on her brothers to provide a living for him and his wife. But should my brother find that he is manly ["good"] and able to support his wife in honor, then there will be no delay on the part of myself and our brother Barnard,—may he live,—in helping her with all she needs for her establishment, as far as we are able to do it. Also I beseech you to see that he shall remain a little longer in . . . (?) till he has become steady and got rid of his old foolishness and made up his mind seriously ["about a career"?]. I have never had him in mind. When we were in India, he was very miserable, but we can only smile at what is past forever. I hope that you now find yourself better, according to the letter of our brother,—may he live. That will rejoice me. And it is a pleasure to me to hear about our sister, Gitel,—may heaven bless her,—that she has her support, even if she has nothing to lay aside. I hope that in a little while everything will improve. The world was not made in a day.

I can inform you of our brother Barnard, that he will establish himself well in Philadelphia, for he is concerned with a great merchant of London, and he behaves himself well. He is honest and a good worker.

I heartily rejoice also, that our family, praise the Lord, are all in good circumstances, as I am told, and I hope that it will always be better in the future. My brother writes to me about a watch for himself. I turned the commission over to the kotzin, our cousin Solomon, and he will attend to it when he has the opportunity. I beg that you will pardon me for not writing more now. I am in a great hurry now, as I must prepare for the voyage.

Illinois Business "Turning Out to Great Advantage"

August 21, 1769. Michael Gratz in Philadelphia wrote to his brother, Barnard, in London, of his business venture beyond the Alleghenies.

A few days ago, I received a letter from Mr. William Murray, of the Illinois, who refers us to letters by Colonels . . . ., Mr. Burk and Mr. Morgan; but none of these have arrived here as yet. He relates in regard to the goods he had with him turning out to great advantage, and hopes we have sent the like goods by first batteaus on our joint account with him, or else we will be only the poorer for it. However, there is a little fear of an Indian war, by what letters I saw from Mr. Milligan. The Seneca Indians are much discontented on account of the purchase money that was given at the last treaty to the nether Indians, and their share not yet received *by* them, which makes them very insolent and daring, though it is thought they want nothing but presents and rob, if they can, *in the* mean time. So *I* am *in* no ways sorry that we did not send any more, as I am much afraid of what we have there already, if an Indian war should happen, though nothing is thought of one at present by the generality of people. Mr. Callender has sustained a loss of about 300 Pounds by the Black Boys, (The "Black Boys" were backwoodsmen painted like Indians, who treated goods for the Indians as contraband, if they included arms.) as they call them, stopping 24 horse loads of Indian goods on the road to Fort Pitt, a little this side of Bedford, where they pretended to burn the goods, but the chief was carried off by them, for which he will receive but little satisfaction, though he is after them. Mr. Croghan has wrote a letter to you, wherein he promises to be here in September or October, when perhaps he will want some goods. However, I shall be glad to see him here, whether he does or not.

Business at present is very dull, owing to the scarcity of money; none yet received from Mr. Callender, Mr. Hart, or St. Clair and Limes [? perhaps "Symmes"], all which injures our trade much and keeps my hands tied. Have called on Mr. Thomas Lawrence, but can get no satisfaction of him as yet. Mr. T. White says he has no occasion to pay Mr. Russell's share, as he settled his account and paid him without deducting your account, which he had not until you went away, and that he should not advance it; also 5 Pounds, which he paid and was not credited for. However, you should look over the account again and see. So I would have you speak to Mr. Russell, who went to London also in June, I think with Captain Falkner, when you may hear how it is and know what to *advise* on your return, please God, of which I should be glad to hear when it is to be and what success you meet with. Mr. Ae. Mackay wrote us also and wishes you a safe and satisfactory return; have wrote to him a few days ago; received last week a letter from Mr. M. Hays, who informs me that all the Holland bill will be paid, which I wish may be true; and should be glad to have you inform yourself about Mr. Jacob Polock and one Mr. Manley, of Newport, Rhode Island,—if they succeeded in bringing out large cargoes of dry goods.

I am informed since my last to you, that there is nothing done yet in regard to B., W. and Co. [Illinois?] Land affairs being confirmed, so that there can be nothing done in what I mentioned to you about Mr. Joseph Simon. However, I hope you will be able to settle *on* a good correspondent for a small cargo of Indian goods and the other articles of East India goods, which I am in hopes we will be able to make quick and good returns of, with the assistance of the great run and our friends. Especially when the goods are laid in on good terms, *I* think they cannot fail. And no doubt the difficult Acts will be on their repeal before you leave England; so that *I* would not omit bringing some goods, even if they *were* to be stored here for a little time till we have account of the repealing of those Acts . . . However, I would do nothing in case there is no prospect of the Acts being repealed, which you are to judge, as you are on the spot. I should be glad if you would get in with the Levy family and try if they would ship those East India nankeens, etc., as there we might do something profitable for them and ourselves too. I find there is a lottery this year; so *I* must desire you to concern me in a ticket *or in* one-half or a quarter in two tickets and send me them.

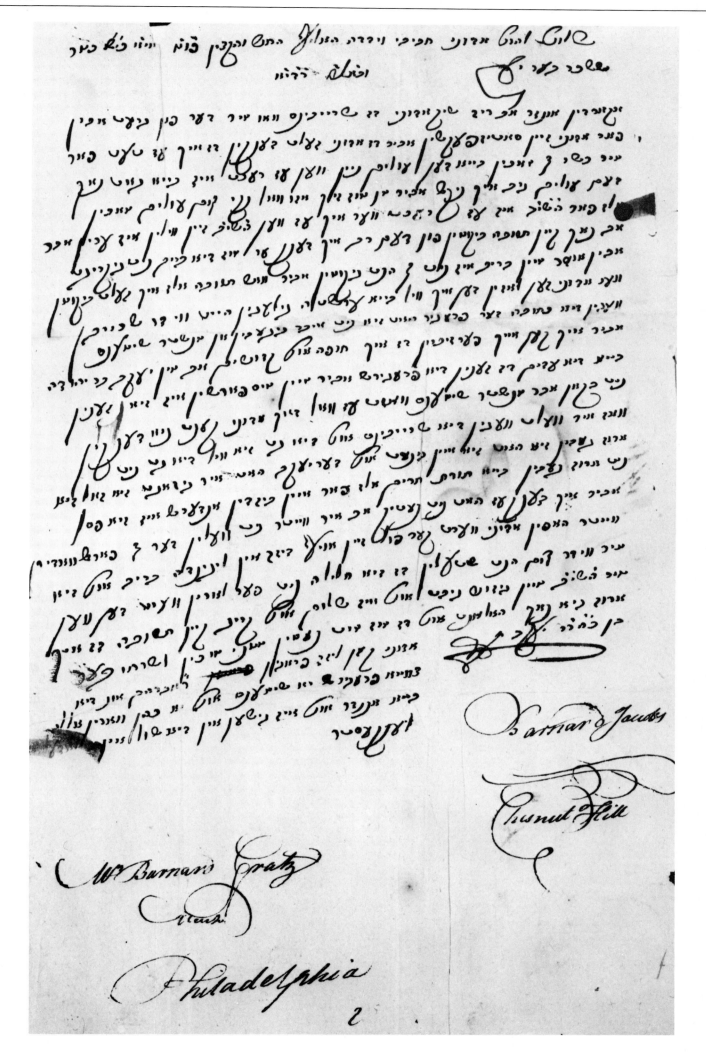

Yiddish Letter, 1768: Yiddish letter from Barnard Jacobs of Chestnut Hill, Pennsylvania to Barnard Gratz of Philadelphia. *Credit:* LCP

The least of the Disciples of JESUS, Ezra Stiles wisheth Satiety of Delights unto the illustrious and Venerable Hocham the great Rabbi Haijm Isaac Carigal; who daily & without ceasing lifteth up his Eyes unto the Things on high, and is enlightened with the Dew of Lights from Jehovah, and has been initiated into the secrets of understanding and sublime Knowledge, and perfected in the hidden Mystery of the סוד at the mouth of the Masters of the Law, and by the Tradition of the wise Men of all ages. Amidst the Darkness of the present ages, may the Lord shine upon thee, and lead thy going in the Path of Perfection; until thou shalt be laid up on high among the chosen Ones of Righteousness in the Crown of the Hosts which croud around the Throne of the Lord; and so be immersed in the mysterious סוד, to behold the Beauty of the Lord, and be swallowed up in the Splendor of his Glory. Amen.

Let the Thoughts & Meditations of my heart be acceptable upon the Messiah and the Greatness and Glory of his Kingdom. All kings shall bow down to him, and all Nations shall serve him. Ps. LXXII. 11.

Who is this great King of Glory? He is my Beloved and I am his. I will sing a Song unto my Beloved. How beautiful art thou, how pleasant for delights? But where is he to be found whom my soul loveth? shall we seek him among the Lilies, among the Souls and pure minds in the Garden of Eden? He is mighty and more exalted than the Multitude of the Princes of Hosts; and amidst the Ten Saphirots he hath reigned from Eternity, and shall reign over all the Sons of the Mighty the Aralim and the Hashmalim, and over all the holy Beings; and unto him all the superior Powers bow down with one accord all as one. Amen.

Letter of Ezra Stiles to Rabbi Haim Isaac Carigal, 1773: Ezra Stiles, a Christian minister in Newport who later became President of Yale College, wrote this letter on July 19, 1773, to Rabbi Haim Isaac Carigal of Hebron, Palestine, who was visiting the American colonies at that time. Stiles, like many Christians at this time, was enamoured of Hebrew and introduced Hebrew in the midst of his English letter. *Credit:* LCP

Rabbi Haim Isaac Carigal, undated: Religious leaders from the Holy Land often visited this country to collect funds for the Jewish communities in Palestine. Dr. Haim Isaac Carigal of Hebron delivered a sermon in Spanish in Newport, Rhode Island in 1773 which was later translated into English and published as the first Jewish sermon to appear in print in North America. Portrait by unknown artist. *Credit:* Mrs. Richard Prouty and Yale University Library

Colonel Isaac Franks, 1802: The son of Moses and Sarah Franks of New York, he served under George Washington in the Revolutionary War. Later he moved to Germantown, Pennsylvania. Portrait by Gilbert Stuart. *Credit:* PAFA

Mordecai Sheftall Describes his Capture by British Troops

December 29, 1778. Mordecai Sheftall, born in Savannah, Georgia, in 1735, was a successful merchant and outstanding civic leader who joined the Revolutionary Army. He described his capture and the fall of Savannah to the British.

This day the British troops, consisting of about three thousand five hundred men, including two battalions of Hessians, under the command of Lieutenant-Colonel Archibald Campbell, of the 71st regiment of Highlanders, landed early in the morning at Brewton Hill, two miles below the town of Savannah, where they met with very little opposition before they gained the height. At about three o'clock, P.M., they entered, and took possession of the town of Savannah, when I endeavoured, with my son Sheftall, to make our escape across Musgrove Creek, having first premised that an intrenchment had been thrown up there in order to cover a retreat, and upon seeing Colonel Samuel Elbert and Major James Habersham endeavour to make their escape that way; but on our arrival at the creek, after having sustained a very heavy fire of musketry from the light infantry under the command of Sir James Baird, during the time we were crossing the Common, without any injury to either of us, we found it high water; and my son, not knowing how to swim, and we, with about one hundred and eighty-six officers and privates, being caught, as it were, in a pen, and the Highlanders keeping up a constant fire on us, it was thought advisable to surrender ourselves prisoners, which we accordingly did, and which was no sooner done than the Highlanders plundered every one amongst us, except Major Low, myself and my son, who, being foremost, had an opportunity to surrender ourselves to the British officer, namely, Lieutenant Peter Campbell, who disarmed as we came into the yard formerly occupied by Mr. Moses Nunes. During this business, Sir James Baird was missing; but, on his coming into the yard, he mounted himself on the stepladder which was erected at the end of the house, and sounded his brass bugle-horn, which the Highlanders no sooner heard than they all got about him, when he addressed himself to them in Highland language, when they all dispersed, and finished plundering such of the officers and men as had been fortunate enough to escape their first search. This over, we were marched in files, guarded by the Highlanders and York Volunteers, who had come up before we were marched, when we were paraded before Mrs. Goffe's door, on the bay; where we saw the greatest part of the army drawn up.

From there, after some time, we were all marched through the town to the coursehouse, which was very much crowded, the greatest part of the officers they had taken being here collected, and indiscriminately put together. I had been here about two hours, when an officer, who I afterwards learned to be Major Crystie, called for me by name, and ordered me to follow him, which I did, with my blanket and shirt under my arm, my clothing and my son's, which were in my saddle-bags, having been taken from my horse, so that my wardrobe consisted of what I had on my back.

A Request for Gunpowder to Defend his Schooner

June 27, 1779. Isaac Moses, one of the leading Jewish merchants in New York, requested gunpowder from the Continental Congress for his ship.

To the Honorable the Congress of the United States of North America:

The petition of Isaac Moses, now of the city of Philadelphia, merchant, most humbly sheweth:

That your petitioner, having loaded a schooner, letter of marque, and fitted her with every necessary but gun powder, in a warlike manner, has made all the search in his power for that article, but finding himself every where dissappointed, is now under the dissagreeable necessity of troubling Your Honours, and to pray that you would be pleased to spare him, out of the public stores, two or three hundred weight of powder.

He flatters himself his principals as a true Whig and friend to the liberties of this country are so well known to some of your members, that it is needless to mention them here, or to remind your body of the assistance he has afforded these United States from time to time in the importation of divers articles which he spared them, but particularly when he and his partners spared these states upwards of twenty thousand dollars in specie, in exchange for Continental dollars, at the time the Canada expedition was on foot, and for which they received the thanks from or through your then president, the Honourable John Hancock, Esq.

Your petitioner submits to your honourable House to consider how unsafe it would be in him to risk his property at these times on the high seas without having proper means of defence with it, and pledges himself either immediately to pay for the powder, or to reemburse the public with an equal quantity of that article, and that either on the return of his vessel, or at the time that she ought to return.

Your petitioner therefore flatters himself your honourable House will be pleased on these considerations to grant him his request.

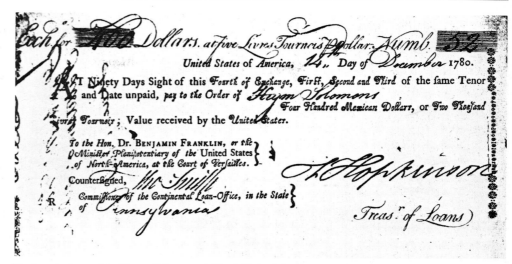

Bank note issued to Haym Salomon, 1780: A United States government bank note issued to Haym Salomon in the amount of 400 dollars. After emigrating from Lissa, Poland in 1752, he later established himself in New York. He aided the Revolutionary cause and was captured by the British. Escaping from confinement, he moved to Philadelphia where he assisted the Continentral Congress in borrowing money to finance the Revolution. *Credit:* AJHS

A Peddler Wins and Loses

1753. During the 18th, 19th and early 20th century, being a peddler in a rural area served as one of the first economic opportunities for immigrant Jews. This news item appeared in the Pennsylvania Gazette *of March 13, 1753.*

A Jew pedlar went into a house where he offered his goods for sale, but the good man being out, and all his family, except his wife, who told the pedlar that she could not buy any thing, for her husband had got the key of the money. The pedlar, then, finding that the woman was entirely alone, offered to make her a present of a piece of calicoe upon condition of her giving up her charms to him. The bait was very alluring, for the thoughts of sporting with a young man, and having a new gown in the bargain, made her readily yield to his desires.

He accordingly gave her the calicoe and, after taking a repast in the banquet of love, went about his business, but had not gone far before he met with her husband, and having some knowledge of him, said: "Sir, I have sold your wife a very cheap piece of calicoe, and on six months' credit." With that the poor man stood amazed, and said: "I wonder at my wife's ill conduct in running me in debt, when she knows that I have a considerable sum of money to pay in a few months' time, and can't tell how to make it up." He then persuaded the pedlar to go back and take his piece of calicoe, which he readily consented to, and, when they came to the house, he [the husband] ordered his wife to give the pedlar his calicoe again, which she did, after privately concealing a coal of fire in it.

The pedlar took the calicoe and put it up in his pack (which was a wallet slung across his shoulders) [and] so marched off, pleased with the thoughts of his success. But for his sweet meat he soon found sour sauce. He, not suspecting the cheat, jogged along till he met with a countryman, who, seeing his pack on fire (and which was then just ready to blaze), cryed: "Hay, friend, from whence came you?" *"From Hell,"* replied the pedlar. "So I perceive," says the countryman, "by the flames at your back." The pedlar then looked behind him, and to his great surprize found all his goods on fire, which made him stamp and rave like a mad man and curse his folly in cuckolding the poor man.

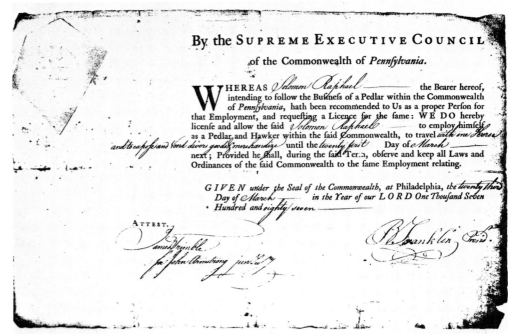

Peddler's License, 1787: License issued to Solomon Raphael "to follow the Business of a Pedlar within the Commonwealth of *Pennsylvania,*" signed by Benjamin Franklin. *Credit:* AJHS

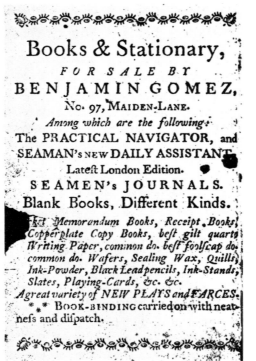

Advertisement for Benjamin Gomez, 1791: The first American Jewish bookseller and publisher opened his shop in New York in 1791. Benjamin Gomez was the descendant of a Spanish Jewish family that arrived in this country at the beginning of the 18th century. Like other members of his family who were successful New York merchants, he was an active member of Congregation Shearith Israel and served as both its treasurer and president. *Credit:* AJHS

Ship's Journal of Solomon Moses, 1798: Page for February 18, 1798 from Solomon Moses' journal as seaman aboard the Sansom with Madras and Calcutta, India as destinations. *Credit:* AJHS

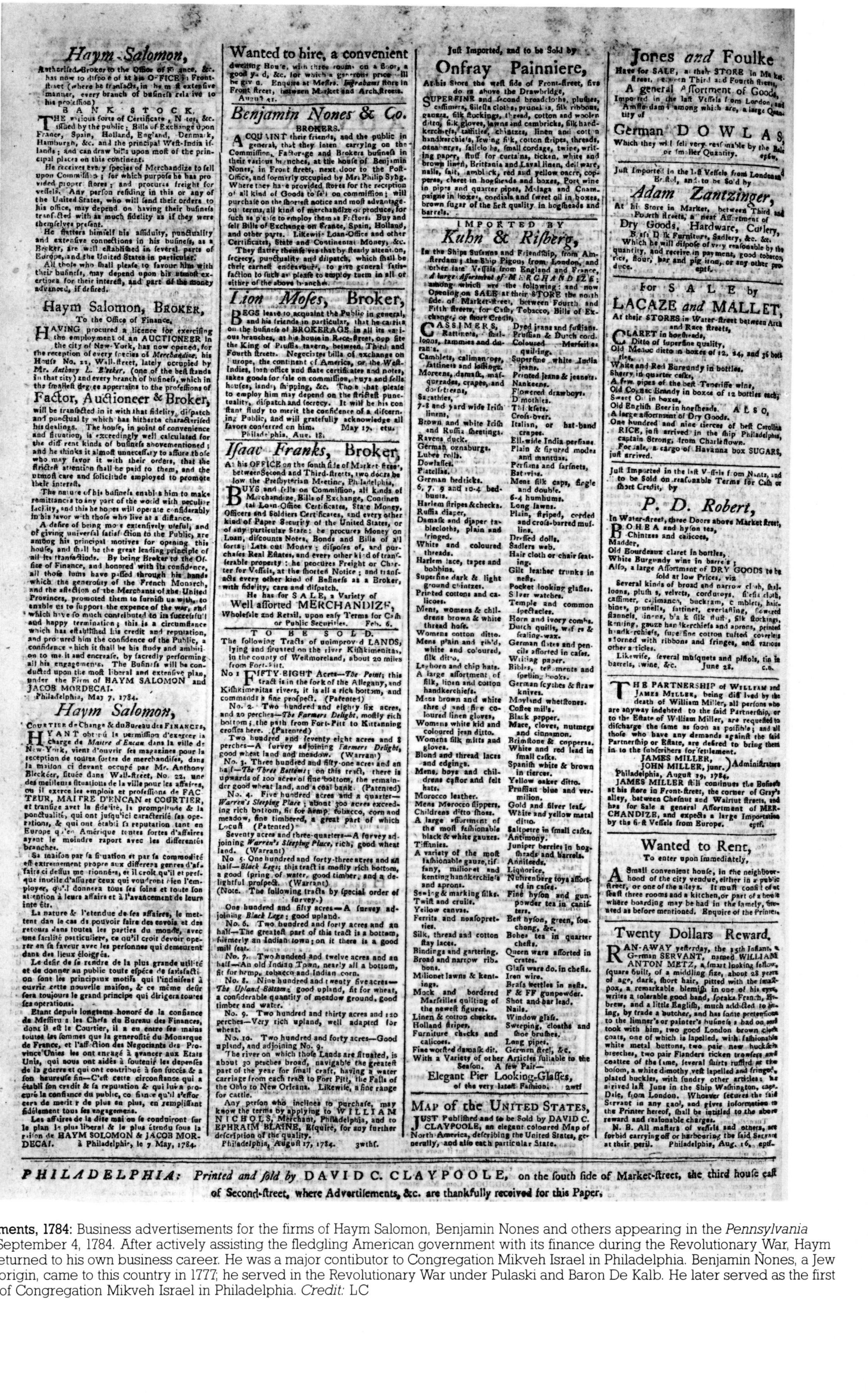

Haym Salomon,

Authorised Broker to the Office of Finance, &c. has now to dispose of at his OFFICE in Front-street (where he transacts, in the most extensive manner, every branch of business relative to his profession)

BANK STOCK,

THE various sorts of Certificates, Notes, &c. issued by the public; Bills of Exchange upon France, Spain, Holland, England, Denmark, Hamburgh, &c. and the principal West-India islands; and can draw bills upon most of the principal places on this continent.

He receives every species of Merchandize to sell upon Commission; for which purpose he has provided proper stores; and procures freight for vessels. Any person residing in this or any of the United States, who will send their orders to his office, may depend on having their business transacted with as much fidelity as if they were themselves present.

He flatters himself his assiduity, punctuality and extensive connections in his business, as a Broker, are well established in several parts of Europe, and the United States in particular.

All those who shall please to favour him with their business, may depend upon his utmost exertions for their interest, and part of the money advanced, if desired.

Haym Salomon, BROKER,

To the Office of Finance,

HAVING procured a licence for exercising the employment of an AUCTIONEER in the city of New-York, has now opened, for the reception of every species of Merchandize, his House No. 22, Wall-street, lately occupied by Mr. Anthony L. Bleeker, (one of the best stands in that city) and every branch of business, which in the smallest degree appertains to the professions of

Factor, Auctioneer & Broker,

will be transacted in it with that fidelity, dispatch and punctuality which has hitherto characterised his dealings. The house, in point of convenience and situation, is exceedingly well calculated for the different kinds of business abovementioned; and he thinks it almost unnecessary to assure those who may favor it with their orders, that the strictest attention shall be paid to them, and the utmost care and solicitude employed to promote their interest.

The nature of his business enables him to make remittances to any part of the world with peculiar facility, and this he hopes will operate considerably in his favor with those who live at a distance.

A desire of being more extensively useful, and of giving universal satisfaction to the Public, are among his principal motives for opening this house, and shall be the great leading principle of all its transactions. By being Broker to the Office of Finance, and honored with its confidence, all those sums have passed through his hands which the generosity of the French Monarch, and the affection of the Merchants of the United Provinces, promoted them to furnish us with, to enable us to support the expence of the war, and which have so much contributed to its successful and happy termination; this is a circumstance which has established his credit and reputation, and procured him the confidence of the Public, a confidence which it shall be his study and ambition to merit and encrease, by sacredly performing all his engagements. The Business will be conducted upon the most liberal and extensive plan, under the Firm of HAYM SALOMON and JACOB MORDECAI.

Philadelphia, May 7, 1784.

Haym Salomon,

COURTIER de Change & du Bureau des FINANCES,

HAYANT obtenu la permission d'exercer la charge de Maitre d'Encan dans la ville de New-York, vient d'ouvrir ses magazines pour la reception de toutes sortes de merchandises, dans la maison ci devant occupé par Mr. Anthony Bleeker, située dans Wall-street, No. 22, une des meilleurs situations de la ville pour les affaires, ou il exerce les emplois et professions de FACTEUR, MAITRE D'ENCAN et COURTIER, et tranfige avec la fidelité, la promptitude & la ponctualité, qui ont jusqu'ici caracterisé ses operations, & qui ont établi sa reputation tant en Europe qu'en Amérique toutes sortes d'affaires ayant le moindre raport avec les differentes branches.

Sa maison par sa situation et par sa commodité est extremement propre aux differens genres d'affaires ci dessus mentionnés, et il croit qu'il et presque inutile d'assurer ceux qui voudront s'en l'employer, qu'il donnera tous ses soins et toute son attention à leurs affaires et à l'avancement de leurs interêts.

La nature & l'etendue de ses affaires, le mettent dans le cas de pouvoir faire des envois et des retours dans toutes les parties du monde, avec une facilité particuliere, ce qu'il croit devoir operer en sa faveur avec les personnes qui demeurent dans des lieux éloignés.

Le desir de se rendre de la plus grande utilité et de donner au public toute espéce de satisfaction sont les principaux motifs qui l'induisent à ouvrir cette nouvelle maison, & ce même desir sera toujours le grand principe qui dirigera toutes ses operations.

Etant depuis longtems honoré de la confiance de Messieurs les Chefs du Bureau des Finances, dont il est le Courtier, il a eu entre ses mains toutes les sommes que la generosité du Monarque de France, et l'affection des Negociants des Provinces Unies les ont engagé à avancer aux Etats Unis, qui nous ont aidés à soutenir les depenses de la guerre et qui ont contribué à son succès & a son heureuse fin—C'est cette circonstance qui a établi son credit & sa reputation & qui lui a procuré la confiance du public, ce sera qu'il s'effor cera de merit r de plus en plus, en remplissant fidélement tous ses engagements.

Les affaires de la dite mai on se conduiront sur le plan le plus liberal & le plus étendu sous la raison de HAYM SOLOMON & JACOB MORDECAI. à Philadelphie, le 7 May, 1784.

Wanted to hire, a convenient

dwelling House, with three rooms on a floor, a good yard, &c. for which a generous price will be given. Enquire at Messrs. Ingraham store in Front street, between Market and Arch streets. August 21.

Benjamin Nones & Co.

BROKERS.

ACQUAINT their friends, and the public in general, that they intend carrying on the Commission, Factorage and Brokers business in their various branches, at the house of Benjamin Nones, in Front street, next door to the Post-Office, and formerly occupied by Mr. Philip Syng. Where they have provided stores for the reception of all kind of Goods to sell on commission; will purchase on the shortest notice and most advantageous terms, all kind of merchandize or produce, for such as please to employ them as Factors. Buy and sell Bills of Exchange on France, Spain, Holland, and other parts. Likewise Loan-Office and other Certificates, State and Continental Money, &c.

They flatter themselves that by steady attention, secrecy, punctuality and dispatch, which shall be their earnest endeavour, to give general satisfaction to such as please to employ them in all or either of the above branches.

Lion Moses, Broker,

BEGS leave to acquaint the Public in general, and his friends in particular, that he carries on the business of BROKERAGE in all its various branches, at his house in Race-street, opposite the King of Prussia tavern, between Third and Fourth streets. Negociates bills of exchange on Europe, the continent of America, or the West-Indies, loan office and state certificates and notes, takes goods for sale on commission, buys and sells houses, lands, shipping, &c. Those that please to employ him may depend on the strictest punctuality, dispatch and secrecy. It will be his constant study to merit the confidence of a discerning Public, and will gratefully acknowledge all favors conferred on him. May 17. etu.

Philadelphia, Aug. 18.

Isaac Franks, Broker,

At his OFFICE on the south side of Market street, between Second and Third streets, two doors below the Presbyterian Meeting, Philadelphia,

BUYS and sells on Commission, all kinds of Merchandize, Bills of Exchange, Continental Loan-Office Certificates, State Money, Officers and Soldiers Certificates, and every other kind of Paper Security of the United States, or of any particular State: he procures Money on Loan, discounts Notes, Bonds and Bills of all sorts; Lets out Money; disposes of, and purchases Real Estates, and every other kind of transferable property; he procures Freight or Charter for Vessels, at the shortest Notice; and transacts every other kind of Business as a Broker, with fidelity, care and dispatch.

He has for SALE, a Variety of Well assorted MERCHANDIZE, Wholesale and Retail, upon easy Terms for Cash or Public Securities. Feb. 6.

TO BE SOLD,

The following Tracts of unimproved LANDS, lying and situated on the river Kiskiminetas, in the county of Westmoreland, about 20 miles from Fort-Pitt.

No 1 FIFTY-EIGHT Acres—The Point; this tract is in the fork of the Allegany, and Kiskiminetas rivers, it is all a rich bottom, and commands a fine prospect. (Patented)

No. 2. Two hundred and eighty six acres, and 20 perches—The Farmers Delight, mostly rich bottom, the path from Fort-Pitt to Kittanning crosses here. (Patented)

Two hundred and seventy eight acres and 8 perches—A survey adjoining Farmers Delight, good wheat land and meadow. (Warrant)

No. 3. Three hundred and fifty-one acres and an half—The Three Bottoms; on this tract, there is upwards of 100 acres of fine bottom, the remainder good wheat land, and a coal bank. (Patented)

No. 4. Five hundred acres and a quarter—Warren's Sleeping Place; about 300 acres exceeding rich bottom, fit for hemp, tobacco, corn and meadow, fine timbered, a great part of which Locust (Patented)

Seventy acres and three-quarters—A survey adjoining Warren's Sleeping Place, rich, good wheat land. (Warrant)

No. 5. One hundred and forty-three acres and an half—Black Legs; this tract is mostly rich bottom, a good spring of water, good timber, and a delightful prospect. (Warrant)

(Note. The following tracts by special order of survey.)

One hundred and fifty acres—A survey adjoining Black Legs; good upland.

No. 6. Two hundred and forty acres and an half—The greatest part of this tract is a bottom, formerly an Indian town; on it there is a good mill seat.

No. 7. Two hundred and twelve acres and an half—An old Indian Town, nearly all a bottom, fit for hemp, tobacco and Indian corn.

No. 8. Nine hundred and twenty five acres—The Upland Bottom; good upland, fit for wheat, a considerable quantity of meadow ground, good timber and water.

No. 9. Two hundred and thirty acres and 120 perches—Very rich upland, well adapted for wheat.

No. 10. Two hundred and forty acres—Good upland, and adjoining No. 9.

The river on which those Lands are situated, is about 30 perches broad, navigable the greatest part of the year for small craft, having a water carriage from each tract to Fort Pitt, the Falls of the Ohio to New Orleans. Likewise, a fine range for cattle.

Any person who inclines to purchase, may know the terms by applying to WILLIAM NICHOLS, Merchant, Philadelphia, and to EPHRAIM BLAINE, Esquire, for any further description of the quality.

Philadelphia, August 17, 1784. 3wthf.

Just Imported, and to be Sold by

Onfray Painniere,

At his Store the west side of Front-street, five doors above the Drawbridge,

SUPERFINE and second broadcloths, plushes, cassimers, Silesia cloths, prunellas, silk ribbons, gauzes, silk stockings, thread, cotton and woolen ditto, silk gloves, lawns and cambricks, silk handkerchiefs, taffities, chintzes, linen and cotton handkerchiefs, sewing silk, cotton stripes, threads, osnaburgs, failcloths, small cordage, twine, writing paper, stuff for curtains, ticken, white and brown linen, Brittania and Laval linen, delf ware, nails, salt, lampblack, red and yellow oacre, copperas, claret in hogsheads and boxes, Port wine in pipes and quarter pipes, Malaga and Champaigne in boxes, cordials and sweet oil in boxes, brown sugar of the first quality in hogsheads and barrels.

IMPORTED BY

Kuhn & Risberg,

In the Ships Susanna and Friendship, from Amsterdam; the Ship Pigou from London, and other late Vessels from England and France,

A large Assortment of MERCHANDIZE;

among which are the following: and now Opening on SALE at their STORE the north side of Market-street, between Fourth and Fifth streets, for Cash, Tobacco, Bills of Exchange, or short Credit,

CASSIMERS, Rattinets, shalloons, tammies and durants,
Camblets, calimancoes, sattinets and lastings,
Moreens, damask, masquerades, crapes, and dorsteens,
Sagathies,
7-8 and yard wide Irish linens,
Brown and white Irish and Russia sheetings,
Ravens duck,
German oznaburgs,
Lubec rolls,
Dowlasses,
Platillas,
German hedricks,
6, 7, 9 and 10-4 bedtuns,
Harlem stripes & checks,
Russia diaper,
Damask and diaper tablecloths, plain and fringed,
White and coloured threads,
Harlem lace, tapes and bobbins,
Superfine dark & light ground chintzes,
Printed cottons and calicoes,
Mens, womens & childrens brown & white thread hose,
Womens cotton ditto,
Mens plain and rib'd, white and coloured, silk ditto,
Leghorn and chip hats,
A large assortment of silk, linen and cotton handkerchiefs,
Mens brown and white thread and fine coloured linen gloves,
Womens white kid and coloured jean ditto,
Womens silk mitts and gloves,
Blond and thread laces and edgings,
Mens, boys and childrens castor and felt hats,
Morocco leather,
Mens Morocco slippers,
Childrens ditto shoes,
A large assortment of the most fashionable black & white gauzes,
Tiffanies,
A variety of the most fashionable gauze, tiffany, milinet and kentinghandkerchiefs and aprons,
Sewing & marking silks,
Twist and cruils,
Yellow canvas,
Ferrits and nonsopretties,
Silk, thread and cotton stay laces,
Bindings and gartering,
Broad and narrow ribbons,
Milionet lawns & kentings,
Mock and bordered Marseilles quilting of the newest figures,
Linen & cotton checks,
Holland stripes,
Furniture checks and calicoes,
Fine worsted damask dit.
Dyed jeans and fustians,
Prussian & Dutch cord,
Coloured Marseilles quilting,
Superfine white India jeans,
Printed jeans & jeanets,
Nankeens,
Flowered drawboys,
Dimothies,
Ticklefets,
Cross-over,
Italian, or hat-band crapes,
Ell-wide India persians,
Plain & figured modes and mantuas,
Persians and sarsnets,
Batavias,
Mens silk caps, single and double,
6-4 humhums,
Long lawns,
Plain, striped, corded and cross-barred muslins,
Dressed dolls,
Sadlers web,
Hair cloth or chair seating,
Gilt leather trunks in nests,
Pocket looking glasses,
Silver watches,
Temple and common spectacles,
Horn and ivory combs,
Dutch quills, wafers & sealing-wax,
German slates and pencils assorted in cases,
Writing paper,
Bibles, testaments and spelling books,
German scythes & straw knives,
Moyland whetstones,
Coffee mills,
Black pepper,
Mace, cloves, nutmegs and cinnamon,
Brimstone & copperas,
White and red lead in small casks,
Spanish white & brown in tierces,
Yellow oaker ditto,
Prussian blue and vermilion,
Gold and silver leaf,
White and yellow metal ditto,
Saltpetre in small casks,
Antimony,
Juniper berries in hogsheads and barrels,
Anniseeds,
Liquorice,
Nuhrenberg toys assorted in cases,
Fine hyson and gunpowder tea in canisters,
Best hyson, green, souchong, &c.
Bohea tea in quarter chests,
Queen ware assorted in crates,
Glass ware do. in chests,
Iron wire,
Brass kettles in nests,
F & FF gunpowder,
Shot and bar lead,
Nails,
Window glass,
Sweeping, cloaths and shoe brushes,
Long pipes,
German steel, &c.

With a Variety of other Articles suitable to the Season. A few Pair—

Elegant Pier Looking-Glasses,

of the very latest Fashion. 2wtf

MAP of the UNITED STATES,

JUST Published and to be Sold by DAVID C. CLAYPOOLE, an elegant coloured Map of North America, describing the United States, generally, and also each particular State.

Jones and Foulke

Have for SALE, at their STORE in Market-street, between Third and Fourth streets,

A general Assortment of Goods,

Imported in the last Vessels from London, and Amsterdam; among which are, a large Quantity of

German DOWLAS,

Which they will sell very reasonable by the Bale or smaller Quantity. ep6w.

Just Imported in the last Vessels from London and Bristol, and to be Sold by

Adam Zantzinger,

At his Store in Market, between Third and Fourth streets, a neat Assortment of

Dry Goods, Hardware, Cutlery,

Brass Desk Furniture, Sadlery, &c. &c.

Which he will dispose of very reasonable by the quantity, and receive in payment, good tobacco, rice, flour, bar and pig iron, or any other produce. eptf.

For SALE by

LACAZE and MALLET,

At their STORES in Water-street between Arch and Race streets,

CLARET in hogsheads,
Ditto of superfine quality,
Old Medoc ditto in boxes of 12, 24, and 36 bottles,
White and Red Burgundy in bottles,
Sherry in quarter casks,
A few pipes of the best Teneriffe wine,
Old Cogniac Brandy in boxes of 12 bottles each;
Sweet Oil in boxes,
Old English Beer in hogsheads. ALSO,
A large assortment of Dry Goods.
One hundred and nine tierces of best Carolina RICE, just arrived in the ship Philadelphia, captain Strong, from Charlestown.
For sale, a cargo of Havanna box SUGARS, just arrived.

Just Imported in the last Vessels from Nantz, and to be Sold on reasonable Terms for Cash or short Credit, by

P. D. Robert,

In Water-street, three Doors above Market street,

BOHEA and hyson tea,
Chintzes and calicoes,
Madder,
Old Bourdeaux claret in bottles,
White Burgundy wine in barrels,
Also, a large Assortment of DRY GOODS to be sold at low Prices, viz.

Several kinds of broad and narrow cloth, shalloons, plush s, velvets, corduroys, fustian cloth, cassimer, calimanco, buckram, cambleis, hairbines, prunells, sattinet, everlasting, flowered flannels, linens, black silk stuff, silk stockings, kenting, gauze handkerchiefs and aprons, printed handkerchiefs, superfine cotton tufted coverlets adorned with ribbons and fringes, and various other articles.

Likewise, several musquets and pistols, tin in barrels, wine, &c. June 28. c.o.

THE PARTNERSHIP of WILLIAM and JAMES MILLER, being dissolved by the death of William Miller, all persons who are anyway indebted to the said Partnership, or to the Estate of William Miller, are requested to discharge the same as soon as possible; and all those who have any demands against the said Partnership or Estate, are desired to bring them in to the subscribers for settlement.

JAMES MILLER, JOHN MILLER, junr. Administrators

Philadelphia, August 19, 1784.

JAMES MILLER still continues the Business at his store in Front-street, the corner of Gray's alley, between Chesnut and Walnut streets, and has for Sale a general Assortment of MERCHANDIZE, and expects a large Importation by the first Vessels from Europe. eptf.

Wanted to Rent,

To enter upon immediately,

A Small convenient house, in the neighbourhood of the city vendue, either in a public street, or one of the alleys. It must consist of at least three rooms and a kitchen, or part of a house where boarding may be had in the family, situated as before mentioned. Enquire of the Printer.

Twenty Dollars Reward.

RAN-AWAY yesterday, the 15th Instant, a German SERVANT, named WILLIAM ANTON METZ, a smart looking fellow, square built, of a middling size, about 28 years of age, dark, short hair, pitted with the small-pox, a remarkable blemish in one of his eyes, writes a tolerable good hand, speaks French, Hebrew, and a little English, much addicted to lying, by trade a butcher, and has some pretensions to the limner's or painter's business, had on and took with him, two good London brown cloth coats, one of which is lapelled, with fashionable white metal buttons, two pair new buckskin breeches, two pair Flanders ticken trowsers and coattee of the same, several shirts ruffled at the bosom, a white dimothy vest lapelled and fringed, plated buckles, with sundry other articles. He arrived last June in the Ship Washington, captain Dale, from London. Whoever secures the said Servant in any gaol, and gives information to the Printer hereof, shall be intitled to the above reward and reasonable charges.

N. B. All masters of vessels and others, are forbid carrying off or harbouring the said Servant at their peril. Philadelphia, Aug. 16. eptf.

PHILADELPHIA: Printed and sold by DAVID C. CLAYPOOLE, on the south side of Market-street, the third house east of Second-street, where Advertisements, &c. are thankfully received for this Paper.

Advertisements, 1784: Business advertisements for the firms of Haym Salomon, Benjamin Nones and others appearing in the *Pennsylvania Packet* of September 4, 1784. After actively assisting the fledgling American government with its finance during the Revolutionary War, Haym Salomon returned to his own business career. He was a major contibutor to Congregation Mikveh Israel in Philadelphia. Benjamin Nones, a Jew of French origin, came to this country in 1777; he served in the Revolutionary War under Pulaski and Baron De Kalb. He later served as the first president of Congregation Mikveh Israel in Philadelphia. *Credit:* LC

Letter of Haym Salomon to a Relative, 1783:
This letter of July 10, 1783 was written to a relative planning to emigrate to the United States. Salomon suggests seriously considering the move to this country because the relative cannot expect him to provide a yearly allowance for his support. *Credit:* AJHS

I Do Not Want to Bring Up My Children as Gentiles

1791. Rebecca Samuels, living in Petersburg, Virginia, wrote to her parents in Germany describing the difficulties involved in maintaining Jewish traditions in rural America.

I hope my letter will ease your mind. You can now be reassured and send me one of the family to Charleston, South Carolina. This is the place to which, with God's help, we will go after Passover. The whole reason why we are leaving this place is because of [its lack of] Yehudishkeit [Jewishness].

Dear parents, I know quite well you will not want me to bring up my children like Gentiles. Here they cannot become anything else. Jewishness is pushed aside here. There are here [in Petersburg] ten or twelve Jews, and they are not worthy of being called Jews. We have a shohet here who goes to market and buys terefah [nonkosher] meat and then brings it home. On Rosh Ha-Shanah [New Year] and on Yom Kippur [the Day of Atonement] the people worshipped here without one sefer torah [Scroll of the Law], and not one of them wore the tallit [a large prayer shawl worn in the synagogue] or the arba kanfot [the small set of fringes worn on the body], except Hyman and my Sammy's godfather. The latter is an old man of sixty, a man from Holland. He has been in America for thirty years already, for twenty years he was in Charleston, and he has been living here for four years. He does not want to remain here any longer and will go with us to Charleston. In that place there is a blessed community of three hundred Jews.

You can believe me that I crave to see a synagogue to which I can go. The way we live now is no life at all. We do not know what the Sabbath and the holidays are. On the Sabbath all the Jewish shops are open, and they do business on that day as they do throughout the whole week. But ours we do not allow to open. With us there is still some Sabbath. You must believe me that in our house we all live as Jews as much as we can.

As for the Gentiles [?], we have nothing to complain about. For the sake of a livelihood we do not have to leave here. Nor do we have to leave because of debts. I believe ever since Hyman has grown up that he has not had it so good. You cannot know what a wonderful country this is for the common man. One can live here peacefully. Hyman made a clock that goes very accurately, just like the one in the Buchenstrasse in Hamburg. Now you can imagine what honors Hyman has been getting here. In all Virginia there is no clock [like this one], and Virginia is the greatest province in the whole of America, and America is the largest section of the world. Now you know what sort of a country this is. It is not too long since Virginia was discovered. It is a young country. And it is amazing to see the business they do in this little Petersburg. At times as many as a thousand

hogsheads of tobacco arrive at one time, and each hogshead contains 1,000 and sometimes 1,200 pounds of tobacco. The tobacco is shipped from here to the whole world.

When Judah [my brother?] comes here, he can become a watchmaker and a goldsmith, if he so desires. Here it is not like Germany where a watchmaker is not permitted to sell silverware. [The contrary is true in this country.] They do not know otherwise here. They expect a watchmaker to be a silversmith here. Hyman has more to do in making silverware than with watchmaking. He has a journeyman, a silversmith, a very good artisan, and he, Hyman, takes care of the watches. This work is well paid here, but in Charleston, it pays even better.

All the people who hear that we are leaving give us their blessings. They say that it is sinful that such blessed children should be brought up here in Petersburg. My children cannot learn anything here, nothing Jewish, nothing of general culture. My Schoene [my daughter], God bless her, is already three years old, I think it is time that she should learn something, and she has a good head to learn. I have taught her the bedtime prayers and grace after meals in just two lessons. I believe that no one among the Jews here can do as well as she. And my Sammy [born in 1790], God bless him, is already beginning to talk.

I could write more. However, I do not have any more paper.

Establishing a Fund for the Sick and Poor

1799. Following a long established Jewish tradition, members of Congregation Shearith Israel in New York, agreed to create a fund to help less fortunate members of the Jewish community. At this time the synagogue functioned as the center for most aspects of Jewish life.

Several members of the congregation (Shearith Israel in New York) being assembled in the *sucah* ["booth"] the hazan requested their attention to what he had to propose, which was nearly in the words following: That it had been suggested by some of our congregators to establish [a] fund abstractedly [apart] from the *sedaha* [treasury] to assist such poor or sick persons of our society as might be in want during the time our trustees should be absent from the city; and as the power vested in the *segan* [vice president] were very inadequate to any extraordinary matter, it would be necessary to appoint at least two members from the congregation [at large?] to be his associates in council, to superintend the direction of this institution; that the hazan had written to his brother Benjamin and had informed him of the problem[?], that he, Mr. Benjamin Seixas, had mentioned it to Mr. Moses, the parnas presidente of the congregation, who had written to the hazan; that he had no objection to such an institution being established, provided that the[re] should be but one offering only made to that fund;

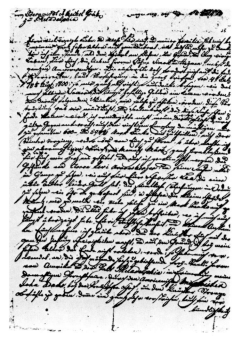

Letter to Jonas Bluch, 1801: Jonas Hirschel Bluch of Langendorff, Germany, wrote in German to his brothers-in-law, Barnard and Michael Gratz of Philadelphia. *Credit:* AJHS

and in order to commence a fund for that express purpose, he would give five pounds thereto; and that he had nominated Mr. Samuel Lazarus as a proper person to be joined in the direction, upon which Mr. Lazarus was nominated and approved of unanimously. Mr. Isaac Abrahams was then proposed for the other associate and was also approved of unanimously. Mr. Barnard Hart, the *segan*, having likewise approved of the institution, he desired the hazan to ask the members chosen if they would accept of their appointment. They having replied in the affirmative, the following conditions were discussed and agreed to unanimously *viva voice [voce]*.

Conditions made and entered into by the members of our congregation assembled this day (as before recited) to establish an institution for the assistance of the poor or sick of our society:

1st. That every person be allowed to make one single offering at any proper time in the synagogue to any amount, or for any particular appreciation.

2dly. That the gentlemen appointed to act in counsel with Mr. B. Hart, the *segan*, be a committee to appropriate any sum or sums of money of the fund to such purposes as they judge proper, without being accountable to the contributors for their expenditures, and [that] the said committee continue in office untill the trustees of our congregation return to the city and be enabled to form a quorum.

3dly. If the trustees, when assembled, do not approve of the institution and should deprive them of the liberty of offering in the synagogue, then the contributors should meet and determine by a majority of voices in what manner the residue of the money which shall then be in stock shall be disposed of.

4thly. That the committee meet by themselves and chose one of themselves to be their cashier, and any two of them be competent to determine in all cases, and any one of the three be allowed to dispend any sum not exceeding twenty shillings for any charitable purpose without being obliged to consult the other two, provided it be a case of emergency, and to draw on the cashier for that amount.

The whole of the preceeding was unanimously agreed to and G. Seixas offered his service to keep the account of offerings made to the fund and to collect the monies and pay such sums to the cashier, which was accepted of by the members.

Advertising Packet Boats from Pittsburgh to Cincinnati

October 14, 1793. Jacob Myers announced in the Pittsburgh Gazette *that he was offering passage on the Ohio River to Cincinnati.*

Two Boats for the present will set out from Pittsburgh for Cincinnati, and return to Pittsburgh in the following manner, viz:

First Boat will leave Pittsburgh on Monday next, the 21st inst., at eight o'clock in the morning, and return to Pittsburgh, so as to be ready to sail again in four weeks from the above date.

Second Boat will leave Pittsburgh on Monday, the 5th of November next, and return to Pittsburgh in four weeks as above.

And so on regularly, each boat performing the voyage to and from Pittsburgh once in every four weeks.

Two boats in addition to the above, will shortly be completed and regulated in such manner that one boat of the four will set out weekly from Pittsburgh to Cincinnati and return in like manner.

The Proprietor of these Boats having maturely considered the many inconveniences and dangers incident to the common method, hitherto adopted of navigating the Ohio, and being influenced by a love of philanthropy and desire of being serviceable to the Public, has taken great pains to render the accommodations on board the boats as agreeable and convenient as they could possibly be made.

No Danger need be apprehended from the Enemy, as every person on board will be under Cover, made proof against rifle or musket balls and convenient portholes to fire out of. Each of the Boats are armed with six pieces, carrying a pound ball; also a number of good musquets, amply supplied with necessary ammunition, strongly manned with choice hands, and the Masters of approved knowledge.

A separate cabin from that designed for the men is partitioned off in each boat for accommodating the Ladies on their passage. Conveniences are constructed in each boat so as to render landing unnecessary, as it might be at times attended with Danger.

Rules and regulations for maintaining Order on board and for the good management of the boats, and tables accurately calculated of the rates of freightage for passengers and carriage of letters to and from Pittsburgh to Cincinnati; also a table of the exact time of the arrival and departure to and from the different places on the Ohio, may be seen on board each boat. Passengers will be provided with provisions and liquors of all kinds of the first quality at the most reasonable rates possible. Persons desirous of working their passage will be admitted on finding themselves, subject, however, to the same order and directions from the Master of the boat as the rest of the working hands of the boat's crew.

An office of insurance will be kept at Pittsburgh, Limestone and Cincinnati, where persons desirous of having their property insured, may apply. The rates of insurance will be moderate.

For freight or passage, apply at the Insurance Office or to the Master on Board.

To the Hebrew Congregations in the Cities of Philadelphia, New York, Charleston and Richmond.

Gentlemen,

The liberality of sentiment towards each other, which marks every political and religious denomination of men in this country, stands unparalleled in the history of Nations. — The affection of such a people is a treasure beyond the reach of calculation; — and the repeated proofs which my fellow citizens have given of their attachment to me, and approbation of my doings, form the purest source of my temporal felicity. — The affectionate expressions of your address again excite my gratitude, and receive my warmest acknowledgment. —

The Power and Goodness of the Almighty were strongly manifested in the events of our late glorious revolution; and his kind interposition in our behalf has been no less visible in the establishment of our present equal Government. — In war he directed the Sword; and in peace he has ruled in our Councils. — My agency in both has been guided by the best intentions, and a sense of the duty which I owe my Country: — And as my exertions have hitherto been amply rewarded by the approbation of my fellow Citizens, I shall endeavour to deserve a continuance of it by my future conduct.

May the same temporal and eternal blessings which you implore for me, rest upon your Congregations. —

G. Washington

The Blessings of Living in the United States

1798. Gershom Mendes Seixas, the outstanding hazan (minister) of Congregation Shearith Israel in New York, spoke favorably of Jewish life in America.

It hath pleased God to have established us in this country where we possess every advantage that other citizens of these states enjoy, and which is as much as we could in reason expect in this captivity, for which let us humbly return thanks for his manifold mercies, and sincerely pray for a continuance of his divine protection: Let us not be deficient in acknowledging his power and his goodness, and with one heart supplicate him to promote the welfare of these states, the United States of America; to grant wisdom, knowledge and understanding to the rulers and administrators of the government, and enable them to persevere in the paths of rectitude, so as to procure peace and safety to the citizens, both in their persons and their properties; that every man may sit under his own vine and under his own fig-tree, when ye shall have beaten your swords into plough shares and your spears into pruning hooks.

The many marvellous deliverances that we have experienced since the time of our redemption from Egypt, are manifest evidences of our being under the providential care of the God of Israel; for "had it not been that the Lord was on our side," where should we have been now? Perhaps not in existence (as a peculiar people among all nations); for of all of the ancient nations that were famous in the world at the time of our being settled in our own land, there is none remaining but us, who I am confident are reserved to answer the particular purpose of infinite mercy. He it was who led our fathers through the Red Sea on dry land: He it was who fed them with manna in the wilderness for forty years: By his direction they were settled in the holy land: He it was that destroyed the enemies of our faith, and subdued those that rose up against us, and he it is who hath preserved us alive, even as at this day.

For all those benefits, what can we return but an humble acknowledgement of our dependence on him, and by a steady observance of his holy law, endeavor to retain his protection and mercy; for we know ourselves to be deficient in good works; but, as it is said in Jer. ch. 14, "Oh Lord, though our iniquities testify against us, do thou it for thy name's sake, for our back-slidings are many. We have sinned against thee," and again it is said in holy writ, "He who confesseth and forsaketh his sins shall have mercy."

Letter of President George Washington, 1790: Three letters of congratulations were sent by Jewish communities in the United States to President George Washington on his election. In response, he sent a letter to the Hebrew Congregations of Philadelphia, New York, Charleston and Richmond in 1790. *Credit:* CMIP

Letter to George Washington and His Response, 1790: When President Washington visited Newport, Rhode Island, local groups addressed letters to him and he responded. The letter from the Hebrew Congregation of Newport and his reply were printed in *The Providence Gazette and Country Journal* on September 18, 1790. *Credit:* LC

The Providence Gazette and Country Journal.

(Nº 38, of Vol. XXVII.) SATURDAY, *September* 18, 1790. (Nº 1394.)

Publiſhed by *JOHN CARTER*, at the Poſt-Office, near the State-Houſe.

The following ADDRESSES *were preſented to the* PRESIDENT *of the* UNITED STATES, *at* NEWPORT.

ADDRESS *from the* CITIZENS *of* NEWPORT.
To the PRESIDENT *of the* UNITED STATES *of* AMERICA.

SIR,

IMPRESSED with the livelieſt ſentiments of gratitude and affection, the citizens of Newport ſalute you on your arrival in this State, and wiſh to expreſs their joy on this intereſting occaſion.

The preſent circumſtances of this town forbid ſome of thoſe demonſtrations of gratitude and reſpect, which the citizens of our ſiſter States have diſplayed on a ſimilar occaſion; yet we rejoice in this opportunity of tendering the richeſt offering which a free people can make—hearts ſincerely devoted to you, and to the government over which you preſide.

We anticipate with pleaſing expectation the happy period, when, under the auſpicious government of the United States, our languiſhing commerce ſhall revive, and our loſſes be repaired—when commerce at large ſhall expand her wings in every quarter of the globe, and arts, manufactures and agriculture, be carried to the higheſt pitch of improvement.

May kind Providence long continue your invaluable life; and in the progreſſive advancement of the United States in opulence, order and felicity, may you realize the moſt glorious proſpect which humanity can exhibit to an enlightened and benevolent legiſlator; and when you ſhall ceaſe to be mortal, may you be aſſociated to the moſt perfect ſociety in the realms above, and receive that retribution for your diſintereſted and extenſive ſervices, which the JUDGE of all the earth will beſtow on the friends of piety, virtue and mankind.

By Order,
H. MARCHANT, Moderator.

The ANSWER.
To the FREEMEN *of the Town of* NEWPORT.

GENTLEMEN,

I RECEIVE with emotions of ſatisfaction the kind addreſs of the citizens of Newport on my arrival in this State.

Although I am not ignorant how much the worthy inhabitants of this town have been injured in their circumſtances, by their patriotic ſufferings and ſervices; yet I muſt be allowed to ſay, that nothing on their part has been wanting to convince me of their affection to myſelf, and attachment to the government over which I am appointed to preſide.

I requeſt, Gentlemen, you will be perſuaded that I take a due intereſt in your particular ſituation; and that I join with you in anticipating the happy period, when, in our country at large, commerce, arts, manufactures and agriculture, ſhall attain the higheſt degree of improvement.

My expreſſions would but faintly communicate my feelings, ſhould I enlarge beyond the proper limits of an anſwer to your addreſs, in evincing my ſenſibility of your affectionate wiſhes for my felicity in the preſent and future ſtate of exiſtence.—It will be a better proof of my zeal for the proſperity of the inhabitants of this town, and their fellow-citizens of this State, to loſe no opportunity of attending to the advancement of their intereſts, in combination with the general welfare of the community.—This I ſhall do with unfeigned ſatisfaction.—And may all the happineſs be theirs, which can reſult, in their ſocial character, from the uniform practice of induſtry, virtue, fraternal kindneſs, and univerſal philanthropy.

G. WASHINGTON.

ADDRESS *from the* CLERGY.
To GEORGE WASHINGTON, PRESIDENT *of the United States of America.*

SIR,

WITH ſalutations of the moſt cordial eſteem and regard, permit us, the Clergy of Newport, to approach your perſon, intreating your acceptance of our voice, in conjunction with that of our fellow-citizens, to hail you welcome to Rhode-Iſland.

Shielded by Omnipotence, during a tedious and unnatural war—wiſe, as a meſſenger ſent from Heaven, in conducting the councils of the cabinet—and, under many embarraſſments, directing the operations of the field; Divine Providence crowned your temples with unfading laurels, and put into your hand the peacefully-waving olive-branch. Long may you live, Sir, highly favoured of GOD and beloved of men, to preſide in the Grand Council of our nation, which, we truſt, will not ceaſe to ſupplicate Heaven, that its ſelect and divine influences may deſcend and reſt upon you, endowing you with "grace, wiſdom and underſtanding," to go out and in before this numerous and free people; to preſide over whom, Divine Providence hath raiſed you up.

And therefore—before GOD, the Father of our Lord Jeſus Chriſt, in whom all the families both in heaven and earth are named, according to the law of our office, and in bounden duty—we bow our knee—beſeeching him to grant you every temporal and ſpiritual bleſſing—and that, of the plenitude of his grace, all the families of theſe wide-extended realms may enjoy, under an equal and judicious adminiſtration of government, peace and proſperity, with all the bleſſings attendant on civil and religious liberty.

SAMUEL HOPKINS, *Paſtor of the 1ſt Congregational Church.*
GARDNER THURSTON, *Paſtor of the 2d Baptiſt Church.*
FREDERICK SMITH, *Paſtor of the United Brethren.*
WILLIAM BLISS, *Paſtor of the Sabbatarian Baptiſt Church.*
WILLIAM SMITH, *Rector of Trinity Church.*
MICHAEL EDDY, *Paſtor of the 1ſt Baptiſt Church.*
WILLIAM PATTEN, *Paſtor of the 2d Congregational Church.*

The ANSWER.
To the CLERGY *of the Town of* NEWPORT, *in the State of Rhode-Iſland.*

GENTLEMEN,

THE ſalutations of the Clergy of the town of Newport, on my arrival in the State of Rhode-Iſland, are rendered the more acceptable, on account of the liberal ſentiments and juſt ideas which they are known to entertain, reſpecting civil and religious liberty.

I am inexpreſſibly happy, that, by the ſmiles of Divine Providence, my weak but well-meant endeavours to ſerve my country have hitherto been crowned with ſo much ſucceſs, and apparently give ſuch ſatisfaction to thoſe in whoſe cauſe they were exerted. The ſame benignant influence, together with the concurrent ſupport of all real friends to their country, will ſtill be neceſſary, to enable me to be in any degree uſeful to this numerous and free people, over whom I am called to preſide.

Wherefore I return you, Gentlemen, my hearty thanks for your ſolemn invocation of Almighty GOD, that every temporal and ſpiritual bleſſing may be diſpenſed to me; and that, under my adminiſtration, the families of theſe States may enjoy peace and proſperity, with all the bleſſings attendant on civil and religious liberty.—In the participation of which bleſſings, may you have an ample ſhare.

G. WASHINGTON.

ADDRESS *from the* SOCIETY *of* FREE-MASONS.
To GEORGE WASHINGTON, PRESIDENT *of the United States of America.*

WE the Maſter, Wardens and Brethren, of King David's Lodge, in Newport, Rhode-Iſland, joyfully embrace this opportunity to *greet* you as a Brother, and to *hail* you welcome to Rhode-Iſland.—We exult in the thought, that as Maſonry has always been patroniſed by the wiſe, the good and the great, ſo hath it ſtood, and ever will ſtand, as its fixtures are on the immutable pillars of faith, hope and charity.—With unſpeakable pleaſure, we gratulate you as filling the Preſidential chair, with the applauſe of a numerous and enlightened people—whilſt, at the ſame time, we felicitate ourſelves in the honour done the Brotherhood, by your many exemplary virtues and emanations of goodneſs, proceeding from a heart worthy of poſſeſſing the ancient myſteries of our craft; being perſuaded that the wiſdom and grace with which Heaven has endowed you, will ever *ſquare* all your thoughts, words and actions, by the eternal laws of honour, equity and truth; ſo as to promote the advancement of all good works, your own happineſs, and that of mankind.—Permit us, then, illuſtrious Brother, cordially to ſalute you, with *Three* times *Three*, and to add our fervent ſupplications, that the Sovereign Architect of the Univerſe may always en-*compaſs* you with his holy protection.

MOSES SEIXAS, Maſter, } *Committee.*
HENRY SHERBURNE, }

By Order,
WILLIAM LITTLEFIELD, *Sec'ry.*

The ANSWER.
To the MASTER, WARDENS *and* BRETHREN, *of* KING DAVID'S LODGE, *in* NEWPORT, RHODE-ISLAND.

GENTLEMEN,

I RECEIVE the welcome which you give me to Rhode-Iſland with pleaſure—and I acknowledge my obligations for the flattering expreſſions of regard contained in your addreſs with grateful ſincerity.

Being perſuaded, that a juſt application of the principles, on which the maſonic fraternity is founded, muſt be promotive of private virtue and public proſperity, I ſhall always be happy to advance the intereſt of the Society, and to be conſidered by them as a deſerving Brother.——My beſt wiſhes, Gentlemen, are offered for your individual happineſs.

G. WASHINGTON.

ADDRESS *from the* HEBREW CONGREGATION.
To the PRESIDENT *of the* UNITED STATES *of* AMERICA.

SIR,

PERMIT the children of the ſtock of Abraham to approach you, with the moſt cordial affection and eſteem for your perſon and merits—and to join with our fellow-citizens in welcoming you to Newport.

With pleaſure we reflect on thoſe days—thoſe days of difficulty and danger, when the GOD of Iſrael, who delivered David from the peril of the ſword, ſhielded your head in the day of battle:—And we rejoice to think, that the ſame ſpirit, who reſted in the boſom of the greatly beloved Daniel, enabling him to preſide over the provinces of the Babyloniſh Empire, reſts, and ever will reſt, upon you, enabling you to diſcharge the arduous duties of Chief Magiſtrate in theſe States.

Deprived as we heretofore have been of the invaluable rights of free citizens, we now (with a deep ſenſe of gratitude to the Almighty Diſpoſer of all events) behold a government erected by the MAJESTY OF THE PEOPLE—a government which to bigotry gives no ſanction—to perſecution no aſſiſtance; but generouſly affording to ALL liberty of conſcience, and immunities of citizenſhip—deeming every one, of whatever nation, tongue or language, equal parts of the great governmental machine. This ſo ample and extenſive federal Union, whoſe baſis is philanthropy, mutual confidence, and public virtue, we cannot but acknowledge to be the work of the great GOD, who ruleth in the armies of Heaven and among the inhabitants of the earth, doing whatſoever ſeemeth him good.

For all the bleſſings of civil and religious liberty which we enjoy under an equal and benign adminiſtration, we deſire to ſend up our thanks to the Ancient of Days, the great Preſerver of men—beſeeching him, that the angel who conducted our forefathers through the wilderneſs into the promiſed land, may graciouſly conduct you through all the difficulties and dangers of this mortal life; and when, like Joſhua, full of days and full of honour, you are gathered to your fathers, may you be admitted into the Heavenly Paradiſe, to partake of the water of life, and the tree of immortality.

Done and ſigned, by order of the Hebrew Congregation, in Newport, Rhode-Iſland, Auguſt 17, 1790.

MOSES SEIXAS, Warden.

The ANSWER.
To the HEBREW CONGREGATION *in* NEWPORT, RHODE-ISLAND.

GENTLEMEN,

WHILE I receive with much ſatisfaction your addreſs, replete with expreſſions of affection and eſteem, I rejoice in the opportunity of aſſuring you, that I ſhall always retain a grateful remembrance of the cordial welcome I experienced in my viſit to Newport, from all claſſes of citizens.

The reflection on the days of difficulty and danger which are paſt, is rendered the more ſweet, from a conſciouſneſs that they are ſucceeded by days of uncommon proſperity and ſecurity. If we have wiſdom to make the beſt uſe of the advantages with which we are now favoured, we cannot fail, under the juſt adminiſtration of a good government, to become a great and a happy people.

The citizens of the United States of America have a right to applaud themſelves, for having given to mankind examples of an enlarged and liberal policy—a policy worthy of imitation. ALL poſſeſs alike liberty of conſcience, and immunities of citizenſhip. It is now no more that toleration is ſpoken of, as if it was by the indulgence of one claſs of people, that another enjoyed the exerciſe of their inherent natural rights: For happily the government of the United States, which gives to bigotry no ſanction—to perſecution no aſſiſtance, requires only that they who live under its protection, ſhould demean themſelves as good citizens, in giving it on all occaſions their effectual ſupport.

It would be inconſiſtent with the frankneſs of my character not to avow, that I am pleaſed with your favourable opinion of my adminiſtration, and fervent wiſhes for my felicity. May the children of the ſtock of Abraham, who dwell in this land, continue to merit and enjoy the good will of the other inhabitants; while every one ſhall ſit in ſafety under his own vine and fig-tree, and there ſhall be none to make him afraid. May the Father of all mercies ſcatter light and not darkneſs in our paths, and make us all in our ſeveral vocations uſeful here, and in his own due time and way everlaſtingly happy.

G. WASHINGTON.

State of Rhode-Iſland and Providence Plantations.
IN GENERAL ASSEMBLY. Sept. Seſſion, A.D. 1790.
An ACT regulating the Inſpection of Beef, Pork, pickled Fiſh and Tobacco, and for other Purpoſes therein mentioned.

WHEREAS for the want of proper regulations in this State, relative to the packing and inſpecting of beef, pork, pickled fiſh, and tobacco, the prices of thoſe articles exported from this State are conſiderably diminiſhed in foreign markets r

Replying to Anti-Semitic Slander

August 11, 1800. Benjamin Nones, a Jew of French origin who had settled in Philadelphia and fought in Revolutionary War under Pulaski and Baron De Kalb, became involved in a political situation in which he was the focus of a personal attack published in the Federalist paper, Gazette of the United States. *He addressed an eloquent response to Caleb F. Wayne, printer of that journal, which Wayne refused to print. Nones then approached the editor of* The Philadelphia Aurora, *a Republican journal, who agreed to publish it.*

I *am a Jew.* I glory in belonging to that persuasion, which even its opponents, whether Christian, or Mahomedan, allow to be of divine origin—of that persuasion on which christianity itself was originally founded, and must ultimately rest—which has preserved its faith secure and undefiled, for near three thousand years—whose votaries have never murdered each other in religious wars, or cherished the theological hatred so general, so unextinguishable among those who revile them. A persuasion, whose, patient followers, have endured for ages the pious cruelties of Pagans, and of christians, and persevered in the unoffending practice of their rites and ceremonies, amidst poverties and privations—amidst pains, penalties, confiscations, banishments, tortures, and deaths, beyond the example of any other sect, which the page of history has hitherto recorded.

To be of such a persuasion, is to me no disgrace; though I well understand the inhuman language of bigotted contempt, in which your reporter by attempting to make me ridiculous, as a Jew, has made himself detestable, whatever religious persuasion may be dishonored by his adherence.

But I am a Jew. I am so—and so were Abraham, and Isaac, and Moses and the prophets, and so too were Christ and his apostles, I feel no disgrace in ranking with such society, however, it may be subject to the illiberal buffoonery of such men as your correspondents.

I am a *Republican!* Thank God, I have not been so heedless, and so ignorant of what has passed, and is now passing in the political world. I have not been so proud or so prejudiced as to renounce the cause for which I have *fought,* as an American throughout the whole of the revolutionary war, in the militia of Charleston, and in Polafkey's legion, I fought in almost every action which took place in Carolina, and in the disastrous affair of Savannah, shared the hardships of that sanguinary day, and for three and twenty years I felt no disposition to change my political, any more than my religious principles.—And which in spite of the witling scribblers of aristocracy, I shall hold sacred until death as not to feel the ardour of republicanism.—Your correspondent, Mr. Wayne cannot have known what it is to serve his country from principle in time of danger and difficulties, at the expence of his health and his peace, of his pocket and his person, as

I have done; or he would not be as he is, a pert reviler of those who have so done—as I do not suspect you Mr. Wayne, of being the author of the attack on me, I shall not enquire what share you or your relations had in establishing the liberties of your country. On religious grounds I am a republican. Kingly government was first conceded to the foolish complaints of the Jewish people, as a punishment and a curse; and so it was to them until their dispersion, and so it has been to every nation, who have been as foolishly tempted to submit to it. Great Britain has a king, and her enemies need not wish her the sword, the pestilence, and the famine.

In the history of the Jews, are contained the earliest warnings against kingly government, as any one may know who has read the fable of Abimelick, or the exhortations of Samuel. But I do not recommend them to your reporter, Mr. Wayne. To him the language of truth and soberness would be unintelligible.

I am a Jew, and if for no other reason, for that reason am I a republican. Among the pious priesthood of church establishments, we are compassionately ranked with Turks, Infidels and Heretics. In the *monarchies* of Europe, we are hunted from society—stigmatized as unworthy of common civility, thrust out as it were from the converse of men; objects of mockery and insult to froward children, the butts of vulgar wit, and low buffoonery, such as your correspondent Mr. Wayne is not ashamed to set us an example of. Among the nations of Europe we are inhabitants every where—but Citizens no where *unless in Republics.* Here, in France, and in the Batavian Republic alone, we are treated as men and as brethren. In republics we have *rights,* in monarchies we live but to experience *wrongs.* And why? because we and our forefathers have *not* sacrificed our principles to our interest, or earned an exemption from pain and poverty, by the direliction of our religious duties, no wonder we are objects of derision to those, who have no principles, moral or religious, to guide their conduct.

How then can a Jew but be a Republican? in America particularly. Unfeeling & ungrateful would he be, if he were callous to the glorious and benevolent cause of the difference between his situation in this land of freedom, and among the proud and privileged law givers of Europe.

But I am *poor,* I am so, my family also is large, but soberly and decently brought up. They have not been taught to revile a christian, because his religion is not *so old* as theirs. They have not been taught to mock even at the errors of good intention, and conscientious belief. I hope they will always leave this to men as unlike themselves, as I hope I am to your scurrilous correspondent.

I know that to purse proud aristocracy poverty is a crime, but it may sometimes be accompanied with honesty even in a Jew. I was a bankrupt some years ago. I obtained my certificate and I was discharged from my debts. Having been more successful afterwards, I called my creditors together, and eight years after-

wards unsolicited I discharged all my old debts, I offered interest which was refused by my creditors, and they gave me under their hands without any solicitations of mine, as a testimonial of the fact (to use their own language) as a tribute due to my honor and honesty. This testimonial was signed by Messrs. J. Ball, W. Wister, George Meade, J. Philips, C. G. Paleske, J. Bispham, J. Cohen, Robert Smith, J. H. Leuffer, A Kuhn, John Stille, S. Pleasants, M. Woodhouse, Thomas Harrison, M. Boraef, E. Laskey, and Thomas Allibone, &c.

I was discharged by the insolvent act, true, because having the amount of my debts owing to me from the French Republic, the differences between France and America have prevented the recovery of what was due to me, in time to discharge what was due to my creditors. Hitherto it has been the fault of the political situation of the two countries, that my creditors are not paid; when peace shall enable me to receive what I am entitled to it will be my fault if they are not fully paid.

This is a long defence Mr. Wayne, but you have called it forth, and therefore, I hope you at least will not object to it. The Public will now judge who is the proper object of ridicule and contempt, your facetious reporter, or . . .

Rebecca Gratz Writes to her Brother in Kentucky

March 7, 1819, Rebecca Gratz, a leading member of the Philadelphia Jewish community, wrote to her brother, Benjamin, who went to Lexington, Kentucky, to seek his fortune.

I am always delighted My dear Ben, to receive your letters but do not feel any mortification at your silence. When your letters to our brothers assure me of your health I am grateful for the blessing, and am too sensible of the amiable sensibility of your heart to doubt your constant affection for your family. The bond of sympathy will I trust never be broken, which has been such a source of happiness to our family—and you are cherished with the fondest remembrance of all, even the little children of our sisters enquire with interest for letters & receive your messages with delight. Miriam was much gratified by your flattering notice of her letter and looks forward to the fulfilment of your promise as a thing of great importance. You must not fail to write to her.

I have never been apprehensive of your becoming attached to a wandering life, but that some project of interest would induce you to fix your residence abroad, and I have considered few things in life worth the sacrifice of the society and habits of home, and the cherished associations of early life—at least few that could be obtained in the western wilds. If objects to advance your prospects opened in any city where you could enjoy such advantages as you are accustomed to whether in the new or old world I believe I could submit to separation easier, because I should still believe you surrounded by friends & comforts, but the *ideal good* which of late has been so inticing to our young men of clearing land, building huts—cultivating soil with the sweat of their brows, and waiting till it should grow into a populous city and seeing themselves great proprietors of lots and the wealth of ages is too chimerical for realization, and I could not bear that you should waste the flower of your days—(which can never bloom again) in such vain experiments. You have had a delightful season for your travels, the winter has been like a continued autumn—and spring has returned before we have felt the rigours of a months cold weather. I hope you will be as well pleased with the remainder of your tour. I have written to our friend Maria, and am quite ashamed of having neglected her so long—everybody I see from Kentucky speaks of her in terms of deserved praise . . . . The amusements of the season have conformed very much to the weather—they have had very little dancing and until lately few parties—the Theatre has been more fashionably attended and as there has been a succession of good actors here—the dramatic taste of the citizens revived—the streets exhibited a great deal more gaiety than usual—fine weather & good walking brought out belles in handsome walking dresses. Your studies in your Chestnut street office would have been constantly interrupted—and what the girls have lost by your windows being shut is hardly to be calculated—but this genial weather does not seem to have quickened the growth of sentiment—there are no new matches on the tapis—at least none that come under this description. . . . .

Jo is still at Washington—Hyman returned last week and I hope to have the remnant of the family collected—it has been very small all winter. The 10th of April is Passover would I might expect you to keep it with us, when you went away I did certainly hope to see you at that time—you must at least let me know where you will be at that period—on Thursday next is Purim no longer a mirthful festival with us—it passes away without celebration—but more solemn feasts are more permanently observed. It is difficult to fix a time to be happy and tho' we feel grateful for the deliverance this feast commemorates as nothing is required of us but to be glad and merry, we are not always able to do so. Accept the affectionate love of all the family, My dearest Ben, and believe me always with the sincerest prayers for your health prosperity and happiness your Most truly Attached Sister RG.

Will Religion Affect Admission to Harvard?

May 21, 1815. In this letter to his sponsor, William Meredith, Nathan Nathans asks if his religion will present a problem regarding admission to Harvard College.

There is one thing that I neglected mentioning in my last letter. I would wish to know wether it is your wish for Doctor Allen to prepare me, for the Cambridge College or the University at Philada as I think there will be some difficulty about my religion at Cambridge, as I understand they are very strict; I think that it will be much better for me, to be prepared for the University at Philada as it will be much more agreeable to myself & family. & I therefore hope it will meet your approbation. Give my best respects to Mr. Gratz, & be pleased to write me soon as school will commence the 29 this month.

A Prospect of the Colledges in Cambridge in New England

Harvard College, about 1740: Located in Cambridge, Massachusetts, engraving by William Burgis. *Credit: LC*

Max Guggenheimer, Jr., undated: Born in Hurben, Bavaria in 1842, he arrived in New York in 1856 with his parents and they moved to Lynchburg, Virginia where his family operated a department store. He was a member of the Confederate Army. He married Bertha Rosenbaum in 1877. This is likely to be either an engagement or wedding photograph. *Credit:* LBI

Bertha Rosenbaum Guggenheimer, undated: Born in Richmond, Virginia in 1857, she married Max Guggenheimer, Jr. in 1877. This is likely to be either an engagement or wedding photograph. *Credit:* LBI

Creating a Jewish Presence

In 1820, there were 9,600,000 inhabitants in the United States, of which an estimated 20,000 were Jews. Barely sixty years later, in 1880, there were more than fifty times that number of Jews, 250,000, while the total population of the United States had increased only five-fold.

The dramatic growth of the American Jewish population was the result of the arrival of vast numbers of Jews from German-speaking countries. The flood of immigrants following the unsuccessful revolutions throughout Europe in the 1840's altered the character and composition of the Jewish community.

When the German Jews arrived in America, their brethren were established and thriving in colonial communities along the Atlantic seaboard. The extent to which Jews had become integrated into American society was reflected by playwright and politician Mordecai Manuel Noah, as he offered asylum to the Jews of the world in a place "where they can enjoy the peace, comfort and happiness . . . denied them through the intolerance and misgovernment of former ages . . ." That asylum was "in the state of New York, the greatest State in the American confederacy." The city was dubbed "Ararat," after the fable mountain on which Noah found refuge after the flood.

Although the city of Ararat never materialized, many of the German Jewish refugees who arrived in America found asylum and opportunity in locations other than the established communities on the Eastern seaboard. They tended to settle in the burgeoning commercial and industrial cities of Cincinnati, St. Louis, Chicago, Detroit and San Francisco. Joseph Jonas described the first Jewish settler's life in Cincinnatti in the year 1817: "The city then contained about six thousand inhabitants . . . Solitary and alone he remained for more than two years; and at the solemn festival of our holy religion, in solitude was he inclined to commune with his maker." Although Jews tended to settle in communities, many struck out on their own in the spirit of entrepreneurs. Other Jews settled in small frontier towns across the country peddling goods from town to town, opening general stores in rural communities. It was from such humble beginnings in Talbotton, Georgia that the Straus family went on to buy the controlling interest in Macy's, which , under their leadership, became one of the world's most prestigious department stores.

The Gold Rush in the 1850's drew Jews westward. Writing in 1851, Abraham Abrahamsohn captured the contagious excitement of the times: "Everywhere the astonished eye saw people, who coming from there, showed large chunks of gold or carried them braggingly around their necks, and who lived in grand style." In vivid detail Abrahamsohn described his four-month journey via the Isthmus of Panama, arriving finally in San Francisco, where he elaborated on the finer sights in town: ". . . large gambling houses . . . beautiful girls, for the most part French, but also brown, black-eyed Mexicans, with perfumed flowers in their hair . . . and in each gambling hall they offered to everyone . . . ale, port, various wines . . . bread, butter, cheese, all of it for free."

"If somebody is thrifty and active," wrote another Jewish immigrant to his relatives in Bamberg, Germany, "he can go pretty far in this country." Many Jews followed that dictum, thus becoming an integral part of both the economic and social life in San Francisco and Los Angeles. Some peddled goods to the prospectors and homesteaders who settled the small towns which sprung up in the wake of the new wealth. The miners of these towns were the first customers of the now-famous denim pants manufactured by the immigrant Levi Straus under the trademark, "Levis." Another Jewish immigrant, Adolph Sutro from Germany, began as a cigar and tobacco vendor in San Francisco in the 1850s. He later constructed tunnels in Nevada to facilitate the mining of the Comstock Lode, and then topped off his varied and lucrative career by becoming the mayor of San Francisco in 1894.

This was the stuff the American dream was made of. Rags to riches stories crossed the Atlantic. Rumor had it that the

1820-1880

streets of America were paved with gold. It was, according to some accounts, almost impossible to fail. In an autobiographical account, German immigrant David Hyman described how after failing in one business he attended Harvard Law School and then made his fortune through a lucky investment in Colorado mining ventures.

Until the 1840s, Jews were spread out in self-sufficient separate communities. Centralized organization did not exist for the synagogue as did its European counterpart, attended to communal needs. But with the expansion of the Jewish population and its movement westward, individual synagogues were no longer the central force in the Jewish community. Earlier, in 1830, the prominent physician Daniel Peixotto, speaking on behalf of the Society for the Education of Orphan Children and Relief of Indigent Persons of the Jewish Persuasion, stressed the need to carry on the tradition of Jewish philanthropy: "The proudest badge of any sect is, and should be, that none of its members are dependents on the public eleemosynary institutions." Continuing this tradition, twelve men founded B'nai Brith in 1843, the first Jewish fraternal organization in the world. That same year, the outstanding religious leader and educator Isaac Leeser first published his monthly newspaper, *The Occident*. The first Jewish newspaper to provide America's Jews with a national voice, *The Occident* bridged the great distances which now separated Jewish communities.

Despite these distances, American Jews consistently united when confronted by a crisis situation, regardless of where it occurred. In 1840, demonstrations were held in New York, Philadelphia and Richmond to protest the persecution of Jews accused of blood libel in Damascus, and a letter requesting action by the federal government was sent to President Martin Van Buren. Similarly, in 1858, Jewish leaders such as Rabbi Max Lilienthal of Cincinnati mobilized American Jewish action in the case of Edgardo Mortara, a Jewish child from Italy who had been abducted and converted to Christianity. In

response to such crises, the Board of Delegates of American Israelites, representing approximately thirty American congregations, was formed in New York in 1859.

As the Civil War erupted in 1860, Jews and Christians alike took up arms against their brothers. Loyalty was determined by place of residence. An anonymous soldier reporting on his war experience in the Union army wrote he heard of "but a single case in which a Jew was wantonly insulted on account of his religion . . ."

As after most times of armed conflict, a period of restoration and economic expansion followed the Civil War. Jewish merchants in both the North and the South benefited during Reconstruction. Building upon their earlier successes as peddlers, storekeepers and wholesale merchants, German Jews further established themselves throughout the United States. Bankers helped to finance the expansion of the national transportation system. German Jews who prospered surpassed the financial successes of their colonial predecessors.

Although the economic status of the Jews had risen during the Civil War and Reconstruction, socially and politically Jews remained vulnerable to anti-Semitic incidents. In 1862, General Grant expelled all Jewish traders from the territory which he commanded. His infamous "General Orders Number 11" was later cancelled by President Lincoln. Nevertheless, the matter served as a harsh reminder to Jews that they were subject to discrimination. Although Jews were actively involved Masons and many partook of the lavish life, Joseph Seligman, a successful banker, was denied admittance to the Grand Union Hotel in Saratoga Springs in 1877. The general press joined America's Jewish communities in protest of the incident, but the exclusion of Jews from privileged social circles would remain in practice in America until the mid-twentieth century.

"Equality of Rights to Every Religious Sect"

August 20, 1820. Former President James Madison wrote to Dr. Jacob de la Motta of Savannah on the occasion of the consecration of the synagogue there praising the virtues of the American political system.

I have received your letter of the 7th inst. with the Discourse delivered at the consecration of the Hebrew Synagogue at Savannah, for which you will please to accept my thanks.

The history of the Jews must for ever be interesting. The modern part of it is at the same time so little generally known, that every ray of light on the subject has its value.

Among the features peculiar to the political system of the U. States is the perfect equality of rights which it secures to every religious sect. And it is particularly pleasing to observe in the good citizenship of such as have been most distrusted and oppressed elsewhere, a happy illustration of the safety and success of this experiment of a just and benignant policy. Equal laws protecting equal rights, are found as they ought to be presumed, the best guarantee of loyalty, and love of country; as well as best calculated to cherish that mutual respect and good will among citizens of every religious denomination which are necessary to social harmony and most favorable to the advancement of truth. The account you give of the Jews of your Congregation brings them fully within the scope of these observations.

Social Gaieties in Philadelphia

December 21, 1821. Rebecca Gratz, a prominent member of the Philadelphia Jewish community, wrote to Maria Gist Gratz, the wife of her brother Benjamin, about the social affairs of the season.

At length My dear Maria, we have the happiness to know that you are at home again, and in health. and I trust your darling boy has not suffered—nor made you suffer during your long and tedious journey—it appears an age since you left us yet we have not ceased to regret you. As the season advances when Phila has most attractions for strangers, we wish your visit had been planned so as to have partaken of its amusements. I called to see Mrs Bayard a few days after a grand ball had been given by Mrs Meade, after enquiring very kindly about you, she lamented that you had not been there— said she could not help thinking what a fine figure you would have made among them. and in her usual style of saying pretty things, passed some of her well timed compliments with so much judgment, that I went away quite charmed with her politeness, and scarcely doubting her sincerity—What a pity thought I, she is a . . . .—one might else have been delighted with such candour—she is very beautiful too, and their house is among the gayest of our fashionables— they have already given one large party

Mizrach, about 1825: A mizrach is a visual ornament with religious significance which hangs on the eastern wall of the house, the direction of Jerusalem. This one was made in Pennsylvania by an unknown artist. *Credit:* Private Collection of Stephen Gemberling

Rebecca Gratz, 1830: Portrait by Thomas Sully of the prominent Philadelphia educator and Jewish communal leader. She is said to have been the model for Sir Walter Scott's Rebecca in his novel *Ivanhoe.* In 1819 she was one of the founders of the Female Hebrew Benevolent Society and in 1838 she established the Hebrew Sunday School Society. *Credit:* DAM

Uriah Phillips Levy, about 1820: First Jew to reach the rank of Commodore in the United States Navy, fought in the War of 1812. *Credit:* AJHS

and are going to have a dance soon. Mrs John Sargeant has invited us to see the old year out at her house—and the Assembly's commence the first week in the new one—but what is all this to you or me? if you were here I should buckle on my old finery again for the pleasure of accompanying you, but as it is, I do not mean to go anywhere, except to matronize Rosa Hays on her debut, for to tell you the truth such scenes are "stale, flat & unprofitable" to me—the companions of former days have either passed away, or have lost their interest in my heart and the idea has so much of melancholy in it to me, that a ball room seems more like a memorial of lost pleasures than an incitement to new ones.

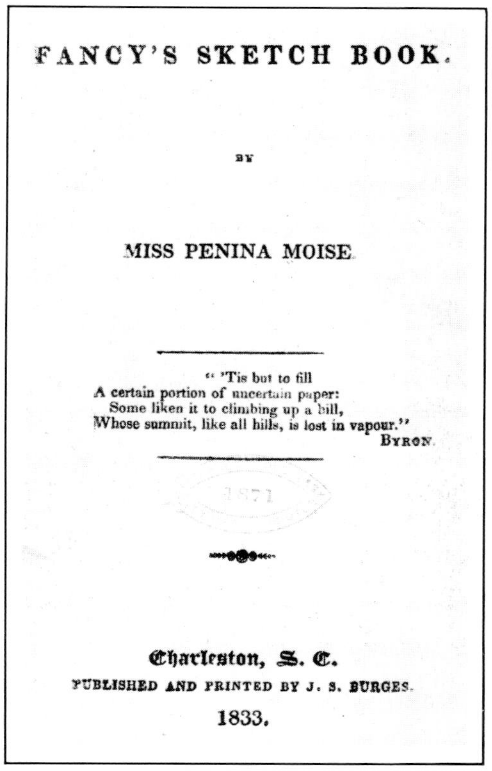

FANCY'S SKETCH BOOK.

BY

MISS PENINA MOISE.

" 'Tis but to fill
A certain portion of uncertain paper:
Some liken it to climbing up a hill,
Whose summit, like all hills, is lost in vapour."
BYRON.

Charleston, S. C.
PUBLISHED AND PRINTED BY J. S. BURGES.
1833.

Fancy's Sketch Book, 1833: Penina Moise lived in Charleston, South Carolina. Her family originated in Alsace-Lorraine, moved to the West Indies and finally settled in Charleston. Her poems were widely published in newspapers and other journals. A collection of them later appeared in book form in 1835 under the title of *Fancy's Sketch Book*, purported to be the first book by a Jewish woman to be published in the United States. *Credit:* LC

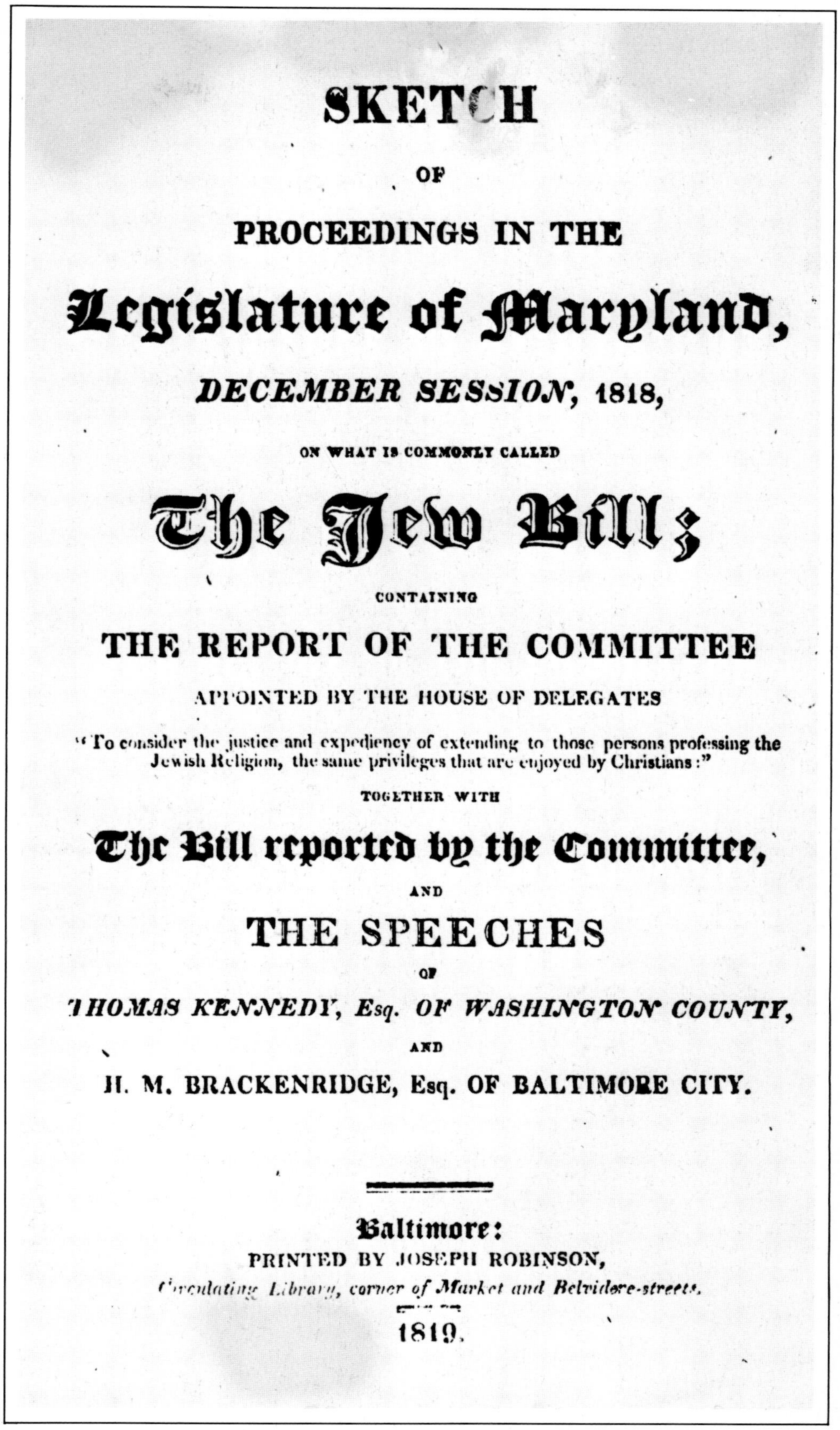

SKETCH

OF

PROCEEDINGS IN THE

Legislature of Maryland,

DECEMBER SESSION, 1818,

ON WHAT IS COMMONLY CALLED

The Jew Bill;

CONTAINING

THE REPORT OF THE COMMITTEE

APPOINTED BY THE HOUSE OF DELEGATES

"To consider the justice and expediency of extending to those persons professing the Jewish Religion, the same privileges that are enjoyed by Christians:"

TOGETHER WITH

The Bill reported by the Committee,

AND

THE SPEECHES

OF

THOMAS KENNEDY, Esq. OF WASHINGTON COUNTY,

AND

H. M. BRACKENRIDGE, Esq. OF BALTIMORE CITY.

Baltimore:
PRINTED BY JOSEPH ROBINSON,
Circulating Library, corner of Market and Belvidere-streets.

1819.

The Jew Bill, 1819-1826: Report of the debate on a bill, published in 1819, to grant equal rights to Jews in Maryland. Seven years later the bill was finally passed. *Credit:* AJHS

Encouraging German Jews to Emigrate

October 16, 1822. Although the "great German and Irish migration" did not begin until later in this decade, the New York Commercial Advertiser *encouraged German Jews to come to this country.*

The wealth and enterprize of the Jews would be a great auxiliary to the commercial and manufacturing, if not agricultural, interests of the United States. A new generation, born in more enlightened times, and having the benefit of education, would be free from those errors generally imputed to the Jews, and participating in the blessings of liberty, would have every inducement to become valuable members of society.—That toleration and mildness upon which the Christian religion is founded, will lend its influence to the neglected children of Israel, who, in the United States, can find a home undisturbed—land which they dare call their own—laws which they will assist in making—magistrates of which they may be of the number—protection, freedom, and as they comport themselves respect and consideration. We shall not be surprised if the views which shall be spread before them should lead to a valuable emigration of these people; and when they perceive one of their brethren honored with the highest executive office of the metropolis of the Union, and exercising a jurisdiction over Christians with Christian justice, they will be satisfied of the practical utility of those institutions which proclaim equal freedom and privileges to all.

Ketubah, 1823: This ketubah recorded the marriage of Eveline Leon to Joseph B. Nones on July 23, 1823. It was written by Moses Levy Peixotto. *Credit:* Private Collection of Joseph Lyon Andrews, Jr. M.D.

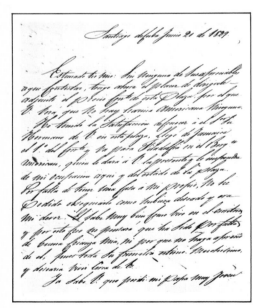

Spanish Letter, 1829: To David B. Nones from a nephew in Cuba discussing heavy immigration from Europe to America. *Credit:* AJHS

The Benefits of White Sulphur Springs

July 26, 1824. S. Jacobs of Richmond wrote to his brother-in-law, David B. Nones in Philadelphia, encouraging him to "take the cure."

I am preparing to go to the White Sulphur Springs in the western part of this state, the state of my system, blood & skin, *require it.* These springs *I know* to be *certain* cure of eruptions—(?)—You still have time to reach them in good season. Pass by way of Fredericktown, Maryland—Winchester & Staunton in Virginia. By all means push out there if not entirely cure—2 weeks will cure you get there by 7th to the 15th August. I have (?) the effects of them. There are no others in this country so efficacious in (?) disorders & cleaning the blood system.

Dedication of the New Synagogue for Mikveh Israel in Philadelphia

February 27, 1825. Rebecca Gratz wrote to her brother, Benjamin, in Lexington, Kentucky, describing the ceremonies dedicating the new building.

I am surprised you have no account of the consecretion except from the newspaper as it was a subject engaging universal attention—the article you mention was written by your old friend Tom Wharton who was a spectator on the occasion. I have never witnessed a more impressive or solemn ceremony or one more calculated to elevate the mind to religious exercises—the shool is one of the most beautiful specimens of ancient architecture in the city, and finished in the Stricklands best manner—the decorations are neat yet rich and tasteful—and the service commencing just before the Sabbath was performed by lamp light—Mr Keys was assisted in the service by the Hazan from New York Mr Peixotto a venerable learned & pious man who gave great effect to the solemnity—the doors being opened by our brother Simon and the blessing pronounced at the entrance—the processions entered with the two Reverends in their robes followed by nine copies of the Sacred Rolls—they advanced slowly to the Tabah while a choir of five voices chanted the appointed psalms most delightfully when the new Hazan had been inducted into his office and took his place at the desk. Mr P. in slow and solemn manner preceded the Sephers in their circuit round the area of the building between the desk and the ark—whilst such strains of sacred songs were chanted as might truly be said to have inspiration in them—between each circuit, the prayers appointed (as you will see in the book our brother sent you) to be performed by the Hazan and the congregation were said and among the most affecting parts of the service—Mr Keys in a fine full voice and the responses by Mr Peixotto in a voice tremulous from agitation and deep feeling. I have no hope of conveying by description any idea of this ceremony—you must have seen the whole spectacle—the beautiful

Mikveh Israel Synagogue, undated: Mikveh Israel Synagogue was organized in Philadelphia in 1747. The interior of its building on Cherry Street designed by William Strickland and dedicated in 1825 is illustrated here. *Credit:* AJHS

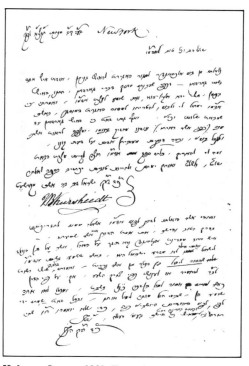

Hebrew Letter, 1831: From Israel Baer Kurshedt to Rabbi Solomon Hirschel in London on matters relating to Jewish law. *Credit:* AJHS

ark thrown wide open to receive the sacred deposit, with its rich crimson curtains fringed with gold—the perpetual lamp suspended in front with its little constant light like a watchman at his post—and with the humble yet dignified figure of the venerable Mr P. as he conducted the procession in its seven circuits and then deposited the laws—after which Mr Keys recited with an effect amounting almost to eloquence that impressive prayer of King Solomon—the whole audience was most profoundly attentive and tho' few were so happy as to understand the language—those who did—say they have never heard the Hebrew so well delivered as by Mr Keys—the bishop expressed this opinion—and all who were there acknowledge there has never been such church music performed in Phila—you will wonder where "these sweet singers in Israel" were collected from—the leader, teacher and principal performer is Jacob Seixas and his female first voice his sister Miriam, they were fortunately on a visit to their sister Mrs Phillips and induced a class to practice for some weeks—Miriam and Becky Moses contributed very considerably and all in the congregation who Mr S. found teachable assisted—he is now resident here and we hope by his assistance to keep up a very respectable class of singers in the synagogue. The service continues to be finely performed and the congregation behave with the utmost decorum and propriety during the service.

Mordecai Manuel Noah, about 1820: Mordecai Manuel Noah was a man of varied talents and accomplishments. In 1808, his first play, *The Fortress of Sorrento,* was written. In 1813 he was appointed Consul to Tunis by President James Madison, the first Jew appointed to a high diplomatic post. In 1825 he attempted to establish a Jewish colony in Ararat, near Buffalo, New York. *Credit:* AJHS

Broadside, 1828: Mordecai Manuel Noah, who had also been High Sheriff of New York City, was known for his outspoken public statements and acts. This broadside testifies to this side of his personality. *Credit:* AJHS

Introducing a Messenger from the Holy Land

April 13, 1833. It was common for religious leaders from the Holy Land to visit American congregations to collect funds. Mordecai Manuel Noah of New York wrote this letter of introduction to Zalegman Phillips of Philadelphia.

Dear Sir, Rabbi Zundal a missionary from Jerusalem has been with us nearly a year and in conformity with his instructions proceeds to Philada to receive whatever aid the Congregation in that City may please to afford The Rabbi is a learned and intelligent man and his conduct and deportment is that of a gentleman I should be happy to learn that he has succeeded & beg you to give him the names of such of the Congregation disposed to aid him & shew him any civilities in your power I am Dear Sir very truly yrs . . .

Ararat, A City of Refuge for American Jews

September 25, 1825. Mordecai Manuel Noah, one of the most well-known Jews of his generation, proposed to create "a city of refuge for the Jews" on Grand Island in the Niagara River near Buffalo.

Therefore, I, Mordecai Manuel Noah, citizen of the United States of America, late Consul of the said States to the City and Kingdom of Tunis, High Sheriff of New York, Counsellor at Law, and by the grace of God, Governor and Judge of Israel, have issued this my Proclamation, announcing to the Jews throughout the world, that an asylum is prepared and hereby offered to them, where they can enjoy that peace, comfort and happiness which have been denied them through the intolerance and misgovernment of former ages; an asylum in a free and

powerful country remarkable for its vast resources, the richness of its soil, and the salubrity of its climate; where industry is encouraged, education promoted, and good faith rewarded, "a land of milk and honey," where Israel may repose in peace, under his "vine and fig tree," and where our people may so familiarize themselves with the science of government and the lights of learning and civilization, as may qualify them for that great and final restoration to their ancient heritage, which the times so powerfully indicate.

The asylum referred to is in the State of New York, the greatest State in the American confederacy. New York contains forty-three thousand, two hundred and fourteen square miles, divided into fifty-five counties, and having six thousand and eighty-seven post towns and cities, containing one million, five hundred thou-

sand inhabitants, together with six million acres of cultivated land, improvements in agriculture and manufactures, in trade and commerce, which include a valuation of three hundred millions of dollars of taxable property; one hundred and fifty thousand militia, armed and equipped; a constitution founded upon an equality of right, having no test-oaths, and recognizing no religious distinctions, and seven thousand free schools and colleges, affording the blessings of education to four hundred thousand children. Such is the great and increasing State to which the emigration of the Jews is directed.

The desired spot in the State of New York, to which I hereby invite my beloved people throughout the world, in common with those of every religious denomination, is called Grand Island, and on which I shall lay the foundation of a City of Refuge, to be called Ararat.

An Immigrant Writes to Relatives in Germany

1835. Local Jewish newspapers in Germany printed glowing accounts of life in America. This one appeared in Das Füllhorn, *published in Bamberg.*

I presume you know through my last letter from England how I lived in England and how I felt. Now, about two years ago my lucky star directed me, like many another young man, to go West and I travelled with a friend from London to New York. Arriving here safely after a long and difficult journey, I got a job in a store where I remained 55 months, and saved a nice sum of money; during this time I met an English girl outstanding in every respect who to my good fortune consented to marry me. We live an extremely happy and contented life and six months ago were blessed with a healthy, pretty little daughter. I own a well-stocked clothing store here and live quite happily among my friends and the relatives of my wife and as part of a circle of many respectable Israelites, for more than 2,000 Israelites live here, most of whom are religious observers. There are three synagogues here. One large German one, which is very beautiful and has a tower with a clock, and then an extremely beautiful and richly decorated Portuguese one and further a small German synagogue. The Israelites living here come from various countries: Americans, Englishmen, Dutchmen, Portuguese and German. Everybody can choose freely whether or in which synagogue he wants to be enrolled. In general the Israelites here live completely free and without restrictions like all the rest of the citizens, and many immigrants still come to America from Germany and from our region, and among these to my happy surprise [I met] last week our friend, Dr. Nordheimer (of Memmelsdorf) who arrived here safely from Hamburg. How conditions and prospects in America are in general I shall describe in the letter to my dear brother." This [letter] now reads as follows:

You will have learned from my previous letter to our dear relatives what my domestic conditions are like here and what my general situation here is so that I have now only to add a general description of America. It is a little difficult though to write about this point since so much has already been written about it and America is praised in one work and blamed in another; for this reason I shall only tell the truth as I see it. When I look at America in general terms I can in truth maintain that in spite of its shortcomings it is nevertheless much better than Europe because not only is there no difference in the civic relations between Christians and Jews and everybody can do what he wishes, but what is more everybody who is ready to exert himself only a little can easily find work and his efforts in every trade are rewarded. Thus for instance all

Naturalization Papers, 1848: Naturalization papers of Frederick Tedesco issued in New York City, 1848. *Credit:* LBI

Naturalization Papers, 1848: Naturalization papers of Elias Wolf issued in Tuscarawas County, Ohio, 1848. *Credit:* Edwin Wolf, 2nd

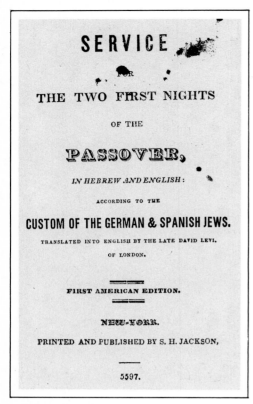

SERVICE

FOR

THE TWO FIRST NIGHTS

OF THE

PASSOVER,

IN HEBREW AND ENGLISH:

ACCORDING TO THE

CUSTOM OF THE GERMAN & SPANISH JEWS.

TRANSLATED INTO ENGLISH BY THE LATE DAVID LEVI.

OF LONDON.

FIRST AMERICAN EDITION.

NEW-YORK.

PRINTED AND PUBLISHED BY S. H. JACKSON,

5597.

Passover Service, 1837: Title page of Passover service in English and Hebrew, published in New York, 1837. *Credit:* AJHS

craftsmen whose trade is not in competition with factory production are very well off and every one can live well and still lay aside a nice sum of money. Thus for example tailors, shoemakers and carpenters earn 20 fl. a week with little effort. One can live quite decently for half and thus save forty fl. a month. There will never be too many tailors and shoemakers coming here, since such are demanded in the newspaper every day. A girl that is ready to sew earns 7–10 fl. a week. Boys are accepted with pleasure in any trade whatsoever and don't have to pay the master as in Germany but get board and room and 100–120 fl. even in the first year, in the second year and in various trades even 200–250 fl. You will probably think this exaggerated but it is the purest truth. Those who come here to trade have much greater difficulties, since business is overcrowded and most of those who come here are not yet acquainted with the English language, and is able to get a job in a store, he could easily manage through a recommendation to get into a store where he receives 70–80 fl. a month aside from board and room, which is not much yet, since a good bookkeeper ordinarily gets 150 fl. a month. Now, if somebody is thrifty and active, he can go pretty far in this country. That many a man has already been deceived in his hopes may have various reasons; this much is sure, however, that no craftsman who is ready to work will have anything to regret if he comes to America.

A Letter to President Van Buren Regarding the Damascus Affair

August 24, 1840. This resolution, approved at a protest demonstration in New York was sent to the President. There were other demonstrations and protests in Richmond and Philadelphia against persecution of Jews in Damascus accused of blood libel. The Secretary of State replied that the American government had taken action already.

At a meeting of the Israelites of the City of New York held on the 19th last for the purpose of uniting in an expression of sentiment on the subject of the persecutions of their Brethren in Damascus, the following Resolution was unanimously adopted "Resolved that a Letter be addressed to his Excellency the President of the United States respectfully requesting, that he will direct the Consuls of the United States in the Dominions of the Pasha of Egypt to cooperate with the Consuls or other agents accredited to the Pasha. in endeavoring to obtain a fair & impartial trial for our Brethren in Damascus"

In transmitting the same to your Excellency we beg leave to express what we we are persuaded is the unanimous opinion of the Israelites throughout the Union, that you will cheerfully use every possible effort to induce the Pasha of Egypt to manifest more liberal treatment towards his Jewish Subjects not only from the dictates of humanity but from the obvious policy and justice by which such a course is recommended by the tolerant spirit of the age in which we live.

The Liberal & enlightened views in relation to matters of faith, which have distinguished our Government from its very inception to the present time have Secured the sincere gratitude and kind regard of the Members of all religious denominations and we trust that the efforts of your Excellency in this behalf will serve to render yet more grateful & to impress more fully on the minds of the Citizens of the United States, the Kindness and liberality of that Government under which they live.

With the best wishes of those in whose behalf we address you, for your health & happiness and for the glory & honor of our common Country We have the honor to be Your Excellency's Obedient Servants

I B Kursheedt Chairman&c
Theodore J. Seixas Secy.
&c

Beth Elohim Synagogue, Charleston, undated:
In 1749 the first Jewish congregation was
organized in Charleston. In 1794 this synagogue was dedicated; it was destroyed by
fire in 1838. The print is after a drawing by
Solomon N. Carvalho. *Credit:* AJHS

**Beth Elohim Synagogue, Interior, Charleston,
undated:** This print, made after a drawing by
Solomon N. Carvalho, depicts a typical interior arrangement for an Orthodox synagogue.
Credit: AJHS

Mrs. Hyam Harris, undated: Silhouette by Augustin Edouart. *Credit:* AJHS

August Belmont, 1839: A German immigrant who changed his name from Schönberg, Belmont came to this country as the representative of the House of Rothschild. He became one of the leading financiers of his generation. Silhouette by Augustin Edouart. *Credit:* AJHS

Moss Family, undated: Mr. and Mrs. Samuel Lyons Moss with their children and slave boy. Silhouette by Augustin Edouart. *Credit:* AJHS

Judah Touro, about 1854: Judah Touro was a New Orleans merchant and philanthropist who donated generously to the establishment of synagogues, hospitals and libraries in New Orleans, New York, Boston and Newport. Daguerreotype by Anderson & Blessing. *Credit:* AJHS

Henry Hendricks, about 1860: One of three sons of Harmon Hendricks who built the first copper rolling mill in America in Soho, New Jersey. The Hendricks family remained active in the copper industry for 175 years. *Credit:* AJHS

Captain Jonas Phillips Levy, about 1855: He served with the U.S. Navy during the Mexican War. He worked for civil rights for Jews abroad and helped to establish the first synagogue in Washington of which he was president. Daguerreotype. *Credit:* AJHS

Establishing a Jewish Community West of the Alleghenies

December 25, 1843. Joseph Jonas, the first Jew to settle in Cincinnati in 1817, recounted his personal experiences while this city was still a frontier community.

It was in the month of October, 1816, that a young man arrived in New York from the shores of Great Britain, to seek a home and a residence in the New World. This individual's name was Joseph Jonas, from Plymouth, in England. He had read considerably concerning America, and was strongly impressed with the descriptions given of the Ohio river, and had therefore determined to settle himself on its banks, at Cincinnati. This he was encouraged in by a relative he met with in New York. On arriving at Philadelphia, he was persuaded to settle in that city, and took up his residence for a short time with the amiable family of the late Mr. Samuel Joseph, (peace be unto him.) He here became acquainted with the venerable Mr. Levi Philips, who took a great interest in him, using many persuasive arguments not to proceed to Ohio. One of them was frequently brought to his recollection: "In the wilds of America, and entirely amongst gentiles, you will forget your religion and your God."

But the fiat had gone forth, that a new resting place for the scattered sons of Israel should be commenced, and that a sanctuary should be erected in the Great West, dedicated to the Lord of hosts, to resound with praises to the ever-living God. The individual solemnly promised the venerable gentleman never to forget his religion nor forsake his God: he received his blessing, and taking leave of the kind friends with whom he had resided, departed for Pittsburg on the 2d of January, 1817. On his arrival, he found the navigation of the Ohio stopped by being frozen over. He procured profitable employment during the winter, being a mechanic, and at the breaking up of the ice was wafted on the bosom of this noble river to the then rising city of Cincinnati, where he arrived on the 8th day of March 1817. The city then contained about six thousand inhabitants, but the only Israelite was himself. With the assistance of the God of his ancestors, he soon became established in a lucrative and respectable business, and his constant prayer was, that he might be a nucleus around whom the first congregation might be formed, to worship the God of Israel in this great western territory. Solitary and alone he remained for more than two years; and at the solemn festivals of our holy religion, in solitude was he obliged to commune with his Maker. Before proceeding further, permit me to make a few remarks: from the period of the arrival of the first Israelite in Cincinnati to this date, the Israelites have been much esteemed and highly respected by their fellow-citizens, and a general interchange of

Cincinnati, about 1850: Jews moved westward with the expanding frontier. A Jewish community was established in Cincinnati in 1824. This city on the Ohio River became the hub of a Jewish dry goods trade with a network of merchants and peddlers. *Credit:* CINHS

Joseph Jonas, about 1860: The first Jew to settle in Cincinnati came from Plymouth, England via New York, Philadelphia and Pittsburgh. He became parnas of the first congregation. *Credit:* AJA

civilities and friendships has taken place between them. Many persons of the Nazarene faith residing from 50 to 100 miles from the city, hearing there were Jews living in Cinncinnati, came into town for the special purpose of viewing and conversing with some of "the children of Israel, the holy people of God," as they termed us. From the experience which we have derived by being the first settlers of our nation and religion in a new country, we arrive at the conclusion, that the Almighty will give his people favour in the eyes of all nations, if they only conduct themselves as good citizens in a moral and religious point of view; for it is already conceded to us by our neighbours that we have the fewest drunkards, vagrants, or individuals amenable to the laws, of any community, according to our numbers in this city or district of country; and we also appreciate the respect and esteem those individuals are held in, who duly conform to the principles of our religion, especially by a strict conformity to our holy Sabbath and festivals.

The original founders of our congregation were principally from Great Britain, and consequently their mode of worship was after the manner of the Polish and German Jews; but being all young people they were not so prejudiced in favour of old customs as more elderly people might have been, and especially as several of their wives had been brought up in Portuguese congregations. We therefore introduced considerable chorus singing into our worship, in which we were joined by the sweet voices of the fair daughters of Zion, and our Friday evening service was as well attended for many years as the Sabbath morning. At length, however, large emigrations of our German brethren settled amongst us; again our old customs have conquered, and the sweet voices of our ladies are seldom heard.

During the months of May, June and July, we sold seats in our new Synagogue to the amount of four thousand and five hundred dollars, which enabled us to finish the interior of the building in much superior style than we originally in-

Cleveland, about 1850: A Jewish community was established in Cleveland in 1839. *Credit:* LC

tended. The edifice is erected with a handsome Doric front, a flight of stone steps over the basement, with a portico supported by pillars. The building is eighty feet in length by thirty-three in breadth, including a vestibule of twelve feet. It has a very handsome dome in the centre ornamented with panels and carved mouldings in stucco. On entering the building from the vestibule, the beholder is attracted by the chaste and beautiful appearance of the Ark situated at the east end; it is eighteen feet in front, surrounded by a neat low white balustrade, ornamented by four large brass candlesticks; it is ascended by a flight of steps handsomely carpeted; the entablature and frieze are composed of stucco work, supported by four large fluted pillars of the Corinthian order; the doors are in the flat, sliding into the sides; when opened, the interior appears richly decorated with crimson damask; the curtain is handsomely festooned in front of the doors; between the pillars on each side are two marble painted slabs containing the Decalogue in gold letters; the entablature and frieze contain suitable inscriptions; the whole is surmounted by a large vase in imitation of the pot of incense. Near the west end is the Taybah; it is a square surrounded on

three sides by steps imitating marble, with seats enclosed for the Parnassim in front; it is handsomely painted, as well as all the seats, in imitation of maple: the balustrade of the Taybah is surmounted on the four corners by four large brass candlesticks; on the platform is the reader's desk, neatly covered, and supported by two small columns. The gallery, with a neat white front, is over the vestibule, supported by pillars, with six rows of seats. The seats in the area are placed four in a row, fronting the ark, on each side of the Taybah. The ceiling is handsomely finished, with five circles of stucco work, from which are suspended five large brass chandeliers. The edifice, when finished, was much admired, and the Building Committee received a vote of thanks from the congregation for their unremitted attentions in procuring the necessary funds and materials, and for the time and trouble bestowed by them in superintending the erection of the building. The 9th of September, 1836, corresponding to the 27th of Elul, 5596, was appointed for the consecration. The day having arrived, the crowd of our Christian friends was so great that we could not admit them all. We therefore selected the clergy, and the families of those gentlemen.

Chicago, 1845: A Jewish congregation was established in Chicago in 1845. *Credit:* LC

Joining the "Gold Rush" to California

1851. Abraham Abrahamsohn recounted his experiences in traveling from the East Coast, across the Isthmus of Panama, and to San Francisco.

Steamer Golden City, about 1849: This paddle wheel steamer was typical of the ships which carried passengers from the West Coast of Panama to San Francisco. *Credit:* BL

Everywhere, everywhere one heard the fame of the newly discovered land of gold, and how so many people had quickly and easily become rich there. Everywhere the astonished eye saw people who, coming from there, showed large chunks of gold or carried them braggingly around their necks, and who lived in grand style. I still had nine hundred dollars worth of goods and one hundred fifty dollars in cash. I packed the goods in boxes and sent them insured, on a sailing ship around Cape Horn to San Francisco. On January 13, 1851, I myself went aboard the steamer *Christian City,* and after a good trip I reached Chagris on the Isthmus of Panama, which joins North and South America. Our trip was not to go around the southern tip of America. Cape Horn, but over said Isthmus of Panama to the Pacific or Great Ocean, where we were sure to find ships to transport us to California. The heat affected us very strongly in Chagris, and Indians who live there in huts made of sugar cane, took us in canoes made from hollowed logs upstream to Grakun, where there also are Indians living in cane huts. Worn out from the difficulties of the trip and the glowing heat, we fell asleep in the alleys

of the village, but were woken up in the night by dreadful cries and noises. Several huts were going up in flames and after a few minutes the whole place. The copper-red Indians were running around like black goblins, trying to save what they could of their miserable possessions. After a quarter-hour the whole village was in ashes. This was at the beginning of March.

In the morning forty of us took off on mules, the rent of which cost some eight dollars, and went over rocky mountains to Panama. A really hellish heat lay over the Spanish-built town with its stone houses and flat roofs, and yellow fever was raging. To increase our sorry state, there was no ship in the harbor to transport us. We had to wait there three

weeks, and several hundred people from almost all nations of the world with us. Thus it happened that food supplies were very expensive and when the longed-for ships finally arrived, I no longer had enough money for the passage. Although I carried glass and my diamond with me, I was unable to earn anything, as none of the houses there had any windows, only wooden venetian blinds. I was in a desperate situation, and for a long time I went fruitlessly onto the ships, trying to find work for my fare. Finally I had the great luck of finding a place as dishwasher and bootblack for first class, on the steamer *Golden Gate,* with eighty passengers travelling on it.

About Panama, I just wish to mention a large magnificent Catholic church, which

"The Way They Go to California," 1849: A contemporary lithograph depicting the Gold Rush to California. A considerable number of Jews were among the first to arrive in San Francisco. *Credit:* BL

"The Way They Cross The Isthmus," 1849: To get to California there was the choice of going by boat to Panama and crossing The Isthmus or going around Cape Horn. This contemporary lithograph, as well as depicting the hazards of the trip includes racial slurs directed toward the local population. Numerous Jews such as Abraham Abrahamsohn and Adolph Sutro took this route to San Francisco. *Credit:* BL

K. Heller, undated: K. Heller, a native of Bavaria, came to San Francisco with his wife, Esther, about 1851. *Credit:* WHJC

Esther Heller, undated: Esther Heller, a native of Bavaria, came to San Francisco with her husband about 1851. *Credit:* WJHC

Mokelumne Hill, 1855: One of the many mining towns in the hills of California where Jewish businessmen provided necessary services. *Credit:* BL

Levinson Brothers & Co., 1855: One of the Jewish merchants in Mokelumne Hill, California. *Credit:* BL

Boston Fancy Store, 1855: A. Straus was the proprietor of this general merchandise store in Mokelumne Hill, California. *Credit:* BL

Downieville, 1856: One of the many mining towns in the hills of California where Jewish businessmen provided necessary services. *Credit:* BL

had so much gold, silver and precious stones glowing in its rooms, that the eyes of the beholder hurt.

In a few days we left the harbor and sailed northward toward California. I was kept extraordinarily busy. After I had worn myself out during the day with plates and other cooking utensils, I had to spend every night cleaning so many shoes. But I was treated well and I had plenty to eat from the left-overs and enough to give to other steerage passengers, for which they gladly helped me with my work. During the storm-free trip an old Jew died and was buried at sea according to Jewish religious customs. The Captain took charge of his belongings and later sent them to the family in St. Louis.

On April 8, 1851, the morning sun shone with such golden glow on the partly bare, partly green, very high mountains with magnificent cedars on them behind San Francisco, that we greeted them jubilantly in the happy certainty of the riches they contained. At ten o'clock the anchor was dropped while we yelled "Hurray" and the cannon were shot off. We were among a large number of ships from almost all the seafaring nations, and with warm memories of our homeland we greeted the flags of merchants from Bremen and Hamburg, which were fluttering gaily in the fresh morning breeze. The customs officers soon appeared in a steamer, to collect the dues for declarable items, and the doctor to examine our health. All

the passengers went ashore on the same day, but I still had dishes to wash and followed the next morning.

On all the faces of the people I saw, as well as in their demeanor and their busy work, I clearly read the desire to become rich quickly in order to leave their Eldorado even more quickly. Many people were proudly and triumphantly wandering through the streets with large pieces of gold, which looked like yellow iron dross, or with bags full of gold grains in their hands. They had come from the mines in order to lose their either hard or easily acquired winnings in the gambling halls in one night, and then have the pleasure of grubbing again for the yellow metal in the mountains.

Los Angeles, 1857: Although they were few in number, Jews were among the early settlers in Los Angeles at this time. *Credit:* BL

Billiards and Saloon, 1858: C.L. Weiss operated this establishment in North San Juan, California. *Credit:* BL

J. Meier, 1856: A Jewish merchant who operated a dry goods store combined with a cigar and tobacco store in Downieville, California. *Credit:* BL

A. Wolf & Brothers, about 1855: A dry goods store in Sonora, California. *Credit:* BL

The city was filled to excess with large gambling houses, whose presence was indicated by loud music. They sought to make the passerby curious with drums, trumpets, violins, flutes and guitars, and those that entered were tempted with piles of silver and especially gold coins. Whenever these instruments made a deafening noise, one became downright cheerful. Many of my compatriots appeared in such houses as musicians, especially on the flute and the guitar. Beautiful girls, for the most part French, but also brown, black-eyed Mexicans, with perfumed flowers in their hair and on their bosom, flirted with word, smile and look, and in each gambling hall they offered to everyone who entered, ale, port, various wines, punch and grog, white bread, butter, cheese, all of it for free. The games were faro, twenty-one, dice, roulette and monte, a Mexican game resembling lansquenet.

The gambling places, like the restaurants, fancy-goods stores, coffee houses and fine bakeries were for the most part run by Frenchmen. Among the many Germans there were several respectable stores. Jews generally were in the clothing business, and the Chinese, of whom there were not a few, ran eating places which were heavily patronized due to their respectability and cheapness. The population of the city, the majority of which is from the United States, could not be determined due to the coming and going. But while I was there it must have been around 30,000 souls.

Labor, rent and food were enormously expensive. A day laborer received six dollars a day, a workman ten to eighteen, and a waiter over one hundred dollars a month. A wooden partition called a room cost twenty to thirty dollars, storage for a trunk one to two dollars, and one was lucky to find oneself under a roof, that is, under a canvas cover. The price of goods and food stuffs varied according to sometimes large, sometimes scant supplies, but was always high, and one can imagine the rest when one knows that I had to pay one dollar for an egg.

Levi Strauss, about 1870: He began his career by selling clothing and dry goods. Later he began to manufacture blue denim pants for miners in San Francisco which have since become the most popular item of American clothing. *Credit:* WJHS

Adolph Sutro, undated: Born in Westphalia, Germany Adolph Sutro was among the first Jews to arrive in San Francisco in 1850. His flamboyant career included many enterprises, among them a cigar and tobacco store. Later he was involved in silver mining and eventually elected mayor of San Francisco in 1894. *Credit:* LC

Residence of Isaias N. Hellman, Los Angeles, 1880: He came to Los Angeles at the age of fifteen from Bavaria and worked as a clerk in a dry goods store operated by a relative, before establishing his own dry goods firm. In 1868 he entered banking; later he organized the Farmers and Merchants Bank, the first incorporated bank in Los Angeles. His residence was said to be one of the finest in the state outside of San Francisco. *Credit:* LC

Newmark Block, Los Angeles, 1880: H. Newmark was born in Prussia in 1834 and came to Los Angeles in 1853. He founded H. Newmark & Co. in 1853, dealers in groceries, hardware, hides, wools, etc. In 1877 he purchased the Temple Block for one hundred and thirty thousand dollars; the building was subsequently renamed. *Credit:* LC

Exploring the West

1857. Solomon Nunes Carvalho, an artist and photographer, accompanied John Charles Fremont on his fifth expedition across the Rocky Mountains. Several years later he published his record of the trip.

The crossing of the Grand River, the eastern fork of the Colorado, was attended with much difficulty and more danger. The weather was excessively cold, the ice on the margin of either side of the river was over eighteen inches thick; the force of the stream always kept the passage in the centre open; the distance between the ice, was at our crossing, about two hundred yards. I supposed the current in the river to run at the rate of six miles an hour. The animals could scarcely keep their footing on the ice, although the men had been engaged for half an hour in strewing it with sand. The river was about six feet deep, making it necessary to swim our animals across; the greatest difficulty was in persuading them to make the abrupt leap from the ice to the roaring gulph, and there was much danger from drowning in attempting to get on the sharp ice on the other side, the water being beyond the depth of the animals, nothing but their heads were above water, consequently the greater portion of their riders' bodies were also immersed in the freezing current.

To arrive at a given point, affording the most facilities for getting upon the ice, it was necessary to swim your horse in a different direction to allow for the powerful current. I think I must have been in the water, at least a quarter of an hour. The awful plunge from the ice into the water, I never shall have the ambition to try again; the weight of my body on the horse, naturally made him go

under head and all; I held on as fast as a cabin boy to a main-stay in a gale of wind. If I had lost my balance it is most probable I should have been drowned. I was nearly drowned as it was, and my clothes froze stiff upon me when I came out of it. Some of the Delawares crossed first and built a large fire on the other side, at which we all dried our clothes standing in them.

It is most singular, that with all the exposure that I was subjected to on this journey, I never took the slightest cold, either in my head or on my chest; I do

not recollect ever sneezing. While at home, I ever was most susceptible to cold.

The whole party crossed without any accident; Col. Fremont was the first of our party to leap his horse into the angry flood, inspiring his men, by his fearless example to follow.

"Julius Caesar crossed the Rubicon with an immense army; streams of blood followed in his path through the countries he subdued, to his arrival at the Eternal City, where he was declared dictator and consul."

Sigmund Shlesinger, Frontier Fighter, 1870: He was one of fifty mounted scouts who held off almost a thousand Native Americans at the Battle of Beecher's Island in 1868. *Credit:* AJA

Solomon N. Carvalho, undated: A talented and adventurous artist, he crossed the Rocky Mountains with John Charles Fremont's expedition in 1853. Silhouette by Augustin Edouart. *Credit:* AJHS

From Otterberg, Bavaria to Talbotton, Georgia

1845–1864. Isidor Straus, one of the brothers who made Macy's the world's preeminent department store, recounted his family's journey from Europe to America.

I was born in Otterberg, Palatinate of Bavaria (Rheinpfalz), February 6th, 1845—if I mistake not, in the same house where my father was born. The Straus family resided there, or in the immediate vicinity, for several generations. My father, Lazarus Straus, was the eldest son of Jacob Straus, who was the eldest of three brothers, all residing in the same town of Otterberg. My grandfather's two brothers were named Lazarus and Salomon, the latter being the father of my mother and the youngest of the brothers. My father was born in Otterberg, April 25th, 1809. My mother whose maiden name was Sara Straus, was also born in Otterberg, January 14th, 1823.

The three brothers, Jacob, Lazarus and Salomon, all lived in Otterberg. If they were not born there, they were born in close proximity. I have an idea that they may have been born within five miles, at a place called Minchweiller. The name Straus figured among the prominent Jewish families of that section. The Jews of the Palatinate adopted family names when Napoleon took possession of that part of the country. My great-

grandfather, whose name was Jacob Lazar, was one of the members of the great Sanhedrin assembled in Paris in 1807 by Napoleon to aid in making laws so as to harmonize the status of the Jews, who were accorded equal rights with the professors of other religious sects. I assume that his name was Jacob ben Lazar, for up to the time that the Jews adopted family names it was customary for them to be identified in this wise: Jacob, son of Lazarus.

My great-grandfather had contracts with Napoleon's Army for the delivery of supplies for the horses—my impression is as a sub-contractor, for I have heard my father speak of a lawsuit which he recalls as a boy was being carried on by his father and uncles against a Fould family of Paris growing out of some of those contracts. I never knew my grandfather on my father's side, as he died when my father was a young man, but I well remember the other two brothers, Lazarus and Salomon, the latter being my grandfather on my mother's side. They were both cultured and educated gentlemen. They spoke French as fluently as German. Neither one was engaged in any regular business. They were land owners, and, I believe, when the crops were harvested, they bought the wheat, oats, clover and clover seed, which were the principal crops of that section, from their neighbors and then sent them to the market of Kaiserslautern

and Mannheim, the chief commercial towns of the section.

The Jewish burial ground at Mehlingen (about 5 miles from Otterberg) contains the graves of several generations of Strauses, there being no Jewish cemetery at Otterberg.

Up to 1848, Otterberg was a very thriving town, containing perhaps 40 Jewish families. After that they began to emigrate, and at this writing not a single Jewish family remains. They had a nice synagogue and school house which were both yet actively occupied when I visited them in 1863. But after the death of my grandfather about 1873 or 1874, who seems to have been the last prop of the Jewish community, it rapidly disintegrated, so that when I again visited there in the early eighties, both buildings were demolished and the religious relics which the synagogue contained had been removed to Kaiserslautern.

My father, who was active in the revolution of 1848, finding life burdensome after the collapse of the movement, long contemplated emigrating, but his ties were so many that he found it most difficult to tear himself away, and not until the spring of 1852 could he bring himself to take this decisive step. I believe he landed at Philadelphia and there met a number of former acquaintances who had preceded him to this country, some of whom were established in business in different parts of the country. He was

The Peddler's Wagon, about 1850: Newly arrived German Jewish immigrants began their lives in the United States as peddlers, moving from town to town with a wagon load of merchandise. As time went on, some established small stores while others created wholesale firms and remerchandising networks. *Credit:* LC

advised to go south to make a start in business, and I believe Oglethorpe, Georgia, proved to be his destination. There he met some acquaintances from the old country through whom he made a connection with two brothers, Kaufman, who were the owners of a peddler's wagon which circulated with an assortment of dry goods, Yankee notions and the like through several adjoining counties. In those comparatively primitive days, when that state was yet sparsely settled, the rural parts, through the existence of slavery, segregated on the large plantations, contained a population equal to, and often greater than, the nearest villages. The itinerant merchant filled a want, and hence his vocation was looked upon with much favor by the people and he was treated by the owners of the plantations, which he usually visited at regular periods, with a spirit of equality that it is difficult to appreciate at the present day. Another feature which helped to lift the plane of this vocation in the southern states was the existence of slavery, as this drew a line of demarcation between the white and the black race and was largely instrumental in giving every white man a sort of status of

equality which probably did not prevail in sections where slavery did not exist.

Thus, if the peddler proved to be an honest, upright man, who conscientiously treated his customers with fairness and made no misrepresentation as to his wares, he was, during his sojourn at the house (for he slept and took his meals with the family who was his customer) usually one night at a house, treated as an honored guest and his visits were looked forward to with real pleasure. Another feature, which almost sounds like fiction, respecting the relationship between even the wealthiest and most aristocratic families and the comparatively humble peddler, was the chivalrous spirit of hospitality that refused to take any pay for board and lodging of the man and made only a small charge for the feed of the horses, which gives an idea of the view entertained by the southern people regarding the proper conduct towards the stranger under his roof. The peddler in return usually reciprocated by making some suitable present, either to the lady or her daughter, and he frequently provided himself with articles for the purpose, with the view of ascertaining at one visit what

particular item might prove especially welcome at the next, and thus a bond of friendship sprang up which in this part of the country and at this time seems difficult to understand.

In the course of these journeys my father happened to reach Talbotton, Georgia, which town made such a favorable impression on him, owing to the air of refinement which its appearance gave evidence of, as compared with all other points he had visited, that the idea struck him that it was a place in which he would like to settle. He was fond of relating that this little town was the first one which made him feel that he had gotten away from the uncouth, primitive and frontier-like conditions which characterized every other settlement he had passed through. The houses looked well kept and neat, attractively painted, nice gardens, flowers and cultivated shrubbery abounded, and then he found that these external signs were borne out by other conditions; splendid schools, both for boys and girls, and the people appeared as a whole to be of a finer type than he had met with anywhere else.

Talbotton is the county seat of Talbot

Store and Livery Stable of A. Levi, about 1873: Store and livery stable of A. Levi, located in Julian, San Diego County, California. *Credit:* SDHS

County, and while Georgia was termed the Empire State of the South, Talbot was called the Empire County of the state. Father's judgment, therefore, was not astray. It happened to be court week when he reached there, which always brings many people to the town, and it therefore was at its best so far as activity goes. This no doubt also had its influence in impressing my father, for during court week business is active and the town has a comparatively festive appearance.

Another factor must not be lost sight of. Peddlers had to take out a license in each county in order to do business, and this had to be obtained at the county seat. So his first step was to go to the Court House to ascertain the cost of a license. It proved to be very high—so high that my father was in doubt whether the business which he might do would justify the outlay. So in leaving the Court House the idea occurred to him that he might find a store where he could unpack his goods and take advantage of the opportunity which so many strangers presented (visitors, not permanent residents, were in town) to test the business calibre of the place. He found that the only tailor in the village occupied a store

which appeared to be too large for his needs, and a short interview developed the fact that he was willing to have my father share its occupancy, at a price which seemed attractive, I believe my father said less than a license to ply his trade as an itinerant would have cost. So he promptly accepted, and immediately unpacked and displayed his wares. The results proved so satisfactory that after a few weeks his stock was so depleted, and the first impression of the town turned out to be so fully justified, that he proposed to his partner, Kaufman, to try to rent a store in the town and settle there. They succeeded in finding one, and my father arranged to leave for Philadelphia to lay in a stock of goods. His partner doubted the wisdom of the move, for he feared that the Oglethorpe merchant who had heretofore supplied them with their merchandise might put his veto on their settling down to store keeping, instead of peddling, and as they were beholden to the Oglethorpe merchant, and were indebted to him for most of the merchandise they possessed, the fear was not entirely unfounded. He further doubted my father's ability to procure sufficient credit in Philadelphia

to enable them to secure sufficient merchandise in the comparatively large space (large only in comparison to the wagon which theretofore constituted their place of business) to make a display which the rented store required.

When my father reached Philadelphia, he immediately began to look around to ascertain what prospects he had towards accomplishing the purpose of his mission. He found several wholesale houses, in different lines of merchandise that he required, who either knew him personally or knew the family reputation, as it happened that there were in Philadelphia many former residents of that part of Germany from which my father came. He had no difficulty in establishing credit solely on the strength of the character and reputation which he bore in the old country, for he had neither capital nor business experience in the new country which justified any basis for the same. There were some branches in which this did not prevail, and to these he was recommended by the ones who knew him. Naturally all the merchants rested their credit on faith in his honesty entirely, but there was one line of merchandise which required more capital

J.S. Mansfield's Pioneer Newstand, about 1875: Founded in 1870, his Tuscon, Arizona store was the first newspaper agency in the territory. In addition to maintaining a circulating library, he sold stationery and toys. *Credit:* AHS

ADOLPH SUTRO & CO.

DEALERS IN

FINE HAVANA CIGARS

AND MANUFACTURERS OF FINE

CHEWING & SMOKING TOBACCO

Keep on hand a full assortment of

GENUINE MEERSCHAUM PIPES,

MATCHES, SNUFF, ETC.

Corner of Montgomery and Sacramento Streets,

SAN FRANCISCO.

Adolph Sutro & Co., about 1855: Soon after arriving in San Francisco, Adolph Sutro became a cigar dealer and tobacco merchant. *Credit:* LC

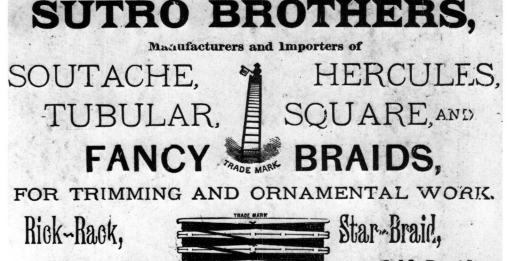

Advertisement, 1860: Advertisement for Mark Levy & Brothers, stationers, New York. *Credit:* SI

Advertisement, about 1870: Advertisement for Sutro Brothers, New York. *Credit:* SI

Advertisement, undated: Advertisements for D. Danziger of New Orleans. *Credit:* SI

Feustmann & Kaufmann, about 1860: In addition to being involved in retail trade, Jewish Merchants were active in wholesale dry goods in cities along the Eastern Seaboard, the Midwest and the California coast. Firms such as this one in Philadelphia often supplied peddlers that traveled by foot with packs or with horses and wagons to rural areas. *Credit:* AJHS

than any German immigrant seemed to have been able to accumulate—dry goods and domestics, as it was known. This branch was entirely in the hands of native Americans, and it was therefore the most difficult branch in which an unknown man, without an established credit, could obtain a foothold. It is necessary to add that it might have been about June when my father reached Philadelphia, before fall stocks were ready, so that the moment assortments were complete my father began making his selections and shipping the merchandise, and by the time the other merchants from the south began to arrive, my father had nearly completed his business. Among these merchants my father found more acquaintances from the old country. One of these, when he learned from my father that he had completed his purchases excepting domestics and dry goods, for which line he had not the courage or knowledge to seek a connection, this newly-found friend offered to introduce him, and in this way he succeeded in carrying out the plan he had laid out for himself, for in the country stores, such as Talbotton had, it was necessary to embrace all lines of merchandise, and "dry goods and domestics," as this brand was designated, constituted the most important.

My father was about ready to return to Georgia when there arrived in Philadelphia the merchant from Oglethorpe

whose house had previously supplied him with goods. He was astonished and evidently displeased with the discovery that he would lose a customer, and intimated that he would see to it that the necessary credit to enable my father to obtain his supplies would be withheld. When, however, he discovered that it was too late to accomplish his jealous end, he changed his tune, as it seems that he feared that my father's influence might prove sufficient to turn the tables against him, and so he expressed the hope that the heretofore friendly relations would not be disturbed.

The most astonished individuals my father found were his partners on his return to Talbotton. How my father, an utter stranger in Philadelphia, without capital and without any known record, as they supposed, could succeed in stocking a store with a general assortment of merchandise, was beyond their comprehension.

This episode must have occurred in the summer of 1853 and as my father was naturally anxious to have his family join him as soon as he was satisfied that he had found a foothold, he began to make plans to this end, and he wrote to my grandfather, the father of my mother, that he expected to be able to take care of them the following summer. The means which my father left behind him in Otterberg were sufficient to keep the family in comfort during the period that he was

preparing a home for them in the new country. He therefore was struggling with the problem only of providing the new home, which he succeeded in doing by the following summer.

My mother with her children (Isidor, Hermine, Nathan and Oscar) left Otterberg August 24th, 1854, on her journey to join my father. We were accompanied to Havre only by my mother's youngest brother, Jacob (a half-brother). Our grandfather accompanied us from Otterberg—he on horseback and the rest of us, together with a nursemaid, in a carriage, to Kaiserslautern, where we took the railroad train to Ferbach, which at that time was the French frontier town, and there we remained one night. In those days, I assume, this was considered a long enough journey for a mother with little children to take in a single day.

On the following morning we left for Paris, where we remained until August 29th, when we started for Havre, where we took the steamer "St. Louis," on her maiden trip, for New York. We arrived in New York on September 12th. Before the steamer had fastened to the dock my mother recognized my father impatiently pacing up and down, and I clearly recall the lengthened minutes, which seemed like hours, that elapsed between his first recognition and the time when we could be embraced in his arms.

Our trip to Talbotton was postponed for several weeks, owing to yellow fever

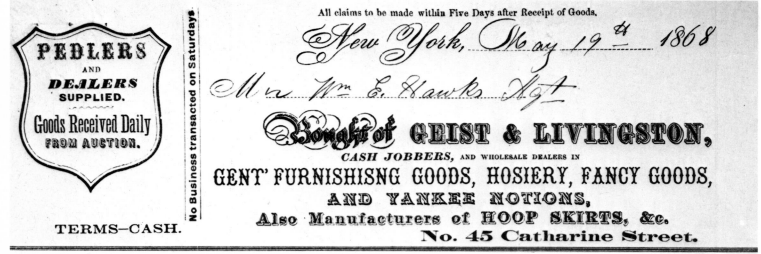

Billhead, 1868: This firm described itself as "cash jobbers and wholesale dealers" who supplied peddlers and did not transact business on Saturdays. *Credit:* SI

raging in Savannah. We remained in New York a few days and then departed for Philadelphia. There we spent several weeks, until it was considered fairly safe to take the steamer for Savannah. To the best of my recollection the steamer arrived at Savannah in the morning, and as it was considered safer not to enter the city, we spent the day, until evening, when the train started, at the shanty called the station, which I believe was on the outskirts of the town.

On arriving at Talbotton, which was five miles from Geneva, the railway station, which part of the journey was made by stagecoach, we found a comfortably furnished home. I recall that soon after reaching there I ran around the grounds on an inspection tour, and coming back to the house to say that our house was built on stilts—the style of construction being no cellar, but open air space, pillars of wood, perhaps twelve feet apart, forming the foundation which supported the building.

After attending a preparatory school, I entered Collingsworth Institute, a sort of high school, which was well known throughout the South and attracted students from many states. There I received practically all the schooling I have enjoyed. My attendance covered the period between 1856 and 1861. In the latter year, owing to the breaking out of the Civil War, and my father's partner having joined the army, I was withdrawn

from school to assist in the business. Even prior to this period I was accustomed to help my father in the evenings, the store being closed to enable my father to go home for the evening meal, then called supper, and opened again after that until about 9:30. There was economy in this program, for the store was lit by kerosene lamps, which was a luxury that the home did not afford, and therefore furnished a better light for the preparation of my lessons, which I always did during these hours. It may sound strange, but economy was practised by my mother, who was a most systematic and circumspect housekeeper, to such an extent that the log fire in the evening was made to do service as light after the evening meal was disposed of, during the winter, while in the summer the outdoor life dispensed largely with the need of light indoors. Candles were in those days the illumination, which were manufactured largely in the household. I can well recall assisting in this industry, the material for which was gathered from the tallow that the cooking material threw off.

My father's partner boarded with us, and this money enabled my mother to defray her outlay for groceries, which was about all of the table necessities that it was necessary to purchase. Vegetables came from our garden. Chickens were also raised, and the principal other meat consisted of smoked bacon, that

was laid in for the whole year during the annual hog-killing season, and generally cured or smoked in our own smoke house. Fresh meat was a rare delicacy in that part of the world. Such a thing as a butcher did not exist in our little town. Whenever a farmer of the county saw fit to slaughter an ox or a sheep, he would bring the carcass to town, exhibit it in a building, or rather shanty, on the public square, called a market, which in reality was only a market for that particular occasion, for at other times it was an empty building, ring a bell which was hung there, and thus announce that some fresh meat was for sale. This scarcely happened oftener than once in two or three weeks, during the cold portion of the year. Ice being a very scarce commodity, a great luxury in fact, which had to be shipped from distances of many miles, was, as I recall it, only brought once in a great while by a confectioner when he wanted to offer the townspeople the opportunity of ice cream treats.

L.J. Levy & Company, about 1857: In 1842 Adam Gimbel opened the first department store in Vincennes, Indiana.   The L.J. Levy & Company dry goods store was in Philadelphia. *Credit:* HSP

Beginning a Business Career

1860–1880. David M. Hyman, for whom Hyman Street in Aspen, Colorado, was named as a result of his mining ventures, later described his years in this country.

I was born at Demmelsdorf, which is a small village in Bavaria, on March 9th, 1846. My father died when I was two years old and my mother married again a few years afterward. I was well treated by my step-father, whose name was Jacob Herman, but from infancy, and as long as I can remember, it was my desire to emigrate to America and to seek my fortune there. At the age of eleven years, I left home in company with an uncle named Gabriel Simon, who was paying a visit to my parents, and I arrived in this country in July, 1857, and went to Cincinnati to live with this Uncle. I entered school the following August and had no knowledge whatsoever of the English language, but I went through what is known as the District School, which included the Fifth Reader, in one year, then went through the intermediate school in two years and the Woodward High School in four years, graduating in 1864.

From the year 1860, I lived with my Uncle Benjamin Simon in Cincinnati, and I was always treated as one of the children. At that time there were five children—three daughters, Caroline, Nanny and Tillie, and two sons, Edward B. and Alexander B. No one certainly was more fortunate than I was in the kind treatment that I uniformly received from relatives. My uncles, Benjamin Simon and Ezekiel Simon, were as devoted to me as though I were their son, and there was nothing that they were not willing to do for me, and I shall remember and appreciate their kindness to me to my dying day. After my graduation from the High School, they proposed to send me to Harvard University to receive a college education. I felt I was old enough to earn my own living, and I declined to accept their kind offer. This I have regretted constantly during my long life for no one appreciates the value of a college education more than the one who has not received it.

I concluded to earn my living and I went to Memphis, Tenn. in the fall of 1864, which was during the Civil War, and I entered the employ of Messrs. Iglauer & Pritz, who were conducting a retail dry-goods store in Memphis.

Mr. Pritz was the father of Sidney E. Pritz and Mattie Freiberg, Carl Pritz and Mildred Meyer. I entered their employ as entry clerk and remained there until after we ended the Civil War, which followed the surrender of Richmond in April 1865. I was in Memphis during the great excitement that followed the assassination of President Lincoln in April 1865. I thought that the South furnished a good field for business enterprise after the end of the war, and I asked my uncles Benjamin & Ezekiel Simon to start me in business because I believed that I could make my fortune somewhere in the South.

I was then nineteen years old, had no experience whatsoever in business except this short one to which I have referred, and I think as I look back upon it today it was almost an insane request, but it was more of an insane act on the part of my uncles to comply with it. I was absolutely ignorant about the business. I knew nothing about the value of goods and, as I said before, I had no experience whatsoever. They, however, consented to my request, and I went south during the latter part of the summer of 1865 to look for a location, and I picked out Montgomery, Ala. as being a promising point where I expected to make my fortune. I had no money whatsoever. I did not pretend to have any, but my uncles furnished me with a large stock of goods and obtained credit for me from the other merchants, everyone of whom knew just exactly my condition and were taking their chances with me. My uncles who at that time composed the firm of Simon & Co., leading dry-goods merchants of Cincinnati, furnished me even the necessary money to pay freights and the incidental expenses connected with the opening of a new store, and I started in at a time when all goods were still very high on account of the depreciation of our currency due to the Civil War and when goods were declining almost daily, so that immediately after you had purchased a stock of goods, there was already a loss before you could ever expose them for sale. I, however, continued for several years and did quite a large business, but the decline in the goods was so great that it was impossible to make any money, and a loss was inevitable each month and each year, with no capital to start with and the business losing money constantly. In the spring of 1867 it became evident that it was useless to continue any longer. My creditors, the principal of which was my uncles' firm, knew this as well as I and they sent me a proposal of their own accord that I was to surrender everything that I had and that they would release me from all obligations; and in addition to that, they would pay all my local debtors in full so that I would not lose my name. The only condition they made was that I was to dispose of all of the goods in the following fall because springtime was not opportune for the sale of the fall & winter goods of which there were the greater quantity. This was all done before I was twenty-one years of age.

I came back to Cincinnati in the spring of 1867, and my uncles then said that I had had experience enough in business, and they insisted then upon my studying law and offered to send me to the law school of the Harvard University and give me a thorough education in the law. I yielded to their request and entered the law office of Bartley & Burnett, Mr. Burnett being the General Burnett who afterwards came to New York and was U.S. District Attorney there for eight years. I stayed with them until the fall of 1867, when I went to Montgomery and disposed of the balance of the goods on hand, which took about two months, and then returned and remained in that office studying law until the fall of 1868 when I entered the law school of Harvard University.

Having failed in business and recognizing that I could not afford to make another failure, I went to work in real earnest and studied hard in order to acquire a knowledge of the law. I may say that my work at Cambridge was very painstaking and thorough and that I occupied a very high position amongst the students of the law school. The professors who were then connected with the law school were Theophilus Parsons, Emery Washburne, and Nathaniel Holmes. All three took a very great interest in me, and I had the benefit of social relations with them that helped me very much. I had strong letters of recommendation from them when I left, and through them I became acquainted with Judge Bellamy Storer who was at that time the nestor of the Bar of Cincinnati and who was one of the judges of the Superior Court of Cincinnati. He came to Cambridge to visit a brother who was living there, and I met him at the house of Prof. Parsons, and he took quite an active interest in my welfare.

I returned to Cincinnati in January, 1870 having received my degree of Bachelor of Laws and immediately entered the firm of Cox. Burnett & Follette in Cincinnati, Ohio.

The year 1879 was a period of great excitement in Colorado on account of the wonderful discoveries that had been made in Leadville and in that mining district, and there was a regular mining craze all over the United States. About that time I had been very successful for a young lawyer and had accumulated in the neighborhood of $40,000, which I had invested principally in paying real estate in Cincinnati. When I made this arrangement with Mr. Hallam, I had no idea of engaging in mining but thought I would take a little flier in the way of speculation and either make or lose in the neighborhood of $5,000. I never contemplated that under any circumstances I would abandon the law, for I was much attached to my profession, and I had no reason whatsoever for changing my business career.

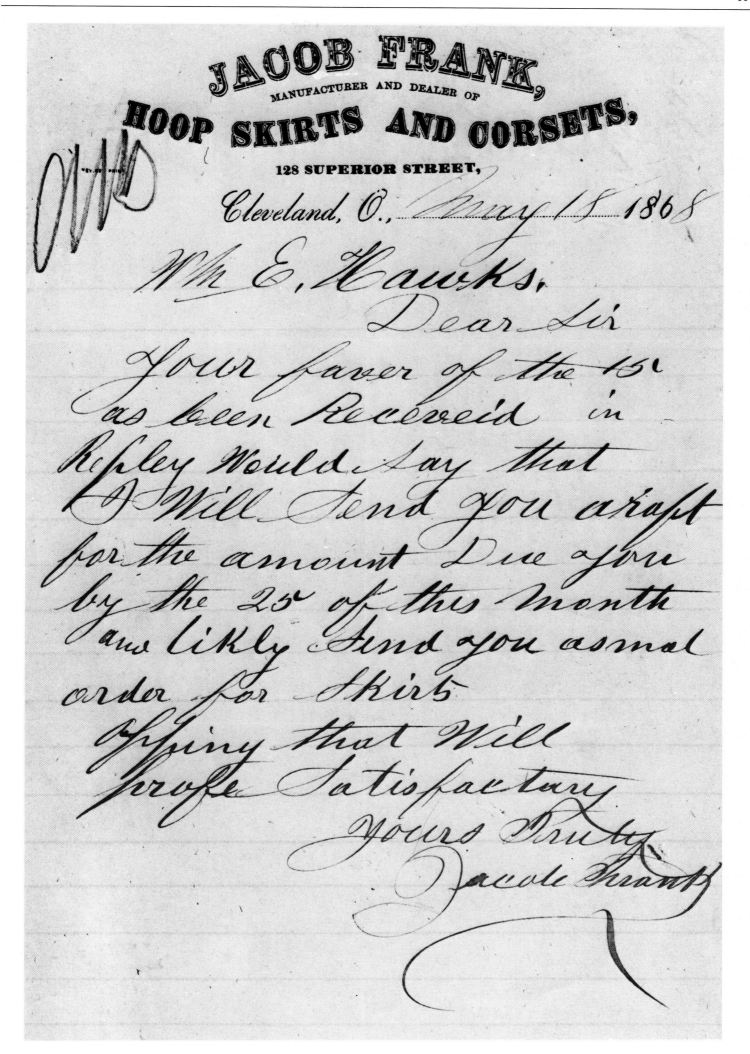

JACOB FRANK,
MANUFACTURER AND DEALER OF
HOOP SKIRTS AND CORSETS,
128 SUPERIOR STREET,

Cleveland, O., May 18 1868

Wm E, Hawks,

Dear Sir

Your favor of the 15.
as been Received in
Repley Would Say that
I Will Send you a draft
for the amount Due you
by the 25 of this month
and likly Send you a smal
order for Skirts

Hoping that Will
profe Satisfactary

Yours Truly

Jacob Frank

Billhead, 1868: Credit: SI

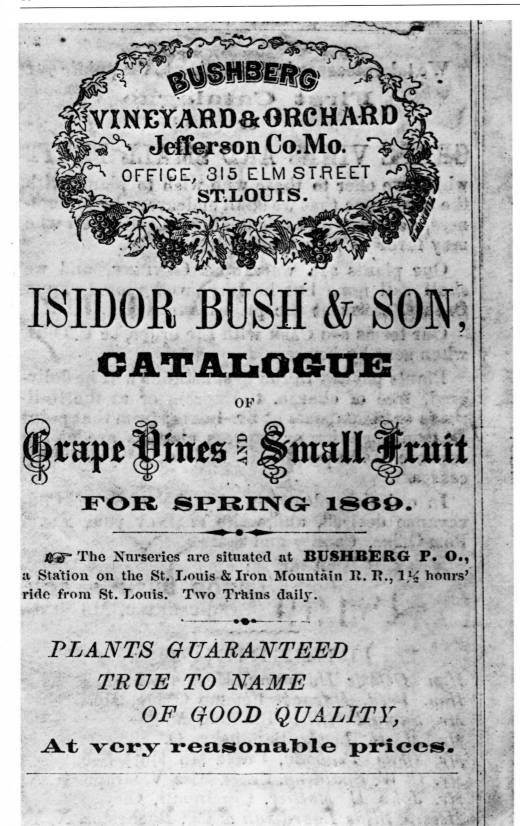

Catalogue Cover, 1869: Cover for the catalogue of Isidor Bush & Son of St. Louis, Missouri. Isidor Bush, a successful viti-culturist, publisher for the abolitionist cause, was also a member of the Missouri State Convention during the Civil War. *Credit:* MIHS

Mr. Hallam went to Colorado and remained there for a number of months before undertaking to acquire any property. He attempted to post himself about the different districts and finally associated himself with one who was called Prof. B. C. Wheeler.

In this connection I want to pay a tribute of respect to the memory of Charles A. Hallam. He was a man of great ability and of the highest integrity and was intensely loyal and devoted to me, and in all our subsequent litigation, which grew out of the purchase of a property that I made through him, he was a most valuable aid to me, and I could always count upon him to make any sacrifice that was necessary in order to help me.

Prof. Wheeler was a man who was unknown to me, a man of wonderful energy, of great professions, but whose character I never admired and whose knowledge of mining matters was not at all equal to his profession.

On the morning of January 22, 1880, if I remember correctly, about three o'clock in the morning, I was awakened by the delivery of a telegram, which was sent from Leadville, Colo. and was signed by Charles A. Hallam and B. C. Wheeler in substance, as follows.

"There is a tide in the affairs of men which if taken at its flood, leads on to fortune. We congratulate you. We have drawn upon you at sight for five thousand dollars."

And that was the commencement of what proved to be a long, eventful, troublesome, and finally successful career, in connection with the acquisition of what were known as the Aspen properties.

I had no knowledge of what the transaction was until I received letters from both Mr. Hallam and Prof. Wheeler which gave me the first outline of what they had done.

It appears from these letters and papers that they took a lease and bond upon seven and a half mining locations situated in what was known as the Roaring Fork Mining District, Gunnison County, Colorado. The names of the claims were:

The Smuggler mining claim

The Hoskins, Monarch, Iron, and Mose mining claims

The Durant mining claim

The Thousand-and-One mining claim

An undivided half of the Steel mining claim

These claims were located in what had heretofore been known as the Ute Indian Reservations, which were only open for settlement and location in 1879, and these locations were the first locations ever made in that section because it had been heretofore occupied and been the property of the Indians. The locators of these claims were experienced and well known prospectors.

Their names were:
Almon C. Fellowes
Debois C. Tooker
Charles H. Bennett
Silas E. Hoskins
Steven W. Keen
Walter C. & Geo. W. Clark

For the first time when I got the letters heretofore mentioned, I learned that Messrs. Wheeler and Hallam had bought these properties for the sum of $165,000, five thousand of which was to be paid in cash and for which they made a draft on me, and $160,000 was to be paid on the 1st day of June. I never contemplated involving myself in a transaction of that kind, and I was horrified when I learned the terms of it, for I did not consider that it was possible in the short time intervening between the first and last payment that I could raise any such sum of money, and especially under the circumstances connected with the location of these properties. They were far away from any railroad transportation, involving the crossing of the main range of the Rocky Mountains and at the season of the year when it was impossible to reach them except upon snow shoes. This was especially true of 1879 and 1880 when they had the heaviest snows that were ever known in Colorado.

I, however, paid the $5,000 and concluded to trust to luck to see what I could do. I knew that in some way the terms of the bond must be changed or I would have to sacrifice my $5,000. I went to Colorado for the first time in my life in February, 1880 and, of course, I heard the wildest reports and rumors about the value of these properties. Nothing could be done, as I said before, because it was impossible to reach them except upon dangerous trips on snow shoes for a distance of some sixty miles and as these claims were covered by probably ten feet of snow, it was impossible to make any examination of them until the snow

had disappeared.

Messrs. Wheeler and Hallam, accompanied by a party of five other men, however, attempted the journey from Leadville on snow shoes and from subsequent reports I learned that they had reached the place in safety, and Mr. Wheeler attempted to make a report to me at Cincinnati on the value of the claims and sent me a telegram stating that each of the four claims—the Smuggler, Durant, Monarch and Iron—were worth more than the amount that I was paying for all of them.

I found myself in a situation which I had never contemplated. When I carelessly said to Mr. Hallam that I was willing to put some money into a venture with him, it was with no expectation that it would involve any change of vocation or of conditions on my part, and here I suddenly found myself confronted by an entirely new experience. I felt that in some way it was necessary to change the terms of the bond and lease Messrs. Wheeler and Hallam had taken upon the property, but how it was to be accomplished I did not know. Sometime in the early Spring of 1880, some gentleman by the name of Miller came into my office in Cincinnati and wanted to know if I was the Mr. Hyman that was interested in some properties in Colorado that were located over the range. I told him I was, and he told me that he was associated with one Abel D. Breed, who was then living in New York, and that he had been requested by Mr. Breed to come and see me and to make an appointment to meet Mr. Breed in New York, as he wanted to see me in relation to these mining claims.

Mr. Breed was then interested in Cincinnati in the big coffin factory of Crane, Breed & Co., and also in some patent medicine and had formerly lived in Cincinnati. He was also well known throughout the country on account of the

sale of a mining claim in Boulder, Colorado, known as the "Caribou" which he had sold in recent years to some Dutch people for one million dollars, and he had quite a reputation as a mining man in consequence of that fact. He was also known as a man of very considerable means. I made an arrangement to meet Mr. Breed in New York and went there for that purpose sometime in the month of April. The first thing that he said to me was "Young man, I want to congratulate you, for you are the first man that I have known who struck a fortune in the very first venture. You have acquired a wonderful property and I want to become interested with you." Of course, this furnished the solution to my difficulties, and I immediately entered into an agreement with him. He asked me how much money I was out and how much money I had contracted to expend and I told him that it was about $16,000. He said, "If I pay you back that amount of money, how much of an interest will you give me with you?" And I told him I would give him one-third of an interest and he said he would agree to help furnish the necessary money to carry the enterprise through. Of course. I had every faith in him and in his ability to do what he had agreed to do, and I drew up an agreement in accordance with our understanding, and he gave me a check for $16,000 to my order. I had a right to use this money as I pleased, but I concluded to use it in connection with the enterprise. This is the first time that I felt that I really had acquired a valuable property and had laid the foundation of a fortune for myself and those associated with me, and it was soon heralded around Cincinnati that Mr. Breed had become interested with me and that I had made a fortune in the acquisition of a valuable mining property in Colorado.

Business Card, about 1875: Credit: SI

Business Card, about 1875: Credit: SI

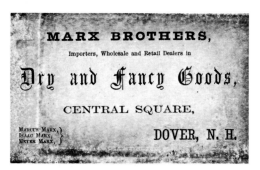

Business Card, about 1875: Credit: SI

Business Card, about 1875: Credit: SI

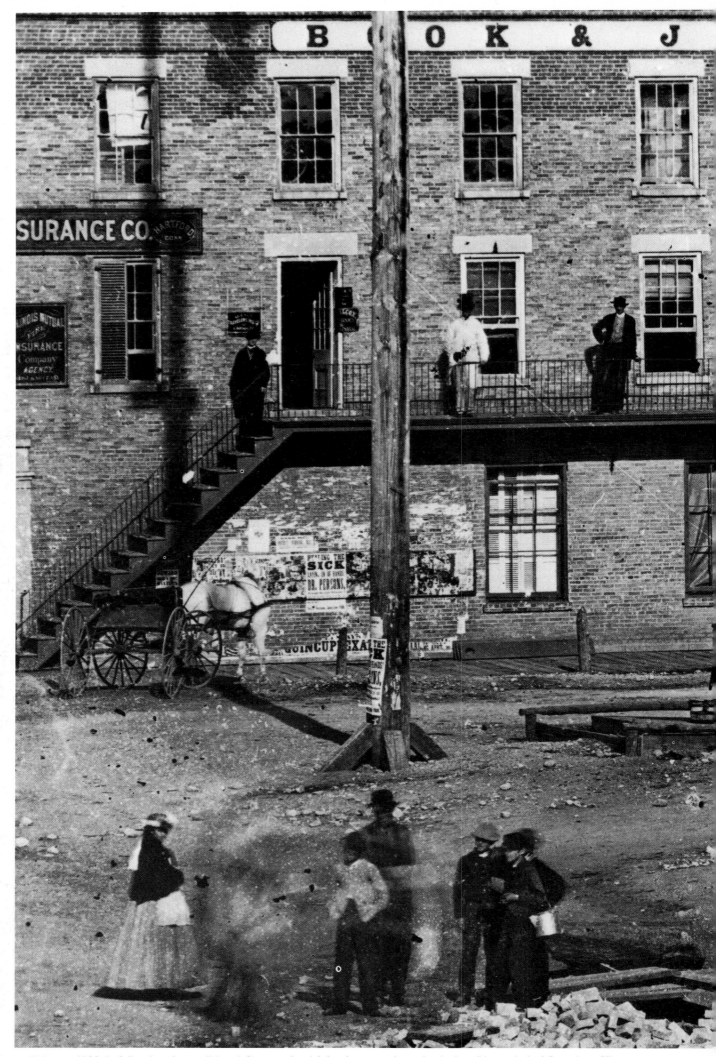

Adler & Brothers, Chicago, 1866: In following the traditional German-Jewish businessman's cycle during this period of American History, a

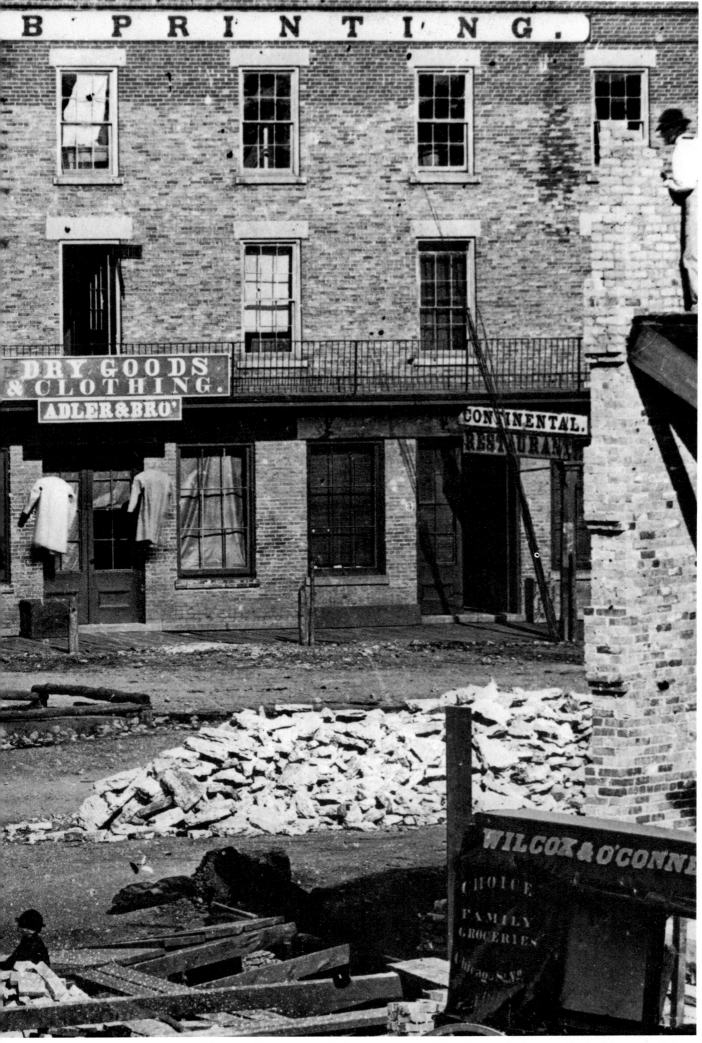

man would begin as a peddler. After acquiring some capital, he would establish a dry goods store similar to this one in Chicago. *Credit:* CJA

A Call to Action Concerning the Mortara Affair

October 22, 1858. Rabbi Max Lilienthal of Cincinnati called upon American Jews to appeal to their government to protest to the Pope regarding the forced abduction and conversion of Edgardo Mortara in Italy.

The forced abduction of the child of Mr. Mortara in Rome, Italy, by order of the Catholic clergy has created throughout the civilized world a cry of horror and indignation. Religious liberty is set at naught by the fanaticism of the Roman Inquisition. The Israelites throughout Europe have taken energetic measures, to have the decision of Rome revoked. The Central Consistory of France, the Board of Jewish deputies of England, the Consistory of Sardinia have addressed their respective governments in behalf of down-trodden religious liberty. The same was done by the Israelites in Germany. Let us follow their example! Call meetings in your congregations! Address remonstrances and Petitions to our government in Washington, that the President and his secretaries may throw their influence too in the scale of this important case. We rise, not only for our cause but for one of the highest principles of our enlightened age, Religious liberty, and no clerical inquisition!

Congregation Temple Emanu-el, 1866: This large San Francisco synagogue located on Sutter Street symbolized the prosperity of the recently established Jewish community in that city. Posen-born Dr. Elkan Cohn, a scholar and advocate of Reform Judaism, became its rabbi in 1860. *Credit:* LC

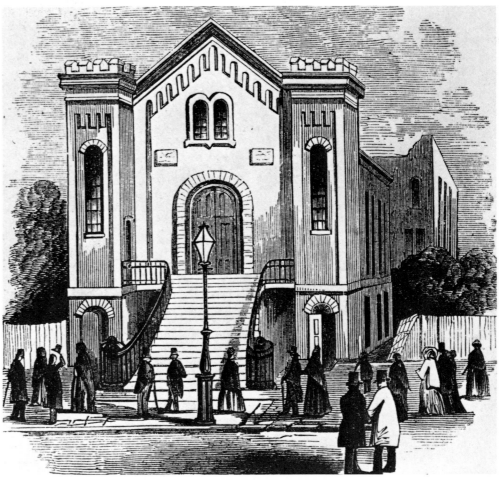

Rodeph Shalom Synagogue, New York, 1853: In 1825 members of Congregation Shearith Israel in New York seceded and formed a new congregation. This opened the door to the formation of other congregations, like Rodeph Shalom on Clinton Street in New York which was primarily German. *Credit:* LC

Washington Hebrew Congregation Synagogue, about 1875: The Washington Hebrew Congregation Synagogue was converted from a Methodist church in 1860 located at 8th and Eye Streets, N.W. In the 1890s it was torn down. *Credit:* WHC

Temple Emanu-El, New York, 1868: Interior of the temple at the dedication ceremony on September 11, 1868. *Credit:* LC

Temple Emanu-El, New York, 1868: Construction of this large and impressive synagogue at the corner of Fifth Avenue and 43rd Street in New York reflected the financial success of the German-Jewish members of the community. It contained 1,800 seats on the main floor and 500 in the gallery; the cost of construction was estimated to be $800,000. *Credit:* LC

New Jewish Settlements

1846. Isaac Leeser, the most influential Jewish leader in the pre-Civil War period, reported on the increased observance of Judaism as he experienced it in his travels.

We constantly hear of new incipient congregations springing up in every direction, and every year the worship of the God of Israel is extending into towns where formerly the One had no adorers. Far and near the sons of Jacob are diffusing themselves over the area where liberty of conscience is the inalienable right of all the inhabitants, and glad are we that they are remembering the God of their fathers in the new homes which they possess in peace and security.

Whilst lately on a short tour through a portion of Virginia, we stopped a day [in the fall of 1846] at Norfolk, and were rejoiced to find that the Israelites assembled there during the last holydays for worship, having at the same time a sepher [scroll] out of which to read the word of the Lord. One of the people has kindly undertaken to kill [slaughter cattle and fowl] twice a week so that kosher meat can be procured by all; and we are pleased to learn that several, who before the settlement of Mr. Umstetter did not keep strict [a strictly kosher] house, now do so, availing themselves of the services of this worthy Israelite. We should not be surprised to hear that in the course of a little while a permanent synagogue were organized in Norfolk, especially as many individuals are scattered in the towns of eastern North Carolina, Newbern, Elizabeth City, Edenton, etc., as also at Suffolk, Va., and hence they can easily unite with those in Norfolk for the promotion of public worship.

In Petersburg there are several families, but they have not yet united into a congregation, and are contributors to some

Isaac Leeser, undated: Isaac Leeser was one of the foremost leaders of American Jewry of his time. Born in Germany, he arrived in this country in 1824. He became the religious leader of Congregation Mikveh Israel in Philadelphia in 1829. Among his many accomplishments were an English translation of the Old Testament and making English sermons a regular feature of the Sabbath morning service. In 1843 he initiated publication of *The Occident and American Jewish Advocate* and in 1867 he established Maimonides College in Philadelphia. *Credit:* LC

THE OCCIDENT,

AND

AMERICAN JEWISH ADVOCATE.

VOL. I.]   **NISSAN 5603, APRIL 1843.**   **[No. 1.**

INTRODUCTORY REMARKS.

IT is a time-honoured custom, that when an Editor appears for the first time before the public, he is to state something of the course he means to pursue, and of the subjects he intends laying before his readers. In our case, this is hardly necessary, since the name of "Jewish Advocate" amply shadows forth that we mean to devote our pages to the spread of whatever can advance the cause of our religion, and of promoting the true interest of that people which has made this religion its profession ever since the days of the great lawgiver, through whom it was handed down to the nation descended from the stock of Abraham. But this general view may, perhaps, not be sufficiently detailed for many whom we would gladly number among our readers; and we will therefore briefly state our object in assuming the editorship of this new periodical, and of the course it is our firm determination to pursue.

With regard to our object, we state candidly, that the plan of a religious periodical did not originate with ourself, nor did we approve of it when it was first suggested to us. We thought then, and still think, that newspaper knowledge is at best but superficial; or, to make a paper or magazine really interesting to the general public, (and for such a one it is our duty to labour in our present vocation,) much matter must be admitted which is more pleasing in its nature than instructive, and the variety, which is to be constantly furnished, will naturally prevent long and continuous articles being given, although they might be extremely rich in information, even such as the people stand most in need of. We dreaded, moreover, that despite of the greatest care which we could bestow, articles might at times gain admission which

VOL. I.   **1**

The Occident and American Jewish Advocate, 1843: Title page of the first issue. *Credit:* AJHS

extent to the Portuguese *kahal* ["congregation"] at Richmond. In Richmond there are two congregations. The minister of the Portuguese body is the Rev. Ellis Lyons, and Rev. Max Michelbacher is the minister of the German brethren. Mr. Michelbacher is also the teacher for his congregation and also preaches to them in German. He informed us that he meant soon to preach in the English language, which we do consider far more useful in America than a resort to an idiom which only can be allowed here on account of the want of knowledge of the vernacular by the emigrants from Europe, . . .

An American Judaism

About 1860. Isaac Mayer Wise, leader of Reform Judaism, stressed the relationship between the Reform movement and Americanization.

But why have Jews so little regard for one another that they revile and traduce each other? How is it that a highly honored public applauds loudly whenever literary rowdies squabble like street gamins, and throw mud at decent people? Whence comes this wretched imitation of Christian customs, good and bad, by Jews; this cringing to every Christian fashion; this eager association with, this humble attitude towards, every Christian, even though he be a knave, for no other reason than that he is not a Jew? Whence this disgusting phenomenon?

I could find but one answer to these questions: The century-long oppression has demoralized the German and Polish Jew and robbed him of his self-respect. He has no self-respect, no pride left. The hep! hep! [attacks on Jews] times still weigh him down; he bows and scrapes, he crawls and cringes. The Jew respects not the fellow man in another Jew, because he lacks the consciousness of manhood in himself. He parodies and imitates, because he has lost himself. After diagnosing the evil, I set myself to seeking a remedy.

The Jew must be Americanized, I said to myself, for every German book, every German word reminds him of the old disgrace. If he continues under German influences, as they are now in this country, he must become either a bigot or an atheist, a satellite or a tyrant. He will never be aroused to self-consciousness or to independent thought. The Jew must become an American, in order to gain the proud self-consciousness of the free-born man.

From that hour I began to Americanize with all my might and was as enthusiastic for this as I was for Reform. Since then, as a matter of course, the German element here, as well as in Germany, has completely changed, although Judaeophobia and uncouthness have survived in many; but at that time it appeared to me that there was but one remedy that would prove effective for my coreligionists, and that was to Americanize them thoroughly. We must be not only American citizens, but become Americans through and through, outside of the synagogue. This was my cry then and many years there after.

The Israelite, 1854: First issue of Rabbi Isaac Mayer Wise's publication which became his device for promoting the platform of Reform Judaism in this country. *Credit:* AJHS

Plum Street Temple, Cincinnati, undated: This synagogue in the Moorish style was built for Congregation B'nai Yeshurun in Cincinnati in 1866. Isaac Mayer Wise was the religious leader of the congregation at the time and this synagogue became the focal point for his activities as the predominant leader of Reform Judaism. *Credit:* LC

Isaac Mayer Wise, undated: Isaac Mayer Wise was one of the most important Jewish leaders in the post-Civil War period. Born in Bohemia in 1819, he arrived in this country in 1846. After settling in Albany, New York as minister to Congregation Beth-El, he initiated his prolonged campaign for religious reform in America, stressing the need to adapt Judaism to American conditions. In 1854 he moved to Cincinnati which then had the third or fourth largest Jewish community in this country. In the same year he started publication of *The Israelite*, the journal that he used to promulgate his ideas. In 1855 he initiated publication of *Die Deborah* in German; thus he was able to communicate with Jewish households through the two dominant languages. Among his major contributions were the establishment of the Union of American Hebrew Congregations in 1873 and Hebrew Union College in Cincinnati in 1875. *Credit:* AJA

CHOICE GROCERIES FOR PASSOVER,

פסח

AT D. BEHRMAN'S NEW STORE,
172 BOWERY
Opposite Delancy Street, NEW-YORK·
Which will be Superintended by L. M. RITTERBAND.

The subscriber begs to inform you, that he has made the necessary arrangements for the ensuing holydays, and will keep a full assortment of Groceries, also, every other article suitable for the occasion ; and guarantees the same to be of the most superior quality, and at the lowest market prices, delivered free of expense to any part of the city. The goods will be ready for sale on the 3d of April, to which the subscriber respectfully solicits your custom.

D. BEHRMAN,
172 BOWERY, *Opposite Delancy Street.*

☞ Orders received immediately if required ☜

הגדה של פסח In Hebrew and English For Sale.

Groferies für פסח.

Der Unterzeichnete eröffnet am 3ten April seine Niederlage von Groferies, von befter Qualität für die zukünftigen Feiertage פסח, unter der Aufficht von L. M. Ritterbänd,

Es wird alles zum billigften Preife verkauft und koftenfrei zu irgenb einem Theil der Stadt gefandt.

D. Behrman,
172 Bowery, gegenüber Delancy Street.

☛ Orders werden jetzt angenommen wen man es verlangt.

JACKSON, Cheap Printer, 190 Houston Street, and 203 Bowery.

PASSOVER GROCERIES,
פסח
At D. BEHRMAN'S 72 BOWERY.

		Sh.	pence
Lb.	Butter,		
"	Holland Cheese,		
Gal.	Santa Croix Rum,		
Bot.	Cordials,		
Gal.	White Wine Vinegar		
"	Cider,		
Lb.	Havanna Sugar,		
"	Porto Rico do.		
"	N. Orleans do.		
"	Coffee,		
"	Young Hyson Tea,		
"	Gunpowder, "		
"	Black, "		
Box.	Raisins, whole boxes		
"	" half "		
"	" quarter "		
Lb.	Almonds,		
Bot.	Sweet Oil,		
Lb.	Wax Candles,		
"	Sperm "		
"	Spices,		
"	Pepper, ground		
"	" whole,		
"	Ginger, "		
"	" ground,		
"	Cinnamon, "		
"	" whole,		
"	Allspice, "		
Ozs.	Nutmegs,		
Doz.	Lemons		
Qts.	Salt,		

Please to write your Name, Street and Number.

Advertisement for Passover Groceries, 1848: The Passover celebrations date back to the liberation of the Hebrews from Egyptian slavery. Certain types of foods are prohibited from use during Passover and grocers serving a Jewish clientele traditionally make a special effort to provide the basic necessities for these holidays. This advertisement appearing in both English and German reflects the large number of German-Jewish immigrants at that time. *Credit:* AJHS

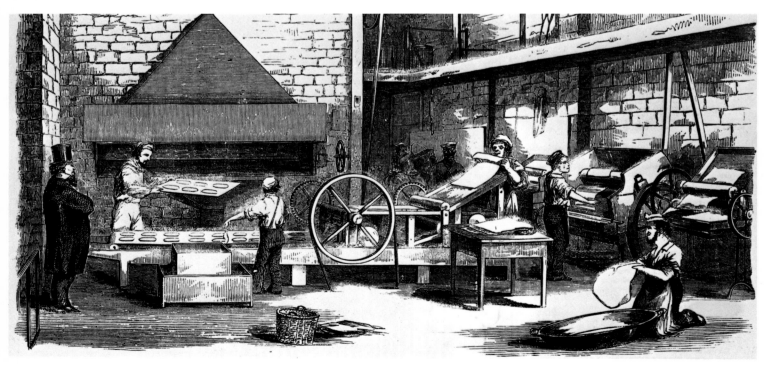

Preparing and Baking Matzoth, 1858: When Jews first arrived in this country, Passover matzoth were baked in the synagogue. As other aspects of traditional life were influenced by conditions in America, the making of matzoth became a factory process and the distribution became a commercial enterprise. However, a rabbi had to be present at all times during their preparation to guarantee that the finished product would be kosher. *Credit:* LC

Purim Ball, 1865: Balls and dances are sometimes organized during this festival of redemption commemorating the events recounted in *The Book of Esther.* This costume ball took place at the Academy of Music in New York on March 14, 1865. *Credit:* LC

The Weekly Gleaner, 1857: A Jewish communal publication which commenced in 1857, a short time after the first settlers arrived in San Francisco. *Credit:* LC

A Soldier's Civil War Experiences

1862. A Jewish member of the Union Army reported his experiences in an anonymous letter to The Jewish Messenger. *Thousands of Jews participated in the Civil War in both the Union and Confederate armies as both officers and infantrymen. Their loyalty was determined by the region of the country in which they resided.*

A friend of mine, who has special facilities for ascertaining the extent of the Jewish element in the army, and has devoted considerable time to that inquiry, informs me, that, although it is extremely difficult to obtain correct statistics, yet he believes that there are no less than five thousand Jews in our army. He attempted, by a twofold process, to arrive at a correct estimate of their member [sic—number?], first by requesting the Quartermasters of each regiment, to ascertain how many Jews there were in each company, and secondly, by calling upon the Jewish soldiers in general, to send in their names to his address, in both of which, he signally failed. This want of success on his part may be traced to various causes, but principally to the fact that few people feel disposed to give an account of their religious principles, when no practical object is to be attained, and inquiries of this nature are generally regarded as unbecoming, and even insulting. As a general rule, the Jews do not care to make their religion a matter of notoriety, as it would at once involve them in an intricate controversial disquisition with the Christian Chaplains, for which they do not always feel themselves qualified, and which, of course can, under no circumstance, afford them any thing but annoyance. Some of our brethren fear that, were they known as Hebrews, it would expose them to the taunts and sneers of those among their comrades who have been in the habit of associating with the name of Jew, everything that is mean and contemptible; but I must say, and it redounds much to the credit of the army, that in the course of my experience in the camps, which has been considerable, I have heard but of a single instance in which a Jew was wantonly insulted on account of his religion, and that was by a drunken Scotchman, who commenced damning in every variety of language and motion, when he learned that he was addressing an Israelite, declaring them all to be cheats and thieves. His wrath was, however, of short duration, for the soldiers who were present, finding him incorrigible, after having repeatedly warned him to desist, at last resolved to inflict summary punishment, and collectively flung him into a certain capacious receptacle for liquid matter, from which, let us hope, he emerged a wiser and a cooler man.

My friends found his estimate of the number of Jewish soldiers on the

Dr. Jacob Da Silva Solis-Cohen, about 1862: Dr. Jacob Da Silva Solis-Cohen, at one time, was Acting Fleet Surgeon to the South Blockading Squadron of the Union forces. He later became a prominent Philadelphia physician. *Credit:* AJA

fact, that according to his observation, at least, one in every hundred soldiers is a Jew, and supposing the army to consist of half a million of men, the Jews must number at least five thousand. This estimate, he believes to be supported by other calculations, for, supposing the Jews to have enlisted in the same proportion as the rest of the population, which is two and a half per cent. this would make them reach the above figure, as it is generally supposed that there are two hundred thousand Jews in this country. Without, however, insisting on the accuracy of this estimate, we may safely assert, that they are largely represented in the army, not only among the privates, but also among the commissioned officers. There are at least five Jewish colonels, as many lieutenant colonels and majors, and quite a host of captains, lieutenants, and quartermasters among the volunteer regiments, but in the regular army I know of no Jew holding a higher rank than that of captain. Some of the Jewish officers and privates told me that they had taken part in the Crimean, Hungarian and Italian wars, and that they followed the profession of arms from inclination, but not liking the dull routine of a soldier's life in times of peace, they eagerly avail themselves of every opportunity to return to their tents and the battlefield. This was the first time I had ever heard of the existence of such a class of military adventurers among our people.

Judah P. Benjamin, undated: Judah P. Benjamin, who served as Secretary of War and then Secretary of State for the Confederacy, became the popular scapegoat for the South's military failures. As a result of his role as Secretary of War, he was called "Judas Iscariot" Benjamin. From a daguerreotype by Matthew Brady. *Credit:* LC

Confederate War Bond, 1862: Carried a portrait of Judah P. Benjamin. *Credit:* AJHS

Reactions to General Grant's General Orders No. 11

1862. General Grant's father, Jesse, was involved with the Mack Brothers of Cincinnati in a plan to buy and ship cotton from Union occupied territories in Tennessee under his son's command. When General Grant learned of this, he was indignant and mortified. As a result, he issued his infamous order to expel all Jewish traders from the area under his command. Although Army officers might have assumed that all traders in this area were Jewish, this was not the case. Protests such as this one from Jews in Paducah, Kentucky, to President Lincoln were effective. General Grant's Orders No. 11 was rescinded.

General Orders, No. 11, issued by General Grant at Oxford, Miss., December the 17th, commands all post commanders to expel all Jews, without distinction, within twenty-four hours, from his entire department. The undersigned, good and loyal citizens of the United States and residents of this town for many years, engaged in legitimate business as merchants, feel greatly insulted and outraged by this inhuman order, the carrying out of which would be the grossest violation of the Constitution and our rights as good citizens under it, and would place us, as outlaws before the whole world. We respectfully ask your immediate attention to this enormous outrage on all law and humanity, and pray for your effectual and immediate interposition. We would respectfully refer you to the post commander and post adjutant as to our loyalty, and to all respectable citizens of this community as to our standing as citizens and merchants. We respectfully ask for immediate instructions to be sent to the commander of this post.

Confederate Two Dollar bill, 1862: Carried a portrait of Judah P. Benjamin. *Credit:* AJHS

Jewish Union Soldiers in Georgia, about 1865: Thousands of Jewish soldiers fought on both sides during the Civil War. Here we can see Jewish soldiers who were members of the Union Army being visited by some of their Southern Jewish relatives in Dougherty County, Georgia. *Credit:* Louis Schmier

August Bondi, undated: A German Jewish immigrant who arrived in the United States in 1848, he was associated with liberal causes and was active as an abolitionist. *Credit:* LC

Philanthropy and Jewish Community Life

1830. At the celebration of the anniversary of the founding of the Society for the Education of Orphan Children and Relief of Indigent Persons of the Jewish Persuasion, Dr. Daniel L.M. Peixotto spoke of the tradition of Jewish philanthropy and its application to this country.

Imbibing this spirit, in its most active influences, from the great Law which was announced to them, amidst the awful thunders of Sinai, by the Creator Himself, the Israelites have never been found wanting in yielding their ready assistance to promote and extend its operations. It may, however, be urged against them, that their benevolence is confined in its exertions to themselves; and the very title of this Society would seem to lend countenance to the charge. It is not, however, founded in fact. The ear of the Israelite can never be deaf to the cry of the sufferer; his heart can never refuse to sympathise with the distresses of his fellow-man; nor can his door ever be closed to the hospitable reception of the destitute, whatever be their creed, origin, or complexion. The first law impressed on his heart, and engraved upon his memory, by his religious teacher, is to love his neighbour as himself, and not to afflict the stranger that is within his gates.

If it then be asked, why are the objects of *this* Society limited? The answer is ready: Not from any illiberality of feeling have the founders of this institution circumscribed the sphere of their exertions, but from an honest conviction that charity, to be efficient, must be limited to a definite number of objects, and of those objects only with whose peculiar claims and wants it is best acquainted. An indiscriminate and vague dispensation of relief is ever destructive of its own end. It is a received law in moral and political economy, that the first duty which a citizen owes to the community of which he is a member, is to provide for his own wants; in other words, to prevent those wants from becoming a burden to the public. After these wants are satisfied; after this first duty has been discharged, then it will be time to assume new responsibilities and charges. Now, the same rule which applies to individuals will also apply to *associations* of individuals, or to sections of the community. *Their* first duty is to protect their own body from suffering; and, if they succeed in doing this, if they subtract all the evil that falls within their own immediate sphere from the general charge, they will, in reality, do more to contribute to the public good, than if they were, with utopian zeal, to attempt to grasp the universe in their ideal benevolence. The proudest *badge* of any sect is, and should be, that none of its members are dependants on the public

Mount Sinai Hospital,
No. 232 West Twenty-eighth street.

Mount Sinai Hospital, New York, undated: Mount Sinai Hospital was incorporated as the Jews' Hospital in 1852. This building, located at 232 West 28th Street, was occupied from 1852 to 1872. The lot upon which the hospital was located was donated by Samson Simson and the trustees received a bequest of $20,000 from the estate of Judah Touro of New Orleans. *Credit:* NYPL

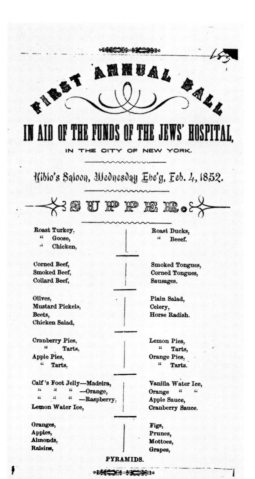

Mount Sinai (Jews' Hospital) Ball, 1852: Menu and toasts for the first fundraising dinner and ball for the new hospital. *Credit:* AJHS

eleemosynary institutions. Not then, I repeat it, from illiberality does the limitation
of our benevolence proceed; but from a
sincere desire of rendering that good
which is in our power, efficient and conducive to the general weal. It is not in the
United States of America that a Jew can
cherish illiberality. It is not in the land
where the very term toleration is exploded, and which acknowledges him as
equal of his fellow-creature man, that the
Jew can regard that fellow-creature with
indifference, or a contracted spirit.

Dentist's Diploma, 1872: William Sach, Jr.'s
degree from the College of Dentistry,
University of Pennsylvania, 1872. *Credit:* LBI

HOSPITAL FOR ISRAELITES
IN PHILADELPHIA.

WHEREAS, A Jewish Hospital has been found to be a necessity in the cities of New York and Cincinnati, and in the large
cities of Europe, and
WHEREAS, All the causes that make such an institution a
necessity there, are in full operation here, and
WHEREAS, Within the last six months three Israelites of this
city have died in Christian hospitals, without having enjoyed
the privilege of hearing the ישראל שמע, the watchword of their
faith and nation, and
WHEREAS, It reflects the greatest discredit on so large a
Jewish population as that of Philadelphia, to force friendless
brothers to seek, in sickness and the prospect of death, the
shelter of un-jewish hospitals, to eat forbidden food, to be dis-
sected after death and sometimes even to be buried with the
stranger. Therefore be it
Resolved, That the District Grand Lodge No. 3, of the Independent Order of the Benai Berith, acting on that Benevolence
and Brotherly Love, which are the motto of the Order, take
immediate steps to secure the co-operation of all Jewish societies
and individuals for the purpose of founding a Jewish hospital,
and be it further
Resolved, That the whole subject be and is hereby refered to
a special committee of seven, to be called the Hospital Committee.

In consequence of our appointment as a provisional Committee to promote the founding of a Jewish hospital in or near the city of Philadelphia,
at a meeting of the Grand Lodge of the Benai Berith, held on Sunday,
the 14th of August, we now appeal to you for your active sympathy and
co-operation, to carry out the idea embraced in the above proceedings.

                 M. Thalheimer, *Chairman,*
                 Isaac Leeser, *V. Chairman,*
                 A. Sulzberger, *Secretary,*
     Provisional   S. Hofheimer,
     Hospital Committee.   R. Teller,
                 L. Ellinger,
                 S. Weil.

Philadelphia, August 18th, 1864.
     Menachem 16th, 5624.

NOTICE.—The Grand Lodge in taking the initiative do not design to
forestall public action, but desire to defer the plan to a general meeting
of committees from various public bodies and individual Israelites, to be
held at the earliest possible date.

Spital für Israeliten
in Philadelphia.

In Erwägung, daß die Gründung jüdischer Spitäler in den Städten
New-York und Cincinnati, sowie in den größern Städten Europas sich
als Nothwendigkeit herausstellte,

In fernerer Erwägung, daß das Bedürfniß eines solchen Institutes
in der hiesigen Stadt eben so dringend ist,

In fernerer Erwägung, daß während der jüngsten sechs Monate, drei
hiesige Israeliten in christlichen Spitälern starben, denen der Todeskampf
nicht durch Vernehmung der Worte: ישראל שמע erleichtert wurde,

In fernerer Erwägung, daß es einer so zahlreichen jüdischen Bevöl-
kerung wie der Philadelphia's zur großen Unehre gereicht, für ihre verlasse-
nen Brüder während ihrer Krankheit und ihrer Todesstunde nicht zu sorgen,
so daß diese unglücklichen Brüder zu nicht-jüdischen Spitälern ihre Zu-
flucht nehmen, und dort verbotene Speisen genießen müssen, nach ihrem
Tode auch oft secirt und auf nicht-jüdischen Begräbnißplätzen beerdigt
werden; daher sei es

Beschlossen, Daß die Distrikts-Groß-Loge No. 3, des Unabhäng-
igen Ordens Bene Berith, treu ihrem Wahlspruche der Wohlthätigkeit
und brüderlichen Liebe, ungesäumt die nöthigen Schritte thue, um die
Mitwirkung aller jüdischen Gesellschaften und Individuen zur Gründung
eines jüdischen Spitals zu sichern; und sei es ferner

Beschlossen, Daß der ganze Gegenstand einer Spezial-Committee
von sieben, die den Namen "Spital-Committee" führt, übertragen werde,
und somit übertragen ist.

In Folge unserer Ernennung, bitten wir Sie, Ihr reges Mitgefühl
und Ihre Mitwirkung der Ausführung des vorstehenden Plans zu schenken.

                 M. Thalheimer, *Vorsitzer,*
                 Isaac Leeser, *V. Vorsitzer,*
                 Abraham Sulzberger, *Secretär,*
    Provisorische   Solomon Hofheimer,
    Spital-Committee.   R. Teller,
                 L. Ellinger,
                 S. Weil.

Philadelphia, den 18ten August, 1864.
     16ten Menachem, 5624.

Jewish Hospital Announcement, 1864: Announcement of creation of a committee to
establish a Jewish hospital in Philadelphia.
Both English and German appear in recognition of the considerable number of German
speaking Jewish immigrants who had just
arrived in this country. *Credit:* LCP

B'nai B'rith Charter, 1874: In 1843 B'nai B'rith was organized in New York as the first Jewish fraternal organization in the world. Lodge No. 228 was chartered in Lancaster, Pennsylvania in 1874 when about 30 Jewish families were living there. *Credit:* Lancaster Jewish Community Archives and B'nai B'rith Lodge No. 228

Master Mason Certificate, 1858: The Masons have been one of the few traditional American organizations to readily accept Jewish members. Isaac Adler became a member in Cairo, Illinois. *Credit:* Harriet Rauh

A Lavish Philadelphia Wedding

1880. The wedding of Joseph Cohen to Clotilda Florance at the Mikveh Israel Synagogue was one of the largest and most fashionable in years.

Both parties move in the elite of Philadelphia society, and the event had been looked forward to in upper-ten circles for many months. The groom is President of the Mikveh Israel congregation, a prominent member of the Young Men's Hebrew Association, and is noted for his liberality toward Jewish institutions and movements. Nearly one thousand invitations had been issued, and a large number of friends of the family came on from New York, Montreal, Canada, and Savannah, Georgia, to participate in the happy occasion.

Four o'clock was the time fixed for the ceremony. Soon after three, however, every seat was occupied, and the late comers could not find even standing room. The aisles were crowded and the galleries jammed, not less than 1,800 people being crowded into a space which would not comfortably hold more than three-fourths that number. The gentlemen and a majority of the ladies were in full dress, and the rich costumes, combined with the flashing of diamonds from nearly every nook and corner, made the scene a brilliant one. On the floor in the centre of the edifice stood a magnificent "Chuppa" or canopy, of white silk, with embroidered hangings of the

Master Mason, about 1875: Master Mason in full regalia, Georgia. *Credit:* Louis Schmier

same material. This had been made expressly for the occasion. The steps leading to the ark were covered with exotic and choice growing plants, while the space usually occupied by the reading desk was filled with the choicest gems of the hothouse, which sent their fragrance throughout the building. On the west side a temporary orchestra had been erected for the accommodation of Hassler's Band, which gave some suitable selections before and after the ceremony. This was the first time that the strains of music had ever been heard inside of the synagogue. According to the customs of this congregation no musical instruments are allowed to be used in the religious exercises, and the innovation of yesterday was intended as a recognition of the relation of the groom to the church and congregation.

The buzz of voices was suddenly hushed when the doors were thrown open for the bridal party. Eight groomsmen led the way. These were followed by a similar number of bridesmaids, each attired in white cashmere costumes, elaborately trimmed with swan's down, and white felt hats adorned with an ostrich feather. Behind, leaning on the arms of their sons, came the mothers of the bride and groom, the one wearing a plum-colored velvet costume trimmed with point lace, and the other a heavy black silk. Rabbi Morais, in a sombre black gown, came next, and the two whose lives were to be linked together brought up the rear. The bridal costume was of white gros grain silk, short sleeves, low corsage and adorned with point lace, the whole being entirely covered with a tulle veil. The couple took their places under the canopy, the bride standing between her mother and future mother-in-law, facing west, and the groom confronting her, while the groomsmen and bridesmaids ranged themselves in a circle. Then the shoulders of the groom were covered with an embroidered "tallith", or scarf, and the ceremony was commenced after the old Portuguese orthodox style. Rabbi Morais first delivered a short address in English, in which he dwelt upon the high and the noble aims of the married state, and then chanted a blessing in Hebrew. Then a glass of wine was handed to the bride to sip, and the groom, after following suit, placed the wedding ring upon her finger; another blessing was chanted, another glass of wine sipped and then the glass having been placed on the floor the newly-made husband planted his foot upon it and crushed it into fragments. This is a Jewish custom which signifies that the bond of union cannot be more easily broken than the glass can be made whole. After this the nuptial kiss was exchanged and the ceremony was at an end. In the evening the wedding banquet was given at the residence of the bride's mother, and later the happy couple left town for their honeymoon.

Allemenia Club, Cincinnati, about 1875: Exterior of the Jewish social club in Cincinnati. *Credit:* CINHS

Cartoon from *Puck*, 1877: Joseph Seligman, the prominent Jewish banker, was refused admittance to the Grand Union Hotel in Saratoga, New York, because he was a Jew. This cartoon from *Puck* depicts the event. *Credit:* LC

Levy Family, Philadelphia, about 1890: This family portrait was taken on Marshall Street, a German-Jewish neighborhood. From left to right: Beulah, Harry, Jan and Dell. *Credit:* HSP

Finkelstein Family, Cleveland, 1910: A family portrait taken in the Woodland Avenue section, an area where newly arrived Eastern European Jews settled. From left to right, children in the front row: Jerome Gleitz, Elmer Brown, Morton Scheingold, in the second row: Edward Fink, Aaron Finkelstein, Toba Finkelstein, Mr. Steers, the former property owner, Marie Gleitz, back row, William Zorach and unidentified man. *Credit:* Author

Contrasts: The Established Germans and The Eastern European Immigrants

There were two dominant features of American Jewish life between 1881 and 1919: the outstanding economic success of some German Jews in the fields of banking, merchandising, and manufacturing; and the arrival of over two million impoverished East Europeans in the largest wave of Jewish immigration in American history.

With the arrival of the East European Jews, the Jewish community was divided between the haves and the have-nots. German Jewish families were among the notables in banking: the Goldmans, Kahns, Kuhns, Lehmans, Loebs, Schiffs, Seligmans and Warburgs. They were found at the helm of major department stores: the Altmans, Gimbels, Kaufmanns, Lazaruses, Magnins, Marcuses, Mays and Strauses. The son of a German Jewish immigrant, Julius Rosenwald improved Sears Roebuck's mail order merchandising. In men's clothing Hart, Schaffner, Marx, Kuppenheimer and Levi Strauss became household names.

German Jewish creative enterprise not only transformed established businesses, but also fostered a new economic democracy in America. With the development of department stores, the expansion of mail order merchandising, and the manufacturing of low-priced ready-to-wear garments, Jewish entrepreneurs made available to farmers, workers and their families products and services previously accessible to only the wealthy.

While the established Jews were "making it" in America, many of the Eastern European Jews were struggling to survive. Arriving at a time when cheap labor was sorely needed in America's urban centers, they joined millions of other European immigrants who had flocked to the "Golden Land" in search of their fortune. Crowded into cheap dwellings they became the urban poor, the sweatshop workers in the garment factories owned by the German Jews. They had exchanged the ghettos of Europe for the American urban ghetto.

The Eastern European migration brought a broad cross section of people, sophisticated Jews from Moscow and Odessa and those from small towns and villages. They carried with them from the old country a strong admixture of socialism and anarchism—a sense of social justice which originated in a Jewish idealism rooted in the Prophets of the Old Testament.

In the first decade of the 20th century, Clara Lemlich, a leader of a shirtwaist makers strike, offered a first hand account of the terrible conditions which most garment workers endured: long hours, unsanitary conditions and poor lighting. Reported Lemlich, the bosses "yell at the girls," treating them worse "than I imagine the Negro slaves were in the South . . . At the beginning of every slow season, $2.00 is deducted from our salaries."

Following the Triangle Shirtwaist Company fire in which 143 women employees, most of them Jewish, lost their lives, Rose Schneiderman, a leader in the Hat and Cap Makers' Union declared: "Too much blood has been spilled . . . it is up to the working people to save themselves." Reacting to such exhortations as well as to their economic plight, Eastern European Jews working in the garment trade sweatshops started to organize unions, which finally emerged as the International Ladies' Garment Workers' Union and the Amalgamated Clothing Workers' Union. Both contributed an enlightened form of unionism which later had considerable impact on the New Deal and progressive labor legislation.

Having come from the total environment of the *shtetl,* adapting to the American way of life often proved to be a

1881-1919

traumatic experience for the immigrants. They were faced at once with a new language, different social mores, and a unique American invention—a dominant Christian yet secular culture. The established members of the Jewish community developed and financed institutions designed to assist their brethren in adjusting to their new life in America.

German Jewish response to its East European counterpart was complex. Impelled by an ethical precept which held Jews responsible for one another's welfare, they sought to "Americanize" the newcomers as quickly as possible, sometimes at much human cost to the immigrants. Reacting to the huge swell of immigration following the pogroms in Eastern Europe, the Industrial Removal Office was established to disperse Jewish immigrants from congested cities such as New York to smaller towns where employment was available. Leo Stamm, a client of the Removal Office, wrote from Meridian, Mississippi in 1906: "For an honest working man the South is a very good place to live in, and here I send my advise to the enslaved Jews of New York to leave the town as quick as they can and come here to get the benefit of the good climate and to conduct a good living." The Galveston Plan, initiated by Jacob Schiff in 1907, directed Jewish immigrants to areas of the South and West where labor was scarce.

Due to the fact that many of the new immigrants were originally from different areas of Eastern Europe, their only common language was Yiddish. It was spoken in the home, in the workplace, in the synagogue and at union meetings. In an era of the burgeoning ethnic newspaper, the Yiddish press blossomed. It became a vital force in the Jewish community, unifying the thousands of dispersed Jews throughout the land as well as Americanizing them in the process by informing them about life in America. What would life be without the personal ads, the advice to the lovelorn, the social debates that raged on the pages of the Yiddish newspaper? Abraham Cahan's column in the Jewish Daily Forward became the mainstay of many an immigrant's life.

But the dominance of Yiddish was short-lived. The immigrants felt the pressure to Americanize. In order to advance you had to learn English. Taking advantage of America's vast educational opportunities, immigrant parents eagerly enrolled their children in the public school system. Not surprisingly, English soon came to replace Yiddish as the everyday language of the second generation Jews.

While Eastern European Jews were undergoing the trials and tribulations of the Americanization experience, the "uptown" Jews, as German Jews came to be called, in contrast, were partaking of the good life that was to be had in America. Family portraits of the Kuhns, the Sterns, the Frohmans at the turn of the century convey an air of gentility and well-being. Photos of the period show a galaxy of handsome men and women in a variety of poses at a Philadelphia "coming out" party, attending a Versailles inspired costume party, and visiting the Egyptian pyramids.

Yet despite their integration in the social and economic life of America there was still little Jewish presence in government or in the expanding industrial and commercial corporations. The sudden influx of millions of immigrants perceived as low class, vulgar, and threatening had produced an anti-foreign sentiment from earlier arrivals. In the wave of zenophobia anti-Semitism flourished. Jews, irrespective of their cultural origins, found limitations on their ability to attain the upper reaches of the political, social, and cultural institutions.

From Vilna to New York

1882. Alexander Harkavy, along with a group of idealistic young Russian Jews, planned to emigrate to America with the hope of becoming farmers. Although Harkavy did not fulfill that objective, he became the first great Yiddish lexicographer in this country. He was also responsible for immigrant-aid books which assisted Eastern European Jews in learning to speak, read and write in English.

The day set for our departure from Vilna arrived, and we were ready to go. At ten in the morning every member of our group was supposed to gather by the railway. When the moment came to separate from Vilna, love for my native land welled up within me, and I lamented to myself my decision to set out for America. But everything was set: there was no turning back. Brokenhearted, I parted from my relatives who owned the press and from the auditors in the office of accounting, and I made my way to the railway where members of the group had gathered. Our first destination was a small city in Lithuania near the Prussian border. We arrived there after noon, and turned in at a hotel outside the city. There we found a Jew engaged in border crossing [smuggling]. We contracted with him to cross us into Prussia at a price of three rubles a head. Toward evening the man brought a large wagon which took us as far as the border district. There we got off the wagon, and the man left us alone. He went off to bargain on our behalf with one of the district's residents. No sooner did he leave than we began to fear for our lives. We were terrified that army border-

Statue of Liberty, 1894: Photograph by J.S. Johnston. *Credit:* NYPL

Emma Lazarus, undated: In 1883 Emma Lazarus, a thirty-four year-old poet native and resident New Yorker, wrote a sonnet, *The New Colossus,* describing the plight of the immigrant masses, as her contribution to a fund to pay for a base for the Statue of Liberty. In 1903, her sonnet was inscribed on a bronze plaque and placed on the pedestal of the statue. *Credit:* LC

North German Lloyd Passenger Ship, about 1881: Many Eastern European Jews managed to make their way to German ports where they embarked on their transatlantic voyage to America. *Credit:* SI

Entertainment and Ball

In Aid of the
RUSSIAN JEWISH REFUGEES,
Under the Auspices of
Chebra "Ohavai Shalom,"
—AT—
B'NAI B'RITH HALL,
Wednesday Evening, April 19th, 1882.

PROGRAMME.
PART FIRST.

Accompanist, ... **Madame SAVENIER**

1. Piano Duet, ... Master SUNDLAND & ABE SICHEL
2. Recitation, ... Miss NELIA SMART
3. Song, "My Love's a Rover," .... Miss REGINA GANS
4. Comic Song, ... JOSH DAVIS
5. Operatic Selection. .... Miss LOUISE LESTER
   The Accomplished Prima Donna, by Kind Permission of
   JOSEPH KRELLING, Esq.
6. "The Haunted House," .... by the TWO HARRYS
   Assisted by Mr. N. G. GOODWIN.
   Mr. Hunter .... N. G. GOODWIN
   Jake .... HARRY ALEXANDER
   Julius .... HARRY ANKLE

PART SECOND.

1. Recitation, ... Miss SARAH WOLFF
2. Denticon Solo, "or Musical Teeth," .... SAM THORS
3. Duet, "When I Behold," from La Mascott, ...
   .... Miss LOUISE LESTER and Mr. JOSH DAVIS
4. Piano Solo, ... Miss RACHEL WOLFF
5. Selection from Richard III "Battle Scene," ....
   .... Master RICHARD LOUIS and KOSSUTH LEVY
6. Closing Address, ...Chairman of Committee ISADORE WOLFF

DIRECTOR, ... **JOSH DAVIS.**

Aid for Russian Refugees, 1882: A fund raising entertainment and ball to aid Russian Jewish refugees held in San Francisco. *Credit:* WJHC

guards would see and catch us. After an hour, our border crosser returned with a Christian man and both quietly ordered us to come along. Trembling mightily we followed them. They led us into Prussia. The border area was filled with wells of water and slime, and we grew impatient at our pace. Finally, after wandering about for half an hour, we came to the city of Eydtkuhnen in Prussia. The short time had seemed to us like an eternity. When told by the men that we were no longer in Russia, our joy knew no bounds.

We arrived in Eydtkuhnen after midnight and made straight for the hotel. There we feasted on bread and ale: we were happy and in high spirits. We were pleased both to have safely succeeded in crossing the border of our cruel native land, and to have placed the soles of our feet down on the soil of Germany— which excelled in higher education and in a legal system designed to benefit its citizens. After having eaten, we lay down to rest from the ardors of our journey. We slept very well indeed. Next morning we woke joyfully, and went out walking to see the city and its inhabitants. We found groups of people and spoke with them about the quality of Germany, and the relationship of its citizens to the government. The residents whom we asked praised both their leaders and their way of life. They told us that Germans were pleased that their government extended human rights to all citizens. I asked one about the relationship of Jews to the army: did some of them try to escape this obligation? The man replied that every one of them enters military service willingly: not only that, they yearn for it even if not admitted. To support his words he told me the story of how in Eydtkuhnen there was a Jew who was not admitted to military service on account of some deformity which was found in him. This man, according to the storyteller, spent a great deal of money in order to be admitted, but he didn't succeed and was terribly disappointed. This was astonishing to me. I told myself: "see how great the difference is between Germany and Russia."

We remained in Eydtkuhnen for twenty-four hours, and then travelled on to Hamburg. We remained in this port city for two days. At that time there was in Hamburg a Jewish committee to support Russian emigrants who came there by the thousands on their way to America. We turned to this committee with the request that it purchase for us tickets on an English boat at the special rate offered charitable societies. The committee filled our request, and in this way we saved the treasury of our group some money.

From Hamburg, we travelled over the North Sea to the city of Hartlepool in England, and from there via train to the port city of Liverpool. There we were to wait until the Am Olam from Kiev arrived so that we might go down to the ship along with them. Four days later the group arrived. Great joy filled our hearts

Steerage Deck, 1893: Aboard the S.S. Pennland. The mass of immigrants arriving from Europe during the last quarter of the 19th century and first quarter of the 20th century were compelled to travel under miserably crowded conditions in steerage class. Photograph by Byron. *Credit:* MCNY

The Battery, New York, 1893: Castle Garden, the point of arrival for immigrants prior to the construction of Ellis Island. *Credit:* NYHS

when we learned that our allied group had made it. In high spirits we rushed to greet them. After a meeting between the leaders of our two groups, the creation of a legal union was announced: henceforward, we were like brothers of a single society. The Kiev group with which we had joined had seventy members, men and women. Most were young intellectual men, dreamers just like we were. Among its members was the late poet, David Edelstadt, then about eighteen years old. Our two groups met up with one another on the afternoon of May 15th. That very day, the ship "British Prince" stood at the harbor ready to accept passengers for America. It was destined to take us as well. Just an hour after our union we went down to the ship together. That evening the "British Prince" hoisted anchor, and began to transport us to our ultimate destination: the new world.

The boat "British Prince" was like a city floating on water, so great was the number of its passengers. All its passengers were Russian immigrants: all, save members of our group, were travelling to America as individuals, seeking to improve their position by their own brains and brawn; this one through handiwork, that one through peddling. Members of our group saw themselves as superior to this multitude. "The other passengers are not like us." said we to ourselves, "we are not merely going to America for simple comfort, we are idealists, eager to prove to the world that Jews can work the land!" In our imagination, we already saw ourselves as land-owning farmers dwelling on our plots in the western part of the country. So certain were we that our aims in the new world would be achieved that even on the boat we began to debate which kind of community institutions we would build, which books we would introduce into our library, whether or not we would build a synagogue and so forth (with regard to the synagogue, most of the views were negative). We danced and sang overcome with joyous expectations of what America held in store for us. In spite of seasickness, storms, and tempests which visited us on our journey, we were happy and lighthearted. All the days of our Atlantic voyage were filled with joy.

On May 30th, fifteen days after our boat set sail from Liverpool, we arrived safely at the North American shoreline and disembarked onto dry land. Our boat stood at the port of Philadelphia in the state of Pennsylvania. Our destination, however, was New York where the Hebrew Emigrant Aid Society was centered, and the next day we were taken there by railroad. Upon our arrival we were brought to a place then known as Castle Garden where we rested from the wearisome journey. Our leader, the head of the Kiev group, went to the administration office of H.E.A.S. on State Street to inform them of our arrival, and to ask them what they planned to do for us.

Barge Office, New York, about 1900: This building at the foot of Manhattan was the point at which newly arrived immigrants were released from the control of immigration authorities. They were often met by relatives or representatives of immigrant aid organizations. *Credit:* LC

Ellis Island, about 1910: Newly arrived immigrants were brought into this great hall on Ellis Island, located in New York's harbor, for processing

prior to their being permitted to enter the United States. *Credit:* NYPL

Between the time that our group was founded and the time of our arrival large numbers of our brethern had emigrated from Russia and come to New York. So great were their numbers that the shore officers had found it necessary to erect large wooden shacks around Castle Garden to provide them with cover and a place to sleep. The Castle Garden Plaza was filled from one end to the other with immigrants. On the adjoining streets--State Street, Greenwich Street, and even at the top of Broadway— women sat on the ground, babies in hand, for want of a home. Owing to the flood of Russian immigrants, the aid society was short of means and couldn't undertake great projects on their behalf. All it could do was arrange that the mass of people be provided with bread until such time as the incoming flood would diminish and they could do somewhat more for their benefit.

The officers of the Society received our leader politely, but informed him that in the existing circumstances they could do not a thing for our group. They continued to say, however, that since we had come to America trusting in the Society, they would agree to provide us at the first opportunity with food and lodging. After a short while our leader returned to our camp and told us everything that the Society's officers had said. Our spirits sank. "No more hope of working the land! Our dreams had come to naught! Alas that we have reached such a state!" After a time, however, we calmed down a bit and our spirits improved. When we saw what troubles faced the rest of our brethren wandering about outside, we made peace with our lot and were grateful for the Society's promise to feed us for the time being.

The Hebrew Emigrant Aid Society at that time owned a refugee station on Greenpoint, Long Island, near New York. There they gave immigrants food and lodging for a short time so that they might renew themselves after the ardors of their journey. We were taken to this house on the day we arrived in New York, and stayed there for about a week. We originally thought that we would be maintained there for several weeks, but after just one passed we were informed that the time had come for us to leave. This seemed wrong to us, and we said that we would stay on notwithstanding the demands of the society's lackeys. When the superintendents of the station saw that they could not force us, they set about deceiving us. On the eighth day of our stay, two men came in the name of the New York Society and gently asked us if we would be so kind as to accompany them to the bathhouse to clean ourselves off. Feeling grimey from the boat voyage, we went along gladly. The men brought us on the ferry to New York, and there, right in the middle of the river, told us that there was no more room for us on Greenpoint. As the saying goes, "they had taken us for a ride."

I cannot let pass in silence our own actions at the refugee station. In spite of

Examining Eyes, Ellis Island, 1913: U.S. Immigration Service inspectors customarily examined all arriving immigrants for a variety of diseases. Those who were rejected were either put in quarantine or compelled to return to the country from which they had emigrated. *Credit:* LC

Russian Jewish Immigrant, 1900: Arriving in New York with all of his belongings. Photograph by R.F. Turnbull. *Credit:* LC

Jewish Immigrants, Galveston, 1907: Due to the overcrowding of Jewish ghettos in Eastern cities resulting from the arrival of hundreds of thousands of new immigrants, Jacob H. Schiff initiated the Galveston Plan to divert some immigrants to the South. These Jewish immigrants are seen on their arrival in Galveston in July 1907. *Credit:* Archives of Temple B'nai Israel, Galveston, Texas, from a copy at University of Texas, Institute of Texan Cultures

our idealism we did not act honorably.
The reason for this was that the house
rules were very strict. The superinten-
dent was a pious old German Jew whose
devotion to every rule was absolute.
Since we couldn't follow every detail of
every rule there were always arguments
between us. Many in our group would
arouse this man's anger in very strange
ways; for example, at night when he was
in bed one would begin to yell, another
to dance, another to screech like a
chicken, another to sing like a cantor,
another to sermonize like a preacher,
another to spin rhymes like a jester and
so forth. When our behavior was brought
to the attention of the Society's overseers
in New York, they sent several honorable men out to reprove us. But this had
no effect at all: the men did as they had
earlier, renewing their pranks even
more strongly than before.

The superintendents of the immigrant
aid society did not abandon us, however.
They felt themselves obligated to extend
a helping hand until such time as we
could depend on ourselves. Once we
were brought from Greenpoint to New
York, they allocated enough money to
support us for a month (which by their
estimation was time enough for us to be
able to find work), and they rented a
large room for us on 4½ Division Street
where we could live. They also bought
us a stove for cooking, so we could fix
ourselves meals. Responsibility for running our house lay with us and we chose
among ourselves a cook and food pro-
curer. Cooking was the only work we
did in the house. We paid no attention to
cleaning which we considered unnecessary. Our furniture consisted of an oven,
pots and dishes, a long table, and long
wooden benches. We bedded down on
the packs which we had carried with us
and which were spread over the floor.
Since the room was too narrow to ac-
commodate us all, the women and one or
two of the men took beds for the night in
one of the nearby hotels.

So long as we lived in our group
lodging, we paid no attention to the fact
that in a short time we would have to go
out on our own. We didn't worry ourselves about tomorrow; we spent our
time at home. Between meals somebody
would pace up and down the width of
the room with a book on the syntax of the
Russian language reading great rapture
examples of that language's classical
poetry. Some other member was pacing
the breadth of the room with a volume
by the Polish poet Adam Mickiewicz
which he read moving his lips lustily.
Another sat quietly in a corner writing a
poem or an article. Near the stove stood
a group of boys fighting with the cook
over the small portions he gave them at
mealtime. On the floor, on top of our
scattered bundles, several people were
lying on their backs, hands folded, looking upward and yawning. The same
scenes could be seen in our Division
Street room almost every day.

One day, while we were living in this
apartment, a fine looking guest ap-

Young Russian Jew, 1905: Recently arrived
Russian Jewish immigrant at Ellis Island.
Photograph by Lewis Hine. *Credit:* NYPL

Armenian Jew, about 1917: Recently arrived
Armenian Jewish immigrant at Ellis Island.
Photograph by Lewis Hine. *Credit:* NYPL

Orchard Street, 1898: New York's Lower East Side was the first destination for many of the
newly arrived Eastern European Jews. Photograph by Byron. *Credit:* MCNY

peared before us: Abraham Cahan of Vilna who had arrived in America about six weeks after we had. He would come by our home to spend his time, being as miserable as we members of Am Olam were. Who could have predicted that this man would have risen to the station which he commands today? It is worth mentioning here that one of the members of our group was the widow, Mrs. Anna Bronstein from Kiev who later [December 11, 1886] became his wife.

Several of the men among us became exceptions to the rule: they decided to seek their livelihood by their own sweat and blood, and set out in search of some sort of job. Two or three became independent peddlers, and several others, myself among them, decided to seek salaried employment. In those days it was easy to find work unloading ships, since the stevedores had called a strike. We at that time did not understand the meaning of "strikes" and "scabs", and sought jobs on the ships without knowing whether we would succeed in finding any or not. The supervisors of the loading dock accepted us willingly and put us to work. Our job consisted of wheeling wheelbarrows to the bridges of the ship, loading them up with boxes or sacks full of merchandise, and transporting them to the warehouse next to the harbor. It was very difficult work, and on our first day we returned home totally exhausted, not an ounce of strength left in us. By the second day we had grown accustomed to our work and we didn't strain so hard at it.

The boxes and sacks that we unloaded from the boat were filled with produce from various kinds of trees: almonds, nuts, figs, dates, raisins and others. While working with this merchandise we were overcome with the desire to enjoy some of it. Unable to contain ourselves, we treated the merchandise as one does his own goods: we opened sacks and crates and ate as much as we liked without being disturbed, as there was nobody watching over us. We earned $1.70 a day, but the number of days we spent at the work was few. The original workers, striking for higher wages interfered. After our first week of work, on the day we were to get paid, we were told to be prepared for a settlement of the strike. When we left the supervisors' office there stood in our path groups of strikers lying in wait for "the scabs." They fell upon us. Loading dock supervisors were forced to call out the police to accompany us on our way. After that, we did not go back to work.

"Straight to Lafayette, Indiana"

1891. Israel Elkin, like many Eastern European Jewish immigrants, did not make the Eastern Seaboard his first stop. Mrs. Spector, the wife of a man with whom he had done business in Russia, persuaded him to accompany her and her children on the trip to rejoin her husband who had already settled in Lafayette, Indiana.

I traveled to Cracow and then to Hamburg. Mrs. Spector and her daughters took the ship at Hamburg, but for some reason Oscar Sadock and I could not go on the same boat. A day or two later Oscar took sick. I had to take him to a hospital. After he was better, I left and he came a month later. I had to go to Amsterdam for my ship. The passage was quite stormy, the food not very good for I traveled third class in one of the fifty bunks in a large so-called dormitory. I felt fine until the sixth day; then I had an upset stomach. The doctor said he couldn't do anything for me. I suffered for six days and finally on the thirteenth day we landed: June 15, 1891. We landed at Castle Garden, and after the necessary preliminaries, I took the train straight to Lafayette, Indiana, where Mr. Spector had settled. I was well received by Mr. Spector and as soon as I was taken into the home which he had provided for his family, I realized that in his enthusiasm for the new country and the desire to have his family with him, he had exaggerated the wonders of America and allowed his imagination to go rampant. Instead of having a large department store, he had walked to the country with a pack on his back, selling dry goods and notions. Now he was extremely affluent: with two old horses and a wagon, he peddled junk. When I saw this I was petrified. Just think, a man like Mr. Spector, a *Bolobus* at home in Russia, with a fine business, deliberately gave up all of this and came here to struggle. My heart sank. That meant that I would have the same fate. What should I do? My own thought was to run back. But after all I was a grown man with a family. I couldn't give up so easily. So I decided to try here for a while anyway. Through the good graces of Mr. Spector, the Loeb and Hene Department Store extended credit to me, and I too carried a pack of dry goods and notions on my back and went to the surrounding country to induce the farmers' wives to buy my wares. The degradation of this menial business and the language difficulties which I encountered nearly drove me insane. One day I was so disgusted that I threw my pack in the mud, only to pick it up again, realizing that that was not the solution to the problem. Even with a heavy heart, I realized that I could make a living doing this, and it would be merely a stepping stone to something better.

For the first few days I'd come back to the city every night. After a week I became ambitious and decided to save time by going out for a whole week instead of coming in every night. This meant that I would have to stay in some farm house overnight, and also spend each night in a different place. Having great difficulty in expressing my thoughts and desires in English, I asked Jake Salzman what to say when evening came and I wanted to ask for a place to stay overnight. He told me what to say, and incidentally thought he would play a good joke on me. That night when it was getting dark and I was hungry and weary of foot, I stopped at a farm house, knocked on the door, and spoke to the farmer's wife: "Lady, can I sleep with you?" For a moment she looked dismayed; then, realizing that I was a "greenhorn," she took no offense at my question and I stayed overnight in her home.

In order to get to my bedroom, I had to go through the bedroom of the farmer and his wife (at present we would call this room the master bedroom). Going up was all right, for they were still up, but during the night, I had to get up. The toilet was out of doors. Imagine my dilemma: What should I do? If I went through their room it would not have been polite. Necessity makes one do many things. I took a new handkerchief from my bundle—I remember to this day, it was a lovely new bandanna, something like the one Aunt Jemima wears. I made use of it, hid it under the bed, and the next morning disposed of it. My only sorrow was that I had to lose the bandanna.

The next evening I stopped at another home, and for supper they served something that was as big around as a plate, looked doughy, and had something oozing out of the little slits on top. I couldn't imagine what it was, had never seen anything like it before. It was passed to me first, and not knowing exactly what to do, I cut half of it with my knife and slipped it on my plate. I ate it and it was quite good. The remaining half was passed all around the table. No one touched it, and finally it came back to me. Thinking maybe the rest of it was meant for me, I slipped the rest of it on my plate and finished it. Not a word was said and I didn't know I had made any kind of a social error until I came home and asked Jake Salzman, "What was this thing which was dough, the size of a whole plate, and had fruit between?" He said that was called a "pie." I told him how peculiar it was that no one touched it, that I took one half, then the other. He was convulsed with laughter. He said each one was to take a small piece, and here I had taken the whole thing. You can well imagine my mortification, for I've always had a very sensitive soul, and was so chagrined to think I had made such an error and deprived the rest of the family of their food. Even to this day when I eat pie, this picture comes before my mind's eye.

Hester Street, New York, about 1890: The Lower East Side in New York was an area where newly arrived Jewish immigrants settled; Hester Street was a center of activity. Photograph by Jacob A. Riis. *Credit:* MCNY

Maxwell Street, about 1905: Although New York's Lower East Side has come to symbolize the environment in which most Eastern European Jews found themselves on their arrival to this country, it had its smaller equivalents in other large urban centers. Maxwell Street was the center of Chicago's Eastern European Jewish community at the beginning of this century. *Credit:* CHS

Hester Street, 1900: On New York's Lower East Side. *Credit:* MCNY

Maxwell Street, 1906: Second hand clothes being sold on the street in Chicago. Photograph by C.R. Clark. *Credit:* CHS

Maxwell Street, 1906: Selling kitchenware on the street in Chicago. Photograph by C.R Clark. *Credit:* CHS

A Russian Immigrant's Odyssey

1892. Like many others who arrived at the peak of immigration, A. B. Cohen experienced the travails of an illegal border crossing, a delayed departure from Europe, a miserable ocean crossing, quarantine on arrival and difficulties in finding steady employment.

In May of 1892, I left Birzai to go to America. I had to board a ship in Hamburg, but before reaching there, had to pass through Germany. It was illegal for anyone to leave Russia without having special permission from the Government. Owing to the fact that I left Russia before I served my military term, I was obliged to pass the border from Lithuania to Germany in an illegal way. There were people specializing in that. In fact, of all the people who left Russia for America, every one passed over the border in an illegal way as none was able to get the special passport.

When we passed the border from Urbrich to Germany our first stop was Koenigsburg. There we met a committee from the *Judische Hilfsvereine* (Jewish Relief Society) and they told us that because there was an epidemic of cholera in Russia, the German government would not permit us to go through, and special *SOPES* (concentration camps) had been set up for the immigrants.

In Hamburg we were also sent to the *SOPES* in which there were approximately three thousand people waiting for ships. There were bunks or berths in which three or four people could sleep. The meals were provided in soup kitchens and we would have to line up early in the morning with our plates to get a dish of soup or whatever there was.

Among the people who were in the *SOPES*, I noticed a middle-aged man dressed in striped pants, frock coat and a silk hat. I became acquainted with him and he told me he was from Friederstadt in Kurland: like Lithuania, Kurland belonged to Russia. His name was Jacobson, and he told me that in Friederstadt he had owned a factory, making knitted goods. He appeared very prosperous, but his family (two sons and one daughter) lived in Baltimore and it was their desire that he should join them. He told me that he was going to travel either first or second class and his plan was to buy this passage in Germany, but he was trapped in the *SOPES*, and when he reached Hamburg it was too late to get a ship with first or second class accommodations; he was obliged to go third class with the rest of the immigrants.

In the *SOPES* there was a building where the German officials were housed. They weren't very kind to the immigrants and the only person who had some influence with them was Jacobson. He was kept busy day and night, advising those immigrants who needed guidance. On my third day I discovered that Mr. Jacobson bunked on the top level of the fourth berth, and it was very hard for him to climb. My bunk was in another section of the *SOPES*, but I was lucky to

Hester Street, 1898: Street vendors on New York's Lower East Side. Photograph by Byron. *Credit:* MCNY

910 South Fifth Street, Philadelphia, 1915: Street scene in Philadelphia's Jewish immigrant section. *Credit:* PCA

get a lower berth. So I exchanged with him and that made us very close to each other.

People, seeing our relationship, started to ask me if I would intervene for them with Mr. Jacobson. He suggested to me that he would be my uncle and I his nephew so that our relationship would be closer. So anytime people wanted to go near him, they would call on me and ask me to intervene for them with my uncle. I must say that I was treated much better by the German officers than the rest of the immigrants because of my relationship with "Uncle" Jacobson.

We stayed in that camp almost three weeks. We were supposed to embark on a Saturday morning, and on Friday representatives of the *Judische Hilfsverein* called on us and asked us if we needed anything as they would be willing to go to town for anything we wanted. They took our money, but they never came back.

I will never forget that Saturday. The ship on which we were to embark was named Scande, and a group of seven hundred fifty people were designated to leave the *SOPES* on it. We were all told to face a certain gate, and a group of doctors was there examining us. In order not to lose too much time, we were told to be ready for the examination. They wanted to examine our eyes, inspect our vaccinations and our tongues. This was a sight to see—we took off our glasses, took off our jackets, rolled up our sleeves and stuck out our tongues. Because we were so afraid we would be rejected, we stood there for hours with our tongues out.

In later years, in New York City, I ran into one of my so-called ship brothers, a man named Stein; we talked about the experiences of the *SOPES* and when we remembered the examination we had a big laugh looking at each other with our tongues out.

Our real troubles began on the ship. It took us about fifteen days to cross the Atlantic. During that time, thirty-two people died of cholera and were buried at sea. The rumor was that the doctors didn't diagnose the cases correctly and any weak spell would be considered cholera, and no effort was made to save the patient. Of course, this was only a rumor and the truth was never known.

Going through Germany we were not permitted to stop in any cities, and when we did stop, we were put in concentration camps. But on the ship, we mingled with non-Jewish people coming from the same parts of Lithuania and Russia as we did and, to our great surprise, none of the non-Jews had been kept in concentration camps. It was the opinion of some of the Jews on the ship that the Germans did not want us to stop for fear that we would settle there.

The food aboard ship was terrible; practically all of the time our diet consisted of bread and tea and sometime a herring. The drinking water was so bad that we couldn't even drink it after we became thirsty from eating herring.

As we neared America the ship was anchored off shore. We discovered the reason after two days: there was a question as to whether or not we would be permitted to land because of the cholera epidemic.

We were on the decks of the ship for fifteen days, but during that time some of the immigrants were able to communicate with their friends in New York as we were getting mail every other day. We were also getting newspapers and there we discovered our danger. However, a few days later, we were a little encouraged by the report that some committee in New York was trying to save us from being sent back and finally we were ordered to Hoffman's Island and there we stayed for about five weeks. This was supposed to be the quarantine test to see whether or not any one of us was infected with cholera.

When we landed on Hoffman's Island all our clothes were taken away from us, put in bags and fumigated for twenty-four hours. In the meantime, we were supplied with blankets to cover ourselves against the chilly air.

I had a very bad experience myself. When I had reached Koenigsburg I was able, only for a little while, to go through some stores to buy some things which I needed. I bought myself a derby hat thinking this would be more American style. But when they took all my clothes at Hoffman's Island, my hat went along; of course they weren't particular about how the clothes were put in the bags and when I got back my bag the heat had ruined everything. My poor hat—it looked like a Napoleon hat; I could hardly put it on my head and the whole thing was so stiff it was just like steel.

On the second day we took a walk to examine the island and at the banks there was a group of sailors drinking beer. When I passed by, one of the sailors took up a bottle of beer and hit me over the head with such force that my hat was actually wedged against my scalp. My head was bleeding all around and when they took me down to the dispensary the doctor had an awful job taking off my hat. He said: "You ought to be thankful for your funny hat; it was so stiff that it protected your scalp against a very dangerous condition." I could then understand why "We have to praise God for any misfortune that may befall us the same as we praise God for any goodness he bestows upon us."

The rest of the immigrants had similar experiences with their clothes; practically all of the garments fell to pieces on account of the heat. Somebody—the government or the ship company—supplied us with new clothes. They were all very cheap and the officers of the ship company weren't particular as to the sizes we got—they used their own judgment. However, we were all glad we had something to wear.

Rosh Hashana was to be spent on Hoffman's Island and we worried because we didn't have a prayer book or a Torah to read. From the newspapers we found there was a Rabbi, very famous in those days, by the name of Hillel Klein. So we sent him a letter signed by a dozen people and asked him to provide us with prayer books and a Torah. He was very prompt to answer, and we received a box with about one hundred prayer books and a small Torah. He requested us to return the Torah.

After going through inspection again, the government permitted us to land. This was about two days before Yom Kippur, on the tenth of October; I remember the exact date, as on the twelfth the people in this country were celebrating Columbus Day.

In those days, Castle Garden was the place where all the immigrants landed. We didn't have to go through any further hardship. I had all my tools and I remember that when asked what I was going to do in America, I said I was a goldsmith. A committee from H.I.A.S. (Hebrew Immigrant Aid Society) was there to meet us. They were very kind and told us what street cars to take. As it happened, my brother had just moved and we couldn't contact him. I had an address on Clinton Street where his father-in-law lived, so I showed them this address and they put me on a horse car and told the conductor where to let me off. The car stopped about three blocks from Mr. Horwitz, and it was hard to find the right number. I had a lot of fun looking, though! The committee in charge of asking Dr. Klein for the prayer books and the Torah had assigned to me the job of returning the Torah. People stopped to look at me and wondered

what was going on—a young boy walking the streets with a Torah. However, I soon reached my brother's father-in-law. He sent word to my brother who called for me that evening to take me to his home at 336 E. 106th Street.

I arrived in New York on October 10, 1892. After resting for a few days, I started to look for a job and got one with a man by the name of Garfinkle at 56 Suffolk Street. My salary was four dollars a week and after lunches and traveling, I was left with one dollar and ninety cents. This was hard to get along on especially since I had an obligation to send some money home, and therefore I decided to look for another job.

Henry Anselowitz sold tools, materials and accessories for jewelers and watchmakers. His business was at 110 Canal Street, and it was an assembling place for jewelers and watchmakers who had just come to this country. He was very kind to all of them, freely giving advice and encouragement.

He advised me to watch the newspapers carefully to see if there was an opening for a goldsmith. One morning I read in the paper that a concern called Eisenson and Marx, a jewelry factory in Newark, was looking for a goldsmith. When I arrived in Newark, I was told that they had needed only one extra goldsmith, and the job was taken.

While I was standing there in great disappointment a messenger from a jewelry store brought in a link button and said that the jeweler wanted to have another button made to match it. The messenger was told that this would require a special die and it would never pay to do it. However, after examining the button, I said I would make a button to match this one if I could get a job afterward. The foreman asked me how I could do it without any die and I told him that where I learned my trade, in addition to manufacturing jewelry, we also had to be tool makers and therefore I could make any tool required without depending on dies. I was promised that if I could make the button, I could get a steady job.

The factory was not very large as there were only twenty jewelers employed there. I will never forget the curiosity of the men watching me make the button. After spending more than a day, I succeeded in making a button to match as nearly as possible. My work pleased the foreman very much and I got the job. However, after I worked three days, the men left their jobs to strike for higher wages. So this was the end of my second job.

Mr. Anselowitz advised me to peddle in my neighborhood to repair jewelry and clocks. This was customary for practically all the newcomers—to knock on doors and ask if there was any jewelry or clocks to be repaired. I succeeded in getting a couple of jobs in the beginning, but the trouble was that people didn't like to trust their valuables to be taken by a jeweler and it was impossible to do the work at their homes.

Robinowitz Tobacco Store, 1898: Located on Maxwell Street in Chicago. Members of the family from left to right: Sholom Baer, Ira Robbins, Ida Devoretsky, Goldie Shapiro, Alex Shapiro, Jean Devoretsky, Sarah Devoretsky, Jack Devoretsky, Annie Robins Mansfield, Annie Robinowitz (grandmother), Ida Robins Reisberg, Rose Michelsen, Celia Robins Kantor, Grandfather and Sam Devore. *Credit:* CJA

Maxwell Street, about 1905: A store front tobacco factory in Chicago's Jewish immigrant neighborhood. *Credit:* CHS

Tailor Shop, about 1905: Adler's tailor shop in a Chicago Jewish immigrant neighborhood. *Credit:* CJA

Division Street, about 1912: Wholesale and retail stores selling clothing and millinery were traditional Jewish businesses. Division Street on New York's Lower East Side was a center for this activity. Photograph by Lewis Hine. *Credit:* NYPL

The jewelers or the watchmakers who were peddling for repair jobs used to carry little satchels with their tools and the face of a clock attached to the front to signify their trade. One day I was sitting on the bench in the park and an old gentleman was sitting alongside me. Looking at my satchel with the face of the clock, he asked me if I was from Switzerland as he was a great believer in the Swiss watchmakers. I told him I was from Lithuania, but to him it was the same thing. He told me that he was a school director in charge of schools in that neighborhood. He told me there were about thirty clocks in the schools but none of them kept time; the clocks had been sent to different watch-making shops but it appeared that they couldn't do anything with them. So he asked me if I could take a job of this kind.

I told him that before I would answer, I would like to see the clocks. After I finished my lunch, he took me to one of the schools and while I was not a watch-maker, I could still see the trouble. They were wall clocks and I presumed they weren't hanging straight. I told him that I would be very glad to take the job. I called on Mr. Anselowitz and told him my problem and he told me he knew a watchmaker who was an expert but he was just as green as I was, having been in the United States for only a month. He recommended that I get in touch with that man so that he would do the actual repair work.

I got hold of the man and after examining the clocks he found I was right. All the clocks were wound by key and it appeared that the man that was winding them moved them from the right position. The two of us worked for two weeks straightening out the clocks and putting tacks on the sides so that their positions would not be disturbed again. We were told that we should wait an-other couple of weeks and that if the clocks kept time we would get paid. While both of us were very anxious to get the money as we needed it badly, we had to wait until the man was satisfied.

I asked Mr. Anselowitz how much I should charge for the job and he told me to leave it to the school director. Because I was the so-called contractor, I should give my assistant five dollars a week or ten dollars for the job and he would be perfectly satisfied.

After two weeks I called on the school director and I got a check for one hundred fifty dollars. So I told Mr. Anselowitz that because the watchmaker actually did the work I would give him twenty-five dollars; this gave me over one hundred dollars for myself net. This was more money that I would have made working in the factory for a whole month.

I continued peddling and while I wasn't a big success, I made enough money to pay my living expenses and also had a little money to send home. I remember one Sunday night, after buy-ing some material, I found that I had spent all my money and didn't have five cents left for carfare. If I hadn't been bashful, I could certainly have gotten

Division Street, about 1910: Jewish businesses on New York's Lower East Side. *Credit:* LC

Delancey Street, New York, 1901: Jewish restaurant on New York's Lower East Side. *Credit:* NYHS

716-718 Race Street, Philadelphia, 1915: Street scene in Philadelphia's Jewish immigrant section. *Credit:* PCA

Second-hand Clothes, undated: A typical street scene on New York's Lower East Side. *Credit:* LC

Tenement Yard, about 1910: In 1895 New York's tenement districts had the highest population density of any city in the world: 143.2 persons per acre. These buildings were jammed one alongside the other with scarcely any daylight or fresh air penetrating the crowded rooms, and the children had nowhere to play. *Credit:* NYCPD

some money from Mr. Anselowitz, but I thought that I would rather call on one of my friends on the East Side. However, wherever I called I was very embarrassed. This was Chanukah and they were all playing cards. When I came in I was invited to take a hand in the game—which was not my purpose in visiting them. Finally, I decided to go back to 110 Canal Street and ask Mr. Anselowitz to lend me some money for carfare. But when I got there I found the place was already closed. I was obliged to walk home to 106th Street and this was an experience which I will never forget; it was practically one hundred and fifteen blocks. It was a journey which took me over three hours. When I told my experience afterwards to some of my friends, they all laughed at me and said that I would never be successful if I was too sensitive to ask for help.

"A Baptism of Fire" on The Lower East Side

1893. Lillian Wald, daughter of a well-to-do German-Jewish family established the first visiting nurse service on New York's Lower East Side to minister to the needs of the newly arrived immigrants living in miserable conditions.

From the schoolroom where I had been giving a lesson in bed-making, a little girl led me one drizzling March morning. She had told me of her sick mother, and gathering from her incoherent account that a child had been born, I caught up the paraphernalia of the bed-making lesson and carried it with me.

The child led me over broken roadways—there was no asphalt, although its use was well established in other parts of the city, over dirty mattresses and heaps of refuse—it was before Colonel Waring had shown the possibility of clean streets even in that quarter—between tall, reeking houses whose laden fire-escapes, useless for their appointed purpose, bulged with household goods of every description. The rain added to the dismal appearance of the streets and to the discomfort of the crowds which thronged them, intensifying the odors which assailed me from every side. Through Hester and Division streets we went to the end of Ludlow; past odorous fish-stands, for the streets were a marketplace, unregulated, unsupervised, unclean; past evil-smelling, uncovered garbage-cans; and—perhaps worst of all, where so many little children played—past the trucks brought down from more fastidious quarters and stalled on these already overcrowded streets, lending themselves inevitably to many forms of indecency.

The child led me on through a tenement hallway, across a court where open and unscreened closets were promiscuously used by men and women, up into a rear tenement, by slimy steps whose accumulated dirt was augmented that day by the mud of the streets, and finally into the sickroom.

All the maladjustments of our social and economic relations seemed epitomized in this brief journey and what was found at the end of it. The family to which the child led me was neither criminal nor vicious. Although the husband was a cripple, one of those who stand on street corners exhibiting deformities to enlist compassion, and masking the begging of alms by a pretense at selling; although the family of seven shared their two rooms with boarders—who were literally boarders since a piece of timber was placed over the floor for them to sleep on—and although the sick woman lay on a wretched, unclean bed, soiled with a hemorrhage two days old, they were not degraded human beings, judged by any measure of moral values.

In fact, it was very plain that they were sensitive to their condition, and when at the end of my ministrations they kissed my hands (those who have undergone similar experiences will, I am sure, understand), it would have been some solace if by any conviction of the moral unworthiness of the family I could have defended myself as a part of a society which permitted such conditions to exist. Indeed, my subsequent acquaintance with them revealed the fact that, miserable as their state was, they were not without ideals for the family life and for society of which they were so unloved and unlovely a part.

That morning's experience was a baptism of fire. Deserted were the laboratory and the academic work of the college. I never returned to them. On my way from the sickroom to my comfortable student quarters my mind was intent on my own responsibility. To my inexperience it seemed certain that conditions such as these were allowed because people did not *know*, and for me there was a challenge to know and to tell. When early morning found me still awake, my naïve conviction remained that, if people knew things—and "things" meant everything implied in the condition of this family—such horrors would cease to exist, and I rejoiced that I had had a training in the care of the sick that in itself would give me an organic relationship to the neighborhood in which this awakening had come. . . .

Idealism from Russia Transferred to America

About 1895. Abraham Cahan, author and outstanding editor of the Jewish Daily Forward *described some of his first experiences in this country.*

With the coming of the new immigrants one began to hear Russian spoken on the streets of the East Side. Once, a woman passing by as a friend and I were conversing in Russian on East Broadway, turned on us with disgust and spat out: "Tfu! The nerve, actually talking Russian! Wasn't it bad enough that you had to hear that dirty language in Russia?"

Even the uneducated immigrants could speak Russian, although they preferred Yiddish. But the intellectual minority spoke only Russian among themselves. This was a new thing in New York and it was because we were the first Russian-Jewish intellectuals in the United States.

We had brought something more than just this new way of conversing. In our hearts we also brought our love for enlightened Russian culture. We had transported from Russia the banner of idealism, scarred and bloodstained in the Russian revolutionary movement.

We could feel the resistance of the old-fashioned Suwalki Jews to the spirit of our new movement. They considered us to be atheists and lunatics; we intellectuals thought of them as ignorant, primitive people.

We were a small minority. Most of our own fellow immigrants shared the suspicions felt by the Suwalki Jews. The Jewish masses in the old country knew little about socialism. Socialist ideas were fenced in by a wall of guns and gallows, by censorship and the fear of the police. The formation of the Jewish Workers' Bund in Vilna was still fifteen years off. A mere handful of Jewish workers in Vilna had grasped the meaning of socialism—and almost all of this handful had come to America.

After my arrival it took me just three days to realize that the establishment of commune colonies was not really my dream. I was not fascinated by village life, by the prospect of laboring on the soil. On the contrary, I felt strongly drawn to the life of the city. My heart beat to its rhythms, and as the heart feels so thinks the head.

More than feeling was involved when one weighed the chances of a communist farm colony in the United States. I expressed my opinion on this so sharply that I found myself quarreling about it with some of my idealistic friends.

Several years earlier William Frey, a Russian revolutionary follower of Chernishevsky, became converted to idealistic communism as opposed to revolution by force. He gave up his career and came to America where he soon became an advocate of Auguste Comte's "religion of humanity." In line with that "religion," he preached against every revolutionary movement, even against the workers' struggle for higher wages and a shorter work week.

In the 1870s, the revolutionary Russian journal, V*period*, published in Switzerland, contained a long letter from Frey about communist colonies in the United States. The letter had been sent from Kansas where Frey and his followers were operating a commune on a farm.

The editor of V*period* had replied in the same issue and had argued that the instrument for overthrowing the capitalist system was a great mass movement, not ineffective, small communist colonies. The editor complimented the communards for their hard work and their devotion but said that their colony was like a plant being nurtured under glass by artificial means. The fate of humanity could not be made to depend on such artificial means. Revolution must proceed by natural means.

I read this exchange in V*period* long after it had occurred, and it opened my eyes. I remembered the fable I had read in a Russian reader for children about the fool who tries to clinch the sale of a house by offering a brick as a sample.

Socialism could not be achieved through sample colonies. What did such a colony prove as it struggled to survive, surrounded by a vast capitalist country, dependent on capitalist transportation and capitalist banks and capitalist stores and competing with capitalist farmers? An entirely new structure was needed. What good was a sample brick?

In my arguments with followers of the commune idea I cited all the previous attempts in the United States to establish commune farms and noted that only the Quakers had succeeded.

I told my friends, sometimes in heated arguments, that they were wasting their time and their energy on an impossible dream. I counted myself out of the group for I had begun to feel around me the seething life of a great American city. Formerly I had only read about capitalism. Now it surrounded me on all sides.

New York had a German-language socialist daily newspaper called the *New Yorker Volkszeitung*. For us it was a real treasure. In Russia such a publication was a secret and dangerous enterprise, circulated underground and issued irregularly. But here it was issued regularly every day and openly circulated!

This newspaper was the reason some of us learned German even before we learned English. It played a major role in our intellectual development. Every day we could read in its pages challenging Marxist interpretations of the news.

In the old country we had been limited to the few booklets and pamphlets that had circulated secretly. But in the United States we received through the *New Yorker Volkszeitung* a daily Marxist commentary on life and politics. And every day the unreal nature of commune colonies became increasingly clear to me.

I also began to attend the German-language meetings addressed by the editors of the *New Yorker Volkszeitung*. I remember the first German workers meeting I attended in a hall on Second Avenue near Houston Street. In a fever of excitement, I followed as best I could the inspiring German talks by editors Sergius Schevitsch and Alexander Jonas. Schevitsch was a German baron from Latvia. He had been educated in Russia and could speak and write French, Italian and English as well as Russian and German. He was married to Elena von Racowita for whom Ferdinand Lassalle died in a duel.

I have no words sufficient to describe the deep excitement this first meeting stirred in me. How could I even think of deserting this seething, stimulating life in the midst of the struggles of the workers and take off, instead, for some far-off puny colony which had as much chance

Pushcart Peddler, undated: A typical street scene on New York's Lower East Side. *Credit:* NYPL

Street Vendor, about 1910: Selling food on New York's Lower East Side. *Credit:* NYPL

Kibitzers, 1920: On New York's Lower East Side. Photograph by Lewis Hine. *Credit:* NYPL

Anti-immigrant Cartoon, 1882: With the arrival of hundreds of thousands of immigrants from Southern and Eastern Europe in the last quarter of the 19th century, native Americans manifested anti-immigrant sentiments. This cartoon from *The Judge* included Jews among the hordes of immigrants who were crowding cities across the country. *Credit:* AJHS

of overthrowing capitalism as a fly has of pushing over an elephant? The dream of an instant earthly paradise dissolved. The *New Yorker Volkszeitung* and the German-language socialist meetings took its place.

I felt America's freedom every minute. I breathed freer than I had ever breathed before. But all the time I was saying to myself, "All of this is a capitalist prison." And the confusion in my brain was compounded by the fact that in the first few months in America I worked like a slave at my first jobs.

From Russia, where distribution of socialist literature was a secret task evoking the terror of Siberian exile, I had brought the notion that to be dedicated to the cause required the underground performance of such prohibited tasks. Therefore I planned to print socialist propaganda leaflets, to post myself in the street in front of the shops and factories and to distribute them to the workers. This had the taste of underground conspiracy, although there was no risk in doing it here.

I longed to persuade myself that by distributing such socialist leaflets I would be leading the life of a Russian revolutionary in the United States. The word "leaflet" had a sacred sound. It was "forbidden fruit" even though it was not forbidden. In years to come, hundreds of others, for the same reason, experienced the same illusion. And because there was no secret socialist movement in the United States, they looked upon the native movement with contempt.

What kind of socialism could it be without conspiracy? What good was the fruit if it wasn't forbidden? The power of deeply rooted beliefs is greater than the power of logic and common sense. Socialism itself teaches that the special circumstances of each time and each place must be taken into account in formulating tactics. But the romantic stimulation of danger is powerful. If all is permissible and danger is absent, socialism becomes diluted and revolutionary heroism becomes impossible.

In the Park, about 1912: On New York's Lower East Side. Photograph by Lewis Hine. *Credit:* NYPL

Working in a Sweatshop

1909. Clara Lemlich, leader of a shirt-waist makers strike, described the miserable working conditions in the shops.

First let me tell you something about the way we work and what we are paid. There are two kinds of work—regular, that is salary work, and piecework. The regular work pays about $6 a week and the girls have to be at their machines at 7 o'clock in the morning and they stay at them until 8 o'clock at night, with just one-half hour for lunch in that time.

The shops. Well, there is just one row of machines that the daylight ever gets to—that is the front row, nearest the window. The girls at all the other rows of machines back in the shops have to work by gaslight, by day as well as by night. Oh, yes, the shops keep the work going at night too.

The bosses in the shops are hardly what you would call educated men, and the girls to them are part of the machines they are running. They yell at the girls and they "call them down" even worse than I imagine the Negro slaves were in the South.

There are no dressing rooms for the girls in the shops. They have to hang up their hats and coats—such as they are—on hooks along the walls. Sometimes a girl has a new hat. It never is much to look at because it never costs more than 50 cents, but it's pretty sure to be spoiled after it's been at the shop.

We're human, all of us girls, and we're young. We like new hats as well as any other young women. Why shouldn't we? And if one of us gets a new one, even it it hasn't cost more than 50 cents, that means that we have gone for weeks on two-cent lunches—dry cake and nothing else.

The shops are unsanitary—that's the word that is generally used, but there ought to be a worse one used. Whenever we tear or damage any of the goods we sew on, or whenever it is found damaged after we are through with it, whether we have done it or not, we are charged for the piece and sometimes for a whole yard of the material.

At the beginning of every slow season, $2 is deducted from our salaries. We have never been able to find out what this is for.

The Cloakmakers' Strike

1910. Meyer London, one of the leaders of the cloakmakers, was active in the great strike of 1910. He later became a lawyer, was a founder of the Socialist Party and in 1914 was elected to Congress from The Lower East Side for the first of two terms.

We offer no apology for the general strike. If at all we should apologize to the tens of thousands of the exploited men and women for not having aroused them before.

The cloak trade at present is the trade par excellence in which the "survival of the fittest" has come to mean "the survival of the meanest." Among employers the manufacturer who is merciless in reducing wages and in stretching out the hours of labor, the manufacturer who disregards in dealing with his employes all laws human and divine is most likely to succeed. The employer who neglects all sanitary requirements, who does business with money taken from the workmen under the guise of security and who levies a tax upon the employees for the use of electricity, is a danger not only to the employees but to every reputable employer in the trade.

We charge those employers with ruining the great trade built up by the industrious immigrants. We charge them with having corrupted the morale of thousands employed in the cloak trade.

The man who licks the boots of his employer, the individual who works without regard for time and for conditions is promoted in the factory. Treachery, slavishness and espionage are encouraged by the employers as great virtues of the cloakmakers.

This general strike is greater than any union. It is an irresistible movement of the people. It is a protest against conditions that can no longer be tolerated. This is the first great attempt to regulate conditions in the trade, to do away with that anarchy and chaos which keeps some of the men working 16 hours a day during the hottest months of the year while thousands of others have no employment whatever.

We cannot trust ourselves to the kind mercies of the employers. To our sorrow we have trusted them long enough. We ask for humane treatment; we demand the right to live; we refuse to be annihilated. We realize that we must be united; we know that we have the sympathy of every man that deserves the name. We know that organized labor throughout the country will applaud our efforts. We appeal to the people of America to assist us in our struggle.

How the New York Cloak Union Started

1903. Joseph Barondess, leader of the cloakmakers and one of the founders of the Socialist Party, described the struggle between the workers and the clothing manufacturers.

The first attempt to organize the cloakmakers on a real trade union basis was made in the year 1889.

I called the first meeting to order, as the secretary of the United Hebrew Trades, and from that time on remained at the head of the organization, which assumed the name "Operators and Cloakmakers Union of New York and Vicinity."

From the first day of its existence the Operators and Cloakmakers Union was a militant organization, and we achieved one victory after the other and our power for good grew to immense proportions.

The manufacturers, frightened at our power, organized a manufacturers association, and in the month of October 1889, all of them locked out all of our members, who then numbered about 10,000.

This lockout lasted for nearly six months, during which time we succeeded in entering into a treaty with the outside contractors.

Aside from our victory, we also succeeded in compelling the manufacturers to pay to the Cloak and Suit Cutters somewhat near $20,000 for loss of time.

Strikes followed one after the other on the least provocation. We did not understand at that time that in the labor movement as well as in any other branch of activity and reform, things must develop by the process of evolution, and that reforms and improvements can only have a lasting influence where they have been achieved gradually.

Our employers saw fit to invoke the aid of the courts and the police force in order to break up our union. Most of the prominent members of the Executive Board, including myself, were arrested on all sorts of charges, thereby compelling us to spend all our means and energies to defend ourselves instead of assuming the aggressive position against the unscrupulous employers as a labor organization.

It was then that we became convinced that no matter how powerful an individual organization might be, it must have the backing of a national union which would aid it in its struggles, and also influence the consuming public to stand by it against the atrocities of mean and oppressing employers.

Striking Cloakmakers, New York, 1916: There was a continuing struggle to overcome miserable working conditions in the garment trades. In 1900 the International Ladies' Garment Workers' Union was formed. In 1909 the "uprising of the 20,000," occurred in New York and was considered a turning point in the union-management struggle. Jacob H. Schiff believed that Jewish workers and bosses should not be antagonists. *Credit:* LC

Sweatshop, about 1910: With few job opportunities for the unskilled immigrants, many were compelled to accept employment in sweat-shops and to work in crowded and unhealthy conditions for between twelve and eighteen hours a day. *Credit:* ILGWU

Men's Clothing Factory, New York, about 1912: The shop of Moe Levy & Company, manufacturers of men's clothing. Photograph by Byron. *Credit:* MCNY

I.W.W. Demonstration, New York, about 1910: Daniel De Leon, socialist trade union organizer, addressing an International Workers of the World demonstration in Union Square, New York. Although the I.W.W. stressed organizational drives among the unorganized workers, there was some limited support among the Jewish trades. *Credit:* LC

Women Workers on the March, 1909: The Shirt Waistmakers' Strike of 1909 was a milestone in labor history as workers began to organize against the owners. Thousands joined the picket lines refusing to work without improved conditions. *Credit:* Culver

Celebrating Strike Victory, 1915: Sidney Hillman, center with glasses, leading Amalgamated Clothing Workers union in a celebration after winning their strike against Hart, Schaffner & Marx in Chicago. *Credit:* CHS

How to "Relieve the Tremendous Congestion in the Seaboard Cities"

October 15, 1891. Jacob H. Schiff, who became one of the most prominent and influential Jewish financiers and philanthropists, arrived in this country from Germany in 1865. Like many other successful German Jews, he was concerned about the impact of the huge numbers of impoverished Eastern European Jews who began to flood New York and other East Coast cities. In this letter to Baron Maurice de Hirsch, who had established a fund to aid Russian and Romanian Jews, Schiff suggested that the Eastern European immigrants should be encouraged to go west of the Rocky Mountains and engage in agriculture.

I agree entirely with you that any plan, whatever it may be, must be carried out on business-like principles, and if on this point we do not succeed in New York, it will be mainly because the influx for many months has been so enormous that no systematic arrangement can possibly be effected to take proper care of the arrivals. It is difficult enough to deal on business principles with people who come almost naked and helpless, but even if it were feasible with a few individuals or with a small number, it is entirely impossible when it is a matter of ten thousand per month. We here find ourselves very hard-pressed, but that is apparently an unalterable situation. We have been called by Divine Providence to stand guard, and we must perform the possible and the impossible, so long as present conditions continue. Since we must provide even the barest necessities for the immense number of refugees who come to our shores, and since even the small sums required involve, in the aggregate, great financial sacrifices on the part of American Jewry, we cannot collect the large sums which would alone make possible in this country a colonization scheme that would yield results. In the last analysis the United States remains the best field for colonization, and if we only had the necessary capital, much could still be done here, especially in the states west of the Rocky Mountains. What we are now doing, as you know, is to organize trial colonies, through which we hope to awaken in our Russian co-religionists a desire to engage in agriculture, and in this manner to induce those who are already here to relieve the tremendous congestion in the seaboard cities.

I hope that you will have an opportunity to confer with Dr. Julius Goldman, the honorary secretary of your Trust Fund here, who sailed last week for the conference in Berlin. He understands the situation in all its phases, and has displayed a truly admirable devotion to the cause. He will be able to explain many things to you about which you will want to know more, and in which you are certainly interested. You will also doubtless have an opportunity to meet Mr. Jesse Seligman during his extended stay in Europe. He is particularly in a position to be able to explain the position taken by our Government in the question of Russian emigration.

Reaction to the Triangle Fire

1911. Rose Schneiderman, a leader in the Hat and Cap Makers' Union, spoke of the need for the workers to organize and protect themselves from tragedies such as the fire at the Triangle Shirtwaist Company in which 146 women employees, mostly Jewish, lost their lives.

I would be a traitor to these poor burned bodies if I came here to talk good fellowship. We have tried you good people of the public and we have found you wanting. The old Inquisition had its rack and its thumbscrews and its instruments of torture with iron teeth. We know what these things are today; the iron teeth are our necessities, the thumbscrews are the high-powered and swift machinery close to which we must work, and the rack is here in the firetrap structures that will destroy us the minute they catch on fire.

This is not the first time girls have been burned alive in the city. Every week I must learn of the untimely death of one of my sister workers. Every year thousands of us are maimed. The life of men and women is so cheap and property is so sacred. There are so many of us for one job it matters little if 146 of us are burned to death.

We have tried you citizens; we are trying you now, and you have a couple of dollars for the sorrowing mothers, brothers and sisters by way of a charity gift. But every time the workers come out in the only way they know to protest against conditions which are unbearable the strong hand of the law is allowed to press down heavily upon us.

Public officials have only words of warning to us—warning that we must be intensely peaceable, and they have the workhouse just back of all their warnings. The strong hand of the law beats us back, when we rise, into the conditions that make life unbearable.

I can't talk fellowship to you who are gathered here. Too much blood has been spilled. I know from my experience it is up to the working people to save themselves. The only way they can save themselves is by a strong working-class movement.

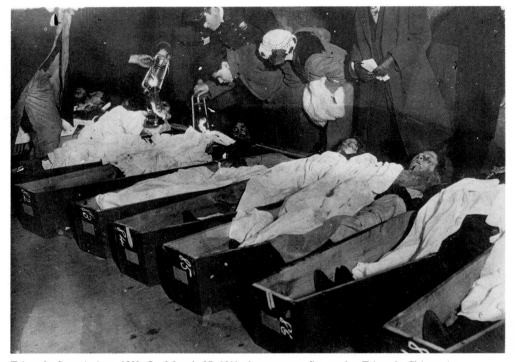

Triangle fire victims, 1911: On March 25, 1911, there was a fire at the Triangle Shirtwaist Company at the corner of Washington Place and Greene Street in New York. One-hundred and forty-six workers, mostly young Jewish women, perished and scores of others were permanently injured. This lead to the enactment of strong legislation dealing with working conditions in the garment factories. *Credit:* BB

Furriers' Strike Notice, 1917: Notice of a fur workers strike in Chicago. *Credit:* CHS

Strike Notice, about 1919: This notice appeared during the Amalgamated Clothing Workers' organizational drive in Philadelphia. *Credit:* UATU

The Beginnings of American Socialism

1890's. Morris Hillquit, an active force in the Socialist Labor Party and later in the Socialist Party, described the early years of American socialism.

A definite change in the policies and methods of the Socialist Labor Party came with the advent of Daniel De Leon, who joined the party in 1890.

De Leon represented a new type of leadership in the Socialist movement of America.

Born in Curaçao, in the Dutch West Indies, he came to the United States as a young man. He studied in Holland, Germany, and at Columbia Law School in New York, and later lectured at Columbia University on international law and diplomacy. He had actively supported Henry George in his mayoralty campaign and subsequently developed a growing interest in the Socialist and labor movements. For a decade he exerted a determining influence in the Socialist Labor Party. In fact he was the first and probably the only man who occupied the position of the traditional political boss in the Socialist movement of America.

Daniel De Leon was intensely personal. Almost immediately upon his entry in the Socialist arena he divided the movement into two antigonistic camps—his devoted admirers and followers and

his bitter critics and opponents. Now, almost twenty years after his death, it is still not easy to formulate a just and objective evaluation of his personality and of the part he played in the history of American Socialism.

De Leon was unquestionably a person of great erudition, rare ability, and indomitable energy. He served the cause of Socialism, as he saw it, with single-minded devotion. He had unshakable faith in Socialism and its future, but his greater faith was in himself. He never admitted a doubt about the soundness of his interpretation of the Socialist philosophy or the infallibility of his methods and tactics. Those who agreed with him were good Socialists. All who dissented from his views were enemies of the movement. He never compromised or temporized outside or inside the Socialist movement. "He who is not with me is against me" was his motto and the invariable guide of all his political relations and practical activities.

Daniel De Leon was a fanatic. A keen thinker and merciless logician, he was carried away beyond the realm of reality by the process of his own abstract and somewhat Talmudistic logic.

Of small stature, mobile features, and piercing black eyes, he was a distinctly southern type. He was a trenchant writer, fluent speaker, and sharp debater. For his opponents he had neither courtesy nor mercy. His peculiar traits and methods were not due entirely to his personal temperament and character. In part at least they were the logical expression of his social philosophy. De Leon was not a social democrat with the emphasis on the "democrat." He was strongly influenced by the Blanquist conception of the "capture of power," and placed organization ahead of education, politics above economic struggles, and leadership above the rank and file of the movement. He was the perfect American prototype of Russian Bolshevism.

Having unsuccessfully attempted to "capture" the Knights of Labor and the American Federation of Labor, he organized a rival trade-union body under the name of Socialist Trade and Labor Alliance, thus provoking an open breach with the organized labor movement of the country.

His policy of antagonizing the trade unions and his régime of despotism and intolerance resulted in strong and organized opposition to him. The final breach came in 1899, when the party split into two antagonistic factions, each claiming title to the party name and property.

The split was preceded by a long and bitter fight within the party, in which the administration faction of Daniel De Leon was supported by the official party papers, *The People* in English, and the *Vorwärts* in German, while the opposition rallied around the daily *Volkszeitung*.

I was chosen by my comrades for the strenuous task of leading the opposition. There was never much love lost between Daniel De Leon and me. I was

repelled by his dictatorial demeanor, so utterly misplaced in a voluntary and democratic movement, and I considered his trade-union policy as suicidal to the party. When the Socialist Trade and Labor Alliance was organized and officially sanctioned by the party at its national convention in 1896, I could not accept it and for a time retired from active party work. But I soon realized that retirement was no solution and returned to the harness determined to make an open fight on the spirit and practices that had come to be known among us as Deleonism.

I was given ample opportunity to fight. In the columns of the party papers, at the meetings of the "Sections," and in numerous private conferences, the battle raged on both sides with evergrowing asperity, and I took part in all of it. Daniel De Leon proved a formidable antagonist. He excelled any person I ever knew in unscrupulousness of attack, inventiveness of intrigue, and picturesqueness of invective. But in spite of his vigorous methods of combat, or perhaps because of them, the opposition grew constantly. While the official title to the party name was awarded by the courts to the De Leon faction, the secessionists clearly represented the numerical majority.

In the meantime reinforcement came to American Socialism from unexpected quarters. In the Middle West an indigenous though somewhat vague Socialist movement sprang up as a sort of cross between certain surviving radical elements of Populism and the remnants of the American Railway Union shattered by the ill-fated Pullman strike. The movement crystallized in the organization of the "Social Democracy of America" in 1897. One year later the new party split in two. The organization remained in control of a group of romantics, who proposed to introduce Socialism by the spread of coöperative colonies, while the followers of the modern Socialist program formed the "Social Democratic Party of America."

It was to this party that the insurgent faction of the Socialist Labor Party turned for unity and coöperation.

Formal negotiations for the merger of the two organizations were opened at the national convention of the Social Democratic Party held in Indianapolis in March of 1900.

I attended the convention as a member of a committee delegated by the organization opposed to De Leon to offer our hands and hearts to our Social Democratic comrades. Associated with me on the committee were Job Harriman, a California lawyer of rare eloquence, deep sincerity and irresistible personal charm, and Max Hayes, a printer of Cleveland, equally prominent and popular in the Socialist and trade-union movements.

It was on this occasion that I first met the two main leaders of the new party who were destined to play such important parts in the later history of American Socialism, Eugene V. Debs and Victor L. Berger.

Library, New York, about 1898: Young Jewish immigrant readers in the library of the Educational Alliance on East Broadway on New York's Lower East Side. *Credit:* NYPL

Arbor Day, New York, 1908: Leon Berman, class orator, on Arbor Day in a public school on New York's Lower East Side. *Credit:* LC

Reading with Librarian, about 1912: A library on New York's Lower East Side. Photograph by Lewis Hine. *Credit:* NYPL

Cutting and Designing Class, about 1910: Training for employment in the women's clothing industry at the Chicago Hebrew Institute. *Credit:* CHS

Sewing Class, about 1915: Sewing class for women at the Chicago Hebrew Institute. *Credit:* CHS

Band Practice, 1919: Chicago Hebrew Institute. *Credit:* CHS

Cooking Class, about 1915: Chicago Hebrew Institute. *Credit:* CHS

Ceramics Class, about 1910: Chicago Hebrew Institute. *Credit:* CHS

Sewing Class, about 1911: Jewish Manual Training School in Chicago. *Credit:* CHS

Woodworking Class, about 1911: Jewish Manual Training School in Chicago. *Credit:* CJA

Swimming Pool in the River, about 1890: Vacation school at a swimming pool constructed in New York City's East River. Photograph by Jacob Riis. *Credit:* MCNY

Indoor Pool, about 1915: Swimming pool at the Chicago Hebrew Institute. *Credit:* CHS

Exercise Class, about 1911: Jewish Manual Training School in Chicago. *Credit:* CJA

Rosh Hashanah, New York, about 1910: Boy with *tallis* (traditional Orthodox Jewish prayer shawl) celebrating Rosh Hashanah on New York's Lower East Side. *Credit:* LC

Immigrant *Seder,* about 1910: HIAS (Hebrew Immigrant Aid Society) was active in providing assistance to Jewish immigrants at home and abroad. This Passover *seder* was organized by HIAS for newly arrived immigrants in New York. *Credit:* YIVO

Religious School, about 1890: Coming from Eastern European communities where religion was a major factor in daily life, immigrant Jews established a variety of religious institutions and schools on New York's Lower East Side to maintain continuity with their past. Photograph by Jacob Riis. *Credit:* MCNY

Rosh Hashanah, New York, about 1910: Getting shoes shined for the holidays on New York's Lower East Side. *Credit:* LC

Jewish New Year's card, about 1910: This folding three-dimensional greeting card was printed in Germany and distributed in the United States by the Hebrew Publishing Company for Rosh Hashanah. *Credit:* Author

Rosh Hashanah, New York, about 1910: Young couple celebrating *Tashlich* (a ceremony usually associated with Rosh Hashanah) on the Brooklyn Bridge near New York's Lower East Side. *Credit:* LC

Grand Theater, New York, about 1900: Exterior of the Grand Theater on Grand Street on New York's Lower East Side. Jacob P. Adler, the head of the great Yiddish theatrical family, appeared in *The Broken Hearts.* Photograph by Byron. *Credit:* MCNY

Cast of "The Broken Hearts," about 1900: Jacob P. Adler and his wife, stars of "The Broken Hearts," on stage at the Grand Theatre with the cast. Photograph by Byron. *Credit:* MCNY

Yiddish Theater Poster, 1915: Yiddish theater came to the United States with the tide of Eastern European Jewish immigration during the last quarter of the nineteenth century. It was one of the most popular forms of entertainment for newly arrived immigrants. Boris Thomashefsky was one of the leading actors in the Yiddish theater. *Credit:* AJHS

The Yiddish Theater

1902. In his classic study of Jewish life on New York's Lower East Side, The Spirit of the Ghetto, *Hutchins Hapgood provided a sensitive interpretation of the most popular form of entertainment available to the immigrant population.*

In the three Yiddish theaters on the Bowery is expressed the world of the ghetto—that New York City of Russian Jews, large, complex, with a full life and civilization. In the midst of the frivolous Bowery, devoted to tinsel variety shows, "dive" music halls, fake museums, trivial amusement booths of all sorts, cheap lodginghouses, ten-cent shops, and Irish-American tough saloons, the theaters of the chosen people alone present the serious as well as the trivial interests of an entire community. Into these three buildings crowd Jews of all ghetto classes—the sweatshop woman with her baby, the day laborer, the small Hester Street shopkeeper, the Russian-Jewish anarchist and socialist, the ghetto rabbi and scholar, the poet, the journalist. The poor and ignorant are in the great majority, but the learned, the intellectual, and the progressive are also represented, and here, as elsewhere, exert a more than numerically proportionate influence on the character of the theatrical productions, which, nevertheless, remain essentially popular. The socialists and the literati create the demand that forces into the mass of vaudeville, light opera, and historical and melodramatic plays a more serious art element, a simple transcript from life, or the theatrical presentation of a ghetto problem. But this more serious element is so saturated with the simple manners, humor, and pathos of the life of the poor Jew that it is seldom above the heartfelt understanding of the crowd.

The audiences vary in character from night to night rather more than in an uptown theater. On the evenings of the first four weekdays the theater is let to a guild or club, many hundred of which exist among the working people of the East Side. Many are labor organizations representing the different trades, many are purely social, and others are in the nature of secret societies. Some of these clubs are formed on the basis of a common home in Russia. Then, too, the anarchists have a society; there are many socialist orders; the newspapers of the ghetto have their constituency, which sometimes hires the theater. Two or three hundred dollars is paid to the theater by the guild, which then sells tickets among the faithful for a good price. Every member of the society is forced to buy, whether he wants to see the play or not, and the money made over and above the expenses of hiring the theater is for the benefit of the guild. These performances are therefore called "benefits." The widespread existence of such a custom is a striking indication of the growing sense of corporate interests among the laboring classes of the Jewish East Side.

On Friday, Saturday, and Sunday nights the theater is not let, for these are the Jewish holidays, and the house is always completely sold out, although prices range from twenty-five cents to a dollar. Friday night is, properly speaking, the gala occasion of the week. That is the legitimate Jewish holiday, the night before the Sabbath. Orthodox Jews, as well as others, may then amuse themselves. Saturday, although the day of worship, also has a holiday character in the ghetto. This is due to Christian influences to which the Jews are more and more sensitive. Through economic necessity Jewish workingmen are compelled to work on Saturday, and, like other workingmen, look upon Saturday night as a holiday, in spite of the frown of the Orthodox. Into Sunday, too, they extend their freedom, and so in the ghetto there are now three popularly recognized nights on which to go with all the world to the theater.

On those nights the theater presents a peculiarly picturesque sight. Poor workingmen and women with their babies of all ages fill the theater. Great enthusiasm is manifested; sincere laughter and tears accompany the sincere acting on the stage. Peddlers of soda water, candy, and fantastic gewgaws of many kinds mix freely with the audience between the acts. Conversation during the play is received with strenuous hisses, but the falling of the curtain is the signal for groups of friends to get together and gossip about the play or the affairs of the week. Introductions are not necessary, and the Yiddish community can then be seen and approached with great freedom. On the stage curtain are advertisements of the programmes, and circulars distributed in the audience are sometimes amusing announcements of coming attractions or lyric praise of the "stars."

Yiddish Theater Poster, Philadelphia, 1917: Poster for the Arch Street Theater in Philadelphia announcing the *Russian Jew in America. Credit:* AJHS

My German-Jewish Family Life

Irma Levy Lindheim grew up on New York's Upper East Side around the turn of the century. Having been raised in a family which had already made economic progress, she was an "Uptown Jew," a vivid contrast to the newly arriving Eastern European immigrants.

I was born into an unexceptional family, began my life in a period in which only change was exceptional, and grew in an unexceptional environment.

Ours was a middle-class existence, well to do, well behaved, complacent. When I was born, in the last month of 1886, our house was brownstone, with a high stoop, on Ninety-fourth Street near Lexington Avenue in New York City. It was a great pleasure to me as a child to watch, from our front windows, a family of goats and their kids frisking over a patch of rocks the size of a square city block.

Twice a year my sisters and I were taken by horsecar for shopping expeditions in the big stores on Thirty-fourth Street, or farther south on Fourteenth Street. After a spree of buying we ate our lunch in a public restaurant, an adventure so unimaginably satisfying that we felt no need to envy Marco Polo or even Hannibal with all his elephants.

My father, Robert Levy, born in Hesse-Cassel, Germany, of German-Jewish parents who died in their own country without my ever knowing them, was an importer of nettings and veilings, who climbed slowly but steadily to affluence in this country.

To his family he was first and foremost a businessman, virtually a slave to his success in pursuit of security for his family. In the rare instances when he tore himself away from success, to relax and be friendly with his wife and children, he showed himself invariably to be a man of superb charm. But there was little time, really, for learning to know his children, or we him.

His America was an America of expansion, a solid, planned, conservative world, demanding the closest attention, where opportunity was unlimited for those who had energy and the industriousness to grasp it. The only kind of man considered worthwhile carefully conserved what he acquired, and built on it what he wanted for the future. Cash in the bank, or invested in the business, was the acid test of a man's value. Our father had the prejudice of many men of German-Jewish origin against Jews born "east of Berlin." I can only speculate on his feelings, had he lived to see—when German-Jews sought refuge in Palestine—that it was the Russian and the Polish Jews who were first to welcome them with open hearts and hospitality, doing everything humanly possible to ease their difficult adjustment to a new home. I can imagine only too well how he would have felt when, in time, I was to choose as my dearest friends and closest associates, people who stemmed from the very background he abhorred.

Residence in Oakland, California, about 1900: While the newly arrived Eastern European Jews were living in tenements, the established German Jews had already moved to commodious dwellings in attractive neighborhoods. The Levy family standing in front of their house on Adeline Street. *Credit:* WJHC

Adelson Sisters, New York, about 1880: May Adelson on the left with her sister Eva. *Credit:* Mrs. Richard Rodgers

Dell Levy, about 1890: In the yard of the Levy family residence on Marshall Street, Philadelphia. *Credit:* HSP

May Adelson, New York, about 1898: In costume for an amateur show. *Credit:* Mrs. Richard Rodgers

Professor and Mrs. Jastrow, about 1888: In their rooms in Ladies Hall, University of Wisconsin, Madison. Rachael Szold Jastrow was the sister of Henrietta Szold, founder of Hadassah. Mrs. Jastrow established the second chapter of Hadassah. *Credit:* SHSW

Benjamin F. Feiner, 1898: On his graduation from New York University Law School. He married May Adelson, and their daughter Dorothy became the wife of Richard Rodgers, the composer. *Credit:* Mrs. Richard Rodgers

Kuhn Family portrait, about 1905: The children of Samuel Kuhn and Regina Wise Kuhn of Cincinnati with their respective husbands and wives. From left to right, back row: Simon Kuhn, Morris Loeb, Eleanor Mack Kuhn, Charles Kuhn, Robert Kühn, Minnie Strauss Kuhn, Max Senior, Eleanor Feiss Kuhn; front row: Amelia Senior Kuhn, Settie Swarts Kuhn, Edward Kuhn, Eda Loeb, Clarence Kuhn, Louis Kuhn and wife. *Credit:* AJA

Family picnic, 1897: The Stern family picnic in Golden Gate Park, San Francisco. *Credit:* BL

Dr. Joseph Ransohoff, 1894: In his study, Cincinnati. *Credit:* Daniel J. Ransohoff

May Adelson, New York 1900: . *Credit:* Mrs. Richard Rodgers

Frohman Family Portrait, 1889: Children and grandchildren of Mr. and Mrs. Albert Frohman of Cincinnati. *Credit:* Daniel J. Ransohoff

Rauh Family Portrait, about 1908: Grandparents, parents and children in Cincinnati. *Credit:* Harriet Rauh

Coming Out Party, Philadelphia, 1911: *Credit:* Private Collection

Stern Family Portrait, about 1900: Sigmund Stern and Rosalie Meyer Stern of San Francisco with their daughter, Elise. *Credit:* WJHC

Golden Wedding, 1897: Anniversary of Adolph Godchaux and Sophia Wollhoff Godchaux in San Francisco. *Credit:* WJHC

Newmark Family, 1881: From left to right, Joseph Newmark, Estelle Loeb as child, Mrs. Leon Loeb and Mrs. Harris Newmark, Los Angeles. *Credit:* Norton B. Stern

Rodgers Children with Nurse, 1903: Mortimer and Richard Rodgers with their nurse, Stella, near their home in Mount Morris Park, New York City. *Credit:* Mrs. Richard Rodgers

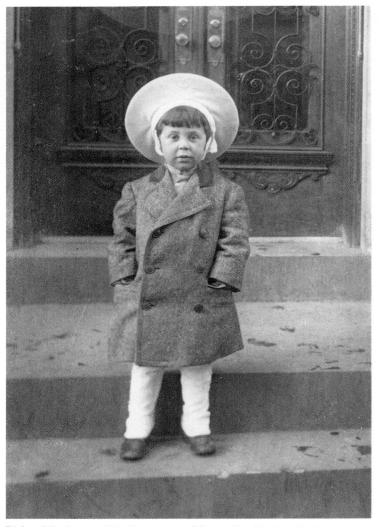

Richard Rodgers, 1905: At the age of three. *Credit:* Mrs. Richard Rodgers

Rodgers Children, 1905: Mortimer and Richard Rodgers. *Credit:* Mrs. Richard Rodgers

Dorothy Feiner, 1911: With baby carriage at the age of two. *Credit:* Mrs. Richard Rodgers

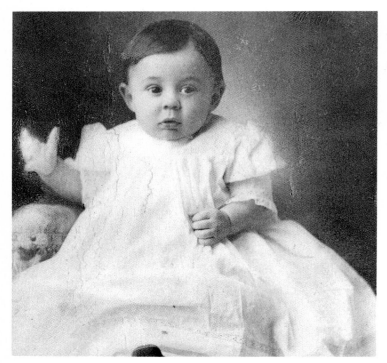

Richard Rodgers, 1902: . *Credit:* Mrs. Richard Rodgers

It was his fixed and unalterable belief that neither politics nor religion were fit subjects for family conversation. Even so important a topic as the Dreyfus case was proscribed, as a dinner table incident showed. It took place the evening of his arrival from a business trip in Europe.

With rage and indignation he described rioting he had seen in Paris, and how he had barely been rescued from the hands of a mob yelling "Down with Dreyfus! Down with the Jews!" While an attack on my father was too unbelievable to be real, what I could not comprehend at all was that, suddenly in the middle of a sentence, he put his finger to his lips with the sharp exclamation, "Hush!" when the Irish maids came in to change the plates.

Was the word "Jew" something not to be mentioned in front of servants? I did not understand. All I knew was the distressing shame and embarrassment I felt for something incomprehensible in my father who, I always told myself, could do no wrong.

The only other time I remember seeing him give vent to fury in connection with politics was at the time William Jennings Bryan delivered his startling "Cross of Gold" speech, at the Democratic National Convention in 1896. When the full force of Mr. Bryan's ideas struck him, my father shouted, "Why, that shameful demagogue!"

My feelings about my father were ambivalent. I dearly loved him, and he was not really the tyrant he appeared at times to be. With me he was downright indulgent—my middle sister said overindulgent—perhaps because his "baby" was the only one in the family with no fear of him. And yet often his authority and domination affected me in ways exactly opposite to his wishes or expectations. In time I came to see, for all I loved him, that I learned from him more of what I wanted *not* to be and do, than *to* be and do.

My mother had no interest whatever outside her husband, her children, and her home, and was completely content for it to be so. Not all women, eternally doing for their loved ones, are able at the same time, to create an atmosphere of tranquillity. Giving herself up solely and completely to the needs and wants of her family, she crowned it all with unity and peace.

Her parents had emigrated to Pittsburgh from Nuremburg, Germany. Our maternal grandparents Morganstern prospered until their sons, educated beyond such mundane practicality, took over the family's thriving shoe business and ran it quickly into the ground. The disaster had one happy effect at least; it brought our mother's parents to New York to live with us.

Of the experiences of my childhood only one influence was to have a clear effect on the course of my future; even so, it long lay dormant.

In a line of direct descent from my maternal grandmother and through my mother to me had come a passionate

Costume Party, Cincinnati, about 1910: Alfred Friedlander in the center and Emma Kuhn Fischer, second from the left. *Credit:* Daniel J. Ransohoff

A Cincinnati Family Visiting Egypt, about 1900: From left to right: Eugene F. Westheimer, Mrs. M. Schulofer, Morris F. Westheimer, Hattie H. Westheimer and Pauline E. Westheimer. *Credit:* Daniel J. Ransohoff

Aunt Sallie's Cow, 1895: In her backyard in Avondale, Cincinnati. *Credit:* Daniel J. Ransohoff

Johanna Haas Westheimer, about 1890: Wife of Samuel Westheimer of St. Joseph, Missouri. *Credit:* Jane Steinfirst

Samuel Westheimer, about 1890: Resident of St. Joseph, Missouri. *Credit:* Jane Steinfirst

Dr. SACHS'S
COLLEGIATE INSTITUTE FOR BOYS,
38 West 59th St.,

Thorough preparation for College, scientific schools and business; pupils specially fitted for Columbia and Harvard. German and French form important features of regular curriculum. Building new and approved by sanitary experts, gymnasium with elaborate apparatus connected with the School.

Mrs. Leopold Weil's,
ENGLISH, GERMAN, FRENCH & HEBREW

Boarding and Day School
FOR YOUNG LADIES,
AND KINDERGARTEN
75 West 55th Street,

Bet. 5th and 6th Avenues,

F.·rmerly 57 and 59 West 55th Street,
NEW YORK.

Advertisements for Private Schools, 1882: These advertisements appeared in *The American Hebrew* describing two prominent private schools in New York which prepared their students for Ivy League colleges. *Credit:* AJHS

Schwartz Family, 1911: Ray, Viola and Claire Schwartz in Brooklyn, New York. *Credit:* WJHC

Jewish consciousness. With one exception, my grandmother's sister, we were the only ones to possess it. So intrinsic in nature was it, so indivisible, that, in spite of being negated and suppressed in me, taking many, many years to rediscover, it remained alive.

My grandmother's Jewishness was more active than my mother's; it was my mother's quiet way to live her convictions without, however, obtruding them on those around her.

I used to sit every day on a footstool at my grandmother's feet, listening in rapt attention to stories she told me from the Bible. She sat very tall and straight in a high-backed Victorian chair but in some wonderful way her hazel eyes, with bronze specks in them, brought her down close to me. Mine, and my mother's eyes were like hers, only hers had more crinkles around them because she was old.

She would rest her hand tenderly on my head as she told the stories. I loved everything about her; the soft, billowy folds of her black silk dress, the way her white lace cap with the black ribbon bows set on her wavy brown-gray hair, her face shining with love for me as she stroked my hair.

More than anything I remember the day—though I was only five when she died—when, taking my face in her hands, and looking deep, deep into my eyes, she said, "Never, never, my darling, forget you are a Jew."

Always after they were gone, my grandmother and my mother were identified in my mind as one.

My confirmation was the tremendous event of my youth. For a while I felt an acute regret that I was not a man, and therefore could not become a rabbi. I felt almost suffocated with wonder and joy at the moment when, before the open ark, my rabbi placed his hands on my head and blessed me. To myself I vowed that my life would forever be dedicated to my people.

What happened between that moment of exaltation, set to the deep, majestic tones of Handel's "Largo," and the time, only a few short years later, when there seemed nothing left of the burning faith that had been mine but the ashes that

Samuel Lehman Family, 1914: Husband, wife and daughter of the Samuel Lehman family of New York. *Credit:* LC

Lloyd Dinkelspiel, about 1907: The prominent San Franciscan in his youth. *Credit:* WJHC

Loew Family, about 1900: With their carriage in Central Park, New York. *Credit:* LC

Bridesmaids, 1916: Attendants at a Warburg family wedding in New York. *Credit:* LC

appeared to be without ember or spark?

Somehow the longing questions of a seriously inquiring child had been answered without affirmations she could accept. Could I, I wondered persistently to myself, be a Jew merely because of having been born a Jew?

Before doubts and questions assailed me, I loved going to temple with my mother on Saturdays, the only one of the children who really wanted to go. My father attended service only on the high holidays, and then merely to please my mother. He could make me laugh with funny things he would say, but I did not really like his saying them because everything in temple was to me too solemn and beautiful. When the organ

poured forth its wonderful sound, and the choir sang, I felt myself lifted right up to heaven.

Because she was so devoted to us, mother was a worrier. It made for almost too cushioned a kind of life for us, overprotected. No matter how many servants there were—in time nurses, governesses, cooks, waitresses, chambermaids, finally a lady's maid, our darling, fat, French Marie—all picking up after us and tending to our slightest needs—our mother was always ready at any time to hurry to the kitchen and cook our favorite dishes as she knew that *we* knew only she could cook them; to sew for us, to knit beautiful stockings and sweaters for us, as later she would do for

our children; to help us with our homework; from morning to night to add in whatever way she could to our happiness and wellbeing.

She taught us varied skills; though I could never seem to do very well at the drudgery of household cleaning jobs which in her wisdom she believed that we should master, in later years I could never be grateful enough that she had insisted that we learn them. Only long after she was gone, when I had allowed myself to grow rusty at such tasks, did I feel fortunate that I was able to call back some of the things she had taught me. However, I never learned the art of scrubbing a floor, and it took many grueling tries and much kindly direction

Fridolyn Gimbel, 1910: Daughter of Mr. and Mrs. Ellis Gimbel of Philadelphia. This photograph was taken prior to her marriage to David T. Fleisher, also of Philadelphia. *Credit:* LC

Miss M.E. Kahn, about 1914: Daughter of Mr. and Mrs. Otto Kahn of New York. *Credit:* LC

William Loeb, 1907: A member of the Loeb family of New York. *Credit:* LC

before I could clean the floor of my tiny one-room shack in the kibbutz [collective settlement] and know that there was not more mud on it after I had worked than there had been before I started.

In view of our well-tended household life, it may seem paradoxical to say that before my sisters and I were grown there was never any extravagance in our home. Certain standards and amenities obtained, but they were based on fitness, not show. My mother knew instinctively how to husband material resources, utilizing them for necessary purposes; she was thoroughly in sympathy with my father's passion for saving to provide for our future, in healthy fear of a family being left unprotected, to face

want.

This passion for saving to protect the future was altogether characteristic of German Jews of that period; indeed to this day it is considered something of a crime to spend more than one receives as interest on money. Capital is to be used only for investing.

The business was the big thing in life; the more money ploughed into it, the more profit would be stored up to take out later.

But when it came to our education, nothing was saved.

Contrary to everything which seemed so conducive to happiness and security, I was a lonely little girl, for a reason as painful and baffling to me as it was to my

parents and the doctors.

I had been blessed in being born with the gift of a happy nature. My mother said I awakened to each new day with a smile. Regularly I was told that I was pretty. It was mentioned also that I was lucky, because of being "born in the caul," which I was happy to believe must be something exceptional. People said this brought luck to even those around me, and my father made me feel proud and important by telling me that it was when I was born that his real success in business began.

"I Married Wyatt Earp"

1882. Josephine Sarah Marcus of San Francisco was the common-law wife of Wyatt Earp, the frontier hero. She described their travels through the West. When Earp died in 1929, he was buried in a Jewish cemetery.

I left Tombstone with a sense of relief, glad that Wyatt had got safely away, and relieved to be away from the dreadful place myself. It had come to mean nothing but suppressed terror to me.

Following the killing of Ringo, Wyatt picked me up in San Francisco and we traveled back to Gunnison by way of Salt Lake City and Denver. Bat Masterson was one of the first people we saw on our stop-over in Denver. I had never before met him. He was a handsome, happy-go-lucky sort of person. One wouldn't expect him to hold a reputation as one of the deadliest gunfighters in the West. When I got to know him better he confided to me, "Most of that is hot air. If you ever have the bad luck to have to kill someone, the tall tales will grow about you. Even the tough ones hesitate to go up against you if they think you've knocked off a couple of dozen hard cases just like them. Wyatt would tell you the same thing. It's all part of the game."

In addition to Bat we soon ran into Doc Holliday, who looked us up as soon as he heard Wyatt was in town. As I've already mentioned, the trouble in Arizona had made national headlines, so the news got around that Wyatt Earp and Doc were in Denver. He and Doc were both plagued by a great deal of hero-worshipping curiosity on the part of the crowd who hung around the gambling halls.

Through Bat Masterson I came to realize that I had married a very unusual man, one who bore a reputation for fearless law enforcement as a deputy marshal in Dodge City when it was considered the toughest town in the West. Later I was to see Dodge City and meet many of Wyatt's old friends there, who bore out in almost every particular what Bat had told me.

Meanwhile Colorado was an idyll. Wyatt prospected considerably, as did his brother Warren. Sometimes he took me with him on trips to the hills. Other times I was left behind to amuse myself as best I could. Very often it was the mining magnate H. A. Tabor and his wife Baby Doe who helped keep me occupied during Wyatt's absences. We partied, went riding, had sumptuous dinners, played genteel card games, gossiped, did the shops and generally had a very good time together.

Wyatt never struck it rich or even made a promising find; however, he always managed to make a good enough living through investments or gambling. He often financially backed games of chance run for him by others.

Wyatt also worked for Wells Fargo on occasions, just as he had in Arizona. He continued to investigate for the company off and on until the turn of the century. Jim Hume, the chief investigator for

Family Outing, 1910: The Moritz Bernstein family of Walsenberg, Colorado, visiting Seven Falls, Manitou Springs, Colorado. *Credit:* RMJHS

Family Picnic at Country Cabin, about 1885: The Gans, Goldbergs, Sobles, Marks and Sands families with Rabbi Shulkin at a picnic in Montana. *Credit:* MOHS

Wells Fargo, was a life-long friend of Wyatt. I might point out that this is a strong refutation of the lies alleging that the Earps were stage-robbers in Tombstone.

Gradually my prospecting jaunts with Wyatt taught me to enjoy the outdoor life. We also went on hunting and fishing trips. I remember one campout with John O'Toole, his wife and Bat Masterson. We hired a big covered wagon and set out for the Laramie River. The wagon carried our bed rolls and camping supplies, and I made sure personally that it was amply supplied with good things to eat.

"What are you going for?" Wyatt teased me. "You can't shoot a gun. I'll bet you don't even know which end the bullet comes out of. Furthermore you can't bait a fishhook."

I told him, "I'm going along to see that you great hunters and fishermen don't have to depend on your own kills for something to eat!"

Wyatt decided he'd better make a rifle-shooter of me anyhow, just to justify my presence. He showed me how to hold and shoot the gun and explained the fine points of aiming to me. He then encouraged me to put the rifle to my shoulder and aim at a knot on a tree. Standing by ready to laugh was Bat Masterson, who didn't do a thing for my self-possession.

"Don't get in a hurry to shoot," Wyatt explained. "Concentrate on holding the gun on the target and squeeze the trigger easy till she lets go."

"And get ready to pull leather when she bucks!" Bat added. That did it. I'd seen guns kick up when the men shot them. The thought of the kick from the gun was too much for me. I'd heard men use such expressions as "She kicks like a mule!" I dropped the gun and ran for our tent. Mrs. O'Toole was sympathetic, but the men just roared. Wyatt never tried to teach me to shoot again, although I learned to get by passably in an emergency.

I'm sure many will be disappointed to find my story of our life filled with so

Russian Jewish Immigrants in Colorado, about 1883: At E.S. Hart's store in Cotopaxi, Colorado. *Credit:* AJHS

Alaskan Trading Post, about 1900: S. Ripinsky's store in Chilkat, Alaska. *Credit:* AJHS

Solomon Yaekel, about 1882: California resident. *Credit:* BL

Fur Trading Post, about 1888: Albert N. Rose, extreme left, at Edmonton, Alaska fur trading post. *Credit:* AJA

With Fur Traders, about 1888: Albert N. Rose, with straw hat, meeting fur traders in Alaska. *Credit:* AJA

Posing with Guns, about 1880: Charles M. Strauss, posing here with an unidentified boy, was Boston-born and elected mayor of Tucson, Arizona in 1883. *Credit:* AHS

many of these commonplace incidents, but this was largely the way it was. After leaving Tombstone, Wyatt desired nothing more than to renounce completely the life of a lawman. Therefore the reader will have to content himself with the fairly mild diet of our everyday life. For me, it held just the right amount of excitement.

For example, one day we were trying to get from Ouray, Colorado, to Silverton. These are mining camps high in the Rocky Mountains. It was early spring, and the snow was still deep. We left Ouray in a buckboard but had not gone far when we found the snow too heavy to proceed and returned to the hotel at Ouray. But Wyatt was determined to reach Silverton; he got a mule for me to ride while he walked.

"You'd better put on overalls," he told me. "Those skirts will be wet before we get halfway to Silverton." But I was ashamed to wear men's clothes. Wyatt finally convinced me they were the only sensible things to wear.

The mule was frisky, and I was so bundled up I could hardly manage him. As a matter of fact, I was afraid of him. When we reached a little camp called Iron Mine we got a burro for me to ride in place of the mule.

The snow was deep, but we were able to get along on the rocky ridges where it was thinner. As we topped the summit we met three men coming up from Silverton. Two were reporters from a Chicago paper and the third a Denver newspaper man.

"We can't believe our eyes!" said one. "Here we've been trudging through this upended wilderness of snow all day without seeing a soul!" Obviously they were surprised to find a woman way up there.

We talked for awhile and they took our name and address. They were interested when they heard Wyatt's name, and one of them said, "I never realized before that Wyatt Earp was a real flesh-and-blood man." This reporter had read some of the lurid hogwash written concerning my husband, Bat Masterson, Wild Bill Hickock and their type.

Store, Trinidad, Colorado, about 1890: Jaffa Brothers Mercantile Company of Trinidad, Colorado. *Credit:* AJA

Gertrude Strauss, about 1880: Advertising stoves in Tucson, Arizona. *Credit:* AHS

Cigar store, Tucson, Arizona, about 1900: Sam Drachman's cigar store on the main corner in Tucson, surrounded by saloons and gambling halls, became a gathering place. Sam Drachman served as lay rabbi, leading services and conducting marriages. From left to right: Sam Katzenstein, Sam Drachman and Owen T. Rouse. *Credit:* AHS

American Grocery Co. store, about 1880: Isidore Gotthelf operated this store in Tucson, Arizona. From left to right: Adolph Steinfeld, Dr. Adler, Isidore Gotthelf, unknown and Joseph Ferrin. *Credit:* AHS

I.E. Solomon Commercial Store, about 1896: Located in Solomonville, Arizona, this was I.E. Solomon's second store, built in 1895. Bricks for construction were brought from El Paso, Texas. *Credit:* AHS

Fruit Dealer, Pueblo, Colorado, about 1910: Max Stein with his fruit wagon. *Credit:* RMJHS

Some time later we received in the mail a copy of the Chicago newspaper with a glowing account of our chance meeting on a remote mountain summit. The article went something to the effect of: "The prettiest sight we have ever seen—the snowy mountain wilderness, the brown-eyed goddess, the blond Apollo who turned out to be none other than the famous Wyatt Earp, tamer of wild western desperados" and several other such flowery phrases. Some more hogwash, in other words.

Sometime after we got to Colorado I recall Wyatt saying, "In her heyday there was probably never any place like Dodge!" The first time I saw the town in 1883 I would have been hard put to see why there was never any place like it. It looked like all the other rundown prairie towns.

Wyatt must have been attracted to it by memories. I could tell by his reminiscing that he was considering a visit back to his old stamping grounds. But in the end it was circumstances that called us back to Dodge. The event was a testimonial to the stature of my husband in the eyes of the people of that city.

It seems that Luke Short, an old friend of Wyatt and Doc, was in trouble with the city fathers. Bat, who had been sheriff at Dodge when Wyatt was deputy marshal, had gone back to see if he could help Luke. Bat was highly regarded by most of the people of Dodge, but he also had made enemies. These were strong in the city government of which Luke had run afoul.

The best face that can be put on the affair is to admit that both Bat and Luke were run out of Dodge at gunpoint. As Bat later said, "Those old boys were downright serious. I looked down a double barrel that was about right for a narrow-gauge railroad tunnel and decided to keep right on going while I still had a whole skin. All around I was damn glad to see that iron hoss pull out of the station."

Bat wrote Wyatt regarding the situation. Reading the letter, Wyatt observed to me, "We may have to take a little trip to Dodge. How would that suit you?"

"Fine," I told him. I was always ready to see new scenery. Besides I recalled stories Bat had told me of Wyatt's lawing days in Dodge City. I had sometimes wondered though if Bat were not over enthusiastic in his estimate of Wyatt. On this trip I became satisfied that perhaps he was not. People in Dodge whose integrity was above question told me eyewitness stories that verified what Bat said.

If they all told the truth, then Wyatt certainly must have possessed, as Bat put it, "a strange power over men." He had again and again without touching a weapon walked up to men known to be dangerous outlaws, some of whom had their six-shooters in their hands, and cooly requested them to hand their weapons to him. Whatever the reason may have been, these bad men tamely handed over their arms and were placed

Policeman, Pueblo, Colorado, about 1900: Max Stein, mounted policeman, with his horse in Pueblo, Colorado. *Credit:* RMJHS

Kosher Picnic, 1895: This picnic was sponsored by the National Council of Jewish Women, Denver Section. *Credit:* RMJHS

under arrest. Bat said, "It takes more guts to arrest a desperate man peaceably than to shoot him and discuss the case later. No *other* man I ever heard of did such things day after day as Wyatt did and lived. It often seemed to me he led a charmed life."

Luke's trouble was not of his own making, but he hadn't realized the extent of the forces allied against him and had played into their hands. A policeman by the name of Hartman had arrested some of Luke's employees. When Luke sought to obtain bail, he ran into Hartman, and they ended up shooting at each other. Luckily neither was hit. I suppose Luke was pretty hot under the collar over being pushed around. At any rate, he put himself in deep with the law by firing on an officer.

He used his shotgun to stand off the policemen who came to arrest him, sitting in his locked saloon till the next morning, but he had to come out sometime. When he finally negotiated with the officers, they promised a trip to justice court and said that the matter would end there.

Unbeknownst to Luke, the city administration had other plans in mind for him. When he was finally disarmed and helpless they escorted him to the jail, where he was given either of two choices—the eastbound or westbound train. He went east to Kansas City and promptly contacted Bat Masterson, with the final result being our trip to Dodge.

The upshot of our coming was that the city in crowd, having a healthy respect for Wyatt and his friends, allowed Luke to return to Dodge. Wyatt arranged this through a meeting with the city council. Luke arrived, accompanied by Bat, a few days after our arrival.

Now that the odds were more in Luke's favor, the city's shotgun posse was not in evidence. Still he decided that it wouldn't be healthy for him to remain in Dodge after Wyatt and his friends pulled out again, so he sold out his interest. He moved to Fort Worth, where he was living when next we saw him.

While Luke was winding up his affairs, a group known as the Dodge City Peace Commission was formed to maintain peace in the city. Mr. Moonlight, the adjutant general of Kansas, was the chairman, and the members consisted of Wyatt and several trusted friends of his and Luke's.

The trouble all blew over as quickly as it started, no one was injured and I'm glad I got to see Dodge City before it became a small farmers' market type of commercial village. It was still wild enough for anyone's taste in those days, though by no means as bad as it had been.

We returned from Dodge to Colorado, soon to embark on several years of wandering in the West. We made a trip to Texas later that same year. In our travels it turned out that Wyatt knew someone in almost every town we came to.

Agricultural Colony, 1882: There was a return to the land movement underway among Russian Jews, some going to the United States to establish agricultural colonies, others to farm in Palestine. This colony was established by 20 families near the town of Bismarck, North Dakota. Each family had a claim of 160 acres of government land. After six years of difficulties most of the original settlers left. *Credit:* AJA

Rural Family, North Dakota, about 1900: Aaron Barony and family of Ong, North Dakota. *Credit:* YIVO

Farmers, Woodbine, New Jersey, about 1900: Erecting a fence for a chicken yard. *Credit:* AJA

Agricultural colony, Woodbine, New Jersey, 1897: Throughout the 19th century a number of Jewish agricultural colonies were established in different locations in the United States. In 1891 the Baron de Hirsch Fund created the Woodbine colony. Farmers are seen here with their fourth crop of corn. *Credit:* BHF

Woodbine, New Jersey, about 1900: In addition to farming, this agricultural colony maintained small factories and educational programs such as this chemistry class. *Credit:* BHF

Produce Exhibition, 1909: Vegetables from the Jewish Agricultural School on display. *Credit:* LC

Woodbine, New Jersey, about 1900: The fire department. *Credit:* BHF

Woodbine, New Jersey, about 1900: The band. *Credit:* BHF

"My First Big Deal"

1898. Bernard Baruch, who had a spectacular career on Wall Street and served as an advisor to seven presidents from Wilson to Eisenhower, described the daring with which he managed this financial coup.

I was spending the July Fourth week end with my parents at Long Branch, New Jersey. Late on Sunday night, Arthur Housman telephoned to say that a newspaperman had told him that Admiral Schley had destroyed the Spanish fleet at Santiago. Coming after Dewey's victory at Manila Bay, the news foretold a speedy end to the Spanish-American War.

The next day being the Fourth of July, the American exchanges would be closed. But the London exchange would be open. Sizable profits could be made by placing orders for American stocks on the London Exchange when it opened. To do that we had to get to New York and be on the cables by daylight.

At that hour on Sunday night, however, no trains were running. Routing out some railroad people, I hired a locomotive and tender with a coach attached to carry me to the ferry on the Jersey shore of the Hudson. It could not have been much more than two in the morning when Clarence Housman, my brother Sailing, and I were hurtling through the darkness on our way to New York.

That was my first ride on a "special" train. What a thrill it was! As our special roared past sleeping towns and hamlets it seemed to me that I was repeating on a smaller scale the financial feat which legend ascribed to Nathan Rothschild at the Battle of Waterloo.

In honoring Wellington's drafts when the English government was unable to do so, Rothschild had staked his fortune on the overthrow of Napoleon. Wellington's campaign in Belgium started badly, which depressed English securities. Rothschild, who had crossed the Channel to get first news of events, is said to have been on the field of Waterloo when the tide of battle turned against Napoleon. By getting word of this to London a few hours in advance of the official couriers he enabled the Rothschilds to make large purchases before shares rebounded.

As our train sped through the dark, it seemed that history was repeating itself. Thinking of how American arms had been victorious on land and sea from Cuba to the Phillippines, halfway around the world, I felt the surge of empire welling within me. No thought entered my head of the problems and responsibilities that an "American Empire" might bring in years to come.

When we got to our office in lower Manhattan, I found that in my haste I had forgotten the key. Fortunately the transom was open. Sailing weighed only about a hundred and fifty pounds so I boosted him through. Before sunrise I was on the cable.

A few minutes after the London market opened the essentials of the picture

Clothing Manufacturing Building, about 1885: At the corner of Broadway and West Houston Street in New York, this building housed clothing manufacturers and retailers. *Credit:* NYHS

LOUIS ADLER, Manufacturer of Cloaks, 127 & 129 Market Street, CHICAGO, ILLS.
PRICE LIST ENCLOSED.   Do not fail to Visit us when in the Market. We offer Great Inducements to Buyers.   POST CONSPICUOUSLY.

Advertisement, 1885: In the last quarter of the 19th century Chicago was one of the centers of Jewish activity in the manufacture of men's and women's clothing. *Credit:* CHS

Advertisement for Kosher Butcher, 1886: From *The American Hebrew. Credit:* LC

Advertisement, 1886: From *The American Hebrew. Credit:* LC

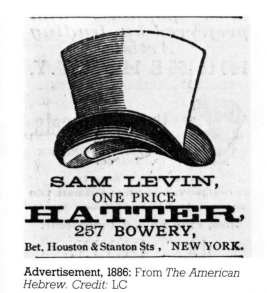

SAM LEVIN,
ONE PRICE
HATTER,
257 BOWERY,
Bet. Houston & Stanton Sts , NEW YORK.

Advertisement, 1886: From *The American Hebrew. Credit:* LC

were before us. Arthur Housman, who arrived at the office a bit later, cranked the telephone, interrupting the holiday slumbers of our customers. Always an optimist, he was made for the job. Snatches of his excited phrases drifted over to where I was busy with the cables. "Great American victory . . . United States a world power . . . New possessions . . . New markets . . . Empire rivaling England's . . . Biggest stock boom in years . . ."

We got an order from nearly everyone he called. We made large purchases of American stocks in London to fill these orders and to hold for ourselves. The next morning when the Exchange in New York opened, stocks advanced all along the line. Our London purchases showed good profits immediately. We had scored almost a clean beat on the other New York houses. In addition to the quick profits, which were large, the coup gave A. A Housman & Company the name of being an alert firm which knew when to act.

Business Card, about 1900: For a men's tailor in San Francisco. *Credit:* BL

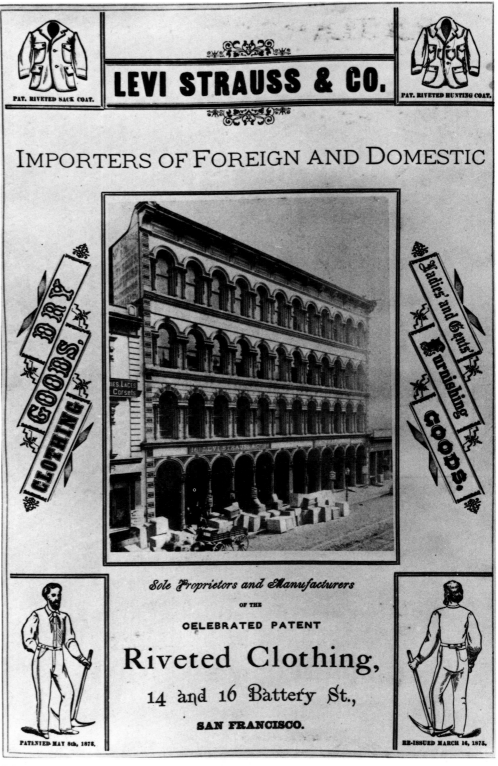

Advertisement, undated: Advertisement for Levi Strauss & Co. of San Francisco. *Credit:* BL

Poster, 1912: The A.B. Kirschbaum Co., a leading manufacturer of men's clothing was located in Philadelphia. At a time when many manufacturers were mixing cheaper materials with their woolens, firms with national reputations felt it necessary to emphasize that their clothing was made of 100 percent wool. *Credit:* SI

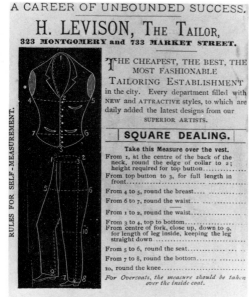

Advertisement, about 1900: For a men's tailor in San Francisco. *Credit:* BL

Business Card, about 1900: For a shoe store. *Credit:* BL

Business Card, about 1900: For a shoe store. *Credit:* BL

Cigar box label, about 1910: The "five cent cigar" was an American tradition. Jews continued to be active in the cigar making industry both as entrepreneurs and as workers. *Credit:* SI

Advertisement, 1882: Appearing in a synagogue Purim ball program. *Credit:* SI

Advertisement, about 1890: An established San Francisco firm. *Credit:* BL

Advertisement, about 1890: Jewelry stores were a common form of Jewish enterprise. *Credit:* BL

Sears, Roebuck & Co. catalogue cover, 1897-1898: In 1895 Julius Rosenwald acquired an interest in the recently established mail order firm of Sears, Roebuck & Company. Eventually, it became the largest retail merchandising organization in the world. *Credit:* SI

Fan, 1902: Advertisement for R.H. Macy & Co., the New York City department store which was purchased by Isidor and Nathan Straus in 1887. *Credit:* SI

Anti-Semitic Cartoon, 1882: This cartoon from *The Judge* caricatures Jewish businessmen who were taking over stores formerly operated by gentiles. *Credit:* AJHS

Kaufmann's, Pittsburgh, about 1910: The creative enterprise of Jews assisted in the growth and expansion of department stores across the country. *Credit:* SI

Our splendid store renders shopping a pleasure. Our low prices for elegant goods are the magnets that attract crowds from all parts. Our Genuine Alaska Seal Sacques from .... $85 00 Plush Sacques................. .... 11 95 Beautiful Manchester Plush Sacques........................ 18 95 and numerous other styles at equally startling prices.

BLOOMINGDALE BROS.

3d Ave., 59th & 60th Sts.,
NEW YORK.

Bloomingdale's, New York, 1885: From an advertisement in *The American Hebrew. Credit:* LC

The Boston Store, Omaha, about 1890: Department stores made available to farmers and workers merchandise which had been previously reserved for the more well-to-do. *Credit:* NSHS

Lazarus Store, Columbus, about 1890: German Jewish merchants created successful retail stores. S. Lazarus Sons & Co. of Columbus, Ohio, was
Credit: OHS

the starting point for what has become Federated Department Stores, one of the largest department store chains in the United States.

"The South is a Very Good Place to Live"

1906. The Industrial Removal Office was established to assist Eastern European Jews find their ways to cities throughout the country. Leo Stamm, who got to Meridian, Mississippi, wrote to express his appreciation. (His original letter was in Yiddish; the English translation appears here.)

Dear Sir: With a feeling of thankfullness I am writing to you this letter in which you will recognize one of the clients of the Removal Office by the name Leo Stamm.

It is five months since I have arrived to Meridian and with pleasure will describe to you the condition in which the Jewish Immigrants are around this neighborhood. The city of Meridian where I am living consists of about 75 Jewish families which are here for the last 8–10 years and are all well to do. The most part of them are very rich doing business in millions. Three quarters of them are German Jews and the rest of them are Russian Jews, but every one of them is trying to get the title of a German Jew. The most business of the town is in the hands of the Jews and they are growing very rapidly in both power and richess. The christian population is very friendly to the Jews and the antisemitism is very low, because the Jews in this town are very honest and doing business on a business principal, but here is a little exception with the the Russian Jews in this matter, being there was some crimes committed by them to a few natives of this city, because some misfortune happened with a peddler who stole from a farmer a gold watch and chain and the other one was a clerk who escaped with a hundred dollars from his employer. And that what is usually done here in New York every day is unexpected in a small town like this and the natives of this city recollected very often that this crime was done by a Russian Jew. For a honest working man the South is a very

Peddler with Wagon, 1910: Peddling with either a pack or a wagon was a common Jewish enterprise in all parts of the country. Ben Taylor is seen here with his horse and wagon in Quilman, Georgia. *Credit:* Louis Schmier

Isaias Hellman, about 1895: He came to Los Angeles from Germany and entered banking in 1868. He organized the first incorporated bank in Los Angeles and was later associated with the Wells Fargo Bank. *Credit:* AJA

Ludwig Vogelstein, about 1915: In his office in New York City. *Credit:* LBI

S. Kuhn & Sons Bank, Cincinnati, about 1890: This firm, established in Cincinnati, was the forerunner of Kuhn Loeb & Co. of New York. *Credit:* Daniel J. Ransohoff

Bank, about 1900: The D. & A. Oppenheimer Bank on Commerce Street, San Antonio, Texas. *Credit:* Dan Oppenheimer, from a copy at University of Texas, Institute of Texan Cultures

Barbary Coast Clothing Store, about 1900: This clothing store was located in San Francisco's Barbary Coast area. *Credit:* WJHC

good place to live in, and here I send my advise to the enslaved Jews of New York to leave the town as quick as they can and come here to get the benefit of the good climate and to conduct a good living. To you I send my gratefulness for your kindness to the people who are applying to the Removal Office, for help I will never forget that the Immigrants on their difficult way are meeting such people like you. My wife is in New York yet. She would be here long ago, if not the arrival of my friends whom we are waiting every day. I think, that also they will be obliged to apply for the help of the office and that their impression will be the same as mine. The family of Davidson send their intimate regards to you whom you rejected hither a few months ago. They settled themselves very well as I expected. They remembered you as the one who helped their leaving New York. Especially they are very thankfully for sending them by the way of Washington. It saved them the way almost from 35–55 hours. I hope you are all well as upon your own wishes.

Yours very respectfully,
(Signed)
Leo Stamm.

Lazarus Dinkelspiel & Co., about 1900: Located in San Francisco. *Credit:* WJHC

Liquor Store, New York, about 1910: The Glatzer family liquor store at 506 Amsterdam Avenue. The family lived in an apartment in the same building. Mrs. Glatzer is seen here with a relative. *Credit:* Daisy Marks

Jewelry Store, Fort Worth, about 1900: Sam Kruger in his jewelry store, Fort Worth, Texas. *Credit:* Bert Kruger Smith, from a copy at University of Texas, Institute of Texan Cultures

Levi Strauss & Co., about 1890: Levi Strauss began as a dry goods merchant and later began to manufacture denim pants for miners which have since become one of the most popular items of clothing throughout the world. *Credit:* WJHC

Rose Brothers Fur Co., St. Paul, 1911: Blackfoot Indians posing with the four Rose brothers: Albert, Isaac, Nathan and Isidore, along with James Hill, who was responsible for bringing the Indians to the winter carnival. Standing directly in front of Mr. Hill is "Two Guns White Calf," whose likeness appeared on the "Indian Head" nickel. *Credit:* AJA

Cooperage, Los Angeles, 1912: From left to right: John Vlah, the driver, Hyman Levine, owner, and Frank Rubassa, employee. "Daisy" next to Mr. Levine was a wild range horse that he and Jake Levy caught in 1906 in Saugus, California. She was broken to become a dray horse and

pulled his small wagon until he bought a second one to make a team to pull this larger wagon. This load of used barrels was for the Union Oil Company. *Credit:* Sid Levine

We Need a "First Class Dry Goods Store"

August 7, 1912. Stanley Watson, representative of the Frisco Lines railway in Kingsville, Texas, wrote to the Industrial Removal Office in New York requesting their assistance in getting a Jewish merchant to move to their town.

August 7, 1912

Mr. Samuel Cohen
Industrial Removal Office
174 Second Avenue
New York, N.Y.

Dear Sir:

Through the Industrial Removal Office I learn that you wish to find a business opening and I wish to call your attention to the town of Blessing, Brazeria County, Texas. By reference to a railroad map of Texas, you will find that Blessing is located on the St. Louis, Brownsville & Mexico Railway and the Palacios branch of the Southern Pacific Railway, 109 miles south-west of Houston.

Blessing has no first class dry goods store, and I believe that a store carrying an up to date stock of goods would do a splendid business there. The town has a population of five hundred people, is surrounded by a good farming country, and is growing rapidly. It will be in a few years a town of fifteen hundred or two thousand people and all of the farming lands around it will be closely settled. The climate is much more pleasant than that of New York, and while the thermometer goes higher, it is not so hot in summer, because of the breeze coming off the Gulf of Mexico which is only about twenty miles away. The winters are very mild and pleasant. The country is healthful, and I believe that you and your family would prosper and enjoy good health in Blessing.

There has just been completed there a handsome two story brick store building. The upper floor being used for offices and the one half of the lower floor now being occupied by a modern drug store, with quite handsome plate glass front, and would be leased to you at a reasonable rate.

I am requesting Mr. A. B. Pierce, the banker in Blessing, who has this property in charge, to write to you and unless the building has been taken and a dry goods store put in in the last few days, you ought to hear from him at an early date. If this information does not reach you too late, I want to urge you to make a thorough investigation of this proposition at once, because I believe it is a good opportunity. If, however, someone beat you to it, I will try to find another location for you. You can get information as to rates and train service from our representative offices No. 385 Broadway.

Yours truly,
Stanley H. Watson

Jewelry Store, about 1910: Located in San Francisco, this jewelry store was typical of small businesses operated by Jews. *Credit:* WJHC

Department Store, San Francisco, about 1915: Glove department of The White House (Raphael Weill & Company) department store in San Francisco. *Credit:* WJHC

1301-1307 Race Street, Philadelphia, 1915: Manufacturing lofts with Jewish businesses: men's and women's clothing. *Credit:* PCA

Jacob H. Schiff, 1917: A German Jewish immigrant who arrived in this country in 1865, he became one of the most influential members of the Jewish community in his generation. He entered the firm of Kuhn, Loeb and Company in 1875 and participated in its growth to become one of the largest private banking houses in the United States. As a philanthropist, his benefactions encompassed most of the major American Jewish organizations and cultural institutions. *Credit:* LC

Senator Simon Guggenheim, about 1908: A member of the distinguished family of bankers, mine operators and industrialists, Simon Guggenheim was Republican Senator from Colorado between 1907 and 1913. He founded the John Simon Guggenheim Memorial Foundation in 1925 which makes annual grants to benefit the "educational, literary, artistic and scientific power of this country, and also to provide for the cause of better international understanding." *Credit:* LC

Otto H. Kahn, 1909: Born in Mannheim, Germany, in 1867, he came to New York in 1893. In 1896 he married Addie Wolff, daughter of Abraham Wolff, a partner in Kuhn, Loeb and Company, and joined the firm the following year. He became known as a successful banker, arts patron and philanthropist. From 1903 to 1917, he was Chairman of the Board of the Metropolitan Opera Company and one of its principal benefactors. *Credit:* LC

Mrs. Simon Guggenheim, about 1908: Wife of Senator Simon Guggenheim of Colorado and a patron of the arts. She was an early member of the board of The Museum of Modern Art and benefactor of the Museum collections. *Credit:* LC

Mrs. Otto Kahn, 1912: Her son Roger Wolff Kahn became a well known band leader. *Credit:* LC

Louis Marshall, 1908: One of the leading constitutional lawyers of his generation, he was also one of the outstanding Jewish communal leaders of his time. In response to persecution of Jews in Russia, he was active in the organization of the American Jewish Committee in 1906. He was a delegate to the Versailles Peace Conference in 1919 where he represented Jewish interests. Photograph by Lewis Hine. *Credit:* James Marshall

Louis D. Brandeis, 1919: Outstanding lawyer and champion of social justice, he was instrumental in overcoming industrial unrest in the garment trades. In 1916 he was appointed Associate U.S. Supreme Court Justice, the first Jew to hold this position. He is seen here on his way to the Versailles Peace Conference. *Credit:* LC

Lillian Wald, about 1910: Lillian Wald, a German Jew, arrived in New York's Lower East Side in 1893 and established the first Visiting Nurse service in the city; it ministered to the basic health needs of recently arrived immigrants who were living in miserable conditions. From her activities the Henry Street Settlement, an outstanding community center, emerged. *Credit:* LC

Fannie Hurst, 1914: Born in St. Louis the daughter of a German-Jewish family, she moved to New York where she became one of the country's leading novelists and short story writers. *Credit:* LC

Isidor Straus, 1908: In 1887 Isidor and Nathan Straus became the sole owners of Macy's in New York. Under their management, Macy's became the largest department store in the world under one roof. They introduced many innovations to retail merchandising. He died on board the *Titanic. Credit:* John W. Straus

Ida Straus, 1908: She and her husband Isidor Straus were aboard the *Titanic* when it struck an iceberg. Given the opportunity to go into one of the lifeboats, they stated that as they had lived happily together for over forty years; younger people should take preference. They went down with the ship and have become legendary heroes. A crowd of 40,000 gathered to honor them at the Educational Alliance on East Broadway. *Credit:* John W. Straus

Nathan Straus, about 1910: With his brother Isidor, Nathan Straus participated in a successful management of Macy's. Nathan Straus was a dedicated proponent of the pasteurization of milk, establishing the Straus Milk Fund which distributed pasteurized milk at less than cost to the needy and later helped to found health centers in Jerusalem and Tel Aviv. *Credit:* LC

Sheet Music, 1919: Commemorating the heroic death of Isidor and Ida Straus aboard the *Titanic* in 1911. *Credit:* AJHS

Cyrus L. Sulzberger, 1908: Prominent foreign affairs columnist of *The New York Times* and first cousin of Arthur Hays Sulzberger, publisher of *The New York Times* from 1925 to 1961. *Credit:* LC

M.H. De Young, 1881: Journalist and publisher of the *San Francisco Chronicle. Credit:* BL

Abraham Cahan, about 1910: In 1896 Abraham Cahan published "Yekl," the first of a series of novels on the urban Jewish experience. Under Cahan's editorship beginning in 1903, the *Jewish Daily Forward* became the most widely read Yiddish newspaper in America with a circulation of 200,000 and 11 local and regional editions. In addition to being a novelist and editor, he was an outspoken socialist. *Credit:* BB

Dr. Simon Baruch, about 1900: Simon Baruch emigrated from Posen, Prussia, and settled in South Carolina in 1855. As a medical doctor he spent three years in the Confederate Army and in 1881, moved to New York City to become professor at the College of Physicians and Surgeons of Columbia University. He is credited with being the first to diagnose and remove a ruptured appendix. His son, Bernard Baruch, the financier, became a counselor to American presidents. *Credit:* AJA

Dr. Abraham Jacobi, about 1905: Born in Westphalia, he came to the United States in 1853. When the College of Physicians and Surgeons of Columbia University appointed him professor of infant pathology and therapeutics in 1860, the first systematic instruction in that field commenced. In 1862 he established the first pediatric clinic in this country. *Credit:* AJA

Dr. Jacob Da Silva Solis-Cohen, about 1890: Born in New York in 1838, he was educated in public schools in Philadelphia. He received his medical degree from Jefferson Medical College of the University of Pennsylvania in 1860. In the Civil War he served as Acting Fleet Surgeon of the Union forces. Resuming his medical practice in Philadelphia in 1866, he rapidly became identified with the successful diagnosis of diseases of the throat and chest. Recognized as an international authority in his field, he was both a teacher and lecturer. *Credit:* AJA

The Mount Sinai Hospital Staff, New York, 1914: The senior members of the medical staff included an outstanding group of physicians, surgeons and specialists who were distinguished for their intellectual caliber, cultural attainment and sheer brilliance of scientific productivity. From left to right they are doctors, front row: Fred S. Mandelbaum, Mayer, Brettauer, Julius Rudisch, Abraham Jacobi, Arpad Gerster, Bernard Sachs, Howard Lilienthal, Carl Koller, Nathan Brill, Leo Buerger, second row: S. Oppenheimer, Charles Elsberg, Albert A. Berg, Fred Whiting,

Charles May, Goldenberg, R. Weil, Edwin Beer, Emanuel Libman, W. Brickner, Leviseur, third row: Aranson, Abrahamson, Alexis
Moschcowitz, S. Wiener, Epstein, Robert Frank, J. Wolff, A. Wiener, H.W. Berg, Lewisohn, Celler, L.B. Meyer, Louis Hauswirt, fourth row:
J. Wiener, Roberts, A. Hyman, Sidney Yankauer, Davison, Bernard Oppenheimer, Abraham Wilensky, John Gerster, Ware, Heist, Schwartz,
Heiman and unidentified.. *Credit:* AJA

Bertha Kalich, 1910: Well-known actress of the Yiddish theater. *Credit:* LC

Alice B. Toklas, about 1900: Lifetime intimate friend of Gertrude Stein. Photograph by Arnold Genthe. *Credit:* BL

Dankmar Adler, 1885: Born in Stadtlengsfeld, Germany, Dankmar Adler came to America at an early age. Trained as an architect he established a successful practice which Louis Sullivan joined in 1881. The firm designed some of the most advanced buildings of the period, such as the Auditorium Building in Chicago, the Transportation Building at the Chicago Columbian Exposition in 1893 and the Wainwright Building in St. Louis. *Credit:* AJA

Gertrude Stein, about 1900: The author as a college student. Before going to Paris in 1902, she studied psychology under William James at Radcliffe College and attended medical school at Johns Hopkins University. *Credit:* BL

Morris Hillquit, about 1905: Born in Riga, Latvia, Morris Hillquit arrived in New York City in 1886 and became a leading activist in the labor movement and the Socialist Party, helping to organize the United Hebrew Trades in 1888. In 1917 he ran for the office of Mayor of the City of New York on a peace platform but was defeated. *Credit:* AJA

Emma Goldman, about 1911: Born in Kovno, Lithuania, Emma Goldman came to the United States in 1885. An advocate of anarchism, she opposed conscription during World War I, was imprisoned, and her publication, *Mother Earth*, was banned from the mails. In 1919, she was deported to the Soviet Union where she remained for two years. *Credit:* LC

Mr. and Mrs. Samuel Gompers, about 1905: Born in London, the son of Jewish parents of Dutch origin, Gompers' family settled in New York's East Side in 1863. At the age of 13 he began work in a cigar factory; later he became head of the cigarmakers' local union. He played a major role in the creation of the Federation of Organized Trades and Labor Unions in 1881, and its successor, the American Federation of Labor in 1886. *Credit:* LC

Congregation Anshe Mayriv, Chicago, 1891:
This synagogue, designed by Dankmar
Adler, partner of Louis Sullivan, was dedi-
cated on June 11, 1891. Adler's father had been
the rabbi of this congregation in 1861.
Credit: AJA

**B'nai Abraham Synagogue, Philadelphia,
about 1910:** This Orthodox synagogue in the
Moorish style was dedicated in 1910 on
Lombard Street near Sixth in Philadelphia.
Credit: LCP

Rabbi Solomon Schechter, about 1910: Research scholar and teacher, he was invited to come
from England in 1901 to serve as president of the Jewish Theological Seminary of America, the
center for training rabbis for the Conservative movement. He founded the Teachers' Institute
in 1909 and the United Synagogue of America, an affiliation of Conservative congregations.
Credit: AJHS

Synagogue, Omaha, Nebraska, about 1900: Temple Israel in Omaha. *Credit:* NSHS

Cemetery, about 1910: Man visiting his mother's grave. *Credit:* LC

Confirmation class, Washington, about 1900: Confirmation class of Washington Hebrew Congregation. *Credit:* WHC

Confirmation class, Galveston, 1905: Rabbi Henry Cohen with confirmation class in Galveston, Texas. *Credit:* Archives of Temple B'nai Israel, Galveston, from a copy at University of Texas, Institute of Texan Cultures

Orphan Asylum, Cleveland, about 1890: Main building of the Jewish Orphan Asylum on Woodland Avenue in the Jewish immigrant section of Cleveland. *Credit:* WRHS

Purim Gazette, 1887: Purim celebrations have been a long established Jewish tradition. Balls were often organized as fund raising events. On this occasion the Metropolitan Opera House in New York was the center of activity. *Credit:* SI

Purim ball menu, 1885: Elaborate dinners often accompanied Purim Balls. *Credit:* SI

Ambulance, Philadelphia, undated: Horse-drawn ambulance in use at Mt. Sinai Hospital, Philadelphia, later the Albert Einstein Medical Center, Southern Division. *Credit:* AEMC

Zionist Provisional Committee Meeting, 1915: Henrietta Szold, founder of Hadassah, with leaders of the World Zionist Organization in New York. Included in the photograph are Rabbi Stephen S. Wise, Jacob de Haas, Joseph Kesselman, Louis Lipsky, Charles A. Cowen, Shmarya Levin and Meyer Berlin. *Credit:* Hadassah

"Girl of the Golden West," 1905: David Belasco's long-running New York theatrical production with Blanche Bates and Robert Hilliard. Belasco, born in San Francisco, came to New York to become one of the leading playwrights, directors and producers of his day. He was responsible

for nearly four hundred plays including minstrel shows, melodramas, tragedies, fairy tales and musical comedies. As a theatrical innovator, he introduced electrical lighting to the stage. Photograph by Byron. *Credit:* MCNY

Orchestra, undated: At the Chicago Hebrew Institute. *Credit:* CHS

Charity Bazaar Play, about 1905: For the benefit of a Chicago organization. *Credit:* CHS

FAT FOLKS REDUCED

by a harmless treatment administered by a practicing physician. Read the following testimonial from an "American Jewess." Thousands of others equally good.

Troy, N. Y., Aug. 3, 1895.

DR. SNYDER, Sir:—
       I have taken your treatment three months and have lost forty-one pounds, and my general health is greatly improved. The following table shows my reductions to the present time:

	Weight	Bust	Waist	Hips
Before	221 lbs.	42½ in.	32½ in.	54 in.
Now	180	38	28	46

The above can be verified by addressing me with postage.   (Miss) RAY BERNSTEIN.

PATIENTS TREATED BY MAIL.
For circulars with full information, address with stamp **Dr. Snyder,** 347 McVicker's Theatre, Chicago, or Room 6 J, 907 Broadway, New York City.

Advertisement, 1896: This advertisement appeared in *The American Jewess* magazine, April 1896. *Credit:* AJHS

Business Card, about 1915: . *Credit:* Alan Teller

Baby Contest, 1915: At the Chicago Hebrew Institute. *Credit:* CHS

Tableau, 1919: Depiction of "The Jewish Rebirth," Poale Zion Chasidim pageant, Milwaukee, Wisconsin. *Credit:* SHSW

Pageant, 1917: Esther Berman of the Chicago Hebrew Institute Players. *Credit:* CHS

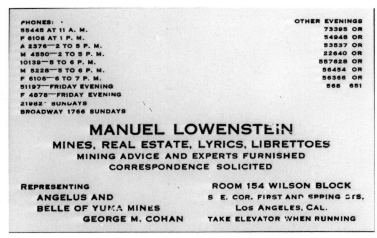

Business Card, about 1915: . *Credit:* Sylvan Cole

Boxing Club, about 1915: At the Chicago Hebrew Institute. *Credit:* CHS

Wrestling Club, about 1915: At the Chicago Hebrew Institute. *Credit:* CHS

Joseph Alexander, 1919: Left guard and captain of Syracuse University's football team. He was chosen twice on Walter Camp's All-American teams and was elected to the Football Hall of Fame. *Credit:* AJA

Fencing Team, about 1915: At the Jewish People's Institute, Chicago. *Credit:* CHS

Chicago Hebrew Institute, about 1910: Located on Taylor Street from 1908 to 1925, the Chicago Hebrew Institute conducted various activities, including an extensive sports program. *Credit:* CHS

Baseball Team, about 1912: The Cook's Baths baseball team, Denver, Colorado. *Credit:* RMJHS

Women's Fencing Team, about 1919: At the Jewish People's Institute, Chicago. *Credit:* CHS

Gym Club, 1915: At the Chicago Hebrew Institute. *Credit:* CHS

A Family's Fortunes Rise and Fall

About 1910, Henry Hurwitz described his family's successes, failures and moves from Boston to Gloucester to Worcester and back to Gloucester. He later became the distinguished editor of The Menorah Journal.

One day at last, Uncle Sam, mother's young brother, came from distant America, bearing those magical *billeten* from father—the steamship tickets to Paradise on the other side of the ocean. For the long journey on land and sea mother had prepared a store of food in pots and jars; how could we touch a crumb of unkosher food on the way? And we took along the family bedding—pillows, *perenes* (feather-beds), linens. And the pair of silver candlesticks. And the large brass samovar (which now graces my dining-room in New York).

A crowded room some time later flashes into my memory. The company is congenial, very gay, they are friends enjoying the proverbial Marks-Bailie hospitality in our new home. We are settled on the first floor of Number 2 Crescent Place, in the West End of Boston. The men are seated around the long table in the dining room, under the lighted and domed gas-jets, at their garrulous game of cards ("okkie"), with glasses of hot tea before them, and many plates of kichlach. Mother and her cronies, wives of the men at play, hover over them, filling their glasses from the steaming, pleasantly whistling samovar on a side-table. All is jovial and mock-serious as this man or that throws down his cards bemoaning his ill luck. I duck about with a pinch on my cheek here and a pulling of my ear there, and many a penny pushed into my hand by victory in the deals.

The family fortune was flourishing. Father had a successful ladies' wrapper factory on Hanover Street. We moved to larger quarters at 72 Leverett Street, one flight up. The adjacent apartment was occupied by the Chatskel Goldman family, old friends from Baltermantz, leather merchants. A slim dark young son of that family, Abba Koppel (Albert) by name, began courting the pretty blond eldest daughter of the Hurwitz family—Julia. (Our family had been recently augmented by the birth of another daughter, the "Amerikannerke"—Marcia (May)).

Then a terrific blow fell upon us. Father's partner in the factory—a kinsman but a scoundrel—absconded with the money. The factory went under. Father was ruined. Nothing for him now but to put the pack on his back again and return, after a short interlude of being a "boss," to his peddling in Gloucester, where he had so laboriously, after many struggling years, made the money to open up the business in Boston. For a while there was the effort to keep the family in the city, father returning from "the country" for Shabbas every week. Though our "front room" had been let out to a pale pharmacy student, the dread decision had to be made—to pull up stakes in the city and

Henry Hurwitz, about 1917: *Credit:* AJA

move out to "the country," away from shul, from heder, and from friends. Thus the day came when mother took me again to heder, but this time to tell the rebbe that I must leave. She broke down and wept. I had never heard her sob so heartbreakingly, except once before, when a cablegram from the old country came announcing the death of her mother.

What a dreary rainy March day it was, the day Mr. Reed's tired old nag finally pulled up to 11 Harold Avenue in Gloucester, with all our worldly goods. Mother and the children had arrived before by train. Despite rain and ruin, what spacious quarters were now ours. A whole half house, with three floors, seven rooms, and both a porch and a cellar all to ourselves, and a big yard. The way from the kitchen door to the outhouse (there was no toilet within the house) was not long. It was a white frame house, partitioned in the middle from roof to cellar. The rent was twelve dollars a month.

Kerosene lamps and candles provided the light at night, the water came from a large cistern in the cellar. It was rainwater, flowing down into the cistern through outside pipes from the roof. An iron hand pump in the kitchen sink pulled the water up. For Mr. Modgkins, the tall gangling Yankee who owned the house and taught us how to work the pump, it was a toy. For mother, who had to pump the water constantly for washing, cooking, drinking, it was often a backbreaking instrument of torture. Yet the pump was perhaps the least of her troubles.

Those were the years of direst poverty. Father trudged about all day, under his pack or with large bundles; and at night mother would wash his swollen feet. The two older girls worked at various jobs; mother cooked midday dinners for itinerant peddlers (at 35 cents a full meal); and some men would be put up over-night.

One permanent boarder we had was such a sweet old man—Reb Yossel Borofsky. I shared the front attic with him. He had been the bookkeeper in father's wrapper factory, and when the crash came he would not leave us and voluntarily went with us into "exile." He was a learned man, and during the High Holy Days, as well as on Sabbath mornings, he led the congregational prayers. He would not hear of leaving us in our time of trouble, and insisted on sharing our portion and paying his part. He loved little May, who grew up on his knees. Father gave him the headship of our table, and mother fed him as royally as she could, washed his linen and mended his socks.

Doubtless she had a selfish motive, for Mr. Borofsky took the place of heder for me; he taught me *Chumash* and *Nach* with Rashi, and even a little Talmud. This gentle old man, accustomed all his life to poring over books, now took upon himself another yoke: peddling. Over his bent narrow shoulders he would lug five or six rugs as he trudged from door to door, his long beard incongruous to the business. But you should have seen him in our attic Friday afternoon, preparing himself to greet the Princess Sabbath. He washed himself carefully from a basin, put on fresh linen and a black string tie, tended his fingernails, combed his long iron-gray beard lovingly like a vain woman at her coiffure, all the while humming his Sabbath tunes. Meticulously he would don his black glossy Prince Albert coat, with the black velvet yarmulke on his head. Shoulders erect, he would take his place of honor at the dining-room table and, after a courteous bow to father, intone the kiddush with flourishes, and drink the wine with *geshmack* from a large silver cup.

But he had a wife in the Old Country, in Bialystok; and inevitably the time arrived when he yielded to her entreaties to "come home" and spend his last days with her. With a handshake ceremony over that dining-room table, Reb Yossele "sold his customers" to father, handing him a record-book in return for a wad of greenbacks, and that same day our faithful friend parted from us forever.

Somehow or other, father built himself up again. One day a large loft full of shiny new fixtures and tables heaped with men's clothing opened for business on the second floor of 70 Main Street, fronted with a big plate glass window bearing the letters CAPE ANN SUPPLY COMPANY for all Gloucester to behold. I don't recall how soon after the grand opening the crash came, but misfortune stalked us again. What was left of the goods, after the creditors seized all they could, was installed in the back attic at home. There, on more than one night, I would hold up a small lamp while father trussed a yokel into a suit and exclaimed over the wonderful "fit."

Mother, it seemed, could not rest until my Jewish education was resumed. She got wind of a young shochet in Boston, a lamdan, pious and yet modern, who knew modern Hebrew, and could teach *dikduk* (grammar). The girls in particular, for some reason or other, had set their hearts on my learning *dikduk*. So, by methods still obscure to me, Mr. Marcus was lured from Boston and ensconced in the better part of our front attic.

If you would like to know how Mr. Marcus looked, just go and see El Greco's marvellous portrait of Fra Palavicino in the Boston Museum of Fine Arts. Mr. Marcus's little black beard was pointed rather than squarish as in the portrait, but the other features—the eyes, the nose and nostrils, the thick fleshy lips, especially the eyes, black, glowing, fanatical—belonged to my tutor also. And the long, strong fingers of his shapely hands, as they held the pen writing his beautiful Hebrew script, were the swords of his mind. He was apt to rush his spoken Yiddish or Hebrew in the heat of his strong emotions, just as he walked with quick short steps; yet his whole life seemed curiously impersonal, almost abstract, fired wholly by his love of Hebrew and Palestine. He rose at dawn, put on tefillin and prayed devoutly, and was at his books and writing before breakfast. Regularly I watched him from my cot in the shadows. He was an extraordinary combination—as I came to realize only much later, and he was the only exemplar of the combination I was ever to meet—of the Haskalah renaissance with strict Orthodox rabbinic practice.

In addition to his ritual doing-in of chickens for the Jewish families of Gloucester and neighboring villages, mother also contrived to find him a few other youngsters to teach Hebrew or prepare for bar-mitzvah. What with one thing and another, it was usually toward sunset—in winter after dark—when he came home and mother served him his dinner. He was a hefty eater, unlike Mr. Borofsky; but mother saw to it that he was well fed, as well certainly as any member of the family, except herself. I fear that she herself often went supperless to bed.

Usually I would also be at the dining-room table doing my school homework, and right after Mr. Marcus ate we set to together on our Hebrew books and exercises for a couple of hours. In the year or two Mr. Marcus was with us, he also introduced me to Jewish history and inoculated me with his fervent Zionism. Mr. Marcus himself achieved his heart's desire by going to live in Palestine. Some years later I received a book from him, a Hebrew work he had written and published in Palestine, on various abstruse themes in Talmudic theology and the rise of Christianity.

Things were becoming brighter for the family again. Father had been gradually paying off his creditors with his "customer peddling" and that little attic-store. He wanted passionately to recover his "name," so he could do business in his own name again instead of mother's. There was another driving motive, I think, an even stronger one. He was proud of his reputed descent—the *yichusbrief*, the documentary evidence, had been destroyed in one of those recurrent fires in Baltermantz—from the famed sixteenth century rabbi Isaiah Hurwitz, author of *Shnei Luhot ha-Brit*, and known in Jewish history as the "Shelah." That name must never be under a cloud. In time father, honorably discharged from bankruptcy, got back his "name."

Still, though he continued to keep his head above water and was even able to put aside some savings for the future, father kept up the treadmill of his customers' route every day, either collecting the week's installment of a dollar or trying to sell them something new; there was also no letup in mother's grind at home. So a bright idea occurred to Uncle Sam Wolfson, the uncle who had fetched us from Baltermantz some twelve years before.

Uncle Sam had always been devoted to us, regarding mother almost as a second mother to himself. A dapper man with bright blue eyes and a bristling blonde mustache, Sam had married a

Family Photograph, about 1905: Children of Mr. and Mrs. Nathan Eckert, Fort Worth, Texas. *Credit:* Thelma Strickler

On Her Wedding Day, about 1895: Becky Eckert Silverman, Fort Worth, Texas. *Credit:* Thelma Strickler

young woman from Newark, New Jersey,
a niece of our Mr. Borofsky, and was now
living proudly as a pillar of the Jewish
community in Worcester, Massachusetts.
He had a flourishing ladies' comb factory
and owned a spacious richly-furnished
house on top of the hill on Providence
Street. Generous to a fault, he was
helping out a good many people (with or
without Aunt Gussie's knowledge). In
later years he fell upon hard days—was
it because women cut off their hair and
didn't need so many combs any more, or
was it due to imprudent investments?
That was the time another man from
Worcester, the dramatist S. N. Behrman,
chose to publish a snide, cheaply clever
portrait of him in *The New Yorker*.

Back in 1904, however, when he was
riding high, Uncle Sam proposed to
mother and father to move to Worcester,
where father, investing his savings, could
take it easy just supervising some of the
work at the factory, and my sister Bessie
could become a bookkeeper and meet
some eligible young men of the city. To
be sure, Worcester wasn't Boston, to
which both father and mother hankered
to return, yet certainly with opportunities
for Jewish social life above the level of
the second-hand clothing merchants and
junk peddlers of Gloucester. I had just
finished high school and was to leave
home to enter Harvard College in the
fall. So we moved to Worcester.

But it didn't work out. After less than a
year the family was back in Gloucester,
this time settled in a more modern house
at Number 4 Exchange Street, opposite
the railroad depot. Father, with his
money fully returned to him by Uncle
Sam, resumed his former "customer-
business."

Family Portrait, 1919: The Glatzer family; Sigmund (father, seated) Willie, Daisy, Cornelia (mother) and Harold. *Credit:* Daisy Marks

Richard Rodgers, 1918: The composer at the age of 16, prior to entering Columbia University. *Credit:* Mrs. Richard Rodgers

Family Portrait, 1908: The Glatzer children: Willie, Daisy and Harold in New York City. *Credit:* Daisy Marks

Jewish Soldiers, 1918: Jewish soldiers assembled at an Army base in Augusta, Georgia, to attend holiday services organized by the Jewish Welfare Board. The Board was organized in 1917 to meet the religious needs of Jews in the US Armed Forces. *Credit:* NA

Tent Exhibit, 1918: A Jewish Welfare Board exhibit at the Iowa State Fair, Des Moines. *Credit:* AJA

Three Generations, Cincinnati, 1918: Dr. Joseph Ransohoff, seated; Dr. Louis Ransohoff; and Joseph Ransohoff, who followed the family tradition and became a medical doctor. *Credit:* Daniel J. Ransohoff

Passover Services, 1918: Seder at Camp Upton, Rabbi Blechman, Jewish Chaplain in the U.S. Army, officiated. *Credit:* NA

Patriotic Demonstration, 1918: At the Chicago Hebrew Institute. *Credit:* CHS

Ambulance Driver, 1918: Francis Nathan Solis-Cohen in the uniform of the ambulance service. *Credit:* AJA

Rabbi Stephen S. Wise and son, 1918: As their contribution to the war effort, Rabbi Wise and his eighteen year-old son spent their vacation as laborers in the shipbuilding yards of Luder Marine Construction Co. in Stamford, Connecticut. *Credit:* NA

Meeting of Joint Distribution Committee, 1918: Members of the American Joint Distribution Committee met in New York to administer relief funds collected from the Jewish community for European Jews affected by the ravages of World War I. Participants attending included Cyrus Adler, Sholem Asch, Arthur Lehman, Jacob H. Schiff and Felix M. Warburg. *Credit:* NA

Post-war conference, 1919: Bernard Baruch on the far left and Herbert Hoover on the far right attending a conference in Brussels. *Credit:* AJA

Princeton University, 1907: The center of the campus. *Credit:* LC

Woodrow Wilson on Admission to Princeton

September 23, 1904. In this excerpt from a letter to his classmate, J. Ridgway Wright, Woodrow Wilson explained that Princeton students were not anxious to see Jews on the campus. Wright sponsored a Jewish student who was later admitted.

You were mistaken in regard to my own feelings or wishes in such a case as that of your young friend J----- C------, and you may be sure that I will do whatever I can to make matters smooth for him, but alas I fear what I can do is very little—there matters do not fall under authority, but settle themselves and I fear it must be admitted that the students in general do not welcome Jews to Princeton. We have thought over the matter a great deal, but have felt that in such a thing purely social in character we had no power at all.

I hope that you will see to it that the boy is sent to call on me so that I may form my own impression of him, and if possible find out some way in which I can give him counsel and guidance. I will do that with the greatest possible pleasure.

The Lynching of Leo Frank

In 1915 Leo Frank was lynched by a mob in Georgia after his conviction of the murder of a female employee in the factory that he managed. Louis Marshall, one of the founders of the American Jewish Committee and an outstanding lawyer, provided a detailed record of this frightening anti-Semitic event in his letter to the Editor of The Boston Herald *twelve years later. (Recent testimony by one of the prime witnesses has exonerated Frank completely.)*

The letter of William B. Stoneman which appeared in one of your recent numbers, in which he contends that Leo Frank, who was lynched in Georgia in 1915, was guilty of the crime of murder, should not remain unnoticed.

Speaking from the record, I say without the slightest mental reservation that never was there a greater crime against justice perpetrated than the condemnation of this innocent man for a crime which he did not commit. I have before me the record of the case, which shows that he was the victim of insane prejudice and of the virulent animosity of Tom Watson and the shameless articles published from day to day in The Jeffersonian with the avowed purpose of arousing antipathy. Conley, the Negro whose testimony was relied upon, had a criminal record at the time when he was sworn. The letters which were found on the body of Mary Phagan were written by him and demonstrated to a certainty that Frank had no part, directly or indirectly, in the murder of this unfortunate girl. At various times Conley gave at least five different conflicting versions of his story. After Frank's tragic death Con-

ley was convicted of the crime of burglary and sentenced for a long term in State prison. It is said that while there he confessed that Frank had nothing to do with the murder. Another of the principal witnesses against Frank was subsequently convicted of blackmail in the State of Tennessee.

Under the laws of Georgia, Frank could not be sworn as a witness in his own behalf, although he made an unsworn statement denying all participation in the crime. His character was beyond reproach. He was a graduate of Cornell University, and a number of the members of the faculty and of his fellow-students testified to his unblemished reputation, as did various leading citizens of Atlanta.

The trial was a travesty on justice. The record shows that while it was in progress the windows of the court room looking out upon the adjourning streets were open and that large and boisterous crowds were gathered in the streets and were engaged in noisy demonstrations plainly audible in the court room, which was also crowded, and those assembled within its walls, as well as those outside, applauded whenever the State's attorney scored a point. Those outside cheered, shouted and hurrahed, while those within the court room evidenced their feelings by applause and other demonstrations. During his arguments and when he made objections the counsel for the prisoner was jeered by those present.

As the trial proceeded Judge Roan, who presided, became apprehensive as to whether it could be safely continued. While upon the bench and in the presence of the jury, he conferred with the chief of police of Atlanta and with the Colonel of the Fifth Georgia Regiment stationed at Atlanta who were well known to the jury. The public press of Atlanta, apprehending danger if the trial continued, on the Saturday prior to the submission of the case to the jury united in a request to the court that the proceedings should not continue on Saturday evening. While the State's attorney was engaged in summing up there was frequent applause, and when he left the court room he was carried on the shoulders of the mob in triumph. While the jury was deliberating the presiding justice called before him the counsel for the defendant and impressed them with the probable danger of violence which the defendant as well as his counsel would incur if they were present in the court on the rendition of the verdict in the event that the verdict was one of acquittal or disagreement. He requested counsel to agree to absent themselves from the court room when the jury was polled and that the defendant should be kept out of the court at that time, and yielding to this urgent request the defendant was not represented in court when the verdict was rendered. When it was announced that the jury had agreed upon a verdict a signal was given from within the court room to the crowd outside to that effect, and as the polling

of the jury proceeded the crowd cheered vociferously. After the first juror had been polled the noise was so loud and the confusion so great that the further polling of the jury had to be stopped so that order might be restored. The tumult was so great that it was difficult for the presiding Judge to hear the responses of the jurors while they were being polled, although he was only ten feet distant from them. Sheriff Mangum informed me personally that while the trial was proceeding he supplied the defendant's counsel with weapons with which to defend themselves against what he feared might be an onslaught upon them by the mob.

Several months after the rendition of the verdict a motion was made for a new trial, and in denying the motion Judge Roan said that he had thought about the case more than any other that he had ever tried and was not certain of the defendant's guilt; that with all the thought that he had devoted to the case he was not convinced that he was guilty. When the case came before the Supreme Court of Georgia two of the Justices of that tribunal dissented. Subsequent to the affirmance of the conviction an application was made for a writ of habeas corpus in the United States District Court, which was denied, and an appeal to the Supreme Court of the United States from that determination was allowed by Mr. Justice Lamar, a Justice of that Court and a resident of Georgia. Because of technical objections as to procedure the Supreme Court affirmed the denial of the writ of habeas corpus, but Mr. Justice Holmes and Mr. Justice Hughes dissented from that decision in an opinion written by the former which has become a legal classic. After reciting the facts above set forth as to the atmosphere in which the trial was conducted, this memorable utterance was made:

"Whatever disagreement there may be as to the scope of the phrase 'due process of law,' there can be no doubt that it embraces the fundamental conception of a fair trial, with opportunity to be heard. Mob law does not become due process of law by securing the assent of a terrorized jury. We are not speaking of mere disorder, or mere irregularities in procedure, but of a case where the processes of justice are actually subverted. * * * This is not a matter for polite presumptions; we must look facts in the face. Any judge who has sat with juries knows that in spite of forms they are extremely likely to be impregnated by the environing atmosphere. And when we find the judgment of the expert on the spot, of the judge whose business it was to preserve not only form but substance, to have been that if one juryman yielded to the reasonable doubt that he himself later expressed in court as the result of most anxious deliberation, neither prisoner nor counsel would be safe from the rage of the crowd, we think the presumption overwhelming that the jury responded to the passions of the mob."

Presenting Petitions, 1915: This group of men, including Samuel Goodman with a suitcase, presented petitions on behalf of Leo Frank at the Boston Federal courthouse. Leo Frank was convicted of the murder of a female employee in the factory that he managed in Georgia. There were serious questions about the evidence and testimony on which he was convicted. He was later lynched by a mob. Subsequent evidence has demonstrated his innocence. *Credit:* AJHS

In commenting upon this case in The New York Times on June 22, 1915, I said: "I also prophesy that the day will come when the dissenting opinion of Justices Holmes and Hughes will become the law of the land." It is not often that a prophesy of this sort is so soon verified as this was, because in 1923 in the case of *Moore v. Dempsey*, 261 U.S. 86, the Supreme Court adopted and applied that very principle in the very terms in which it was laid down in the Frank case.

After the courts had declined to give relief to Frank an application was made to Governor Slaton for a commutation of sentence, and after an elaborate review of all the evidence that distinguished jurist granted the application and indicated that the evidence did not justify the conviction and that in his opinion Frank was innocent. It was one of the most courageous acts ever performed by a high public official in this country. He knew that his life and the lives of his family were imperiled if his determination was favorable to Frank. A mob of ten thousand men marched upon his country home. It attacked the troops that were stationed there for his protection. He was hanged in effigy. And yet, appreciating this menace, he acted in accordance with the dictates of his con-

science. I have it from his own lips that after he had reached the conclusion that Frank was innocent he felt it his duty to tell his noble wife of what he had in mind and of the jeopardy in which he would place his family by acting in accordance with his convictions, and that she declared that if that was his belief she would despise him if he hesitated in the performance of his duty. Today he stands as one of the most respected men in the South because of his courage and his manhood. And yet Mr. Stoneman is seeking to cast a slur upon this man who has reflected glory upon Georgia, and to intimate that he was swayed by improper motives. He charges that a large fund was raised in the country for Frank. There is no foundation in fact for such a statement. As one of his counsel I can say that even the ordinary expenses of that part of the litigation in which I was engaged were paid out of my own pocket and that I never received or charged a penny for my services, regarding it to be my solemn obligation as a citizen to defend the laws of my country and the cause of justice.

To indicate the state of mind which designing men had fostered by criminal methods for the undoing of Frank, let it be remembered that after he had been

lodged in the State prison of Georgia one of his fellow-prisoners cut Frank's throat while asleep. Before the wound had healed a mob entered the State prison of Georgia—not a mere jail, not an insecure structure, but a fortified place—seized Frank, carried him by automobile seventy-five miles across country, and hung him to a tree. The account of this execution shows that Frank was the only dignified human being present. He did not whimper, but asserted his innocence so persuasively that many of those present were convinced, but they had carried him away under such conditions that they did not have the decency to refrain from the murder and the treason to their State upon which they had embarked.

And yet Mr. Stoneman has the hardihood to intimate that Frank had a fair trial, that his lynching under those circumstances was but the act of riff-raff, and that "mob violence is a crime which the good people of Georgia do not tolerate." And this in the face of the well-known fact that there have been more lynchings in Georgia than in any other State of the Union. Every statement here made is borne out by the official record. It would have been wiser for Mr. Stoneman had he remained silent.

MENAUHANT HOTEL

💲💲💲💲💲💲💲💲💲💲💲 **MENAUHANT. MASS.** 💲💲💲💲💲💲💲💲💲💲💲💲

MENAUHANT WHARF.

THIS House, is situated in Falmouth Township, on the South Shore of Cape Cod, at the confluence of Nantucket and Vineyard Sounds, it is directly on the beach, and is nearly surrounded by water; it is owned and managed by Mr. Floyd Travis, and will be open for the season of 1906, on June 16th.

Date of Opening

A great many conditions combine to make Menauhant the most delightful summer resort on Cape Cod.

We have no HEBREW patronage.

Advertisement, 1906: *Credit:* AJHS

ע פריינד

Family Reunion, about 1920: The Freund family reunion demonstrates the process of acculturation in America. It is possible to see differences
Credit: YIVO

in three generations, those who retained their European traditional appearance and those who accepted the contemporary American style.

Americanization Becomes Evident

Although the first World War interrupted the flow of Eastern European Jews across the Atlantic, it was the restrictive immigration laws passed after the war which ended the mass immigration of Jews to the United States. The huge influx of immigrants from Eastern and Southern Europe during the first two decades of the century resulted in severe limitations on future immigration. In 1921, the first "Quota Law" was passed, followed by the "Closing of the Gates" which went into effect in 1924.

The war years and their aftermath deeply affected those Eastern European Jews already in the United States prior to the closing of the gates. For them, it was a time to establish and cultivate roots in their new homeland. This process was greatly accelerated by the entry of 250,000 American Jews into the United States Armed Forces during World War I. While the army was a powerful agent of acculturation, it was the incredible prosperity of the postwar period which allowed a number of Eastern European Jews to leap into America's middle class. More Jews could now afford to move out of the tenements of the immigrant ghettoes and into the houses of the more prosperous neighborhoods.

In the larger cities, upward mobility was measured by one of two forms: moving into the neighborhoods recently vacated by the ethnic group next in the hierarchy; or moving into new luxury apartment houses. In the smaller cities, prosperity meant the purchase of a single family dwelling in an established neighborhood. Better housing, however, was only a part of acculturation. The single most influential instrument of Americanization was the public school system.

Traditionally, one of the principal functions of America's public education system had been to prepare predominantly Christian children of farmers and immigrants for their roles in the burgeoning American economy. Overnight, these schools were called upon to Americanize the Yiddish speaking children of Eastern European Jews. Noted historian Theodore H. White, the son of an immigrant, vividly described his experience growing up in the hustle-bustle atmosphere of Boston's Dorchester. Recounting his progress through the public school system, White spoke of the neighborhood elementary school where "the Irish had replaced the Yankee school marms," stating that his love of history began with his history teacher, Mrs. Fuller, who ". . . was probably the first Protestant I ever met . . . the first person who made me think I might make something of myself."

Ahead of her time, Mrs. Fuller had her students act out historical events such as Thanksgiving: "The recently arrived immigrant children played the game of being 'Indians' for a few minutes," wrote White, "then fell into Yiddish pretending it was Indian talk." Significantly, it was Mrs. Fuller who persuaded White's mother to allow her son to attend the prestigious Boston Latin High School, the gateway to Harvard. But the death of his father and the onslaught of the Depression delayed White's matriculation at Harvard for two years. In September of 1934, Theodore H. White became a "meatball" (scholarship or day student) at Harvard University. Among his classmates were Caspar Weinberger, John King and Arthur M. Schlesinger.

Theodore H. White was not an exception. It became commonplace for Eastern European Jews to attend college and professional schools, and a sizable Jewish professional class consisting of doctors, lawyers, accountants, educators and scientists emerged. In addition, traditional Jewish businesses such as retailing and manufacturing continued to provide avenues of success.

With each succeeding generation, the immigrant heritage disappeared. Children spoke English more fluently than they did Yiddish, and grandchildren seldom spoke Yiddish at all. A photograph of the Freund family reunion in 1920 captured the process of acculturation to America; whereas the elders clung to their European garb and whiskers, the clean-shaven young members looked like any other American youth.

Similarly, second-generation neighborhoods were a far cry from such immigrant enclaves as the Lower East Side. The affluence of the new Jewish middle class permitted the construction of splendid synagogues in the new neighborhoods, which, more often than not, were Reform or Conservative rather than Orthodox. In response to such changes in the lives of

1920-1945

America's Jews, the rabbi and philosopher Mordecai Kaplan espoused the need for Jewish community centers which offered social and religious programs.

Eastern European Jews joined either the established Jewish community organizations founded by the earlier German arrivals, or they formed their own mutual aid organizations. In the former instance, their participation often widened the scope of the organization, forcing it to adjust to the needs of the new immigrants as well as providing yet another American experience—membership in an organization. Many of the newcomers, particularly those with secular and socialist orientations, joined already established groups such as the landsmanschaft, based upon one's town of origin, or the Workmen's Circle which administered to its members' needs from birth until death.

By the 1920's, Jews were in the mainstream of American culture and began to produce entertainers with mass appeal. With the advent of radio and sound films, Jewish actors, singers and comedians such as Eddie Cantor, Al Jolson, Fanny Brice and the Marx Brothers become national celebrities. Louis B. Mayer, Sam Goldwyn, the Warner Brothers, Jesse L. Lasky and Irving Thalberg laid the foundations for the motion picture industry. Imported from the East, Elmer Rice, a Jewish playwright, described those early days of Hollywood when the industry was in its infancy. Rice presented a graphic account of the studio system, its galaxy of stars and the stages of the Hollywood script writing process. Writing about another infant industry, William S. Paley, the founder of CBS, described how he left the family's cigar manufacturing business because of his fascination with the potential of radio.

Despite their success, Jews did not escape new and continuing forms of anti-Semitism. Admissions quotas at some colleges were openly acknowledged, and certain industries deliberately excluded Jews. Social anti-Semitism was evident in the restrictions placed on Jewish membership in many clubs.

Even with the persistence of anti-Semitism, however, the 1920's was a decade of prosperity and opportunity. In direct contrast, the 1930's were bleak years for Jews in the United States. The Depression wiped out newly made fortunes as wide-spread unemployment became a fact of life. Some Jews, influenced by economic conditions and social consciousness, became active in the Socialist and Communist parties. The majority, however, were attracted to the progressive policies of Franklin D. Roosevelt.

Despite economic hardships during this period, America's Jews in the early thirties were able to look back upon a 275-year history in the United States free of massacres and pogroms. But the rise of Nazi Germany unleashed a new wave of anti-Semitism in Europe which demonstrated that a civilized nation was capable of barbaric persecution. At home, the German-American Bund, Father Coughlin's weekly radio diatribes and the American First Movement were nightmares within the American dream.

Throughout the thirties there were attempts to create an awareness of what was happening in Hitler's Germany. Rabbi Stephen S. Wise's prescient speech of 1933 warned of future dangers both to Jews and Christians. Fearing that Jews would retreat from their high social and ethical ideals in the face of the Nazi threat, Wise exhorted: "Shock troops we are, the shock troops in the army of civilization." In conclusion, he called upon the civilized people of the world to repudiate "neo-paganish Hitlerism."

The civilized world did not heed Rabbi Wise's warning as a period of darkness descended. Those European Jews capable of escaping made their way to America's shores. This new wave of immigration brought with it a large number of German Jewish professionals as well as a number of the leading intellectuals of Europe, Albert Einstein among them. Many of these immigrants went on to make enormous contributions to American science and the arts. Looking back at the appeals of such individuals as William Stricker, the odyssey and separation of Dr. Mechner and his family, and the hazardous escape of composer Darious Milhaud, we are reminded of the distress and torture which refugees were forced to endure even if they were fortunate enough to find a haven in America.

Growing Up in Boston in the Twenties and Thirties

Theodore H. White, one of our most emminent journalists and contemporary historians, has described with vivid detail his experiences in the neighborhood in which he grew up, going to public school, the impact of the Depression and later his days as a student at Harvard.

Erie Street was my street school. It was then a bustling market street, ancillary to the main shopping artery of Dorchester—Blue Hill Avenue. Storekeepers had transformed Erie Street from the quiet residential neighborhood my grandparents had sought as Jewish pioneers in the district into a semipermanent bazaar. Whatever you wanted you could buy on Erie Street. Or else someone could get it for you. Herrings were stacked in barrels outside the fish stores, and flies buzzed over the herrings. Fresh-caught fish lay on slabs, and little boys were allowed to keep the fishhooks for the trouble of extracting them. All butcher shops were kosher, sawdust on the floor, chopping blocks scrubbed clean every day, unplucked chickens piled in flop heaps in the store window, from which housewives squeezed and prodded, then picked and chose. There were four grocery stores, several dry-goods stores, fruit and vegetable specialists, hardware stores, mama-papa variety stores, penny candy stores.

But it was the peddlers who gave the street its sound and motion. The banana man was Italian, but all other peddlers were Jewish. Early in the morning, the peddlers would go to their stables, hitch up their horses, and proceed to Faneuil Hall or the Fish Pier to bring back the day's glut in the city market. Then, leading their horse-and-wagons through Erie Street, they would yodel and chant their wares. For each peddler another chant: the fish man would sing in a special voice, *"Lebediker fisch, weiber, lebediker fisch";* the secondhand-clothes merchant would chant otherwise; the Italian banana man would chorus only "Bananas, bananas, bananas," hawking a fruit previously unknown to Eastern Europeans . . .

I tried my hand at the peddling business. One summer I sold ice cream. For several winters, with my across-the-street friend Butsy Schneiderman, I peddled tin horns at New Year's Eve. Another entire summer Butsy and I sold stuffed dates from door to door in Quincy and Wollaston, of which venture I remember two things: the Quincy police drove us out, for they did not want adolescent Jewish peddlers in the neighborhood; and the best quick ice cream and hot dogs in the neighborhood came from a small counter stand run by a Swede named Howard Johnson. Howard Johnson's stores later expanded across the nation. But so did one of the local grocery stores on Erie Street, Rabinowitz's, which later grew into a chain of supermarkets now listed on the New York Stock Exchange. And Sammy Rosenzweig, my classmate who had a job as a soda fountain clerk in one of Erie Street's drugstores, later made his own drugstore chain the largest in New England.

But this out-migration into the larger community was all to come later. Erie Street was the hub of a self-contained neighborhood, and it was a safe street. The mothers all watched each other's children. No one was ever struck or mugged or threatened, even late at night; and "late at night" meant ten o'clock on weekdays, eleven o'clock on Saturdays . . .

Whatever the general theory of the Boston School Committee was, in the state in which Horace Mann had first broached the idea of free public education, its practice, when I was going to school, was excellent.

As the Boston public-school system absorbed me, it was simple. Each neighborhood had an elementary school within a child's walking distance—kindergarten through third grade. At the level of the William E. Endicott School, where I began, the Irish had replaced the Yankee schoolmarms and my teachers were Miss Phelan, Miss Brennan, Miss Murray, Miss Kelly. They were supposed to teach us to read, write (by the Palmer method) and add. They also made us memorize poetry, and the poetry was all New England—Henry Wadsworth Longfellow, James Russell Lowell, John Greenleaf Whittier. But memory was essential, as it was in Hebrew school, where one memorized the Bible.

Each neighborhood also had an intermediate school—in my case, the Christopher Gibson School. There segregation began, boys separated from girls for special periods. In the fourth grade, boys had special periods to learn carpentry, girls to learn sewing. In the fifth grade, it was electricity and wiring for boys, cooking for girls. Vocational and book learning were taught in the same building. I can still tell a ripsaw from a crosscut saw by what was taught me (by a lady carpentry teacher, Miss Sprague) in the fourth grade. I can still wire lamps in series or in parallel, insulate or install cutoff switches by what was taught me in the fifth grade. But—most importantly—I first became aware of the word "history" in the sixth grade at the Christopher Gibson School—and my teacher was Miss Fuller.

How can I say what a ten-year-old boy remembers of a schoolteacher lost in time? She was stout, gray-haired, dimpled, schoolmarmish, almost never angry. She was probably the first Protestant I ever met; she taught history vigorously; and she was special, the first person who made me think I might make something of myself. She was the kind of teacher who could set fire to the imaginations of the ordinary children who sat in lumps before her, and to do so was probably the chief reward she sought.

Her course in American history began, of course, at a much later date than the history we were taught at Hebrew school. In Boston, history began in 1630—when the Puritans came. It then worked back and forth, but every date had to be impeccably remembered; Columbus was 1492, Cabot was 1497. Cortés was 1519, as was Magellan; and so on, moving through Jamestown, 1607; New York, 1614; Plymouth Colony, 1620; then other dates that led up to the settlement of Boston—1630! 1630! 1630! We also had to know the names in the tests: William Penn, Sir George Carteret, King James (which had to be written King James I, or else you were marked wrong).

Miss Fuller did not stop with names and dates. First you had to get them right, but then they became the pegs on which connections between events were to be hung. In this she was far ahead of most of the teachers of her day. For example: Thanksgiving. How did it come about? What would you have thought that first winter in Plymouth, if you had come from England, and survived? How would you invite the Indians to your feast? She decided we would have a play the day before Thanksgiving, a free-form play in the classroom, in which we would all together explore the meeting of Puritans and Indians, and the meaning of Thanksgiving. She divided the class, entirely Jewish, into those children who were American-born and spoke true English, and those who were recent arrivals and spoke only broken English or Yiddish. I was Elder William Bradford, because I spoke English well. "Itchie" Rachlin, whose father was an unemployed trumpet player recently arrived from Russia, and who spoke vivid Yiddish, was Squanto, our Indian friend. Miss Fuller hoped that those who could not speak English would squawk strange Indian sounds while I, translating their sounds to the rest of the Puritans, all of us in black cardboard cone hats, would offer good will and brotherhood. "Itchie" and the other recently arrived immigrant children played the game of being "Indian" for a few minutes, then fell into Yiddish, pretending it was Indian talk. Miss Fuller could not, of course, understand them, but I tried nevertheless to clean up their Yiddish vulgarities in my translation to the other little Puritans, who could not help but giggle. (*"Vos is dos vor traef?"* said Itchie, meaning: "You want us to eat pig food?" and I would translate in English: "What kind of strange food is this before us?") Miss Fuller became furious as we laughed our way through the play; and when I tried to explain, she was hurt and upset. Thanksgiving was sacred to her.

But she was a marvelous teacher. Once we had learned the names and dates from 1630 to the Civil War, she let us talk and speculate, driving home the point that history connected to "now," to "us." America for her was all about freedom, and all the famous phrases from "Give me liberty or give me death" to the Gettysburg Address had to be memorized by her classes—and understood.

She was also a very earnest, upward-striving teacher. I realize now that she might have been working for an advanced degree, for she went to night school at Boston University to take education courses. This, too, reached from outside to me. One day she told my mother about a project her night-school seminar was conducting in how much independent research a youngster of ten or eleven could do on his own—one of those projects now so commonplace in progressive schools. Would my mother mind, she asked, if I was given such an assignment, and then reported on it to her seminar? My mother said yes after Miss Fuller promised to bring me home herself afterwards.

My assignment was to study immigration, and then to speak to the seminar about whether immigrants were good or bad for America. Her seminar mates would question me to find out how well I had mastered the subject. The Immigration Act of 1924—the "Closing of the Gates"—had just been passed; there was much to read in both papers and magazines about the controversy, but my guide was my father. He put it both ways: the country had been built by immigrants, so immigrants were not bad. He had been an immigrant himself. On the other hand, as a strong labor man, he followed the A.F. of L. line of those days. The National Association of Manufacturers (the capitalists) wanted to continue unrestricted immigration so they could sweat cheap labor. But the American Federation of Labor wanted immigration restricted to keep the wages of American workingmen from being undercut by foreigners. This was a conundrum for my father: he was against the capitalists and for the A.F. of L.; but he was an immigrant himself, as were all our friends and neighbors. He helped me get all the facts, and I made a speech on the platform of a classroom at Boston University Teachers College at nine one night, explaining both sides of the story and taking no position. I enjoyed it all, especially when the teachers began asking me questions; I had all the dates and facts, and an attentive audience, but no answers then just as I have none now. I must have done well, for Miss Fuller kissed me and bought me candy to eat on the streetcar. It became clear to me, as we talked on the way home, that immigrants were history, too. History was happening now, all about us, and the gossip of Erie Street and the problem of whether someone's cousin would get a visa back in the old country and come here were really connected to the past, and to Abraham Lincoln, Henry Clay, Sam Adams, Patrick Henry and the elder William Bradford.

If I went on to the Boston Public Latin School, I think it was because of Miss Fuller and my mother; it was Miss Fuller who persuaded my mother that there was something more than a lump in the boy, and pointed me in the direction of the Latin School.

The Boston school system offered then

Citizenship Class, New York, 1920: Immigrants attending a citizenship class at the HIAS (Hebrew Immigrant Aid Society) building in New York. *Credit:* YIVO

English Class, Chicago, 1920: Graduation photograph of an English class at the Chicago Hebrew Institute. *Credit:* CHS

Young American Patriots, about 1928: Bert and Aaron Kruger of Wichita Falls, Texas, dressed in patriotic costumes. *Credit:* Bert Kruger Smith from a copy at University of Texas, Institute of Texan Cultures

Grandfather and Grandson, Denver, about 1932: Robert Lazar Miller, on horseback, with his grandson, Stanley Stein, at the Denver Stockyards. *Credit:* Ira M. Beck Memorial Archives, Rocky Mountain Jewish Historical Society of the Center for Judaic Studies, University of Denver

what seems to me still a reasonable set of choices after intermediate school. You could go to a local high school—Charlestown High School, Roxbury Memorial High School, South Boston High School. Or, if your parents chose, you could go to a "downtown" high school. Today these central schools would be called "magnet schools," "enrichment schools," "elite schools." They served the entire Boston community—a Commerce High School to learn bookkeeping and trade, a Mechanic Arts High School to learn blueprints, welding, machining, and, at the summit, the Boston Public Latin School, the oldest public school in America, founded in 1635. It was free choice: you could walk to your local community high school, or you could go downtown to the central, quality schools. There were no school buses then, so if you did want to take the half-hour trolley ride to a downtown school, you bought student tickets, beige-brown tabs at five cents each, half the price of the dime fare for a regular rider on the Boston transit system. Ten cents a day, five days a week, for carfare was a considerable sum. You had to *want* to go.

My mother, my father, myself all agreeing, I chose the Latin School.

The Boston Public Latin School reeked of history. Harvard had been founded only in 1636, a year after the Latin School, because, so the school boasted, there had to be a college to take its first graduates. The school had sat originally on Beacon Hill, before being moved ultimately to the Fenway, where it was when I attended. The original school on the hill had given its name to the street which is still there: School Street in Boston. We learned that the legendary boys who had outfaced the British on the hill, and thrown snowballs at the Redcoats who put cinders on the icy streets where they sleighed, were Latin School boys. They were the first recorded student demonstrators in American history. In our Latin School assembly hall, the frieze bore proudly the names of boys who had graduated to mark American history. From Franklin, Adams and Hancock, on through Emerson, Motley, Eliot, Payne, Quincy, Sumner, Warren, Winthrop—the trailblazers pointed the way. The frieze might later have listed a Kennedy, a Bernstein, a Wharton. But all this history translated quite precisely to the immigrant parents of Boston. The Latin School was the gateway to Harvard—as much so in 1928, when I entered, as it had been for hundreds of years before. No longer is it so.

In my day, the Latin School was a cruel school—but it may have been the best public school in the country. The old Boston version of "Open Admissions" held that absolutely anyone was free to enter. And the school was free to fail and expel absolutely anyone who did not meet its standards. It accepted students without discrimination, and it flunked them—Irish, Italians, Jewish, Protestant, black—with equal lack of discrimination. Passing grade was fifty, and to average

eighty or better was phenomenal. Our monthly tests were excerpts from the College Board examinations of previous years—and we learned "testmanship" early, beginning at age fourteen. The entire Latin School was an obstacle course in "testmanship," a skill which, we learned, meant that one must grasp the question quickly; answer hard, with minimum verbiage; and do it all against a speeding clock. If you scored well in Latin School classroom tests in arithmetic, the College Boards held no peril—you would do better in those exams; and at Harvard, almost certainly, you would qualify for the advanced section of Mathematics A.

The Latin School taught the mechanics of learning with little pretense of culture, enrichment or enlargement of horizons. Mr. Russo, who taught English in the first year, had the face of a prizefighter—a bald head which gleamed, a pug nose, a jut jaw, hard and sinister eyes which smiled only when a pupil scored an absolute triumph in grammar. He was less interested in the rhymes of *The Idylls of the King* or "Evangeline," or the story in *Quentin Durward*, than in drubbing into us the structure of paragraph and sentence. The paragraph began with the "topic sentence"—that was the cornerstone of all teaching in composition. And sentences came with "subjects," "predicates," "metaphors," "similes," "analogies." Verbs were transitive, intransitive and sometimes subjunctive. He taught the English language as if he were teaching us to dismantle an automobile engine or a watch and then assemble it again correctly. We learned clean English from him. Mr. Graetsch taught German in the same way, mechanically, so that one remembered all the rest of one's life that six German prepositions take the dative case—*aus-bei-mit, nach-von-zu*, in alphabetical order. French was taught by Mr. Scully. Not only did we memorize passages *(D'un pas encore vaillant et ferme, un vieux prêtre marche sur la route poudreuse)*, but we memorized them so well that long after one had forgotten the title of the work, one remembered its phrases; all irregular French verbs were mastered by the end of the second year.

What culture was pumped in came in ancient history, taught by Mr. Hayes; American history taught by Mr. Nemzoff, who enlarged on what Miss Fuller had taught in the sixth grade; and Latin itself, taught by "Farmer" Wilbur. "Farmer" Wilbur was a rustic who raised apples on his farm outside Boston and would bring them in by the bushel to hand out to the boys who did well. Latin was drudgery; one learned Caesar, one groaned through Cicero, one went on to Virgil. I did badly in Latin, although ancient history fascinated me; and not until I came many years later to American politics did I realize how much of "Farmer" Wilbur's teaching of Caesar and Cicero had flaked off into the sediment of my thinking.

Yet, though the choice had been my

own, my first three years at the Latin School were an unrelieved torment. I barely managed a sixty average, which put me somewhere in the lower third of my class. But then in June 1931 my father died, and I was plunged into an education that remains for all men and women of my generation their great shaping experience—the lessons taught by the Great Depression.

One reads now that the 1920s were boom years, that the Great Depression did not begin until the stock market crash of October 1929.

For those of us of the underclass, the Depression had begun long before then. I had started a schoolboy diary the same year I entered the Latin School, in 1928. On historic Black Friday, October 29, the day of the great Wall Street crash of 1929, my diary makes no mention of the event. It says: "No money all week, Pa brought home $2.00 today, Mama is crying again."

The two years after that, the two years during which my father's heart was broken, come back at me again and again like a nightmare.

This was our country.

I was, by then, an American history buff. But even a teen-ager could see that this country was not working for us. There were no clothes—literally no new clothes for over four years in the family, all of us wore hand-me-downs. We traded at a delicatessen store where, occasionally, I had to ask Mr. Schiff if he could slice an *achtel* (an eighth of a pound) of corned beef into six slices, one for each of us in the family. Mr. Schiff could perform that butcher's miracle, and a slice of a sixth of an eighth of a pound of corned beef was so paper thin that you could see the light through it if you held it up—but if you held it up, it shredded in your fingers. For a passing delicacy, I would walk a mile to the baking plant of Drake's Cakes, and there, at the factory, could buy two pounds of day-old stale cake for ten cents. A mile the other way was a chocolate factory. For a dime, you could buy old and moldy chocolates about to be thrown out; but such a dime for chocolate was an extravagance. Movies vanished entirely from the family budget—so the children read books instead. I began to walk back and forth to the Latin School, four miles away, whenever the weather was fair, to save the nickel fare. And as one walked to school by Roxbury Crossing and through the factory district, one saw that the shoe plants were closed down, no workers going in and out, no smoke from the cold smokestacks that silhouetted my route. The year I entered Latin School, in 1928, there were 948 shoe factories in Greater Boston; a year later, only 817. By 1930, in the city of Boston there were only eight thousand shoe workers; by 1940, only half that number.

What I saw and what I felt had no connection at all with what I had learned of American history. The evidence before me said that Papa was right—

Bathgate Avenue, Bronx, New York, 1936: A "second settlement" Eastern European Jewish urban area in New York to which first generation immigrants moved away from the crowded "first settlement" tenements on the Lower East Side. Photograph by Arthur Rothstein. Credit: LC

East 105th Street, Cleveland, about 1925: This is a "second settlement" Eastern European Jewish urban area. *Credit:* The Jewish Community Federation of Cleveland

Apartments, Boston, about 1925: These three-decker apartments were typical of "second settlement" Jewish neighborhoods in Boston. *Credit:* AJHS

The Jewish Center and Synagogue, Cleveland, about 1930: Located on East 105th Street in the "second settlement" Eastern European Jewish community, Congregation Anshe Emeth was a Conservative synagogue with an associated Jewish Center. *Credit:* Park Synagogue, Cleveland

capitalism had ruined us. Capitalism did not care what happened to us. No one cared what happened to us. I worked on off-school days and during the school vacations for a house renovator, a small-time contractor who had me on the job from eight in the morning until the house was scraped of its old wallpaper, its crumbling plaster gouged out and re-spackled; for a twelve-hour day I was paid two dollars, and glad to have it. I was lucky—until the little contractor went broke, too, and that was the end of that job. People hungered. Lives ended.

The Depression was too immense an event to grasp. Our streets and my friends hived with young adolescents who were joining either the Young People's Socialist League (YPSL), or the Young Communist League (YCL) or the Young Worker Zionists, whose song ran: "Off we go to Palestine—the hell with the Depression." American politics seemed to offer nothing. When I was sixteen or seventeen, I visited the local Democratic Party storefront on Blue Hill Avenue, the first political headquarters I ever entered. I might get a job, I thought, by getting into politics—and a thug grabbed me by the shoulders, kicked me so hard that the base of my spine still tingles at the memory, and said that they didn't want any goddamn kids around this place. It must have been the year that Franklin D. Roosevelt was building his 1932 campaign for the Presidency; I now know he had Curley and the Boston machine with him; but from where I walked the streets, I could not see what Franklin Roosevelt would do, and I loathed the whole system. Revolution, only revolution, would save us—but how did you connect revolution with what Miss Fuller and Mr. Nemzoff taught of American history?

It was worse when my father died. I was sixteen then. My diary records a one-line sentence, June 16, 1931: "Pa died today." And the memory of the year after he died I cannot, despite every effort, bring back. I pushed it out of mind long ago. I know, technically, that my mother let me finish my last year of school before I went to work—I was to graduate in the class of 1932 at the Boston Latin School. But in dignity the price of my finishing the Latin School, instead of going out to hunt work, was crushing. We were on home relief.

It was shameful—we, of a learned family, on home relief. With my father's death, we were five left. And for five people the city of Boston gave eleven dollars a week. We survived on eleven dollars a week, for my grandmother, upstairs, had ceased demanding that we pay rent. But to get home relief, in those days, my mother had to take a streetcar (ten cents each way) downtown to the relief office. And there, after standing in line for hours, she would receive a five-dollar greenback and six ones. Each week she made the trip, each trip brought her home desolate. It was intolerable. My marks at school rose spectacularly in the last year of misery. If there was no father left, I had to make it on my own. If I wanted to go to college, I would have to do it by scholarship, and scholarship meant getting good marks. Given this need, my marks jumped from a sixty to a ninety average. My final College Board examinations brought marks then called "highest honors." And immediately after graduation, there was an acceptance to Harvard. But the acceptance carried no scholarship money; no stipend, nothing but the right to enroll. And so the certificate became a trophy to put away in a drawer. The problem was how to get off relief—and yet survive.

The struggle to survive spared no one. My sister, Gladys, a woman of extraordinary gifts, had to leave college after her first year to find a job as a library assistant. My two younger brothers—Robert, then nine, and Alvin, twelve—were conscripted to sell newspapers at the corners before going to school. That meant they had to be roused from bed before six each morning, and thrust out into the winter cold. And I woke at five each morning, for I had won from the local news wholesaler the right to run the streetcars on the tough ride from Franklin Park to Egleston Square, peddling papers . . .

Newspapering lasted for over a year. I would scream the headlines; and occasionally, when I saw an old Latin School friend taking the trolley in town to Boston University or Massachusetts Institute of Technology, I would scream the headlines in Latin. I could sell almost as many papers, if I put emotion into the call, by shrieking, *"Quo usque, O Catilina, tandem abutere patientia nostra, quem ad finem nos eludet iste furor tuus . . ."* as I could by shrieking anything else. But my old schoolmates of the Latin School ignored me. I was a dropout, they were college day students . . .

And then, in the fall of 1934, when I was two years out of Latin School, confused, angry and on my way to nowhere, two things happened. Harvard College gave me a scholarship of $220 and the Burroughs Newsboys Foundation gave me a college grant of $180 (I still ran a newspaper route). Two-twenty and one-eighty came to four hundred dollars—which was the exact fee for a year's tuition at Harvard, and so I could try that for a year. Harvard then required a bond that a freshman would do no property damage there, and luckily, our neighbor, Mrs. Goldman, who owned a house down the street, was willing to sign such a bond. So in September of 1934, cutting a corner here and amplifying a hope there, I took the subway into Harvard Square to enroll.

I have, in the years since, served as an overseer of that majestic institution Harvard University, a member of the Honorable and Reverend Board of the most ancient corporation in the Western world, the chosen thirty who tip their silk hats as they file, two by two, past the statue of John Harvard on Commencement Day in the Yard. But it was a better Harvard I entered in the 1930s than it was later, when I sat on its Board of Overseers, or than it is today.

One emerged, as one still does, from the subway exit in the Square and faced an old red-brick wall behind which stretched, to my fond eye, what remains still the most beautiful campus in America, the Harvard Yard. If there is any one place in all America that mirrors better all American history, I do not know of it . . .

Students divide themselves by their own discriminations in every generation, and the group I ran with had a neat system of classification. Harvard, my own group held, was divided into three groups—white men, gray men and meatballs. I belonged to the meatballs, by self-classification. White men were youngsters of great name; my own class held a Boston Saltonstall, a New York Straus, a Chicago Marshall Field, two Roosevelts (John and Kermit), a Joseph P. Kennedy, Jr. The upper classes had another Roosevelt (Franklin, Jr.), a Rockefeller (David, with whom I shared a tutor in my sophomore year), a Morgan, and New York and Boston names of a dozen different fashionable pedigrees. Students of such names had automobiles; they went to Boston deb parties, football games, the June crew race against Yale; they belonged to clubs. At Harvard today, they are called "preppies," the private-school boys of mythical "St. Grottlesex."

Between white men above and meatballs at the bottom came the gray men. The gray men were mostly public-high-school boys, sturdy sons of America's middle class. They went out for football and baseball, manned the *Crimson* and the *Lampoon*, ran for class committees and, later in life, for school committees and political office. They came neither of the aristocracy nor of the deserving poor, as did most meatballs and scholarship boys. Casper Weinberger, of my class of 1938, for example, was president of the *Crimson* and graduated magna cum laude; he later became Secretary of Health, Education and Welfare, but as an undergraduate was a gray man from California. John King, of the same class of 1938, was another gray man; he became governor of New Hampshire. Wiley Mayne, an earnest student of history, who graduated with us, was a gray man from Iowa, later becoming congressman from Sioux City. He served on the House Judiciary Committee that voted to impeach Richard Nixon—with Wiley Mayne voting to support the President. The most brilliant member of the class was probably Arthur M. Schlesinger, Jr., who defied categorization. Definitely no meatball, Schlesinger lacked then either the wealth or the savoir-faire of the white men. Indeed, Schlesinger, who was to go on to a fame surpassing that of his scholar father, was one who could apparently mingle with both white men *and* meatballs. In his youth, Schlesinger was a boy of extraordinary sweetness and generosity, one of the few on campus who would be friendly to a Jewish meatball, not only a liberal by heredity, but a liberal in practice. Since Wiley Mayne, Arthur Schlesinger and I were all rivals, in an indistinct way, in the undergraduate rivalry of the History Department, I followed their careers with some interest. Mayne was a conservative, tart-tongued and stiff. I remember on the night of our Class Day Dance, as we were all about to leave, he unburdened himself to me on "Eastern liberals who look down their long snob noses on people like me from the Midwest." Over the years Mayne grew into a milder, gentler, warmer person until in his agony over Nixon, wrestling with his conscience on whether to impeach or not, he seemed to be perhaps the most sensitive and human member of the Judiciary Committee. Schlesinger, by contrast, developed a certainty about affairs, a public tartness of manner associated with the general liberal rigidity of the late sixties that offended many—and yet, for all that, he remained as kind and gentle to old friends like myself, with whose politics he came profoundly to disagree, as he had been in boyhood. Both Schlesinger and Mayne, the liberal and the conservative, were always absolutely firm in their opinions. I, in the years starting at Harvard, and continuing in later life, wandered all through the political spectrum, and envied them both for their certainties.

I find some difficulty in describing what a "meatball" was. Meatballs were usually day students or scholarship students. We were at Harvard not to enjoy the games, the girls, the burlesque shows of the Old Howard, the companionship, the elms, the turning leaves of fall, the grassy banks of the Charles. We had come to get the Harvard badge, which says "Veritas," but really means a job somewhere in the future, in some bureaucracy, in some institution, in some school, laboratory, university or law firm.

Conant was the first president to recognize that meatballs were Harvard men, too, and so he set apart a ground floor room at Dudley Hall where we could bring our lunches in brown paper bags and eat at a table, or lounge in easy chairs between classes. The master of this strange enclave of commuting Irish, Jewish and Italian youngsters from Greater Boston was a young historian named Charles Duhig, whose argument was that the most revolutionary force in history was the middle class. Duhig had contempt for the working class ("slobs"), disdain for the upper class. His theory held that modern history is carried forward chiefly by the middle class, their children, and what moves them to the future. In us, his wards, he had a zoo of specimens of the mobile lower middle class and he enjoyed watching us resist Communist penetration.

Dudley Hall was plowed regularly by Harvard's intellectual upper-class Communists, who felt that we were of the oppressed. Occasionally such well-bred, rich or elite Communist youngsters from the resident houses would bring a neat brown-paper-bag lunch and join us at the round tables to persuade us, as companions, of the inevitable proletarian revolution. Duhig, our custodian, welcomed their visits because he knew his scholarship boys could take care of such Communists in debate as easily as they could take care of the Republican youngsters who staffed the *Crimson*. We were Duhig's own middle class in the flesh—hungry and ambitious. Most of us, largely Boston Latin School graduates, knew more about poverty than anyone from Beacon Hill or the fashionable East Side of New York. We hated poverty; and meant to have no share in it. We had come to Harvard not to help the working classes, but to get out of the working classes. We were on the make. And in my own case, the approach to Harvard and its riches was that of a looter. Harvard had the keys to the gates; what lay behind the gates I could not guess, but all that lay there was to be looted. Not only were there required courses to be attended, but there were courses given by famous men, lectures open to all, where no one guarded the entry. I could listen. There were museums to be seen, libraries and poetry rooms of all kinds to tarry in—and stacks and stacks and stacks of books. It was a place to grab at ideas and facts, and I grabbed at history.

IV/3

The Jewish Heritage in America

1920's. Morris Raphael Cohen, distinguished professor of philosophy at the City College of New York, gave his personal interpretation of Jewish adaptation to conditions of life in the United States.

So long as the Jews were shut up in their ghettos and excluded from the universities they had no chance to make significant contributions to the life of science. But when ghetto gates and university doors were opened there were special factors which led the Jews to make extraordinary contributions to the development of modern science.

In the first place the pursuit of science depends to a large degree on communal respect for the scientist. In this the Jews have the advantage of a highly favorable tradition. Ever since the synagogue has taken the place of the temple the Jews have always regarded the scholar with great reverence. This traditional respect for scholarship readily transforms itself under new conditions into a respect for intellectual life, of which the pursuit of science is a part.

A second element in the scientific endeavor is the element of zest or adventure. The Greeks, when they made their great contribution to science, were a commercial people traveling from one country to another and thus liberating their minds from complete subservience to customary or inherited views. So it has

Family Portrait, about 1940: Residents of a small town in Connecticut. *Credit:* LC

Cowboy Suits, 1937: Walter and Peter Marks wearing costumes given to them by their Aunt Rosie. *Credit:* Daisy Marks

Returning from the Hunt, 1932: Albert Weinberg returning to his home in Detroit with a deer that he shot in Northern Michigan. *Credit:* Merrill Winton

been with the Jews, who since the end of the eighteenth century have been a people on the move. Breaking away from old routines, the Jews have been spiritual explorers ready to appraise and enter new realms of thought. It is thus that they entered the field of science as a result of the enlightenment which began with Mendelssohn. It is thus that the Russian Jews in the liberal days of Alexander II flocked to the universities. Something of this sort is now going on in this country despite many obstacles, external and internal.

In this connection it is interesting to note the prominent part that Jews have taken in new and revolutionary movements in science. Jews such as Einstein, Levi-Civita, Minkowsky, Michelson, and Ehrenfest, in relativity, quantum and statistical mechanics, and atomic research, Jacques Loeb in biology, Peano and Sheffer in mathematical logic, Boas, Lowie, Sapir, Kroeber, Goldenweiser, Durkheim and Lévy-Bruhl in anthropology, Ricardo and Marx in economics, and, in the fields of jurisprudence, Brandeis, Cardozo, Ehrlich, Stammler, Kantorowicz, Hohfeld and Freund, are not merely great names but identified as explorers in hitherto uncharted realms.

Such being the fact, and believing as I do that science has done much to lighten human life, spiritually as well as physically, I have not been able to embrace the assimilationist idea that Jews should give up as quickly as possible all those characteristics which distinguish them from their non-Jewish neighbors. Of course if all Jews were to retire to farms their "visibility" in American life would diminish and points of irritation leading to anti-semitism would also diminish. If we should cease to value higher education, the number of Jews in the professions would decline and a common source of rabble-rousing would lose whatever statistical base it now has. But why should good Americans object to our Norwegian immigrants, with their great maritime tradition, supplying more than their proportionate numbers to American shipping? Or why should we object to the concentration of Scottish immigrants in the engineering profession, or to the fact that the Irish have more than their proportional share in our police forces, where their loyalty and courage contribute conspicuously to the public good? If the traditional Jewish love of learning is of value to a liberal civilization, is it not better for the Jews to maintain it, and perhaps transmit it to other portions of the population, rather than retreat from it as a source of danger?

I have always sympathized with the feelings, if not with the arguments, of those who oppose assimilation as an ideal. Of course everyone living in this country and seeking to share fully in its life and in the responsibility of citizenship must try to assimilate American ways of earning a living, dressing, eating, recreation, newspaper reading, and use of the English language. Even con-servative Jewish rabbis have introduced the sermon as a regular part of their religious services, though that was not the custom of the Orthodox before they came to this country. In that literal sense of the word we are all assimilationists. On the other hand, it seems an entirely vain and undignified attitude to attempt to imitate the manners or mores of those about us, if that means ignoring our own past experience and traditions which have molded us. Not only does self-respect militate against such an attitude but we can be better Americans, if, instead of being blind imitators, we approach American civilization critically and try to contribute something distinctive to the general fund of its spiritual goods.

What that contribution shall be cannot be fixed in advance. I am myself inclined to believe that the Jewish tradition of high respect for, and internal interest in, the intellectual life for its own sake—derived from the Hebrew idea that study is a form of divine worship—is a valuable influence mitigating the American acquired habit of glorifying narrowly practical values. Others think that the Jewish zeal for social reform or social justice, or for the arts and sciences, will probably be our most valuable contribution. But this issue can be resolved only by time. Today we can only say that if the Jew has any distinctive gifts or historically inherited traits, he will show them to the best advantage if he has an opportunity to choose freely from the elements of both the Jewish and the American traditions.

To the extent that such opportunity is held open, the process of assimilation is, to quote a phrase of Justice Holmes's, "only a necessity and not a duty." Assimilation is a poor ideal, but it cannot be denied as a fact, at least a long-range fact.

I am no longer shocked to see a Reform rabbi eat ham. Nor am I shocked by intermarriage, which so many of my Zionist friends exemplify. Yet I am less than enthusiastic about a good many of the changes in Jewish attitudes that mark the process of assimilation. For two thousand years the Jews have admired scholarship and have looked up to the *Talmud Chocham* (the scholar or searcher after wisdom) as a leader in the community. It seems to me that this Jewish tradition, under which you find scholars among shoemakers, is worth preserving. The people of Neshwies, in the days of my childhood, wore rags on their feet and ate white bread only on the Sabbath, but no child went without schooling. That subordination of material things to spiritual values has made it possible for Jews to survive unprecedented calamities with dignity and self-respect. But in this country, which has relatively recently been conquered from nature, and where people have had to build anew the physical basis of civilized life, it has been the practical man who has been most admired. The result is that the scholar, the contemplative per-son, is often regarded as a nut (I think that is the official name).

I remember a professor of my college—to be sure, a professor of military training, but I think he was typical of American instructors—addressing the student body one day and saying, "If you want to be a he-man, go in for football; if you want to be a nut like Einstein, stick to the books."

Practically, this means that in American national life scholars are not accorded a very high place. We do not even trust them to run our educational institutions, but usually put men of property on the supreme governing boards. A recognition in recent years of the need of scholars in government was quickly followed by a reaction against "brain trusters."

We Jews in imitation of American ways have gone much farther and have made no room at all for the scholar in our communal affairs, leaving the communal will to be determined entirely by gifted orators, journalists, or men of affairs whose philanthropies give them deserved distinction. I do not doubt that many of these leaders are possessed of a good deal of shrewd wisdom. But a man may be a persuasive orator or well informed and wise in business affairs and yet not have the requisite insight into issues that require long historical and other study. Moreover, while we cannot ignore the lessons of experience which men of affairs accumulate, it is not good to be guided in practical affairs entirely by practical people. For the man who has his nose to the grindstone in the marketplace cannot usually see far enough. We need also other-worldly people who look ahead and are not too enmeshed in the immediate situation. This, historically, has been the role of the rabbi. But today the Jewish people are divided with regard to religion, and even those who derive comfort from the rabbi's ministration will often question his authority to pass on the crucial social, political and economic problems which face us.

Despite the process of assimilation, the Jews will, for a long time to come, continue as a distinct group. This is inevitable because of the natural force of social cohesion. Jews are more likely to associate with other Jews than with Gentiles. The majority of Jewish boys are likely to keep company with and marry Jewish girls and thus group cohesion will continue and group traditions be perpetuated. The highest rate of intermarriage ever known in the heyday of German liberalism was fourteen per cent. Even if centuries of assimilation in an atmosphere of tolerance were unbroken by waves of anti-semitism, it would probably be at least eighty generations before the Jews would disappear as a distinguishable people upon the American scene. It is probable that for many centuries the Jewish group will continue to show some characteristics which will differentiate it from the rest of the population, and so long as there are differences between groups there are bound to be elements of friction. I do not regard this as necessarily evil. It is, according to the liberal philosophy, a good thing for a Christian community to have its faith challenged, as my revered teacher Thomas Davidson used to put it, by the presence of those who hold that the tradition of the Old Testament has been properly continued in the Talmud rather than in the New Testament, and *vice versa*, just as it is good for both to be challenged by the presence of agnostics and atheists. It might be even better if all of these were challenged by the resurgence of some form of polytheism such as William James preached at times, to which as a pluralist I am benevolently inclined. The Greeks were able to make their unprecedented contributions to civilization precisely because there were so many differences among them. The Jews as well as the Scots resemble them in this respect. The cause of liberal civilization in twentieth-century America will not be served by wiping out the cultural values of any minority.

Hadassah Nurses, 1922: First graduating class of Hadassah nurses in Jerusalem with Henrietta Szold in the center. *Credit:* Hadassah

The Early Struggles of Hadassah

1922. In these letters, Henrietta Szold, founder of Hadassah, the Women's Zionist Organization of America, described the precipitous state of the organization in its early years. She discussed the American Zionist Medical Unit which reached its destination during the summer of 1918; however, four years later it was still in jeopardy.

Jerusalem, January 11, 1922
At present the Medical Unit is again hanging in the balance. That means primarily that we are not getting our budget money regularly or fully. Daily Dr. Rubinow and I ask each other: what are we going to do? I am in mortal terror that Dr. Rubinow is going to throw up the job and leave me to grapple with the problems of the break-up. So I ask myself day in and day out: will the Unit live, will it die? As soon as that question is settled, and no matter which way it is settled, I shall begin to make my preparations for homegoing.

It's time for me to be going back, spiritually and physically. I want to get back to you all, I need the atmosphere in which I am taken for granted among those whom I take for granted. And I am in tatters! You will remember that I equipped myself at a time when everything was frightfully expensive, and as shabby in quality as it was expensive in price. Sometimes, lately, I have given my imagination freedom to shape my life when I get home. What am I going to do? How am I going to live?

S.S. Esperia, October 22, 1922
Somehow or other, or rather no way or other, I feel that I shall find some amelioration of conditions. Perhaps the Joint Distribution Committee has relented and will continue its subsidy

another year. Perhaps a miracle has uncovered new resources for Hadassah to tap. Perhaps somebody has died and left his fortune for the upkeep of the medical work. So many things may have happened—or not. Curiously enough, it is home news that I am always least sanguine about. In anticipation I already feel the tremor running through me which always makes me hold a letter from one of you in my hand for a moment before I pluck up the courage to open it. You see, I am still as sentimental as before.

Well, one more confession. About the Unit I am cultivating optimism; about you I force myself to be calm—to pretend that I have no tremors, when I have heard nothing from you since August; but I have neither optimism nor calm to summon to my support when I think that Dr. Rubinow is going to leave Palestine in a short month from now; and that, it appears, the whole administration of the Unit will rest upon my shoulders. Admit: it is too much for a woman of my age and disposition to face. I am not ashamed to admit that I am a coward about it. Perhaps I may still have to do what I felt like doing in Paris—decamp to America and you.

Jerusalem, December 3, 1922
Two days ago Dr. Rubinow decided to take passage on a vessel leaving Jaffa on December 10. In seven days more I shall have to carry the Unit. The task seems insupportable. We are practically bankrupt. We have completely exhausted our credit. The Zionist Organization of America continues to send us cables bidding us not to lose courage. A cable today even says some hopeful words about Joint Distribution Committee possibilities. But can we hold on until the situation in America clears up? I cannot get it out of

my head—we—that is, Hadassah here—shall be like the patient who dies after a successful operation. We have all but made up our minds that we must liquidate at once. But we haven't the money even to let go. We can't pay off salaries or tradesmen. It's appalling. And such a situation as once more I have to face with the doctors. Just as it was when I came out here two and a half years ago. They are out of bounds—at least their leaders are.

Jerusalem, December 2, 1922
I can't believe my record—that I haven't written to you for nearly four weeks. Probably it is correct, for during these four weeks Dr. Rubinow left. He fortunately could carry one bit of good news with him. By this time it has probably become known in America that Mr. Nathan Straus cabled me $20,000. In his message he said nothing about the use to which the princely sum was to be put. He simply said: "We have placed at your disposal for immediate use $20,000."

We are about £20,000 out. I know the agony of an honest bankruptcy. Hour by hour I sit in the office and count and calculate. To no purpose! I feel like a hunted animal. Can you imagine what Mr. Straus's generous cable meant? It may still save us—these $20,000 of his. If only we use them ourselves. The question is to pay salaries or to pay suppliers. Soon nobody will let us have drugs, bread, milk, and eggs on credit. And we can't even shut down any of our hospitals. Liquidation is more expensive than hanging on.

Besides Mr. Straus's cable, there is another ray of sunshine: Dr. Magnes. He has put himself entirely at my disposal. He is at the office daily, and with him I discuss every problem. He knows the Joint Distribution Committee inside out. He has a good head for figures and accounts. He has conceived for our work almost as much affection as we have ourselves. He is an excellent mediator.

Another ray of sunshine: the head office, the clerks, accountants, etc., are wonderfully loyal. They have rallied around me like an army devoted to its chiefs. And even a few of the doctors are coming out true blue in the crisis.

One of Rachel's wishes for me is: "I hope something pleasant will happen to make you happy on your birthday—a rich man leaving the million or so you need for the Unit in his will." Mr. Straus's gift almost realizes the wish, doesn't it? At least in its unexpectedness, for I should tell you that it came wholly unsolicited. I had written the Strauses a long letter about the Unit—that events had proved me not a pessimist but a prophet: witness my interview with Baron Rothschild, which I described in detail.

My guess is that my letter produced the $20,000. At all events, I do know that I did not ask for the money; of this I can be sure, for I never do. I don't remember any more what *was* in the letter. If it really produced the result, I am sorry I haven't a copy of it. I'd like to try it on a few other millionaires.

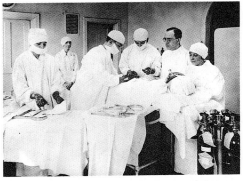

Operating Room, Philadelphia, about 1925: Mt. Sinai Hospital, Philadelphia. *Credit:* Albert Einstein Medical Center, Philadelphia

Hospital Solarium, Philadelphia, 1931: Tenth floor solarium at Mt. Sinai Hospital in Philadelphia. *Credit:* Albert Einstein Medical Center, Philadelphia

Wilshire Boulevard Temple, about 1938: This Los Angeles synagogue was typical of those being built across the country in metropolitan areas with sizeable Jewish populations during the 1920's and 1930's. *Credit:* AJA

Rural Synagogue, Newton, Connecticut, 1940: This typical American wooden clapboard building in a rural New England landscape is adapted for use as a synagogue. It serves a congregation of 15 families. Photograph by Jack Delano. *Credit:* LC

Is There a Jewish Point of View?

1934. Dr. Albert Einstein, the leading scientific genius of the 20th century, described his position on Jewish life.

In the philosophical sense there is, in my opinion, no specifically Jewish point of view. Judaism seems to me to be concerned almost exclusively with the moral attitude in life and to life. I look upon it as the essence of an attitude to life which is incarnate in the Jewish people rather than the essence of the laws laid down in the Torah and interpreted in the Talmud. To me, the Torah and the Talmud are merely the most important evidence of the manner in which the Jewish concept of life held sway in earlier times.

The essence of that conception seems to me to lie in an affirmative attitude to the life of all creation. The life of the individual only has meaning in so far as it aids in making the life of every living thing nobler and more beautiful. Life is sacred, that is to say, it is the supreme value, to which all other values are

subordinate. The hallowing of the supra-individual life brings in its train a reverence for everything spiritual—a particularly characteristic feature of the Jewish tradition.

Judaism is not a creed: the Jewish God is simply a negation of superstition, an imaginary result of its elimination. It is also an attempt to base the moral law on fear, a regrettable and discreditable attempt. Yet it seems to me that the strong moral tradition of the Jewish nation has to a large extent shaken itself free from this fear. It is clear also that "serving God" was equated with "serving the living." The best of the Jewish people, especially the Prophets and Jesus, contended tirelessly for this.

Judaism is thus no transcendental religion; it is concerned with life as we live it and as we can, to a certain extent, grasp it, and nothing else. It seems to me, therefore, doubtful whether it can be called a religion in the accepted sense of the word, particularly as no "faith" but the sanctification of life in a supra-personal sense is demanded of the Jew.

But the Jewish tradition also contains something else, something which finds splendid expression in many of the Psalms, namely, a sort of intoxicated joy and amazement at the beauty and grandeur of this world, of which man can form just a faint notion. This joy is the feeling from which true scientific research draws its spiritual sustenance, but which also seems to find expression in the song of birds. To tack this feeling to the idea of God seems mere childish absurdity.

Is what I have described a distinguishing mark of Judaism? Is it to be found anywhere else under another name? In its pure form, it is nowhere to be found, not even in Judaism, where the pure doctrine is obscured by much worship of the letter. Yet Judaism seems to me one of its purest and most vigorous manifestations. This applies particularly to the fundamental principle of the sanctification of life.

It is characteristic that the animals were expressly included in the command to keep holy the Sabbath day, so strong was the feeling of the ideal solidarity of all living things. The insistence on the solidarity of all human beings finds still stronger expression, and it is no mere chance that the demands of Socialism were for the most part first raised by Jews.

How strongly developed this sense of the sanctity of life is in the Jewish people is admirably illustrated by a little remark which Walter Rathenau once made to me in conversation: "When a Jew says that he's going hunting to amuse himself, he lies." The Jewish sense of the sanctity of life could not be more simply expressed.

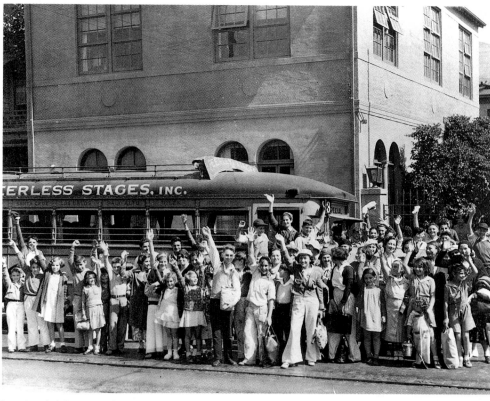

Leaving for Summer Camp, about 1933: Children's summer camp organized by the Oakland California Jewish Community Center. *Credit:* WJHC

CRISCO RECIPES

for the
JEWISH HOUSEWIFE

PROCTER & GAMBLE
Cincinnati, Ohio

Copyright 1933
The Procter & Gamble Co.

Crisco Recipes, 1933: Packaged food manufacturers like Procter & Gamble prepared special recipe books to encourage Jewish housewives to use their products. *Credit:* AJHS

Inspecting Passover Wine, Brooklyn, 1945: Rabbi S. Cohen at the Manischewitz Winery in Brooklyn inspecting Passover wine. *Credit:* LC

Confirmation Class, Denver, 1921: Confirmation class of Congregation Beth Hamedrosh Hagadol, Denver. *Credit:* Congregation Beth Hamedrosh Hagadol and Rocky Mountain Jewish Historical Society

Confirmation Class, Philadelphia, 1925: Confirmation class of Congregation Beth Shalom, Philadelphia. *Credit:* YIVO

Country Club Dinner, 1921: The Losantville Country Club continues to be the citadel of Cincinnati's German Jewish society. At this formal dinner in 1921 members of some of the most prominent German Jewish families were present: Fechheimers, Freibergs, Friedlanders, Josephs, Macks, Ortons, Pollaks, Ransohoffs, Seasongoods, Sterns and Westheimers. *Credit:* Daniel J. Ransohoff

Wedding, New York, 1932: Daisy Glatzer and Duke Marks being married in the chambers of Judge William S. Evans on April 23, 1932. *Credit:* Daisy Marks

Wedding, New York, 1942: Amy Jacobs and Eugene Lynn were married in the Hotel Pierre on March 20, 1943. Her daughter, Robin, was married in the same room in the same dress in 1974. *Credit:* Robin and Larry Blumberg

Wedding, New York, 1930: Dorothy Feiner on the day of her marriage to Richard Rodgers. *Credit:* Mrs. Richard Rodgers

Wedding, Fort Worth, Texas, 1924: Wedding of Labe H. Golden and Bessie Antweil in Forth Worth, Texas. *Credit:* Mr. and Mrs. L.H. Golden, Corsicana, Texas, from a copy at University of Texas, Institute of Texan Cultures

Silver Wedding Anniversary, New York, 1926: Cornelia and Sigmund Glatzer celebrating their 25th wedding anniversary at the Biltmore Hotel. It was a grand affair with marvelous food and music. Mrs. Glatzer wore a sequined dress from Saks Fifth Avenue and her daughter, Daisy, wore a dress that she had made herself. *Credit:* Daisy Marks

Mr. and Mrs. Adolph Ochs, Madrid, about 1925: Mr. and Mrs. Ochs on the left are seen leaving the royal palace after an audience with the king. Adolph Ochs rose from newsboy and printer's apprentice to become publisher and controlling owner of *The New York Times* in 1896. It was under his aegis that the newspaper achieved its standards of excellence which continue to be maintained by family descendants. *Credit:* AJA

Charles Lindberg and Harry Guggenheim, 1928: Charles Lindberg, who had completed his solo transatlantic flight the previous year, seen here with Harry Guggenheim, a member of the highly successful mining family, arriving at Bolling Field to attend the International Civil Aeronautics Conference. *Credit:* AJA

Max Baer, 1933: Max Baer on the left with Max Schmeling of Germany, former heavy weight champion. In 1934, Baer beat Primo Carnera of Italy to become the world heavy weight champion, a title that he retained until the next year. *Credit:* AJA

Mr. and Mrs. Julius Rosenwald, 1926: Mr. and Mrs. Rosenwald arriving on the S.S. Aquitania in New York. At that time he was Chairman of the Board of Directors of Sears, Roebuck & Company. In 1895, he had acquired an interest in the firm which had then recently been established as a mail order business. Eventually, it became the largest retail merchandising organization in the world. *Credit:* LC

Justice Benjamin Cardozo, about 1925: He was born in New York City where his ancestors had settled before the Revolutionary War. A distinguished lawyer and judge; President Herbert Hoover appointed him to the U.S. Supreme Court in 1932. During his term on the court, he provided a bulwark in defense of New Deal legislation. *Credit:* AJA

Ellis Gimbel, about 1925: A leading member of the Philadelphia family which operated department stores along the East Coast. *Credit:* LC

Rabbi Epstein, 1927: Rabbi M.M. Epstein of Tulsa, Oklahoma. *Credit:* LC

"Mode of the Moment" Dresses

1199
A NEW and unusual fabric, Velcherie, with a pronounced self-stripe, is kit fox and black. The cuffs, the tunic and skirt openings are edged with brocaded silver cloth. Chenille tassels emphasize the straightness of the silhouette.
$45.00

1205
CHIFFON velvet in brown or black, with panels made from heavy Italian silk lace shawls. The fur-edged collar and cuffs are also made of this lace, and a fur-edged cabochon at the waist adds interest to the back of the dress.
$59.50

Individualized Style

IN the handling of the rich and stately fabrics which dominate the mode for late Fall, Moshontz again displays the creative resourcefulness of the inspired designer.

Unequalled in his mastery of the prevailing straight-line silhouette, Moshontz brings to his creations a piquant and vivacious individuality which is eloquently expressive of the American woman in this light-hearted era.

The two Moshontz models here illustrated are typical — but there are many others, at similar and at lower and higher prices, now on display at leading stores and shops.

THE MOSHONTZ BROS. COMPANY
CLEVELAND
New York Office, 141-145 West 36th Street

N·SOBEL·INC
22-24 WEST 27th ST.
NEW YORK

The Secret of Our Success
is that
WE CAN SUPPLY AT ALL TIMES
THE MANUFACTURING FUR TRADE
THE CLOAK AND SUIT TRADE

with

**THE RIGHT KIND OF FURS
AT THE RIGHT TIME
AT THE RIGHT PRICES**

We respectfully invite you to seek the proof in our store when next you are in need of raw or dressed skins

CHICAGO OFFICE
PALMER HOUSE

Printzess
COATS AND SUITS

Look for the label. It is the identification of a smart garment, and your assurance of quality. Ask for Printzess apparel by name.

PRINTZ offers this interpretation of the new blouse wrap. This is but one of the many Printzess models which a leading merchant in your city is featuring this Fall. His store also features Printzess-Travechure wraps for travel and sport wear, and Printzess-Petite for the requirements of the shorter figure. The Printz-Biederman Company, Cleveland and New York.

DISTINCTION IN DRESS — SINCE 1893

"A Garment is no finer than its Fabric"

For Summer Evening Wear
Haas Brothers'

Modern Elegance Chiffon Prints

are translated into gowns of sheerest charm

Produced by

Haas Brothers
FABRICS CORPORATION

These fabrics by the yard at retail silk departments— also in made-up garments

Fifth Avenue
New York

Monte Carlo
FLOCK
VOILE
Registered

A New Dress Delight for Summer Days

ADD to the crisp daintiness of fine voile a design that is a delicate tracery of tiny dots that look like Pearls—and you have this new and delightful fabric. Here is a voile both beautiful and practical—in a dozen distinct and unusual patterns—in an endless variety of bright summer colors — washable, serviceable. You can use it for the whole dress or combine it with plain color voiles.

Ask for Monte Carlo Flock Voile by name at the fabric counters of good stores everywhere and in made up garments that bear the Monte Carlo Flock Voile label to assure you of lasting style and service.

Write for Style Booklet

MAX SCHWARZ TEXTILE CO.
122-124 FIFTH AVENUE
NEW YORK

YOU can't enjoy Fall Sports unless you're comfortably dressed...and you might as well stay home if you're not smart... So we've sketched four Crystal Creations that will help you start the season right. ¶ Each costume is developed in a combination of soft imported woolens, giving you a choice of the new romantic color contrasts brought out at the last Paris Openings. ¶ You'll find them at your favorite shop priced from thirty-nine fifty to fifty-nine fifty. ¶ If you have any difficulty, be sure to advise us.

DAVID CRYSTAL
530 SEVENTH AVENUE
NEW YORK

Advertisements, 1923-1931: Jewish entrepreneurs became principals in numerous firms associated with the women's garment industry in the 1920's and 1930's. This selection of such company ads appeared in fashion magazines. *Credit:* Costume Institute, The Metropolitan Museum of Art

Truck, about 1925: Truck belonging to Harry Lipsky, who sold furniture and pianos in Lynn, Massachusetts. *Credit:* LC

Dry Goods Store, Texas, about 1936: David M. Wolff's dry good store in Lockhart, Texas. *Credit:* Herbert H. Wolff, San Antonio, Texas, from a copy at University of Texas Institute of Texan Cultures

Grocery Store, San Francisco, about 1928: Goldberg, Bowen and Lebenbaum, located in downtown San Francisco, was one of the finest grocery stores in the nation, laden with every possible quality food imaginable. *Credit:* CALHS

Department Store, San Francisco, about 1925: H. Liebes and Company was one of San Francisco's most fashionable stores at this time. *Credit:* CALHS

David Sarnoff and others, 1921: David Sarnoff, front row, second from the left, a founder of RCA and the National Broadcasting Company, demonstrating RCA's experimental transoceanic communications station at New Brunswick, New Jersey, with a group of distinguished scientists, including Dr. Albert Einstein and Dr. Charles P. Steinmetz. *Credit:* RCA

The Early Days in Hollywood

1920's. Elmer Rice, who later developed an outstanding reputation as a Broadway writer and director, was invited by Sam Goldwyn to join a group of accomplished writers in Hollywood and prepare scripts for his films which he hoped would give his film company supremacy over Jesse Lasky's Famous Players.

For the fourth successive year I went to New Hampshire, hopeful that a summer by the quiet waters of the lake would free me from my negativism and enable me to develop a constructive work program. I had hardly arrived there when I was asked to come to New York to discuss with Samuel Goldwyn the possibility of joining his scenario department. Goldwyn told me he felt that the rapidly expanding motion picture industry was relying too much on the personality of actors and not enough on story material. He had acquired exclusive rights in the works of a group of well-known novelists. To adapt these books for the screen, he wanted writers skilled in dramatic construction and not conditioned by Hollywood routines. I listened with considerable skepticism, but he meant what he said; throughout his long, highly successful career he has given greater recognition to the writer's contribution than has any other Hollywood producer.

Some weeks later, he offered me a five-year contract, which I accepted mainly because I felt that a complete change of scene and a wholly new activity might pull me out of the bog in which I was floundering. If Goldwyn really wanted new ideas and fresh material there might be opportunities to use the motion picture medium creatively. I was curious, too, about the workings of this strange new industry that was beginning to compete with the theatre. Moreover, the prospect of seeing the Far West appealed strongly to my appetite for travel. Finally, there was the economic

Adolph Zukor, 1921: Born in Ricse, Hungary, he came to the United States in 1888. He began his career by opening a group of movie houses. In 1912, he founded the Famous Players Company. In 1917, he joined Jesse L. Lasky to form Paramount, of which he was President and Chairman of the Board. *Credit:* FD

George Cukor, about 1930: Born in New York City in 1899, he established a reputation as a director on Broadway in the 1920's. In Hollywood, when sound film was introduced he began as a dialogue director. He was noted director of such stars as Greta Garbo and Katherine Hepburn. Some of his most notable films were *Dinner at Eight* and *Little Women* in 1933, *Camille* in 1936, the *Philadelphia Story* in 1940, *Born Yesterday* in 1951, *A Star is Born* in 1955 and *My Fair Lady* in 1969. *Credit:* FD

situation. Another baby was expected and I wanted to avoid drawing too heavily upon reserves. The starting salary of one hundred and fifty dollars was not lavish in Hollywood terms even then, but it was substantial in terms of purchasing power, and it advanced by stages to six hundred. I was reluctant to bind myself for so long, but I was sure that if I wanted a release I could get it, since no producer would want to go on paying an unwilling writer.

Goldwyn insisted that I report for work in mid-August, only four weeks off. We had to hurry back to New York, make arrangements for storage of our belongings, wind up personal and business matters, work out travel plans. I decided to take along my mother, who was still keeping house for Grandpa and Uncle Will. I felt that after thirty years of devotion to my family and his family she should be released from responsibility. I told my wealthy widowed Aunt Fannie that it was about time she looked after her father. An indolent, pampered woman, she was not pleased, but she could not very well refuse.

We set off at last on the four-day journey, exhausted but eager. It was our first trip beyond the Mississippi; we spent most of it on the platform of the observation car, gazing at the spectacular Western scenery. As soon as we reached Los Angeles, I called the studio. Goldwyn took the announcement of my arrival calmly; he told me to report next day. When I asked him how to get out there, he replied, "Well, listen, find out how you get out here." It was not a heartwarming welcome. As I soon discovered, it would have made no difference if I had arrived a month or two later.

Next day I did find out how to get to the studio. Goldwyn, a little more cordial now, turned me over to the scenario department, with the suggestion that I take my time about looking around and getting acquainted. Jack Hawks, head of the department, made the same recommendation. When I told him that I had to find a place to live, he assured me that I need not worry about getting down to work until I was comfortably settled.

Very quickly we found a house on Crenshaw Boulevard, then on the outskirts of the city but now in its very heart. A trolley line at the corner took me right to the gates of the studio. To my relief, the rental was not excessive. I was determined not to adopt the extravagant scale of living characteristic of Hollywood. I did not intend to become a permanent resident and hoped to add to my savings. We were pleased with the house. The front lawn and the back yard were safe playgrounds for Bobby, now nearly three. There were a lemon, an orange and a fig tree, rose hedges, fuchsias and bougainvillaea, Palm trees shaded the quiet street, beyond whose distant end rose the wooded hills behind Hollywood. It was all new and strange and interesting, quite unlike the sidewalks of New York or the pinewoods of New Hampshire.

I had wanted to avoid buying a car. But the trolley service turned out to be infrequent and irregular; further, without a car we could not go anywhere on the long weekends. So after a few weeks I reluctantly bought one. Never having attempted to drive and conspicuously lacking in mechanical aptitude, I took two or three lessons from the car dealer, applied for a license, and obtained one without being asked to pass a test. How I managed to preserve my life and the lives of others, I do not know, but except for a few crumpled fenders there were no mishaps. In time I learned to drive competently enough, but I have never learned to enjoy it. Living in the country,

Irving Thalberg, 1933: General Manager of Universal Pictures at the age of twenty-four, he later became Chief of Production at MGM and guided that studio through its transition from silent to sound film. *Grand Hotel* and *Mutiny on the Bounty* are two of his most celebrated films. He brought many stars, including Marx Brothers, Greta Garbo, Clark Gable and Joan Crawford, to fame. *Credit:* FD

Jesse L. Lasky, about 1925: After completing a transcontinental trip with his Stutz sportscar. Before entering the motion picture industry, he was a newspaper reporter, gold prospector and vaudeville promoter. In 1911, he entered a partnership with Cecil B. De Mille. With Samuel Goldwyn, they produced *The Squaw Man* in 1913. He joined Adolph Zukor to form Paramount in 1917, and was later associated with Twentieth Century Fox, RKO-Radio Pictures and Warner Brothers. *Sergeant York, Adventures of Mark Twain* and *Rhapsody in Blue* are among his most notable films. *Credit:* MOMA

I find a car a necessity, but I also find it and everything connected with motoring a great bore.

Compared to the Metro-Goldwyn-Mayer plant which superseded it, the Goldwyn studio in Culver City was a modest establishment. There were, of course, none of the great soundproof stages that came in with the talkies. The administration building, the commissary and the dressing rooms were jerry-built wooden structures, shabby by comparison with the elegant temples that replaced them. The greater part of the "lot" was vacant land, on which outdoor sets—those Western frontier streets!— were sometimes erected. The industry, as its apologists were fond of saying, was still in its infancy, though it was an infancy not unlike Gargantua's.

The studio, of course, had its galaxy of stars, only two of whom, Pauline Frederick and Madge Kennedy, had, as far as I know, been exposed to dramatic training. The others included Mary Pickford's brother Jack; her former husband's brother, Tom Moore; Olive Thomas, a great beauty; and Mabel Normand, who had graduated from Mack Sennett's

Paramount Studios, about 1928: Jews played a decisive role in the birth of the motion picture industry. Jesse L. Lasky and Adolph Zukor founded Paramount. Louis B. Mayer and Samuel Goldwyn formed Metro-Goldwyn-Mayer. Albert, Harry and Jack Warner created Warner Brothers. William Fox was the founder of Twentieth Century Fox and Marcus Loew established an extensive chain of movie theaters. *Credit:* MOMA

slapstick comedies. Most important of all, perhaps, was Will Rogers, the gum-chewing, rope-twirling, wisecracking cowboy, who had made a great reputation in the Ziegfeld Follies. He never pretended to be an actor, but relied upon his engaging personality. Personality, looks, sex appeal: these have always been the chief Hollywood assets. A skillful, patient director can extract a passable performance from almost any well-built boy or girl, however innocent of talent.

Goldwyn, in pursuit of his new policy, had challenged Jesse Lasky's Famous Players by organizing his Eminent Authors: Basil King, Gertrude Atherton, Rupert Hughes, Gouverneur Morris and Rex Beach. To adapt their works, he had made an even greater break with tradition by engaging a group of writers from the East, all of whom had had some connection with the theatre. The newcomers were Clayton Hamilton, to whom I have referred in connection with *On Trial;* Louis Sherwin, able dramatic critic of the New York *Evening Globe*; and the playwrights Charles Kenyon, Cleves Kinkead and Thompson Buchanan.

George Mooser, Mary Pickford and Douglas Fairbanks, 1923: George Mooser was a San Francisco theatrical impresario; he is seen here on a Hollywood set with two leading film personalities of the 1920's. *Credit:* WJHS

Louis B. Mayer on the set of *Ben Hur*, about 1925: Louis B. Mayer, second from the left, was one of the film industry pioneers. Here he is seen on the set of *Ben Hur,* an extravaganza with a cast of 150,000 extras and which took three years to produce. Fred Niblo, the director is to his left. Mayer was born in Russia in 1885. He operated a burlesque theater where he showed films. Later he moved to Hollywood and formed his own production company which became part of Metro-Goldwyn-Mayer. An exponent of the "star system," he is credited with discovering Greta Garbo. For seven years he was the highest paid executive in this country. *Credit:* MOMA

Ernst Lubitsch Telling a Joke, about 1935: From left to right: King Vidor, David O. Selznick, Ernst Lubitsch and Ben Hecht on a set in Hollywood. David O. Selznick was the son of Lewis Selznick, a film production pioneer. In 1939 he produced *Gone With the Wind.* Ernst Lubitsch was born in Berlin in 1892. First directing films in Germany, he was brought to Hollywood in 1923 and became one of the most successful directors of comedy, initially at Paramount and later at MGM where he made *Ninotchka.* Ben Hecht, newspaper reporter, co-authored *The Front Page.* In the 1930's he went to Hollywood to write film scripts. *Credit:* MOMA

Kenyon's crude but forceful *Kindling* was one of the first American plays with a "social" theme: a poverty-stricken woman turns thief to provide for her newborn child. Kinkead, the year after *On Trial*, had written *Common Clay*, a courtroom melodrama in which Jane Cowl made a great hit. Buchanan was the author of several successful melodramas and sentimental comedies.

The new contingent did not supplant the existing staff; it merely augmented it. Jack Hawks, head of the department and a veteran of the infant industry, was an energetic, unlettered, likable, alcoholic extrovert, well versed in all the routines and clichés of film making, and not without a certain instinct for dramatic construction. The other six or eight members of the old staff were former newspapermen, or youngsters who had "grown up" in pictures and had had no other writing experience.

Learning the ropes was not too difficult. Apart from its photographic technology, in which I took no interest and which will forever be a mystery to me, I found that picturemaking was merely a greatly simplified form of playmaking. The absence of dialogue and the rather limited aesthetic and intellectual capacity of the mass audience for whose entertainment films were designed necessitated a concentration upon scenes of action: melodramatic, comic, erotic. Wit and poetry were, of course, excluded; nuances of characterization and subtleties of motivation were not attempted; ideological conflicts were rarely and warily presented, and always with strictly orthodox resolutions.

Scenario writing, therefore, was an exercise in dramatic craftsmanship rather than a literary art, the writers often working in pairs. First came the story outline, a straight narrative based more or less upon a book or play, seldom upon original material. After much discussion and revision, the outline was turned over to a continuity writer, who broke it up into "camera angles" or "action shots"—in other words, detailed stage directions. Since the camera was still stationary, the movement had none of its present-day fluidity; each scene was rather static and self-contained. The director often used the continuity merely as a sort of general guide, improvising as he went along.

The third element in the development of the scenario was the writing of subtitles, those informative bits flashed on the screen to indicate locales and time lapses, to identify characters and establish relationships, and to supply snatches of dialogue whenever the action was not self-explanatory. The early Chaplin films are brilliant examples of kinetic storytelling that requires no verbal amplification. In most pictures, however, considerable visible dialogue was required. Sometimes the actors spoke the lines that appeared on the screen. More frequently they just improvised, or ad-libbed; or, if their spirits were high, they spoke words that were wholly at variance with the emotions they were portraying. Theatregoers who had mastered the art of lip reading discovered to their horror or delight that what was being said was not always fit for home consumption. Protests poured in and the exuberance of the players was checked.

After the filming was completed, subtitles often had to be substantially revised to make them conform to changes in action, or even in story line, made in the course of production. These revisions were made by a specialist called a title writer, whose contribution was sometimes the most important writing element. The whole impact of a picture could be changed if, at a crucial moment, a character said "Yes" instead of "No." Yet this drastic alteration could be effected merely by substituting one title card for another.

I had a hand in one of these title-writing metamorphoses. The studio made a picture based upon Wallace Irwin's *Trimmed with Red*, a heavy-handed "satire" on "parlor Bolshevism," a fashionable term that implied that any intellectual—particularly a Greenwich Villager—who was sympathetic to the Russian experiment was either a hireling or a dupe of the Kremlin. The picture was so bad that Goldwyn asked me to try to find a way to make it distributable so that some of the production cost could be recouped. In running the cuts, which amounted to more footage than had survived, I found that many of the castoff scenes dealt with the silly heroine's hobby of collecting animals. There were lovebirds, canaries and cockatoos, white mice and chameleons, fish and frogs, even a baby alligator in the bathtub. Brooding over this zoological abundance, I threw out parlor Bolshevism entirely and invented a new religion, Neo-Pythagoreanism, which posited the transmigration of human souls into the bodies of animals. The story now dealt with the excesses into which the lady's adherence to this exotic creed led her. I recut the whole picture, eliminating all political scenes and restoring all scenes in which animals appeared. Then I wrote a series of explanatory introductions and appropriate bits of dialogue, none of which bore any relation to the original story, but which managed to suggest the new plot. It was still a bad picture, but was now releasable. It must have brought in many times my total earnings at the Goldwyn studio.

Mr. and Mrs. Samuel Goldwyn, about 1930:
Standing at the entrance to their home in
Hollywood. *Credit:* MOMA

Mr. and Mrs. Samuel Goldwyn with their Son, about 1925: An outstanding independent film
producer, Samuel Goldwyn has emerged as a legendary personality. Born in Warsaw, Poland,
he came to this country at the age of thirteen. He entered motion pictures in 1913 in association
with Jesse L. Lasky and Cecil B. de Mille to create *The Squaw Man* which is considered to be
the first feature length film made in Hollywood. His films were elaborate and noted for the
distinguished writers whom he engaged to prepare film scripts. *Credit:* MOMA

Edward G. Robinson, about 1939: Born in
Bucharest in 1893, he came to this country at
the age of ten. Established in the theater, he
moved to Hollywood in the late 1920's. His
role as a gangster in the 1931 film, *Little
Caesar,* immortalized him as "the little tough
guy," and he appeared in 150 films. An avid
art collector, he is seen with one of his prized
paintings, Grant Wood's *Daughters of
American Revolution. Credit:* MOMA

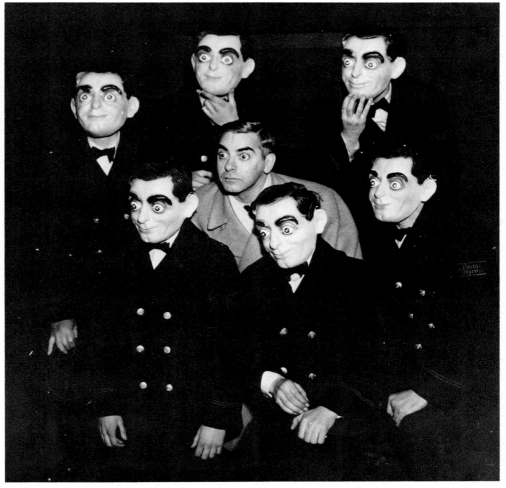

Eddie Cantor with Postal Telegraph Boys, about 1933: On his return from Hollywood to New
York, Eddie Cantor was greeted by a group of Postal Telegraph boys wearing "pop eye"
masks. Born on New York's Lower East Side in 1892, he won a musical hall amateur contest in
1907 and began touring with a black face comedy act. He starred in the *Ziegfeld Follies* of 1917,
1918 and 1919 and *Kid Boots,* a musical which opened on Broadway in 1923 and ran for three
years. His films include *The Kid from Spain* in 1933 and *Roman Scandals* in 1935. For many
years his radio and television programs were regular weekly fare. *Credit:* MOMA

Sophie Tucker, about 1925: Popular singer born in Russia in 1884 and raised in Hartford, Connecticut. She began in vaudeville with an act that mixed Yiddish and English. Her successful career lasted for nearly 50 years. Described as big, brassy and flamboyant, she became known as "the last of the red hot mamas." *Credit:* FD

Fanny Brice Arriving in Hollywood, about 1927: Being greeted by Archie Mayo, the director, on her left, and producer Jack L. Warner, one of the Warner brothers, on her right. *Credit:* MOMA

Fanny Brice, about 1925: Born in New York City in 1891, she began her career acting in Brooklyn, later she appeared in Manhattan vaudeville shows as a singer and dancer. From 1910 to 1923 she was a star in the *Ziegfeld Follies.* Brooklyn dialect became the essence of her comedy routine. On radio, she was famous as "Baby Snooks." Her life was immortalized in the Broadway production, *Funny Girl,* in 1968 and the film, *Funny Lady,* in 1975. Barbra Streisand appeared in both the play and film. *Credit:* MCNY

Fanny Brice, about 1925: In her New York apartment. *Credit:* MOMA

Warner's Theatre, New York, 1927: Crowds outside Warner's Theatre in New York waiting to see Al Jolson in *The Jazz Singer,* the first sound motion picture. *Credit:* SI

Marx Brothers on the MGM Lot, about 1935: Legendary comedians, the Marx Brothers were born in New York. They started touring vaudeville shows and made their Broadway debut in 1924. Their films which include *Animal Crackers,* 1930, *Horse Feathers,* 1932, *A Night at the Opera,* 1935 and *A Day at the Races,* 1937, are masterpieces of wild non-sequitur humor. From left to right: Harpo, a mute who relied on honks, whistles and pantomime, Groucho, the plot instigator, and Chico, who spoke with a thick Italian accent. *Credit:* MOMA

The Jazz Singer, 1927: Al Jolson appearing in *The Jazz Singer. Credit:* FD

Harry Houdini, 1926: The world-famous magician and escape artist, Harry Houdini, is seen emerging from an airtight coffin in which he was submerged in New York's Shelton Hotel swimming pool for 90 minutes. Houdini was born in Budapest and came to this country in his youth. He became famous for his extraordinary feats, escaping from shackles, ropes, chains and handcuffs while suspended head down in a tank of water, buried alive or thrown into an icy river, and he was the most popular and highest paid performer of his day. *Credit:* LC

Al Jolson, about 1927: Born in 1886, the son of a cantor, his career as a singer and film star began in circuses, minstrel shows and vaudeville. His first Broadway success occurred in 1911; his appeal was phenomenal; the Schuberts named a theater in his honor in 1921. Hollywood found his hearty, exuberant style well suited to the early talkies. He is seen here departing from Grand Central Station in New York on his way to California to appear in *The Jazz Singer. Credit:* MOMA

How the Columbia Broadcasting System Began

1928. William S. Paley's family had been successful in cigar manufacturing, but it was the new field of radio braodcasting which fascinated him. He described the origins of CBS, of which he was Chairman and chief operating officer for over fifty years.

The first radio I ever saw was a primitive crystal set. A friend clamped the earphones on me and I was dumbfounded. It was hard to believe that I was hearing music out of the air and I never got over the surprise and the fascination. I quickly found someone to build such a set for me, because there were no ready-made radio sets at the time. As a radio fan in Philadelphia, I often sat up all night, glued to my set, listening and marveling at the voices and music which came into my ears from distant places. A few years later I became a sponsor.

While my father and uncle were on a trip in\Europe, leaving me more or less in charge, I bought an hour program to advertise La Palina cigars on the local station WCAU. Cost? The munificent sum of $50 per broadcast. But when they returned, my uncle upon going over the books immediately spotted the new expenditure. "What kind of foolishness is this?" he demanded. "Cancel it right now." Reluctantly, I followed instructions.

A few weeks later at a luncheon, my father remarked, "Hundreds of thousands of dollars we've been spending on newspapers and magazines and no one has ever said anything to me about those ads, but now people are asking me 'What happened to the *La Palina Hour?*' " A feeling of vindication rose within me, for I had argued about advertising on radio with my uncle, and to my surprise, my uncle now agreed. He admitted to my father that he had ordered me to cancel the program and that he had since been asked about the program by friends. So, he said, perhaps he had been wrong.

At about the same time, my father was approached by one of his very close friends, Jerome Louchheim, a well-known and highly successful building contractor in Philadelphia, with a personal appeal that Congress Cigar advertise its La Palinas on a small radio network in which he had recently bought a controlling interest. The network, called the United Independent Broadcasters, was still in financial difficulties in New York City and Louchheim asked for my father's advertising as a token of his personal friendship. So, my father agreed to advertise and put me in charge of organizing a program. I put together a program called *The La Palina Smoker*, a half-hour show that featured an orchestra, a female vocalist whom we called "Miss La Palina," and a comedian as a master of ceremonies. It turned out to be a pretty good show.

Over the next six months I made frequent trips to the United Independent Broadcasters' offices in New York and

William S. Paley, about 1928: Although he began his business career in his family's cigar manufacturing company in Philadelphia, he was captivated by the opportunities in the newly born radio industry of the late 1920's. He created the Columbia Broadcasting System and has been a dominant force in radio and television broadcasting for nearly fifty years. *Credit:* UPI

became rather well acquainted with this little network and its activities. UIB had been formed by Arthur Judson, the celebrated concert manager, and a few associates, as a vehicle for putting the classical musicians he represented on the air. Incorporating the network on January 27, 1927, Judson had arranged with the Columbia Phonograph Company that in exchange for its financial backing, the network would be known on the air as the Columbia Phonograph Broadcasting System. He had managed over that first year to sign up sixteen stations as network affiliates, each of which would receive ten or so hours of air time a week from the network.

Arthur Judson and his associates had a lot of trouble getting on the air. But after eight months of strenuous preparations, the network made its debut on Sunday, September 18, 1927, with its own twenty-two-piece orchestra. That same evening, it put on an ambitious performance of the Deems Taylor—Edna St. Vincent Millay opera, *The King's Henchman*, featuring artists from the Metropolitan Opera Company. It was a gala première and a great achievement, but at a cost they were unable to bear. The UIB group

went broke and was unable to meet its payroll. Hearing of the network's financial distress, Isaac and Leon Levy, who owned station WCAU in Philadelphia, an affiliate of UIB, brought the wealthy Jerome Louchheim to the rescue. Louchheim bought an interest in the network and was elected chairman of the board of directors on November 7, 1927, and the Levys bought a smaller portion of its stock.

Shortly afterward, the Columbia Phonograph Company withdrew its participation, accepting free advertising time in payment for its interest. UIB then dropped the word "Phonograph" but continued to use the name Columbia Broadcasting System on the air. In its first full year of operation, UIB had taken in $176,737 in net sales and had paid out $396,803, for a net loss of $220,066. Louchheim had failed in all his efforts to turn the company around.

Some ten months after taking over and having bought the controlling interest in the company, he approached my father and offered to sell the network to him, saying, "Sam, why don't you buy it from me? You at least have a cigar to advertise and you can make some use out of it. I can't use it; I have nothing even to try to sell over it." My father later repeated the gist of this conversation to me, as well as his answer: he had no interest in the matter whatsoever. Louchheim had told him he had bought "a lemon," that the network's books were a mess, and that he wanted out. But my father did not want to invest *his* money in such a venture.

I became tremendously excited at the prospect and the network's shaky condition did not deter me. It was the great promise of radio itself that impelled me to act and to act immediately. I did not know what it would cost to buy control of UIB or whether Louchheim would sell it to me. But I had the money to buy it. I had about a million dollars of my own and I was willing to risk any or all of it in radio.

The source of that million dollars was a family affair. When I went to work for Congress Cigar in 1922, my father put a block of its stock in my name. As the company was privately owned by the Paley family (except for a modest amount of stock owned by Willis Andruss), Congress Cigar stock then had no known market value. Financially speaking, my shares did not impress me at the time. But in 1926, Congress Cigar went public with the sale of 70,000 shares, and the company was listed on the New York Stock Exchange. After the sale, 280,000 shares remained privately held. The following year my father arranged to sell 200,000 shares to the Porto Rican-American Tobacco Company, and my father and Uncle Jay entered into an employment contract to continue running the company for a number of years (they retired in 1931). Some of my stock went with these sales and so I came to have on my own account a little over a million dollars. This was the money I always regarded as sacrosanct, not to be spent

George Jessel, 1930: Star of musical comedy, stage and screen, George Jessel appeared on the Fleischmann Radio Hour as a guest artist. A natural story-teller, he had an endless repertoire. Born in New York in 1898 he began his career as a boy singer in vaudeville at the age of ten. *Credit:* FD

Jack Benny, about 1940: A consummate comedian, he projected the image of a self-deprecating, violin-playing, wisecracking miser; his style was based on perfect timing and supreme use of the pause. He was born in Chicago in 1894 and raised in Waukegan, Illinois. His professional career began as a violinist at the age of fifteen. After appearing in touring vaudeville shows he made films and was featured on his own regular radio and television shows for nearly thirty years. His films included: *Broadway Melody of 1935, Big Broadcast of 1938, Charley's Aunt,* 1942 and *George Washington Slept Here,* 1945. *Credit:* MOMA

or invested without my father's approval.

Nevertheless, on my own I went to see Louchheim whom I had long known as a family friend. He was much older than I, rich, and an important figure in Philadelphia, a man who did not waste words. A bit in awe of him and in view of my youth, I feared that he might think I was not serious about what I had to say. But I told him straight out: I wanted an option to buy his UIB stock, or a substantial amount of it.

Louchheim, it turned out, owned about 60 per cent of the shares in the company. I asked for just over 50 per cent, that is, just enough to secure absolute control. We settled on 50.3 per cent. He asked for $200 a share, though I had no real way to judge the value of the stock. That came to $503,000, and I must say I did not blink an eye. I was satisfied because the sum came to only about half of my personal fortune. I knew that I would have to put in more, perhaps all of what I had when I got into the network. Indeed as part of the deal with Louchheim, I agreed also to place $100,000 in acceptable securities with the American Telephone & Telegraph Company as a bond for its wire services, in place of the similar bond which Louchheim had put up. UIB itself still did not have sufficient funds for the bond. In exchange, I got Louchheim to agree to place his remaining shares in a voting trust for five years—with the important provision that the Voting Trustee would vote for directors whom I nominated—an arrangement that further secured my control and made sure that my management policies in UIB would be stable at the directors' level.

Louchheim, for his part, drove a conventional hard bargain. The price of the option he said would be $45,000, to be applied to the purchase price when I picked up the option, to be forfeited if I did not. The option was to run ten days. I am able to be so precise about these terms because I still have in my possession a copy of that option-contract. It is dated September 19, 1928. I was still in my twenty-sixth year.

I cannot recall just when I went to my father to ask his approval. Ours was an old-fashioned relationship in which he was the authority figure, especially when it concerned money I had received from Congress Cigar stock. But in this instance there was another ticklish question. The problem was how my desire to go up to New York and run UIB might affect my position as his heir-apparent in the cigar company. The fact that as a family we no longer held the controlling stock in Congress Cigar, and that my father and Uncle Jay had a limited contract to manage the business, left me somewhat freer than I might have been otherwise. Nevertheless, it was still my intention to continue in my father's footsteps. I would promise only to take a leave of absence for a few months to put the network in shape and then to leave it to be operated by a professional management while I returned to my career in the cigar business. I knew my father

expected to pass the management of the business on to me, so I had to explain my intentions to him.

On the other hand, I realized that my father would be disturbed if he thought his disapproval would embarrass me. I was troubled even by the thought of possibly disturbing him. Our relationship was then a crucial thing in my life. Family tradition, going back to my childhood, prevented either of us from knowingly giving offense to the other. It was also in our style to be polite and somewhat formal with each other. My father had always believed in giving me or letting me take responsibilities, even in fields where I had little experience. I was very conscious as a young man of my father's confidence in me. It was not an uncomplicated confidence. We had our differences in philosophic outlook. My father, a self-made man who had known adversity, was far more cautious than I and, despite his confidence in me, he thought me rather rash. He also had a strong preference for tangible things: land, factories, physical products. UIB had nothing but office furniture; no radio station of its own, no tangible properties; just prospects. So, with considerable trepidation in my heart, my plans hanging in the balance, I approached my father. I put it to him straight: did he think I should do it or not?

He asked for a day to think it over and then he surprised me. "Yes, I would do it," he declared. And he went further: he and the family would relieve me of some of the burden; they would join me in buying some of Louchheim's stock. They took approximately $100,000 worth of stock, leaving me with about $400,000 worth. Later, I asked him why he was so congenial about it and he explained: "Well, I figured that if it were a failure, you'd lose some money, but you'd have gained a lot of experience. And if it were a success, what you were going into seemed to be more interesting. It would give you a more interesting world to work in than the field I was in. So, on balance, I didn't think it was a bad risk." He also anticipated something I didn't: that if I made a go of it, I would not come back.

On September 25, I closed the deal and on the next day, September 26, 1928, was elected president of a patchwork, money-losing little company called United Independent Broadcasters.

I left Philadelphia for New York unaware that I was starting a new life. I moved into an apartment in the Elysée, a smart little hotel on Fifty-fourth Street between Madison and Park, which had one of the best French restaurants in town. The economy was booming, the stock market had begun its last wild rise before the crash, and the theatrical district, through which I passed on the way to work, was in its glory. The marquees read *Strange Interlude, Show Boat, Animal Crackers, George White's Scandals, This Thing Called Love, The Front Page* and a score of others. I attended the theater many evenings during the 1928–29 season.

Elmer Rice, about 1935: Successful playwright of the pre-World War II period, first known for his experimental play *The Adding Machine*. *Street Scene*, a tragedy of New York slum life, won a Pulitzer Prize in 1929 and was later made into a film. *Credit:* AJA

Clifford Odets, 1937: As a playwright, he, more than anyone else of his generation, expressed the hardships of the depression. *Waiting for Lefty*, a one-act play about a taxi strike brought him success in 1935. *Golden Boy*, 1937, was the story of a musician turned prize fighter. Born in Philadelphia and raised in the Bronx in New York City, he began acting at the age of fifteen. Photograph by Carl Van Vechten. *Credit:* LC

Lillian Hellman, about 1930: Born in 1905, she first worked for a publishing house and then wrote short stories. She turned to theater and some of her successes include: *The Children's Hour*, 1934, *The Little Foxes*, 1939 and *Watch on the Rhine*, 1941 which was inspired by her personal experiences during the Spanish Civil War. Recently she has written several volumes of her memoirs. *Credit:* LC

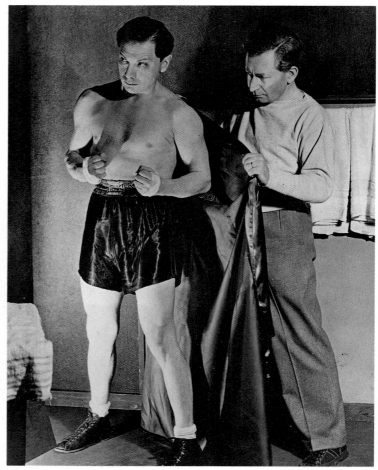

Golden Boy, 1937: A play by Clifford Odets which is the story of a musician who becomes a prize fighter, with Luther Adler, son of Jacob P. Adler of Yiddish theater fame, in the starring role. *Credit:* MCNY

Of Thee I Sing, 1931: The first Broadway musical comedy to win a Pulitzer Prize with book by George S. Kaufman and Morrie Ryskind, directed by George S. Kaufman, music by George Gershwin and lyrics by Ira Gershwin. *Credit:* MCNY

You Can't Take It With You, 1936: Original Broadway production of this comedy by Moss Hart and George S. Kaufman, directed by George S. Kaufman. *Credit:* MCNY

Sheet Music, 1931: Music by George Gershwin and lyrics by Ira Gershwin for the musical comedy, *Of Thee I Sing. Credit:* MCNY

Porgy and Bess, 1935: The original Broadway production of what has since become an American classic with music by George Gershwin, libretto by Debose Hayward, lyrics by Dubose Hayward and Ira Gershwin and directed by Rouben Mamoulian. *Credit:* MCNY

Carousel, 1945: The original Broadway production with music by Richard Rodgers, book and lyrics by Oscar Hammerstein 2nd, dances by Agnes de Mille and directed by Rouben Mamoulian. *Credit:* MCNY

Oklahoma, 1943: The original Broadway production of this musical which became an American classic with music by Richard Rodgers, book and lyrics by Oscar Hammerstein 2nd, dances by Agnes de Mille and directed by Rouben Mamoulian. *Credit:* MCNY

Jerome Kern, about 1930: Composer of popular music, born in New York City in 1885. *Show Boat,* 1927, was his greatest success. He wrote nearly one thousand songs for at least one hundred stage shows and films. *Ol' Man River* and *Smoke Gets In Your Eyes* are two of his all-time favorites. *Credit:* FD

George Gershwin and Irving Berlin, about 1926: George Gershwin was one of the outstanding musical talents of his generation whose creative career was terminated by his early death. He composed for both Broadway and symphony orchestras. His *Rhapsody in Blue,* 1924, made jazz respectable. *An American in Paris,* premiered in 1928, remains a popular piece of serious music. His Broadway musicals, *Of Thee I Sing,* 1931, and *Porgy and Bess,* 1935, have become American classics. Irving Berlin was born in Russia in 1888 and arrived in New York City at the age of five. Although he had no musical training, he has composed some of America's most popular music including: *Alexander's Ragtime Band,* 1911, *Easter Parade,* 1948 and *God Bless America,* 1950. He has composed music for numerous Broadway shows and Hollywood films. *Credit:* FD

Lorenz Hart, about 1940: Lyricist who collaborated with Richard Rodgers on many musicals including *Babes in Arms,* 1936, *The Boys from Syracuse,* 1938 and *Pal Joey,* 1940. *Credit:* FD

Around the Piano, about 1932: Composer Harold Arlen, singer Lee Wiley and band leader Leo Reisman. *Credit:* FD

Gus Arnheim Orchestra, 1932: One of the big traveling bands at the Ambassador Hotel in Los Angeles. *Credit:* FD

Benny Goodman Orchestra, 1939: His radio show, *Lets Dance* in 1934 and 1935 established Benny Goodman as the "King of Swing." Five years later his band appeared on the *Camel Caravan* radio program. Born in Chicago of immigrant parents, he became the most famous clarinetist and band leader of the 1930's and 1940's. He took music lessons as a child at the local synagogue and at Hull House, the famous settlement house. He started performing full time at the age of fourteen and formed his own band in 1933. His talent as both a jazz and classical musician is universally recognized. Here he is standing to the far right playing the clarinet. *Credit:* FD

Roger Wolff Kahn Orchestra, about 1927: Roger Wolff Kahn sixth from the left, was the son of Addie Wolff Kahn and Otto H. Kahn, the financier. *Credit:* FD

Artie Shaw and Benny Goodman, 1939: Artie Shaw and Benny Goodman, two of the leading jazz band leaders of the day at the Waldorf. Benny Goodman was the undisputed "King of Swing." Artie Shaw was a talented clarinetist and successful band leader in the 1930's and 1940's. Born in 1910 in New York, he was raised in New Haven, Connecticut. At the height of his success he withdrew from the limelight; although he continued to perform he never achieved his former prominence. *Credit:* FD

Ben Pollack Band, 1929: At the Park Central Hotel in New York. Benny Goodman is the fifth from the right. *Credit:* FD

Eddie Duchin, about 1935: A popular pianist and band leader in the 1930's and 1940's who was known for his unique piano introductions to band numbers. Military service between 1942 and 1945 interrupted his career and he was never able to regain his former popularity. *The Eddie Duchin Story,* a 1956 film, told the story of his life. His son, Peter, is a popular society pianist-band leader. *Credit:* FD

Ben Bernie Orchestra, 1932: Ben Bernie, eighth from the left, was the leader and vocalist of this group which was popular on radio in the early 1930's. *Credit:* FD

Buddy Rich and Ziggy Elman, 1941: Buddy Rich on the drums and Ziggy Elman on the cornet were two of the outstanding jazz soloists of the 1940's. Here, they appeared with the Dorsey band. *Credit:* FD

Helen Forrest, 1940: Vocalist who appeared with Benny Goodman, Artie Shaw and several other swing bands. *Credit:* FD

Lillian Roth, 1929: Actress and singer whose career was wrecked by alcoholism and eight divorces. Born in Boston in 1910, she was in show business at the age of six, billed as Broadway's "youngest star." She appeared in Earl Caroll's *Vanities* and Florenz Ziegfeld's *Midnight Frolics* as well as a number of successful Hollywood films. By the late 1930's she had disappeared from prominence. Her autobiography, *I'll Cry Tomorrow,* 1954, was an international best seller. *Credit:* FD

Abbe Lane, about 1940: Vocalist who appeared with the popular bands of the 1940's. *Credit:* FD

Kitty Kallen, about 1940: Vocalist who appeared with leading bands of the day. *Credit:* FD

Belle Baker, about 1935: Vocalist who appeared with a number of the leading swing bands of the 1930's and 1940's. *Credit:* FD

American Art and Artists in the Early Thirties

William Zorach, a leading sculptor, described his personal experiences with artists, dealers and collectors.

It was in 1930 that I had my first sculpture exhibit at Edith Halpert's new gallery on Thirteenth Street. The depression had not yet settled down over the country. I had known Edith Halpert back in 1915. She was an attractive young thing working at Macy's to help support her widowed mother and studying art nights in Leon Kroll's class at the National Academy. Sam Halpert fell in love with Edith, and although he was a man twenty years older than she, Edith, being very young and very much impressed with art and artists, married him. Sam's art was too modern for his time and there was only the Daniel Gallery to show his work. Edith went to work every day—she was then an efficiency expert at Strauss's bank. Sam stayed home and painted. He seldom sold a picture. Edith got the idea that she could sell paintings if she tried. Through friends she arranged an exhibition in a hotel lobby. It was no place for an exhibition, but she did sell a few paintings and this encouraged her. That was in 1930.

The next summer Edith and Sam went to Ogunquit, Maine. This was quite an art colony in those days—not so many summer people but lots of artists and lots of antique shops. All of us were picking up early-American furniture and antiques. Not only were they more beautiful than the regular manufactured products but they were much cheaper, and a lot of us had acquired houses and had very little to furnish them with. Hunting antiques was great sport and lots of excitement. Edith got the idea of picking up antiques and opening a little shop in New York with Bea Goldsmith, a sister of Leon Kroll's. They bought an old house on Thirteenth Street—I think Bea put up most of the money. They converted the basement into a shop and gallery. They hung Sam Halpert's pictures and Marguerite and I let them have some or ours. Gradually more artists had their work there. At first they expected the antiques to carry the art, but Edith found she could sell contemporary art; she did not need the antique business. Later on, with the help of Holger Cahill she collected and built up a market for Harnett and early-American art—folk art. She went in for Americana on the side, promoted it from the art angle, and became quite an authority. When the Rockefellers were re-creating Williamsburg, she was a great help to them and found all manner of fine and interesting folk art for them.

What to name the gallery?

Edith and Bea thought of "Our Gallery," but I said, "After all, the other galleries are all uptown. Why not call it the Downtown Gallery?"

And that is what it became. Edith was full of ideas. In order to get people into the gallery and used to coming there, she had evening talks and gatherings of artists and people interested in art and she served coffee. The critics came and the reputation of the gallery grew. A gallery thrives by the quality of its shows and the enthusiasm and personality of the dealer.

As Edith and Bea became more and more involved in gallery affairs and the business of selling, this created difficulties for their husbands. Both were older men—lethargic, and used to being taken care of. They regarded the gallery as a pleasant club and sat around there afternoons and evenings playing cards and checkers and smoking big cigars. Not only did this embarrass the girls, but they were always in the way of the customers. Finally Sam got a job teaching painting in Detroit. That solved the problem, and shortly after Edith sued for a divorce. The day the divorce came through, Edith got a telegram that Sam had died of spinal meningitis. Later Edith and Bea separated and Edith carried on alone.

One evening a man came in, looked around, and asked where they served the drinks. This was in the days of prohibition and many village speakeasies were hidden behind a pretense of business. Edith persuaded him that this was a legitimate art gallery. It seems he was very much interested in art and he became very much interested in Edith. He asked Edith if she had any Arthur B. Davies lithographs. She told him she would have some in a few days. She rushed up to the Weyhe Gallery on Lexington and Weyhe let her have a number of Davies. This man was Duncan Chandler. He became a regular visitor and customer for small things at the gallery. One day Edith told him that if she could only get a hold of a Winslow Homer somewhere she would put on a show of American watercolors and show collectors that there were men today that would hold up with Winslow Homer.

Ernest Bloch, about 1925: Composer, conductor and educator. He was born in Geneva, Switzerland and came to this country in 1916. In 1920 he organized the Cleveland Institute of Music and in 1925 became director of the San Francisco Conservatory of Music. *Credit:* AJA

Homer was selling for $10,000 and contemporary watercolors were selling for a few hundred. Chandler said he would borrow a Homer for her and he did.

One day a tall, aristocratic lady came in to see the watercolor show. Edith told her she did not know who owned the Winslow Homer, but she was sure if the person who owned it could see the contempory watercolors of Marin, Demuth, and Zorach hanging alongside the Homer, he would want to own them too.

The lady said, "I think you are perfectly right. I own the Homer and I would like to buy the other watercolors."

This was Mrs. John D. Rockefeller, Jr. and it turned out that Duncan Chandler was the Rockefeller architect. I believe Mrs. John D. was fascinated by Edith. Edith was attractive, lively, with real intelligence, and full of enthusiasm for modern art. She also sensed that Edith was not out to take advantage of her. There was a period when Mrs. John D. would come down to the gallery before Edith was up, ring the bell, and wait for her on the doorstep.

Edith built a beautiful little one-story exhibition gallery in the back yard at Thirteenth Street with a small patio between it and the front gallery. We all participated. I did the grilles and doors and Marguerite designed the floor in colored concrete in a handsome abstract pattern. The light was beautiful for sculpture as well as for paintings.

I had finished my "Mother and Child" and had my first sculpture show in this gallery in 1930. The show made quite a sensation in the art world. I exhibited all my carvings. I had about ten pieces besides my design for the frieze for the Los Angeles City Hall and the wood carving of the Schwarzenbach doors. In art and in other things I guess every dog has his day. This was my day. The publicity and appreciation was tremendous. Fame and recognition had come to me. I was under the illusion that there was a permanence in this; I did not realize that a new order would take its place and there would be new gods. I think I sold a few things. I only remember the sales that did not go through. Edith asked thirty thousand dollars for the "Mother and Child." A Mr. Bixby wanted to buy it for his garden. He had no qualms about the price but he wanted his landscape architect to see it first— most rich people are controlled by decorators and landscape architects. He wired his architect to come back from Cuba. He came and he didn't approve. He told someone afterwards that he liked the sculpture all right but he wasn't going to have Edith Halpert horning in on his customers. He persuaded Mr. Bixby to buy a classical garden piece from an English collection—the conventional garden sculpture for a rich man. So the sale didn't go through. Now I am glad it didn't. I am much happier to have it in the Metropolitan Museum, which is where it belongs—for all people to see and enjoy; but they didn't buy it until 1955.

Yehudi Menuhin, about 1924: One of the most famous prodigies of all time who has remained throughout his entire career an inestimably respected violin virtuoso. Born in New York in 1916, he was raised in San Francisco. At the age of five he began to study the violin and three years later appeared with the San Francisco Symphony Orchestra. In 1927 he studied with Adolph Busch, the German violinist, and performed in New York at Carnegie Hall to critical acclaim. Since that time he has continued to captivate audiences around the world. *Credit:* AJA

Artur Rubinstein, about 1945: The legendary virtuoso pianist. Born in Lodz, Poland, he first appeared in Berlin in 1897 at the age of eleven. His debut in the United States was with the Philadelphia Orchestra in 1906. During the next two decades he became universally recognized. Since 1937 he lived both in the USA and in Europe and continued to perform until his 90th year, both in concert and on record. *Credit:* FD

Jascha Heifetz, 1939: To musicians and laymen alike, Heifetz' name has been synonymous with the ultimate in violin virtuosity. His legendary performances have set standards which others attempt to achieve. Born in Vilna, Lithuania, in 1901, he started to play the violin at the age of three and made his debut with the Berlin Philharmonic at the age of eleven. At the outbreak of the Russian Revolution his family emigrated to the United States. From the 1920's through the 1960's Heifetz toured frequently here and abroad and fulfilled numerous recording commitments. He is seen in the Samuel Goldwyn film, *They Shall Have Music. Credit:* FD

Sol Hurok, about 1940: For decades he was America's preeminent impresario. Born in Russia in 1890, he came to this country in 1906. He managed Anna Pavlova, Isadora Duncan and Martha Graham. He brought the Sadler's Wells Ballet and Bolshoi Ballet to this country for the first time. *Credit:* FD

Vladimir Horowitz, about 1935: Brilliant and eccentric, Horowitz is considered to be one of the world's leading pianists. Born in Kiev, Russia, in 1904, he remained there until 1925. For the next two years he performed throughout Europe to wide acclaim. His American debut occurred with the New York Philharmonic at Carnegie Hall in 1928. Throughout his career he has gone into periodic retirement emerging again to demonstrate his phenomenal technique to enthusiastic audiences. President Carter invited him to perform at The White House and called him a "true national treasure." *Credit:* FD

Oscar Levant, about 1960: A fine pianist who became widely known as a panelist on radio and television shows. Born in Pittsburgh in 1906, he played the piano in his youth. Musical erudition brought him his first success when he appeared on the *Information Please* radio show as an expert. Later he moved to Hollywood and made some film appearances. Idolizing George Gershwin, he was acknowledged as the composer's definitive interpreter. *Credit:* FD

Jan Peerce, about 1950: The acclaimed tenor who was a principal of the Metropolitan Opera Company from 1941 until 1967. Born on New York's Lower East Side in 1904, he sang in the Attorney Street Synagogue choir. For fourteen years he performed as a violinist and singer in Borscht Belt resorts. In 1932 he began an eight-year association with Radio City Music Hall in New York. Through his performances and radio broadcasts of Music Hall programs he became known to millions. When traveling, he will often enter a local synagogue and volunteer to officiate as cantor. *Credit:* LC

Yiddish Art Theatre's *Stempenyu,* **1929:** When Jacob Adler, the actor, and Jacob Gordin, the author, arrived in New York in the 1890's, Yiddish theater in America took on a new life. Maurice Schwartz's Yiddish Art Theatre, active in the 1920's and 1930's, stimulated a second burst of activity. Lazar Freed, Celia Adler, wife of Jacob Adler, and Maurice Schwartz are seen here in Sholom Aleichem's *Stempenyu. Credit:* MCNY

Yiddish Writers, about 1925: A group of Yiddish writers in Chicago. H. Leivick is third from the left in the back row. *Credit:* YIVO

American Matchmaker, 1940: A Yiddish film comedy starring Leo Fuchs telling the story of a frustrated bachelor who was engaged eight times but never married. *Credit:* NCJF

Yiddish Film Poster, about 1930: There was a lively Yiddish film industry located in the United States which produced numerous films in the 1930's and 1940's. Ludwig Satz was one of the leading actors; here he appeared in the first Yiddish talking picture. *Credit:* AJHS

Motel, The Operator, 1940: A Yiddish film that tells the sad story of a garment trade worker. Motel, played by Chaim Tauber, is injured by strikebreakers when he leads a strike of cloakmakers for better conditions. His wife offers their child to wealthy people for adoption. By the time Motel is released from the hospital, his wife has died and he is unable to locate his son, but twenty years later the two are reunited. *Credit:* NCJF

Catskill Honeymoon, 1949: A Yiddish film in which a Jewish resort hotel celebrates the return of a couple of oldtimers on their second honeymoon by staging an old-fashioned Borscht Belt vaudeville show, with song, dance and comedy. *Credit:* NCJF

The Three Little Businessmen, 1924: Although many of the performers in the Yiddish theater were talented actors, productions were often highly stylized. From left to right: Rudolph Schildkraut, Boris Thomashefsky, Ludwig Satz and Regina Zuckerberg. *Credit:* MCNY

Tevye, 1939: A Yiddish film directed by and starring Maurice Schwartz which is an adaptation of Sholom Aleichem's familiar story in which one of Tevye's daughters, Khave, falls in love with the intellectual son of a local Russian peasant. Twenty-five years later this same story served as the theme for the Broadway success, *Fiddler on the Roof.* *Credit:* NCJF

What to Do About the Depression

1931. The United States established a committee which held a series of hearings on the effects of the great depression. Franklin D. Roosevelt's New Deal later gave expression to some of the ideas proposed at these hearings. Sidney Hillman, President of the Amalgamated Clothing Workers of America gave this testimony.

The Chairman. You do not agree, then with Mr. Swope's plan, which is based on the theory, as I understand it, that trade associations within individual industries can achieve the stabilization of the industries?

Mr. Hillman. Not only do I disagree, but I believe that is not feasible from the whole recorded experience of industry; which gives proof that it is impossible for any industry to meet its own problems, apart from other industries. . . .

Industry has failed to cope with the situation. In the clothing industry we have been unusually resourceful in seeking and putting into effect methods to bring about stabilization. We have gone beyond other industries in putting up employment reserves and employment exchanges. These have helped greatly in stabilizing the industry in normal times.

But even in normal times we did not succeed in achieving complete and real stabilization.

. . .

No one industry can stabilize itself. Its prosperity is dependent upon the general state of industry and of agriculture.

. . .

The problem confronting us today is to find jobs for people out of work, and to maintain a standard of living to match our productive capacity. We cannot possibly achieve this through planlessness which in the very nature of things must again lead to chaos. Economic national planning is essential to any constructive program.

. . .

Let us take the question of technological unemployment. Suppose an economic council had been set up in 1920. If it had studied the data, later covered by a report of the Committee on Recent Economic Changes, under the direction of President Hoover, they would have found an increase in productivity per person, from 1920 to 1929, of 40 per cent.

We would not have had to wait until 1929 to find that we were facing a problem. If they had taken the other figures given by the same study, they would have found that in the period of prosperity from 1923 there was not a year until 1927 when our number of unemployed was less than a million and a half, going up to over 2,000,000 in 1927.

These facts, interpreted by a committee or council responsible for bringing them to public attention, together with its recommendations, would have given us a program before 1929 . . .

The Chairman. . . . considering the proposal which is before the committee for a council which relies entirely upon voluntary coöperation, have you come to any conclusion as to whether such a council should be representative in character, or whether it should be composed of men who might be called experts in the various phases of our economic life?

Mr. Hillman. It all depends on who the experts are. If you will tell me the group of experts I can answer your question, because there is no such thing as a race of mere experts. They all have their prejudices and their own philosophy of things. I would say that whether it is composed of experts or other people, it should be representative of different interests in the country . . .

The Chairman. Would you care to outline for the committee some of the factors which you think contributed to producing the present depression?

Mr. Hillman. As I view it, the fundamental trouble is lack of planning. Assuming that we would go ahead in the province of construction, suppose we should try to put up a building such as the Empire State Building, over 100 stories high, and use the same engineering that we would use in putting up a barn on a farm, what would happen? Why, as we put up the building it would topple over. . . .

Assuming that all the industries should put in employment reserves, which I believe in, it would not have any real effect outside of just helping a little, unless we come down to the question of planning. We know that we have a population of so many; we have capacity to produce things on a certain scale, and we should run industry accordingly. I do not believe that that takes away anything from our individual theory of running industry, any more than traffic regulation takes away from our individual initiative. Anyone who wants to cross Forty-second Street and Broadway with no regard for traffic regulation will soon find no particular use for individual or any other initiative. . . .

Unless we can get planning, we are bound to have these depressions; and I certainly do not at all share the point of view of some people who accept these things as inevitable, who say they have always been so and always will continue so. That is a theory of despair. It is the same kind of theory that was held centuries ago, when they had plagues. I can visualize almost the same kind of a committee appearing when the plague broke out, and some of the representative citizens saying, 'Well, nothing can be done. It is an act of God. We will just have a third of the population carried off, and in another 10 or 20 years we will make it up, and wait for the next plague.'

. . . Those who are afraid of dictatorship—and I do not believe that the greater part of the community would like to accept any kind of dictatorship—should realize that this kind of drift may bring us into a dictatorship. The surest road to a dictatorship is just not attending to things that have to be done, or at least not finding out what has to be done. That may result in our drifting into something that none of us will be able to control.

Farm Mother, 1936: Mrs. Cohen, was the wife of the farm manager at a New Jersey U.S. Resettlement Administration Project. Photograph by Dorothea Lange. *Credit:* LC

Chicken Farmer, 1940: Mr. Swartz at the door of his chicken house in West Haven, Connecticut. Photograph by Jack Delano. *Credit:* LC

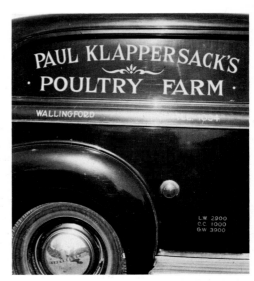

Farm Truck, 1940: Paul Klappersack's farm truck, Wallingford, Connecticut. Photograph by Jack Delano. *Credit:* LC

President Roosevelt and Judge Rosenman, 1943: Judge Samuel Rosenman, long-time advisor to President Franklin D. Roosevelt, became special counsel to the Chief Executive. They are seen posing with his certificate of office. *Credit:* NA

Roosevelt's friends and associates, although the general public had heard little or nothing of it. Howe knew all about it by this time, and he did not like the idea. One day, in conversation with the Governor, he referred to the group as "your brains trust." Shortly thereafter on a day when we were expected at Hyde Park for a conference, the Governor told the newspaper men that a group was coming up to see him. Although Howe's reference to us had been derisive, the Governor in talking with the newspaper men referred to the group by the same term, "brains trust." One of the reporters used the phrase in his news article the next day—and it stuck. The "s" of "brains" was soon dropped, and the phrase Brain Trust continued to be applied to advisers of the President even after the original group had been completely disbanded.

It was in that little suite in the Roosevelt Hotel that a good part of the spadework, gathering of material and initial drafting of campaign speeches was done. From here the material was forwarded to Roosevelt's campaign train or taken up to Albany for discussion with him.

The following letter, which the President took the time and trouble to write long after the campaign, on March 9, 1933, when the banks were all closed, when he was as thoroughly busy and occupied as at any time during his Presidency, shows what he thought of the work of the Brain Trust and the assistance it had been to him.

Working with Roosevelt

1932. As Governor of New York State Franklin D. Roosevelt included Jewish advisors among his intimates. When he was elected President, some of them including Judge Samuel Rosenman, continued their association. Although he was not immediately involved in Roosevelt's first administration, Rosenman was recognized as one of the President's principal speech writers. Here, Rosenman described events during the election campaign.

Shortly after the acceptance speech the Brain Trust set up its own headquarters in the Roosevelt Hotel in New York City. The headquarters consisted of a living room, working office, and one bedroom where we used to put up visitors who came to see us from out of town. In this suite we used to gather for dinner three or four nights a week to discuss various issues. From time to time we invited people in Washington of practical experience in government to come to talk with us about national subjects. Senator Key Pittman of Nevada and the Senator from South Carolina, James F. Byrnes, were among our visitors. Hugh Johnson became one of the regular group after

the convention. We did not always see eye to eye on all issues; often the discussions became very heated, lasted far into the night, and had to be adjourned to the next night. Robert K. Straus acted as secretary of the group and spent most of his time there during the day, co-ordinating activities, supervising mail, taking care of all the mechanics.

My own part in the work of the group was limited by my court engagements, and Moley continued to act as chairman and supervisor. That summer he was a frequent visitor at my home in Dutchess County, where we used to go over things together before driving over to Hyde Park, a short distance away.

Our headquarters were kept quite separate from those of the Democratic National Committee, which were across the street in the Biltmore Hotel. We did not attempt to participate in their political activities, and they scrupulously refrained from interfering with us in any way.

It was after the nomination that the group acquired its strange name, which like "new deal" was to catch popular fancy and become a common phrase. News of our activities had spread among

The White House
Washington, March 9, 1933

Dear Sammy:

I am waiting to hear what the Congress will do with my first bill. We worked until two o'clock this morning preparing it and it seemed queer to do this kind of work without you. After four years of such close association it is not easy to work with others.

I want you to know how grateful I am for the fine loyalty you have shown and for the unselfish service you gave me during the campaign. Even though you were not with me all the time I knew how hard you were working behind closed doors in smoke-filled rooms, and your contribution of Ray and Rex was probably the best that anyone made during the whole campaign.

I hardly need tell you that I want you to feel perfectly free to telephone or come to see me at any time. If I can be of help to you please let me know. I do hope that we will see you and Dorothy here in Washington often. Our contact has been too close to need constant correspondence or conversations. I just want you to know of my feelings toward you and my gratitude for all that you did.

As ever yours,
/s/ Franklin D. Roosevelt

Roosevelt and Lehman Election, 1936: In 1936 Franklin D. Roosevelt ran for President and Herbert Lehman for Governor of New York State on the Democratic Party ticket. They were both endorsed by the American Labor Party; this announcement appeared in *Justice*, the International Ladies' Garment Workers' Union paper. *Credit:* ILGWU

Growing Up Radical

1940's. Vivian Gornick described her family's involvement with left-wing politics. Although raised in this environment, she later became disenchanted with communism.

My father stood upright on the floor of a dress factory on West 35th Street in New York City with a steam iron in his hand for thirty years. My uncle owned the factory. My father was Labor, my uncles were Capital. My father was a Socialist, my uncles were Zionists. Therefore, Labor was Socialism and Capital was Nationalism. These equations were mother's milk to me, absorbed through flesh and bone almost before consciousness. Concomitantly, I knew also—and again, as though osmotically—who in this world were friends, who enemies, who neu-

trals. Friends were all those who thought like us: working-class socialists, the people whom my parents called "progressives." All others were "them"; and "them" were either engaged enemies like my uncles or passive neutrals like some of our neighbors. Years later, the "us" and "them" of my life would become Jews and Gentiles, and still later women and men, but for all of my growing-up years "us" and "them" were socialists and non-socialists; the "politically enlightened" and the politically *un*enlightened; those who were "struggling for a better world" and those who, like moral slugs, moved blind and unresponsive through this vast inequity that was our life under capitalism. Those, in short, who had class consciousness and those *lumpen* or bourgeois who did not.

This world of "us" was, of course, a many-layered one. I was thirteen or

fourteen years old before I consciously understood the complex sociology of the progressive planet; understood that at the center of the globe stood those who were full-time organizing members of the Communist Party, at the outermost periphery stood those who were called "sympathizers," and at various points in between stood those who held Communist Party membership cards and those who were called "fellow travelers." In those early childhood years these distinctions did not exist for me; much less did I grasp that within this sociology my parents were merely "fellow travelers." The people who came to our house with the *Daily Worker* or the Yiddish newspaper *Der Freiheit* under their arms, the people at the "affairs" we attended, the people at the *shule* (the Yiddish school I was sent to after my public-school day

DON'T VOTE FOR PIKE,

HE'S A KIKE.

VOTE FOR A REAL AMERICAN

William J. Morris, Jr.

FOR JUSTICE - MUNICIPAL COURT

5th District

Election Campaign Literature, New York, 1932: This anti-Semitic piece of election campaign literature was distributed in the Rockaway Beach section of New York City. *Credit:* AJHS

was over), the people at the rallies we went to and the May Day parades we marched in, the people who belonged to the various "clubs" and were interminably collecting money for the latest cause or defense fund—they were all as one to me; they were simply "our people." Of a Saturday morning, the doorbell in our Bronx apartment would ring, my father would open the door, and standing there would be Hymie, a cutter in my father's shop, a small, thin man with gnarled hands and the face of an anxious bulldog. *"Nu,* Louie?" Hymie would say to my father. "Did you see the papers this morning? Did you see—a black year on all of them!—what they're saying about the Soviet Union *this* morning?" "Come in, Hymie, come in," my father would reply. "Have a cup of coffee, we'll discuss it." I did not know that there was a difference between Hymie, who was also only a "fellow traveler," and my cousins David and Selena, who were YCLers, or my uncle Sam, who was always off at "a meeting," or Bennie Grossman from across the street who had suddenly disappeared from the neighborhood ("unavailable" was the word for what Bennie had become, but it would be twenty years before I realized that was the word). It was, to begin with, all one country to me, one world, and the major characteristic of that world as I perceived it was this:

At the wooden table in our kitchen there were always gathered men named Max and Hymie, and women named Masha and Goldie. Their hands were work-blackened, their eyes intelligent and anxious, their voices loud and insistent. They drank tea, ate black bread and herring, and talked "issues." Endlessly, they talked issues. I sat on the kitchen bench beside my father, nestled in the crook of his arm, and I listened, wide-eyed, to the talk. Oh, that talk! That passionate, transforming talk! I understood nothing of what they were saying,

but I was excited beyond words by the richness of their rhetoric, the intensity of their arguments, the urgency and longing behind that hot river of words that came ceaselessly pouring out of all of them. Something important was happening here, I always felt, something that had to do with understanding things. And "to understand things," I already knew, was the most exciting, the most important thing in life.

It was characteristic of that world that during those hours at the kitchen table with my father and his socialist friends I didn't know we were poor. I didn't know that in those places beyond the streets of my neighborhood we were without power, position, material or social existence. I only knew that tea and black bread were the most delicious food and drink in the world, that political talk filled the room with a terrible excitement and a richness of expectation, that here in the kitchen I felt the same electric thrill I felt when Rouben, my Yiddish teacher, pressed my upper arm between two bony fingers and, his eyes shining behind thick glasses, said to me: "Ideas, dolly, ideas. Without them, life is nothing. With them, life is *everything.*"

Sometimes I would slip off the bench and catch my mother somewhere between the stove and the table (she was forever bringing something to the table). I would point to one or another at the table and whisper to her: Who is this one? Who is that one? My mother would reply in Yiddish: "He is a writer. She is a poet. He is a thinker." Oh, I would nod, perfectly satisfied with these identifications, and return to my place on the bench. *He,* of course, drove a bakery truck. *She* was a sewing-machine operator. That other one over there was a plumber, and the one next to him stood pressing dresses all day long beside my father.

But Rouben was right. Ideas were everything. So powerful was the life

inside their minds that sitting there, drinking tea and talking issues, these people ceased to be what they objectively were—immigrant Jews, disenfranchised workers—and, indeed, they became thinkers, writers, poets.

Every one of them read the *Daily Worker,* the *Freiheit,* and the *New York Times* religiously each morning. Every one of them had an opinion on everything he or she read. Every one of them was forever pushing, pulling, yanking, mauling those opinions into shape within the framework of a single question. The question was: Is it good for the workers? That river of words was continually flowing toward an ocean called *farshtand,* within whose elusive depths lay the answer to this question.

They were voyagers on that river, these plumbers, pressers, and sewing-machine operators. Disciplined voyagers with a course to steer, a destination to arrive at. When one of them yelled at another (as one of them regularly did) "Id-yot! What has *that* to do with anything? Use your brains! God gave you brains, yes or no? Well, use them!" he was, in effect, saying: Where will that question take us? Nowhere. Get back on course. We're going somewhere, aren't we? Well, then, let's go there.

They took with them on this journey not only their own narrow, impoverished experience but a set of abstractions as well, abstractions with the power to transform. When these people sat down at the kitchen table to talk, Politics sat down with them, Ideas sat down with them, above all, History sat down with them. They spoke and thought within a context that had world-making properties. This context lifted them out of the nameless, faceless obscurity of the soul into which they had been born and gave them, for the first time in their lives, a sense of rights as well as of obligations. They had rights because they now knew who and what they were. They were not simply the disinherited of the earth, they were proletarians. They were not a people without a history, they had the Russian Revolution. They were not without a civilizing world view, they had Marxism.

Within such a context the people at my father's kitchen table could place themselves; and if they could place themselves—compelling insight!—they could *become* themselves. For, in order to become one must first have some civilizing referent, some social boundary, some idea of nationhood. These people had no external nationhood; nothing in the cultures they had left, or the one to which they had come, had given them anything but a humiliating sense of outsidedness. The only nationhood to which they had attained was the nationhood inside their minds: the nationhood of the international working class. And indeed, a nation it was—complete with a sense of family, culture, religion, social mores, political institutions. The people in that kitchen had remade the family in the image of workers all over the world, political institutions in the image of the

Communist Party, social mores in the image of Marxist allegiance, religion in the image of the new socialized man, Utopia in the image of the Soviet Union. They sat at the kitchen table and they felt themselves linked up to America, Russia, Europe, the world. Their people were everywhere, their power was the revolution around the corner, their empire "a better world."

To see themselves as part of an identifiable mass of human beings with a place and a destiny in the scheme of civilized life—when until now they had left only the dread isolation that is the inevitable legacy of powerlessness—was suddenly to "see" themselves. Thus, paradoxically, the more each one identified himself or herself with the working-class movement, the more each one came individually alive. The more each one acknowledged his or her condition as one of binding connectedness, the more each one pushed back the darkness and experienced the life within. In this sense, that kitchen ceased to be a room in a shabby tenement apartment in the Bronx and became, for all intents and purposes, the center of the world as that center has ever been described since the time of the ancient Greeks. For, here in the turmoil and excitation of their urgent talk, the men and women at the kitchen table were involved in nothing less than an act of self-creation: the creation of the self through increased consciousness. The instrument of consciousness for them was Marx. Marx and the Communist Party and world socialism. Marx was their Socrates, the Party was their Plato, world socialism their Athens.

Hitler's Challenge to Civilization: Attack on World Jewry

November 24, 1933. Rabbi Stephen S. Wise, who had been president of the American Jewish Congress and Zionist Organization of America, was one of the most esteemed religious leaders of his times. This address drew attention to the seriousness of the Jewish situation in Germany at an early date.

It is not to be thought that the tragedy of the Jew is a new or unknown thing in Jewish history. The tragedy of the Jew is become the commonplace of commonplaces. The tragedy of the Jew is none other than the paradox of the servant despised and rejected of men.

The Jew has been a bringer of blessings to the world, yet is he accursed. The Jew has been a light to the nations, yet is he doomed to darkness. The Jew has not dared to be himself and yet has not been free to be other than himself. The Jew has a genius for at-homeness, yet always and everywhere is regarded and treated as if he were an alien. The Jew is a victim in every generation, yet is he victor through the ages.

Wherein lies the tragedy of the Jew in this hour in Germany? In this—that the German Jews were unprepared in every

Ford Motor Company

ROUGE PLANT

DEARBORN, MICHIGAN

January 7 1942

Mr Sigmund Livingston
160 North LaSalle Street
Chicago, Illinois

Dear Sir:

In our present national and international emergency, I consider it of importance that I clarify some general misconceptions concerning my attitude toward my fellow-citizens of Jewish faith. I do not subscribe to or support, directly or indirectly, any agitation which would promote antagonism against my Jewish fellow-citizens. I consider that the hate-mongering prevalent for some time in this country against the Jew, is of distinct disservice to our country, and to the peace and welfare of humanity.

At the time of the retraction by me of certain publications concerning the Jewish people, in pursuance of which I ceased the publication of "The Dearborn Independent," I destroyed copies of literature prepared by certain persons connected with its publication. Since that time I have given no permission or sanction to anyone to use my name as sponsoring any such publication, or being the accredited author thereof.

I am convinced that there is no greater dereliction among the Jews than there is among any other class of citizens. I am convinced, further, that agitation for the creation of hate against the Jew or any other racial or religious group, has been utilized to divide our American community and to weaken our national unity.

I strongly urge all my fellow-citizens to give no aid to any movement whose purpose it is to arouse hatred against any group. It is my sincere hope that now in this country and throughout the world, when this war is finished and peace once more established, hatred of the Jew, commonly known as anti-Semitism, and hatred against any other racial or religious group, shall cease for all time.

Sincerely yours,

Henry Ford

Letter from Henry Ford, 1942: In 1920 Henry Ford initiated publication of violent attacks on Jews in his *Dearborn Independent*. This ended in 1927 when he issued an apology to Louis Marshall, President of the American Jewish Committee. In 1942 Ford wrote to the national chairman of the Anti-Defamation League disclaiming responsibility for continued circulation of the anti-Semitic *The International Jew*, which he originally sponsored. *Credit:* Anti-Defamation League of B'nai B'rith

sense, unprepared inwardly and outwardly, though some of us foresaw and foretold what would happen. The Jew is doubly unprepared insofar as he was unprepared for the worst that the world could inflict upon him because he was uprooted and unanchored in the best of his own tradition. The Jew who had so long denied the reality and the authenticity of the people Israel finds himself at last denied a place in Germany. If it be true that all things are ready if our minds be so, then were the German Jews tragically unready for the awful hour that came upon them. The tragedy of the Jew cannot be stated nor yet summarized in mere facts. And still the truth is that German Jewry presents the picture of a people on the rack. I have seen torture chambers in the course of the summer in European castles very near to Germany. Germany is a torture chamber for the Jewish people.

The tragedy of the Jew lies in the two-

fold purpose of the new rulers of the German Reich—to exterminate on the one hand and, in the meantime, to degrade on the other. As if economic, industrial extermination were not enough, degradation, humiliation are ceaselessly inflicted. They of the intelligentsia who ought to stand apart from the band of Jewish torturers identify themselves with the unfaith and the misdeeds of their people. The tragedy of the Jew lies in the Nazi threat to Jewish children. Not only are the children wounded in their souls from day to day, but Germany is preparing for a future of hatred, of reprisal, of unrelieved shame.

There is another and still greater Jewish tragedy, and that is the tragedy of the Jew in the rest of the world. We Jews outside of Germany are just as little prepared as were the Germans—unprepared in the matter of understanding of the forces that have evoked this tragic hour. Again there is no union of Jewish

Father Charles E. Coughlin, Cleveland, 1936: Through his weekly radio programs and his magazine, *Social Justice*, Father Charles E. Coughlin, a Catholic priest, preached anti-Semitism. He was supported by the *Boston Pilot* and *Brooklyn Tablet*, official archdiocesan publications. *Credit:* WW

Anti-Hitler Protest, 1933: A crowd of 10,000 persons: Jews, Catholics, Protestants, clergy and laity, assembled in Cleveland's Public Hall to demonstrate against Hitler's treatment of the Jews in Germany. *Credit:* NA

die for these things is not to make a vain sacrifice. No vain sacrifice is made by them that battle for eternal causes as we have done throughout the generations. Let not Hitlerism, Nazism, achieve the triumph over us of moving us to forswear the things by which and for which our fathers lived. Whatever may be the suffering which Jews must endure in Germany, whatever tortures may be visited upon them, Jews may not, dare not forswear their highest faith and their loftiest ideals. Israel disloyal to itself is Hitlerism triumphant; Israel unimpairably and indeflectibly loyal to its faith in and its power of sacrifice for its divine and eternal ideals is the doom of a thousand Hitlerisms.

Grave and destructive as is the attack of Hitlerism upon German Jewry, one thing if possible is graver even in its origins and consequences than the Hitler persecution of German Jews. The still graver evil is the avowed purpose of Hitlerism, the destruction of world Jewry. I limit myself at this time to pointing out that the persecution of German Jews by the Hitler government is a moral, indeed religious problem for all men to whom spiritual and ethical values mean something.

But the Hitler war upon world Jewry as announced again and again by the representatives of the Third Reich is more if possible than a moral and religious problem. The formulated and indeed initiated war upon world Jewry is more than cause for alarm to Jews wherever they may dwell. It constitutes the most solemn warning to the nations that forces are at work in the world, which are resolved to end understanding between Jew and Christian, to set the world of Christendom against the Jew and to mark this holy year by beginning a crusade of death against Jews everywhere.

How shall the Hitler challenge to the ideals and standards and hopes which comprise civilization be met? We who are Jews are resolved to meet it as men, to dare do all that doth become men, to defend ourselves in every honorable, peaceable and just way. Better that Jews nobly perish than ignobly survive, that is to say, unresistingly accepting Hitlerism. Christianity, too, must accept the challenge. The real conflict in the world is between the Hitlerism or Aryan and neo-Aryan paganism with its rejection of the moral and spiritual ideals associated with the Jewish and Christian covenants and that Western world point of view which is oftenest designated as Christianity.

Civilization must accept the challenge of Hitlerism, unflinchingly rejecting every doctrine which threatens human liberty, which would undermine the ancient moralities. Civilization must reaffirm the principles and ideals, the standards and hopes by which mankind has arisen out of the darkness of the past and to the repudiation of which it will not suffer itself to be driven by neo-paganish Hitlerism.

forces. There is no large planning, no statesmanlike envisagement, no setting up of great purposes with a view to bringing help and healing to our people. All of which means that there is a woeful unreadiness on the part of Jews really and freely to share in the, alas, involuntary sacrifices of our people in Germany.

Over and above all the Jewish tragedy for us lies in the danger of Jews forswearing their ideals, ideals by which and for which they have lived, not the ideal of religious loyalty for, happily, a religious disloyalty and infidelity do not avail to save the faithless. The real danger is that under the pressure of the

Nazi movement, Jews may be moved consciously and deliberately to surrender their ideals, such high and abiding ideals as the ideals of democracy, of the forward-looking human collectivity, of war-resistance. In a word, the tragedy is being enacted before our eyes of the current and urgent Jewish need which is for an hour leading us to surrender ideals which are eternal. We are not fighting for ourselves alone in all the great battlefield to which the Third Reich has summoned us. We are battling for the world's ideals, for the ideals of democracy and liberalism, human peace and cooperation. To battle and even to

Appeals for Help

1938–1939. Wilhelm Stricker, originally of Vienna, contacted Rabbi Stephen S. Wise for assistance in making it possible for him, his wife and his father to emigrate to the United States. The following correspondence describes their ordeal. Although the father never got to the United States, he fortunately was able to reach Israel.

Prague, August 2, 1938

Dear Rabbi Wise,

Returning from Vienna, where I spoke with Rabi Dr. Goldberg, I come to you again with a great petition, this time for myself.

Since this time I am in Prague (5 month) it was not possible—in spite of best relations—to get an employment, and also the future gives only very little hope. I don't say, that it will happen here in Czechoslovakia like in Germany, but we have all signs, that there comes a numerous clauses for the Jews like in Hungaria. The economic concessions to our Sudeten-Nazi must be a damage to the positions of the Jews.

Now I beg You to write me, if it would be possible, that I and my wife may immigrate to America.

Please don't mind my asking you again to do something for me, but really I don't see any other way to settle down somewhere and to find an existece.

I heard in Vienna that my father is healthy, but he is obliged to travel the whole day with sheard hair and beard on the field. I'm sure, I mustn't tell you, what this means for a 59-years old, ill man.

I thank you very, very much for all the troubles you had with my father and me and I hope the won't be without a success.

I remain, dear Mr. Wise, once more with my best thanks

Yours truly,
Wilhelm Stricker

September 1, 1938

Mr. Wilhelm Stricker
℅ Dr. Robitschek
Dlouha 47
Prague

Dear Mr. Stricker:

Yes, I know about your visit to Vienna and your meeting with my friend, Rabbi Dr. Goldberg.

I will send the affidavits today. I could not get them ready before.

As for your dear father, my dear friend, I have done what I could. More I cannot do. When you come to America with your wife I will explain to you. I cannot in writing.

Hoping that we shall soon see you in America and that the independence and

Mass Meeting to Save Jews, 1944: A crowd of 40,000 gathered in New York City in an effort to save as many Jews as possible from atrocities in Germany and German-controlled countries. The mass meeting was presided over by Rabbi Stephen S. Wise and messages were read from President Roosevelt and Governor Dewey. *Credit:* NA

Anti-Hitler Protest Parade, 1933: An estimated 100,000 people, both Jews and non-Jews, marched to Madison Square in New York City to demonstrate against the policies of Nazi Germany. *Credit:* NA

integrity of Czechoslovakia may be preserved, I am

Faithfully yours,
Stephen S. Wise

The Jewish Agency for Palestine

London
August 31st, 1938

Dear Dr. Wise,

Many thanks for your letter of the 18th inst., with regard to Stricker. I informed the Executive of the contents of your letter, and they are very grateful indeed for everything you have done in the matter. Dr. Nahum Goldmann is also doing whatever he can. Let us hope that it will soon be possible to have Stricker released. I do not know whether you have heard that he had to undergo three months solitary confinement.

With kindest regards,
Yours very sincerely,
J. Linton

New York City
September 9, 1938

Mr. J. Linton
The Jewish Agency for Palestine
77 Great Russell Street
London

Dear Linton:

In strictest confidence I send you a copy of a statement that has just come to me from an Aryan American lawyer who has been in Vienna and who is dealing with the Str. situation. You will note what he says about the possibility of getting Str. released. No, I did not know that he had to undergo three months solitary confinement.

It might interest you to know that, although I have never seen Str's children, I have given my personal affidavits to his son and his son's fiance or wife.

It was interesting to note with what warmth and earnestness the "New Judea" in its August number welcomed Dr. Goldmann, my successor, and dealt with the two terms of my own administration as President of the Zionist Organization of America and Chairman of the United Palestine Appeal.

Faithfully yours,
Stephen S. Wise

Park Lane Hotel
Piccadilly
W.1 London

25th February 1939.

Mr. William Stricker,
Hotel Sherman Square,
Broadway 70–71st Street,
New York City, U.S.A.

Dear Mr. Stricker

Your letter has come and I need hardly say that I share your hopes over your father's complete release. I did try my best and moved in the highest quarters, of which I shall tell you, to effect his release, but now, as you know, Dr. Goldmann has succeeded in seeing to it in a certain way and I was happy to bear my share of the rather large expense in effectuating what all of us desire. I am sorry to think you and I will not be able to see your father before he leaves for Palestine, but the important thing is that he is free. I heard many startling and characteristic things about Father from his fellow victim in a concentration camp,—Dr. Maximilian Reich: a guard at the camp stuck a pistol into the mouth of Reich and he admitted "I trembled and was silent." Then he went to your father and stuck the pistol far down his throat, and Father laughed defiantly, whereupon the officer said to him: "Why do you laugh, don't you know that I can shoot you?" Father answered with the pistol in his mouth: "Of course you can, but you would not be coward enough to shoot me, unable to defend myself," and the guard walked off. I need not tell you how typical of your father's unshakeable courage that is. When I get home as I shall within a fortnight, I will write to him, assuming that at that time you will know his address in Palestine, and he will have left, as Nahum Goldmann says he will be permitted to leave, after a month or two in Vienna. I earnestly trust this is so, for his sake and for the sake of all who love him.

I presume you know that your hotel is just a stone's throw from my office in 68th street. Telephone to me if you please on the Monday or Tuesday morning at 11 a.m. after my return on Thursday, March 9th.

Faithfully yours,
sgned. Stephen S. Wise.

July 19, 1939.

Dr. William Stricker
2023 Broadway
New York.

Dear Dr. Stricker:

A letter has come to Dr. Wise from Dr. Goldman, in which occurs this reference to your Father:

"Thank you for the money for Stricker. He is in not too bad health and will come in a week or two to Switzerland, from where he will go to Palestine. I am very happy that we could save him at least. The strength of his character helped him to leave the concentration camp unbroken in health and spirit."

Sincerely yours,
Berta Willig
Secretary to Dr. Wise

From Vienna to Havana and Finally to New York

1938–1944. Escaping Nazi persecution in Austria, Dr. Adolph Mechner, his wife and two children hoped to emigrate to the United States together, but they were separated. Dr. Mechner managed to get to Cuba and was later joined by their son. Mrs. Mechner and their daughter reached New York in 1939. All four members of the family were reunited in New York in 1944. In his memoirs Dr. Mechner recounted their experiences.

A few days later, we were in Havana, Cuba. The whole voyage had taken 14 days. The disembarcation took a very long time, as an officer of the immigration department examined the papers of each passenger very thoroughly. While this was going on, a man from the Joint Distribution Committee came on board and explained the situation, in which refugees from Europe will find themselves in Cuba, and what the chances of getting visas for the immigration to the United States were. He explained the quota system and the waiting period for people from different countries of origin. For me, this man had very bad news. I had expected that I would have to wait a few weeks or perhaps months, but he told me that it will take years, since I was born in Romania, and the Romanian quota was very small, only 375 per year. I was shocked, and fell for the next few days into deep despair. All my plans had suddenly come to naught.

. . . I was receiving letters from Hedy and also from Lisa and Francis and had written to them frequently. Pictures, which I had sent them, showing me in a white suit with a straw hat seemed to have impressed them very much. In one of the letters Hedy wrote that the Nazis had come to look for me on the day after the so called Crystal-Night from the 9th to the 10th of November, 1938, when they had put on fire 17 temples and 61 Houses of Prayer in Vienna and the other cities in Austria and had arrested and sent to concentration camps 7800 Jews. In Germany they had also destroyed by fire innumerous temples and arrested 26,000 Jews. That was 40 days, after I had left Vienna. How lucky I was!

. . . I had enough reason for grave worries for the lives of Hedy, Johanna, Hedy's parents, Lisa, and Francis. I thought that I will now be completely cut off from them, and that I will never see them again. It took me some time to see this was a special kind of war, affecting, at least for some time only Eastern Europe. The Germans had occupied within 4 weeks one half of Poland, at which time the Russians, to the astonishment of the whole world, invaded Poland from the East, occupied the other half of that country, and met the Germans in the area of Brest Litowsk, where they shook hands with the Germans.

At about that time my worries abated a little, when I received letters from Hedy from Vienna, and one of them made me especially happy, in which she wrote that she had received the American visa for herself and Johanna, and that she was now trying to get the tickets for a boat. So, it was a special kind of war, in which it was possible to send letters from Austria to Cuba, and in which it was possible to leave Vienna and to go on a voyage to the United States. It finally really happened that they got tickets for the boat "Rotterdam" and could go to Holland and leave for the United States.

. . . The great disappointment was that Francis did not get the American visa in France. The American consul in Vienna had told Hedy that he will send all the papers for Francis to the American consul in Paris, so that he could get the visa there. But the American consul in Paris was not willing to write the visa for Francis, gave as the excuse that there was not enough time to write it, although there would have been plenty of time. He said that the mother should leave without him and that Francis could follow here with another boat. When Hedy came to Amsterdam, she was, of course, terribly disappointed, that Francis was not there, did not know what had happened.

. . . Anyway, I was happy to learn that Hedy and Johanna had left by boat from Rotterdam—it was on the 12th of December, 1939—and that they had safely arrived in New York, 12 days later. I had written in the meantime to Hedy's cousin, Dr. Johanna Hilkowicz, and had asked her to rent a little apartment for them, and that she should put there in a vase a bunch of flowers. I also sent her a check of $30—to give to Hedy, so that she would have a little money right away. That was probably all I had at that time.

Department Of State
Washington 25, D.C.

December 17, 1943

Mrs. Hedwig Mechner,
721 Carroll Street,
Brooklyn, New York.

Madam:

With reference to your interest in the visa case of your husband Adolf Mechner and son Franz Gerhart, I have pleasure in informing you that after further consideration of the case in the light of existing regulations, the Department has given advisory approval for the issuance of immigration visas to the American Embassy at Habana.
Notification of this action has been sent by air mail.

Very truly yours,
H. K. Travers
Chief, Visa Division

. . . We took a plane for Miami, and our immigration procedure and examina-

Mechner Family Reunion, 1944: After a five-year separation in their attempt to seek refuge in the United States, the Mechners were finally reunited in New York. They are seen in front of their new home in Brooklyn. From left to right: Johanna, Hedy, Francis and Adolph. *Credit:* Dr. Adolph Mechner

tion by the immigration officers was smooth and there was no difficulty. I was pleased to be told that my English was quite good. After a stay of two days in Miami, where we visited our good friend Mrs. Else Wagner and where I met for the first time Mr. Spielmann, we took the train for New York, where Hedy had already a nice furnished apartment prepared for all of us at 408 Garfield Place in Brooklyn. I was overwhelmed already in Miami and then again in New York by the entirely different world, into which we had come, the enormous buildings, the well regulated traffic, the clean streets, etc.

When we arrived in New York, Hedy had a job. She had to paint ties, which were modern at that time, and she had to leave early in the morning and came home late in the afternoon when it was already dark. Johanna went to public school, only a few blocks from our home, and I had to pick her up every day after school. Francis was at that time already 13 years old and we thought it would be nice for him to be put in the Ethical Culture School. . .

. . . I had to start to prepare myself for the State Board examination, which consisted of two parts, an English language examination and an examination of medical subjects.

. . . There came the time of my examination on October 1st, and I studied at the end all night and slept only one or two hours. Dr. Hirschfeld, our tutor, told me that I was very well prepared, the best in the whole group. The examinations were in writing, starting in the morning at 9 and ending at 12 noon, and then starting again at 1 P.M. and ending at 4. Each day 2 subjects for 4 days. Each time when I came home in the late afternoon, I could say that I was sure I

had passed the examination. After sleeping for 1 hour, I started again to study, ending at 6 in the morning, sleeping then for one hour and then getting up to take the subway to Manhattan, to get there in time before 9 o'clock. That went on for 4 days. After coming home on the 4th day, I went to bed and slept for almost 2 days, completely exhausted.

Darius Milhaud's Escape from France

1940. Darius Milhaud, the composer, his wife and son, were able to get out of France before the German armies arrived. He described the ordeal of going from Paris to Lyon, to Aix, across the border, to Lisbon and finally by boat to New York.

. . . Next day we had news of the invasion of Holland. Hélène Hoppenot implored me to go back to Aix, and insisted that we should leave by car. I took a taxi to Lyon, where we picked up our little Fiat. Madeleine, Marcelle Carmona, and I gazed at the countryside, torn between sadness and wonder. Never had it seemed more beautiful or more sublime.

The days that followed passed swift and slow, and implacably the Battle of France was fought. All the roads were jammed with refugees, all of whom seemed to be wanting to get to Aix, both those from Holland and the north fleeing before the Germans, and those coming from the south and abandoning the coastal areas for fear of the Italians. The fall of Paris, the advance of the Germans, Marshal Pétain's decision to stop the fighting, came to rend our hearts as we sat in a little bistro in the Vieux-Port at Marseille. All around us people wept in despair. On our way back to Aix we met an uninterrupted line of trucks carrying away the men of the R.A.F.

I had had too many contacts with German, Austrian, Czech, and Italian refugees not to have a good idea of what an occupation would mean. I realized clearly that the capitulation would prepare the soil for fascism and its abominable train of monstrous persecutions. Madeleine proposed that we should leave the country. I was powerless, incapable of running away, or even of hiding if need be, but such a decision was a bitter pill to swallow. When one of our young friends, who was later to become a very gallant member of the Resistance, said to Madeleine, who was confiding in him how much she was worried: "All we've got to do is to drop England and sign a fifty-year pact with Germany," she realized the full horror of our situation and set to work immediately to organize our departure. Already all the consulates were besieged by a tightly packed crowd of British citizens trying by every means possible to get out of France. At Cook's, where we reserved seats on the clipper, we met the Werfels, who were in despair because they had been refused visas in view of their being Czechs. In desperation, they took a taxi for Bordeaux, where they hoped to get their papers. Sadly and with foreboding we took our leave of them. For us, however, everything went off well. I had in my possession all my correspondence with my manager and pre-war newspaper articles announcing my symphony, so that the American visa was granted immediately. As for the Portuguese visa, the official at the consulate was kind enough to give it to me without even telegraphing his government. At the last moment the driver who had undertaken to take us to the frontier refused to go. Madeleine loaded up the little Fiat, and we said good-by to our relatives. We set out in an exceptionally violent thunderstorm. We were stopped several times along the way for our papers to be examined. The road-blocks grew more and more numerous because the Minister of the Interior had just put a ban on all movements by road. We had to explain our position and show our passports and our tickets for the clipper.

Some soldiers were hard to convince—the Senegalese, for example. We drove on till late at night, and when we came to a square in Narbonne the blackout was solid—you could see exactly nothing. Madeleine asked a passer-by the way to a hotel. "You won't be able to find room anywhere, dear," said a woman's voice. "You'd better come home with me." The good woman, a market-gardener, gave us her bed, made us some coffee, and insisted on giving us breakfast before we left. We carried away with us a warm memory of her open-hearted hospitality.

At Cerbère we left the car in a garage and crossed the frontier. We were searched by young Falangists wearing scornful and triumphant expressions on their faces. We nearly missed the train because they insisted on weighing every tube in our stock of homeopathic remedies and looking up every name in the dictionary. The trains were not running regularly, and there was only a limited number of seats. We should have preferred to buy through tickets to Lisbon, but were not allowed to do so. The tickets were issued only by sections, and no one was able to give us even an approximate idea of what the total cost would be. We traveled third-class, with goodhearted peasants who marveled at Daniel, who never stopped drawing. They all insisted on sharing their food with us. We reached Madrid about midnight and suddenly, to our horror, noticed that Daniel had disappeared. Panic-stricken, Madeleine ran off to find the entrance to the station, but there were several of these. She came back to me, and I went on shouting his name at the top of my voice. This is what saved the lad. He heard me and found his way back to us. Half asleep, he had been following a lady whom he took to be his mother.

We stayed two days at a little hotel,

waiting for the train to Lisbon. It was then that we learned that we should not be allowed to take any Spanish money out of the country. We therefore decided to spend all our pesetas, much to Daniel's amazement, for he had never had so many presents before in his life. We traveled in a sleeper, and what a relief it was to cross the Portuguese frontier! The officials were kindly and sympathetic. At Lisbon, we rushed to the clipper office, but our tickets were no longer valid. They had been paid for in Marseille, and the franc had lost its value. We had no means of making up the difference in price, having brought out only the sum authorized by the government—namely, twelve thousand francs for the three of us. We had not even enough money to take passage by boat. While we waited on events, we moved into a little hotel. I wrote letters to Kurt Weill, to my manager, to Mrs. Claire Reis, to Pierre Monteux, and to Mrs. Coolidge. I told them where we had got to, and these good friends set about organizing a future for me in America. Antonio Ferro, the Minister of Propaganda, let us know that the Portuguese government would be responsible for all our expenses while we stayed in Lisbon. Ernesto Halffter, Falla's favorite pupil, together with his Portuguese wife, came to see us with offers of assistance. I conducted a radio concert organized by Freitas Branco. I conducted *La Cantate de l'Enfant et de la Mère*, recited by Madeleine. I also gave a lecture on Poetry and Music at the Conservatoire. Several of our friends attended it. How apt Péguy's saying: *"Il faut qu'une sainte réussisse!"* (a holy woman is bound to succeed) seemed to me then!

The Baronne de Goldschmidt-Rothschild, who had managed to escape from France with her children in a little car into which she had packed some of the pictures from her amazing collection—works by Van Gogh, Manet, Cézanne, Cranach—was in Estoril at the time, and told me how disappointed she had been when the bank had refused to let her send some money to her gardener in Toulon. I saw in this a way of salvation for us. I got my father to send the money, and she paid me, so in that way I was able to leave.

On board the *Excambion*, I was handed a telegram from Mills College offering me a teaching post, my name having been put forward by my friends Pierre Monteux, Robert Schmitz, and the members of the Pro Arte Quartet. It was only then, after the wrench of departure, that I realized I was entering on a new phase in my existence. I should find new copies of my orchestral works in America. Deiss was the only publisher engraving my scores, and he had sent copies regularly to his agent Elkan Vogel in Philadelphia. But the agent for Universal Edition would not have many of my works in stock. I should have to start work afresh to cope with any demands that might be made by concert societies. Lying in a deck-chair beside my wife

and son, I felt how privileged I was to be able to be working with them at my side, and I can never be grateful enough to Providence for not having parted me from them at this time of ordeal.

That was a gloomy crossing. There were a few Frenchmen on board: Jules Romains and his wife, Robert de Saint-Jean, Lévy-Strauss, the Duviviers, and the American writer who is such a Frenchman at heart, Julien Green. Like ourselves, all were filled with inconsolable grief. I remember now the desperate, profound sadness that fell upon us on that July 14, 1940, when we for-gathered in my cabin.

When we arrived in New York next day, my faithful friends Kurt Weill and his wife were standing on the dock to greet us.

How "Refugees" Adapted in Baltimore

1930's and 1940's. Gertrude Hirschler managed to flee from Germany and arrive in the United States. She described the experiences of German Jewish refugees in Baltimore.

Unlike the earlier Jewish immigrants who had come to Baltimore from Russia and Poland thirty, forty and fifty years before, the "refugees" did not settle "downtown," in the "ghettos" of South or East Baltimore, where many Jewish families of East European origin were then still living. They congregated in the "midtown" area, which was then considered a good middle and upper-middle-class section. Located in northwest Baltimore, this area was bounded by West North Avenue on the south, Bolton Street on the east, upper Eutaw Place on the west, and Lake Drive on the north. Here, scattered among the dignified apartment buildings that housed wealthy, aging descendants of the German Jews who had arrived in the city nearly a century before, and handsome homes owned by prosperous Russian Jewish families that had moved up from "downtown," there were more modest apartments, some of them in the "row houses" for which Baltimore is famous, where rents were scaled to lower-income budgets.

Next, and equally important, were the problems entailed in settling down and making a living. Most of the "refugees" who arrived in Baltimore during the late 1930s and early 1940s had little or no money, for by that time the Nazi authorities had already cut to a ridiculous minimum the funds that Jews could legally take out of Germany or Austria. Only a very few of the relatively well-off had been able surreptitiously to build up "nest eggs" abroad so that, once in Baltimore, they could establish themselves in business, or make a down payment on a small home in a modest neighborhood with spare rooms or apartments that could be rented out for immediate income. Except for a very small minority indeed, most of the "refugees" in Baltimore could not even afford to take a few weeks to "look around" for work that fitted their skills and experience. Unfortunately, just at that time jobs were scarce. Baltimore, along with the rest of the country, was only beginning to recover from the prolonged depression of the early 1930s. As a result, even simple work that required no great proficiency in English was hard to find. Wages and salaries were correspondingly low. During the months immediately preceding and following America's entry into World War II, a family of four—two adults and two children—could live, albeit very frugally, on $25.00 a week, but many of the "refugees" in the beginning earned no more than $15.00 for a week's work. As a consequence, wives, and in some cases even teenage children, had to work to supplement the family income, and many "refugee" families were forced to turn to Baltimore's Associated Jewish Charities for financial support.

It is true that the immigrants of an earlier era, notably the Jews from Eastern Europe, had also had to contend with extreme poverty when they first arrived in the United States. But they, for the most part, had been young and had seen their early struggles on New York's Lower East Side or in East Baltimore merely as the beginning of a slow but steady upward climb in America, the *goldene medina*, the land of unlimited opportunities. By contrast, most of the "refugees" of a generation later had passed their years of enthusiasm and had come, if not from lives of wealth, then at least from settled circumstances. Now in the autumn of life they had to begin all over again from the lowest rung of the ladder.

For cases in point, we need only think of the men who comprised the "Planning Committee" for the meeting at Schanze's Hall. These were all men in their mature years, none below early middle age. Back in Germany, Jacob Fuld and Abraham Wartensleben had each owned prosperous dry goods stores; in Baltimore, Fuld was doing heavy physical work at a chemical plant, and Wartensleben was a handyman in the furniture department of the Julius Gutman Company. Willy Brill, formerly a cattle dealer, was now a laborer in a winery. Adolf Straus, who had been in the wholesale millinery business in Germany, had found a job as a shipping clerk, Fred Baer, who had been in the metal business, had acquired a truck and from it sold fruit and vegetables to housewives who would wait out in the street for the "Gemuesebaer" to arrive. Alfred Loebenberg had been a well-to-do businessman who had had time to be active in the Jewish war veterans' organization in Frankfort. In 1941 he was past sixty and had been working variously as a night watchman and a bricklayer. He had not lasted long at either job and eventually began to sell kosher, German-style cold cuts and *Wuerstchen*, im-

Fund Raising Poster, 1944: A campaign to raise funds for Jews to emigrate to the United States. *Credit:* AJHS

ported from New York, personally delivering his wares to his customers in large shopping bags.

These six men, along with most of the other "refugees" who had been fortunate enough to be able to leave Hitler's Europe before Auschwitz and Majdanek, could not view their sudden, plummeting descent down the economic and social scale—as they saw it—as an adventure or even as an interesting challenge to their resourcefulness. Unlike an earlier generation in Russia and Poland, the "refugees" from Nazi Germany and Austria had never before had to accept physical or economic persecution as an ever-present threat or fact of life; when they suddenly found themselves deprived of their civil and personal rights in a country where they had lived for generations, that loss came to them as a fearful psychological shock. The "refugees" who landed in America before the Holocaust descended in full force upon European Jewry had not lived through those horrors which caused the "displaced persons" of only a few years later to point to their naked survival as a personal victory over death and destruction. After an initial sense of relief at having left Nazi Europe behind, many a "refugee" of the period before the death camps could feel only bewilderment and a deep sense of insecurity. Husbands and fathers who found themselves confronted in middle age with the prospect of starting all over again in a strange new country were shaken in their self-assurance and in their feeling of personal worth. Wives and mothers saw themselves chained to a seemingly never-ending routine of household drudgery, coupled in many cases with hard work at some outside job, an existence of unremitting toil, unrelieved by the diversions, the social events, and the other little pleasures of life to which they had been accustomed back in Europe but for which they now had neither the time nor the money.

An American Jewish Soldier's Encounters in Europe

1944. YIVO Institute for Jewish Research conducted a contest requesting that Jewish soldiers write recollections of their experiences in World War II. In this fascinating contest entry, we learn of the incredible encounters of this soldier while the American Army was liberating sections of France and Germany.

The time was November, 1944. My outfit was crossing the Channel en route to France. We were sitting in the Officer's Lounge playing pinochle to pass the time. One would imagine that it should take no more than one day to cross the Channel from England to France. But here it was the third day and we were still on the boat. After the trip from the States to England, our patience was beginning to run out at the slow crossing. You probably recall that worn out, listless, purposeless, beaten feeling that overcomes you during a long trip. Travelling with us "reinforcements" from England was a Free French Corps outfit, which included General De Gaulle's military band. The officer in charge of the band sensed the general listless attitude of his fellow American travellers, and asked the pianist and violinist of the band to play some interlude music for us. I was absorbed in the card game, and paid little attention to the music, other than to appreciate its presence. Suddenly, I heard a familiar tune. The violinist was playing "Yiddishe Mamma." Was it possible?

My curiosity was aroused. After the "concert", I spoke to the violinist, who was a sergeant. My three years of high school French (plus the guide book) enabled me to ask the name of the first song in the medley. In perfect Yiddish diction, he replied, "Yiddishe Mamma." "Bist ein Yid?" I inquired in my "Workmen Circle" dialect. "Of course," he replied, with an air of "what else?" in his voice. I don't recall the conversation verbatim, but to the best of my recollection, this is his story.

Aaron Kahn was born in Romania forty-six years ago. When he was two, his family moved to Paris. Aaron devoted his time to music, studying the violin, and training in the best conservatories of music in France. He played in various orchestras in Paris, and finally organized his own unit. He also composed music and acquired a valuable library of original compositions. In pre-war days, he was the musical director for the leading Jewish theatre in Paris. In his capacity as director he played host to the prominent Jewish actors and actresses who toured the continent and stopped in Paris. He knew Ludwig Satz, Molly Picon, Maurice Schwartz, Menasha Skulnick, the Adlers, Goldenberg. He built a home for his wife and only daughter in the suburbs of Paris which cost 300,000 pre-war francs. Throughout Parisian music circles, he was well-known and recognized as an artist. He enjoyed the richness of a full life after early years of struggle for security. Then came 1939. Mobilization. Aaron Kahn was a reservist and went into the lines with a field artillery unit. France fell in June, 1940. Aaron Kahn, the Jew, was demobilized and imprisoned in a concentration camp. His mother and daughter were shot by the Nazis after Paris fell. His wife disappeared. After a year in the concentration camp, Aaron Kahn plotted his escape. He succeeded in breaking out, travelled through Southern France into Spain and then to North Africa. In Oran, he joined the De Gaullists, and re-entered the Army, this time in the Medical Corps. He served with a combat unit and was cited for bravery under fire in the North Africa campaign.

In August, 1944, the unit sailed for England. They toured the United Kingdom for two months, and were returning to France to join De Gaulle's headquarters in Paris. Each man was to receive a 30 day leave to visit home after reaching Paris. Aaron was going to Paris to seek his wife and other members of his family. He was returning to his home to secure his music library. He intended to remain in the Army for the duration. When the war was over, he planned to visit America and settle there. His desire was to start life anew. He asked specific questions about life in the States, and I clarified some of his distorted notions about the American community. During the conversation, Aaron failed to explain his reason for playing "Yiddishe Mamma" for his audience. When I put the question to him, he answered simply, "It was my Mother's favorite." He didn't add to the remark; it was apparent that he preferred to drop the subject. We exchanged addresses, and promised to write. A few weeks later, while at the front, I received the reply to my first letter. He wrote in English as follows:

"Dear Friend!

I receive just now the letter you sent me to Paris.

About my next meet, I think it will be difficult because I am always travelling, but I will be very happy if we have the chance to meet in Paris. Write me at the same address when you are going, and it will be a pleasure for me to make you visit the town, if you can.

About my family, men and women were all deported and shooted, the rest it is impossible to learn at this time.

I hope all is right for you, and you receive good news from your family. Good luck.

Aaron."

. . . While I was resting on the steps of a bombed out church, the Pastor of the Church approached. He was a dignified looking Catholic priest with friendly blue eyes and a soft, gentle manner. He was silent for a while and then asked if anyone spoke German. I introduced

Commemorating the Warsaw Ghetto Uprising, 1944: On the first anniversary of the "Battle of the Warsaw Ghetto" in which a small number of Jews held off the German army for five weeks in the Polish capital a memorial service was held in New York City. Participating were Dr. Isaac Rubinstein, Chief Rabbi of Vilna, and Mayor Fiorello H. La Guardia. *Credit:* NA

Passover Seder, 1943: Passover seder at Great Lakes Naval Training Station near Chicago during World War II. *Credit:* CJA

myself. He greeted me cordially. He volunteered the information that all the German soldiers had departed on the previous day, and hence we should meet little resistance. This was my first encounter with German civilians and my sociological curiosity was aroused. As the Pastor seemed anxious to talk, I decided to ask him some questions. He proved to be a very informative conversationalist. He spoke about the morale of the German people, life under Nazi domination, and the terror of Allied bombings. After we had talked for about fifteen minutes, I asked the question, "Are there any more Jews in Cologne?" To my astonishment, he replied, "Yes. Those few who have survived are in hiding."

It seemed incredible that German Jews could have survived in Germany. I asked the Pastor for an explanation. The Pastor told me that when the 1938 laws were instituted, the Bishop of Cologne had created a special fund which was available to local pastors to aid in feeding and caring for the Jews. The Pastor said that he was still aiding two families who were hiding out near the church. I asked if I could meet these Jews. For the first time in our conversation, the Pastor hesitated. It were as if he had something to say which he thought would displease me. Cautiously, he looked at me and said, "Herr Officer, I would like to oblige, but I vowed not to violate the trust put in me when I promised not to reveal the location of these people. I am a religious man and believe in the sanctity of my vows." I explained to the Pastor that I appreciated his position, and inquired if he would ask these Jewish people if they wanted to meet me. Would the Pastor explain to them that I was an American officer of Jewish faith who desired to help them in every possible way? The Pastor indicated his agreement to visit these Jewish families and get their reaction.

Within ten minutes, the Pastor returned with two elderly men. They were both pale, hollow-eyed, and emaciated looking. For a few seconds, they stared at me in bewilderment. Then Mr. Rothberg, the younger, less timid of the two, extended his hand and said quietly, "Sholem Alechem." "Sholem," I answered softly. Words are inadequate to describe the emotional reactions of these two men. To them, the events that were transpiring appeared unbelievable. They wondered if it were true that the Messiah had come. During the ensuing conversation, Mr. Rothberg and his friend, Mr. Jacobs, gave me an eyewitness account of their trials and sufferings under Nazism. They repeated the story told by the Pastor of how the church had assisted them. Mr. Rothberg confided that his wife was working as a practical nurse for the nuns in a convent home.

Broome Street, New York, 1942: Window of a store selling Jewish religious articles during World War II. *Credit:* LC

Graveyard, France, 1945: Cemetery and memorial for World War II American soliders who participated in battles in Normandy. The cemetery is located in St. Laurent, Calvados, France. *Credit:* American Battle Monuments Commission

Park Synagogue, Cleveland, 1961: After World War II Jews moved to the suburbs and built a whole new breed of synagogues that were no longer modest in architectural design, but flamboyant in their proclamation of Jewish identity. Eric Mendelsohn, the eminent German-Jewish

architect who emigrated to this country to escape Nazi persecution, designed this outstanding structure for Congregation Anshe Emeth Beth Tefila in Cleveland in 1948. *Credit:* Park Synagogue

In the Mainstream

The end of the Second World War ushered in a new era of opportunity and achievement for Jews in the United States. Two separate but related phenomena occurred: in the wake of Hitler's defeat and the subsequent disclosure of Nazi atrocities, there was widespread condemnation of anti-Semitism; and concurrently, the participation of minority groups in the armed forces demanded greater equality for all groups. These two factors served to lessen discrimination against American Jews in education, housing and employment. As doors were increasingly opened, American Jews distinguished themselves in new fields of endeavor.

In the field of education, the number of Jews holding academic positions in American colleges and universities rose rapidly, and a flock of Jewish-American writers emerged, attracting a wide literary following: novelists Saul Bellow, Bernard Malamud and Norman Mailer; poets Delmore Schwartz, Karl Shapiro and Allen Ginsberg; and playwright Arthur Miller all attained prominence in the 1950s. American Jews had become part of the mainstream as Jewish poets and writers tapped into the American soul. As in previous decades, Jews continued to play a major role in the fields of business, law, medicine, science, communications, theater and film. Now, however, a new Jewish intelligèntsia began to make significant contributions to the intellectual and cultural aspects of American life.

Writer and editor Norman Podhoretz acutely described his journey from humble origins to mainstream prominence. ". . . I started on the road many years before I realized what I was doing, and by the time I did realize it I was for all practical purposes already there." Podhoretz's guide was his English teacher, Mrs. K., "an old fashioned kind of patrician" anti-Semite obsessed with getting Podhoretz to attend Harvard University. Forever badgering him, Mrs. K's efforts were not wasted, for Podhoretz went on to become the editor of *Commentary,* one of the outstanding intellectual forums in the United States.

Norman Mailer found his own path to success in America at the age of twenty-five with his best seller, *The Naked and The Dead.* Writing several years later on the effect of his early success, Mailer stated: ". . . I spent the next few years trying to gobble up the experiences of a victorious man when I was still no man at all, and had no real gift for enjoying life." Continued Mailer the existentialist: "Success had been a lobotomy to my past, there seemed no power from the past which could help me in the present, and I had no choice but to force myself to step into the war of the enormous present, to accept the private heat and fatigue of setting out by myself to cut a track through a new wild."

Texas businessman Stanley Marcus introduced innovations in his management of Nieman-Marcus which have transformed the store into a legend in the annals of American business. Others pursued success in the arts and sciences and in academia. By the 1960's, many Jews had attained high positions in both the corporate world and in government.

As did their fellow Americans, Jews adapted to the social and geographic mobility of the times. While first and second generation Jews preferred to live in cities with sizeable Jewish populations, Jews in the 1950's joined the middle class exodus to the suburbs. Nathan Glazer examined the impact of this departure from the inner cities on the traditional values of Jewish life, while sociologists Marshall Sklare and Joseph Greenblum noted the changes which occurred over twenty years in Lakeville, a renamed suburban community in the midwest. In their study, they found that Jews who had been a minority in the 1950's became a majority by the 1970's. Interestingly, there had been no organized attempt to make Lakeville a Jewish suburb. On the contrary, Lakeville's Jewish residents had preferred to retain their minority status. However, the continued influx of Jews and the resulting outflow of gentiles rapidly transformed Lakeville into a Jewish community.

American Jewish life was profoundly affected by the establishment of the State of Israel in 1948. Although some Jewish leaders, such as the Conservative rabbi and author Arthur Hertzberg, expressed concern over the dilemma which a Jewish state posed for American Jews, the granting of statehood to Israel united America's diverse Jewish population by reinforcing a sense of group identity and pride. Support for Israel and concern over its fate became the shared responsibility of the entire American Jewish community. In the aftermath of the Six Day War, Milton Himmelfarb took a hard look at the way in which the war affected American Jews: "We learned the old truth that you can depend only on yourself."

History repeated itself. As the sage Hillel had questioned thousands of years ago: "If I am not for myself, who is for me? And when I am for myself, what am I?" In this tradition of social concern and idealism, many American Jews became active participants in the student demonstrations, the civil rights movement and the anti-Vietnam wave of protests in the 1960's. The criticisms held by Americans of their values and lives as expressed in the poems by Allen Ginsberg are representative of the views of many American Jewish protestors in the sixties.

As the sixties progressed, it was expected that second and third generation Jews would experience a concomitant abandonment of their religious practices as they entered the American mainstream. However, sociologist Nathan Glazer's research pointed to the opposite. Synagogue affiliation among America's Jews had increased in the 1950's, with Conservative

After 1946

Judaism showing the largest growth, and by the 1960's, Orthodox, Conservative and Reform congregations could be found in any American city with a sizeable Jewish population. Even a small town with a modest Jewish community was able to boast that it, too, had the three denominational branches of American Judaism. Furthermore, with the exodus of many Jews from the urban centers, elaborate new synagogues were built in the suburbs. Many of these functioned as social and recreational centers for the community.

In the decades following the Second World War, Orthodox Judaism ceased to be identified with the shtetl and the immigrants in the "ghettos" of the larger cities. Orthodoxy acquired a new following among the middle class and American-born. From the years 1950 through 1980, the number of Orthodox Jewish day schools has increased eightfold. William Helmreich examined this phenomenal growth in his study of the yeshiva movement. Even among Jews raised in nonreligious or assimilated homes, there had been a rekindling of interest in the Jewish tradition. Paul Cowan's rediscovery of his "ancestral legacy" reflected this trend. He, as did many others, sought to "synthesize [his] . . . Old World heritage with the America that has shaped [his] . . . consciousness."

It is inconceivable to survey contemporary American life without mention of the Women's movement whose impact on the way we live and think is one of the most important social phenomena of the last fifteen years. Jewish women have been represented in large numbers among its leadership and activists. Betty Friedan, the founder of NOW, and author of *The Feminine Mystique,* was an early leader in the feminist movement. Former Congresswoman Bella Abzug named the third most influential member of Congress by her colleagues was appointed by President Carter to head the National Commission on the Observance of International Women's Year. Dr. Ruth Weiner describes how she got her doctorate, raised a family, and the subsequent university hiring barriers she encountered when both she and her husband applied as scientists to teach in the same university.

It is fitting that this final chapter which documents the American Jewish experience speak once again to the issue of immigrants, for that remains the essence of the United States of America—a nation of immigrants. After World War II, Jewish immigration, limited by the quota system, consisted largely of European survivors of the Holocaust.

The immigration laws today are much more flexible. In their study examining current patterns of Jewish immigration, sociologists Drora Kass and Seymour Martin Lipset found that the past ten years reflect a higher immigration rate for all peoples than any other ten-year period in American history. This upswing in immigration includes large numbers of Jews who have been permitted to emigrate from the Soviet Union and have chosen to settle in the United States, where they have established ethnic enclaves in several cities. In addition, a large number of Israelis have moved to the United States, where even those who are long-term residents maintain close ties with their homeland. Commented Kass and Lipset on the recent wave of Jewish immigrants: "One out of every ten to twelve Jews in the United States is a recent arrival who has been here less than ten years."

While overt anti-Semitism is not as prevalent in contemporary America as it has been in the past, there have been periodic episodes of anti-Jewish prejudice, including synagogue fires, thefts and desecrations, which have been attributed to a small minority. Generally, while they recognize a need for continued vigilance, Jews look upon America as a safe country in which to live.

The diverse memoirs, narratives and analyses presented here are not meant to be read as a crystalization of current American Jewish life. Rather, they are an attempt to capture a segment of American society which is alive, vital and changing. Much to the concern of Jewish professionals and members of the rabbinate, assimilation and marriage outside of the faith have been increasing within the Jewish community. At the same time, however, there appears to be a growing emphasis on traditional Jewish values and a seeking-out of community.

American Jews reflect the changes which are occurring all around them. Recent events in Israel have generated controversy and dissension where previously none existed. Similarly, as the structure of American family life is rapidly being transformed away from a nuclear unit, Jews, whose ties to family life are just short of proverbial, apparently are not immune to the forces at work.

America has been a unique experience for Jews. In this new nation, a nation unencumbered by the feudal and hierarchical traditions of Europe, free of century-old ties between church and state, and home to a wide variety of ethnic and religious groups, Jews have flourished. They have been active participants in the American experiment, and an integral part of the American experience. There is a fine line between integration and assimilation, and thus far, Jews have managed to retain their identity in a process that is the American encounter.

Albert Einstein, 1953: One of the most influential scientists in history, physicist, discoverer of the theory of relativity, Nobel Prize Winner. Born in Ulm, Germany in 1879, he came to the United States in 1933 to escape persecution in Nazi Germany. He was associated with the Institute for Advanced Studies at Princeton and became an American citizen. Although his discoveries lead to the development of nuclear weapons, he urged outlawing atomic and hydrogen bombs. Photograph by Trude Fleischman. *Credit:* LBI

Making It: From Brownsville to Columbia

Late 1940's. Norman Podhoretz, a leading writer and editor, described some of his first experiences in being exposed to a wider world than the one in which he grew up.

One of the longest journeys in the world is the journey from Brooklyn to Manhattan—or at least from certain neighborhoods in Brooklyn to certain parts of Manhattan. I have made that journey, but it is not from the experience of having made it that I know how very great the distance is, for I started on the road many years before I realized what I was doing, and by the time I did realize it I was for all practical purposes already there. At so imperceptible a pace did I travel, and with so little awareness, that I never felt footsore or out of breath or weary at the thought of how far I still had to go. Yet whenever anyone who has remained back there where I started—remained not physically but socially and culturally, for the neighborhood is now a Negro ghetto and the Jews who have "remained" in it mostly reside in the less affluent areas of Long Island—whenever anyone like that happens into the world in which I now live with such perfect ease, I can see that in his eyes I have become a fully acculturated citizen of a country as foreign to him as China and infinitely more frightening. . . .

Given the fact that I had literary ambitions even as a small boy, it was inevitable that the issue of class would sooner or later arise for me with a sharpness it would never acquire for most of my friends. But given the fact also that I was on the whole very happy to be growing up where I was, that I was fiercely patriotic about Brownsville (the spawning-ground of so many famous athletes and gangsters), and that I felt genuinely patronizing toward other neighborhoods, especially the "better" ones like Crown Heights and East Flatbush which seemed by comparison colorless and unexciting—given the fact, in other words, that I was not, for all that I wrote poetry and read books, an "alienated" boy dreaming of escape—my confrontation with the issue of class would probably have come later rather than sooner if not for an English teacher in high school who decided that I was a gem in the rough and who took it upon herself to polish me to as high a sheen as she could manage and I would permit.

I resisted—far less effectively, I can see now, than I then thought, though even then I knew that she was wearing me down far more than I would ever give her the satisfaction of admitting. Famous throughout the school for her altogether outspoken snobbery, which stopped short by only a hair, and sometimes did not stop short at all, of an old-fashioned kind of patrician anti-Semitism, Mrs. K. was also famous for being an extremely good teacher; indeed, I am sure that she saw no distinction between the hopeless task of teaching the proper

use of English to the young Jewish barbarians whom fate had so unkindly deposited into her charge and the equally hopeless task of teaching them the proper "manners." (There were as many young Negro barbarians in her charge as Jewish ones, but I doubt that she could ever bring herself to pay very much attention to them. As she never hesitated to make clear, it was punishment enough for a woman of her background—her family was old-Brooklyn and, she would have us understand, extremely distinguished—to have fallen among the sons of East European immigrant Jews.)

For three years, from the age of thirteen to the age of sixteen, I was her special pet, though that word is scarcely adequate to suggest the intensity of the relationship which developed between us. It was a relationship right out of *The Corn Is Green*, which may, for all I know, have served as her model; at any rate, her objective was much the same as the Welsh teacher's in that play: she was determined that I should win a scholarship to Harvard. But whereas (an irony much to the point here) the problem the teacher had in *The Corn Is Green* with her coal-miner pupil in the traditional class society of Edwardian England was strictly academic, Mrs. K.'s problem with me in the putatively egalitarian society of New Deal America was strictly social. My grades were very high and would obviously remain so, but what would they avail me if I continued to go about looking and sounding like a "filthy little slum child" (the epithet she would invariably hurl at me whenever we had an argument about "manners")?

Childless herself, she worked on me like a dementedly ambitious mother with a somewhat recalcitrant son; married to a solemn and elderly man (she was then in her early forties or thereabouts), she treated me like a callous, ungrateful adolescent lover on whom she had humiliatingly bestowed her favors. She flirted with me and flattered me, she scolded me and insulted me. Slum child, filthy little slum child, so beautiful a mind and so vulgar a personality, so exquisite in sensibility and so coarse in manner. What would she do with me, what would become of me if I persisted out of stubbornness and perversity in the disgusting ways they had taught me at home and on the streets?

To her the most offensive of these ways was the style in which I dressed: a tee shirt, tightly pegged pants, and a red satin jacket with the legend "Cherokees, S.A.C." (social-athletic club) stitched in large white letters across the back. This was bad enough, but when on certain days I would appear in school wearing, as a particular ceremonial occasion required, a suit and tie, the sight of those immense padded shoulders and my white-on-white shirt would drive her to even greater heights of contempt and even lower depths of loving despair than usual. *Slum child, filthy little slum child.* I was beyond saving; I deserved no better

than to wind up with all the other horrible little Jewboys in the gutter (by which she meant Brooklyn College). If only I would listen to her, the whole world could be mine: I could win a scholarship to Harvard, I could get to know the best people, I could grow up into a life of elegance and refinement and taste. Why was I so stupid as not to understand?

In those days it was very unusual, and possibly even against the rules, for teachers in public high schools to associate with their students after hours. Nevertheless, Mrs. K. sometimes invited me to her home, a beautiful old brownstone located in what was perhaps the only section in the whole of Brooklyn fashionable enough to be intimidating. I would read her my poems and she would tell me about her family, about the schools she had gone to, about Vassar, about writers she had met, while her husband, of whom I was frightened to death and who to my utter astonishment turned out to be Jewish (but not, as Mrs. K. quite unnecessarily hastened to inform me, *my* kind of Jewish), sat stiffly and silently in an armchair across the room, squinting at his newspaper through the first *pince-nez* I had ever seen outside the movies. He spoke to me but once, and that was after I had read Mrs. K. my tearful editorial for the school newspaper on the death of Roosevelt—an effusion which provoked him into a full five-minute harangue whose blasphemous contents would certainly have shocked me into insensibility if I had not been even more shocked to discover that he actually had a voice.

But Mrs. K. not only had me to her house; she also—what was even more unusual—took me out a few times, to the Frick Gallery and the Metropolitan Museum, and once to the theater, where we saw a dramatization of *The Late George Apley*, a play I imagine she deliberately chose with the not wholly mistaken idea that it would impress upon me the glories of aristocratic Boston.

One of our excursions into Manhattan I remember with particular vividness because she used it to bring the struggle between us to rather a dramatic head. The familiar argument began this time on the subway. Why, knowing that we would be spending the afternoon together "in public," had I come to school that morning improperly dressed? (I was, as usual, wearing my red satin club jacket over a white tee shirt.) She realized, of course, that I owned only one suit (this said not in compassion but in derision) and that my poor parents had, God only knew where, picked up the idea that it was too precious to be worn except at one of those bar mitzvahs I was always going to. Though why, if my parents were so worried about clothes, they had permitted me to buy a suit which made me look like a young hoodlum she found it very difficult to imagine. Still, much as she would have been embarrassed to be seen in public with a boy whose parents allowed him to

Senator Jacob Javits, 1978: The former United States Senator seen in his Manhattan office. Throughout his twenty-four years in the Senate he was regarded as one of the house's most valuable people. He consistently supported greater public aid to education, health, housing, the arts, civil rights and the curtailment of nuclear testing. He was born in New York City in 1904 and was raised on the Lower East Side. He joined the Republican Party in 1932 and was identified with its liberal wing. *Credit:* Photograph by Barbara Pfeffer.

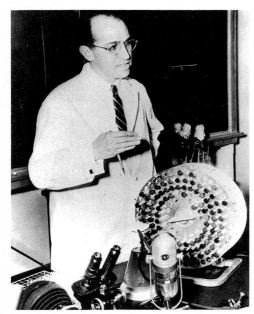

Dr. Jonas Salk, 1955: Epidemiologist and developer of a vaccine which was the first effective weapon against polio. For this accomplishment he was presented with the Congressional Medal for Distinguished Achievement. *Credit:* UPI

Isaac Bashevis Singer, 1974: Born in Poland in 1904. He published in Yiddish and Hebrew publications there from 1926 to 1935, when he came to the United States. He is a contributor in Yiddish to the *Jewish Daily Forward.* Among his most notable books are: *The Family Moskat,* 1950, *Gimpel the Fool,* 1957 and *The Magician of Lublin,* 1960. In 1978 he received the Nobel Prize for Literature. He is seen in his New York apartment. *Credit:* Photograph by Barbara Pfeffer

Erich Fromm, about 1955: Psychoanalyst, social philosopher and author. Fromm pursued an independent road in the publication of psychoanalysis to the problems of culture and society; he believed in the need for a society which recognized man as a responsible individual. Born in Frankfurt, Germany, and trained there, he emigrated to the United States when Hitler came to power. *The Sane Society,* 1955, and *The Art of Loving,* 1956, are among his most widely known books. *Credit:* AJA

Sharon and Michael Strassfeld, 1979: Two of the editors of *The Jewish Catalogue,* an informal yet comprehensive collection of crafts, history, tradition and general information relevant to Jewish life, which first appeared in 1973. They are seen in the backyard of their Upper West Side New York City home. *Credit:* Photograph by Bill Aron

Arthur Miller, 1972: Playwright and author noted for his significantly realistic dramas. Born in New York City in 1915, he became a newspaper editor and began to write in the 1930's. After World War II he acquired an international reputation for his plays, *All My Sons,* 1947, *Death of a Salesman,* 1949, *The Crucible,* 1953, and *A View from the Bridge,* 1957. He received Pulitzer Prizes for both *Death of a Salesman* and *A View from the Bridge. Credit:* Photograph by Charles Harbutt/ARCHIVE

Richard Tucker, about 1965: One of the most beloved and highly regarded operatic tenors since Caruso. Born in Brooklyn in 1913, he, like the children of other Russian immigrant parents, worked in the garment trades. He saved his meager earnings for voice lessons. From a member of a Lower East Side synagogue choir he rose to become a leading soloist at the Metropolitan Opera Company with which he was associated for thirty years. *Credit:* FD

Leonard Bernstein, about 1978: A prodigious talent, he has been acclaimed as one of the most charismatic and gifted personalities in the music of our times. He excels as a conductor, composer of serious and popular music, pianist, lecturer and author. Born in Lawrence, Massachusetts in 1918, he studied musical composition at Harvard, piano in Philadelphia and conducting with Serge Koussevitzky. He was associated with the New York Philharmonic from 1943 to 1969 as Assistant Conductor, Music Director and Conductor. *On the Town* and *West Side Story,* for which he composed the music, were presented on Broadway in 1944 and 1957. Outside the world of music, he has been consistently identified with liberal and humane causes. *Credit:* FD

Philip Roth, about 1960: Novelist who is noted for his incisive and satirical portraits of middle class American Jews. Born in Newark, New Jersey, in 1933, he studied at Rutgers, Bucknell and the University of Chicago. *Goodbye, Columbus,* 1959, was his first success, followed ten years later by *Portnoy's Complaint. Credit:* AJA

Isaac Stern, about 1975: The violin virtuoso who has become one of the most widely acclaimed musicians of his day. He has been described as the complete violinist . . . one who has tone, technique, musicianship and above all the ability to project. Born in the Ukraine in 1920, his family moved to San Francisco the next year. In 1931 he performed with the San Francisco Symphony conducted by Pierre Monteux. He is the first world famous violinist to receive all of his musical training in the United States. When developers wanted to raze Carnegie Hall, he lead the movement to save it. *Credit:* CBS Records

wear a zoot suit, she would have been somewhat less embarrassed that she was now by the ridiculous costume I had on. Had I no consideration for her? Had I no consideration for myself? Did I want everyone who laid eyes on me to think that I was nothing but an ill-bred little slum child?

My standard ploy in these arguments was to take the position that such things were of no concern to me: I was a poet and I had more important matters to think about than clothes. Besides, I would feel silly coming to school on an ordinary day dressed in a suit. Did Mrs. K. want me to look like one of those "creeps" from Crown Heights who were all going to become doctors? This was usually an effective counter, since Mrs. K. despised her middle-class Jewish students even more than she did the "slum children," but probably because she was growing desperate at the thought of how I would strike a Harvard interviewer (it was my senior year), she did not respond according to form on that particular occasion."At least,"she snapped, "They reflect well on their parents."

I was accustomed to her bantering gibes at my parents, and sensing, probably, that they arose out of jealousy, I was rarely troubled by them. But this one bothered me; it went beyond banter and I did not know how to deal with it. I remember flushing, but I cannot remember what if anything I said in protest. It was the beginning of a very bad afternoon for both of us.

We had been heading for the Museum of Modern Art, but as we got off the subway, Mrs. K. announced that she had changed her mind about the museum. She was going to show me something else instead, just down the street on Fifth Avenue. This mysterious "something else" to which we proceeded in silence turned out to be the college department of an expensive clothing store, de Pinna. I do not exaggerate when I say that an actual physical dread seized me as I followed her into the store. I had never been inside such a store; it was not a store, it was enemy territory, every inch of it mined with humiliations. "I am," Mrs. K. declared in the coldest human voice I hope I shall ever hear, "going to buy you a suit that you will be able to wear at your Harvard interview." I had guessed, of course that this was what she had in mind, and even at fifteen I understood what a fantastic act of aggression she was planning to commit against my parents and asking me to participate in. "Oh no," I said in a panic (suddenly realizing that I *wanted* her to buy me that suit), "I can't, my mother wouldn't like it." "You can tell her it's a birthday present. Or else I will tell her. If I tell her, I'm sure she won't object." The idea of Mrs. K. meeting my mother was more than I could bear: my mother, who spoke with a Yiddish accent and of whom, until that sickening moment, I had never known I was ashamed and so ready to betray.

To my immense relief and my equally immense disappointment, we left the store, finally, without buying a suit, but it

was not to be the end of the clothing or "manners" for me that day—not yet. There were still the ordeal of a restaurant to go through. Where I came from, people rarely ate in restaurants, not so much because most of them were too poor to afford such a luxury—although most of them certainly were—as because eating in restaurants was not regarded as a luxury at all; it was, rather, a necessity to which bachelors were pitiably condemned. A home-cooked meal was assumed to be better than anything one could possibly get in the restaurant, and considering the class of restaurants in question (they were really diners or luncheonettes), the assumption was probably correct. In the case of my own family, myself included until my late teens, the business of going to restaurants was complicated by the fact that we observed the Jewish dietary laws, and except in certain neighborhoods, few places could be found which served kosher food; in midtown Manhattan in the 1940's, I believe there were only two and both were relatively expensive. All this is by way of explaining why I had so little experience of restaurants up to the age of fifteen and why I grew apprehensive once more when Mrs. K. decided after we left de Pinna that we should have something to eat.

The restaurant she chose was not at all an elegant one—I have, like a criminal, revisited it since—but it seemed very elegant indeed to me: enemy territory again, and this time a mine exploded in my face the minute I set foot through the door. The hostess was very sorry, but she could not seat the young gentleman without a coat and tie. If the lady wished, however, something could be arranged. The lady (visibly pleased by this unexpected—or was it expected?—object lesson) did wish, and the so recently defiant but by now utterly docile young gentleman was forthwith divested of his so recently beloved but by now thoroughly loathsome red satin jacket and provided with a much oversized white waiter's coat and tie—which, there being no collar to a tee shirt, had to be worn around his bare neck. Thus attired, and with his face supplying the touch of red which had moments earlier been supplied by his jacket, he was led into the dining room, there to be taught the importance of proper table manners through the same pedagogic instrumentality that had worked so well in impressing him with the importance of proper dress.

Like any other pedagogic technique, however, humiliation has its limits, and Mrs. K. was to make no further progress with it that day. For I had had enough, and I was not about to risk stepping on another mine. Knowing she would subject me to still more ridicule if I made a point of my revulsion at the prospect of eating nonkosher food, I resolved to let her order for me and then to feign lack of appetite or possibly even illness when the meal was served. She did order— duck for both of us, undoubtedly because it would be a hard dish for me to manage without using my fingers.

Becoming a Successful Writer

Mid 1950's. Norman Mailer, one of the most outstanding writers of his generation, described his reactions to the success that his first book, "The Naked and The Dead," had brought to him.

Once it became obvious that *The Naked and The Dead* was going to be a best seller, and I would therefore receive that small fame which comes upon any young American who makes a great deal of money in a hurry, I remember that a depression set in on me. I was twenty-five, living in Paris with my first wife, Beatrice, and I had gone through a long leaky French winter in which I discovered once again that I knew very little and had everything still to learn. So I think I probably had been hoping *The Naked and The Dead* would have a modest success, that everyone who read it would think it was extraordinary, but nonetheless the book would not change my life too much. I wished at that time to protect a modest condition. Many of my habits, even the character of my talent, depended on my humility—that word which has become part of the void in our time. I had had humility breathed into me by the war. After four serious years of taking myself seriously at Harvard, the army gave me but one lesson over and over again: when it came to taking care of myself, I had little to offer next to the practical sense of an illiterate sharecropper. Sometimes I think courage is the most exhaustible of the virtues, and I used up a share of mine in getting through the war with my lip buttoned, since it took all of me to be at best a fair rifleman. No surprise then if I was a modest young man when it was all over. I knew I was not much better and I was conceivably a little less than most of the men I had come to know. At least a large part of me felt that way, and it was the part in command while I was writing *The Naked and The Dead.*

But once free of the army, I came back to some good luck. My first wife and I had saved some money during the war, and I did not have to work for a year. She believed in me and my family believed in me, and I was able to do my book. *The Naked and The Dead* flowed—I used to write twenty-five pages of first draft a week, and with a few weeks lost here and there, I still was able to write the novel and rewrite it in fifteen months, and I doubt if ever again I will have a book which is so easy to write. When once in a while I look at a page or two these days, I like its confidence—it seems to be at dead center—"Yes," it is always saying, "this is about the way it is."

Naturally, I was blasted a considerable distance away from dead center by the size of its success, and I spent the next few years trying to gobble up the experiences of a victorious man when I was still no man at all, and had no real gift for enjoying life. Such a gift usually comes from a series of small victories artfully achieved; my experience had consisted of many small defeats, a few victories, and one explosion. So success furnished me great energy, but I wasted most of it in the gears of old habit, and had experience which was overheated, brilliant, anxious, gauche, grim—even, I suspect—killing. My farewell to an average man's experience was too abrupt; never again would I know, in the dreary way one usually knows such things, what it was like to work at a dull job, or take orders from a man one hated. If I had had a career of that in the army, it now was done—there was nothing left in the first twenty-four years of my life to write about; one way or another, my life seemed to have been mined and melted into the long reaches of the book. And so I was prominent and empty, and I had to begin life again; from now on, people who knew me would never be able to react to me as a person whom they liked or disliked in small ways, for myself alone (the inevitable phrase of all tear-filled confessions); no, I was a node in a new electronic landscape of celebrity, personality and status. Other people, meeting me, could now unconsciously measure their own status by sensing how I reacted to them. I had been moved from the audience to the stage—I was, on the instant, a man—I could arouse more emotion in others than they could arouse in me; if I had once been a cool observer because some part of me knew that I had more emotion than most and so must protect myself with a cold eye, now I had to guard against arousing the emotions of others, particularly since I had a strong conscience, and a strong desire to do just that—exhaust the emotions of others. If there I was, with two more-than-average passions going in opposed directions, I was obviously a slave to anxiety, a slave to the fear that I could measure my death with every evening on the town, for the town was filled with people who were wired with shocks for the small electrocution of oneself. It is exhausting to live in a psychic landscape of assassins and victims: if once I had been a young man whom many did not notice, and so was able to take a delayed revenge—in my writing I could analyze the ones who neglected to look at me—now I came to know that I could bestow the cold tension of self-hatred, or the warmth of liking oneself again, to whichever friends, acquaintances, and strangers were weak, ambitious, vulnerable and in love with themselves—which must be of course half the horde of my talented generation.

This was experience unlike the experience I had learned from books, and from the war—this was experience without a name—at the time I used to complain that everything was unreal. It took me years to realize that it was my experience, the only one I would have to remember, that my apparently unconnected rat-scufflings and ego-gobblings could be fitted finally into a drastic vision, an introduction of the brave to the horrible, a dream, a nightmare which would belong to others and yet be my own. Willy-nilly I had had existentialism forced upon me. I was free, or at least whatever was still ready to change in my character had escaped from the social

Norman Mailer, 1948: Novelist and essayist, born in New Jersey in 1923, he grew up in New York City and attended Harvard. He has been described as the most brilliant virtuoso stylist in contemporary American literature having an extraordinary fertile mind with the ability to bring together ideas of a varied political, psychological and philosophical nature. *The Naked and the Dead,* 1948, made him an overnight literary celebrity. He was awarded a Pulitzer Prize in 1969 for *Armies of the Night,* an eye witness account of an anti-Vietnam demonstration in front of the Pentagon. Photograph by Carl Van Vechten. *Credit:* LC

obligations which suffocate others. I could seek to become what I chose to be, and if I failed—there was the ice pick of fear! I would have nothing to excuse failure. I would fail because I had not been brave enough to succeed. So I was much too free. Success had been a lobotomy to my past, there seemed no power from the past which could help me in the present, and I had no choice but to force myself to step into the war of the enormous present, to accept the private heat and fatigue of setting out by myself to cut a track through a new wild.

Now of course this way of describing my past has a protective elegance. I could as well have described the years which followed the appearance of *The Naked and The Dead* by saying that I traveled scared, excited, and nervous, ridden by the question which everyone else was ready to ask and which I was forever asking of myself: had this first published novel been all of my talent? Or would my next book be better?

In a sense, I may have tried to evade the question by writing *Barbary Shore*, but there was no real choice. If my past has become empty as a theme, was I to write about Brooklyn streets, or my mother and father, or another war novel *(The Naked and The Dead Go to Japan)* was I to do the book of the returning veteran when I had lived like a mole writing and rewriting seven hundred pages in those fifteen months? No, those were not real choices. I was drawn

instead to write about an imaginary future which was formed osmotically by the powerful intellectual influence of my friend Jean Malaquais, and by the books I had read, and the aesthetics I considered desirable, but *Barbary Shore* was really a book to emerge from the bombarded cellars of my unconscious, an agonized eye of a novel which tried to find some amalgam of my new experience and the larger horror of that world which might be preparing to destroy itself. I was obviously trying for something which was at the very end of my reach, and then beyond it, and toward the end the novel collapsed into a chapter of political speech and never quite recovered. Yet, it could be that if my work is alive one hundred years from now, *Barbary Shore* will be considered the richest of my first three novels for it has in its high fevers a kind of insane insight into the psychic mysteries of Stalinists, secret policemen, narcissists, children, Lesbians, hysterics, revolutionaries—it has an air which for me is the air of our time, authority and nihilism stalking one another in the orgiastic hollow of this century. I suppose it is a mistake to indulge myself, but I would like to put in some pages of excerpts from the novel, because few people who like my work have read it, and yet much of my later writing cannot be understood without a glimpse of the odd shadow and theme-maddened light *Barbary Shore* casts before it.

Leo Castelli, 1965: Avant-garde art dealer with a painting by Andy Warhol in his gallery on New York's Upper East Side. *Credit:* Photograph by Hans Namuth

William Zorach, 1946: The pioneering modern sculptor and painter in his Brooklyn Heights studio. Born in Lithuania in 1887, Zorach came to this country at the age of four. He was raised in Cleveland; studied there, in New York and Paris. As an early modernist, he exhibited paintings in the famous Armory Show of 1913. He moved from painting to sculpture and developed a personal style in which direct carving in stone and wood became the hallmark of his work and reputation. *Credit:* Photograph © by Arnold Newman, 1983

Louise Nevelson, 1980: Recognized internationally as one of America's leading sculptors, she was born in Kiev, Russia in 1899 and came to this country in 1905. Her family settled in Rockland, Maine. After studying at the Art Students League in New York, with Hans Hofmann in Munich and working as an assistant to Diego Rivera, the Mexican muralist, she began to define her own personal style which is characterized by monochromatic (often all-black or all-white) large reliefs. *Credit:* Photograph by Hans Namuth

Bruno Walter, about 1945: The renowned conductor at a rehearsal for a concert in the Hollywood Bowl. Born in Berlin in 1876, he became Assistant Conductor to Gustav Mahler in Hamburg at the age of eighteen. After a distinguished career as a conductor in Europe, he emigrated to the United States in 1939. From 1947 to 1949 he was Conductor and Musical Advisor to the New York Philharmonic. Considered a classicist, he excelled as an interpreter of Mozart and Mahler. *Credit:* FD

Andre Previn, about 1965: Conductor, composer and pianist. He was born in Berlin in 1929. As a student at the Berlin Conservatory, he was expelled in 1938 because of his religion. His family fled to Paris, arrived in the United States in 1939 and settled in Los Angeles. He began his career as a composer and arranger for films. In 1967 he became conductor of both the Houston Symphony and London Symphony. In 1975 he became conductor of the Pittsburgh Symphony. *Credit:* FD

Arthur Fiedler, about 1970: The recently deceased venerable conductor of the Boston Pops concerts. Although he was born in South Boston in 1894 while his father was a violinist with the Boston Symphony Orchestra, his family moved to Berlin in 1909. Returning to this country in 1915, he later played violin and viola with the Boston Symphony Orchestra. From 1930, his association with the Boston Pops, combining showmanship and musical ability, made the orchestra famous throughout the world. *Credit:* FD

Louise Nevelson Talks about Herself

1976. Louise Nevelson, the internationally recognized sculptor, is known for her eclectic style of dressing. She described her attitude toward clothes in this interview.

I feel the clothes that I have worn all my life have been freedom, a stamp of freedom—because I've never conformed to what is being worn. I remember once in the 1950s . . . I was working very hard at the time and I was living in that lovely house on East 30th Street. So I remember that I would wear, say, a black dress, but I always loved beautiful laces, so I had jackets out of beautiful laces. And black hats. So this man used to take me out and take me to all the night clubs and the smart places. He'd always comment on girls that were coming into these night clubs. The skirt was too short, the shoes didn't match, all of that. And I always thought I dressed special, at least for my kind of thinking, and rather simple. What can you do with black and white? And finally, one day, it struck my sense of humor—we were sitting in a big night club right over the Washington Bridge, where people gambled for high stakes. And finally I turned around and said, "What do you think of my clothes?" And he said, "Dear, *shmattes. Shmattes*" (rags). Well, I looked down and from his point of view, naturally the lace jacket was an antique and was old, so to him, I suppose it did look like rags.

So I never conformed in that sense. But on the other side, in the past, way in the past, artists were always to look poor in America. And they couldn't go into fashion. An artist friend of mine, a painter, said she had her mother's diamond bracelets in the bank and a mink coat, and she said, "I wouldn't be *seen* among artists dressed like that." Why make such a distinction? Isn't it really terribly conventional to think you have to be in a mold? To present a certain thing? Well, I broke that. Let's break tradition. That's exactly why I dress the way I do. Since I have such esteem for the creative mind, I wanted to really open the door. I felt that nothing was too good for anybody if they could recognize it.

I love old robes. I think I was the first person to wear a sixteenth-century Mandarin Chinese robe on top of a blue denim work shirt. Years ago. I still have it and I still do it.

Now I have a shawl that I have had for years, a paisley I paid very little for in Maine, and I decided to have a chinchilla coat made. So I reversed the concept of that. I had the chinchilla put inside and the paisley outside, to make a statement for myself that there is no difference in matter, as such.

I'm a great believer in a person who presents themselves, not too consciously, but that they feel right about their appearance. And they come already with that asset of feeling right. I don't mean that you have to be expensively dressed. It's nice to be informal, it's nice

Mark Rothko, 1964: One of the most prominent artists of The New York School, Rothko was a central figure in the development of abstract expressionism. He was born in Russia in 1903, and studied at Yale and with Max Weber at the Art Students League. After he committed suicide in 1970, his estate became the focus of a prolonged legal battle. *Credit:* Photograph by Hans Namuth

George Segal, 1965: Having established a unique idiom with his sculptures created from plaster casts of living models, George Segal's figures inhabit environments typical of our age incorporating real objects: furniture and machinery. Born in New York City in 1924, he studied at Cooper Union and the Pratt Institute. In 1950 he moved to a chicken farm in North Brunswick, New Jersey where this photograph was taken. *Credit:* Photograph by Hans Namuth

to be formal. I don't see why we have to go to either extreme. There's a place where people are people and confront other people, with dignity and all the niceties that we humans are capable of. But the point is, when I go to a party or I'm invited someplace, I project something. For me clothes and presentation of self is a projection of a total personality.

I recall that I went to a party once. Now it was the Bar Association and my lawyer was in it. And I thought since it was my lawyer, and there were going to be people of that sort, I'll still wear all the trimmings, but I'll play it down a little bit. And I did. And when I got there I couldn't speak. I was a lady. And that wasn't the role. Life is a stage and I

could speak. And I was so unhappy because I couldn't project anything. And I decided to hell with that. I couldn't speak, and I understood Charlie Chaplin.

I don't use anything else: only my eyes. I don't feel dressed without my eyelashes. I don't wear one pair . . . I glue several pairs together and then put them on. I like it and it's dramatic, so why not?

Personally, I'm dramatic, it seems. I like a whole thing, a formal thing—not clothes that show every part of the body and almost naked. I have a feeling maybe my appearance is deceptive. Because if you're going to put on a show like I do, they don't know beneath that facade there's something else. You don't

love a person. You love their position and their possessions . . . if you take away and strip that person to the naked self I don't think there'd be much love, unfortunately. We're caught just the same. Suppose, take me at my age and I didn't have a reputation and this or that and the other. I'd just be an old woman in a corner. And I'll tell you what I'd be doing . . . my chair would be toward the wall so no one could see me and I couldn't see them. Why should I be naked before everyone? Let me put it this way, dear, in life you cannot dig for the truth in every area. Must there be an answer? You take a flower, and you take every petal, and you won't have a flower. Keep the flower.

Louis Kahn: Recognized as one of the most outstanding architects of his generation, Louis Kahn has created major structures in all parts of the world. The Yale Art Gallery, Richards Medical Building at the University of Pennsylvania and Kimball Art Museum are among his most notable projects. Born in Estonia, he came to the United States at the age of four. *Credit:* Photograph by Hans Namuth

Saul Steinberg, 1965: Probably the finest satirical artist that America has produced. He was born in Rumania in 1914 and studied psychology and sociology at the University of Bucharest and Architecture at the University of Milan. He arrived in New York in 1942 and the following year began a continuing association as a cartoonist for *The New Yorker.* He has evolved a highly personal and individual style which embodies a form of short hand notation built on brilliant draughtmanship. *Credit:* Photograph by Hans Namuth

Art Collectors, 1976: Mr. and Mrs. Eugene Schwartz in their New York Park Avenue apartment with their art collection. *Credit:* Photograph by Barbara Pfeffer

Minding the Store

Mid 1950's. Stanley Marcus became President of Nieman-Marcus Co., the Dallas specialty department store, in 1950 and propelled it into a national success story.

After the board meeting at which I was made president, I gathered my brothers together to reiterate the need for continuing family solidarity and to caution us all that the test of this concept was about to begin. Heretofore, we had been held together by the colossal strength of a great man, our father, who was both the head of the family and the controlling stockholder of the company. "Now," I said, "we stand as four brothers with equal shares in the company, with theoretically equal rights as stockholders. I have been named president and chief executive officer and I shall be forced at some time in the future to make decisions which may be contrary to the judgments of one or the other of you. I shall attempt at all times to be fair and objective, but as long as I am the chief executive officer I shall expect you to accept my decisions, even when you may disagree." All three of them recognized my seniority in both age and experience, and pledged their sincere cooperation without reservation.

Being the boss of three brothers with comparable financial stakes and a closeness in age is somewhat different from being the stock-controlling boss of four

sons. No one of us was a shrinking violet, and our egos frequently collided. My father could rule by dictate; I had to administer by persuasion. The situation of four brothers, each separated from the other by only about four years in age, operating within the confines of four walls and under one roof, was not ideal for any of us; yet in some ways we succeeded remarkably well, for a time, at least.

Any successful retail business, in my opinion, must be the reflection of the aims and ideals of the executive director, who sets the basic policies for operations and who vigorously pursues the exection of them. This in no way implies that he does it alone, for he must have the collaboration of scores of able associates, but it does mean that the business cannot function well under a committee management. There must be a head who makes some of the tough final decisions after having heard all the arguments, pro and con, and some of those decisions may prove to be unpopular and even wrong. Nevertheless, he has to make them and make them decisively. My brothers did not always agree, but they did accept my decisions in good spirit. One eventually left the business for personal reasons and I resisted his subsequent attempts to return for business reasons which subjected me to a certain amount of public criticism. This is the type of hard deci-

sion which a chief executive must be prepared to make; it is doubly hard when family considerations come into conflict with sound business judgment. The integrity of management is at stake whenever it displays favoritism to a member of the family, and for that reason I have always insisted that members of the Marcus family conduct themselves in a manner as good or better than other persons in our employ. Nepotism is one of the most debilitating of all business diseases.

Variously I have been described as "the greatest pitchman of them all," "the man who has made more women happy," "the melancholy Plato of retailing," "a maverick," "a left-winger," "a gentleman," "a benevolent dictator of fashion," and "bearded and bald and an inch or two taller than short." Since truth sometimes lies in the eye of the beholder, I presume some of these descriptions of me fit under certain circumstances. I do love to sell, and I make an all-out effort to discover the motivations which make a customer want to say yes. The happiest moments of my day are those involved in devising letters to customers in distant places to inform them of some unusual merchandise offering, or working on a multifaceted advertising program, or leaving my office in response to a call from the selling floor to close a sale on a sable wrap for $50,000, or helping a man select a $10 sweater for his daughter. We have one inviolable rule in our organization—that the customer comes first—and any staff meeting can be interrupted to meet the call of a customer.

Since whoever described me as "the man who has made more women happy" failed to give the full details of what he meant, I must presume that he was referring to the fact that I have tried to create an atmosphere in which women enjoy shopping, that I have brought together the best in fashion and quality from which they can select, and that I have given them honest and candid counsel. That I will admit to. If the writer had anything else in mind, I must take refuge under the fifth amendment!

Women's Wear Daily, with its penchant for pithy labels, hung "the melancholy Plato of retailing" tag on me after a speech I made at the Universty of Southern California on "The Death of Elegance," in which I made some rather acid comments on the state of fashion and the conditions of manufacturing and marketing. I said, The death of elegance was forecast over one hundred and ten years ago by Alexis de Tocqueville, when he visited America and wrote *Democracy in America*. Among other prophetic oberservations, he predicted the inevitable decline of taste in a democratic society. In a stratified society, such as France had at that time, a *fine craftsman has only one set of customers, the aristocracy*. They demand the best

and the craftsman strives to give it to them. . . . But those days are gone forever. Elegance was a product to a large extent of hand labor, not mass production; of low labor cost, not $1.60 per hour minimum pay; of an elegant educated aristocracy, not the Great Society.

Despite my great love and devotion to the specialty store retailing field, I don't regard it as the most important activity of mankind, and I don't mind saying so. I take my business seriously and work extremely hard at it, as I would at any other endeavor which attracted my interest, but I can still take a good philosophical look at it and its relative importance to the world scene.

Bernard Malamud, 1978: Novelist whose work is characterized by use of a dialect of American English mixed with Yiddish and transference of Eastern European culture to the American scene. Born in New York in 1914; he won the Pulitzer Prize for *The Fixer* in 1966. *Credit:* Photograph by Barbara Pfeffer.

Lauren Bacall and Humphrey Bogart, about 1950: Born in New York City in 1924, Lauren Bacall has been a public figure since her 1944 appearance opposite Humphrey Bogart in *To Have and Have Not.* They were married the next year and lived in California until his death in 1957. Although films are her principal vehicle, she has appeared on Broadway on a number of occasions to critical acclaim. *Credit:* MOMA

South Pacific, **1949:** The original Broadway production with Ezio Pinza and Mary Martin. A musical play with music by Richard Rodgers and lyrics by Oscar Hammerstein 2nd. *Credit:* MCNY

Death of a Salesman, **1949:** The original Broadway production of Arthur Miller's Pulitzer Prize winning play.. *Credit:* MCNY

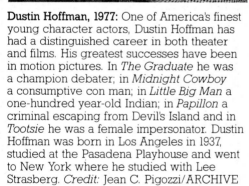

Woody Allen, 1979: Comedian, actor, film director, writer and universal comic genius, Woody Allen has received international acclaim for his books, plays and films. He was born in New York City in 1935 and studied at New York University and City College of New York. He began writing comedy material for television shows while a teenager, later became a night club performer and in 1965 entered film, which seems to be his ideal medium, as both screenwriter and performer. *Annie Hall,* 1978, received an Academy Award for best picture and screenplay. *Credit:* Photograph by Mary Ellen Mark/ARCHIVE

Dustin Hoffman, 1977: One of America's finest young character actors, Dustin Hoffman has had a distinguished career in both theater and films. His greatest successes have been in motion pictures. In *The Graduate* he was a champion debater; in *Midnight Cowboy* a consumptive con man; in *Little Big Man* a one-hundred year-old Indian; in *Papillon* a criminal escaping from Devil's Island and in *Tootsie* he was a female impersonator. Dustin Hoffman was born in Los Angeles in 1937, studied at the Pasadena Playhouse and went to New York where he studied with Lee Strasberg. *Credit:* Jean C. Pigozzi/ARCHIVE

Mel Brooks, 1977: Comedian, film director and television writer, Mel Brooks is recognized as one of the comic genuises of the present generation. Born in the Williamsburg section of Brooklyn in 1926, he began his career in show business as a drummer in Borscht Belt resorts and later wrote for Sid Caesar's television programs. His distinctive brand of mad-cap comedy has made him a cult-hero for younger audiences. Among his films are: *Blazing Saddles,* 1974, *Young Frankenstein,* 1975, *Silent Movie,* 1976, and *High Anxiety. Credit:* FD

Gilda Radner, 1977: While NBC's *Saturday Night Live* was in its prime, Gilda Radner was at her best as a comedienne. Born in Detroit, she appeared with the Second City company in Toronto and later wrote and performed for the National Lampoon radio show. *Credit:* Jean C. Pigozzi/ARCHIVE

Phil Silvers, about 1960: During the late 1950's Phil Silvers became a weekly household television image as the durable Sergeant Bilko. Born in Brooklyn in 1912, he joined Gus Edward's children's vaudeville troupe at the age of twelve as a soprano. When his voice changed, he switched to comedy. Although he started in burlesque, he has appeared frequently on Broadway, in films and on television. *Top Banana,* 1954, and *It's a Mad, Mad, Mad, Mad World,* 1963, are among his film hits. *Credit:* FD

Lenny Bruce, 1963: Described as a brilliant social satirist, people either loved or hated him. His use of profanity was directed at the hypocrisy of our social system with routines that were essentially intimate improvised talks with his audience. Religion, morality, the police and judicial system were the constant focus of his barbs. Wherever he played, his use of off color language got him in trouble with the police. Born in New York City in 1924, he started in the Borscht Belt, developed a stand-up routine for night clubs and came into his own in Greenwich Village clubs. *Credit:* WW

Barbra Streisand, about 1970: Raised in poverty in the Williamsburg section of Brooklyn, she had theatrical aspirations from the age of four. A self-taught singer, she achieved her first success in 1962 at nineteen in David Merrick's Broadway production of Jerome Weidman's *I Can Get It For You Wholesale.* With her vibrant personality and exceptional talent, she has emerged as a superstar entertainer on stage, television, recordings and in films. In 1968 she received the Academy Award for Best Actress for her portrayal of Fanny Brice in *Funny Girl.* *Credit:* FD

Bette Midler, 1977: Outspoken irreverent comedienne, she has described her act as "Trash with flash and sleaze with ease . . . I'm the last of the tacky women, but now I'm getting some class." Born in Hawaii in 1944, she began her career with a bit part in *Fiddler On The Roof.* *Credit:* Jean C. Pigozzi/ARCHIVE

Sid Caesar, about 1955: During the 1950's his *Your Show of Shows* was a highlight of television comedy that has yet to be equalled. With his co-star, Imogene Coca, each week they created hilarious character studies. Woody Allen and Mel Brooks were among his talented writers. Born in Yonkers, New York in 1922, he studied at the Juilliard School of Music and then switched to comedy. After successful appearances on Broadway and in night clubs, he began performing on television. *Credit:* FD

Stephen Sondheim, about 1965: Composer and lyricist for Broadway and motion pictures, born in New York City in 1930. Some of his notable successes have been: *West Side Story,* 1957, *Gypsy,* 1959 and *A Little Night Music,* 1973. *Credit:* FD

Sam Levinson, about 1950: A teacher by profession, he became a raconteur with a gentle folksy approach that appealed to Jewish audiences. Most of his anecdotes were reminiscences of his childhood on the Lower East Side. After appearing at Catskill resort hotels, he became a favorite guest on television shows. *Credit:* FD

Danny Kaye, about 1950: One of the world's most popular entertainers, he has attained extraordinary success on stage, screen, television and in concert halls. He developed a highly individual style which relied on a combination of mime, song, irony and his sunny personality. As permanent ambassador for UNICEF (The United Nations International Children's Emergency Fund), he has toured the world performing for audiences of children and raising funds for this organization. Born in Brooklyn in 1913, his career began as an entertainer in Catskill Borscht Belt hotels. *Credit:* FD

Bob Dylan, about 1965: Born in Duluth, Minnesota in 1941, his family moved to the Canadian border town of Hibbing when he was six. He began to play the guitar at the age of twelve. During a brief interlude at the University of Minnesota he performed with folk groups at coffee houses. He changed his name from Zimmerman to Dylan in recognition of Dylan Thomas, his favorite poet. His exceptional talent was first recognized after his move to Greenwich Village, New York in 1959. He was the undisputed leader of the folk movement from 1963 to 1965 when he turned to rock, becoming in turn one of its superstars. His protest songs were the anthems of social change of the 1960's and his influence on other musicians has been international in impact. *Credit:* FD

Fiddler on the Roof, 1964: Zero Mostel appearing in the original Broadway production of the musical which was based on a story by Sholom Aleichem. Having one of the longest runs on Broadway, this musical has become an American classic. Zero Mostel was born in Brooklyn in 1915. He had a successful career on Broadway and in Hollywood, but was blacklisted as a victim of McCarthyism. In 1958 he returned to Off Broadway in *Ulysses in Nightown.* In addition to his appearances on the stage he made a number of films. *Credit:* MVNY

Rehearsing *Fiddler on the Roof,* 1964: Jerome Robbins, who directed and choreographed this legendary musical, is seen rehearsing with Zero Mostel. Robbins has achieved acclaim as a dancer, choreographer and director. In addition to *Fiddler on the Roof, On the Town,* 1945, derived from his ballet *Fancy Free,* and *West Side Story,* 1957, are considered among Broadway's best musicals. Born in New York City in 1918, he joined the American Ballet Theatre as a dancer in 1940. In 1948 he became associated with the New York City Ballet and is now one of its artistic directors. *Credit:* MCNY

The State of Israel and Its Impact on American Jews

1948. Arthur Hertzberg, religious and communal leader, expressed the dilemmas being faced by American Jews when the State of Israel was established.

My grandfather was not a Zionist, and yet my first experience of Zionism was an act of identification with him—and rebellion against my father. It came right after my Bar Mitzva. My father, who was too much of an old-fashioned Hasid to force the hand of the Messiah, could no longer oppose the new tendencies invading his home, and so finally, rather behind his back, I joined the Gordonia youth group. As its name shows, it was sponsored by the Labor Zionists.

It is always tempting to read back into early adolescence attitudes acquired or clearly formulated later, but I rather think that even then, in a dim sort of way, I was not quite satisfied with the Jewish values of my home. Or, perhaps, as the son of a rabbi I felt left out of things, as indeed was the case, for I was made to study the Talmud during winter afternoons and all day during the summer while others were playing. A child is very lonely with a big folio in front of him—and Henty's stories of the Napoleonic wars, which I read when I was supposed to be reviewing (*iberchazern* is the traditional word), simply made the loneliness more poignant by contrast with such deeds of heroism.

Joining Gordonia was my first independent decision of consequence. It meant the beginning of a Jewish experience of my own. Of course, it was a decision compounded not of ideas but of symbols. My grandfather was still alive in Poland and my memory retained a sort of snapshot image of him. I had been taken to see him in Lemberg when we were leaving for America and I could still see a long gray beard close to my five-year-old head. He was not well off and my parents were too poor to do much to help him or the rest of the family. As Hitler came more and more into my consciousness—and I read more of Jewish martyrology—my grandfather's image acquired deep furrows in the face, a bent back, and troubled eyes. I knew that he was not a Zionist, and yet my Zionism was in large part an act of piety towards him.

It was also, as I said, an act of rebellion. That, too, was crystallized in a symbol, the leader of our group. He was a young man of twenty-two or twenty-four who had a way of life definitely his own. He wore blue, open-collar shirts (the emblem of Hashomer Hatzair) in any weather, did not attend synagogue, and I knew that he ate *trefah*. What he talked of was the new life being created in the *kibbutz*, the Palestinian collective, where he would soon go. I identified myself with him and dreamed of being able to be a new kind of Jew, free and strong and taking part in a life more real than school or Talmud.

Demonstration, Camden, New Jersey, 1948: School children celebrating the founding of the

State of Israel. *Credit:* NA

So I took the Jewish National Fund box in hand and trudged the streets of the east side of Baltimore. It was painful to ask strangers for money, but Grandfather was being saved, I was assuring my independence from my father, and the new Jewish world was being built—all through the little blue box.

Both Zionism and I have changed a bit since those days sixteen years ago. From a minority movement in a rather indifferent Jewish community and a world which did not take it very seriously, Zionism has risen to eminence. It has succeeded in creating a new state and—what is perhaps more difficult—in achieving around itself, at least from 1945 to 1948, a startling unanimity of Jewish opinion. During those three years there was about Zionism the compelling atmosphere of a moral crusade in which all of world Jewry participated. Bevin was the common enemy and the need of the refugees was sore. We all had felt helpless, frustrated, and, in our inmost hearts, immoral during the war as European Jews were being slaughtered. The fight for Israel united us so completely, I suspect, because it was at least a chance to make the world of murderers bend to our will, and also, perhaps, relieve our sense of guilt.

Now that Israel exists, the unity generated by the struggle is fast disappearing. As Oscar Wilde once said: there are two tragedies in the world—one is not getting what you want and the other is getting it. Now that the world Zionist movement has achieved its object, it is in a peculiar and difficult position. In the struggle for Israel, Diaspora Zionism created the greatest élan and the strongest organized instruments in modern Jewish experience. Zionism feels the need to continue its endeavors—certainly all is far from well with the Jewish world, both in Israel and internationally—and yet it is caught in an impasse between its own slogans, platforms, and previous record, and the realities of Jewish life today.

My grandfather is dead—he was killed in Lemberg by the Nazis—and what remained of my family in Europe is now in either Israel or the United States. Of course I know that there are still Arabic-speaking Jews who, even though rather foreign to me, are my brothers, and whom I must help towards Israel. The sense of responsibility for that task does not, however, provide the content for a stirring Jewish emotion. Indeed, it may have an opposite effect. It keeps reminding me that I really am thinking in terms of two categories of Jews—those who feel sufficient pressure to want to leave their homes, and we Americans who, in the vast majority, do not intend to move permanently to Israel. And yet, did not Herzl say in the *Judenstaat* that all of Jewry must return to the homeland? Is this not still an almost unquestioned doctrine of Zionist thinking in Israel?

As a Zionist, I face an impasse. Without passing moral judgment on either myself or Israel, I know that I am

something other than the Israeli, by upbringing, by my allegiance to America, and by my desire to be part of the cultural traditions of the Western world. And yet Zionism has been part of the underpinning of my life, that part which gave it the greatest zeal and vitality. It is not easy to let it go.

What shall I do with my Zionism? I know that I am not alone with this problem, that it is now being much discussed. But I have yet to hear any suggestion that really hits the mark. The attempt to maintain the political character of the movement does not excite me. It is true that a Zionist movement still remains in the political arena, and that Israel is still young and far from secure in the tides of international affairs. Yet the tasks left to bodies other than the Israeli government are of the nature of a political mop-up operation. American Zionist leadership speaks of dangers that may arise for Israel, in the face of which world Zionism must remain strong, standing ever ready on guard; but standing guard, as every soldier knows, is at best only tedious duty.

Indeed, it is becoming increasingly evident that the emergence of the new state will inevitably strip Diaspora Zionism of all political functions. In the heyday of the recent struggle for the state, I had a very real sense of participation. Wires and directives from the Zionist Emergency Council—the joint political high command of all Zionist bodies—were an almost daily occurrence. All this activity took time and pains, and therefore satisfied the heart. It satisfied my heart because I was still, down deep, thinking of my grandfather and of the cousins I had never met. I was helping to build a home for them and for other grandfathers and cousins.

But even Zionists are human beings and not selfless saints. When one builds a home for one's relatives, several emotions are brought into play. Certainly the one that predominates is the sense of kinship and personal responsibility. However, once the home is built, there are also the less creditable desires to receive gratitude, to exercise a continuing right to make the ultimate decisions, or, at the very least, not to be embarrassed or greatly displeased by the decisions that are made. The political direction of the state of Israel has already jarred these emotions and bids fair to deepen very fundamental divisions within world Jewry. I know that this was inevitable and so pass no moral judgment—but a very difficult situation does exist and needs description.

Inevitably, as a Zionist, I will look for content in the direction of cultural endeavor. The homeland has always been envisaged by an important body of Zionist theory as the center which would feed the spiritual energies of Jews the world over. The Hebraic values being revitalized and created by the renascent national culture would provide stimulation for all the Jewish world. This was the

emphasis of Ahad Ha-am fifty years ago, when he struck off the phrase *zarat ha-Yahadut*, the survival of Judaism.

Talk about cultural Zionism is more fashionable today than it has been in many a year. Both the Zionist Organization of America and the Labor Zionist group in the United States have recently held important formal deliberations on the theme. At both these meetings the political and economic sides of Zionism were reaffirmed in the usual way, but cultural notes were sounded more emphatically than heretofore. In the Rifkind report of the ZOA, points 7 and 8 of a suggested program for American and world Zionism read as follows:

"7. To foster among the Jews of America self-awareness and a sense of kinship with Jews everywhere and stimulate Jewish cultural creativity.

"8. To encourage the spread of the Hebrew language and of Jewish culture among the Jewish youth and the Jewish population generally."

In its formal declaration, the National Assembly for Labor Israel also reaffirmed, from its pro-Mapai point of view, the political and economic motifs of Zionism, but in the third paragraph the cultural note was sounded: "Israel and American Jewry both face the necessity of reviving the tradition of Jewish culture in order to integrate into a more meaningful and organic relationship many Jews who are driven together or held together by circumstances. In this endeavor, it is essential for American Jewry to maintain a close bond with the developing culture of Israel, and in turn Jewish culture in Israel can gain in breadth and significance by constant attentiveness to Jewish cultural expression in America."

Celebrating, Los Angeles, 1982: Los Angeles turns out to celebrate the birthday of Israel. *Credit:* Photograph by Bill Aron

United Jewish Appeal Dinner, New York, 1974: Golda Meir, Prime Minister of Israel, being saluted at the United Jewish Appeal dinner at the Waldorf-Astoria. Governor Nelson Rockefeller is applauding on the left. *Credit:* United Jewish Appeal

In the Light of Israel's Victory

1967. Milton Himmelfarb, prominent sociologist, raised questions about the implications of Israel's military success in the Six-Day War.

It's easy to forget. Here we are, some months later, and the news from Israel is of headache and annoyance, trouble and difficulty. We have almost forgotten the joy of unbelievable victory, and all the more our fear and depression in those weeks before the actual fighting broke out, when Nasser was tightening his noose. Political metaphors from thirty years ago kept running through our minds and conversations. We said, Munich; we said, Czechoslovakia; we said, salami tactics. As the days drew on we asked ourselves, "What are they waiting for? Why didn't they jump on Sharm el-Sheikh right away? The longer they wait, the worse it will be."

Some of us surprised ourselves and each other by our concern. Thirty and forty years ago we wouldn't have felt that way. Not to be parochial Jews was our pride. Now there is less of that kind of anti-parochialism than there used to be—not none at all; only less.

In the same way, there is less self-hate than there used to be. The surprise is that some Jews still had to find a reassurance about themselves in the military valor of the Israelis. One would have thought that that had been taken care of in 1948, with the Israeli war of independence. Israel, it then became clear, provided for the Jews of the United States and other countries like it a kind of contemporary pioneer or cowboy ancestry, reassuring us by showing us what we wanted and needed to have shown—that while Jews can be pretty good with a fountain pen and briefcase, they can also if necessary be pretty good with rifle or tank. . . .

In short, the Jews seem to be changing a little; but not as it may have been thought we would. For example, if by Zionism is meant agreement with Zionist ideology, we are no more Zionist than we used to be. Two or three days before the shots were fired, a midwestern professor told me about a plan he had for airlifting Israeli children to the United States, so that they would be out of danger when war broke out. He was sure that he could place five hundred children in his city. That was a personal undertaking. In France it was the offical Jewish community that got ready to receive Israeli children. According to Zionist ideology, this was topsy-turvy: Israel is supposed to be the refuge.

How then shall we describe the change that seems to be taking place among us? What has been happening is a slow bringing into consciousness of a disillusionment that has been going on for a long time now with the characteristic outlook of modern, Enlightened Jews. It is a shift from the general to the particular, from the abstract to the concrete.

The disillusionment is greatest with

Dollars for Israel, Brooklyn, 1981: Collecting money for Israel in an Israeli flag. *Credit:* Photograph by Ricki Rosen

our old idea that our enemies aren't on the Left—which is to say, that all our enemies are on the Right. For most practical purposes, that is where our enemies were, in the 19th century. The French Revolution had equality for the Jews as a corollary. We were for the Revolution and its extension, and the Right was against. Now the location of our enemies is not quite so simple. We have enemies on the Right, but also on the Left; and sometimes it is hard to distinguish between Right and Left. Sometimes our enemies on the Right and Left are happy to cooperate with each other against us. . . .

If we are becoming disillusioned with the Left, that could mean we are becoming more conservative. Hence, perhaps, some of our Gentile neighbors, and friends' irony at our expense during the excitement. The irony wasn't necessarily malicious. In general, it was a way of saying: "Welcome back to common humanity. Your old enthusiasms always seemed strange to us, but your present enthusiasm we can understand very well. Naturally, a Jew would be worried about Israel's danger and rejoice over its victory. That is the point. You Jews are becoming more natural."

More natural, yes; conservative, not quite. In England the Conservatives were said to be the stupid party. (But if the Liberals were so clever, why are they dead?) In the United States the conservatives are the stingy party. The Jews still belong to the generous party, as is proved by the uproar in Wayne, N.J. where we were accused of being liberals, always voting for more liberal school budgets. The Jews of Wayne

didn't attempt to deny it. They said that the purpose and effect of the statement were anti-Semitic, not that its substance was false.

What then are we becoming? To use symbols from the English political tradition, let us say that having been Radicals, we are slowly moving toward the Whigs (left-wing Whigs, of course). Or, to use an American symbolism of persons, we may say that having been partisans of Jefferson, we are growing more friendly to Lincoln.

Maybe it is as Whigs that we are learning new respect for old wisdom—such as that admonition of Oxenstierna's: "My son, if you only knew with how little wisdom the world is ruled." To the degree that we are not incapacitated for living in a practical world, we have always known that to be true, and we have made allowances for it in our own affairs and the affairs of government. We have done what engineers do. We have assigned to future events a Murphy factor—a margin of safety to guard against the accident and error and silliness that are bound to befall any human enterprise. (Engineers, told that a bridge should be able to bear of load of *N* tons, design it to bear 3*N* tons). But here was a case where even an extravagant Murphy factor was not enough to guard against the surprise of human stupidity. Nasser deliberately goads the Israelis into acting militarily. He knows that a shooting war is about to break out, that it must break out. He isn't quite sure whether his men or the Israelis will pull the trigger first, but he knows that someone is about to pull it. Having done all this, and knowing all this, he is then caught with all his planes on the ground.

There is the folk wisdom: too smart is dumb. General de Gaulle was too smart. A machiavellian, he overlooked Machiavelli's caution against being caught practicing machiavellianism in broad daylight. "Put not your trust in princes:" everyone knows that governments will break their word when it suits them. But de Gaulle went too far. Who will now be prepared to give him even the small amount of confidence that earlier might have been given to him? Having so publicly betrayed Israel, how can he expect anyone else to believe him?

An old illusion was that war is good, to which moderns and liberals responded with the illusion that any peace is better than any war. It has been a long time now, at least since Rupert Brooke, that anybody has been able to hear that line of Horace's, *dulce et decorum est pro patria mori*—sweet and fitting it is to die for your country—without gagging or giggling. The proper stance has been black humor: *Catch-22*. But rather less so for the Israelis. Theirs was no artificial state, no absurd Moloch. Its citizens were willing to die for it because they knew that if it died, so would they and their families and their hopes. Not much alienation there. One almost envies them.

It is an old, sad truth: a state acquires

its legitimacy—the opposite of ar-
tificiality—by the blood that its citizens
shed in its defense; as the early Christians said, the blood of the martyrs is the
seed of the Church. An elite acquires its
legitimacy by being prepared to die in a
higher proportion than others. Israel's
elite died disproportionately. The war
dead included many majors and colonels.

Modern, enlightened people, and especially Jews, have generally had a
certain amount of contempt for the military enterprise. Our two great culture-
heroes, Einstein and Freud, were notably contemptuous. What business is war
for an intelligent man? (Note that this is
bourgeois. Engels's friends called him
The General, because of his interest in
military theory; Lenin annotated Claus-
ewitz; Trotsky commanded the Red
Army; Mao made the Long March and
says that power grows from the barrel of
a gun.) Now, for people like us, the
Israeli generals are redeeming the military reputation. It isn't easy to belittle
what they did, or to upstage them.

One reads that the Israelis are a major
military power in the Middle East. One
reads that they have the best tactical air
force in the world. Unbelievable. How
could they have become such good
soldiers? They had no living martial
tradition. Peaceable men can become
warriors because of love of country, and
the roots of the Israeli army today lie in
the more or less underground Haganah
of twenty and thirty years ago; but while
the Haganah could train company commanders, it couldn't train a general staff.
Where does the skill of the Israeli
generals come from? . . .

If our respect for fighting and military
men has gone up, for talking and diplomats it has gone down. Those were
weeks when we couldn't tear ourselves
away from the proceedings at the UN. At
home we compulsively watched television, in our cars we kept the radio on,
to work we brought portables. We had
no mind for anything else, and it wasn't
edifying. You asked yourself how grown
men could sit there and pretend to take
it seriously. Business was transacted
somewhere, off in a corner, but the
diplomats had to be physically present
at the open sessions, pretending to listen
to words—countless words, words innumerable—that were mostly meaningless
and often malignant. It appeared to me
then that the career of diplomat might
not be much superior, for a grown man,
to the career of king. What can a
diplomat learn from that sort of thing that
is better than what the Duke of Windsor
says he learned from his experience as
Prince of Wales and King Edward VIII?
The Duke of Windsor says that he
learned never to pass up a chance to sit
down, or to go to the toilet.

In America the UN has had few
friends more devoted than the Jews.
Now we know not only that the UN can
be no better than the states of which is
composed—including the so-called non-

Demonstration, New York, 1978: Demonstration at the United Nations in opposition to the
resolution condemning Zionism. *Credit:* Photograph by Leonard Freed/Magnum

aligned nations, scurrying about on their
little Soviet errands—but also that the
organization itself, quite apart from the
members, is slightly lower than the
angels. "U Thant's war" is unfair—about
the most that can be said for him. Ralph
Bunche was loyal to Thant—about the
most that can be said for *him.*

We relearned the old truth that you
can depend only on yourself: Israel had
promises and friends, but even if it
hadn't wanted to fight on its own, it
would have had to. We relearned the
old, hard truth that only you can feel your
own pain. Who has really cared about
the Christian Assyrians? Does anyone
know whether any Christian Assyrians
are left alive? More Christian clergymen
worry about the whooping crane than
about the Christian Assyrians. When the
last speaker of Old Prussian died, and
the last speaker of Cornish, did anyone
care? Did any Roman care when the last
speaker of Etruscan died?

Jews who maintain relationships with the
Christian clergy were taken aback by
the generally reserved attitude of official
Christendom toward Israel in its hour of
greatest peril. Why the surprise? Christian ecclesiastics have an interest in the
Arabs, whether institutional or theological. Through the Christians' eyes they
could really not see what through our
eyes we saw as most urgently obvious.
We saw the incommensurability of Israeli and Arab war aims. We saw that the
Arabs wanted to destroy Israel—which
is to say, to destroy the Israelis. They
saw Israeli prowess and Arab refugees.

What I am about to say, a Jew really
shouldn't say to Jews. When we talk

about each other about Arab refugees,
we shouldn't defend ourselves against
charges of heartlessness. We should
leave that to our friends. Among ourselves we should remind each other how
often we are commanded to love the
stranger, not to wrong him and for the
homeborn, because having been strangers in the land of Egypt we know the
heart of the stranger. Having been refugees, we should know what it is to be a
refugee.

But our friends aren't saying it and it
needs to be said. Those who had to flee
Bolshevik Russia or Nazi Germany were
refugees, because there was no other
Russian or German country to receive
them. The Arabs are, or should be, more
like the Greeks from Turkey after World
War I. If the Greeks in Greece had not
received the Turkish Greeks there
would have been a Greek refugee problem, but the Grecian Greeks couldn't
bring themselves to deny refuge to the
Turkish Greeks. After the partition of
India there were Moslem and Hindu
refugee problems, until Pakistan absorbed the Moslems and India absorbed
the Hindus. Neither the Moslems nor the
Hindus could bring themselves to deny
refuge to their fellows from across several borders. Only the Arabs have been
able to do it, for almost twenty years.
Therefore they have had a triumph. The
Arabs turn their backs on other Arabs
and the opinion of the world agrees that
Israelis are at fault: Israel, which receives Jews from the Arab lands, in a de
facto exchange of populations, is condemned for the Arab refugees.

From a certain point of view, the
suspicion of Israelis about the intention of
Israeli Arabs shows greater human respect for them than the liberal urging of
people like us for Arab integration into
Israeli society. Your suspicious Israeli
has enough respect for the Arabs to
believe that their sentiments aren't determined by a comparison of earning
power under an Israeli and an Arab
government.

Now the war has been won and
humanitarians have their fears and worries over Israeli oppression refreshed by
every news report about the looting of a
dozen kerosene stoves. No one stops to
think any more what victorious Arabs
would have done.

Jewish Migration to the Suburbs

Mid 1950's. Nathan Glazer, prominent sociologist, appraised the impact of new communities on established Jewish life and values.

The most striking development of the last fifteen years in American Jewish life has been the "Jewish revival." One hesitates to call it a "revival of Judaism," for if one were to apply the touchstones of Judaism as a religion to the practices and beliefs of American Jews, we should find little to justify any talk about a revival of religion. What we see, specifically, is that Jewish religious institutions are, in relation to the other institutions in American Jewish life, far stronger today than they were in the 20's and 30's; and that Jews no longer take it for granted—as so many did then—that a natural concomitant of Americanization is the abandonment of their religious practices. Indeed, in some families we see the reversal of a process once assumed to be irreversible, with the children seemingly ready to accept more of traditional Judaism than their parents ever were.

It is thus by contrast with the 20's and 30's that the present situation of religion among American Jews strikes one as surprising, and by that contrast alone. Measured against the great ages of faith, what we have today must be called a secular society in which the influence of religion is minor, among non-Jews as well as Jews.

In the 20's and 30's the synagogue and religion offered but one center of life and interest among many on the American Jewish scene. Other specifically Jewish centers of activity, of equal or greater importance, were constituted by philanthropic work, by Jewish politics, and by Jewish culture. The leading figures in these fields were often indifferent when not actually hostile to religion. And so one had a split between what one may call Judaism, the historic religion, and Jewishness—namely, all the activities which Jews come together to carry on without the auspices of religion.

None of the three denominational branches into which American Judaism had become divided showed any great vitality in that period. The strength of Orthodoxy lay in the "ghettos" of the big city. But the prosperity of the 20's brought a mass exodus from these areas, and in many cities they disappeared entirely during the 30's. In the places with the largest Jewish population, however, New York and Brooklyn, the "ghetto" neighborhoods continued to hold many thousands of Jews; and just these were not only the poorer but also the more religious Jews. Religion, almost in its pristine East European form, continued to flourish in these shrunken "ghettos." Here one could still buy kosher food on any street, eat in kosher restaurants, and send children to religious schools conducted in the afternoon, or to all-day schools where half the curriculum was devoted to secular sub-

jects taught in English. Here were Orthodox synagogues of every kind—Ashkenazic, Sephardic, Hasidic, Lithuanian, and Galician. Here, too, were published newspapers and magazines, and books, in Yiddish and in Hebrew. There were by now so many Jews in America that, regardless of over-all statistical trends, enough Orthodox Jews were left in New York and Brooklyn for religious life to flourish.

In the neighborhoods of "second settlement" in the big cities, the predominant type of synagogue was still the Orthodox, with here and there a synagogue calling itself "Conservative" (modified Orthodox, in effect) and now and then a Reform temple. In the smaller cities and towns, where social movements were somewhat abbreviated, the neighborhoods of second settlement contained both Conservative synagogues and Reform temples. In the area of "third settlement"—that is, the expensive residential neighborhoods of the bigger cities—and among the well-to-do of the smaller towns, Reform temples were predominant, but conservative synagogues competed with them. Among well-to-do Jews, the Orthodox became a very small minority.

It was in the areas of second settlement—the Bronx and Brooklyn in New York, Lawndale in Chicago, etc., etc.—that the majority of American Jews lived before 1939. In general, the influence of religion and of religious institutions was very low in these neighborhoods. The synagogues had lost their Old World functions—that is, they were no longer houses of study and daily prayer—and their rabbis and supervisors had not yet developed skill in those functions on which churches of the New World based themselves in large measure—that is, they did not do social work, or serve as social centers; nor were they, for the most part, social institutions of the kind that conferred significant prestige on officers and members. Many of the children of the Jews in these neighborhoods went to college in the 30's, but, whether they went to college or not, in their majority they showed no interest in religion and its observances. Rarely in history, I think, has one come across a group as indifferent to traditional religion.

And yet the social life of these Jews, and of their offspring in the areas of second settlement was confined almost exclusively to fellow Jews. Before the 1880's, there were simply not enough Jews in this country to form the dense concentrations that make an exclusively Jewish social life possible. The "Jewish neighborhood" was born with the arrival of the millions from East Europe.

The relation to Judaism of these almost totally Jewish residential districts was an ambiguous one. While they made it possible for every variant of Judaism to find a minimal number of adherents, they also made possible a varied Jewish social life that was utterly indifferent—in

many cases even hostile—to Judaism. There were organizations that carried on some kind of Jewish activity, but were formally anti- or a-religious, like the Zionist and Yiddishist groups. There were organizations not formally Jewish in their membership, like the Socialists and other radical groups. There were purely social organizations which, whether or not formally Jewish, were altogether Jewish in membership. All this seemed to suggest to some people—notably Horace Kallen—that a specifically Jewish life could survive in the United States with only an incidental relation to religion. The idea was advanced that Jewishness—the complex of characteristics associated with the Jews as a historical group—could be maintained and taught as some kind of cultural whole, with Judaism—the historical religion—forming only a part of it.

This point of view, of course, had meaning only in terms of a larger outlook, that of "cultural pluralism," which looked forward to an America in which the descendants of each immigrant group would retain some of their original cultural peculiarities. Certainly in the 20's and 30's the Jews seemed ideal candidates for a culturally plural America. The problem rather seemed to be whether any of the other immigrant groups was equally eligible.

But after 1945 there could be no doubt as to whether Jewishness or Judaism was to be the basis for Jewish life in America. Jewishness as a program for Jewish life in America—that is, the notion that Jews could survive as a distinctive group in America, their distinctiveness defined not primarily by religion but by secular culture and quasi-national feelings—was seen to be impossible. Indeed, the ground had begun to be cut away from under this "program" by the early 30's. And after the war, with Jewishness already in the decline, Judaism in all its branches began to flourish astonishingly. A few years had wrought an amazing change in American Jewish life.

To consider the institutional side of the matter alone: today the Conservative movement is in process of rapid growth—from about two hundred synagogues at the beginning of the 40's to about five hundred now. The Reform movement is also growing, if not as rapidly—from about three hundred synagogues at the beginning of the 40's to about five hundred now. The congregations have grown in proportion. Even Orthodoxy shows a new vigor that is particularly evident in its all-day schools. These schools, almost all of which are conducted under Orthodox auspices and impose Orthodox religious observances, now have thirty thousand students, about two-thirds of whom are to be found in New York. More of these schools are being started every year. The number of Jewish children getting every kind of Jewish religious education has likewise risen greatly—there were about two hundred thirty thousand Jewish children receiving some form of religious instruc-

Wedding, Los Angeles, 1982: This ceremony was performed at a Conservative synagogue, Valley Beth Shalom. *Credit:* Photography by Bill Aron

Wedding, New York, 1975: Gathering at a Park Avenue apartment after the wedding. *Credit:* Photograph by Joan Liftin/ARCHIVE

Wedding, New York, 1976: A *Havurah* (Jewish commune) wedding of two anthropologists. *Credit:* Photograph by Bill Aron

Wedding, Los Angeles, 1979: This couple was married at home in an informal setting. *Credit:* Photograph by Bill Aron

Wedding, Cleveland, 1975: Dancing at a suburban wedding. *Credit:* Photograph by Jim Brown

Wedding, New York, 1977: The groom raises his foot to break the wine glass, an integral part of the Jewish wedding ceremony. *Credit:* Photograph by Bill Aron

Wedding, New York, 1974: Robin Lynn and Lawrence Blumberg were married at the Hotel Pierre in the same room as Robin's mother and father thirty-one years before. Robin wore her mother's wedding dress. *Credit:* Robin and Lawrence Blumberg

tion (about half in Sunday schools) in 1946; about four hundred thousand (with the same proportion in Sunday schools) were receiving it in 1954. It is hardly likely that the Jewish population of school age rose by something like 73 percent in these eight years.

But leaving aside the matter of figures, it seems to be a fact that the interest in Jewish religion is now greater than it ever was before in this country. People who would never have joined a synagogue fifteen years ago now find themselves (a little sheepishly) members of a congregation. Meantime there is much discussion as to "just what all this means."

The two answers most often heard are: Hitler and Zionism. These explain something, but, to my mind, not much. Certainly the catastrophe in Europe and the crisis in Palestine drew many thousands of Jews into Jewish activities, and into giving vast sums of money for relief and for Israel. This activity was, however, conducted almost exclusively by secular

organizations in which rabbis and religious groups played little part. In fact, the major Jewish fund-raising organizations have generally been indifferent to religion on principle—partly in order to avoid involvement in denominational conflicts, but even more because the leaders in philanthropic and Zionist work have often lacked any personal interest in religion. The temper of the times may well have been such as to bring many Jews back to the temple and synagogue, but I think that if we examine what has happened to the Jewish community in the fifteen years since the beginning of the war, we shall find more cogent explanations for this return.

During the war and after, many Jews in this country became more prosperous than ever before. As a group, they are not on fixed salaries—they do not tend to work for others, whether as manual workers, white-collar employees, or subordinate executives. They are inclined, rather, to be shopkeepers, independent businessmen, and professionals. Such

people were in a better position to take advantage of the war and postwar boom than those on fixed salaries. Businessmen in particular greatly benefited from the tax situation. After the war, one reflection of this new prosperity was the migration of Jews, on a scale unprecedented in this country, out of their old areas of second (and even third) settlement.

It was, in part, the migration of just those Jews who in the past had been most indifferent to religion: the second and third generations of the East European immigrants. The areas of second settlement deserted by these newly prosperous Jews had been, as we said above, the strongholds of Jewish irreligion—and of secular Jewishness. It was in these almost totally Jewish neighborhoods that, paradoxically, Jews could live almost completely out of contact with religion, and that the proportion of synagogue members was always lowest. It was in these neighborhoods, too, that almost any idiosyncratic movement in Jewish life—one, say, combining attachment to Yiddish and socialism with the rejection of Zionism and the insistence on territorial concentration in some area other than Palestine—could be pretty sure to find some adherents. And it was in these neighborhoods, too, that one could live a completely Jewish social life yet have no connection with any Jewish institution, religious or otherwise. It was there, in other words, that one could have none but Jewish friends, eat nothing but Jewish food, unself-consciously act out Jewish mores and culture patterns—and yet have no self-consciousness about being a Jew.

As these neighborhoods broke up under the impact of prosperity, and new settlements of much lower density were created on the outskirts of the metropolitan centers, a number of social influences began to be felt which simultaneously strengthened Judaism and weakened Jewishness.

Let us assume that a typical Jewish family migrating from an area of second settlement to a new suburban development consists of relatively young parents born in this country, and with one or two children of pre-school, or very early school, age. Such a family now become conscious of their Gentile neighbors, and of what they think, in a new way. The few Gentiles (Catholic and Negro janitors and the like) in neighborhoods of dense Jewish settlement were generally of a social status lower than the Jews around them, and as Marshall Sklare points out in his *Conservative Judaism*, they were not "neighbors" of these Jews. New suburban areas that might be considered "largely Jewish" are generally 25 to 50 percent Jewish rather than 75 to 90 per cent, as in areas of second settlement. Neighbors are now of the same or higher social status, and are Protestant rather than Catholic. Children go to school with Protestant children, and when Sunday comes it is embarrassing to have them playing outside while the Protestant children go off to Sunday school and church. The second generation's carelessness about religion—because it lived as it were to itself, away from the scrutiny and heedless of the opinion of the outside (Gentile) world, and under circumstances in which religion was associated with Orthodox narrowness, immigrant foreignness, and poverty—does not sit so easily under the new conditions. The emancipated American Jew now has to reckon with the social consequences of his unself-conscious agnosticism: does he mean it that much?

His children now play with Gentile ones on a level of middle-class respectability that does not generally countenance the simple name-calling and fistfighting of the old slum and the neighborhoods of second settlement, and the children now need *answers* to such questions as "Why am I a Jew?" It is harder to supply such answers in a middle-class suburb where everyone looks alike than in an urban neighborhood where ethnic groups are marked off externally as so many distinct species. The parents are at loss for answers, either because they have had no Jewish education, or because it consisted solely of the inculcation of a few traditional observances and some Hebrew and Biblical lore. None of this supplies the needed answers. A new form of Jewish education becomes necessary, and the modern Sunday school, with modern texts designed to "adjust" children to the fact that they are Jewish is gratefully accepted—relieving parents as it does of a task they cannot perform.

The problems of the third-generation children thus form a major factor in inducing second-generation American

Jewish parents to ask for religious schools. This might have offered the advocates of Jewishness without Judaism a chance to strengthen their position. If the problem faced by the Jewish parents in the suburbs were simply one of getting their children to attend a school on Sunday morning, and there learn some kind of answer to why they are Jews, there would be no reason for the school's being a religious one—it could just as well be secular. Certainly many parents must have considered this a possibility; we know of one case (there are others) in which effort was made to set up a school for the children of suburban Jews where explanations would be offered of what it meant to be a Jew without the inculcation of religious observances.

This proved unfeasible for two reasons. The first was the institutional vigor itself of Jewish religious institutions. Central bodies for each of the major Jewish denominational groups already existed with educational departments, prepared curricula, traveling field advisors, and rosters of qualified teachers. And it proved much easier to resort to such an existing body for help in starting a school than to try to start one oneself, with or without the help of the much smaller groups still maintaining non-religious schools.

Then, too, in each of these communities there tended to be at least a few Jewish families who had belonged to synagogues and who wanted to start one, in any case, in the new community. Those faced with the problem of the Jewish education of their children, but reluctant to allow it to be a religious education, would be confronted, on the

one hand, with an existing congregation—or one about to exist—and its established school, and, on the other hand, with what amounted to a relatively weak and institutionally unsupported feeling in favor of secular Jewish education. In this conflict, there was no question as to which would win out. Moreover, parents who began by sending their children to religious schools would very soon be drawn in themselves, if only by institutional pull. The children of non-members could be barred from the school, or the tuition for non-members' children could be made equal to the regular family membership dues that included children's education.

We began with the children in our attempt to explain how it was that Judaism has developed with such unexpected vigor among second- and third-generation American Jews. The children are not the whole story, but they are indeed a very important part of it. To use Herbert Gans's phrase, the Jewishness of the new suburban areas is "child-centered." The problem of raising children, educating them, and living where they will have the right playmates, takes up a good part of middle-class conversation in this country, and particularly so in the suburbs. Among Jews, the concern with such questions is probably higher than average because they seem more familiocentric than any other element of the population. A higher proportion of Jews marry, a lower proportion get divorced.

We have not yet told the whole story of the role of the children in the revival of Judaism because we are trying to separate those factors which we might call "sociological" from those we might call "religious." We conceive the latter as

Wedding, New York, 1976: This nervous young Hassidic bride is flanked by her mother and future mother-in-law. *Credit:* Photograph by Bill Aron

Educational Program, Scarsdale, 1982: A breakfast for "Scholar's Weekend" at the Westchester Reform Temple in Scarsdale New York. *Credit:* Photograph by Leonard Freed/Magnum

some kind of inner need independent of social surroundings that would lead one to act, if need be, against what one's milieu expects and encourages. The revival of Judaism, as manifested in the increased concern for Jewish education for children, has such aspects too. . .

Certainly the great role played by the children is not the whole story. In urban Jewish neighborhoods, as we have said, one was a Jew without thinking about it, and without having to do anything about it. In the new, middle-class suburban communities to which hundreds of thousands of Jews have moved, it was discovered that, subtly but certainly, American social life moved to a large extent along denominational lines. Gentiles expect the Jew to have a social community of his own, clearly marked off from the Catholic and Protestant ones. This enforced social compartmentalization has had the effect of making the secular Jew a "captive audience" and client of religious, or at least institutional, Jewry.

In urban Jewish neighborhoods, the Jew could choose his social milieu, and in many cases none of his friends or associates would have religious or institutional affiliations. In small towns the Jews had all along been more "exposed" to each other simply because of the smallness of their numbers, and in such circumstances every well-established Jewish institution has won out in the past. In a town like Nashville, Tennessee, for example, with less than 3,000 Jews and three synagogues, half the families are members of more than one synagogue,

and many of all three; even people not particularly attached to the Orthodox synagogue will sometimes give it money. Where Jews are so few that most of them are personally acquainted, it is hard to resist the pressure of those actively engaged in Jewish institutional affairs.

We may take another example from Akron, Ohio, which, because of the working-class origins of most of its Jews, still has two institutions carrying the word "workers" or "workman" in their titles: the Workmen's Circle, which is Socialist, and the Jewish National Workers Alliance, which is Socialist-Zionist. Many an Akron Jewish businessman who is a "capitalist" in the fullest sense of the word will belong to a workers' organization and the B'nai B'rith, a local synagogue, and half a dozen other organizations as well. He simply won't let a Jewish organization die. Of course, this "captive audience," which exists where there is a relatively small Jewish community in which each Jew perforce lives his life among other Jews, is only part of the story in the small cities and the small towns. Some bond of feeling must exist in order to enable the minority of institutionally involved Jews in such communities to play on the sense of obligation (or guilt) of the others. Without this bond of feeling the "captive audience" cannot come into being; it then becomes too easy for one to endure or disregard the disapproval of his fellow Jews.

In small towns, and now in the new suburbs, the majority of the Jewish community tends to surrender to the pressure of its most energetic, aggressive

members. Just who are these? They are the "Judaists," the upholders of Jewish religion, or at least of Jewish religious institutions. There is no question but that since the war the Socialist or Socialist-Zionist or Yiddish-cultural Jews, who were all strenuously anti-religious, have lost heart. The day of their causes is, clearly over. Their simple rationalism, to speak of nothing else, is no longer satisfying. I do not wish to go into all the causes of what the embattled naturalists have called "the new failure of nerve." Certainly the European catastrophe has had something to do with it. In the middle 40's, a fascinating and moving development took place among those Yiddish writers who for generations had been the apostles of simple rationalism. These men, many of them middle-aged and older, returned to religion. It was not rational Reform to which they turned. In typical Jewish style, they underwent no conversions. They did not have visions, or mystical experiences. They decided simply to be "good Jews." One should not exaggerate the scale of this movement: Indeed, to a sociologist it is invisible, for the few Jewish scholars and journalists who returned to traditional religion cause no bulge in any conceivable statistics. Still, what they did was significant in its context.

There was also the general change in the climate of opinion. Almost all recent forms of secular Jewishness have had some kind of Socialist orientation. These tendencies suffered along with the general decline of socialism in America. They were all anti-clerical and even determinedly atheistic; the general fading of militant irreligion in this country, and the growing acceptance of religion as an integral part of Americanism, have made them seem irrelevant. Then, too, the Jewish community, once largely working class, was now almost entirely middle class. How could such a community maintain an attachment to rather exotic and quite foreign-looking secular Socialist movements? And if all these modes of being a Jew were no longer possible, what was left but religion?

And so in the new Jewish communities burgeoning after the war, the naturalist, rationalist, and anti-clericalist were likely to fall silent, or at least become far more reticent than fifteen years before; at the same time the religious Jew, even if his religion was merely nominal, felt distinctly stronger and tended to become more assertive.

Finally, the religious institutions themselves have responded to the needs of the "returning" Jews. In the new synagogue buildings built since the war, the schools and community-center facilities often loom larger than the house of worship itself. The schools are not, as in the city synagogue, housed in a basement. They are fine modern edifices designed by outstanding architects. There are also such installations as nursery schools, clubrooms for teen-agers, meeting places for young married couples, and card rooms for the older people. Following the advice of Mordecai Kaplan consciously or unconsciously, the synagogues have become "synagogue centers." In many cases, the synagogue itself is the last thing a family comes to. The children almost certainly go to the school, the teen-agers very likely go to the dances, the women probably join the sisterhoods, the men possibly join the brotherhoods. Last— and the rabbi often asks himself, does this mean least?—are the services, poorly attended by a core of old-timers and the merest scattering of young people.

In effect, Mordecai Kaplan's view of the future of Judaism, as expressed in the middle 30's in *Judaism* as a *Civilization*, has triumphed. Not that Rabbi Kaplan is himself happy about the result. It was the social needs of the individual Jew and the communal needs of the entire community that the new synagogue met, and as an institution it has flourished in consequence. People asked: Is the new synagogue meeting the religious needs of Jews? Much less seldom did they ask *what* these needs were. Actually, one could have reason to believe that the Jewish religious institutions have won such wide support lately precisely, and merely, because they enable Jews, in the guise of a denomination, to survive as a separate group in America. That this be institutional Judaism's main function was quite directly proposed by one writer, and certainly felt by many other people. C. B. Sherman, a Zionist and a sociologist, pointed out that in America ethnic groups as such do not survive, and considering the make-up of American society there is no reason why they should. Cultural pluralism, which assumed some kind of minority cultural identity, remains unrealized. What, then, of those of us who want to see American Jews survive in their Jewish identity? The answer, said Mr. Sherman, is that we may survive as a religion. For the United States does recognize and grant place to a variety of religions. From a somewhat different point of view, this is what Mordecai Kaplan was saying twenty years before.

Is this the whole story? Does the synagogue survive because it satisfies the social and communal needs of Jews, and, in particular, because it enables them to maintain a somewhat separate identity in a guise appropriate to the American environment? Or does it satisfy real religious needs? Or is the survival of the Jewish people itself a "religious" need?

A Recent Examination of Jewish Suburbia

1979. Marshall Sklare and Joseph Greenblum produced their first sociological study of a Jewish suburban community in 1967. Lakeville, an invented name for an actual suburb of a Midwestern industrial city, served as their focus. Twelve years later they reexamined the situation in Lakeville and reported on it.

While Lakeville has done a first-class job of resisting deterioration, it is nevertheless a far different community today from what it was in the 1950's. The difference resides in the fact that Lakeville is no longer a community dominated by WASP's. In our original study, the Jews were in a minority. By the 1970's, they had become a majority. This is remarkable considering that the Jewish population of the Lake City metropolitan area has declined noticeably in recent decades. Despite this decline, the attraction of Lakeville for middle- and upper-class Jews has been so strong that the area has grown in Jewish population. While some of the more elderly Jews have moved to the Sun Belt or to apartments outside of Lakeville, in the majority of cases their homes have been purchased by young Jews eager to reside in Lakeville and willing to pay a premium price for the opportunity.

The Jewish growth has also been made possible by the fact that White Christians have avoided moving into Lakeville. The exact date when the "tipping point" was reached—that is, when the community became fixed in the public mind as a "Jewish" suburb, when Gentiles began to move away and new Gentile families moving in became fewer—is a project for historians. For our purpose it is enough to note that for some time now, when a Gentile family places their home on the market (assuming that it is located in a desirable residential area), in the majority of cases the home finds a Jewish buyer. Jewish-owned homes placed on the market have generally been purchased by Jewish buyers.

It is noteworthy that the change in the ethnic and religious composition of Lakeville has been a very gradual process. There has not been any panic selling on the part of Gentiles. If anything, Gentiles who have wished to move have been in no hurry to dispose of their property. They have been willing to remain until they could find a buyer willing to meet their price. Indeed, since the community has maintained its excellent facilities and its unique advantages and has even upgraded itself, there has been nothing to motivate panic selling on the part of Gentiles. While crime has increased, it has generally been in the category of home burglary and thus characteristic of many residential communities. In the case of Lakeville, the rise in home burglaries is a tribute to the wealth of its residents and to the standard of living which they enjoy. Street crime has never been a major problem.

In sum, Lakeville has had none of the conditions which would encourage rapid flight of Gentile residents. Nevertheless, at some time a tipping point was reached and Lakeville emerged as a "Jewish" rather than a "Gentile" suburb. Lakeville was in fact identified as a Jewish suburb well before the majority of the population was Jewish. Reaching the tipping point involved two processes: Gentiles avoiding moving into Lakeville and Gentile residents leaving in small but steady numbers.

Movement of Gentiles out of the community appears to have been motivated by the Jewish influx. By the mid-1960's, Lakeville had very few choice building sites available. When new homes were built, they were generally occupied by Jews. Furthermore, the removal of Gentile families occupying older homes was not balanced by an influx of Gentile families moving into Gentile-owned homes.

In the mid-1970's Joseph Manillo, an Italian Catholic who at the time was Lakeville's mayor and leading political figure, told us that he would be the last non-Jewish mayor of Lakeville. He viewed the situation as follows:

I would guess, being very conservative, that the figure today is somewhere between 70 and 75 percent Jewish. And I can't find any other figure. I cannot make it come out any other way. I can't find the other [Gentile] people. I would like to. But I have to say that, of the 33,000, we probably have somewhere in the vicinity of 23,000 people of Jewish descent.

Manillo was acutely aware of the Jewish influx. Each week he received the report of the Welcome Wagon organization which profiled the new residents. Among the items in the profile was religion:

Sometimes a person will say "no re-ligion" or "none." But we know which direction they [the newcomers] are going in, and it's very heavily Jewish. Some weeks it could be 8 to 1, 7 to 2, or 6 to 2; 5 to 3 would be a good week.

Manillo's regret about the new Jewish dominance of Lakeville was just that—regret. He was no lover of WASP's. As a Catholic of working-class origin who was born in Lakeville and grew up there, he found that he was accepted more by Jews than by WASP's. Furthermore, he realized that he could never have achieved his post if the community had remained under WASP domination. Nevertheless, Manillo felt that there were no substantial intergroup relations problems in the community:

I don't think there's any anti-Semitism in the community because of its [Jewish influx]. There may be a slur against anybody. I get it myself. . . . I just think there's a resignation—that this is the way it is in Lakeville, and if you like it, fine, and if you don't, you don't have to stay.

And indeed, true to the Lakeville spirit of preserving community harmony, Gentile neighbors who left Lakeville had a ready battery of rational and inoffensive reasons to explain their removal: they wished to own a smaller house now that their children were grown, they preferred a community with more open space than was available in Lakeville, or they preferred an apartment or condominium where they would be freed from the burdensome responsibilities of home-maintenance. Nevertheless, it was noticeable that when two huge luxury high-rise apartment buildings were constructed on a choice lakefront location close to Lakeville, the majority of the apartments found Jewish rather than Gentile buyers. Gentile buyers tended to purchase in Gentile areas located some distance from Lakeville. This generally meant sacrificing the advantage of a location near the lakefront. Gentiles were willing to forgo the advantage.

Turning to Jewish attitudes and behavior, we should note that there was no organized attempt to make Lakeville a Jewish suburb. In traditional Jewish society the emergence of a Jewish area would be welcome. Not only would Jewish dominance insure greater safety of life and limb, but it would have the advantage of minimizing interaction with the outgroup. However, Lakeville's Jews do not follow the pattern of attitudes found in traditional Jewish society. In fact, a significant segment favored the *status quo*—in effect a Gentile-dominated community. However, they could not bring themselves to take action which would insure continued Gentile dominance. Such action would have necessarily involved some form of exclusion of Jews, or at the very least the placing of the issue on the community's agenda.

Both approaches were highly distasteful to established Jewish residents and were studiously avoided.

The continued influx of Jews is traceable to the fact that the elite of the Jewish community in the metropolitan area is not a miniscule proportion of the total Jewish population but rather is much larger than would be true for many other groups. As a result of the size of this elite, Lakeville had not exhausted its potential by the late 1950's.

Lakeville's emergence as a community where Jews constitute a majority rests upon a further fact: the willingness of some Jews to settle in a community where they are in the majority, or close to becoming one. There is little question that Jewish oldtimers in Lakeville preferred a community where Jews were a minority. But being such a large group, the Jewish elite has several strands of opinion, including one which has no objection to living in a community dominated by Jews. Thus, the fact that Lakeville is, in composition if not in ambience, increasingly like the older Jewish neighborhoods of Lake City as well as like several of the newer suburban areas did not deter some Jews. On the contrary, it increased their interest in moving to the community.

As Manillo put it, those who are unhappy with the changing composition of the community need not stay. Manillo told us that this applied to Jews as well as Gentiles—that over the years he had received calls from Jews as well as from Gentiles about the Jewish influx. He said that one of the Jews who had called him complained that "he was in a worse ghetto now than he had been when he lived in Lake City."

Those Jews who favored stabilizing the community and keeping Gentiles in the majority sought to have the office of mayor of Lakeville occupied by a Gentile. The tradition of retaining a Gentile mayor was supplemented by a further step—that of encouraging Gentiles to take leadership roles in community affairs. The hope was that the occupancy of leadership roles by Gentiles would alleviate Gentile anxieties and prevent the establishment of the image of Lakeville as a Jewish suburb.

There was one area of civic life, however, where Jews did not maintain a low profile. This was the school board, or, more properly, the boards of the various school districts which include the schools of Lakeville and of some of the adjoining communities. The factors which made it difficult for Jews to restrain themselves from running for positions on the school boards include the following: their children constituted a substantial segment of the public-school population; they valued education; they had an affinity for public rather than private education; the Jewish level of education was higher than that of Gentiles; and of college- and university-educated residents, a higher proportion of Jews had attended first-quality institutions. Finally, Jewish familiarity with pub-

lic education, both as professionals and volunteers, exceeded that of Gentiles. In sum, while care was taken to give Gentiles as much representation as possible on Lakeville's recreational commission, civic beautification commission, zoning commission, and similar bodies, the Jews did not cultivate the lowest possible profile in school affairs.

Control of local school boards had a special complication. As the proportion of middle- and upper-class WASP's was diminished by death and removals, and as this segment of the population aged, Lakeville became a community where the two leading components of the student body were Jews and Italians—or, more specifically, middle- and upper-class Jews and working-class and lower-middle-class Italians. An Italian area immediately outside of Lakeville was included in a local school district. The area, which had predated the Jewish influx, was founded by gardeners and construction workers who had helped to build and maintain the homes and gardens of the Gentile upper class. Although Italians slowly moved up the class ladder, the section remained Italian. Italian parents encouraged their children to remain in the area. Thus, the Italian section was a long-established area with firmly-rooted traditions.

While the Italian presence did not disturb elementary schools—each one of which tended to be responsive to local attitudes in respect to curriculum, ambience, and patterns of discipline—the situation was more complicated at the high school with its mixed student body. During the late 1950's and the '60s, much effort was invested in avoiding a confrontation between Italian and Jewish students at the high school as well as a showdown between their parents. Jews were interested in a high school which would produce students who could hold their own in competition with the products of the nation's best secondary schools—students who could score well on the SAT's and thus qualify for admittance to first-class private universities. Italians had no such ambitions, and they saw the high school as insensitive to the needs of the non-college bound or those who were going on to institutions of higher learning which were oriented vocationally rather than to the liberal arts. Jewish parents were also interested in curriculum innovation, whether in science, mathematics, social studies, or English. Italian parents were not similarly interested; they felt that the old methods were still acceptable.

The visibility of Jews in school affairs was more salutary than was realized, however. Dialogue was encouraged between and among students, parents, teachers, and administrators. While community rifts were not entirely bridged, they were placed under scrutiny, and human-relations programs were initiated to build contacts between diverse constituencies.

By the late 1970's, not only did Lakeville have a Jewish mayor but the

low-profile pattern which Jews had established decades earlier had eroded away. While upper-class Protestants still lived in the community, they refused to take part in public affairs. As a long-time resident of German-Jewish background who has been active in civic affairs for several decades explained:

The more involved Jews get, the more the Gentiles retire to their homes and just literally give up, except for a few that we call "show Catholics" and "show Protestants." There are maybe twenty of them, and they will get appointed to every single city-wide thing that goes on, because they'll do it—and they're very capable people. But the others won't even make an effort to come forth.

To all appearances, Lakeville is still the community which it was a few decades ago. During the Christmas season the stores and shopping areas are decorated in the fashion of the old Lakeville. Despite Jewish representation, the Chamber of Commerce still observes a venerable Lakeville tradition: the erection of Santa Claus House. But Gentiles both in Lakeville and in the Lake City metropolitan area know that Lakeville has changed; they identify the community as "Jewish" and thus as far different from the Lakeville of yesterday.

Ketubah Signing, New York, 1979: Rabbi Max Titkin signed the ketubah after the wedding of Richard Siegel and Jeannie Maman. The calligrapher was Joan Mesnick. *Credit:* Photograph by Bill Aron

Wedding, New York, 1979: Richard Siegel is swept up in dancing at his wedding. He collaborated with Michael and Sharon Strassfeld on *The First Jewish Catalogue* and with Michael Strassfeld on the annual *Jewish Calendar. Credit:* Photograph by Bill Aron

National Jewish Organizations, 1981

The American Jewish community is well supplied with a large number of organizations which serve a variety of functions: religious, educational, cultural, community relations, overseas aid, social welfare, social, mutual benefit, Zionist and pro-Israel, professions, women's groups, youth and student groups. This listing was taken from the American Jewish Yearbook, 1981. *Credit: American Jewish Committee and Jewish Publication Society of America*

Community Relations
American Council for Judaism • American Jewish Alternatives to Zionism • American Jewish Committee • American Jewish Congress • Anti-Defamation League of B'nai B'rith • Association of Jewish Center Workers • Association of Jewish Community Relations Workers • Center for Jewish Community Studies • Commission on Social Action of Reform Judaism • Conference of Presidents of Major American Jewish Organizations • Consultative Council of Jewish Organizations • Coordinating Board of Jewish Organizations • Council of Jewish Organizations in Civil Service • Institute for Jewish Policy Planning and Research • International Conference of Jewish Communal Service • Jewish Labor Committee • Jewish War Veterans of the United States of America • National Conference on Soviet Jewry • National Jewish Commission on Law and Public Affairs • National Jewish Community Relations Advisory Council • North American Jewish Youth Council • Student Struggle for Soviet Jewry • Union of Councils for Soviet Jewry • World Jewish Congress

Cultural
American Academy for Jewish Research • American Biblical Encyclopedia Society • American Histadrut Cultural Exchange Institute • American Jewish Historical Society • American Jewish Press Association • American Society for Jewish Music • Associated American Jewish Museums • Association for the Sociological Study of Jewry • Association of Jewish Libraries • Association of Jewish Publishers • Center for Holocaust Studies • Central Yiddish Culture Organization • Conference on Jewish Social Studies • Congress for Jewish Culture • Hebrew Arts School for Music and Dance • Hebrew Culture Foundation • Histadruth Ivrith of America • Jewish Academy of Arts and Sciences • Jewish Book Council of JWB (Jewish Welfare Board) • Jewish Information Bureau • Jewish Music Council of JWB (Jewish Welfare Board) • Jewish Publication Society of America • Judah L. Magnes Memorial Museum (Jewish Museum of the West) • Leo Baeck Institute • Memorial Foundation for Jewish Culture • National Foundation for Jewish Culture • National Hebrew Culture Council • Research Foundation for Jewish Immigration • Society for the History of Czechoslovak Jews • The Jewish Museum • Yeshiva University Museum • Yiddisher Kultur Farband • YIVO Institute for Jewish Research

Overseas Aid
American Council for Judaism Philanthropic Fund • American Friends of the Alliance Israélite Universelle • American Jewish Joint Distribution Committee • American ORT Federation • Association Pour le Rétablissement des Institutions et Oeuvres Israélites en France • Conference on Jewish Material Claims Against Germany • HIAS • International League for the Repatriation of Russian Jews • Jewish Restitution Successor Organization • League for Yiddish • United Jewish Appeal • Women's Social Service for Israel

Religious and Educational
Agudas Israel World Organization • Agudath Israel of America • American Association for Jewish Education • American Association of Rabbis • Association for Jewish Studies • Association of Jewish Chaplains of the Armed Forces • Association of Orthodox Jewish Scientists • Beth Medrosh Elyon (Academy of Higher Learning and Research) • B'nai B'rith Hillel Foundations • B'nai B'rith Youth Organization • Brandeis-Bardin Institute • Cantors Assembly of America • Central Conference of American Rabbis • Central Yeshiva Beth Joseph Rabbinical Seminary • Cleveland College of Jewish Studies • Dropsie University • Gratz College • Hebrew College • Hebrew Theological College • Hebrew Union College—Jewish Institute of Religion • Herzliah-Jewish Teachers Seminary • International Association of Hillel Directors • Jewish Chautauqua Society • Jewish Ministers Cantors Association of America • Jewish Reconstructionist Foundation • Jewish Teachers Association (Morim) • Jewish Theological Seminary of America • Machne Israel • Merkos L'Inyonei Chinuch (The Central Organization for Jewish Education) • Mesivta Yeshiva Rabbi Chaim Berlin Rabbinical Academy • Mirrer Yeshiva Central Institute • National Committee for Furtherance of Jewish Education • National Council for Jewish Education • National Council of Beth Jacob Schools • National Council of Young Israel • National Federation of Jewish Men's Clubs • National Jewish Conference Center • National Jewish Hospitality Committee • National Jewish Information Service for the Propagation of Judaism • Ner Israel Rabbinical College • Ozar Hatorah • P'eylim (American Yeshiva Student Union) • Rabbinical Alliance of America (Igud Harabonim) • Rabbinical Assembly • Rabbinical College of Telshe • Rabbinical Council of America • Reconstructionist Rabbinical College • Research Institute of Religious Jewry • Sholem Aleichem Folk Institute • Society of Friends of the Touro Synagogue, National Historic Shrine • Spertus College of Judaica • Synagogue Council of America • Torah Umesorah (National Society for Hebrew Day Schools) • Touro College • Union of American Hebrew Congregations • Union of Orthodox Jewish Congregations of America • Union of Orthodox Rabbis of the United States and Canada • Union of Sephardic Congregations • United Lubavitcher Yeshivoth • United Synagogue of America • West Coast Talmudical Seminary • Women's League for Conservative Judaism • World Council of Synagogues • World Union for Progressive Judaism • Yavne Hebrew Theological Seminary • Yavneh (National Religious Jewish Students' Association) • Yeshiva University • Yeshivath Torah Vodaath and Mesivta Rabbinical Seminary

Social, Mutual Benefit
American Association for Ethiopian Jews • American Federation of Jewish Fighters, Camp Inmates and Nazi Victims • American Federation of Jews from Central Europe • American Sephardic Federation • American Veterans of Israel • Association of Yugoslav Jews in the United States • Bnai Zion (The American Fraternal Zionist Organization) • Brith Abraham • Brith Sholom • Central Sephardic Jewish Community of America • Free Sons of Israel • Jewish Labor Bund (Directed by World Coordinating Committee of the Bund) • Jewish Peace Fellowship • Jewish Socialist Verband of America • Sephardic Jewish Brotherhood of America • United Order True Sisters • Workmen's Circle

Social Welfare
American Jewish Correctional Chaplains Association • American Jewish Society for Service • American Medical Center at Denver Cancer Research Center and Hospital • Association of Jewish Family and Children's Agencies • Baron de Hirsch Fund • B'nai B'rith International • B'nai B'rith Women • City of Hope (A National Medical Center Under Jewish Auspices) • Conference of Jewish Communal Service • Council of Jewish Federations and Welfare Funds • Hope Center for the Retarded • International Council on Jewish Social and Welfare Services • Jewish Braille Institute of America • Jewish Conciliation Board of America • JWB (Jewish Welfare Board) • Leo N. Levi National Arthritis Hospital • National Association of Jewish Family, Children's and Health Professionals • National Association of Jewish Homes for the Aged • National Association of Jewish Vocational Services • National Congress of Jewish Deaf • National Council of Jewish Prison Chaplains • National Council of Jewish Women • National Jewish Committee on Scouting • National Jewish Hospital • World Confederation of Jewish Community Centers

Zionist and Pro-Israel
America-Israel Friendship League • American Associates of Ben-Gurion University of the Negev • American Committee for Shaare Zedek Hospital in Jerusalem • American Committee for the Weizmann Institute of Science • American Friends of Haifa University • American Friends of the Hebrew University •

American Friends of the Israel Museum • American Friends of the Jerusalem Mental Health Center (Ezrath Nashim) • American Friends of the Tel Aviv University • American-Israel Cultural Foundation • American Israel Public Affairs Committee • American-Israeli Lighthouse • American Jewish League for Israel • American Mizrachi Women • American Physicians Fellowship • American Red Magen David for Israel • American Technion Society • American Zionist Federation • American Zionist Youth Foundation • Ampal (American Israel Corporation) • ARZA (Association of Reform Zionists of America) • Bar-Ilan University in Israel • Brit Trumpeldor Betar of America • Dror (Young Zionist Organization) • Emunah Women of America • Federated Council of Israel Institutions • Fund for Higher Education • Hadassah (The Women's Zionist Organization of America) • Hashomer Hatzair • Hebrew University—Technion Joint Maintenance Appeal • Herut—U.S.A. (United Zionist-Revisionists of America) • Theodor Herzl Foundation • Ichud Habonim Labor Zionist Youth • Israel Music Foundation • Jewish National Fund of America • Keren Or • Labor Zionist Alliance • League for Labor Israel • National Committee for Labor Israel (Israel Histadrut Campaign) • PEC Israel Economic Corporation • PEC Israel Endowment Funds • Pioneer Women (The Women's Labor Zionist Organization of America) • Poale Agudath Israel of America • Rassco Israel Corporation and Rassco Financial Corporation • Religious Zionists of America • Society of Israel Philatelists • State of Israel Bonds • United Charity Institutions of Jerusalem • United Israel Appeal • United States Committee Sports for Israel • Women's League for Israel • World Confederation of United Zionists • World Zionist Organization—American Section • Zionist Organization of America

Professional Associations
American Conference of Cantors • American Jewish Correctional Chaplains Association • American Jewish Press Association • American Jewish Public Relations Society • Association of Jewish Center Workers • Association of Jewish Chaplains of the Armed Forces • Association of Jewish Community Relations Workers • Cantors Assembly of America • Council of Jewish Organizations in Civil Service • Educators Assembly of the United Synagogue of America • International Association of Hillel Directors • International Conference of Jewish Communal Service • Jewish Ministers Cantors Association of America • Jewish Teachers Association (Morim) • National Association of Jewish Center Workers • National Association of Synagogue Administrators, United Synagogue of America • National Association of Temple Administrators, Union of American Hebrew Congregations • National Association of Temple Educators, Union of American Hebrew Congregations • National Conference of Jewish Communal

Service • National Conference of Yeshiva Principals • National Jewish Welfare Board Commission on Jewish Chaplaincy

Women's Organizations
American Mizrachi Women • B'nai B'rith Women • Brandeis University National Women's Committee • Hadassah (The Women's Zionist Organization of America) • National Council of Jewish Women • National Federation of Temple Sisterhoods, Union of American Hebrew Congregations • Pioneer Women, The Women's Labor Zionist Organization of America • United Order of True Sisters • Women's American ORT Federation • Women's Branch of the Union of Orthodox Jewish Congregations of America • Women's Division of Poale Agudath of America • Women's Division of the American Jewish Congress • Women's Division of the Jewish Labor Committee • Women's Division of the United Jewish Appeal • Women's League for Conservative Judaism • Women's League for Israel • Women's Organization of Hapoel Hamizrachi • Yeshiva University Women's Organization

Yeshiva University, New York: The oldest and largest university under Jewish auspices with beginnings in the late 19th century now has an enrollment of approximately 7,000 in its various schools and colleges located in four centers in New York City. Rabbi Isaac Elchanan Theological Seminary, the leading school for the preparation of Orthodox rabbis, is an affiliate. The Joseph and Faye Tannenbaum Hall seen here is one of the main buildings on the Washington Heights campus. *Credit:* Yeshiva University

Jewish Theological Seminary, New York: In 1903, Rabbi Solomon Schechter came from England to serve as president of the newly reorganized Jewish Theological Seminary of America, the central institution of the Conservative movement. Its current home on Broadway and West 122nd Street was built in 1930 and expanded in 1983. *Credit:* Jewish Theological Seminary of America

Youth and Student Organizations
American Zionist Youth Foundation • Atid (College Age Organization, United Synagogue of America) • B'nai B'rith Hillel Foundations • B'nai B'rith Youth Organization • Bnei Akiva of North America (Religious Zionists of America) • Bnos Agudath Israel (Agudath Israel of America) • Dror Young Zionist Organization • Hashachar (Young Women's Zionist Organization of America) • Hashomer Hatzair (Zionist Youth Movement) • Ichud Habonim Labor Zionist Youth • Jewish Student Press-Service (Jewish Student Editorial Projects) • Kadima • Massorah Intercollegiates of Young Israel, National Council of Young Israel • National Conference of Synagogue Youth, Union of Orthodox Jewish Congregations of America • National Federation of Temple Youth, Union of American Hebrew Congregations • Noar Mizrachi-Hamishmeret (Religious Zionists of America) • North American Jewish Students' Appeal • North American Jewish Students' Network • North American Jewish Youth Council • Student Struggle for Soviet Jewry • United Synagogue Youth, United Synagogue of America • Yavneh, National Religious Jewish Students Association • Yugntruf Youth for Yiddish • Zeirei Agudath Israel (Agudath Israel of America)

Hebrew Union College, Cincinnati: Established in 1875 by Isaac Mayer Wise, Hebrew Union College has continued to serve as the training center for rabbis of the Reform movement. Additional campuses are located in New York City and Los Angeles. *Credit:* AJA

Congregation Shearith Israel, New York: The Spanish and Portuguese Synagogue in The City of New York located on Central Park West and 70th Street is the oldest established and continuously functioning congregation in the United States with its roots reaching back to the first half of the 18th century. The current structure was completed in 1897. *Credit:* Congregation Shearith Israel

Welcome to Jewish L.A.

1978. Los Angeles has become the world's third largest Jewish community. Neil Reisner's survey provides an overview of its growth and transformation.

East is east and west is . . . well . . . different. The first thing to understand about Los Angeles is that it's big, very big. And the second thing is that it's new, really new. And the third thing is that it is the frontier of American Jewish life. The vitality, openness, experimentation, youth, and lack of institutionalized tradition which characterize California and provide such ample grist for the stereotyping mills have also led to the emergence of a rich and—in important respects—novel Jewish community.

After New York and maybe Tel Aviv, Los Angeles is the world's largest Jewish community. That community has grown, as has the city itself, without plan. And like the city, it has been easy to dismiss it with contempt. Los Angeles? Palm trees, freeways and crazies. Hollywood, Yorty and rootlessness. A Woody Allen vision, New York as texture, LA as fraud. Scriptwriters rather than poets and novelists, game shows rather than documentaries.

But something's happening in LA, something important. There are 455,000 Jews here (that's the American Jewish Yearbook estimate; others say the number may be as large as 600,000), and more and more of them are seeking each other out, clustering together in a network of institutions, agencies, and chavurot which is characterized by a spirit of cooperation and acceptance that is rare in older Jewish communities, and rarer still in a place which was once termed "a bunch of suburbs in search of a city."

Los Angeles, as Osias G. Goren (General Chairman of this year's United Jewish Welfare Fund campaign) puts it, "is not an urban area. It is a series of villages. But that enables you to have a combination of urban and suburban life which combines the best of both, the camaraderie of the village and the resources of the city."

It's not that LA has Jewish neighborhoods; it doesn't. It has "areas:" Eastern, Western, Southern, and the Valley (that's San Fernando). One can travel 30 miles in any direction (except the Pacific) from the offices of the Jewish Federation-Council and not leave all the areas of significant Jewish settlement behind. For decades, it was that sprawl that seemed to doom the prospect of a real Jewish community. The Jews who were arriving from the Midwest and the East were (by definition) those least tied to the close-knit communities they'd left behind, and even if they'd wanted to connect with "the" Jewish community here in LA, they would have found it exceedingly difficult to do so. Ask a most obvious question, back in 1960—where are the Jewish neighborhoods?—and there was no real answer.

Ironically, however, the sprawl that made LA the butt of so many jokes and that was once the chief impediment to genuine community has contributed much to the vitality of Jewish LA. We have to search each other out. Increasingly, many of us do just that. The sprawl, together with our youth and the fabled Southern California lifestyle, have produced both dynamism and dilemma. From the look of it now, LA may no longer be the place where the rest of the country dumps its misfits; it may, instead, be the cultural R&D center for the nation, the place where new models are tested and then disseminated, our collective future writ small.

It was not always so. Max Vorspan, author of the most complete history of LA Jewry (and Vice President of the University of Judaism) notes that in 1850, according to a Federal census, there were only eight Jews living in Los Angeles—whose total population back then was 1,610. The Jews were all young unmarried men; six were German, and all but one were merchants. They lived next door to one another in a block of storefronts known as Bell's Row, located at what is now the corner of Los Angeles and Aliso Streets, where the Los Angeles Federal Building now stands.

LA was a boom town then, cattle ranchers becoming rich by trading their beef for the gold of Northern California. The Jews who arrived had come to serve the mercantile needs of the growing community.

By 1854, land was purchased for a Jewish cemetery, and eight years later, in 1862, the first congregation was established. Reflecting the flavor of the time, it met for its first ten years in a variety of locations—rented halls, Judge Sepulveda's courtroom, and John Temple's saloon.

The real boom took place between 1880 and 1887, when the population of LA skyrocketed from 11,000 to 100,000. The Jewish community became firmly entrenched during the period, virtually dominating the city's rapid economic growth. And with that growth came the first (and only) major incursion of anti-Semitism in the city's history. As LA changed from frontier-Mexican to big city-provincial, it developed certain airs that led to discrimination—mostly social—against Jews.

This rather predictable development did not inhibit the growth or the development of the Jewish community. By 1900, there were about 2,500 Jews in the city, and two synagogues (one Orthodox, one Reform), two B'nai B'rith lodges, a Hebrew Benevolent Society (which administered the cemetery), a Ladies' Auxiliary, and a downtown social club (The Concordia). And there was the beginning of the inevitable conflict between the established German-Jewish community and the steady influx of East European Jews. In fact, as was the case in so many other cities, it was likely the combination of social discrimination and the German vs. East Euroepan conflict

that started the Jewish community on its way.

The German Jews found the East Europeans an uncomfortable embarrassment. Afraid that the poorer and often sickly newcomers would become a burden on the community-at-large, thus inflaming anti-Semitism still more, and threatening to undermine the status they had managed to achieve, the German Jews did the right thing for the wrong reasons, and established a network of social service agencies to provide aid to the immigrants.

The institutions that were established between 1909 and 1911 form part of the core of today's Jewish Los Angeles: The Hebrew Orphan Home is now Vista Del Mar Child Care Service: Hebrew Free Loan; Kaspare Cohen Hospital is now Cedars-Sinai Medical Center: the Duarte Sanitarium for tuberculosis is now the City of Hope. And in 1912, a Federation of Jewish Charities was organized, to raise funds for all the local Jewish institutions.

As the city and its Jewish population grew, Jewish institutions kept pace, in a pattern that had already become familiar in the older cities of the East. So, too, did Jewish neighborhoods. When the Jews first arrived, they lived in the downtown area surrounding what is now the Civic Center. *Everybody* lived there in the early years; there was no place else to live. Then, as the city grew, Jews followed the traditional pattern of clustering, first fanning south and west of the downtown area, then in the Bunker Hill area north and slightly west of the center of town, and, in the 1920's, with a steady rise in the number of newcomers, in Boyle Heights, east of downtown and in West Adams, south of the city's center.

By World War II, however, these neighborhoods had begun to disappear, and the Beverly-Fairfax area became the primary location of Jewish settlement. Fairfax was once in West Los Angeles, a prime new development, but is now in the urban core (although to an Easterner, what we consider the urban core often looks more like a suburb). Even today, Fairfax is more than 50 percent Jewish, and, with its adjunct to the southwest, the Pico-Robertson district, it is the only neighborhood in LA which still has the "first generation" flavor associated with Jewish neighborhoods. It is the place to go for ethnic foods and ritual objects, for feeling at home.

Once again, LA Jews behaved in familiar ways. The children of the Fairfax settlers didn't stay put. Instead, they moved west to settle in the "I've made it" suburbs of Beverly Hills, West Los Angeles and Pacific Palisades. They went north to the orange groves and vast housing tracts of the San Fernando Valley. They went south to the beach cities with their burgeoning aircraft industry. And some went east, so far east that they were virtually lost to the Jewish community. Fairfax, which might well have disappeared as a Jewish center, retained its character by becoming host to a new generation of Jewish immigrants—Israelis, young people, and more recently, Soviet Jews.

The leap into the future, and away from the familiar, took place after World War II. At the end of the War, there were some 150,000 Jews in LA. By 1951, there were 250,000. And today there are 455,000—or more. Some cities have grown even more rapidly, but the sheer size of the LA community sets it apart from the others. For the fact is that today Los Angeles has more Jews than France or Great Britain, more than the entire continent of Africa, more than Jerusalem and Haifa combined, more even than Tel Aviv (proper). Depending on how you draw the boundaries, Los Angeles may indeed be the second largest Jewish city in the world.

If the pattern of the immediate period had been sustained, the migration of so many Jews to Los Angeles might well have culminated in a Jewish catastrophe, more than 300,000 Jews losing their Jewish identity in the bright sun, hiding their Jewishness in the smog. "I came here to start fresh, not to repeat." But in spite of that ethos, and in spite of the physical vastness, and in spite of the dispersion of the Jewish population, and in spite of the relative ease with which fading away can be accomplished, Jewish LA is making it.

Making it, and then some. What it took was a determination on the part of those who cared the most to develop a style appropriate to the city's dimensions. Back east, Jewish communities are inevitably touched by the shadow of New York. Each city has its own style, to be sure, but none could justify the kind of institutional development which LA, so very far from New York, and big enough to go it alone, has pulled off.

Dr. Lewis Barth is Dean of HUC's Los Angeles facility, and one of the few native Los Angelenos interviewed for this article. (That, of course, is a central aspect of community life here. Relatively few people over 30 come *from* LA; they have come *to* it. The challenge of community building is to develop the sense that one is not a transplant, but is *of* Los Angeles.) Rabbi Barth was one of HUC's first students in LA. He recalls, "There was a sense of excitement about it then, because it was so obviously a real beginning, it was very fresh. We were just becoming aware that Los Angeles was a great Jewish center, one that needed a lot of growth and a deepening of Jewish intellectual and cultural life— and we felt that that was about to happen, that we were on the verge of something very big. We were growing, and we could feel it. Every year, one or another of us—HUC, or UJ or UCLA— would take on an additional faculty person, so we no longer felt that we were in the wilderness. And now we at HUC have one of the finest Jewish museums in the country. . . .

"We do have a programmatic vision which has developed because we're in LA and not in any other community. It combines a very serious commitment to Jewish scholarship with a deep involvement in Jewish community life and concerns. That's very atypical, and we can't say that it can be sustained for a long period of time, but so far we seem to have developed in a way that bridges a number of worlds. So we have really close institutional and personal relations with the Federation, for example."

Barth does not speak for HUC alone when he speaks of the interconnections among LA's Jewish institutions. The building of a Jewish community of LA's scope is necessarily a shared task; the wonder of LA is that the sharing actually happens. And the explanation, of course, is that there is no burdensome history, no ossified tradition to overcome.

Take the Brandeis-Bardin Institute. Located in the Simi Valley (that's one valley over from the San Fernando, about 50 miles from the center of town). Brandeis has moved very far along the road staked out for it by the vision of its founder, the late Dr. Shlomo Bardin. The simple concept of transmitting Jewish knowledge to Jewish lay people by "teaching and touching" has been translated into a major national force which, according to Director Dennis Prager, now reaches as many as 20,000 people each year. It is no longer a surprise, in the Midwest or in the East, to find people who have been exposed to Brandeis-Bardin wondering why their communities cannot learn from what's been done there.

Quoting Bardin, Prager explains the Brandeis success story simply: "West Coast Jews, California Jews, don't know anything, and they know they don't know anything. New York Jews don't know anything, but they think they know everything." And in fact, Bardin had briefly experimented with the Brandeis model in several sites on the East Coast—but met with little success there, and a chilly reception. As Prager puts it, "This was where he found the most fertile and receptive ground, and he was a prophet in that sense. Nobody would have picked the Simi Valley, 35 years

L.A. Plates, 1981: *Credit:* Photograph by Bill Aron

ago, as a likely site for Jewish learning and living."

Learning and living proceed in more conventional ways, as well. There are over a hundred synagogues in the LA area, which may not sound like a very large number until you stop to remember that a synagogue that is more than 30 years old is considered venerable. According to Max Vorspan, the flowering of synagogue life in LA really began only in 1948. "The GI wanted to live in a little home of his own; that was his dream, and out here it was a possible dream. The electronics industry and new businesses began to develop, so the jobs were here, and they came. And, as a result of their experiences, they wanted something Jewish for their children. So they'd put a little ad in the paper and they'd say, 'Kaffee-klatsch at my house to discuss a Sunday School,' and 20 or 30 men and women would show up—and that's how congregations started all over town. It was their particular need that brought them together in the first place. Many of these people were experiencing non-Jewish neighborhoods for the first time; they were often people who had been raised in heavily ethnic Jewish neighborhoods. It was natural for them to want to establish some kind of social or educational setting, not only for their children but also for themselves. So they established 'centers.' Dozens and dozens of them. They had no choice; there weren't any large institutions waiting for new people to join. Small groups had to take responsibility for themselves. So in ten years, a hundred new institutions were born. And each one required its own nucleus of leadership, so you have many more Jews involved in the mechanics of Jewish life.

"It was fascinating to watch it happen. The desire to create a Sunday School for children and a social center for adults wasn't based on ideology or profound religious conviction, and the people involved were pretty limited in their knowledge. So they were open, and went about creating a new tradition based on trial and error. Nobody was there to look over their shoulders and say, 'This is the way it's supposed to be done.' Eventually, they had to develop some kind of ideological conception of what Judaism was going to mean to them. And today, not one of the centers still exists. That is, they all exist, but not one is called a center. Every one of them is today a congregation."

In fact, the recent emergence of a new generation of Jewish neighborhoods can, in some measure, be traced to the development of synagogue life. The case is obvious with respect to Orthodox Jews, who will not drive on Shabbat and hence must live near their shul. But one can also discern a kind of congregational gravity that helps cluster Reform and Conservative Jews in hailing distance of a congregation.

Encino, for example, is an upper middle class neighborhood on the southern flank of the San Fernando Valley. It has had a large Jewish population for some time, with some current estimates going as high as 75 percent. And with the numbers there have now developed the necessary support services: kosher meat, ritual goods, books, the things that make a place a neighborhood, the things that make a neighborhood Jewish. Numbers breed visibility, visibility breeds numbers. And both are encouraged by the presence in Encino of Valley Beth Shalom, a Conservative congregation, and its rabbi, Harold Schulweis. Since Rabbi Schulweis came to Valley Beth Shalom from Oakland, the congregation has grown to 900 families, and, more significant, the concept of the congregation *chavurah* has been so successfully institutionalized that it is now being copied all over the United States.

Rabbi Schulweis explains, "You've got at least 150,000 Jews concentrated in this Valley area. There is tremendous mobility, a shriveled extended family, and a sense of loneliness that's very marked, and all that encourages innovations such as *chavurot*. They're easier to start here than, let's say, even in Boston. We're on the sharp edge of life and what happens, I think, in California, happens back East five to ten years later.

"There is a kind of psychological revolution in which the privatistic needs of people now emerge as central in their agenda, as opposed to the social needs.

"The synagogue could become the most important therapeutic institution imaginable. But that requires a very radical change in the understanding of what is in the proper ken of the synagogue. Instead of saying that the synagogue is the place in which we pursue the ritual celebrations of one's life, rites of passage, festivals, fasts, study, and social action, if we can say that there are problems we have not been attending to, such as existential aloneness, single parenthood, a tremendous increase in divorce, the home which has become a pathogenic institution, and if we can come to understand that it's the synagogue's function to deal with these new kinds of psychological problems, then loneliness and the rest can be, oddly enough, an opportunity.

"The synagogue community has got to prove itself as having something to say in relationship to the moral, spiritual and intellectual needs of a very new kind of Jewish hunger, and that's what the *chavurah* structure—small groups, really cohesive groups, within the synagogue—makes possible."

Camps, schools, neighborhoods, synagogues—and a Federation. The original Federation of Jewish Charities was followed, in 1929, by the establishment of the United Jewish Welfare fund, to do fund raising for both local and overseas needs, and then, in 1933, the Jewish Community Committee, intended to combat anti-Semitism, and the United Jewish Community, concerned with youth, education, and such, were organized. These later merged to become the Los Angeles Jewish Community Council, including the UJWF for fund raising and the United Community Committee (now the Community Relations Committee) as its community relations arm. The latest, and presumably the last, merger took place in 1958, when the Jewish Community Council joined with the Federation of Jewish Charities to become the Los Angeles Jewish Federation-Council.

(There is a story—perhaps apocryphal—that the old Jewish Community building at 590 N. Vermont was built in two wings to facilitate the division of community property should the 1958 merger prove unsuccessful. In 1975, the Federation moved to a more centrally located building at 6503 Wilshire Boulevard. It is a 12 story high-rise with only one wing.)

This merger happened none too soon. With over 500 discrete Jewish organizations and organization chapters in the metropolitan area, *something* has to act as the communal cement. But it's not easy, not only for the same reasons it's not easy anywhere else, but also for some more typically LA reasons.

Thus, Ted Kanner, Executive Director of the Federation, cites problems that go beyond the obvious challenge of geographic size and demographic numbers. He observes that even though most of the Jewish population came here immediately after World War II, there's still a relatively small native population and most people continue to identify home as someplace else—Chicago, Cleveland, Toledo, wherever. And he continues by talking about the weather: "I've come to believe that the warm weather, the climate itself, together with the prevalence of all kinds of recreational opportunities contribute significantly to people taking responsibility less seriously. It's as easy to lie on the beach or pedal your bicycle as it is to go to a meeting, and

At Disneyland, 1981: *Credit:* Photograph by Bill Aron

therefore, we compete with anything that any Federation is up against, plus golf, tennis, the beach and all that. The whole lifestyle ends up stressing the casual rather than the organized. There's real resistance to organized activities.

"That's encouraged," he continues, "by the fact that LA is West Coast, and that means that there's a feeling that people don't have to do what's expected of them. My experience has been that whatever is true of the West Coast is more true in LA, and whatever is true in LA is more true in the Jewish community. The fact that in other parts of the country Jews may hold certain things very dear just doesn't mean that much out here.

"So our job is to take a community that's not deeply rooted, that doesn't respond to the usual public relations, or phone call, or outreach program, and figure out what will make it respond with constructive Jewish behavior. That's a real challenge."

The numbers say that Kanner's right in his assessment. Less than half the Jews of LA appear to maintain even a loose affiliation with the Jewish community. Tom Tugend, writing in *Heritage*, points out that "In 1948, when the Los Angeles Jewish community numbered around 200,000, the Welfare Fund received 54,000 individual or family contributions. Almost 30 years later, with a much wealthier and more than doubled Jewish population, contributors dropped to 49,000." Now, 1948 may be an unfair base-year to use for such a comparison, and the estimates of current donations from within the Federation go as high as 60,000. But even after you make allowances for family size, and add in an estimate for those Jews who maintain organizational affiliation but who do not contribute to the Welfare Fund, you're still hard-pressed to come up with anything over 200,000—and the real figure may be much lower than that. Worse yet, these numbers include many people whose affiliation is absolutely minimal. So what you come up with is that very, very many people—a quarter of a million, maybe more—are functional dropouts from Jewish life.

Calling that a "challenge" is a bit of an understatement.

For that reason, the Federation invests heavily in developing its constituency, supporting a variety of outreach programs. As Kanner explains, "We are attempting to do something highly atypical, by giving power to the people. That's a difficult thing to do, because Federation, in order to be effective, must focus its attention on raising the money that's needed to do all the different things that need to be done. When power is given to the people, that raises expectations for services, for participation, for development of smaller forms of community organization, all of which need to be staffed, all of which cost money. And we know that there isn't necessarily a direct relationship between participation in community organization and giving. We're aware of that, but we're ready to take our chances.

"That's why we're investing heavily in neighborhood councils, grassroots organizations that help people plan for their own neighborhoods. That's a way of enriching Jewish life in the community, even though it may not show in our campaign results."

This trend towards decentralization started with the development of area councils in the Eastern, Western, Southern and San Fernando areas, where professionally-staffed Federation offices were opened, area campaigns were conducted, and fieldworkers from central agencies were assigned on a part-time basis. The trend continued with the development of sub-area councils in Beverly-Fairfax and in the San Fernando Valley. Now, with the growth of storefront agency service centers in Fairfax and the Valley and with increased Federation-synagogue-agency joint-venturing, the trend is growing even stronger.

It's outreach with a new twist. Barbi Weinberg, whose term as Federation president was concluded in December, comments on the change in philosophy: "Federations generally had the attitude years ago that they were secular Jewish institutions. That's a contradiction in terms, of course, but that's what they believed. They saw their responsibility as providing for the health and welfare needs of Jews. We were concerned with widows and orphans and that sort of thing, institutionalizing the older and more personal welfare system. But now we've come to recognize that Jewish life can't be compartmentalized, can't be divided into welfare on the one hand and Judaism on the other. That's why we've developed, in the last few years, a real sense of interdependence between the Federation and the synagogue community.

Our Council on Jewish Life, which has been in operation for several years, includes a Bureau of Synagogue Affairs, whose job is to develop real communication and cooperation between the Federation and the Synagogue. We mean that in mundane ways, such as in saving money by ordering supplies together, and also in searching for opportunities to bring more Jewish knowledge and culture into the Federation. Our goal here is not simply to "Judaize" the Federation, but to overcome the artificial barrier that assigns welfare to one agency and Judaism to another."

The Council on Jewish Life recently coordinated a project designed to increase synagogue affiliation—not exactly your everyday sort of Federation activity. A letter was sent to the entire Federation over Barbi Weinberg's signature encouraging those not affiliated with congregations to seek information on the options available to them. According to Jerry Weber, assistant director of community planning and the professional who works with the Council on Jewish Life, about a thousand people requested information

and were put in touch with the synagogue movements.

Jewish Los Angeles—A Guide was another Council project, a 114-page book that detailed virtually every aspect of Jewish LA from a tour of the Fairfax area to the worship schedule of most congregations. Some 9,000 copies have been sold in the year-and-a-half the *Guide* has been out, and the nicest thing may be that every Jewish couple that gets married in LA receives a copy as a wedding gift from the community. Efforts at outreach and inter-institutional cooperation don't always lead to decentralization. One of the most successful educational programs in town goes in exactly the opposite direction. Sponsored by the Bureau of Jewish Education in conjunction with participating congregations, both Reform and Conservative, Chavurat Noar is designed to give ninth graders, citywide, an intensive Jewish experience, punctuated by six camp conclaves over the course of the year. As Eddie Friedman, the program's director, points out, "We have a whole bunch of little communities, each with its own temple and its own school. And that means that the children are often cut off from any contact with other Jewish children during their early years. So we're trying to create a situation in which they'll get some sense that there's a larger community of which they're a part. Camps are a very important part of that, and I think that camping is much more important to us than to other communities. Camps help to compensate for our geographic dispersion."

Jewish education in general, as elsewhere in the country, is receiving increased attention—and support from Federation. Ten years ago, the total amount allocated to religious schools through the Bureau of Jewish Education was about a quarter of a million dollars. Today, it is closer to a million and a half

Storefront Synagogue, Los Angeles, 1981: Congregation B'nai David on Fairfax Street. *Credit:* Photograph by Bill Aron

dollars. And, for the first time, day schools are making a real impact. There are 14 of them, including one Reform, and of the 14, six have been established within the past 10 years.

If all that sounds as if LA is a Jewish boomtown, remember the 250,000 or so Jews that aren't reached at all. The Anglo-Jewish press (three papers— *Heritage, Israel Today, B'nai B'rith Messenger*) reaches a combined circulation of about 50,000 with a product that leaves many people dissatisfied. (There was quite a flap not long ago when Federation tried to expand its own house organ into a community paper, and, when the issue was finally, more or less, resolved, Herb Brin, editor of *Heritage,* put together a slate of candidates to run for Federation's Board of Directors against the official slate. The insurgent slate was disqualified, and, while there were some very nasty accusations, the end result may be that Federation office is now seen as something worth fighting about.) More important, it is exceedingly difficult for the community simply to keep track of its constituency. One of the sometime results of limited resources and multiple claims on those resources is a tendency to invest huge amounts of time and money in a particular segment of the community for a period of years, and then to move to another, and then still another.

In the late 1960's and early 1970's it was students. Then, for a while, it was the poor and the elderly. More recently, single parent families and young adults have captured the limelight. It's hard to know whether there's a kind of faddism at work here, in which interest in a particular problem area can only be sustained for a limited time, or whether, instead, these shifts in attention are the result of genuine need matched by incredible organizational flexibility.

In the meantime, segments of the community continue, inevitably, to take off on their own. Two current examples are the Orthodox, and the Israeli immigrant community.

Nobody knows exactly how many Orthodox Jews there are in Los Angeles. But there are more than there used to be, and they are far more visible. The reason, says Rabbi Maurice Lamm of the prestigious Beverly Hills Beth Jacob Congregation, is simple: "When I came here in 1972, there was no reliable kashrut in Los Angeles, or very little. For kashrut, we had to get meat from Denver. For yeshivas, we had to send our children to New York. We weren't a community; we were just a few synagogues, and a few schools.

There's still a long way to go, of course. If we can proudly point to a number of innovative achievements and to a special readiness to cooperate across institutional lines, we cannot ignore the areas of gross underdevelopment. There's the entertainment industry, for example, still largely Jewish, and almost wholly irrelevant to Jewish life. With the notable exception of game show host Monty Hall, who is very deeply involved in Jewish affairs, occasional stellar appearances by some others, and perhaps some signatures on a newspaper ad, the creativity, wealth and talent of the world's largest entertainment center simply does not touch Jewish life.

Neither does a good chunk of the old, established Jewish aristocracy. That's been a good thing so far as developing a new and genuinely innovative community, but it's had disastrous consequences for community financing. The $27 million raised in last year's UJWF campaign represent just $60 per Los Angeles Jew, and very little of that derives from the old line wealth that can

be found in this community. The *names* are here, somewhere, but not within the Jewish orbit; LA has made it possible for them to remove themselves without stigma, something that would have been far more difficult in, say, Cleveland.

And there are other groups, whose needs have yet to be met, less dramatically perhaps, which have yet to be fully integrated. For all that the Federation had a female president, women are still under-represented in both lay and professional positions. No one was quite sure last year what to do about the involvement of some Hillel Foundation directors with Breira, and some are not sure what to do this year about Beit Chayim Chadashim, a gay congregation

that participates fully in communal life. And then of course, there are still those 250,000, straights and gays, men and women, rich and poor, who are here, somewhere, hiding or forgotten; uninvolved, counted but not numbered. And the question for us is whether we will be able, as we come to the full realization that we are America's Second Jewish City, to avoid the fate of our East Coast big sister city, where so very many Jews have separated themselves from the community, whether we will be able, as we mature, to retain the sense of Jewish adventure which may yet make us One—and number one, as well. In the meantime, perhaps our motto should be "We are Becoming."

Downtown, Los Angeles, 1980: *Credit:* Photograph by Bill Aron

Dairy Restaurant Menu, 1955: Menu of Ratner's Dairy Restaurant, a landmark on Delancey Street on New York's Lower East Side. *Credit:* AJHS

Delicatessen, New York, 1969: The sausage counter at a delicatessen on New York's Lower East Side. *Credit:* Barbara Pfeffer

Delicatessen, New York, 1976: Bargaining for fish. There are no fixed prices on New York's Lower East Side, that is, if you know how to bargain. *Credit:* Photograph by Bill Aron

Knishes, Brooklyn, 1979: Knish shop on Brighton Beach Avenue, Brooklyn. *Credit:* Photograph by Barbara Pfeffer

Bagel Bakery, New York, 1975: The sign in Yiddish reads, "Not to worry about buying from this store because it is open on Shabbas. The owners are not Jewish." *Credit:* Photograph by Bill Aron

Rise of the Day School Movement

1982. There has been an eight-fold increase in the enrollment of students in Orthodox Day Schools since the end of World War II. Sociologist William Helmreich described this phenomenon.

The traditional value placed on education by Jews is a crucial factor in comprehending the survival and growth of the yeshiva. While this is an important value among all Jews, the Orthodox place greater priority on religious education than on education in general. Immigration therefore accounts for much of the current strength and impressive growth of the day schools and, to a lesser extent, the high schools. The general increase in Jewish identification, spurred largely by the creation of the State of Israel, organizations promoting the yeshivas, the high caliber of the schools themselves, especially in the cities, when compared to public schools, and the general prestige of attending a private school are also important factors in the growth of the day school movement.

Only a minority of children in the day schools are observant (just how many is not known) or continue in religious high schools, and an even smaller number go on to advanced yeshivas. Nevertheless, it is the day school and the *mesivta* that provide the basic education for almost all of those who study at the *beis medrash* level. Without such a background, advanced talmudic study would be impossible for most young men. Table 11-1 indicates the increase up to 1978.

Table 11-1

DAY SCHOOL ENROLLMENT (UNITED STATES)

Year	Number of Schools	Enrollment
1945	69	10,000
1955	180	35,000
1965	323	63,500
1978	463	83,350

HIGH SCHOOL ENROLLMENT (UNITED STATES)

Year	Number of Schools	Enrollment
1944	9	?
1964	83	10,200
1967	105	13,400
1978	150	16,800

Figures are as given in *Tempo*, Report No. 10, June 1979, p. 1, a publication of Torah Umesorah.

The enrollment figures cited in the table include coeducational day and high schools, the vast majority of whose graduates do not continue in advanced yeshivas. Nevertheless, among those who do not are individuals who, having been imbued with a strong Jewish background, provide support for advanced yeshivas. Also, while our focus is on the Strictly Orthodox, it ought to be noted that the majority of those who identify themselves as Modern Orthodox have probably had a yeshiva high school education. Finally, there has always been a good deal of "crossing over"

Outdoor Sabbath Services, 1979: Services at New York *Havurah* (Jewish commune) retreat outside of New York City. *Credit:* Photograph by Bill Aron

Succoth, Milwaukee, about 1958: Succoth, the fall festival commemorating the wandering of the Israelites through the wilderness on their way to the Promised Land, marks the final harvest before the arrival of winter. The temporary festival booth called a sukkah is erected for eating. This group of children is seen with the sukkah erected at Temple Emanuel. *Credit:* SHSW

Bat Mitzvah, New York, 1980: Recently, the bar mitzvah which applied only to males has been adapted to girls when they reach the age of twelve. *Credit:* Photograph by Bill Aron

Scribe, New York, 1978: It takes a scribe nine to twelve months to prepare a Torah scroll. They carve their own pens and quills, and mix their own inks from scratch. Here, one of two scribes on New York's Lower East Side repairs a torah scroll. *Credit:* Photograph by Barbara Pfeffer

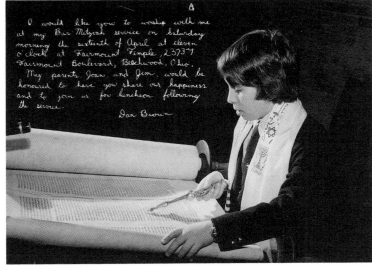

Bar Mitzvah, Cleveland, 1977: A bar mitzvah is a rite of passage which designates the time at which a Jewish male becomes thirteen and is old enough to accept religious duties and responsibilities. In this country the observance has become a family social occasion. *Credit:* Photograph by Jim Brown

Studying Torah, Baltimore, 1974: For religious Jews, the Torah (first five books of the Hebrew Bible: Genesis, Exodus, Leviticus, Numbers, Deuteronomy) is the embodiment of Jewish law and consciousness. Study and comprehension of the Torah is an essential and on-going part of their life and education. *Credit:* Photograph by Joan Liftin

Abbie Hoffman with Bar Mitzvah Photo, 1982: Political activist and writer, Abbie Hoffman has spurned belonging to any established Jewish organization, yet his Jewishness is an essential part of his make-up. After graduating from Brandeis University in 1959, he became involved in the civil rights movement and participated in Freedom Summer in Mississippi in 1964. Later he became a leader of the anti-Vietnam war protest movement. After seven years "underground" as a political fugitive, he has reemerged as an anti-establishment leader of the anti-nuclear pro-civil rights and pro-human rights left. *Credit:* Photograph by Ricky Rosen

between schools characterized as "modern" and those that are "traditional." Parents may find a particular emphasis not to their liking at the elementary school level and compensate for it by sending their children to a different type of high school. In addition, factors such as tuition, friendship networks, and geographic location may impinge upon the true ideological leanings of the families.

Those yeshiva day schools that are oriented toward the approach favored by the advanced yeshivas provide intensive preparation of a sort reminiscent of the strictest European yeshivas. In 1977, for example, Pirchei Agudath Israel, the children's division of the Agudah, sponsored a contest to see how many Mishnas students could recite from memory. (The average Mishna is eight or nine lines long.) More than 1,200 boys competed: "The top finalist . . . knew 2,287 Mishnas by heart. Seven other youngsters memorized more than 1,000 . . . each." Rabbi Nisson Wolpin, a former principal of Yeshiva Ohr Yisroel, a right-wing day school and *mesivta* and now

editor of the *Jewish Observer*, explained the process by which this level of knowledge was achieved:

First you buy talented teachers. Second, it's the long hours and the steady conditioning. As a result they experience success in this area at an early age and they're psychologically ready to go on to mesivta *and* yeshiva gedola.

Thus, we see the crucial role of the day school in socializing the yeshiva *bochur* into the world of the Talmud.

The advanced yeshivas themselves played a crucial role in the development of the day school movement, for it was their leaders who anticipated both the need for and the importance of such education to provide a steady stream of students to the higher schools. The National Society for Hebrew Day Schools (Torah Umesorah), which is involved in almost every aspect of day school education, is staffed primarily by graduated of advanced yeshivas, and is strongly

influenced by a board of *rosh yeshivas* with respect to policy matters. In commenting upon its founding, Dr. Joseph Kaminetsky, its former director, said:

When the lights of Torah went out in Europe, there arose a conviction mainly on the part of Rabbi Mendlowitz that they had to be put on here. He knew that starting more day schools would insure the growth of Torah in America. It could not, however, have been done without the spiritual help and support of Reb Aharon Kotler, Reb Reuvain Grozovsky, Reb Elya Meir Block, and others like them.

Another related development was the establishment of the summer camps which dot the landscape in the Catskill Mountains and elsewhere. As we have noted, they provide continuity with yeshiva education, both by conducting summer classes and by reinforcing the values of family and school.

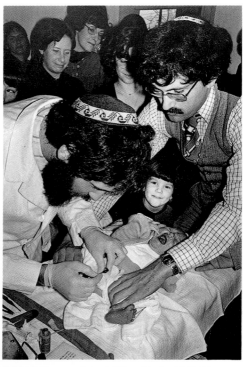

***Briss* (Circumcision), New York, 1977:** The traditional circumcision which takes place eight days after Jewish boys are born is a joyous event attended by family members. *Credit:* Photograph by Bill Aron

***Havdallah,* Boston, 1976:** *Havdallah* marks the end of the Sabbath on Saturday night as soon as three stars have become visible. The ceremony is marked by the lighting of a braided candle, and includes the sniffing of spices and the drinking of wine. Each act is accompanied by a special blessing. *Credit:* Photograph by Bill Aron

***Tashlich,* Los Angeles, 1979:** To throw your sins into the water and say a part of the Bible is symbolic of celebrating the first day of Rosh Hashanah (The Jewish New Year). This group is seen casting their sins into the Pacific Ocean. *Credit:* Photograph by Bill Aron

Celebrating Passover, New York, 1980: Passover, the ancient Jewish festival celebrates the freedom won by the early Hebrew slaves from the Egyptian Pharaoh. The eating of matzoth (unleavened bread) is interpreted as a reminder of the hurried flight of the Israelites from Egypt. The Passover Seder service is the focal point of this holiday; it always takes place in the home and the leader is seated in a comfortable chair. The Seder follows a fixed ritual with everyone seated around a table, and informal celebrations such as this one are not common. *Credit:* Photograph by Bill Aron

Playing with Dreidels, New Jersey, 1975: The custom of spinning dreidels (tops) at Chanukah (festival of lights) is widespread. The tops are four-sided each of which bears a letter: *nun* (N), *gimmel* (G), *he* (H) and *shin* (SH). Chanukah is observed for eight days beginning with the twenty-fifth day of the month of Kislev on the Jewish calendar, which is a lunar calendar and its position on the Gregorian calendar changes each year. *Credit:* Photograph by Bill Aron

Scrabble in Hebrew, Los Angeles, 1982: *Credit:* Photograph by Bill Aron

Hassidim, Brooklyn, 1976: Followers of the Lubavitcher Rebbe, Rabbi Schneerson, listen to their spiritual leader in the Crown Heights section of Brooklyn. *Credit:* Photograph by Barbara Pfeffer

"The Rebbe" on Cable TV, 1982: The Lubavitcher Rebbe (Rabbi Menahem Mendel Schneerson) as he appeared on cable television transmitted by the World Lubavitch Communication Center in Brooklyn. He is the spiritual leader of a group of Hassidic Jews who are actively recruiting new followers. *Credit:* Photograph by Ricki Rosen

Hassidim in Purim Costumes, 1982: For the Purim festival of deliverance it is common to wear costumes. Two members of the large Brooklyn Hassidic community are seen on the street in costume. *Credit:* Photograph by Ricki Rosen

Hassidic Youth, New York, 1975: Blond boy with *peyot* (traditional locks of hair). Hassidism had its origins in Eastern Europe during the 18th and 19th centuries. After World War II a number of ultra-Orthodox groups, including Hassidim, became established in this country. *Credit:* Photograph by Bill Aron

School Bus, Brooklyn, 1975: Students from a Brooklyn Jewish Hassidic community school prepare for a day's outing. *Credit:* Photograph by Leonard Freed/Magnum

School Children, Brooklyn, 1975: On a hot day classes from a Jewish Hassidic community school are held in the park. *Credit:* Photograph by Leonard Freed/Magnum

Bodies of Three Civil Rights Workers Found

1964. The bodies of Michael Schwerner, James Chaney and Andrew Goodman were found in a common grave in Philadelphia, Mississippi. Schwerner and Goodman were Jewish; Chaney was Black. William Bradford Huie, a Southerner, described their participation in the Civil Rights Movement.

Movements are for the young and the crowded. Not for old folks dying around old churchyards. For all my sympathy for Mickey Schwerner, I wish he hadn't led those terrorists to Longdale.

Mickey Schwerner and James Chaney spent three days at Oxford, Ohio, where college students who had volunteered for a summer's work in Mississippi were trained for a week on the campus of the Western College for Women. The National Council of Churches paid training expenses for the group.

Mickey and Rita Schwerner, as well as James Chaney, took part in the widely publicized training program. The students were told:

That they were not to lead or take part in demonstrations but were only to live with Negro families and try to help the Negroes qualify to vote.

That they were to work with school-age Negroes and preschool-age Negroes and try to help them close the educational gap between themselves and the whites.

That they were to try to help Negroes of all ages to qualify for better jobs.

That, by living with Negroes, they were to demonstrate that they did not regard Negroes as Untouchables, or as socially inferior beings, and that Negroes should be admitted to all public places and to all forms of public activity.

That they should expect taunts, verbal abuse, blows, arrests, and jail terms, but that they should respond only and always in a nonviolent manner.

"It was like another holiday for us," Rita told me. "We were housed in a dormitory. The college kids were so enthusiastic; they asked a thousand questions and wanted to talk all night. We met Andy Goodman for the first time, and all of us were delighted with him. He was such a fine, intelligent, unassuming young man. He and I had much to talk about because he was a student at my alma mater, Queens College."

Andy Goodman at twenty, was both like and different from Mickey Schwerner in many ways. His parents, like their parents before them, were humanists in the liberal Jewish tradition. He was not *bar mitzvahed*. He, too, stressed his faith in Man and in social justice in the here and now. Goodman's mother is a psychologist employed by a clinic in Westchester County, New York, and his father is a successful civil engineer and general contractor. Andy was the second of three sons as Mickey was the younger of two.

Demonstration, Selma, Alabama, 1965: Rabbi Abraham Heschel on the far right joined (from left to right in the front row) Ralph Abernathy, Reverend Martin Luther King, Jr. and Ralph Bunche on a civil rights march through Selma. *Credit:* UPI

One difference in the two was in the scope of their commitment to the Movement. Schwerner was a social worker who thought he had found himself in the Movement. Goodman knew that his life had been somewhat sheltered and he believed that his summer in Mississippi would teach him much while at the same time he was determined to make a useful contribution to the Movement. Goodman then, in contrast to Schwerner, the professional reformer, is more representative—if not of the "typical" American—at least of a large group of Americans who recognize an obligation to others, and are willing to work at it but not to devote their entire lives to it, as the professional must.

Goodman's mother explained to me: "Andy knew he had enjoyed most of the good things of life. He was secure in the affections of his brothers, his parents, and his larger family including his grandparents, his uncles, aunts, and cousins. He had been reared in an atmosphere of love, respect, and culture, with books, music, paintings, appreciation of learning, appreciation of individual effort to improve the human personality. He had spent his summers with his cousins and his brothers in our family home in the Adirondacks. He was a happy, well-adjusted, light-hearted young man who knew how and when to be serious. He joined the Movement for two main reasons. He felt it was unfair for him to enjoy so many good things without making some modest effort to help those who are unjustly deprived. And he felt that he had much to learn from the people in Mississippi. He never thought that he had all the answers.

"He had taken part in one demonstration at the World's Fair, and he wanted to work for a summer in Mississippi, after which, had he not been murdered, he would have returned to his studies. He was considering going to Mexico next summer and trying to understand the way of life of the Mexican peasant. Eventually he probably would have wound up as a sociologist or anthropologist, or something in the field of human relations."

Each student going to Mississippi was required to take with him $150 and to have available as much as $500 in bail money.

Goodman's father told me, "I, of course, would gladly have given Andy his money. But he made a point of working for it himself. He wanted his little contribution in Mississippi to be entirely his own."

News of the burning of the church at Longdale reached Mickey Schwerner in Ohio on Wednesday, June 17. It made him anxious to hurry back to Mississippi. He wanted to hold the Freedom School on the site of the burned church, under the scorched trees, with the Negroes sitting on benches which they and workers could build.

Rita Schwerner was urged to remain in Oxford for another week, to help train a second group of summer volunteers. Reluctantly she agreed.

"On Friday night," Rita recalled, "we didn't go to sleep at all. We talked and loaded the station wagon. Four other workers were to travel to Mississippi with Mickey, Jim, and Andy. They left about 3 A.M.—that would be Saturday morning, June 20. They expected to reach Meridian the same day, sometime after dark. Mickey as usual, was impatient to get going, and all of them were excited and anxious to reach their assigned places and get to work."

"Yes," Rita added, "I did wish that I were going with them. But I stayed . . . and that was the last time I saw Mickey."

Journals of the Sixties

1960. Allen Ginsberg, poet and political activist, has been a consistently perceptive critic of American life and standards. He was an outspoken critic of American involvement in the war in Vietnam.

Oct. 1960

Subliminal

One million editorials against Mossadeq
    and who knows who Mossadeq is any
    more?
Me a Democracy? I didn't know my
    Central Intelligence was arming
    fascist, noodnicks in Iran
This true story I got from High Sources
    Check yr local radio announcer.
All I remember's nasty cartoons in N.Y.
    Mirror long-faced Mossadeq
    blubbering in a military court in Persia
looking the opposite of a serious hair'd
    Central Intelligence Agent sipping
    borscht cocktails at a Conservative
    egghead soirée
Whom I wanted for daddy Man of
    Distinction that year
I was working in Market Research.
Who threw poison onion Germs in
    Korea?
Do big fat American people know their
    Seoul from a hole in the ground?
Will Belgians ever get out of Congo so
    King Leopold's ghost stop screaming
    in Hell?
What Civilization the Uranium Addicts
    been selling us niggers?
The Mass Media have taken over Poetry
    U S A
Harold Ickes rushed upstairs to hear
    H.V. Kaltenborn on Pearl Harbor Day.
That is an entity, a single public
    Consciousness, has come
But I am not sure it's really me—"Don't
    make waves?"
Hoover gets up Republican Convention
    1960 says
"Communists beatnicks & eggheads" are
    America's Number 3 Menace
What who me? Is I th'Egghead
    Communist beatnick?
Postmaster General Summerfield
    plastered obscene sex signs all over
    my post office
brought Eisenhower a copy of Lady
    Chatterley's Lover
Eisenhower he's the President of the
    United States in the White House
with all the dirty words underlined Ike
    glances Shrieks agrees
"Terrible . . . we can't have that." Exact
    words quote deadpan my Newsweek
Aint that a National Issue?
How'd an old Fuck like that run my
    Nation?
Who put him in then?
You you dirty son of a bitch I sound like
    Kenneth Rexroth paranoiac—
I asterisked the poetic words in my first
    book to get it printed
and U.S. government seized it when ship
    wafted it over from England
I bit his hand he dropped the case.
But Juvenile vice-cops grabbed it in
    Frisco my publisher had to go to jail
    one afternoon

Allen Ginsberg, 1967: Controversial and innovative poet of the sixties, he received a National Book Award in 1974, and is a member of the National Institute of Arts and Letters. Born in Newark, New Jersey in 1926 and educated at Columbia University, he became the prophet and idol of an entire rebel generation. He has been a civil rights activist, Zen Buddhist and anti-Viet Nam war leader. *Credit:* FD

and Naked Lunch was banned in
    America up yours with a nude yellow
    grapefruit
and I had to rush out to Chicago & ruin
    my stomach orating before mobs
Because the University of Chicago was
    banning Naked Lunch plates from its
    starving Body
U. of C. produces atom bombs & FBI
    men
and when I asked Columbia U why
    doncha invite Kruschef give a speech
    in the Camp David Spirit type days
It said I quote "The State Department
    hasn't asked us to," giggling & bashful
    like it had to pee
Columbia is very Historical, they even
    had Eisenhower for President.
They turn out the cream of the crop,
    fresh young faces that guide the Na-
    tion
O My enemy Columbia University! How I
    would like to strangle you with a
    giraffe's footprint!
Master Kerouac was barred from the
    campus as an "unwholesome element"
    in 1942
Enter the Silent Generation. It got a
    monkey on its back in Korea
and then went advertising, or camped
    back to Columbia to teach the young.
It's all subliminal either you get fucked or
    you don't dearie
That's why American poetry stank for 20
    years.
Not that this is poetry, it's just shoveling
    the Garbage aside for Eternity.
I'm taking a stand! Hot Dog!
It's what's known as being responsible
    even tho it's the sheerest nonsense.
    Just moving my frankfurter!
Crap on all you Critics. You Norman
    Podhoretz, go screw the stars, King of
    the Jews—
you Lionel Trilling get back on the
    Mystic wagon before Infinity chops
    your head off,

and the rest of you, Nat Hentoff, dumb
    Vanden Haag, mute inglorious L.
    Simpson, hypocritic Kazin, Brustein-
    Wechsler, Journalists
attacking Kerouac, Corso & myself,
    snoopers, creeps, hung up idiots, In-
    competents, sneaks & dumbbells,
    quacks,
here, have a piece of my immortality, I
    mention your names.
Some of these are my friends but I have
    been requested to exhibit a sense of
    responsibility
& hitherto have been too tender & kind
    vain egotistical to answer public at-
    tacks.
As for Time Life Daily News the liberal
    Post the Partisan Review
all Yellow Journalism take your filthy
    fathead hands off my genitals, I am the
    Muse!
Go sniff the saintly footprints I left at
    Columbia!
The philistines are running America! Left
    right Center! Shoulder Arms! Onions!
Yes I want riots in the streets! Big orgies
    full of marijuana scaring the cops!
Everybody naked fucking on Union
    Square to denounce the Military Junta
    in San Salvador!
Why did we Crucify Mankind Upon a
    Cross of Gold?
Whatsa matter our secret CIA plot to
    unseat Syngman Rhee
flopped & delayed till Korean students
    rioted & took over the scene?
That's a military secret I'm a prophet I
    know lots of military secrets
I think I'll tell a couple to the Universe
    and go to Jail
I've been investigating— I think I'll be
    unamerican a few minutes
See how it feels like—eek! I just saw FBI
    hiding behind my mother's skull.
This is a private matter between me &
    my conscience
Why those newspapers all staring at me
    like that?
Big eyes on the editorial pages search-
    ing my soul for secret affiliation afflic-
    tions
And pinocchio long noses in literary
    columns sniffing up my ass to smell
    Immutability.
It's only laughing gas dearies. Stick that
    up your dirty old savings account—
and big long mustache headlines waving
    at me in wet dreams & nitemares!
O I just wish I were Mayakovsky! or
    even Neruda!
As it is I'll have to settle for reincarnation
    as a silly Blake.
Walt Whitman thou shdst be living at this
    Hour!
The average American Male & Female
    took over the ship of state
400 of them got smashed up over July 4
    Weekend celebrating!
Democracy! Bah! When I hear that word
    I reach for my feather Boa!
Better we should have a big jewish
    dictatorship full of Blintzes:
Better a spade Fish queen run our
    economics than
Kennedy that tired old man whose eyes
    speed back & forth like taxicabs
rather reptilian what?—

O Nixon's tired eyes! & Kennedy's hurried glance! O that America should be
hung up on these two idiots while I
am, alive!

It's silly but it's serious. What is truth?
said Pilate
Washing his hands in an atom bomb.
If you don't think the Chinese don't hate
us, you're just not Hep.
Get with it, Big Daddy, I been to South
America
Like, it swings there, everybody gets
high on Starvation
Like get with it Cat, you better stash
your wheat,
I hear the sirens of the Fuzz downstairs
in the subconscious
and don't you know, like, Alice Red
Gown she got *Reasons.*

Now where was It I sent my extra little
army in 1917?
I lost it somewhere in my bloomers— O
there it is fighting with General
Wrangle in Siberia
Heavens! What a bad show— you better
tell General MacArthur
shit or Get off the Pot.
    And that Invasion
of Mexico was such a camp! I never had
such a good time fucking all them
bandits and learning how to dance La
Cucaracha!
Let's spend our 50th Wedding anniversary there in Prince Maximilian's Palace.
What'd you say about my United Fruit?
Don't be Nasty you lower class piece

of trade.
I'll show you who's Miss Liberty or Not—
I got what it takes! I got the 1920's (Snap
yr fingers kid!)
I got Nostalgia of Depression! I got
N.R.A.!
I got Roosevelt I got Hoover I got Willkie
I got Hitler I got Franco I got World
War II!
I got the works (cha! cha!) I got the atom
bomb!
I got Cancer! I got Fission! I got legal
Prohibition!
I got the Works! I got the Fuck law! I got
the Junk Law! I got hundred billion
bucks a year!
Yassah! Yassah! I got Formosa! (Catch me
man) I got Chiang Kai-shek!
and I got my Central Intelligence getten
rid of him right now!
I got a million planes flying over Siberia!
I got
10,000,000 upstanding young americans
chargin' on the ricefields of China
Jazzin and waltzen and shootin and hol-
lering all day!
Whoopee! I got crosseye yellow cities in
every corner of the world.
I got the old umph! I got my Guantanamo!
I even got my old Marines!
You'd think I was an old thing way back
from the 19th Century
With Isadora Duncan Oscar Wilde & the
Floradora Sextette!
But I still got my old man, my handsome
lovin blond Marines!
I'm Miss Hydrogen America! I'm Mae in
Cobalt West! I'm the Sophie Tucker of

Plutonium Forever!
I'm the red Hot Mama of Tomorrow! Ain't
nobody gonna burn down my Miami
Hotels!
Didn't they cost 10 million dollars and I
hired the best Architects!
I even built a couple in Havana where
the livin's cheap.
Nosiree I'm up to date I hadda face lift
and got a hot new corset in Los
Alamos
and some airlift brassieres outa Congress and some gold pumps in Texas!
and I gotta boyfriend he's a millionaire
tax collector from Hollywood! He's the
artistic type!
I'm gonna make whoopee next ten years
before I blow my gasket,
I'm gonna take on the whole American
Legion in one night
Just like that cute little Presidential Can-
didate Kennedy Fellow! (He's the intellectual type)
I'm gonna make the Rosicrucians
scream!
Ah, how sad to get hung up in this way,
like on Hungary.
Belinski worried about Russia in 1860!
And Dostoyevsky's hero really worried
about socks.
It'll all pass away and then I'll be
answerable to gloomier onions, we'll
all weep.
I shouldn't waste my time on America
like this. It may be patriotic
but it isn't good art. This is a warning to
you, Futurists, and you Mao Tse-
tung—. . .

Demonstration, New York, 1968: Mark Rudd led Students for a Democratic Society in their "occupation" at Columbia University in 1968. This photograph illustrates a confrontation with the police on the Columbia campus at that time. *Credit:* Ted Cowell/Black Star

Bella Abzug, 1969: Women's rights activist and three-term former Member of the United States House of Representatives, Bella Abzug is seen at a fund raising party on New York's Lower East Side. Her drive, persistence and passionate concern are as well known as her hats. In Congress she emerged as a forceful spokeswoman for peace, full employment, openness in government, equal rights, consumer and environmental protection, aid to cities and aid to Israel. *Credit:* Photograph by Barbara Pfeffer

ERA Demonstration, New York, 1977: Feminist leaders Betty Friedan, far right, and Gloria Steinem, on her left, sign a giant telegram to President Carter supporting the Equal Rights Amendment. Betty Friedan, one of the original leaders of NOW (National Organization of Women) has become one of America's "elder stateswomen" in the battle for equal rights for both sexes. Gloria Steinem, co-founder and editor of MS Magazine, has been active in the feminist movement, civil rights and peace campaigns. In 1977, she was a member of the International Women's Year Committee. *Credit:* UPI

A Woman's Struggle for a Career in Science

1973. Ruth Weiner, described the problems involved in a woman's pursuit of a professional career.

My family background was probably more conducive than most to pursuit of a professional career. I was born in Vienna, Austria; my father holds both an M.D. and a Ph.D. in zoology, and my mother was one of the first women to receive a Ph.D. from the University of Vienna in a science (biology). My two grandfathers were both physicians (my father's father was Mrs. Freud's obstetrician!). In general, my family belonged to the upper-income Jewish society of Vienna; indeed, my paternal grandmother was extremely wealthy. My parents were religious freethinkers, to the extent that they formally disaffiliated with Judaism, and were political liberals. My mother was, until the Anschluss [annexation of Austria to Germany, 1938], a Social-Democrat member of the Vienna City Council.

I am the younger of two half-sibs: my brother is the child of my father's first marriage. It was always assumed that he and I would (1) pursue our education through some graduate degree (preferably in a science), (2) speak at least three languages fluently, and (3) play at least one musical instrument quite well. These, I might add, were the normal expectations for children of the social subgroup into which we were born. Our subsequent forced emigration to the U.S., and life there in moderate poverty for the first decade after immigration, made no difference in these expectations. In fact, we lived up to them. My brother is Dean of the College of Humanities at Montclair State College, New Jersey, and was for several years Chairman of the Department of Comparative Literature at the University of Massachusetts.

It was always assumed that I would pursue a scientific career, since I showed some talent in that direction, and I was strongly pressed to go into my father's field: medicine. I cannot say that I was *encouraged* to have professional aspirations, as much as that it was *assumed* that I would fulfill them. Indeed, throughout childhood I was quite strictly punished for less than superior academic achievement. I was simply too old to change my basic aspirations when I learned that American girls did not, for the most part, share them.

I am a product of the Baltimore, Maryland, public school system, and my recollections are that I fought it every inch of the way. My high school (interestingly, a girls' public high school, one of two such in Baltimore, and with the best academic reputation in the city) discouraged pursuit of scientific professional careers: "Don't you want to go into nursing, instead?" Since I was already on the principal's blacklist because of various political views and general intellectual snobbery and nastiness, this attitude

only encouraged me. At the University of Illinois, I was neither encouraged nor discouraged. I chose physics mainly because it was difficult and challenging, rather than out of any great interest. It never occurred to me until much, much later in life that one could enjoy intellectual pursuits and endeavors that *weren't* difficult.

I married at 18, so that almost all adult professional and social interactions came after marriage for me. My husband also always assumed that I would pursue a professional career, along with him. The question "Was your profession a handicap to love and marriage?" is meaningless for me. I would, however, agree wholeheartedly that marriage has been a handicap to my professional career. The one person who crystallized what is my present professional life is my husband's (and later, my) preceptor for the doctorate, who urged me to do what I wanted and go to graduate school.

The doors began to close to me after graduate school. I am now aware that there is considerable discrimination against women in chemistry at the point of graduate school admissions. I suppose that, at that time, in graduate school, I didn't think about it and accepted it as a normal state of affairs. In my last graduate school year, I did become aware that the reasons given for sex discrimination (girls marry and don't finish; girls don't use their degree even if they do finish; girls have babies and quit) were part of a vicious circle that included inadequate child care and enormous social pressures. I suggested a counseling service for female graduate students—a suggestion that caused considerable hilarity among my colleagues and professors.

My first child was born six months before I began graduate school; my fourth, one year after the Ph.D. Two of my children were contraceptive accidents, and would not have been born had there been any legal abortion available to me. If we can render one service to all women, everywhere, and especially those with professional aspirations, it is to legalize abortion on request by the pregnant woman. As long as the burden of contraception rests primarily on women, this is especially necessary.

Child care was difficult, and enormously expensive. Johns Hopkins University had a good day care center for children from 18 months on, which was my best experience with child care altogether. Other than this one experience, I always employed housekeepers, and was paying, in the last year of graduate school, 75% of my income for child care. Since my youngest child started first grade, I have employed no one for either child care or housekeeping, nor does my husband, now that we live apart. I did experience a great deal of guilt leaving my children to go to work, most of it, I now realize, brought on by comments of nonworking mothers such as those at nursery school: "Don't you think you are ruining your children's lives?" From my present perspective,

now that they are eight through fourteen years old, they seem to be normal children, with a normal relationship toward me and their father. They are, perhaps, more independent and self-sufficient; for example, my thirteen-year-old bicycles to the orthodontist and they *always* walk to school.

As girls, they have perhaps one unique advantage: their father assumes that they have the same aspirations as do boys and that they would undertake no greater household responsibility than nor exhibit markedly different behavior from boys their age. Their attitude toward a professional mother is that this is the normal state of affairs for them. Their behavior and attitudes truly seem to be shaped more by their individual personalities and the way the six of us interact than by whether or not I have a full-time professional job. The two elder ones are extremely "liberated" young women, and are both explicit and vociferous about any sex discrimination that they observe at school or among their friends. I have perhaps been lucky in that they are all sound constitutionally, and are almost never ill. On the other hand, I also encourage them to ignore minor ailments. They have also been, of course, saddled with a mother who could never be "Room Mother," who could not always attend the school Christmas Play, who never made cookies for the bake sale, but does any of this matter in the long run?

I have never made a conscious effort to spend my spare time with my children, but both my husband and I generally do so. We are a close family, and we like to do things such as skiing and traveling as a family. I certainly enjoy my children's company, and this may, in part, be because I have not ever had it for 24 hours a day, day after day after day. Our social life, rather than our children's, is different from that of our colleagues. Because there is little time for household chores (and less inclination to do them) and little interest on either my own or my husband's part in the house and its setting, we live simply and somewhat shabbily. The place is generally a mess; we almost never entertain in the formal sense. Now that we have separate households, this is even more true. Both domiciles are still furnished in "early Salvation Army," and the sum of the two housing payments are about 12% of our combined incomes. If my children could point to one distinguishing feature of their lives as children of professional parents, it is that our housing and life style are well below the expectations in our income level.

When I had completed a year of postdoctoral fellowship, I went with my husband to Denver, where he had found a position at the University of Denver. We had decided that *he* should look for a job, but, if possible, should take one in a place where I would have opportunities also, and Denver seemed like such a place. In looking for an academic position in the Denver-Boulder-Colorado

Sally Jane Priesand, 1978: Ordained by Hebrew Union College-Jewish Institute of Religion in Cincinnati in 1972, she became the first female rabbi in the United States. After her ordination she became assistant rabbi at Stephen Wise Free Synagogue in New York. In 1979 she moved to Congregation Beth El in Elizabeth, New Jersey as head rabbi, being the first woman to serve as head rabbi of a congregation. *Credit:* Photograph by Ricki Rosen

Springs area, I came on very restrictive and very overt sex discrimination. The University of Denver, where my husband was, would not even consider my application (nepotism, although a father and son had been department members in the recent past). The Colorado School of Mines wrote (although their policy has since changed), "We never hire women in the sciences." In general, the attitude toward a person seeking an academic job in a given place because her family is in that place is very negative. I finally got a position at the University of Colorado School of Medicine as a research associate, paid from grant funds. I really got this only because both the chairman and my subsequent coauthor were Johns Hopkins men themselves. After three years, by a stroke of luck, a position as assistant professor of chemistry at Temple Buell College, a woman's college in Denver, opened up. Since CU [Colorado University] would not put me on hard money or a tenure track, I went to Temple Buell. I was considered by my preceptor at Hopkins to be a great success, because I had a tenure-track teaching position at a small college for women, one that is not, in my opinion, first-rate.

My experience at both the Medical School and Temple Buell demonstrated to me that fulfillment involved more interaction with people than was possible in a purely research position and a larger role in policy-making than was possible as a very junior faculty member. At TBC I was, fortunately, able to have positive power in making decisions about curriculum, new faculty, budget, and so on. It is a small college, and a faculty member's role in decision making depends rather heavily on his or her own initiative. The structure of the chemistry major program there is primarily my creation; there was no chemistry major when I went on the faculty.

My experience at TBC demonstrates the enormous importance of women as role models for women students. Prior to my appointment, all the physics, chemistry, and mathematics faculty had been men. The highest professional aspiration voiced by any student then was to become a laboratory technician! Not only was I able to encourage the girls to go on toward a professional career, but I convinced my closest colleague in the Department that encouragement was both necessary and worthwhile. Although he was not himself prejudiced in any way, he had failed to realize that most girls need encouragement to overcome the tremendous internal pressures that have been built up in them.

Shortly after we moved to Colorado, and because I really felt somewhat unfulfilled in my work, I became active in what was then called the conservation movement. We are very active, out-of-doors people and enjoy all sorts of wilderness experiences, and in this sphere, I have developed a deep sense of responsibility of man toward the earth, and see a need to change some fundamental human attitudes. I also saw where, as a scientist, I could render some valuable services to the "lay" citizenry concerned about conservation.

In 1965, a group of us founded the Colorado Open Space Council. I have been on the board since its inception, and have served both as secretary (1966–67) and as vice-president (1970–71). In 1969 I became one of the founders and chairman of Colorado Citizens for Clean Air, and held this post until leaving Colorado in 1971. I served for two years as legislative chairman for the Open Space Council, and was appointed by the Governor of Colorado to the Executive Committee of the Colorado Environment Commission 1970 (one of two women on the 56-member Commission and the 11-member Executive Committee). I have given technical testimony on air- and water-resource problems before innumerable state legislative committees, and five times—twice by invitation—before committees of the United States Congress. I have helped write several laws, including the Colorado Air Pollution Control Act, and have received several state awards for my activity in the field of conservation.

In spring of 1970, while on a speaking tour for the Conservation Foundation, I spoke at a luncheon for a citizens' clean-air group in Miami. One member of the audience (whom I did not meet at the time) was Dean of the College of Arts and Sciences at my present institution—Florida International University. As a result of the speech, I was offered a deanship (which I turned down), and then the chairmanship of the Department of Chemistry, which I ultimately accepted. FIU has made a deliberate effort to hire women for upper-level administrative positions. For this reason, and because of my work in environmental concerns, they wanted me as chairman. My offer from FIU was totally unsolicited by me and came, I might add, as such a complete surprise that I never connected it with the speech I had given there.

What has happened to my family life as a result of my move to Miami has caused a great deal of private and public comment. Having myself been in the position of looking for an academic job while tied to a given geographic location, I did not want to put my husband, now professor of chemistry at the University of Denver, in that position. FIU has no nepotism rule, except that the case where one spouse has direct administrative authority over the other must be considered specially. I felt then, however, and I still feel, that insistence on a "package deal" would be unwise, would set a bad precedent, and would make everyone unhappy. Moreover, we were not sure that we were ready to transfer the entire family permanently from Colorado. Thus, we decided that, for the present, he would remain in Denver with two children, and I would take two with me to Miami.

Our situation certainly focuses a major problem for women (or perhaps one ought to say for married couples) pursuing professional careers. Unless we initiate jobs that are filled by a married couple rather than by a single person, we cannot guarantee a husband and wife equally satisfying professional appointments in the same geographic location, because there are so few positions available. Elimination of nepotism rules is vitally necessary, and will go a long way toward alleviating this situation, but it is no guarantee of good positions for a married couple.

The choice I made is one which a married woman (or man) would make only after many years of marriage, or when contemplating a permanent separation anyway. It has taught me much about the relative roles of married and single people in our society. I am very lonely, but that is largely because almost all social life takes place for couples. In a married society, the woman alone is a social outcast. If we adapted more naturally to the presence of unmarried, mature adults in our social gatherings, they would not be so lonely, and, I am convinced, the present pressure to be married would be greatly alleviated.

I achieved my present position by a fluke, but in part because I had sought and found fulfilment in an area that is now booming: environmental studies. I became an active leader in the conservation movement because opportunities in my chosen professional area—chemistry—were so severely curtailed by sex discrimination. This is the first time since graduate school that I have felt challenged by my job; I enjoy it very much.

The primary advice I would give girls contemplating a professional career is:

1. Be well prepared, but stay flexible. Few women or men end up doing what they had planned while in graduate school.
2. Maintain your humanity in dealing with people and follow your natural instincts, even though some things you do may be labeled "feminine."
3. Be prepared to work very hard, if you plan to have children. Equality in housekeeping roles is something we are still working to attain.
4. Don't sacrifice your ambition, aggressiveness, or intelligence for any of the standard feminine rewards like marriage.
5. Learn to deal casually with, or to ignore, sexism and discrimination.
6. Set high goals for yourself, and set them independently of your sex.
7. If you marry, marry someone in sympathy with those goals.

The Children of Holocaust Survivors

1977. The Holocuast perpetrated by Hitler's Nazi Germany will never be forgotten; however, the children of Holocaust survivors face their own distinct problems. Abraham Peck described his personal experiences in coping with this situation.

Each April, Jews around the world observe Holocaust Day. On this occasion we remember the nearly six million Jews who perished in the era of the Second World War. It is the least that one people can do to perpetuate the memory of so many millions of its own who died more than 30 year ago.

It is proper that the victims of Adolph Hitler's plan to exterminate European Jewry come back into the thoughts of young and old alike. Surely there is no nation on earth, no segment of humanity, which can fail to understand this tragedy as one of the darkest moments in modern history.

In some Jewish homes, this day has an even greater significance. In these homes live the survivors of the Holocaust, the precious few thousands who, by the chance of youth, desire, faith or "luck," survived the likes of Auschwitz, Dachau, Maidanek, and Buchenwald. In those homes, too, live, or have lived, the children of the survivors. Many of them are today in their teens or older. They are of an age where they should have absorbed all that their parents have imparted to them of life and the rules for survival in an increasingly complex society.

What does a concentration camp survivor know of life? Surely more than most, for he or she has seen and lived life in a way that few others have seen and lived it. He has known extended suffering, through physical and mental torture, and witnessed the murder of loved ones, a special kind of torture in itself. Yet he survived.

For the survivors of the camps, however, liberation in 1945 was merely a physical one. From the harrowing experience of being an "individual in the concentration camp," the survivor found himself the victim of the "concentration camp in the individual," a situation where stress and suffering over a sustained period very often left him an emotional cripple. The isolation of captivity in the camps also manifested in some survivors an inner isolation, leaving them unable to respond normally to a "normal" post-camp experience.

Recently, while reviewing a book dealing with survivors in America, I posed some questions meant to come to grips with the problem of the "concentration camp in the individual" "What happens to the concentration camp survivor," I asked, "when the person leaves the 'gates of no return'? How much of the experience has one internalized and to what degree can one adjust to 'normal' life?" I concluded that in the post-war lives of most survivors living in America,

Elie Weisel, 1980: Writer, philosopher, novelist and playwright, he is known throughout the world for his extraordinary efforts to rescue the Holocaust from historical and literary oblivion. Born in Rumania in 1928, he was sent with the other Jewish residents of his town to Buchenwald, the notorious Nazi concentration camp, where he watched his father die. He arrived in New York in 1956 and became an American citizen seven years later. Weisel is Chairman of the U.S. Holocaust Memorial Council, an independent federal agency set up by Congress in 1980 to raise funds to create a Holocaust memorial museum on The Mall in Washington. *Credit:* Photograph by Ricki Rosen

"what emerges is a tale of triumph and sorrow, always tempered by an inability on the part of the survivors to forget or comprehend the tragedy that shaped the remainder of their years.

The Holocaust survivor has been the focus of many studies, both physical and psychological. Some symptoms, common to most survivors, have been diagnosed: pain, recurring nightmares, a loss of religious belief ("If there was a God he could not have allowed such a terrible thing to happen"). Other survivors, however, have drawn even closer to religious orthodoxy, refusing to give up their Judaism, so as not to "give Hitler a post-war victory." Most survivors are bitter that their incredible suffering has been given no meaning—that even if it had, no one would understand ("you have not suffered, you have not survived"). Yet others, such as the distinguished novelist and camp survivor, Elie Wiesel, feel that we are entitled to raise questions about the Holocaust but not to provide answers. Wiesel says it is beyond man's capabilities to provide solutions to an occurrence of such immense moral proportions. Finally, some survivors feel a sense of great guilt at having survived, while their loved ones did not.

Despite these physical and psychological afflictions, the survivors live on, many of them in Israel and America. They have married, borne children and have become professionally successful, steeled by the experience of survival to endure the slings and arrows of the difficult and uncertain world of trade and commerce.

Yet, despite an external sense of

success, the survivors remain a subgroup within their own Jewish communities, preferring to live in close proximity to each other, worship in their own synagogues and participate in their own social organizations. Those survivors living in America have maintained an ambivalence towards the American way of life. They are staunchly patriotic but maintain the right to dismiss some American customs and habits as idiotic, preferring instead to stress the superiority of pre-war European life.

The children of survivors share with them this often unnatural world. Their condition is less well-known than that of the survivors. It is only within the last two or three years that some of these children have begun to come to grips with the reality of their situation. For many, nearing the age of 30, it is the first time these children of survivors have begun to question their own views of life and the effect the Holocaust has had upon that existence.

They have often lived in the eye of a hurricane, surrounded by the shadows of the "war." They know that the "war" is a part of their being, but do not know why. "I've asked next to nothing," writes one survivor's child, "also worried about my own suffering in (my parent's) response. I want to know very badly, yet I dread the moment of having to raise the issue, although I realize that it is my duty to learn and to be able to retell their stories to my children."

Certainly, no two survivors experienced the Holocaust in a similar manner. Neither has every child of survivors formulated his or her views of adolescent experiences in the same way. Yet, I have met enough of them to know that we share similar questions and long for similar answers.

Many of us live with a great and terrible burden, apparent only to those, like myself, who are children of survivors. We have been called a "separate sub-community of Jews," successful, like our parents, externally; we are career-oriented and middle-class in our values, but we bear the traumas of life with the survivor, of life with the "concentration camp in the individual."

Some of the burdens described by others of my generation reflect the process of growing up with survivors of a mythicized event, which the Holocaust has invariably become: "I grew up a mere mortal in a world of martyrs who had suffered (and) heroes who had survived." What was a grandmother to many of us who had never known one, or even an uncle or an aunt?: "The people who were lost (in the Holocaust) have no personalities . . . Childhood memories of Uncle and Aunt are subordinate to adult cries of despair at their loss." Most of us do not know of our parents' early lives: "I never heard about childish games, sibling rivalries, paternal conflict, or any of the things that go to make up a life." And survivors' children have no history. "My parents could not give me their history, because it had been brutally ripped away from them and was no longer theirs to give."

That is why I searched out my roots in the deadness of one of Hitler's most notorious concentration camps—Buchenwald. I had come to Buchenwald, located near the city of Weimar in East Germany, to visit a place where my father, as a Polish Jew, had been a concentration camp prisoner 30 years earlier. I stood in the brutal August heat that day, trying for the first time in my life to understand a part of myself that had been submerged beneath the young adult American I had become. For me, a Jew with a 5000-year history, the world before 1939 did not exist. I could do no genealogical searches, contact no distant or aged relatives. Buchenwald was the only stop on the track of my own personal history—all the others had disappeared.

I often fear that part of the syndrome we labor under is an inability to know when not to blame the Holocaust for misguided or inappropriate deeds. We cannot allow the Holocaust to become convenient as a whipping boy for our actions.

Yet, despite early fears, we continue to seek each other out, enjoying a certain spontaneity we can find with no one else. Most of us, I believe, are seeking a real liberation from our own personal Holocaust. We want to clear away the myths surrounding this terrible time in our parent's lives and confront what has been considered not to be confrontable.

That is why on the Day of Remembrance, I offer a prayer for the dead of the Holocaust and remember those whose lives are still affected by its memory.

Demonstration, Skokie, Illinois, 1978: The American Nazi Party organized a march through Skokie, Illinois, a predominantly Jewish suburb of Chicago. Jewish communal organizations joined many liberal organizations to protest against the decision allowing the Nazi march. *Credit:* Photograph by Ken Love, Atoz Images

Peace Demonstration, New York, 1982: Jewish participants in the massive peace rally held at the United Nations and in Central Park to demonstrate the need for disarmament and an end to the nuclear arms race. *Credit:* Photograph by Ricki Rosen

Demonstration, New York, 1971: Demonstration at Foley Square Courthouse in Lower Manhattan to support freedom for Soviet Jews. *Credit:* Photograph by Charles Gatewood

Jewish Immigration Today

1982. There has been a resurgence of immigration to the United States from all parts of the world in recent years. Since 1973 an increasing number of Jews have migrated to this country. Psychologist Drora Kass and sociologist Seymour Martin Lipset have examined this phenomenon.

Migration remains a Jewish characteristic from the days of Abraham, Isaac, and Jacob. A people of outsiders, Jews have always shown greater readiness to move in search of a better way of life even when anti-Semitism was not a significant factor. Between 1880 and 1952, nearly five million Jews left their country of origin. Close to three million came to the United States, more than half a million migrated to Western Europe, and one and a quarter million, or one out of every five Jews, made aliya to Eretz Yisrael. Although most of the movement to the United States occurred prior to 1924 before restrictive legislation cut off mass immigration, it is estimated that close to half a million Jews reached these shores between 1924 and 1959—roughly a quarter of a million before World War II, and another 200,000 during 1945–59.

Mass immigration to this country, thought of not long ago as predominantly a pre-World War I phenomenon, is once more gaining increased attention from policymakers and the public at large. During the past ten years, the number of immigrants to this country has been close to the highest in any decade in American history (Teitelbaum, 1980). The United States is still by far the world's largest receiver of refugees and other immigrants. America's barriers to entry are less stringent than in other developed countries. It also continues to be its own draw. As one commentator has noted: "It is inherently seductive . . . with all its problems, it remains a country of uncommon freedom and uncommon opportunity."

The recent upswing in immigration to this country has also included a renewed Jewish influx, particularly from 1973 onward—a phenomenon whose numbers appear to be underestimated in offiical community records. Since U.S. government agencies do not inquire into the religious background of immigrants, the major direct source of information is the Hebrew Immigrant Aid Society (HIAS). According to HIAS reports, between 1967 and 1980 the agency assisted in settling over 125,000 Jews in the United States. The bulk of those aided originated from the Soviet Union and other East European countries, with the remainder from the Middle East and Latin America. HIAS records do not include most of the Middle East and Latin America. HIAS records do not include most of the more affluent contemporary Jewish immigrants to the United States from Argentina, Canada, Chile, Colombia, Cuba, Nicaragua, South Africa, and Iran. Nor do they list the several hundred thousand Israelis who have come

here from the land established to put an end to the phenomenon of the wandering Jew.

"Pull" Rather Than "Push"

Unlike past waves of Jewish movement to America which resulted from persecution or severe economic deprivation, contemporary immigration reflects the desire to improve status, widen knowledge and horizons, and exploit greater economic opportunities. "Pull" rather than "push" factors motivate a large number to opt for the United States even when persecution or fear of it affects the decision to emigrate. Many are well educated, highly skilled, and often able to bring economic resources with them or find a well-paid job shortly after their arrival. No strangers to Coca-Cola, rock, Kojak, jeans, and hamburgers, these are individuals with a familiarity, and more often than not prior exposure to American ways through the media, personal contacts, and tourism.

With the exception of Jews who have fled dictatorial or anti-Jewish regimes, emigration no longer implies a sharp break with one's roots. The new arrivals can exercise their nostalgia by going back to their homeland for a visit or by entertaining compatriots in their new homes. The numbers involved are not small. One out of every 10 to 12 Jews in the United States is a recent arrival who has been here less than ten years. Of the 350,000 Israelis living here, the majority have left their poor, more demanding homeland in search of greater educational and economic opportunities. Over 75,000 Soviet Jews have come to these shores since 1972 to escape discrimination and enjoy the benefits of a more

Newly Arrived Soviet Immigrants, 1981: He was a captain in the Red Army and displays some of his medals; she is holding her bacteriologist's diploma. Assisted by a Jewish organization, both are studying English to adapt their skills to life in this country. *Credit:* ISP/Photograph by Charles Steiner

affluent society. The other groups of newcomers, though smaller in number, add much to the kaleidoscope of American Jewry.

Although they do not share cultural backgrounds, Jewish immigrants from South Africa, Latin America, and Canada have similar attributes. Almost all speak English well. They have left their native lands not because of direct persecution but because of survival fears shared by the larger group they were affiliated with—Whites in South Africa, the middle class in Latin America, and the English-speaking community in Quebec—or simply because they saw greater opportunity in the United States. They are more widely traveled than the average Israeli or Russian, and generally more affluent. The choice of location for many is determined by climatic conditions and the presence of a significant Jewish community. Miami, Los Angeles, and Houston seem to answer these requirements more than adequately.

Latin American Jews have always been coming here. Some have bought homes and invested in businesses as a hedge against an uncertain future. "There is no future for the middle class in Latin America, no prospect of a stable democracy," commented one new arrival. "There is a general feeling of malaise, a feeling that we cannot do much to change the inevitable process." A steady stream of young Latin American Jews who come to study in this country have remained here because of a sense of greater social, cultural, scientific, or economic opportunities. Their choice often proves to be an added incentive for their parents' emigration. One recent arrival describes the typical pattern: "Education in Latin America is not too good. People prefer to send their kids to an American university and often they don't come back, so the parents follow. First they visit. Then they buy a house. Then they commute for a period. And then they come to settle permanently."

Miami has been the major recipient of Jews from South of the border: the bulk of the Cuban community who fled Castro and the elimination of private business, Chileans who feared that the Allende regime would prove to be another Cuba, Nicaraguans wary of the pro-PLO politics of the regime which replaced Somoza in July 1979, Colombians disturbed by continuing violence, and Argentinians who have reacted both to fears of anti-Semitism and social and political instability in that country. People are rarely persecuted in Argentina because they are Jewish. But if a Jew is caught in, or suspected of radical politics, as some young Jews are, he or she will be treated more brutally by police, army, or rightist thugs than will a non-Jew.

Canadian migration south in search of a warmer climate and a chance to get a bigger slice from a larger pie is not a new phenomenon. English-speaking North America has come close at times to forming one labor market. Millions of Canadians and hundreds of thousands of Americans have moved across the border in the past century. A disproportionate number of them have been Jews. During the 1920s and for a period following World War II, it was easier for immigrants to get into Canada than into the United States. Hence many Jews who would have preferred to settle in the larger, more affluent society went to Canada (or Latin America), hoping to move to the United States at a later stage.

Most recently, the political triumph of the *Parti Québecois*, the French Canadian separatists, followed by the passage of legislation requiring the use of French in diverse activities, the occasional expression of anti-Jewish sentiments by extremists among the nationalists, and anxiety over that province's economic future, have led some Jews to leave. A survey of Quebec's predominantly Anglophone Jewish community of 115,000, taken before the recent referendum, found that if the province were to become independent, 70 percent of those age 40 and under said they would "probably" or "definitely" leave. Furthermore, over 15 percent of the older respondents reported at least one child who had already moved to another part of Canada, and the offspring over 10 percent of those questioned had chosen to go south rather than west. A 1978 study conducted by the Allied Jewish Community Services of Montreal showed that 40 percent of its respondents did not expect to remain in Quebec upon completion of their studies.

Ruth Wisse and Irwin Cotler of McGill University have described the dilemma facing Quebec's Jews, among whom Holocaust survivors figure prominently: "Quebec's Jews find themselves beset by a *crise de conscience*. On the one hand, they understand, even empathize with the aspirations for self-renewal of the French Canadians. At the same time . . . they wonder at what point their own pluralism . . . will stick in the craw of a nationalist bid for domination." Many feel that while prior to 1976 they were a tolerated and accepted minority, now they share in the antagonism directed against Anglophones in general. Such anxiety is evident in the self-humor of jokes such as: "How does a smart Montreal Jew speak to a dumb one?" "Long distance." With the immediate threat of independence diminished as a result of the 1980 referendum vote against separatism, pressure for emigration may decline.

Another affluent society whose political, ethnic, and racial conflicts have resulted in increased emigration, particularly by Jews, is South Africa. Although in the past South Africans made aliya to Israel or migrated to Britain, many of those who left following the violent race riots of 1976 in the township of Soweto—a Black ghetto on the outskirts of Johannesburg—headed for the United States.

Together with other religious minorities, close to 20,000 Iranian Jews have fled to the United States since the establishment of the Ayatollah Khomeini's fundamentalist Islamic regime. More than any other group of recent arrivals, Iranians still hope eventually to return home, where, under the Shah, they enjoyed equal rights and economic prosperity. Not wanting to foreclose that possibility, very few have sought political asylum in this country.

A Diversity of Jewish Values
All belong to the People of the Book, yet the claim of Jewish newcomers to a common ancestry seems confounded by disparate cultural patterns, a broad range of problems of adjustment to their new home, and varying conceptions of what it means to be Jewish. Russians are the least Jewish—generally irreligious, with little knowledge of Yiddish or of other aspects of Jewish secular culture. Coming from a country in which any form of religious affiliation is considered backward and deviant, and in which Jewish cultural activities have been virtually nonexistent, only a small minority who come to the United States have Jewish interests or strong Jewish identification. On the whole, they do not relate to institutions except to seek help, or sometimes to participate in community programs run by Soviet Jews and tailored to their needs and interests.

To the average Soviet Jew, emigration is simply a struggle for a better personal future. Research conducted in the United States and in Israel (Elizur and Elizur, 1976; Gitelman, 1978) has shown that motives for emigration are general rather than specifically Jewish. These include aspirations for greater vocational and economic opportunities, the wish to join family, the desire for greater freedom, or simply being caught up in a wave of emigration. Yet ethnic proximity and the desire for educational opportunity for their children may eventually establish links, beyond that of patron and client, between newly arrived Soviet Jews and the larger Jewish community.

While almost all Israeli emigrants speak Hebrew fluently and have varying levels of knowledge of Jewish history, culture, and Bible, the large majority are secular. Coming from a Jewish state they have not had to think about being Jewish. Latin American Jews, largely of East European origin and living on the margins of Hispanic-Portuguese-Catholic societies, have maintained a secular Yiddish culture. Their Jewish commitment facilitates their shift from one diaspora community to another. "In Latin America, Jewishness penetrates all spheres of your life," explains Rabbi Gunther Friedlander, who recently settled in Miami, after having held pulpits for twenty-nine years in a number of Latin American countries. "Going to temple is not a weekly affair, but reading the Jewish newspaper is. And then there are frequent visits to Israel. Here Jewishness is mostly a social affair." The largest and

most visible part of Hispanic Jews in the United States, the Cubans, have fitted into their new home as an organized ethnic community whose institutions are an affiliated part of the larger American Jewish society.

Canadian Jews, who have been part of North American English-speaking society, rarely form a distinctive group. They are regarded by American Jews as "in-migrants" rather than foreigners. A greater focus on ethnicity and religion in Canada, which does not separate church and state, has intensified Jewish identity. This background may explain the disproportionate number of ex-Canadians holding American Jewish leadership positions: Edgar M. Bronfman, president of the World Jewish Congress; Bertram H. Gold, executive vice-president of the American Jewish Committee; Norman E. Frimer, former national director of the B'nai B'rith Hillel Foundations and currently executive director of the Memorial Foundation for Jewish Culture; Philip Bernstein, recently retired executive vice-president of the Council of Jewish Federations and Welfare Funds; and Rabbi Wolfe Kelman, executive vice-president of the Rabbinical Assembly (Conservative).

South Africa's 118,000 Jews, living in a society in which people, including Whites, are identified in ethnic terms such as Afrikaaners or English, have always stood out in the diaspora for the intensity of their commitment to and involvement in Jewish activities. They are traditional in their religious orientation. The majority attend Orthodox (equivalent approximately to the American Conservative) synagogues at least a few times a year. Of all diaspora communities they have the highest percentage of children receiving a Jewish education and the largest proportion of Jews affiliated with Zionist organizations. They contribute more to Israel on a per capita basis than any other major community and have sustained the largest rate of aliya from any country which permits free migration.

South Africans continue most of these patterns in their new home. Their strong Jewish identity leads them to settle close to coreligionists and to become rapidly involved in communal activities. They are perceived as a welcome and unproblematic addition to American Jewry. "They're pleasant people whose interpersonal style is familiar," says Sol Brownstein, executive director of the Houston Jewish Federation's Family and Children Service. "And what's more, their Jewish commitment is unquestionable. . . . The Houston Jewish Community is going to be enriched and grow as a result of their presence. They are refined. They are business people. They're the kind of people whom Houstonians can relate to and get along with. The sympathy of the community here has been greater for the South Africans, in terms of their plight certainly, than it's been for the Israelis and in some instances more so than for the Russians."

Russian Jewish Immigrant, New York, 1977: Arrival of Russian Jewish immigrant at Kennedy Airport, New York. Arrangements were made by HIAS (Hebrew Immigrant Aid Society). *Credit:* Photograph by Barbara Pfeffer

The Iranians who have come to this country in the last three years, mostly to Los Angeles, are strongly Jewish in religious terms and proud of their ancient heritage. But they are culturally Iranian; they have no secular Jewish language and they lack the tradition of self-help that characterizes European Jews. American Jewish groups who have tried to assist them often feel frustrated, not knowing how to deal with people who, even when well-to-do as many are, do not contribute to local Jewish federations. Iranians, in turn, resent the stereotype of them as a group which is uniformly wealthy. "Like most middle-class people in Iran, we had very few liquid assets," explains a recent arrival to Los Angeles. "We are forced to leave property behind, and what's more, our finances have suffered from the freeze on Iranian banks in this country. We live in constant fear and uncertainty about our future."

If they shy away from participation in the vast network of secular Jewish ac-

tivities, Iranians do have a role in the more traditional religious community. There are hundreds of Iranian young people studying in various secondary Hebrew day schools and in yeshivoth in Baltimore, Los Angeles, and New York. Rabbi Marc D. Angel of New York's Spanish and Portuguese Synagogue comments: "Iranians have a very strong sense of spirituality when it comes to prayer. They pray with tremendous enthusiasm and devotion." The diverse cultural backgrounds of newly arrived Iranian Jews makes for a wide range of habits, customs, and attitudes which must be adapted to American ways. These vary from basis such as language and adjustment to a value system inherently different from that of the old country to the loss of luxuries such as servants.

The transition of Soviet Jews is by far the most traumatic. They come to the United States often after a lengthy period of "nonperson" status following their application for an exit visa to Israel (a request for any other destination stands

little chance of success). In the words of one Soviet Jew, they "have come from another planet." Of all the recent immigrant groups they are the least familiar with American ways. Though rejecting communist society, Russian Jews have unwittingly accepted much of it as conventional and are startled to find how different things are here. They are accustomed to living in a rigidly regulated, totally statist society, where authorities take responsibility for much that is left here to the individual, such as health care, job placement, and housing. Adaptation to the constant decision making that our system requires is therefore very difficult.

Although native English speakers have the least trouble adjusting, South Africans and Canadians, like transplanted Americans, experience "the typical problems that result from complete separation from the extended family support system," says Sol Brownstein. "Frequently, the sense of isolation they experience as a result of needing to deal with

Grandfather and Grandchildren, New York, 1977: In many families, grandfathers take delight in helping to introduce their grandchildren to Hebrew and Jewish study. *Credit:* Photograph by Bill Aron

everything within the context and re-sources of a nuclear family blows their minds . . . and marital problems that might have been kept under control if relatives were around, erupt."

Israelis in Exile
While we have no precise figures, it seems evident that the bulk of Jewish immigration since the mid-1960s has been from Israel. In December 1980 Israel's Central Bureau of Statistics reported 338,000 Israelis living abroad, the large majority in the United States. Based on discussions with Jewish communal leaders throughout the country, as well as with American immigration officials, we estimate that there are over 350,000 Israelis residing in the United States alone.

Sojourners
Israelis are self-defined sojourners. They are the first group of Jewish immigrants, other than some German refugees in the 1930s, who have come to America in the belief that they will return home. German Jewish émigrés felt that their native culture was superior to anything American, and that once Hitler fell they would return home—sentiments which kept them from assimilating well and participating in local Jewish affairs until World War II.

During the period of mass immigration, i.e. before 1924, Jewish newcomers differed from many other Europeans in that they planned to stay in America permanently. Non-Jews, on the other hand, frequently arrived as sojourners for a limited period. They came to make money or gain a worthwhile skill, and then return to their native land. Of the Jews who came to the United States between 1908 and 1924, only 5 percent left compared to 34 percent of the total immigrant population. Unlike members of other ethnic groups, most could not consider leaving the pluralistic *goldene medineh* tolerant of diversity and free. Some did not have the choice of going back to their country of birth.

Students of the immigrant experience have distinguished between the behavior of "sojourners" and "settlers." Those who come to settle are more likely than sojourner ethnic groups to form communal institutions, get involved in local affairs, claim rights, and seek to advance their own position as a group. For example, the lesser participation in unions or communal institutions by Italians than by Jews before World War I has been explained in part as reflecting the sojourner identity of the Italian working class (Liebman, 1978).

Like other non-Jewish sojourners before them, Israelis cling to their culture and are unwilling to organize as permanent residents in America. Even after many years in this country most never fully assimilate. They face a perpetual dilemma: they do not want to return to Israel until they have accomplished the tasks they set out for themselves—higher education, professional training, and the accumulation of material assets. But as this situation is seldom achieved before developing an extensive personal network of connections and involvements, plans for returning become increasingly complex and vague. Yet Israelis continue to associate almost exclusively with people from their own group. Although they may remain abroad their entire lives, they rarely sever their ties with the homeland. They often go back home for visits, only to return to the country in which, more often than not, they still view themselves as foreigners.

Part of the Israelis' reluctance to admit they have chosen a new home or might be in the process of doing so, results from the stigma attached to anyone viewed as an emigrant from Israel. If aliya, or immigration to Israel, is considered the ultimate Zionist injunction, emigration or *yerida* is looked upon as the ultimate betrayal of the Zionist cause. Furthermore it constitutes desertion at a time when Israel is still struggling for a secure and peaceful existence. This long-standing attitude both on the part of Israeli officialdom and the Israeli public at large, leaves Israelis abroad with an ever-gnawing feeling of guilt and a constant need to justify or rationalize their decision, or else to deny the intention of remaining abroad.

Return to His Jewish Heritage

1982. Paul Cowan, the writer, described the loss of his identity and rediscovery of his heritage.

For more than four years now, I have been embarked on a wondrous, confusing voyage through time and culture. Until 1976, when I was thirty-six, I had always identified myself as an American Jew. Now I am an American and a Jew. I live at once in the years 1982 and 5743, the Jewish year in which I am publishing this book. I am Paul Cowan, the New York-bred son of Louis Cowan and Pauline Spiegel Cowan, Chicago-born, very American, very successful parents; and I am Saul Cohen, the descendant of rabbis in Germany and Lithuania. I am the grandson of Modie Spiegel, a mail-order magnate, who was born a Reform Jew, became a Christian Scientist, and died in his spacious house in the wealthy gentile suburb of Kenilworth, Illinois, with a picture of Jesus Christ in his breast pocket; and of Jacob Cohen, a used-cement-bag dealer from Chicago, an Orthodox Jew, who lost everything he had—his wife, his son, his business, his self-esteem—except for the superstition-tinged faith that gave moments of structure and meaning to his last, lonely years.

As a child, growing up on Manhattan's East Side, I lived among Jewish WASPs. My father, an only child, had changed his name from Cohen to Cowan when he was twenty-one. He was so guarded about his youth that he never let my brother or sisters or me meet any of his father's relatives. I always thought of myself as a Cowan—the Welsh word for stonecutter—not a Cohen—a member of the Jewish priestly caste. My family celebrated Christmas and always gathered for an Easter dinner of ham and sweet potatoes. At Choate, the Episcopalian prep school to which my parents sent me, I was often stirred by the regal hymns we sang during the mandatory chapel service. In those years, I barely knew what a Passover seder was. I didn't know anyone who practiced archaic customs such as keeping kosher or lighting candles on Friday night. Neither my parents nor I ever mentioned the possibility of a bar mitzvah. In 1965, I fell in love with Rachel Brown, a New England Protestant whose ancestors came here in the seventeenth century. It didn't matter the least bit to her—or to me—that we were an interfaith marriage.

Now, at forty-two, I care more about Jewish holidays I'd never heard of back then, Shavuot or Simchat Torah, than about Christmas or Easter. In 1980, fifteen years after we were married, Rachel converted to Judaism, and is now program director of Ansche Chesed, a neighborhood synagogue we are trying to revitalize. Our family lights Friday night candles, and neither Rachel nor I work on the Sabbath. Since 1974, our children, Lisa and Mamu, have gone to the Havurah School, a once-a-week Jew-ish school we started, and at fourteen and twelve they're more familiar with the Torah than I was five years ago. They are very thoughtful children, who have witnessed the changes in our family's life and are somewhat bemused and ambivalent about them. There is no telling whether they'll follow the path we have chosen. But that is true of all children. This past September, Lisa undertook the difficult task of learning enough Hebrew in six months to chant a full Haftorah (a prophetic text) at her bat mitzvah at Ansche Chesed. That day I was as happy as I've ever been in my life.

By now, I see the world through two sets of eyes, my American ones and my Jewish ones. That is enhanced, I suppose, by the fact that my father, who was once president of CBS-TV, who produced "The Quiz Kids," "Stop the Music," and "The $64,000 Question," and my elegant mother, an ardent civil-rights activist, moved easily through all sorts of worlds. Even now, as a journalist, I want to be at once a versatile American writer like James Agee or John Dos Passos and an evocative Jewish one like Isaac Bashevis Singer or Chaim Potok. Sometimes it makes me feel deeply conflicted. Sometimes it makes my life seem wonderfully rich and varied. I do know this: that my mind is enfolded like a body in a prayer shawl, by my ancestral past and its increasingly strong hold on my present. Scores of experiences have caused me to re-create myself, to perceive a five-thousand-year-old tradition as a new, precious part of my life.

I am not alone. Indeed, I believe my story, with all its odd, buried, Old World family mysteries, with its poised tension between material wealth and the promise of spiritual wealth, is the story of much of my generation, Jew and gentile alike.

Sephardic Mother and Child, Los Angeles, 1982: Among the recent immigrants to the Los Angeles area. *Credit:* Photograph by Bill Aron

Grandmother and Grandchild, 1974: *Credit:* Photograph by Abigail Heyman/ARCHIVE

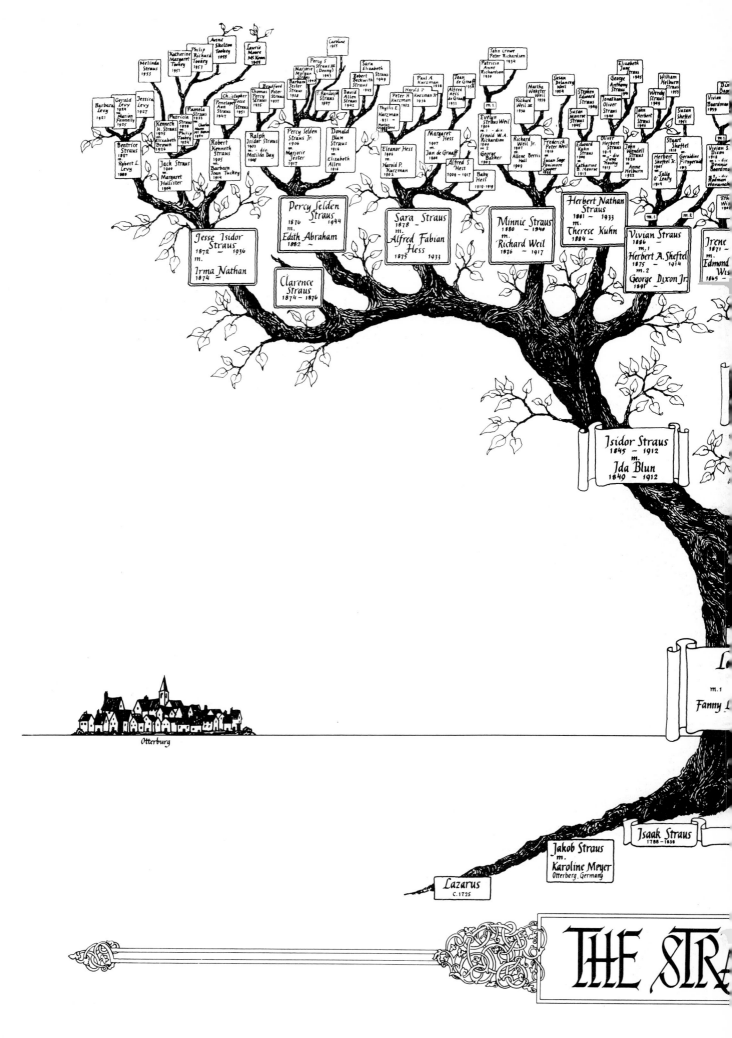

Straus Family Tree, 1955: *Credit:* John W. Straus

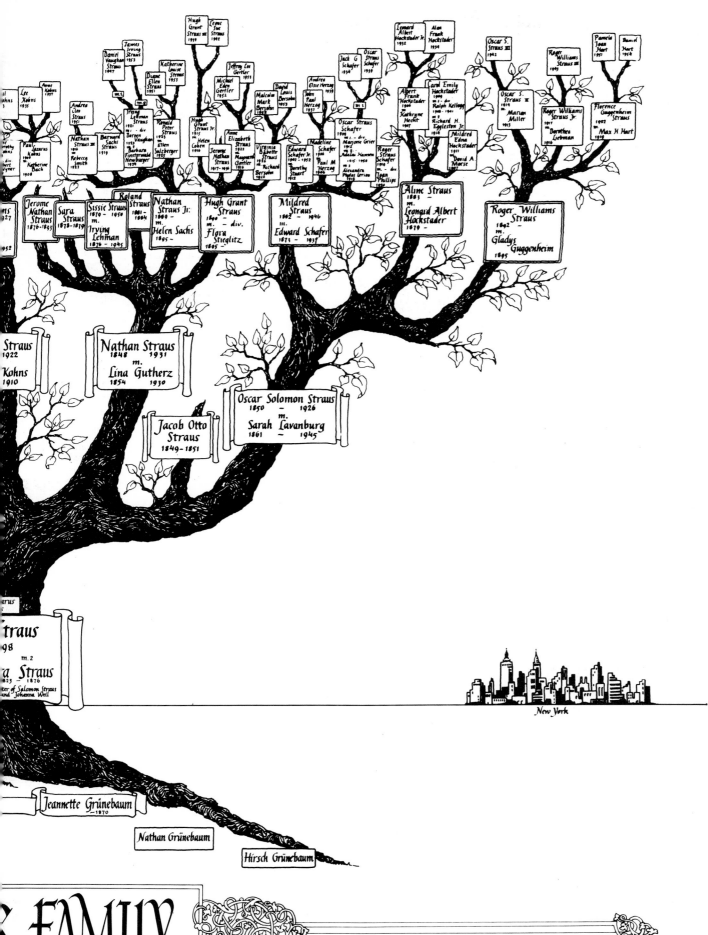

New York

FAMILY

Enid Eder Perkins 1954

Pauline and Max, Los Angeles, 1981: A retired couple living in Los Angeles. *Credit:* Photograph by Bill Aron

Retired Couple, Venice, California, 1981: This retired couple has lived together for so long that they have grown alike in more than their personalities. *Credit:* Photograph by Bill Aron

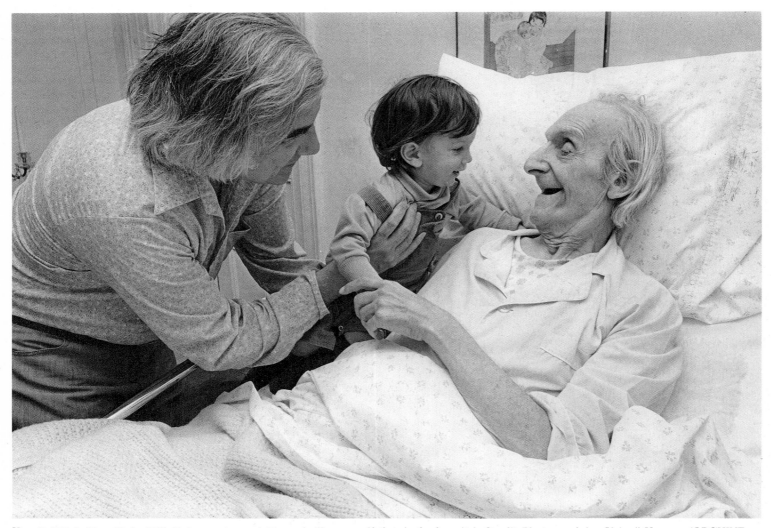

Hospital Visit, New York, 1980: Father and son visiting an ailing grandfather in the hospital. *Credit:* Photograph by Abigail Heyman/ARCHIVE

Hotel, Miami Beach, 1980: The lobby of a senior citizens residence hotel in Miami Beach, Florida. *Credit:* Photograph by Ricki Rosen

Beauty Contest, 1982: Winners of the "Yiddishe Grandma Beauty Contest" in Brooklyn. *Credit:* Photograph by Ricki Rosen

At Grossinger's, 1975: Posing for photographs
at the fabled Catskill resort hotel. *Credit:*
Photograph by Joan Liftin/ARCHIVE

Mah-jongg, 1975: At Grossinger's. *Credit:*
Photograph by Joan Liftin/ARCHIVE

Miami Beach, 1975: A couple enjoying themselves, dancing on the beach at The Fountainbleau. *Credit:* Photograph by Joan Liftin/ARCHIVE

Hillel with Grandparents, Los Angeles, 1981: *Credit:* Photograph by Bill Aron

Father and Son, Los Angeles, 1979: Bill Aron with his son, Hillel. *Credit:* Photograph by Bill Aron

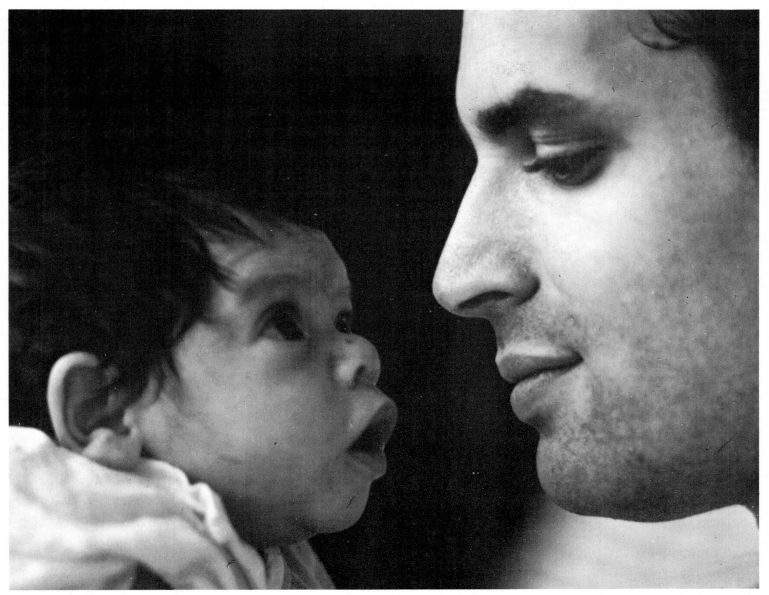

Father and Son, 1979: Lawrence Blumberg with his three-month-old son, Daniel. *Credit:* Robin and Lawrence Blumberg

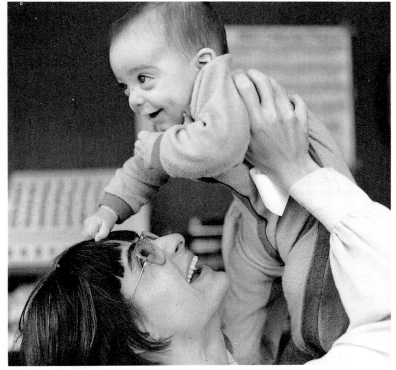

Mother and Son, Los Angeles, 1980: Isa Aron with her son, Hillel.
Credit: Photograph by Bill Aron

Under the Huppa, New York, 1980: The Jewish wedding ceremony is performed under a canopy supported by four poles, the huppa. Historically, wedding ceremonies took place out of doors. To separate the wedding from its surroundings, rabbis in the Middle Ages

sanctioned the use of the huppa, and the custom has been practiced since that time. *Credit:* Photograph by Abigail Heyman/ARCHIVE

Credits for Illustrations and Text Selections

The following abbreviations have been used:

AEMC   Albert Einstein Medical Center, Philadelphia
AJA   American Jewish Archives
AHS   Arizona Historical Society
AJHS   American Jewish Historical Society
ARCHIVE   Archive Pictures
BB   Brown Brothers
BHS   Baron de Hirsch Fund
BL   The Bancroft Library, University of California
CALHS   California Historical Society
CBSR   CBS Records
CINHS   Cincinnati Historical Society
CHS   Chicago Historical Society
CJA   Chicago Jewish Archives
CMIP   Congregation Mikveh Israel, Philadelphia
CULVER   Culver Pictures
DAM   Delaware Art Museum
FD   Frank Driggs Collection
HSP   Historical Society of Pennsylvania
ISP   International Stock Photography
JM   The Jewish Museum
LBI   Leo Baeck Institute
LC   The Library of Congress
LCP   The Library Company of Philadelphia
MAGNUM   Magnum Photos
MCNY   Museum of the City of New York
MIHS   Missouri Historical Society
MOHS   Montana Historical Society
NA   National Archives
NCJF   The National Center for Jewish Film
NSHS   Nebraska State Historical Society
NYHS   New-York Historical Society
NYPL   The New York Public Library
OHS   Ohio Historical Society
PAFA   Pennsylvania Academy of the Fine Arts
PCA   Philadelphia City Archives
RMJHS   Rocky Mountain Jewish Historical Society of the Center for Judaic Studies, University of Denver
RUAG   Rutgers University Art Gallery
SDHS   San Diego Historical Society
SHSW   State Historical Society of Wisconsin
SI   Smithsonian Institution
UATU   Urban Archives, Temple University
UIC   University of Illinois at Chicago, The Library, Manuscript Collection
UPI   United Press International
WHC   Washington Hebrew Congregation
WJHS   Western Jewish History Center of the Judah L. Magnes Museum
WW   Wide World Photos
YIVO   YIVO Institute for Jewish Research

Chapter One / A Few Among the First Settlers / 1654-1819

Peter Stuyvesant Wants Portuguese Jews to Leave New Amsterdam. Oppenheim, *American Jewish Historical Society Publications*, XVIII 1909, pp. 4-5.

A Dutch Priest Complains about the Jews. Oppenheim, *op. cit.,* p. 17.

Amsterdam Jews Petition West India Company on Behalf of the Portuguese Jews in New Netherlands. Oppenheim, *op. cit.,* pp. 9-11.

Permission Granted for Jews to Remain in New Amsterdam. Oppenheim, *op. cit.,* p. 8.

Jews Given Permission to Establish Their Own Cemetery. Oppenheim, *op. cit.,* p. 75.

Abigail Franks Laments Her Daughter's Marriage to a Gentile. Hershowitz, *American Jewish Historical Society Publications,* V, 1968, pp. 116-119.

A Peddler Wins and Loses. *Pennsylvania Gazette,* March 13, 1753. The Library of Congress, Newspaper Collection.

Michael Gratz on his Departure for America. Byars, *B. and M. Gratz Papers,* 1916, pp. 40-41.

Illinois Business "Turning Out to Great Advantage." Byars, *op. cit.,* pp. 100-101.

Mordecai Sheftall Describes his Capture by British Troops. *American Jewish Historical Society Publications,* XVII, 1909, pp. 176-178.

A Request for Gunpowder to Defend his Schooner. The Library of Congress, Division of Manuscripts, Papers of the Continental Congress, 41, VI, p. 141.

Description of a Jewish Wedding. American Jewish Archives.

I Do Not Want to Bring Up My Children as Gentiles. American Jewish Archives.

Advertising Packet Boats from Pittsburgh to Cincinnati. Byars, *op. cit.,* pp. 245-246.

The Blessings of Living in the United States. American Jewish Historical Society.

Establishing a Fund for the Sick and Poor. Congregation Shearith Israel.

Replying to Anti-Semitic Slander. The Library of Congress, Newspaper Collection.

Will Religion Affect Admission to Harvard? Edwin Wolff 2nd.

Rebecca Gratz Writes to her Brother in Kentucky. Philipson, *Letters of Rebecca Gratz,* 1929, pp. 15-17.

Chapter Two / Creating a Jewish Presence / 1820-1880

"Equality of Rights to Every Religious Sect." The Library of Congress, James Madison Papers.

Social Gaities in Philadelphia. American Jewish Historical Society, Rebecca Gratz Papers.

Encouraging German Jews to Emigrate. The Library of Congress, Newspaper Collection.

The Benefits of White Sulphur Springs. American Jewish Historical Society, Nones Papers.

Dedication of the New Synagogue for Mikveh Israel in Philadelphia. American Jewish Historical Society, Rebecca Gratz Papers.

Ararat, A City of Refuge for American Jews. American Jewish Historical Society.

Philanthropy and Jewish Communal Life. American Jewish Historical Society.

Introducing a Messenger from the Holy Land. Congregation Mikveh Israel, Philadelphia.

An Immigrant Writes to Relatives in Germany. American Jewish Historical Society.

A Letter to President Van Buren Regarding the Damascus Affair. National Archives, Martin Van Buren Papers.

Establishing a Jewish Community West of The Alleghenies. *The Occident,* February 1844, April 1844, June 1844.

Joining the "Gold Rush" to California. *Western States Jewish Historical Quarterly,* April 1969, pp. 138-141. Translated by Marlene P. Toeppen.

Exploring the West. Carvalho, *Incidents of Travel and Adventure in the Far West; With Colonel Fremont's Last Expedition Across the Rocky Mountains,* 1857, pp. 97-98.

A Call to Action Concerning the Mortara Affair. American Jewish Historical Society.

From Otterburg, Bavaria to Talbotton, Georgia. *The Autobiography of Isidor Straus,* 1955, pp. 1-10. (privately printed)

Beginning a Business Career. David Hyman, *The Romance of a Mining Venture,* 1981, pp. 1-3. (privately printed)

A Soldier's Civil War Experiences. *The Jewish Messenger,* February 7, 1862, p. 41.

Reactions to General Grant's General Orders No. 11. Markens, *American Jewish Historical Society Publications,* XVII, 1909, p. 117.

A Lavish Philadelphia Wedding. American Jewish Historical Society.

An American Judaism. *Reminiscences of I.M. Wise,* 1901, pp. 330-331.

New Jewish Settlements. *The Occident,* November 1846, p. 404.

Acknowledgements

Since the preparation of this book has taken on encyclopedic proportions, I have obtained assistance from people, organizations and institutions in all parts of the country. I hope that I have not neglected to express my appreciation to anyone. First and foremost, it would have been impossible for me to have completed this book without the American Jewish Historical Society whose archival resources have enriched every aspect of my work and whose staff has been readily available to support my research efforts. In particular I want to thank Bernard Wax, Director, and Dr. Nathan Kaganoff, Librarian, who is a walking encyclopedia of American Jewish history and whom I consider to be a virtual collaborator because of his involvement in every phase of the book's preparation. In addition to providing a stimulating introduction, Dr. Henry Feingold has given me invaluable advice on both concept and details. Conversations with Dr. Marshall Sklare provided insights into American Jewish history which have emerged in various sections of this book.

To locate all of the photographs and illustrations, required extensive research in established archival sources across the country. Diane Hamilton unearthed prize images at The Library of Congress and other Washington sources. Linda Christenson researched the Smithsonian Institution and National Archives. Shari Segel focused on New York City and other locations around the country. Allen Teller made some remarkable discoveries in Chicago. I would also like to thank all those who are unknown to me and who have assisted these individuals in their efforts to help me with the book. I myself visited many archives where members of the staff were of particular assistance: Dr. James Hart, Director, The Bancroft Library, University of California; Anita Friedman, Assistant to Curator of Collections, The Jewish Museum; Dr. J.S. Holliday, Director, California Historical Society; Ruth Rafael Kelson, Archivist, Western Jewish History Center of the Judah L. Magnes Museum; Norman Kleeblatt, Curator of Collections, The Jewish Museum; Miriam Saul Krant, Assistant Director, The National Center for Jewish Film; Dr. Sybil Milton, Archivist, Leo Baeck Institute; Abraham Peck, Associate Director, American Jewish Archives; Marek Web, Archivist, YIVO Institute for Jewish Research; Allen Weinberg, Archivist, Philadelphia City Archives; Edwin Wolff 2nd, Librarian, The Library Company of Philadelphia; and Fannie Zelcer, Archivist, American Jewish Archives.

Numerous friends, relatives and other individuals have been of great assistance in various ways including lending their family photos or procuring them from others. In Cincinnati, Daniel J. Ransohoff had already assembled a great deal of material which he was willing to share with me. Frank Driggs had his own archive of leading personalities in music, film, theater and entertainment. Among the others were: William Friedlander, Daisy Marks, Harriet Rauh, Louis Schmier, Leon Stein, Jane Steinfirst, John W. Straus and Thelma Strickler. The personnel of a number of organizations were particularly helpful including the staff and trustees of the Museum of American Jewish History and Congregation Mikveh Israel in Philadelphia. In addition, Theodore Freedman and Stan Wexler of the Anti-Defamation League of B'nai B'rith have been particularly helpful with advice and counsel as have Morton Yarmon and Sonya Kaufer of the American Jewish Committee. Lily Rivlin provided editorial assistance. The Dartmouth College Library, The Library of Congress and The New York Public Library served as centers for research. Martin Moskof was the graphic designer of this book; however, his dedicated interest in the subject provided me with many concepts which have enriched the completed book. Finally, I want to thank my wife, Mary, my daughter, Rebecca, and my son, Abraham, each of whom has helped me at various times with the endless details associated with the creation of this book.

A.S.

Bibliography

Dr. Nathan Kaganoff, 1981

General Works

Baum, Charlotte, Paula Hyman and Sonya Michel. *The Jewish Woman in America.* New York: Dial Press, 1976. 290 pp.
A study of the adaptation of the Jewish woman immigrant to American life and the role and achievements of Jewish women in American society.

Blau, Joseph L. and Salo W. Baron, eds. *The Jews of the United States 1790–1840: A Documentary History.* New York: Columbia University Press, 1964. 3 vols.
"A . . . collection of public and private documents . . . portraying the character of the Jews of early America."

Dawidowicz, Lucy S. *On Equal Terms: Jews in America, 1881–1981.* New York: Holt, Rinehart and Winston, 1982. 194 pp.
Analytic overview of the last 100 years of American Jewish history.

Feingold, Henry L. *A Midrash on American Jewish History.* Albany: State University of New York Press, 1982. 241 pp.
Thoughtful essays on various aspects of the American Jewish experience.

Feingold, Henry L. *Zion in America: The Jewish Experience from Colonial Times to the Present.* New York: Twayne, 1974. 357 pp.
Stresses the economic, social and political adjustment of the Jew to American life.

Feldstein, Stanley. *The Land that I Show You: Three Centuries of Jewish Life in America.* Garden City: Anchor Press/Doubleday, 1978. 512 pp.
A general history, based on secondary sources and not always reflecting the latest scholarly discoveries.

Glanz, Rudolf. *The Jewish Woman in America: Two Female Immigrant Generations, 1820–1929.* New York: Ktav, 1976. 2 vols.
A study of the role played by the East European and German immigrant Jewish woman in the economic, social and cultural adjustment of the immigrant to life in the New World.

Goren, Arthur A. *The American Jews.* Cambridge: The Belknap Press, 1982. 116 pp.
A comprehensive survey of the history of the Jewish community.

Janowsky, Oscar I., ed. *The American Jew: A Reappraisal.* Philadelphia: Jewish Publication Society, 1964. 468 pp.
A collection of essays dealing with the economic, philanthropic, cultural, organizational and religious aspects of Jewish life in America.

Karp, Abraham J., ed. *The Jewish Experience in America: Selected Studies.* Waltham: American Jewish Historical Society, 1970. 5 vols.
A collection of articles providing a detailed background and excellent overview of American Jewish history.

Korn, Bertram W. *American Jewry and the Civil War.* New York: Atheneum, 1970. 331 pp.
An excellent study of the Jews in the United States from 1861 to 1865.

Learsi, Rufus. *The Jews in America: A History. Epilogue: American Jewry 1954–1971,* by Abraham J. Karp. New York: Ktav, 1972. 422 pp.
An updating of the standard work on American Jewish history.

Lebeson, Anita Libman. *Jewish Pioneers in America, 1492–1848.* New York: Behrman, 1931. 372 pp. illus.
A very fine history of the Jews in America in the period before the Civil War.

Lebeson, Anita Libman. *Recall to Life: The Jewish Woman in America.* South Brunswick: Yoseloff, 1970. 351 pp.
A history of the contributions of women to American Jewish life.

Marcus, Jacob R. *The American Jewish Woman, 1654–1980.* New York: Ktav, 1981. 231 pp. illus.
A history of the activities of the American Jewish woman.

Marcus, Jacob R. *The American Jewish Woman: A Documentary History.* New York: Ktav, 1981. 1047 pp. illus.
A collection of documents depicting the various activities of American Jewish women, published to accompany the author's history of the same subject noted above.

Marcus, Jacob Rader. *The Colonial American Jew 1492–1776.* Detroit: Wayne State. 1970. 3 vols.
A definitive study of the Jewish role in Colonial America.

Marcus, Jacob R., ed. *Critical Studies in American Jewish History: Selected Articles from American Jewish Archives.* Cincinnati: American Jewish Archives; New York: Ktav, 1971. 3 vols. illus.
A collection of articles providing a broad view of American Jewish history.

Postal, Bernard and Lionel Koppman. *American Jewish Landmarks: A Travel Guide and History.* New York: Fleet Press, 1977–1979. 3 vols.
A revised and greatly expanded edition of an earlier work published in 1954 under the title *A Jewish Tourist's Guide to the U.S.,* containing much valuable data on the Jews in the United States.

Postal, Bernard and Lionel Koppman. *Guess Who's Jewish in American History.* New York: New American Library, 1978. 322 pp.
Brief popular biographies of American Jews, some famous and some not well-known, grouped by categories.

Rosen, Gladys, ed. *Jewish Life in America: Historical Perspectives.* New York: Institute of Human Relations Press, 1978. 198 pp.
A collection of essays dealing with various aspects of American Jewish life which were originally presented as a group of lectures sponsored by the American Jewish Committee to commemorate the Bicentennial.

Schappes, Morris U. *A Documentary History of the Jews in the United States 1654–1875.* 3rd ed. New York: Schocken, 1971. 766 pp.
The latest edition of a standard work indispensable for students in the field.

Schappes, Morris U. *A Pictorial History of the Jews in the United States.* New rev. ed. New York: Marzani & Munsell, 1965. 339 pp. illus.
A very useful book, originally published in 1958, which includes new material bringing the narrative up to date.

Siegel, Richard and Carl Rheins, eds. *The Jewish Almanac.* New York: Bantam, 1980. 620 pp. illus. Includes much unusual and generally unknown information about American Jews and American Jewish life.

Stern, Malcolm H. *First American Jewish Families: 600 Genealogies 1654–1977.* Cincinnati: American Jewish Archives, 1978. 419 pp.
A revised and expanded version of the classic work containing the genealogies of American Jews who arrived in the United States before 1840.

Wiernik, Peter. *History of the Jews in America: From the Period of the Discovery of the New World to the Present Time.* 3rd ed. New York: Hermon Press, 1972. 481 pp.
A standard popular study of American Jewish history, originally published in 1931, to which has been added a survey of Jewish life in America from 1932 to 1972.

Regional Studies

Adler, Frank J. *Roots in a Moving Stream: The Centennial History of Congregation B'nai Jehudah of Kansas City, 1870–1970.* Kansas City, Mo.: The Temple, Congregation B'nai Jehudah, 1972. 466 pp. illus.
A very comprehensive and exquisite synagogue history; includes information on the early Jewish community of Kansas City and the role of Eddie Jacobson, a member of the congregation, in the establishment of the State of Israel.

Adler, Selig and Thomas E. Connolly. *From Ararat to Suburbia: The History of the Buffalo Jewish Community.* Philadelphia: Jewish Publication Society of America, 1960. 498 pp.
One of the better written Jewish community studies.

American Jewish Historical Society. *On Common Ground: The Boston Jewish Experience 1649–1980.* Waltham: 1981. 1 vol. illus.
A lavish catalog accompanying the exhibit on Boston Jewry mounted by the Society.

The Architectural League of New York. *Resorts of the Catskills.* New York: St. Martin's Press, 1979. 113 pp. illus.
A very exquisite volume; contains some data on the Jewish hotels and also the Jewish element in the development of the region as a resort area.

Blumin, Stuart M. *The Short Season of Sharon Springs: Portrait of Another New York.* Ithaca: Cornell University Press, 1980. 128 pp. illus.
A photographic study of a village in upstate New York, which serves as a summer resort for Hasidic Jews.

Brandes, Joseph. *Immigrants to Freedom: Jewish Communities in Rural New Jersey since 1882.* Philadelphia: University of Pennsylvania Press, 1971. 424 pp. illus.
A well written and detailed study of the efforts of Eastern European Jewish immigrants to become American farmers.

Brener, David. *The Jews of Lancaster, Pennsylvania: A Story With Two Beginnings.* Lancaster: Congregation Shaarai Shomayim, 1979. 188 pp. illus.
A revised and enlarged version of two studies originally published in 1976: a history of the Jewish community that appeared in the *Journal of the Lancaster County Historical Society* and a history of Congregation Shaarai Shomayim, published by the synagogue.

Elovitz, Mark H. *A Century of Jewish Life in Dixie: The Birmingham Experience (1871–1971).* University, Ala.: University of Alabama Press, 1974. 258 pp.

Elzas, Barnett A. *The Jews of South Carolina: From the Earliest Times to the Present Day.* Spartanburg, N.C.: Reprint Co., 1972. 352 pp. illus.
A reprint of the 1905 edition; an excellent community history covering the period from Colonial times to 1905.

Evans, Eli N. *The Provincials: A Personal History of Jews in the South.* New York: Atheneum, 1973. 369 pp.
Traces the history of Jewish settlement in the South from the eighteenth century to the present.

Golden, Harry. *The Greatest Jewish City in the World.* Garden City, New York: Doubleday, 1972. 236 pp. illus.
Through photograph and text, the "Jewishness" of New York City is expounded.

Gordon, Sarah, ed. *All Our Lives: A Centennial History of Michael Reese Hospital and Medical Center.* Chicago: Michael Reese Hospital and Medical Center, 1981. 210 pp. illus.
A lavishly illustrated history of the hospital, tracing its change from a hospital established for an immigrant community into a major world medical center.

Goren, Arthur A. *New York Jews and the Quest for Community: The Kehillah Experiment, 1908–1922.* New York: Columbia University Press, 1970. 361 pp.
An excellent study on the efforts made by New York City Jewry to create a comprehensive communal structure that would unite the entire Jewish population.

Grinstein, Hyman B. *The Rise of the Jewish Community of New York, 1654–1860.* Philadelphia: The Jewish Publication Society of America, 1945. 645 pp. illus.
A classic, comprehensive study of the early history of the largest Jewish community in the world.

Hapgood, Hutchins. *The Spirit of the Ghetto.* Edited by Moses Rischin. Cambridge, Mass.: Harvard University Press, 1967. 315. pp. illus.
A facsimile reproduction of the classic study of the Lower East Side in New York City, first published in 1902, with a new introduction and notes.

Hertzberg, Steven. *Strangers Within the Gate City: The Jews of Atlanta 1845–1915.* Philadelphia: Jewish Publication Society, 1978. 325 pp.
A comprehensive history, utilizing quantification methodology in addition to traditional documentary sources.

Howe, Irving. *World of our Fathers.* New York: Harcourt Brace Jovanovich, 1976. 714 pp.
A very comprehensive and detailed study of immigrant Jewish life in New York City.

Kaganoff, Nathan M. and Melvin I. Urofsky, eds. *Turn to the South: Essays on Southern Jewry.* Charlottesville: University Press of Virginia, 1979. 205 pp.
A collection of fourteen articles originally presented at a conference on Southern Jewish history held in Richmond, Va., in October, 1976.

Kessner, Thomas. *The Golden Door: Italian and Jewish Immigrant Mobility in New York City 1880–1915.* New York: Oxford University Press, 1977. 224 pp.
A comparative analysis of the two largest immigrant groups in New York City.

Kranzler, George. *Williamsburg—U.S.A.: The Face of Faith; An American Hassidic Community.* Photographs by Irving I. Herzberg. Baltimore: Baltimore Hebrew College Press, 1972. 117 pp. illus.
Photographic essay of the Hasidic community in the Williamsburg section of Brooklyn, N.Y.

Landesman, Alter F. *Brownsville: The Birth, Development and Passing of a Jewish Community in New York.* New York: Bloch, 1969. 418 pp.
A well written and carefully researched study of a community in Brooklyn which contained the largest concentration of Jews in New York City; the author served as the director of the local Hebrew Educational Society for over forty years.

Moore, Deborah Dash. *At Home in America: Second Generation New York Jews.* New York: Columbia University Press, 1981. 303 pp. illus.
A detailed study of the second generation of New York City Jewry's pattern of geographic mobility, education, religious and communal life, and political involvement.

Narell, Irena. *Our City: The Jews of San Francisco.* San Diego, Calif.: Howell-North Books, 1981. 424 pp. illus.
The story of prominent San Francisco Jewish families from the founding of the Jewish community until the present time.

National Council of Jewish Women. Pittsburgh Section. *My Voice Was Heard.* Edited by Ida Cohen Selavan. New York: Ktav, 1981. 278 pp. illus.
A collective oral history of the Jewish immigrant community in Pittsburgh; a continuation of an earlier volume published in 1972 under the title: *By Myself I'm a Book.*

New York. Central Synagogue. *140 Years. A Proud Tradition . . . A Vital Future.* New York: 1979? 31 pp. illus.
A beautifully produced history of the synagogue, whose building has been declared an Historic Landmark.

Pine, Alan S., Jean C. Hershenov and Aaron H. Lefkowitz. *Peddler to Suburbanite: The History of the Jews of Monmouth County, New Jersey from the Colonial Period to 1980.* Deal Park, N.J.: Monmouth Jewish Community Council, 1981. 233 pp. illus.
A well-done local history.

Raphael, Marc Lee. *Jews and Judaism in a Mid-western Community: Columbus, Ohio, 1840–1975.* Columbus: Ohio Historical Society, 1979. 483 pp. illus.
A comprehensive history, utilizing quantification methodology in addition to traditional documentary sources.

Rischin, Moses. *The Promised City: New York's Jews 1870–1914.* New York: Harper & Row, 1970. 342 pp. illus.
A comprehensive study of a significant period in the history of the New York Jewish community; an analysis of the economic adjustment of the new arrivals, their living conditions, relationship to the established community, and their cultural, social and political achievements in the New World.

Rosenbaum, Fred. *Architects of Reform: Congregational and Community Leadership Emanu-El of San Francisco, 1849–1980.* Berkeley: Western Jewish History Center, Judah L. Magnes Memorial Museum, 1980. 241 pp. illus.
A comprehensive history of a leading Jewish congregation in the West.

Rubin, Israel. *Satmar: An Island in the City.* New York: Quadrangle Books, 1972. 272 pp.
A sociological study of the community and culture of the Satmarer Hasidim of the Williamsburg section of Brooklyn, N.Y.

Rudolph, B. G. *From a Minyan to a Community: A History of the Jews of Syracuse.* Syracuse: Syracuse University, 1970. 314 pp. illus.
A fine community study by a non-professional historian.

Schoener, Allon, ed. *Portal to America: The Lower East Side 1870–1925.* New York: Holt, Rinehart and Winston, 1967. 256 pp. illus.
Primarily a collection of newspaper articles and photographs depicting in a very exquisite manner contemporary life on the East Side.

Schultz, Joseph P., ed. *Mid-America's Promise: A Profile of Kansas City Jewry.* Kansas City; The Jewish Community Foundation of Greater Kansas City, 1982. 405 pp. illus.
A collection of essays dealing with the various aspects of the history of the Kansas City Jewish community.

Stern, Zelda. *The Complete Guide to Ethnic New York.* New York: St. Martin's Press, 1980. 312 pp. illus.
Includes a section on "Jewish New York," containing a guide to historic synagogues and landmarks, Jewish restaurants, etc., primarily on the Lower East Side, but with some data on Jewish items of interest elsewhere in the city.

Toll, William. *The Making of an Ethnic Middle Class: Portland Jewry Over Four Generations.* Albany: State University of New York Press, 1982. 242 pp. illus.
A social history of the Portland, Oregon Jewish community.

Vincent, Sidney Z. and Judah Rubinstein. *Merging Traditions—Jewish Life in Cleveland: A Contemporary Narrative 1945–1975; A Pictorial Record 1839–1975.* Cleveland: The Western Reserve Historical Society, 1978. 283 pp. illus.
Primarily a photographic history of the Jewish community, with a brief survey of contemporary Jewish life.

Weinberger, Moses. *People Walk on Their Heads: Jews and Judaism in New York.* Translated from Hebrew and edited by Jonathan D. Sarna. New York: Holmes and Meier, 1982. 137 pp.
Translation of a classic work on Orthodox Jewish life in New York in the 1880's, written by a contemporary but almost completely neglected by historians.

Wolf, Edwin, 2nd and Maxwell Whiteman. *The History of the Jews of Philadelphia: From Colonial Times to the Age of Jackson.* Philadelphia: The Jewish Publication Society of America, 1957. 534 pp. illus.
A very fine study of the Philadelphia Jewish community through the third decade of the 19th century.

Sociological Studies

Bernard, Jacqueline. *The Children You Gave Us: A History of 150 Years of Service to Children.* New York: Jewish Child Care Association of New York, 1973. 186 pp. illus.
A history of the Jewish Child Care Association of New York.

Blaine, Allan, ed. *Alcoholism and the Jewish Community.* New York: Commission on Synagogue Relations, Federation of Jewish Philanthropies of New York, 1980. 365 pp.
A collection of articles, many of which deal with various aspects of alcoholism in the American Jewish community; although statistically much lower among Jews than in the general population, the authors contend that it is a growing problem facing the Jewish community.

Borowitz, Eugene B. *The Mask Jews Wear: The Self-Deceptions of American Jewry.* New York: Simon and Schuster, 1973. 222 pp.
The author describes the American Jews as the "modern Marrano" who has repressed his Jewish identity.

Cohen, Percy S. *Jewish Radicals and Radical Jews.* London: Academic Press, 1980. 224 pp.
A detailed study attempting to explain why Jews are more predisposed to radicalism than non-Jews and how Jewish radicals combine their radicalism and Jewishness; a major portion of the study is devoted to the phenomenon in the United States.

Cowan, Paul. *The Tribes of America.* Garden City, N.Y.: Doubleday, 1979. 311 pp.
A collection of articles that originally appeared in *The Village Voice;* includes articles on Black-Jewish relations in New York City, and Jewish poverty and Orthodoxy on the Lower East Side.

Epstein, Melech. *Jewish Labor in U.S.A.: An Industrial, Political and Cultural History of the Jewish Labor Movement.* New York: Ktav, 1969. 465 + 466 pp.
A reprint of the two-volume 1950–53 edition, which consisted of a study of the Jewish labor movement in America and the impact of Jewish unions on the cultural life of the American Jewish workingman, with a new preface by the author.

Freid, Jacob, ed. *Judaism and the Community: New Dimensions in Jewish Social Work.* South Brunswick: Yoseloff, 1968. 248 pp.
A collection of articles dealing with problems confronting the contemporary American Jew: relations with the community, social welfare, intermarriage, philanthropy and mental health.

Garvin, Philip. *A People Apart: Hasidism in America.* Photographs by Philip Garvin. Text by Arthur A. Cohen. New York: E. P. Dutton, 1970. 192 pp. (chiefly illus.)
An unusual photographic study of Hasidic life in America.

Gillman, Joseph M. *The B'nai Khaim in America: A Study of Cultural Change in a Jewish Group.* Philadelphia: Dorrance, 1969. 168 pp. illus.
A detailed study of the acculturation and adjustment of American descendants of Khaim Kaprov, candle-maker in the Ukraine, their educational and economic achievements, and their attitudes toward matters Jewish and general.

Glanz, Rudolf. *Studies in Judaica Americana.* New York: Ktav, 1970. 407 pp.
Collection of previously published essays, dealing primarily with the German Jew in America.

Goldstein, Israel. *Jewish Justice and Conciliation: History of the Jewish Conciliation Board of America, 1930–1968 and a Review of Jewish Juridical Autonomy.* New York: Ktav, 1981. 252 pp. illus.
A history of the Conciliation Board with examples of the cases it handles in its service to the immigrant Jewish community as a court of arbitration in civil issues.

Goldstein, Sidney and Calvin Goldscheider. *Jewish Americans: Three Generations in a Jewish Community.* Englewood Cliffs: Prentice-Hall, 1968. 274 pp. illus.
A detailed sociological study of the Jewish community of Providence, Rhode Island.

Goodman, Cary. *Choosing Sides: Playground and Street Life on the Lower East Side.* New York: Schocken, 1979. 200 pp.
The author suggests that the development of the organized play movement was a conscientious effort by reformers to acculturate the immigrant to the values of an industrial society and reduce the influence of radical ideas.

Gordon, Albert I. *Jews in Suburbia.* Westport, Conn.: Greenwood, 1973. 264 pp.
A reprint of the 1959 edition; a detailed study of the problems encountered by the Jewish community in the shift from the city to the suburbs.

Harris, Leon. *Merchant Princes: An Intimate History of Jewish Families who Built Great Department Stores.* New York: Harper & Row, 1979. 411 pp.
A collection of family histories.

Kramer, Judith R. and Seymour Leventman. *Children of the Gilded Ghetto: Conflict Resolutions of Three Generations of American Jews.* Hamden, Conn.: Shoe String Press, 1969. 228 pp.
The differing adjustment of second and third generation American Jews in a typical Midwestern city.

Krefetz, Gerald. *Jews and Money: The Myths and the Reality.* New Haven: Ticknor & Fields, 1982. 267 pp.
An attempt to document the popular American myths about Jewish wealth.

Lavender, Abraham D., ed. *A Coat of Many Colors: Jewish Subcommunities in the United States.* Westport: Greenwood Press, 1977. 324 pp.
A collection of articles dealing with Jews in small towns and in the South, the Jewish poor, Hasidic Jews, Black Jews, Jewish women and Sephardic Jews.

Leichter, Hope Jensen and William E. Mitchell. *Kinship and Casework: Family Networks and Social Intervention.* Enlarged ed. New York: Teachers College Press, 1978. 355 pp.
A revised edition of a study of the family relationships of Jewish families, primarily of European origin, conducted among the clients of the Jewish Family Service of New York City.

Liebman, Arthur. *Jews and the Left.* New York: John Wiley, 1979. 676 pp.
In a most comprehensive manner the author traces and attempts to explain how American Jewish affinity for the Left has undergone a major change from the beginning of the century until the present.

Liebman, Charles S. *The Ambivalent American Jew: Politics, Religion and Family in American Jewish Life.* Philadelphia: The Jewish Publication Society of America, 1973. 215 pp.
The author concludes that to ensure Jewish survival in the United States today requires a rejection of the values of integration.

Manners, Ande. *Poor Cousins.* New York: Coward, McCann & Geoghegan, 1972. 318 pp. illus.
A popularly written and amusing account of the conflict between the German and Russian Jew in America.

Metzker, Isaac, ed. *A Bintel Brief: Sixty Years of Letters from the Lower East Side to the Jewish Daily Forward.* Garden City, N.Y.: Doubleday, 1971. 214 pp. illus.
An annotated selection of documents from the famous newspaper column which vividly portray the Eastern European Jewish immigrant experience in America.

Metzker, Isaac, ed. *A Bintel Brief. Vol. 2: Letters to the "Jewish Daily Forward" 1950–1980.* New York: The Viking Press, 1981. 167 pp.
The current volume reflects the different problems facing the members of the contemporary American Jewish community.

Moore, Deborah Dash. *B'nai B'rith and the Challenge of Ethnic Leadership.* Albany: State University of New York Press, 1981. 288 pp. illus.
A study of the factors that have changed the B'nai B'rith from a fraternal order, to one sponsoring various philanthropic programs, to a multi-purpose organization, which includes activities aimed at both Jewish survival and Jewish service.

Rabinowitz, Dorothy and Yedida Nielson. *Home Life: A Story of Old Age.* New York: Macmillan, 1971. 192 pp.
An exploration of the lives of the people in Jewish homes for the aged.

Rosenthal, Gilbert S., ed. *The Jewish Family in a Changing World*. South Brunswick: Thomas Yoseloff, 1970. 367 pp.
Papers from a conference sponsored by the Commission on Synagogue Relations of the Federation of Jewish Philanthropies of New York dealing with the problems facing the Jewish community, including adoption, leisure time, drug addiction, education, the student, intermarriage, philanthropy and the aged.

Rothchild, Sylvia, ed. *Voices from the Holocaust*. New York: New American Library, 1981. 456 pp.
Memoirs of 250 American Jews describing their lives in Europe before and during the Holocaust and their subsequent arrival in America.

Shapiro, Yonathan. *Leadership of the American Zionist Organization, 1897–1930*. Urbana: University of Illinois Press, 1971. 295 pp.
A study of the changing ideological and organizational structure of the American Zionist movement.

Sherman, C. Bezalel. *The Jews within American Society: A Study in Ethnic Individuality*. Detroit: Wayne State University Press, 1965. 260 pp.
A thoughtful and provocative study of the American Jew and the American Jewish community.

Sidorsky, David, ed. *The Future of the Jewish Community in America*. New York: Basic Books, 1973. 324 pp.
A collection of essays dealing with the many facets of the American Jewish community, prepared for the Task Force on The Future of the Jewish Community in America of the American Jewish Committee.

Sklare, Marshall. *America's Jews*. New York: Random House, 1971. 234 pp.
A sociological study analyzing the demography, family and community structure, and education of the American Jew and his relation to non-Jews and to Israel.

Sklare, Marshall, *Conservative Judaism: An American Religious Movement*. New York: Schocken Books, 1972. 330 pp.
An updating of the classic sociological study.

Sklare, Marshall, ed. *The Jew in American Society*. New York: Behrman House, 1974. 404 pp.
A collection of material intended to serve as a source book for the study of the sociology of the American Jew.

Sklare, Marshall, and Joseph Greenblum. *Jewish Identity on the Suburban Frontier: A Study of Group Survival in the Open Society*. 2nd ed. Chicago: University of Chicago Press, 1979. 437 pp.
An updating of a classic study, originally published in 1967, analyzing the internal life of the Jewish suburban community.

Sklare, Marshall, ed. *Understanding American Jewry*. New Brunswick: Transaction Books, 1982. 310 pp.
Papers delivered at a Planning Conference for a Center for Modern Jewish Studies, held at Brandeis University on Oct. 21–24, 1979. The article assesses what we already know and what we still need to know about contemporary American Jewry.

Yivo Institute for Jewish Research. *The Early Jewish Labor Movement in the United States*. Translated and revised by Aaron Antonovsky from the original Yiddish edited by Elias Tcherikower. New York: 1961. 379 pp.
A condensation of the original two-volume work with the addition of new material; a major portion of the study is devoted to the European background of the Jewish immigrant and the American setting to which he came.

Relations With the Overall Community

Barron, Milton L., ed. *The Blending American: Patterns of Intermarriage*. Chicago: Quadrangle Books, 1972. 357 pp.
An anthology of articles on intermarriage including several studies of Jewish intermarriage.

Brotz, Howard. *The Black Jews of Harlem: Negro Nationalism and the Dilemmas of Negro Leadership*. New York: Schocken, 1970. 144 pp.
A description of the life of the Black Jews and their relation to other Jews and Negroes.

Cahnman, Werner J., ed. *Intermarriage and Jewish Life: A Symposium*. New York: Herzl Press, 1963. 212 pp.
Deals with various aspects of the problems of intermarriage with special emphasis on conditions in the United States.

Diner, Hasia. *In the Almost Promised Land: American Jews and Blacks, 1915–1935*. Westport: Greenwood Press, 1977. 271 pp.
A detailed study of how the American Jewish community attempted to utilize the problems faced by Blacks in American society as a means of solving the tensions of American Jewish life.

Dinnerstein, Leonard. *The Leo Frank Case*. New York: Columbia University Press, 1968. 248 pp.
A basic study of the famous incident which provides an analysis of the factors affecting the Southern reaction to the event and the impact of the case on American Jewry.

Dobkowski, Michael N. *The Tarnished Dream: The Basis of American Anti-Semitism.* Westport, Conn.: Greenwood Press, 1979. 291 pp.
The author contends that the negative image of the Jew portrayed in 19th-century American literature was a major factor in the widespread appearance of American antisemitism toward the end of the century.

Forster, Arnold and Benjamin R. Epstein. *The New Anti-Semitism*. New York: McGraw-Hill, 1974. 354 pp.
A useful summary of the contemporary manifestations of an old Jewish problem.

Friedman, Lester D. *Hollywood's Image of the Jew*. New York: Frederick Ungar, 1982. 390 pp. illus.
A survey of how the Jew has been portrayed in film in the last six decades.

Glazer, Nathan and Daniel Patrick Moynihan. *Beyond the Melting Pot: The Negroes, Puerto Ricans, Jews, Italians, and Irish of New York City*. Cambridge, Mass.: M.I.T. Press, 1970. 360 pp.
Includes an analysis of the economic, cultural, communal and political life of the Jewish community in New York and its relationship to other minority groups in the city.

Glock, Charles Y., Gertrude J. Selznick and Joe L. Spaeth. *The Apathetic Majority: A Study Based on Public Response to the Eichmann Trial*. New York: Harper & Row, 1966. 222 pp.
An analysis of a survey conducted in Oakland, Calif. of the public reaction to various aspects of the Eichmann trial and its relation to the overall problem of antisemitism.

Glock, Charles Y. and Rodney Stark. *Christian Beliefs and Anti-Semitism*. New York: Harper & Row, 1966. 266 pp.
The first report of a detailed study on antisemitism by the Survey Research Center of the University of California which revealed that the teachings of the Church is one of the important factors in American antisemitism.

Goodman, Abram Vossen. *American Overture: Jewish Rights in Colonial Times*. Philadelphia: The Jewish Publication Society of America, 1947. 265 pp. illus.
An interesting and very useful account of Jewish rights during our country's early history.

Harap, Louis. *The Image of the Jew in American Literature: From Early Republic to Mass Immigration*. Philadelphia: Jewish Publication Society, 1974. 586 pp.
A comprehensive survey of how the Jew has been portrayed in American literature, both non-Jewish and Jewish.

Harris, Louis and Bert E. Swanson. *Black-Jewish Relations in New York City*. New York: Praeger, 1970. 234 pp.
A very detailed survey of the attitudes of Blacks, Jews, and non-Jewish whites in New York City toward Black-Jewish relations.

Isaacs, Stephen D. *Jews and American Politics*. Garden City: Doubleday, 1974. 302 pp.
A detailed study of the role played by Jews in American politics.

Kanter, Kenneth Aaron. *The Jews on Tin Pan Alley: The Jewish Contribution to American Popular Music, 1830–1940*. New York: Ktav, 1982. 226 pp. illus.
A popular survey.

Kayserling, M. *Christopher Columbus and the Participation of the Jews in the Spanish and Portuguese Discoveries*. 4th ed. New York: Hermon Press, 1968. 189 pp.
A reprint of the London, 1907 edition of a pioneering fully documented study.

Lee, Albert. *Henry Ford and the Jews*. New York: Stein and Day, 1980. 200 pp.
A popular account of a famous American antisemitic campaign.

Lieberson, Stanley. *A Piece of the Pie: Blacks and White Immigrants Since 1880*. Berkeley: University of California Press, 1980. 419 pp.
An attempt to explain why the immigrant groups who arrived in the United States after 1880 have fared better than Blacks; a large amount of the data relates to Jews.

Mayer, John E. *Jewish-Gentile Courtships: An Exploratory Study of a Social Process*. New York: Free Press of Glencoe, 1961. 240 pp.
A study of 25 couples, one or both of whose partners had initially been opposed to intermarriage and the factors that occasioned their change of attitude.

Perlmutter, Nathan and Ruth Ann Perlmutter. *The Real Anti-Semitism in America*. New York: Arbor House, 1982. 303 pp.
The authors maintain that Jews are no longer threatened so much by crude antisemitism as by antisemitic government policies, often promulgated by individuals who are in no way tainted by this evil.

Quinley, Harold E. and Charles Y. Glock. *Anti-Semitism in America*. New York: The Free Press, 1979. 237 pp.
The final "wrap-up" volume, the eighth in a series, providing general observations about antisemitism in America; the studies were based on fifteen years of research conducted by the University of California and funded by the Anti-Defamation League.

Rezneck, Samuel. *Unrecognized Patriots: The Jews in the American Revolution*. Westport: Greenwood Press, 1975. 299 pp.
The most comprehensive study that has appeared to date on the role the Jews played in the Revolution.

Rothman, Stanley and S. Robert Lichter. *Roots of Radicalism: Jews, Christians, and the New Left*. New York: Oxford University Press, 1982. 466 pp.
An attempt to explain the large number of Jews found in the radical student movement of the 1960's and how they differed from non-Jews.

Selzer, Michael, ed. *"Kike!": A Documentary History of Anti-Semitism in America*. New York: World, 1972. 231 pp. illus.
Documents of antisemitism in America from 1654 to the present.

Selznick, Gertrude J. and Stephen Steinberg. *The Tenacity of Prejudice: Anti-Semitism in Contemporary America*. New York: Harper & Row, 1969. 248 pp.
A study conducted by the Survey Research Center of the University of California which indicated that antisemitism continues at a significant level in America and that lack of education is a primary factor in its manifestation.

Snetsinger, John. *Truman, the Jewish Vote, and the Creation of Israel*. Stanford: Hoover Institution Press, Stanford University, 1974. 208 pp.
The author contends that President Truman supported the idea of a Jewish state only when faced with the impending Presidential election of 1948.

Stack, John F., Jr. *International Conflict in An American City: Boston's Irish, Italians, and Jews, 1935–1944*. Westport, Conn.: Greenwood Press, 1979. 181 pp.
A study of the impact of international affairs on the relations of three major ethnic groups in Boston.

Synnott, Marcia Graham. *The Half-Opened Door: Discrimination and Admissions at Harvard, Yale, and Princeton, 1900–1970*. Westport, Conn.: Greenwood Press, 1979. 310 pp.
A very detailed study of how the three most prestigious private universities reacted to the "Jewish invasion" of the children of the East European immigrants.

Volkman, Ernest. *A Legacy of Hate: Anti-Semitism in America*. New York: Franklin Watts, 1982. 358 pp.
A history of antisemitism in America; the major portion of the book is devoted to the contemporary period.

Weisbord, Robert G. and Arthur Stein. *Bittersweet Encounter: The Afro-American and the American Jew*. New York: Schocken, 1972. 242 pp.
A brief historic survey with emphasis on current problems.

Relations Overseas

Avruch, Kevin. *American Immigrants in Israel: Social Identities and Change.* Chicago: University of Chicago Press, 1981. 243 pp.
A detailed anthropological study of why American Jews emigrate to Israel.

Bauer, Yehuda. *American Jewry and the Holocaust: The American Jewish Joint Distribution Committee, 1939–1945.* Detroit: Wayne State University Press, 1981. 522 pp.
A history of the Joint during World War II.

Dinnerstein, Leonard. *America and the Survivors of the Holocaust.* New York: Columbia University Press, 1982. 409 pp. illus.
Despite constant pressure by the American Jewry, it took five years before Congress enacted a bill that enabled the DP's to settle in America.

Feingold, Henry L. *The Politics of Rescue: The Roosevelt Administration and the Holocaust, 1938–1945.* New York: Holocaust Library, 1980. 416 pp.
A classic study on America and the Holocaust, including information on the efforts made by the American Jewish community to save European Jewry; a new edition with new material.

Feinstein, Marnin. *American Zionism 1884–1904.* New York: Herzl Press, 1965. 320 pp.
Primarily based on contemporary newspaper and periodical literature.

Friedman, Saul S. *Amcha: An Oral Testament of the Holocaust.* Washington, D.C.: University Press of America, 1980. 434 pp. illus.
Experiences during the Holocaust recounted by 30 Jews who arrived in America immediately After World War II and who settled in Youngstown, Ohio.

Friedman, Saul S. *No Haven for the Oppressed: United States Policy Toward Jewish Refugees, 1938–1945.* Detroit: Wayne State University Press, 1973. 315 pp.
An attempt to explain America's failure to admit large numbers of Jewish refugees during World War II.

Ganin, Zvi. *Truman, American Jewry and Israel 1945–1948.* New York: Holmes & Meier, 1979. 238 pp.
A meticulous study of the role of American Zionists and Truman in the establishment of Israel.

Glick, Edward Bernard. *The Triangular Connection: America, Israel, and American Jews.* London: George Allen & Unwin, 1982. 174 pp.
A series of short, well-written, intelligent essays concerning, for the most part, American Jews and Israel.

Greenstein, Howard R. *Turning Point: Zionism and Reform Judaism.* Chico, Calif.: Scholars Press, 1981. 186 pp.
A study of the factors that brought about a change in the attitude of Reform Judaism toward Zionism, the issue that most divided the movement in American history.

Halperin, Samuel. *The Political World of American Zionism.* Detroit: Wayne State University Press, 1961. 431 pp.
A sober well-informed and interestingly written study.

Heckelman, A. Joseph. *American Volunteers and Israel's War of Independence.* New York: Ktav, 1974. 304 pp.
An interesting and realistic evaluation of the American military role in the establishment of Israel.

Herman, Simon N. *American Students in Israel.* Ithaca: Cornell University Press, 1970. 236 pp.
A detailed study of American Jewish students in Israel, their reasons for going, the changes in their attitudes and the Israeli reaction to them.

Knee, Stuart E. *The Concept of Zionist Dissent in the American Mind 1917–1941.* New York: Robert Speller, 1979. 268 pp.
An analysis of opposition to Zionism, both Jewish and non-Jewish, in American history.

Safran, Nadav. *The United States and Israel.* Cambridge, Mass.: Harvard University Press, 1963. 341 pp.
Primarily a study of the origins and developments of the State of Israel; includes an analysis of the relationship of American Jewry and its impact on United States foreign policy towards Israel.

Schechtman, Joseph B. *The United States and the Jewish State Movement: The Crucial Decade 1939–1949.* New York: Herzl Press, 1966. 474 pp. illus.
Includes material on the role of American Jews and the Zionist movement in shaping American policy.

Slater, Leonard. *The Pledge.* New York: Simon and Schuster, 1970. 350 pp.
The story of American Jewish underground activity in providing the military needs of the not-yet-established State of Israel.

Szajkowski, Zosa. *Jews, Wars, and Communism.* Vol. 1. New York: Ktav, 1972. 714 pp. illus. Vol. 2. New York: Ktav, 1974. 398 pp. illus.
Vol. 1 covers the attitude of American Jews to World War 1, the Russian Revolutions of 1917 and Communism (1914–1945); vol. 2, the impact of the Red Scare of 1919–20 on American Jewish life.

Thomas, Gordon and Max Morgan Witts. *Voyage of the Damned.* New York: Stein and Day, 1974. 317 pp. illus.
The tragic story of the passenger liner *St. Louis* which left Hamburg for Cuba in 1939 with 937 Jewish refugees who were ultimately refused entry to any country.

Urofsky, Melvin I. *American Zionism from Herzl to the Holocaust.* Garden City: Doubleday, 1975. 538 pp.
A history of the Zionist movement in the United States.

Wyman, David S. *Paper Walls: America and the Refugee Crisis 1938–1941.* Amherst: The University of Massachusetts Press, 1968. 306 pp.
An analysis of the American response to the admission of Jewish refugees from Europe.

Cultural Studies

Agudath Israel of America. *The Struggle and the Splendor: A Pictoral Overview of Agudath Israel of America.* New York: 1982. 172 pp. illus.
An illustrated history of the accomplishments of the Orthodox Jewish organization established in 1922.

Bilik, Dorothy Seidman. *Immigrant-Survivors: Post-Holocaust Consciousness in Recent Jewish American Fiction.* Middletown, Conn.: Wesleyan University Press, 1981. 216 pp.
A critical study of a major theme in contemporary American Jewish literature.

Davis, Moshe. *The Emergence of Conservative Judaism: The Historical School in 19th Century America.* Philadelphia: Jewish Publication Society of America, 1963. 527 pp. illus.
A comprehensive survey of Jewish religious life in the United States in the 19th century.

Doroshkin, Milton. *Yiddish in America: Social and Cultural Foundations.* Rutherford: Farleigh Dickinson University Press, 1969. 281 pp. illus.
A study of the role of Yiddish among the Eastern European immigrants in America.

Ezrahi, Sidra DeKoven. *By Words Alone: The Holocaust in Literature.* Chicago: University of Chicago Press, 1980. 262 pp.
A comprehensive survey of the treatment of the Holocaust in literature.

Fishman, Joshua A., ed. *Never Say Die! A Thousand Years of Yiddish in Jewish Life and Letters.* The Hague: Mouton, 1981. 763 pp. illus.
Includes articles on the role of Yiddish and bilingualism in American Hasidic communities, Chaim Zhitlowsky and American Jewry, the Yiddish secular school and Yiddish press in America and the use of Yiddish among American college students.

Glazer, Nathan. *American Judaism.* 2d ed. Chicago: University of Chicago Press, 1972. 210 pp.
A revised and updated edition of a very thoughtful and well written study of Judaism in the United States.

Gross, Theodore L., ed. *The Literature of American Jews.* New York: The Free Press, 1973. 510 pp. illus.
Contains selections which portray the literary expression of American Jews from the early 19th century until the present day.

Helmreich, William B. *The World of the Yeshiva: An Intimate Portrait of Orthodox Jewry.* New York: The Free Press, 1982. 412 pp.
A detailed study of the advanced yeshiva in America, its development in the United States, its inner life and an effort to assess if it is successful in meeting its objectives.

Kampf, Avram. *Contemporary Syangogue Art: Developments in the United States, 1945–1965.* Philadelphia: The Jewish Publication Society of America, 1966. 276 pp. illus.

Kasnett, Pinchas, ed. *Jerusalem Echoes II: The Ohr Somayach Story . . .* New York: Ohr Somayach Institutions, 1981. 113 pp. illus.
Ohr Somayach maintains a network of schools througout Israel and in New York, providing intensive Jewish study for students with limited backgrounds in Judaism; the volume relates the experiences of many Americans who are involved in the program.

Klaperman, Gilbert. *The Story of Yeshiva University: The First Jewish University in America.* New York: Macmillan, 1969. 301 pp. illus.

Lifson, David S. *The Yiddish Theatre in America.* New York: T. Yoseloff, 1965. 659 pp.
A comprehensive history.

Liptzin, Sol. *The Jew in American Literature.* New York: Bloch, 1966. 251 pp.
A survey of both the image of the Jew in American literature as well as his contribution.

London, Hannah R. *Miniatures and Silhouettes of Early American Jews.* Rutland, Vt.: Charles E. Tuttle, 1970. 154 + 199 pp. illus.
A reprint of two early volumes, amply illustrated, which have become classic works.

London, Hannah R. *Portraits of Jews by Gilbert Stuart and Other Early American Artists.* Rutland, Vt.: Charles E. Tuttle, 1969. 197 pp. illus.
A reprint of the 1927 edition, containing numerous reproductions of portraits and miniatures of early American Jews.

Madison, Charles A. *Yiddish Literature: Its Scope and Major Writers.* New York: Frederick Ungar, 1968. 540 pp.
A comprehensive survey, of which approximately one-half is devoted to Yiddish literature and writers in America.

Noveck, Simon. ed. *Great Jewish Thinkers of the Twentieth Century.* Washington: B'nai B'rith Department of Adult Jewish Education, 1963. 326 pp.
Includes three essays on the theological views of Kaufmann Kohler. Mordecai M. Kaplan and Joseph Soloveitchik as representative of the three groups of contemporary American Judaism.

Plaut, W. Gunther. *The Growth of Reform Judaism: American and European Sources Until 1948.* New York: World Union for Progressive Judaism; Union of American Hebrew Congregations, 1965. 383 pp.
A collection of original source material.

Ribalow, Harold U. *The Tie That Binds: Conversations with Jewish Writers.* San Diego: A. S. Barnes; 1980. 236 pp. illus.
Interviews with prominent American Jewish authors, attempting to discover how they resolve the conflicts between traditional Jewish life and modern society.

Rosenberg, Bernard and Ernest Goldstein. *Creators and Disturbers: Reminiscences by Jewish Intellectuals of New York.* New York: Columbia University Press, 1982. 432 pp. illus.
Interviews with New York Jewish intellectuais on their relation to life in the city.

Rosenfeld, Alvin H. *A Double Dying: Reflections on Holocaust Literature.* Bloomington: Indiana University Press, 1980. 210 pp.
An attempt to reconcile the paradox that such an unprecedented evil as the Holocaust can be the inspiration for such powerful literature.

Sandrow, Nahma. *Vagabond Stars: A World History of Yiddish Theater.* New York: Harper & Row, 1977. 435 pp.
Several of the chapters deal with the Yiddish theater in America and one with the playwright Jacob Gordin.

Schiff, Alvin Irwin. *The Jewish Day School in America.* New York: Jewish Education Committee Press, 1966. 294 pp.
Includes material on the history of the development of the day school in America.

Slobin, Mark. *Tenement Songs: The Popular Music of the Jewish Immigrants.* Urbana: University of Illinois Press, 1982. 213 pp. illus.
A study of the Yiddish sheet music produced by the East European immigrant between 1880 and 1920.

Index

GO TO
...**Eagle Loan Office**...
FOR LOANS ON
Diamonds, Watches, Jewelry, Guns,
Musical Instruments, Etc.

Best Accomodations in the City.
Business Confidential.
Remember the Number.

SOL BRODKEY,
JEWELER AND
DIAMOND BROKER 1301 DOUGLAS ST., OMAHA, NEB

DES MOINES BAKERY

H. LAZRIOWICH, Proprietor
MAKER OF
RYE BREAD
AND ALL KINDS OF
FANCY CAKES
SPECIAL ARRANGEMENTS CAN BE MADE FOR PARTIES
PHONE, AUTO 3086
409 West 7th St.   SIOUX CITY, IOWA

ZIEGLER & BEHREND,
THE BIG
Mail Order Whiskey House,
SOLE DEALERS OF
BRADDOCK PURE RYE
DIRECT FROM DISTILLERY AT DISTILLERY PRICES
Look For Big Demijohn.   Next Door First National Bank.
928 THIRD AVE., HUNTINGTON, WEST VA.

SAM GOLDFINE
PRACTICAL
Boot AND
Shoe Maker
Half Soles, Good Leather
BEST WORK.
REPAIRING A SPECIALTY
925 BROADWAY
Nashville,   Tennessee.

TEL   AUGUST CAPLAN,
GEN. MANAGER.

Midget Auto-Electric Piano Co.
OFFICE & FACTORY.
116 WALKER ST. N. Y.

SPECIALTY NICKEL IN SLOT SELF PLAYING PIANOS.

PIANOS GIVEN ON COMMISSION & ALSO LOANED.

FISCHER BROS.
NEW YORK
LADIES' TAILORS
SUITS, JACKETS AND SKIRTS
MADE TO ORDER   FIT GUARANTEED
PEOPLES PHONE 1575
301 S. 20TH ST., COR. AVE. C   BIRMINGHAM, ALA.

Phone N. W. Cedar 7854

M. OGLANSKY & CO.
DEALERS IN
RAGS, RUBBERS, BARRELS, METALS & BOTTLES

233 E. 14TH. STREET
ST. PAUL, MINN.

B. KARCHMER,   I. KARCHMER,   E. KARCHMER,
ST. LOUIS, MO.   SHERMAN, TEX.   DALLAS, TEX.

The Southwestern Iron and Metal Co.
(Successors to B. Karchmer & Bro.)
WHOLESALE DEALERS IN
Scrap Iron, Metals and Machinery

Sherman (Texas) Branch.   Dallas (Texas) Branch.
411 N. Montgomery   MAIN OFFICE   711-713 Elm Street.
Street,   St. Louis, Mo.   Telephone 1298-1 R
Telephone
SHERMAN, TEXAS.   DALLAS, TEXAS.

Presented by

"FOR PARTICULAR TRADE"
Phone: Main 1679

J. Alpert & Co.
MANUFACTURERS OF
BOYS' KNICKER PANTS

506-508 14th St., N. W.   Washington, D. C.

Telephone 2185 Black.

Oregon Tailoring Company
LOUIS ROSENFELD, Manager
75 Ninth Street, Astoria, Oregon.

Ladies' and Gent's Suits Cleaned, Pressed and Repaired
CLUB RATES $1.50 PER MONTH
First-Class Workmanship   Highest Price Paid for Ladies' and
and Lowest Prices.   Gent's Second Hand Goods.

The Eagle Sheet Metal Works
N LEVIN, PROP.

CORNICE AND   TIN, COPPER, ZINC and   DEALER IN
SKYLIGHT WORK   Galvanized Iron Work   HARDWARE, TIN-
HEATING   Roof Repairing and Roof   WARE, ENAMEL-
and **Ventilating**   Painting   WARE, GLASSWARE
HOTEL, DAIRY & BAKERY work   AND CHINAWARE

ESTIMATES CHEERFULLY FURNISHED
New 'Phone 1261
354 E Commerce St.,   San Antonio, Texas.

BELL PHONE   GOODS CALLED FOR AND DELIVERED

Enterprise
Tailors, Cleaners and Dyers
ED. F. WILLIN, PROP.
SUITS MADE TO ORDER
LADIES' AND GENTS' SUITS DRY AND STEAM CLEANED, PRESSED AND REPAIRED ON SHORT NOTICE
CLEANING, DYEING AND CURLING PLUMES
PORTIERS AND DRAPERIES RENOVATED
LINCOLN AVENUE   OPPOSITE TRAUTMANN'S   McDONALD, PA.

PHILIP LECHER
MOVING VANS

Furniture, Removed to City or Country
Pianos & Safes Hoisted with best Care
324 LIVONIA AVE.
Near Stone Ave.   Brooklyn, N. Y.

פיליפ לעכער
פֿאַרניטשור נעמטסם אין שטאַם אדער קאַנטרי
פּיאַנאָס און סייפס נעהויסטעד זעהר פֿאָרזיכטיג
נירר סטאָן עוו. ברוקלין.   324 ליוואַניע עוו.

ROUMANIAN
כשר
RESTAURANT
19 Richmond St., near Weybosset St.
Telephone Union 5685-J
H. BERCOVITZ, Prop.   PROVIDENCE, R. I.

H. FELDMAN
Dealer in
New & Second Hand
SHOES

Shoes delivered in every
part of the Country
REPAIRING NEATLY Done
552 S. Jefferson St.
CHICAGO

W. FELDMAN, PROPRIETOR
HOME PHONE 3525.

Chicago Fancy Bakery.
BAKERS OF
VIENNA, HOME MADE and BOHEMIAN RYE BREAD.
BUNS, CAKES, CONFECTIONS, ETC.
WEDDINGS AND PARTIES FURNISHED PROMPTLY.
1905 CANTON ST.   TOLEDO, O.

HENRY H. JACOBSON.   SAMUEL JACOBSON.   EMANUEL JACOBSON.

Jacobson Brothers,
Cutters of **DIAMONDS.**
COR. JOHN & NASSAU STS.
(PRESCOTT BUILDING.)
New York

LONDON, 105 HATTON GARDEN.
AMSTERDAM, 2 TULP STRAAT
PARIS, 9 RUE DE CHATEAUDUN.

TELEPHONE, S. B. 4660

L. Klaben
Ladies' Fine Tailor
SEPARATE SKIRTS & TAILOR MADE
SUITS A SPECIALTY
GARMENTS REMODELLED & FURS ALTERED
HIGH GRADE WORKMANSHIP & PERFECT FIT GUARANTEED
307 FREEMASON ST. NORFOLK, VA.
NEXT TO LYNNHAVEN HOTEL